*A Garland Series*

# OUTSTANDING DISSERTATIONS IN THE

# FINE ARTS

# Asher Brown Durand

### His Art and Art Theory in
### Relation to His Times

## David B. Lawall

*Garland Publishing, Inc., New York & London*

*1977*

**HOUSTON PUBLIC LIBRARY**

Copyright © 1977
by David B. Lawall
All Rights Reserved

**Library of Congress Cataloging in Publication Data**

Lawall, David B
    Asher Brown Durand, his art and art theory in relation
to his times.

    (Outstanding dissertations in the fine arts)
    Originally presented as the author's thesis, Princeton,
1966.
    Bibliography: v. 2, p.
    1. Durand, Asher Brown, 1796-1886.  I.  Durand, Asher
Brown, 1796-1886.  II.  Title.  III.  Series.
ND237.D8L33 1977        760'.092'4 [B]        76-23635
ISBN 0-8240-2704-3

Printed in the United States of America

FOREWORD TO THE GARLAND EDITION.

The dissertation on Durand is an attempt to write about
American art rather than an artist's biography--about art in
its relation to life and ideas.  It is offered here without
apology as long as it is understood to be the work of a
younger person writing during the spare moments afforded by
the early phase of a teaching career.  If it were rewritten
today, it would be shorter and the chapter on the religion of
nature would be revised in such a way as to emphasize a continuing current of Deism that finds expression in the archi-
tectonic organization of Durand's studio compositions.  The
Deist strain is vivified by a Pantheist perception of an animating Reason that informs the forest studies painted out-of-
doors and is qualified by a Christian faith in the benevolence
of the Creator, symbolically stated in the church buildings
or steeples that appear with some frequency in the landscape
compositions.  As more American paintings of the nineteenth
century are rediscovered, it may become possible to grasp
more firmly and to state more succinctly the fundamental principles controlling the work of Durand and his followers.  But
the present dissertation, with its perhaps too leisurely
exploration of what may be side-issues of little final importance, raises what I hope may be regarded as the central question:
whether we can see Durand's work, not as the stylish, pictorial
duplication of American faces and places, but as the artist's
effort to stabilize an intuitively formulated and shifting

reality so constituted as to yield significance and dignity to the individual in this world and to impart hope, or at least complacency, to his anticipation of the next.

The text of and notes to the dissertation appear in their original form, but all five appendices comprising volume three of the dissertation--I. Itinerary, II. Catalogue of Paintings Other than Oil Studies from Nature, III. Catalogue of Oil Studies from Nature, IV. Catalogue of Drawings, and V. Portraits of Asher B. Durand Other than Self-Portraits--are here omitted. In consequence, the numerous parenthetical references to these in the body of the text should be ignored. With the exception of portraits and figure studies, the paintings listed in the second and third appendices of the dissertation are listed in a revised and expanded catalogue to be published by Garland under the title Asher B. Durand: a Documentary Catalogue of the Narrative and Landscape Paintings.

David B. Lawall

Charlottesville, Virginia

March 1977

Frontispiece.  Anonymous.  Asher B. Durand.

ASHER BROWN DURAND:

HIS ART AND

ART THEORY

IN RELATION TO

HIS TIMES.


By

David B. Lawall.


Submitted to Princeton University

March, 1966,

in partial fulfillment of the requirements

for the degree of Doctor of Philosophy.

ACKNOWLEDGMENTS.

During the course of my study of American art under Professor Ellen Johnson at Oberlin College and Professor Donald
D. Egbert at Princeton University, it became increasingly clear
to me that a more thorough examination of the art and theories
of Asher B. Durand might yield important insights into the
nature and workings of that curious and seemingly improbable
phenomenon, painting in America; and, that, due to the wealth
of available documentation, some insights might be gained
into the nature of art itself. When their encouragement was
seconded by that of two other very faithful scholars, Miss
Bartlett Cowdrey and Mr. Theodore Bolton, I felt that the
indulgence of my own curiosity in this direction might be
justifiable. From each I have received assistance in the pros-
ecution of my study. In particular Miss Cowdrey placed at my
disposal her accumulated records of paintings by Durand.
Mr. Bolton introduced to me the wealth of Durand material
owned by the Century Association in New York and gave to me
a number of valuable documents from his own files. Professor
Egbert has generously shared his wide knowledge of art, literature, and philosophy; and to his patient suggestions and
criticism the present text owes much of what clarity and
order it may possess.

During the course of my research, conversations with
Messers. William H. Gerdts, Jr., William I. Homer, David Hunting-

ton, Thomas J. McCormick, A. Hyatt Mayor, and Frederick A. Sweet have been both stimulating and fruitful of ideas.

Information regarding particular paintings has been provided by members of the staffs of the following institutions: the Albany Institute of History and Art, Andrew Dickson White Museum of Art of Cornell University, Archives of American Art, Brooklyn Museum, Cleveland Museum of Art, Corcoran Gallery of Art, Frick Art Reference Library, Gemeente Musea (Amsterdam), Georgia Museum of Art of The University of Georgia, Gibbes Art Gallery, Historical Society of Pennsylvania, Isaac Delgado Museum of Art, The John Herron Art Institute, M. Knoedler and Company, The Metropolitan Museum of Art, The Minneapolis Institute of Arts, The Museum of the City of New York, National Academy of Design, The New-York Historical Society, The New York Public Library, Peabody Institute of the City of Baltimore, Pennsylvania Academy of the Fine Arts, Princeton Art Museum, University Galleries of the University of Southern California, Wadsworth Atheneum, The Walters Art Gallery, Witte Memorial Museum, Worcester Art Museum, and the Yale University Art Gallery. But I am especially indebted to Miss Carolyn Scoon and the late Arthur B. Carlson, who made available to me the vast collection of Durand's paintings and drawings at The New-York Historical Society, and to Miss Elizabeth E. Roth and Mr. William Duprey, who performed the same service in respect to The New York Public Library's collection of Durand's

iii

engravings. Messers. Henry M. Fuller, Robert Kennett, and Walter Knight Sturges and Miss Dudley W. Waggoner have kindly provided information about paintings in their ownership.

My research has been facilitated by the Archives of American Art, which was able to provide microfilm copies of the Asher B. and John Durand Papers, owned by The New York Public Library. A Junior Fellowship at Princeton University and a grant from Princeton's Spears Fund offset some of the large initial expenditures for microfilms and photographs.

I can only hope that the reader will discover in what follows something of that spirit of critical enquiry and candor fostered by the faculties of Oberlin College and Princeton University. To the art departments, especially, of these institutions I owe a debt that is a privilege to acknowledge.

The preliminary drafts of the text and appendices were typed by my wife, while the present copy is the work of Mrs. Cynthia Stocking and Mrs. Evelyn Olinger.

David B. Lawall
Charlottesville, Virginia
1966.

# CONTENTS

LIST OF ILLUSTRATIONS.

All works are paintings by Asher B. Durand unless otherwise
noted and are reproduced through the courtesy of the individuals
or institutions indicated.

Frontispiece. Artist unknown. Asher B. Durand. Daguerreotype.
The New-York Historical Society.

12. Musidora. Engraving, 1819. Firestone Library, Princeton University.

13. Winnipiseogee Lake. Engraved after a painting by Thomas Cole, 1830. Prints Division, The New York Public Library, Astor, Lenox and Tilden Foundations.

14. Delaware Water Gap. Engraving, 1830. Prints Division, The New York Public Library, Astor, Lenox and Tilden Foundations.

15. Catskill Mountains. Engraving, 1830. Prints Division, The New York Public Library, Astor, Lenox and Tilden Foundations.

16. James Smillie and Durand, Fort Putnam. Engraved after a painting by Robert W. Weir, 1830. Prints Division, The New York Public Library, Astor, Lenox and Tilden Foundations.

17. Valley with the Catskill Mountains Beyond. Drawing, 1830. The New-York Historical Society.

18. Thomas Cole, River in the Catskills. 1843. Courtesy of the Museum of Fine Arts, Boston. M. and M. Karolik Collection, 1947.

19. Thomas Cole, View on the Catskill, Early Autumn. In the Catskills. 1837. The Metropolitan Museum of Art. Gift in memory of Jonathan Sturges by his children, 1895.

20. Possibly by Durand, Catskill Mountains. Ca. 1831. Present location unknown.

21. The Sisters. Engraved after a painting by Henry Inman. Prints Division, The New York Public Library, Astor, Lenox and Tilden Foundations.

22. Sisters. Engraved after a painting by Samuel F. B. Morse, 1829. Prints Division, The New York Public Library, Astor, Lenox and Tilden Foundations.

23. The Wife. Engraved after a painting by Samuel F. B. Morse, 1829. Prints Division, The New York Public Library, Astor, Lenox and Tilden Foundations.

24. Gipsying Party. Engraved after a painting by Charles R. Leslie. Prints Division, The New York Public Library, Astor, Lenox and Tilden Foundations.

25. Hagar. Drawing, 1827-1829. The New-York Historical Society.

26. John Trumbull, The Saviour and St. John Playing with a Lamb. 1801. Yale University Art Gallery. Trumbull Collection, 1832.

27. John Trumbull, Our Saviour with Little Children. 1812. Yale University Art Gallery. Trumbull Collection, 1832.

28. Portrait of Caroline Durand. Drawing, ca. 1828. The New-York Historical Society.

29. Children of the Artist. 1832. The New-York Historical Society. Gift of the children of the artist through John Durand, 1903.

30. Richard Earlom, Girl with Pigs. Engraved after a painting by Thomas Gainsborough, 1783.

31. Mary and Jane Cordelia Frank. 1834. Collection of the Newark Museum. Gift of Mrs. Helen Thompson Durand, 1935.

32. Thomas Gainsborough, Elizabeth and Mary Linley. Ca. 1772. Reproduced by permission of the Governors of the Dulwich College Picture Gallery.

33. Ariadne Asleep on the Island of Naxos. After John Vanderlyn, ca. 1835. The Metropolitan Museum of Art. Gift of Samuel P. Avery, 1897.

34. Ariadne. Engraved after a painting by John Vanderlyn, 1835. Prints Division, The New York Public Library, Astor, Lenox and Tilden Foundations.

35. Ideal Head, a Suggestion from Life. 1836. The New-York Historical Society. Gift of the children of the artist through John Durand, 1903.

36. Mrs. Asher B. Durand (Mary Frank). Ca. 1837. The New-York Historical Society. Bequest of Mrs. Helen Thompson Durand, 1935.

37. Il Pappagallo. 1840. The New-York Historical Society. Gift of the children of the artist through John Durand, 1903.

38. George W. Flagg, Lady and Parrot. Ca. 1835. The New-York Historical Society.

39. John W. Casilear, The Presidents. Engraving, 1834.

40. Andrew Jackson. 1835. The New-York Historical Society. Gift of the New-York Gallery of the Fine Arts, 1858.

41. James Madison. 1833. The New-York Historical Society. Gift of P. Kemble Paulding, 1870.

42. George Washington. 1835. The New-York Historical Society. Gift of the New-York Gallery of the Fine Arts, 1858.

43. John Quincy Adams. 1835. The New-York Historical Society. Gift of the New-York Gallery of the Fine Arts, 1858.

44. John Quincy Adams. 1835. The Century Association, New York. Purchased from the artist, 1870. Photograph courtesy of the Frick Art Reference Library.

45. James B. Longacre, William Wirt. Engraving, ca. 1836.

46. Aaron Ogden. Engraving, 1834.

47. Luman Reed. 1836. From John Durand, The Life and Times of A. B. Durand, N.Y., 1894, opp. p. 102.

48. Joseph Hoxie. 1839. Present location unknown.

49. William Pitt Fessenden (formerly titled John Fessenden). 1830's. San Antonio Museum Association. Gift of Dr. and Mrs. Frederic G. Oppenheim, 1952.

50. William Cullen Bryant. 1854. Courtesy of Sleepy Hollow Restorations, Tarrytown, New York.

51. Head of a Roman. 1841. The New-York Historical Society. Gift of Mrs. Lucy M. Durand Woodman, 1907.

52. Head of a Roman. 1841. The New-York Historical Society. Gift of Mrs. Lucy M. Durand Woodman, 1907.

53. Alfred Jones and James Smillie, The Capture of Major André. Engraved after a painting by Durand, 1845.

54. The Capture of Major André. Drawing, ca. 1834. Courtesy of the Museum of Fine Arts, Boston. M. and M. Karolik Collection.

55. George W. Flagg, The Murder of the Princes in the Tower. Ca. 1834. The New-York Historical Society.

56. The Pedlar Displaying His Wares. 1836. The New-York Historical Society. Gift of the New-York Gallery of the Fine Arts, 1858.

57. Thomas Rowlandson, Doctor, Syntax Turned Nurse. Etching and aquatint, 1821.

58. William Sidney Mount, The Truant Gamblers. 1835. The New-York Historical Society. Gift of the New-York Gallery of the Fine Arts, 1858.

59. George W. Flagg, Falstaff Enacting Henry IV. Ca. 1834. The New-York Historical Society.

60. The Wrath of Peter Stuyvesant. 1836. The New-York Historical Society. Gift of the New-York Gallery of the Fine Arts, 1858.

61. Thomas Rowlandson, The Death of Punch. Etching and aquatint. 1821.

62. Blind Man's Buff. 1836. The New-York Historical Society. Gift of Dudley Butler, 1940.

63. School Let Out. 1836. The New-York Historical Society. Gift of Dudley Butler, 1940.

64. Boys Playing Marbles. 1836. The New-York Historical Society. Gift of Dudley Butler, 1940.

65. Boy Chasing a Pig. 1836. The New-York Historical Society. Gift of Dudley Butler, 1940.

66. I. W. Bauman, Children on a See-Saw. Engraved after a painting by Thomas Webster.

67. William Sidney Mount, Farmers Nooning. 1836. The Museums at Stony Brook. Gift of Mr. Frederick Sturges, Jr., 1954.

68. William Sidney Mount, Bargaining for a Horse. 1835. The New-York Historical Society. Gift of the New-York Gallery of the Fine Arts, 1858.

69. George W. Flagg, The Chess-Players, Check-Mate. Ca. 1835. The New-York Historical Society.

70. Thomas Cole, Dream of Arcadia. 1838. The Denver Art Museum, Denver, Colorado. Gift of Mrs. Lindsey Gentry, 1954.

71. The Dance on the Battery in the Presence of Peter Stuyvesant. 1838. Museum of the City of New York. Gift of Jane Rutherford Faile through Kenneth C. Faile, 1955.

72. Thomas Rowlandson, Rural Sports. Etching and aquatint, 1812.

73. Sunday Morning. 1839. The New-York Historical Society. Gift of the children of the artist.

74. Robert Hinshelwood, Sunday Morning. Engraved after a painting by Durand.

75. View near Rutland, Vermont. Landscape with Children. 1837. Private collection.

76. James Smillie, Dover Plains. 1850. Engraved after a painting by Durand. The New-York Historical Society.

77. Landscape, View of Rutland, Vermont. 1840. Detroit Institute of Arts. Gift of Dexter M. Ferry, Jr., 1942.

78. Landscape, Sunset. 1838. The New-York Historical Society. Gift of Mrs. Lucy M. Durand Woodman, 1907.

79. Thomas Cole, Summer Sunset. Ca. 1834. The New-York Historical Society.

80. An Old Man's Reminiscences. 1845. Albany Institute of History and Art. Transferred from the Albany Gallery of the Fine Arts, 1898.

81. Henry Inman, Dismissal of School on an October Afternoon. 1845. Courtesy of the Museum of Fine Arts, Boston. M. and M. Karolik Collection, 1948.

82. Omitted.

83. Morning Ride. 1851. Private collection. Photograph courtesy of Vose Galleries of Boston.

84. Thomas Cole, Landscape, the Fountain of Vaucluse. 1841. The Metropolitan Museum of Art. Gift of William E. Dodge, 1903.

85. The Morning of Life. 1840. National Academy of Design. Photograph courtesy of the Frick Art Reference Library.

86. The Evening of Life. 1840. National Academy of Design. Photograph courtesy of the Frick Art Reference Library.

87. Farmyard on the Hudson. 1843. Mr. and Mrs. George J. Arden.

88. View of Oberwesel on the Rhine. 1843. Berry-Hill Galleries, New York.

89. Landscape. 1847. Indianapolis Museum of Art. Gift of Mrs. Lydia G. Millard.

90. Landscape, Progress. 1853. Private collection. Photograph courtesy of Hirschl and Adler Galleries, Inc., New York.

91. The First Harvest. 1855. The Brooklyn Museum. Gift
    of The Brooklyn Institute of Arts and Sciences, 1897.

92. Fenner Sears and Company, A View near Conway, N. Hampshire.
    1831. Engraved after a painting by Thomas Cole.

93. Hudson River, Looking Towards the Catskills. 1847. New
    York State Historical Association, Cooperstown. Gift of
    Stephen C. Clark, 1940.

94. Claude Lorrain, Pastoral Landscape
    1636. The Metropolitan Museum of Art.

95. The Last Interview Between Harvey Birch and Washington.
    1843. From John Durand, The Life and Times of A. B.
    Durand, N.Y., 1894, opp. p. 132.

96. Study of a Tree. Drawing, 1837. The New-York Historical
    Society.

97. Study of a Copse of Trees. Drawing, 1844-1845. The New-
    York Historical Society.

98. Study of a Tree in Foliage. Drawing, 1844. The New-
    York Historical Society.

99. Study of Trees. Drawing, 1848. The New-York Historical
    Society.

100. Study of a Group of Trees. Drawing, 1853. The New-York
     Historical Society.

101. Study of the Branch Structure of Two Trees. Drawing,
     1863. The New-York Historical Society.

102. Study of a Tree. Drawing, 1865. The New-York Historical
     Society.

103. Rural Scene. Drawing, 1827. The New-York Historical
     Society.

103A. Brook, Rocks, and Trees. Drawing, 1836. The New-York
      Historical Society.

103B. Castle of Blonay. Drawing, 1840. The New-York Historical
      Society.

103C. Tivoli. Drawing, 1841. The New-York Historical Society.

103D. Sawmill by a River. Drawing, 1844. The New-York Historical
      Society.

103E. Plain and Mountain Range. Drawing, 1855. The New-York Historical Society.

103F. Lake George and Mountains. Drawing, 1863. The New-York Historical Society.

103G. Lake George. Drawing, 1871. The New-York Historical Society.

103H. Trees and Rocks. Drawing, ca. 1849. The New-York Historical Society.

103I. Study of Rocks. Drawing, 1863. The New-York Historical Society.

103J. Study of the Upturned Roots of a Tree. Drawing, 1870. The New-York Historical Society.

104. Study from Nature. Ca. 1834. The New-York Historical Society. Gift of the children of the artist through John Durand, 1903.

105. Study from Nature. Ca. 1834. The New-York Historical Society. Gift of the children of the artist through John Durand, 1903.

106. Study at Marbletown, N.Y. Ca. 1845. The New-York Historical Society. Louis Durr Fund, 1887.

107. Landscape with a Beech Tree. 1844. The New-York Historical Society. Gift of Nora Durand Woodman, 1932.

108. The Beeches. 1845. The Metropolitan Museum of Art. Bequest of Maria DeWitt Jesup, 1915.

109. Trees by the Brookside, Kingston, N.Y. 1846. The New-York Historical Society. Louis Durr Fund, 1887.

110. Landscape, Composition, Forenoon. 1847. New Orleans Museum of Art. Gift of the Fine Arts Club of New Orleans, 1916.

111. In the Woods. 1847. Amherst College. Purchased, 1947.

112. Woodland Scene. 1850. Private collection.

113. Trees and Rocks. On the Wissahickon. 1850. The Art Museum, Princeton University. Gertrude and John Maclean Magie Fund, 1946.

114. Where the Streamlet Sings in Rural Joy. 1850. Vassar College Art Gallery, Poughkeepsie, N.Y. Gift of Matthew Vassar, 1864.

115. Joseph Vollmering, Landscape. The New-York Historical Society.

116. Joseph Vollmering. Winter-Scene. The New-York Historical Society.

117. Study from Nature: Bronxville. 1856. The New-York Historical Society. Gift of Nora Durand Woodman, 1932.

118. Trees and Rocks. 1856. The New-York Historical Society. Gift of Mrs. Lucy M. Durand Woodman, 1907.

119. Rocks and Trees. 1856. The New-York Historical Society. Gift of Mrs. Lucy M. Durand Woodman, 1907.

120. Interior of a Wood. Study of a Wood Interior. Ca. 1856. Addison Gallery of American Art, Phillips Academy, Andover, Mass. Gift of Mrs. Frederic F. Durand.

121. Bash-Bish Falls. 1861. The Century Association, New York. Purchased, 1862. Photograph courtesy of the Frick Art Reference Library.

122. Landscape with Figures. 1861. Collection of the Walker Art Center, Minneapolis. Gift of the T. B. Walker Foundation.

123. Chappel Pond, Keene Flats, Adirondacks. 1870. The New-York Historical Society. Gift of Nora Durand Woodman, 1932.

124. Chappel Brook. 1871. The New-York Historical Society. Gift of Mrs. Lucy M. Durand Woodman, 1907.

125. Beech and Maples. Landscape. 1855-1857. The Brooklyn Museum. Bequest of Charles A. Schieren, 1915.

126. Group of Trees. 1855-1857. The New-York Historical Society. Louis Durr Fund, 1887.

127. Landscape, a Study from Nature. 1860. Peabody Institute of the City of Baltimore. Gift of John W. McCoy, 1908. On indefinite loan to The Baltimore Museum of Art.

128. Landscape. 1859. Present location unknown. Photograph courtesy of Childs Gallery, Boston.

129. Forest Landscape. 1859. The Brooklyn Museum. Gift of Alfred W. Jenkins, 1930.

130. Mountain and Stream, Shandaken Mountains. 1853. Yale University Art Gallery, New Haven. Gift of Mrs. Frederic F. Durand.

131. *View of the Shandaken Mountains*. 1853. The New-York Historical Society. Gift of Nora Durand Woodman, 1932.

132. Compositional diagram of *Lake George, New York*. 1862. Courtesy of the Museum of Fine Arts, Boston. M. and M. Karolik Collection.

133. Compositional diagram of *The Old Oak*. 1844. The New-York Historical Society. Gift of the New-York Gallery of the Fine Arts, 1858.

134. Compositional diagram of *Vermont Scenery*. 1852. Herbert W. Plimpton. On permanent loan to Amherst College.

135. Compositional diagram of *In the Woods*. 1855. The Metropolitan Museum of Art. Gift in memory of Jonathan Sturges by his children, 1895.

136. *Harbor Island, Lake George*. 1872. The New-York Historical Society. Gift of Nora Durand Woodman, 1932.

137. Compositional diagram of *Harbor Island, Lake George*. 1872. The New-York Historical Society. Gift of Nora Durand Woodman, 1932.

138. *Black Mountain, Lake George*. 1878. The New-York Historical Society. Gift of Nora Durand Woodman, 1932.

139. Compositional diagram of *Black Mountain, Lake George*. The New-York Historical Society. Gift of Nora Durand Woodman, 1932.

140. *Black Mountain, Lake George*. 1874. The New-York Historical Society. Gift of Nora Durand Woodman, 1932.

141. Compositional diagram of *Black Mountain, Lake George*. 1874. The New-York Historical Society. Gift of Nora Durand Woodman, 1932.

142. Compositional diagram of *View of Black Mountain from the Harbor Islands, Lake George*. 1875. The New-York Historical Society. Gift of Mrs. Lucy M. Durand Woodman, 1907.

143. Compositional diagram of *Souvenir of the Adirondacks*. 1878. The New-York Historical Society. Gift of the children of the artist through John Durand, 1903.

144. Thomas Cole, *Tornado in the Wilderness*. 1835. In the Collection of the Corcoran Gallery of Art. Purchased, 1877.

145. James Smillie, *Cover to "The American Landscape."* Engraving, 1830. The center panel is from a "Sketch from Nature by A. B. Durand."

146. Trompe-l'oeil Drawing. 1837. The New-York Historical Society.

147. Thomas Cole, Dream of Arcadia. Trompe-l'oeil oil sketch, 1838. The New-York Historical Society.

148. Landscape, Sunday Morning. Early Morning at Cold Spring. Montclair Art Museum. Lang Acquisition Fund, 1945.

149. John A. Rolph, Evening. Engraved after a painting by Durand, 1845.

150. View in the Catskills. 1844. Courtesy of the Museum of Fine Arts, Boston. Gift of Charles D. White, 1936.

151. Vermont Scenery. 1852. Herbert W. Plimpton. On permanent loan to Amherst College.

152. Brook, Trees, and Mountains, Manchester, Vt. Drawing, 1851. The New-York Historical Society.

153. Trees, a Valley, and Mountains. Drawing, 1851. The New-York Historical Society.

154. High Point, Shandaken Mountains. 1853. The Metropolitan Museum of Art. Bequest of Sarah A. Ludlum, 1877.

155. James Smillie, A Glimpse in New-Hampshire. Engraved after a painting by Durand, 1857.

156. Omitted.

157. The Pedestrian. 1863. Present location unknown. Photograph from the Platt Collection, Princeton University.

158. River Scene. 1861. Present location unknown.

159. Summer Afternoon. 1865. Metropolitan Museum of Art. Bequest of Maria DeWitt Jesup, 1915.

160. Landscape. 1866. Present location unknown. Photograph courtesy of Hirschl and Adler Galleries, Inc., New York.

161. Landscape. 1867. Photograph courtesy of M. Knoedler and Co., Inc., New York.

162. Scene Among the Berkshire Hills. 1872. New Jersey State Museum Collection, Trenton. Gift of the Association for the Arts.

163. View of Black Mountain from the Harbor Islands, Lake George. 1875. The New-York Historical Society. Gift of Mrs. Lucy M. Durand Woodman, 1907.

164. Souvenir of the Adirondacks. 1878. The New-York Historical Society. Gift of the children of the artist through John Durand, 1903.

165. Barend C. Koekkoek, Woodland Scene with Water on a Normal Day. 1849. Amsterdam Historical Museum.

166. Josephine Walters, Pool in the Catskills. The New-York Historical Society.

167. James Hart, At the Ford. Private collection.

168. Woodland Interior. (Formerly titled Primeval Forest.) 1854. Smith College Museum of Art, Northampton, Mass. Purchased, 1952.

169. In the Woods. 1855. The Metropolitan Museum of Art. Gift in memory of Jonathan Sturges by his children, 1895.

170. F. H. Cushman, "...enter this wild wood, / And view the haunts of Nature." Engraved after a design by Robert W. Weir, 1836.

171. James R. Rice, The First Temples. Engraved after a painting by Joseph John, 1870.

172. John Constable, Salisbury Cathedral from the Bishop's Grounds. 1823. Photograph Crown Copyright. Victoria and Albert Museum.

173. Caspar David Friederich. Cloister Graveyard in the Snow. 1810.

174. Carl Gustave Carus, The Churchyard on the Oybin in Winter. Ca. 1828. Museum der bildenden künste, Leipzig, German Democratic Republic.

175. A Primeval Forest. Ca. 1855. The New-York Historical Society.

176. Trees and Brook. Ca. 1855. The New-York Historical Society. Gift of Nora Durand Woodman, 1932.

177. Trees and Brook. 1858. The New-York Historical Society. Gift of Nora Durand Woodman, 1930.

178. Woodland Brook. 1859. The New York Public Library, Astor, Lenox and Tilden Foundations. Gift of Mrs. Robert L. Stuart to the Lenox Library, 1887. On indefinite loan to The New-York Historical Society.

179. A Sycamore Tree. 1858. Yale University Art Gallery. Gift of Mrs. Frederic F. Durand, 1929.

180. A Reminiscence of the Catskill Clove. The Catskills. 1859. The Walters Art Gallery, Baltimore.

181. Landscape. Woodland Scene. 1858. Henry Melville Fuller.

182. Valley Landscape. Drawing, 1859. The Walters Art Gallery, Baltimore.

183. The Edge of the Forest. Primeval Forest. 1871. In the collection of the Corcoran Gallery of Art. Purchased, 1874.

184. The Old Oak. 1844. The New-York Historical Society. Gift of the New-York Gallery of the Fine Arts, 1858.

185. Barend C. Koekkoek, The Way-Side Shrine. 1835. The New-York Historical Society.

186. James Smillie, My Own Green Forest Land. Engraved after a painting by Durand, 1847.

187. Study of Trees. Drawing, 1848. The New-York Historical Society.

188. Landscape. 1849. Collection of the Newark Museum. Bequest of Wallace M. Scudder, 1956.

189. View Toward the Hudson Valley. 1851. Wadsworth Atheneum, Hartford. The Ella Gallup Sumner and Mary Catlin Sumner Collection, 1948.

189A. Study of Trees. Drawing, ca. 1848. The New-York Historical Society.

190. Barend C. Koekkoek, Small Town on a River. 1840. Amsterdam Historical Museum.

191. Shandaken Range, Kingston, New York. 1854. The New-York Historical Society. Louis Durr Fund, 1887.

192. Landscape. 1855. Photograph courtesy of M. Knoedler and Co., Inc., New York.

193. Fishkill Mountains, New York. 1856. Peabody Institute of the City of Baltimore. Gift of John W. McCoy, 1908. On extended loan to The Baltimore Museum of Art.

194. Hudson River, View of the Fishkill Mountains. 1856. The New-York Historical Society. Gift of Mrs. Lucy M. Durand Woodman.

195. Franconia, White Mountains. 1857. The New York Public
Library, Astor, Lenox and Tilden Foundations. Gift of
Mrs. Robert L. Stuart to the Lenox Library, 1887. On
indefinite loan to The New-York Historical Society.

196. Franconia Notch. 1857. The New York Public Library,
Astor, Lenox and Tilden Foundations. Gift of Mrs. Robert
L. Stuart to the Lenox Library, 1887. On indefinite loan
to The New-York Historical Society.

197. Catskill Clove. 1866. The Century Association, New York.
Gift of members, 1866. Photograph courtesy of the Frick
Art Reference Library.

198. Escape of General Putnam. 1844. New York State Historical
Association, Cooperstown. Gift of Stephen C. Clark, 1940.

199. Albert Bobbet and Charles Edmonds, To the Memory of Channing. Wood-engraving after a drawing by Durand, 1849.
Firestone Library, Princeton University.

200. A Tree and a Limb. Drawing, 1848. The New-York Historical
Society.

201. Kindred Spirits. 1849. The New York Public Library,
Astor, Lenox and Tilden Foundations. Gift of Julia
Bryant, 1904.

202. Thomas Cole, Expulsion from the Garden of Eden. 1828.
Courtesy of the Museum of Fine Arts, Boston. M. and M.
Karolik Collection, 1947.

203. Study for Thanatopsis. Classical Landscape. Imaginary
Landscape. 1850. Delaware Art Museum, Wilmington. Gift
of Titus C. Geesey, 1962.

204. Imaginary Landscape, Scene from "Thanatopsis." 1850.
Metropolitan Museum of Art. Gift of J. Pierpont Morgan,
1911.

205. Daniel Huntington, Asher B. Durand. 1857. The Century
Association, New York. Photograph courtesy of the Frick
Art Reference Library.

206. Artist unknown, Asher B. Durand. Wood-engraving after
Gaston Fay, 1870.

INTRODUCTION.

I. Sketch of Durand's Career.

I was born on the 21st day of August, 1796, at a
small village in the township of Springfield, county
of Essex, state of New Jersey. My father was a watch-
maker and silversmith by profession--at least, these
were his principal occupations. He possessed, however,
mechanical talent of great versatility, and could turn
his hand as occasion required to such diverse trades
that it would be difficult to say what he could not
do, so far as the means were within reach. . . . A more
industrious man never lived. Yet with all his industry
and resources he was unable to amass anything beyond
the means for a comfortable living. . . .

My mother was in all respects a suitable helpmate.
She was like him in industry and aptness; there was
no requirement in household economy that she was not
equal to; and for uniform, steady virtues as a wife,
mother, and Christian, more than fifty years of unremitting toil, with many a painful trial, bear witness.

. . . my father was a descendant of the Huguenots,
driven by persecution to this country at the time of
the revocation of the Edict of Nantes. . . . My mother's

1

maiden name was Meyer, of Dutch origin, direct from
the early settlers of New Jersey.[1]

In these terms Asher Brown Durand (August 21, 1796-
September 17, 1886) described his birth and parents.  Born
into a family that had already passed several generations in
the New World and raised in an area of early settlement,
Durand grew up amid a natural environment that had already,
in measure, yielded to the hand of man and in a human context
of European traditions that had already been adjusted to the
task of living in America.  The brutality of man and nature
on the frontier was as remote from his early experience as
was the rapacity of an urban, capitalist economy.  If we
wished to reduce his early world to abstract terms, we might
place it more or less equidistant from the extremes of the
wilderness and the city.  Exempt from the tyranny of nature
as from that of the more advanced economic and political
institutions, the Durand family must, all the same, have
retained a high degree of personal self-consciousness born
of memories of religious persecution in France and, also,
Holland.

Of himself Durand wrote as follows:

> I am the sixth of seven brothers, and, if I may judge
> by earliest recollections, the feebleness of my con-
> stitution was in proportion to the order of succession.
> I remember a keen sense of insignificance compared
> with the rest of my brothers.  I was, indeed, a deli-
> cate child, and, in consequence of this, received a

greater share of maternal solicitude, which circumstance has exercised an important influence on my
feelings and conduct in all the vicissitudes of
life.[2]

His physical frailty, his tendency to contrast himself to
others, and the special attention bestowed upon him by his
mother must have served to heighten an awareness of discrete
existence. While family traditions of ingenuity, industrious-
ness, and self-consciousness may account for the fact that
Durand, like several of his brothers, became a craftsman--an
engraver, the fact that he also became a painter may be the
result of the more intense self-awareness which he developed
owing to the disparity he felt between himself and his
brothers in the early years.

Rapidly Durand rose to preëminence among engravers working in America. At the end of a five-year's apprenticeship
to Peter Maverick (1780-1831) in 1817, he entered into partnership with his former master, and opened an office in New York
City. This partnership lasted until 1820 when Durand received
a commission from John Trumbull to engrave his painting of the
Declaration of Independence, upon which Durand labored for the
next three years. Having finished this--the first large,
multifigure engraving to be executed in America--in 1823,
Durand was free to enter in 1824 into partnership with his
brother Cyrus (1787-1868) and Charles C. Wright (1796-1854)
under the firm name of A. B. & C. Durand, Wright & Co.[3] This
firm, like the one which superseded it--Durand, Perkins &

Co.[4]--was especially concerned with the production of bank-notes. Despite the commercial character of most of Durand's work prior to the dissolution of Durand, Perkins & Co., in 1831, he had by this time published several notable engravings, such as the quarto Musidora of 1825 after his own design and the six topographical views which made up the first number of a proposed annual, The American Landscape, in 1830. After 1831, as an engraver, Durand was principally occupied with engravings for the National Portrait Gallery of Distinguished Americans and with his last large plate, an engraved interpretation of John Vanderlyn's Ariadne Asleep on the Island of Naxos, published in 1835. Because Durand so frequently worked in partnership it would be difficult to form any very exact idea of his total effort as an engraver. However, in 1895 the Grolier Club was able to exhibit some two-hundred and thirty-seven engravings for which Durand himself was largely responsible.[5]

As late as 1839 Durand might still engrave a bank-note vignette,[6] and as early as 1823 he had exhibited a, presumably painted, Portrait of His Child at the America Academy of the Fine Arts.[7] But the year 1835 was the first that he devoted primarily to painting. Of the nineteen engravings executed by Durand for The National Portrait Gallery nine are dated 1834, while only three are dated 1835 or 1836. It was at the beginning of 1835 that Durand commenced the series of portraits and genre paintings for the munificent, New York art-patron, Luman Reed. Most of Durand's distinguished work as

a portrait painter belongs to the period 1832 to 1840, and
during these same years he produced his most ingratiating
genre and historical paintings--The Pedlar Displaying his
Wares (1836, Fig. 56), The Wrath of Peter Stuyvesant (1836,
Fig. 60), and The Dance on the Battery in the Presence of
Peter Stuyvesant (1838, Fig. 71).

Gradually abandoning the several kinds of figure painting,
not until the winter of 1837-1838 did he emerge as a landscape
painter. Already past forty years of age, it was not until
this moment that he rooted himself in a career that he would
pursue for the next forty years. In order to extend his
knowledge of art and nature, he visited England and toured
the Continent in 1840-1841 both to study the paintings of
Constable, Turner, Claude, and the Dutch landscape painters
of the seventeenth century and to acquaint himself with the
scenery of the Old World. Indeed, a far larger portion of his
travel journal records his reactions to scenery than to works
of art. After his return he painted European scenes from the
drawings which he accumulated abroad, but by 1844 these disappear from his work and are replaced by the fruits of his
effort to grasp the native landscape of the north-eastern
United States. Hardly a summer passed between his return to
America and the time he stopped painting in 1880[8] that he did
not travel to the Catskills or Vermont or New Hampshire or to
Lake George and the Adirondacks to draw or paint from nature
itself. The final products of these summer tours--which often
extended into the chill months of autumn--were the composi-

tions elaborated in his New York studio, or after 1869 in the studio-house he built on what had been his father's farm in Jefferson Village, now Maplewood, New Jersey.

While it is Durand's work as an engraver and painter that will be our main concern in the following study, we should not neglect to note here the central position which he held in the New York art world before the Civil War. The several portraits of Durand (see App. V) reveal a man of a gentle and engaging personality, and as such he early won the confidence of artists and patrons alike. In 1825 he was among the leaders of the group of younger artists who, seeking better opportunities for the study of art than were available at the American Academy of the Fine Arts, founded the New-York Drawing Association. Early in the following year he was among the founders of the National Academy of Design, over which he presided from 1845 to 1861. As President of the Academy, Durand was particularly successful in gaining and holding the support of a group of New York merchants, among whom Reed's partner Jonathan Sturges was the most prominent, who provided the funds and advice which insured the perpetuity of the Academy. Aside from the Academy, Durand was an active member of the Sketch Club--a society of artists and amateurs--and a founder of the Century Club.[9]

## II.  Durand Among His Contemporaries.

In no sense was Durand ignored by his contemporaries.
As a man, he won and held their esteem and as an artist received their approbation.  By and large the popular press
picked out his work for favorable comment.  Both William
Dunlap in 1834[10] and Henry T. Tuckerman in 1847[11] and 1867[12]
devoted considerable space to Durand in their biographical-
critical accounts of American art.  William Cullen Bryant,
when invited in 1854 to comment on Durand's landscapes, ranked
both him and Thomas Cole, recently deceased, "among the first
landscape painters of modern times," and added that "there are
no landscapes produced in any part of the world which I should
more willingly possess than his /i.e., Durand's/.[13]  Durand
received not only the verbal praise of his contemporaries but
also the approbation implied by imitation.  As an engraver,
Durand established the use of crisp detail and line, borrowed
from English and Italian engravers of the eighteenth century,
which remained the standard for American engraving until the
steel plate gave way to wood in the 1880's.  Among Durand's
pupils in engraving were George W. Hatch (1805-1867), John W.
Casilear (1811-1893), and Lewis P. Clover, Jr. (1819-1896).

As a painter, Durand may be counted with Thomas Doughty
and Thomas Cole as one of the three founders of the Hudson
River School of American landscape painting--a school that
embraces both a Romantic and a Realist phase and parallels
similar movements in English and Continental art.  But of the

three founders it was Durand who had the widest and largest influence on the development of the school. While securing a firmer hold upon the real forms and scenes of the American landscape than Doughty, Durand was also able to effect a sustained and individual synthesis of the ideal and real qualities which Cole usually relegated to two distinct classes of his work. Durand led the way to a style that substituted a mood of contemplation for the violence of much of Cole's work, that substituted the spiritual for the allegorical, the native for the exotic, the present for the past, and an economical technique for painterly drama. Because Durand normally refused to take pupils, we can name only Samuel Colman (1832-1920) as a proper student. However, the work of a large number of painters--John W. Casilear, John F. Kensett (1816-1872), Sanford R. Gifford (1832-1880), William (1823-1894) and James M. Hart (1828-1901), David Johnson (1827-1908), Worthington Whittredge (1820-1910), George Inness (1825-1894), Alexander H. Wyant (1836-1892), William James Stillman (1828-1901), and others--many of whom worked closely with Durand at one period or another, displays traces of the influence of Durand in matters of technique, subject matter, and mood. Durand's standing among the younger artists in the mid 1850's, when he was at the peak of his career, is suggested by the following passage in a letter to Durand from William James Stillman--probably the most intelligent if not the best painter among the younger men--dated Paris, March 21, 1853:

I must say that for the proper union of that gentle
humility which forgets not the lilies of the field
or the weeds of the roadside, and that inspiring look
above the material to the tokens of that spirit which
animates and vivifies nature--the material and the
moral--the earthly and the heavenly--I have seen
nothing which has given me so much delight as your
own pictures.[14]

III.  Durand's Later Critics.

Later criticism has tended to focus largely, but not exclusively, upon Durand's work as a landscape painter.  And,
in criticisms of his landscapes, detail, feeling, and originality have been the three main foci of comment.

Although in 1867 Henry T. Tuckerman reaffirmed the values
of the Hudson River School by publishing an expanded version
of his 1847 Artist-Life, certain younger men, disciples of
John Ruskin, found reason to dissent from the favorable opinions of Durand's art which had been all but universal in the
1850's.  For example, T. C. Farrer, writing in the Ruskinian
New Path in 1863, could condemn the work of Durand, Thomas
Cole, Washington Allston, and George L. Brown as lacking in
truth to nature.[15]  In 1864 James Jackson Jarves regarded
Durand as an academician and, therefore, confined to a "system
of routine and conventionalism" which would preclude his
achievement of anything great or original.[16]  These early
criticisms, however, represent only the impatience of younger
men who sought to turn the current of American art away from
the Hudson River tradition.

While the doctrines of Ruskin had but little effect upon
American painting after the 1860's, the partial success of
those who advocated a more emotional, selective, and painterly
art, akin to that of Corot and the Barbizon painters, accounts
for the qualified approval of critics in the last three
decades of the nineteenth century.  Eugene Benson (writing in

1870), G. W. Sheldon (1879), S. G. W. Benjamin (1879), and
Sadakichi Hartmann (1902) unanimously discovered redeeming
qualities of feeling in Durand's work. Benson discerned
"a sentiment at once noble and sweet, and a harmony certainly
agreeable and sustained."[17] To Sheldon the paintings of
Durand and the poems of Bryant were "replete with American
woodland feeling, which tells not only of the observant eye,
but also of the sensitive soul."[18] And he found in the work
of both "the expression of the man's sentiments in the presence
of the stillness and solitude of insensible things."[19] Benjamin discovered the "solemn and majestic" especially in
Durand's paintings of trees.[20] Hartmann, who largely copied
from Benjamin, followed his guide in describing a picture of
trees as "poetical and dignified."[21] In all of these critics
except Sheldon, however, one finds the expressed or implied
notion that Durand's paintings were deficient in color and
breadth. To Benson his work lacked "splendor of color or
effect."[22] In speaking of the Hudson River School generally,
Benjamin lamented a lack of ideal and emotional elements, of
subtle suggestions, which appeal to the soul, and decried an
emphasis upon detail rather than masses, upon parts rather
than the whole and the spirit of the scene.[23] But he does
not apply these strictures specifically to Durand. Hartmann
may have been the first to locate the source of an overemphasis on detail in the fact that Durand had been an engraver,
when he copied Benjamin's sentence--"The care he had been
obliged to give to engraving was undoubtedly of great assist-

ance to him in enabling him to render the lines of a composition with truth"[24]--with one slight modification: "The care
he had been obliged to give to engraving was, at times, a
drawback to perfect mastery, but on the other hand also proved
of assistance to him in the composition of lines."[25] That
Hartmann regarded detail as detrimental to "perfect mastery"
is suggested by this statement and by his evident enthusiasm
over a sketch attributed to Durand "as free in its handling
and as fluid in its colour as if a modern Paris or Munich man
had painted it."[26] The notion that an overemphasis on detail
in Durand's work was the result of his prior practice of engraving, an explanation eminently worthy of the superficial
Hartmann, has been repeated frequently by later critics. As
an explanation, of course, it only begs the question by com-
pelling one to ask why Durand sought to incorporate so much
detail into his engravings. In contrast to Benson, Benjamin,
and Hartmann, William James Stillman (1901), who in the 1850's
had been largely responsible for disseminating Ruskin's teach-
ings in America, rather than depreciate the values of Durand's
detailed style, praised his work for just this quality:
". . . he first showed American artists what could be done
by faithful and unaffected direct study of nature in large
studies carefully finished on the spot, though never carried
to the elaboration of later and younger painters."[27] Thus,
except in the 1860's, the critics up to around 1900 continued
to find emotional or moral values in Durand's work. If they

were aware by 1870 of too minute a portraiture, they were
still able to see a living man behind the details.

Before the turning to the more severe criticism of the
first four decades of the twentieth century, we may note the
tokens of esteem called forth by Durand's death in 1886.  In
Daniel Huntington's Memorial Address, published in 1887 by
The Century Club, one finds not a criticism of Durand's work,
but a word-portrait of the man by one who had known him and
worked closely with him in the period of the Hudson River
School's hegemony:

> Durand was endowed with certain traits which com-
> bined to form a great artist.  He was early smitten
> with the love of nature, his native patience was
> strengthened by the severity of his early struggles,
> and to these was added an indomitable perserverance.
> His love of nature was a passion, an enthusiasm al-
> ways burning within him, but it was like a steady fire,
> not a sudden blaze quickly sinking to ashes.  His
> patience enabled him to guide this intense delight in
> beauty into paths of quiet, steady search for the
> result.  It was touch after touch, line upon line, a
> gradual approach to victory.  Added to this was his
> untiring perseverance, which no difficulties could
> overcome, no obstacles affright, or even cold indif-
> ference discourage.
>
> Though full of nervous energy, alive to every
> beauty, keenly sensitive to criticism, and a severe

critic on his own work, he was yet blessed with a
certain serenity of spirit which checked and soothed
the restless fever of the creative brain; a fever
often so violent in the painter or the poet as to
cause a deep and sometimes fatal reaction and depression. Durand formed a habit of working on and on
cheerily till the coveted prize was gained.[28]

We may, at least, raise the question as to whether the value of
Durand's work does not ultimately reside in its revelation of
the man himself. Huntington's Memorial Address was followed
in 1894 by John Durand's _The Life and Times of A. B. Durand_,
which--written under the influence of Hippolyte A. Taine's
concepts of "race," "environment," and "epoch," and dedicated
to Taine--is just what the title promises and offers no critical estimate. In the following year (1895) a comprehensive
exhibition of Durand's work as an engraver was assembled by
the Grolier Club in New York. At this time Durand's eminence
as an engraver was briefly revivified in Charles Henry Hart's
appreciative preface to the catalogue. Here Hart wrote:

It is by no means disparaging to Mr. Durand to
say that his fame as an engraver overshadows his reputation as a painter, and doubtless will not only so
continue, but will become more accentuated by time
. . . As an engraver Asher Brown Durand is _facile
princeps_ among his countrymen and quite the peer of
any of his European contemporaries; while his most

earnest admirers will not claim this place for him
among the painters of this land.[29]

Not only did Hart praise Durand as an engraver in these terms,
but he also had the perspicacity to observe--not that Durand's
work as an engraver was detrimental to his painting--but that
his skill as a draughtsman underlies his success as an engraver: "And it is because Mr. Durand was such a thorough
artist and such an exceptionally skillful draughtsman, that
he became so eminent an engraver."[30] Perhaps the special
quality of Durand's painting may be traced to the same source,
and to the motives that impelled his diligence as a draughtsman, rather than to the fact of his career as an engraver. In
summary, Huntington's Memorial Address, John Durand's biography,
and the Grolier Club exhibition indicate that Durand and his
work had not yet lost their interest in the last years of the
nineteenth century.

Critics in the first four decades of the twentieth century
almost unanimously ignored the question of emotional values in
Durand's landscapes and, instead, looked at his work as having
had as its principal aim the representation, or the "re-presen-
tation," of nature. But viewed against the background of the
broad representation of the Ash Can School and the even more
extreme forms of abstract representation influenced by Fauvism
and Cubism, Durand's detailed, inclusive realism again appeared
to be a defect. The notion that Durand's paintings are representational, more than expressive, was first stated by Samuel
Isham (1905) who, while acknowledging Durand's sincerity, indi-

viduality, and craftsmanship,[31] believed, quite erroneously,
that his mature work consisted exclusively of uncomposed slices
of nature:

> . . . his study from nature forced a new composition
> on him if that may be called composition which is
> primarily lack of it. His pictures are largely great
> sketches or studies from nature. A fine view, a pretty
> fall in a brook, perhaps only a rock or a great tree,
> is taken in its most favorable aspect and enough of the
> contiguous detail added to fill up the canvas. The
> composition never perfectly fits the frame, and some-
> times it does not fit at all.[32]

Although Isham does note that Durand painted details with
"loving interest" and enthusiasm and that his work emits a
feeling of peace and rest, his fundamental ignorance of the
difference between Durand's outdoor studies and his studio
compositions indicates a lack of any real familiarity with
Durand's work as well as a failure to grasp the trans-representa-
tional aims that distinguish Durand's compositions from the
studies.

Affected by the nationalism and naturalism of the early
twentieth century Charles H. Caffin (1907) identified the Hudson River School as a precursor of these attitudes[33] but
deplored the absence in its products of the pictorial values
which American painters later borrowed from the Barbizon
School.[34] Lacking those qualities of "unity and completeness . . . which are the result of selection, simplification,

and organic arrangement" Caffin described a painting by Durand
as "not so much pictorial as panoramic and topographical. It
represents the ordinary way of looking at a landscape rather
than the artist's way."[35] Again, "it is the engraver's rather
than the painter's feeling which is evident throughout the
canvas."[36] What Caffin condemns is not the fact, but the
manner of representation. Believing that the Hudson River
artists were but inadequate representational painters, Caffin
can, of course, find no emotional values at all in their work:
"We are conscious of no condition of feeling but one of purely
intellectual comprehension; we are pretty well answered what
the scene looks like, but not what it feels like."[37]

By the 1920's Durand's landscapes had become virtually a
matter of indifference. In 1923 Ruel P. Tolman published a
lame article, based largely on John Durand's biography, in
which he summarized Durand's career, noted that the Ariadne
engraving "is considered the most important engraving ever produced in America,"[38] that Durand painted portraits, and that

> Truth and love will be found in his paintings. His
> trees are trees and his rocks are rocks and all his
> landscapes are beautifully arranged, true in color,
> carefully drawn and finished, in fact, pictures to
> live with.[39]

In 1927 Frank Jewett Mather, Jr.[40] wrote of the landscapes with
even less enthusiasm:

> He brought to the new task /of landscape painting/ the
> old microscopic eye of an engraver, spent himself in

minute notations of the textures of bark, grass,
rocks--thus frittering away in details the broad
masses of local color . . . The tenacity of his
patient observation excites admiration without giving
much pleasure.[41]

If, however, Mather found little to give pleasure in Durand's
landscapes, he did recall attention to the quality of his work
in other fields. Thus as a portrait engraver his work for The
National Portrait Gallery is described as "the highest American
achievement in this field."[42] And while his landscape and
genre engravings are noted with respect,[43] it is the Ariadne
that evoked his highest praise:

It is throughout executed with a gentle strength, it
is well unified without sacrifice of the rich darks,
it is atmospheric in the landscape through wise utili-
zation of the preparatory etching, it is broadly modeled
and most gracious in mood. It was a calamity for American line engraving when Durand quit such work as this
for forty years of mediocre landscape painting.[44]

Also, Mather noted that Durand "painted a few portraits of extraordinary power" such as that of James Madison (App. II,
no. 20, cf. Fig. 41) which "yields in vividness to no portrait
of its time."[45] Finally, we may observe that when Durand's
work was exhibited in the 1920's his landscapes were generally
omitted in favor of portraits. An age that sought an optimis-
tically clarified vision of the world, expressive of man's

position of efficient command, simply could not abide a perplexing plethora of detail.

In the 1930's there emerged a new interest in Durand,
generated by the trend in American art toward a more literal
representation of the American scene.  But more generally, it
may be supposed that Durand's mature art, born in a period of
aggravated economic disaster, should make its strongest appeal
in later periods of crisis.  Thus, in an essay on "Asher B.
Durand as a Portrait Painter" (1930), Frederick F. Sherman
followed Mather in treating the three branches of Durand's
art--engraving, portraiture, and landscape, acknowledged Dur-
and's preëminence in the first, but controverted Mather's
estimate of the work in the other two fields.  To Sherman,
Durand, as a portrait painter,

> . . . managed only to achieve a modest success.  As
> likenesses his portraits may be acceptable but their
> execution betrays the uncertain touch of a hand not
> sure of itself.  His coloring though generally right
> in its place fails to give life to his canvases and
> his technique is too constrained, save in exceptional
> instances like the Luman Reed /App. II, no. 56, cf.
> Fig. 47/, where the pigment is applied with a certain
> measure of freedom.[46]

Durand's main achievement, in Sherman's opinion, lay in his landscapes:

> Probably one of the chief reasons for his success in
> landscape had to do with his ability as an engraver,

and is to be noted in the perfection with which he
rendered the detail of tree-forms, bark, leaves and
all the other minutiae of nature . . . It is . . .
to his credit that he did not allow the rendering of
detail to interfere with his expression of the dignity
and grandeur of nature. Because of this fact his landscape achieved a vitality that persists to the present
day in face of entirely antipathetic modes such as
impressionism and expressionism.[47]

In this remarkable statement Sherman has suddenly rediscovered
that the engraver's detail does not necessarily make a mediocre
picture and that, despite the detail, Durand's landscapes are
expressive as well as representational.

In the later 1930's Alan Burroughs (1936) found a revelation
of democratic character in Durand's portraits along with sincerity and rather dashing execution.[48] Three years later Lloyd
Goodrich balanced the vices against the virtues of the Hudson
River School in general at the time of the first major exhibition
of nineteenth century American landscape painting. Still
echoing the belief of critics in the earlier years of the century that the Hudson River painters sought to achieve their
aims through representation, Goodrich laments the particular
mode of representation employed:

Cole and the other members of the Hudson River
School believed that the nobler the subject was, the
nobler the picture would be. In the typical Hudson
River landscape the canvas is enormous, the subject

grandiose, the viewpoint panoramic, embracing every natural feature within range of the eye. Yet so minute is the handling that one can see every leaf. The Hudson River painters were convinced that the best way to express their sincere love of Nature was to copy her literally. In this lay the great fallacy of their art. The grandeur of mountains depends on elements--such as light, scale, and distance--that only the greatest artists have been able to translate into plastic terms. The Hudson River method remained that of photographic representation instead of plastic creation.[49]

Goodrich, of course, does not attempt to demonstrate that an artist might express a "sincere love of Nature" more adequately through an act of "plastic creation." If the larger paintings failed to satisfy Mr. Goodrich, the less ambitious products of the School revealed

> . . . a sincerity, a direct communion with Nature, a love of the leafy exuberance of the wilderness, and an engaging romantic sentiment that keep them alive for us today. Their style has a leisurely and spacious completeness, a sense that, in however a provincial a way, they were trying to follow a great tradition. They remain the true pioneers of American landscape painting, and in the work of their most gifted members, Cole, Durand, and Kensett, they left us many canvases that compare with the best of the American School.[50]

Hence, like Sherman, Goodrich was able to respond emotionally
to at least some of the work of the School.

The rediscovery of the Hudson River School that began in
the 1930's accelerated in the 1940's. Annually, during this
decade landscapes by Durand were included in important exhibitions. The most significant of these, as regards Durand,
were the Century Association's "Exhibition of Paintings by
Asher B. Durand, 1796-1886" (1943) and "The Hudson River School
and the Early American Landscape Tradition" (1945) organized by
the Art Institute of Chicago and the Whitney Museum of American
Art.[51] As the title of the latter exhibition suggests, the
Hudson River School in the 1940's was regarded more from the
historical than the critical point of view. By 1945 the work
of Durand and his contemporaries appeared as an historical
phenomenon to be interpreted rather than a dangerous misdirection
still holding its threat for the painter and the public. The
historical point of view has greatly dominated commentary on
Durand during the past twenty years. While the histories by
Samuel Isham and Charles Caffin satisfied readers for the first
four decades of the twentieth century, since the mid-1940's, an
impressive number of books has been devoted to American Romantic
or to American landscape painting. Also there have been two
scholarly articles devoted to Durand himself. Nearly all
recent writers have focused attention primarily upon Durand's
work as a landscape painter. Within the broad range of historical inquiry different authors have focused upon various
problems, such as Durand's life, his place in the development

of American culture, the connection between his art and that of European painters, the development of his style, and the meaning of his work in the light of his own writings. Other writers have, of course, retained a purely critical approach. As these latter are the least interesting, we may glance briefly at them first.

Among the critics the tendency of the earlier writers to bestow some praise and some blame has given way to a tendency simply to praise or condemn. Virgil Barker (1950)[52] believed that Durand reversed the proper order of things in recommending the study of nature prior to the study of the art of the past, and noted in his landscapes too much detail--the result of his practice of engraving--and too little sensitivity to color.[53] John W. McCoubrey (1963) merely classifies Durand with Thomas Doughty as an artist who "almost invariably compromised with traditional methods of landscape painting"[54]--a statement which, purporting to be fact, surely requires demonstration, which this ingenious writer preferred to withhold. Other critics have been equally single-minded in their praise. Thus, Oliver W. Larkin[55] speaks of Durand's "small but exquisite plates"[56] for The American Landscape, admires a portrait of Andrew Jackson,[57] and stresses the "masterly rendering of out-door light" in the mature landscapes.[58] Further, Durand's work as an engraver affected his painting, but this is no longer regarded as a disadvantage since it resulted in fore-grounds that "were patiently studied and then painted with a truthfulness of detail which would have delighted Ruskin."[59]

Larkin is one of the **very few** to have noted that the minute rendering of detail is limited to the foreground of the landscapes, where many earlier writers had implied that separate leaves were distinguishable in the remote distance. It was only Durand's work as a genre painter that Larkin could not appreciate.[60] Edgar P. Richardson (1956),[61] who has written of Durand on several occasions, approved of his work as an engraver and a genre painter,[62] and shared Larkin's view of the landscapes, which display "a painter's eye for light"[63] and "a fine, precise line and a sense of tone" that are the result of his work as an engraver.[64] Finally, we should note that Richardson offers the very astute comment that Durand's "true gift was for observation. What observation meant to the romantic spirit was, however, poetry."[65] The most recent of the exclusively favorable critics is Daniel M. Mendelowitz (1960), who reiterates the Larkin-Richardson view in discovering the influence of engraving in Durand's "trenchant use of line and the crisp clarity of his detail as well as in the fine sense of tone."[66] To this Mendelowitz added the novel idea that Durand had "no other conscious aim than to convey . . . /nature's/ . . . sensuous beauty."[67]

Among the writers who have addressed themselves specifically to historical problems, one may mention Clara Endicott Sears (1947), who sketched a biography of Durand which was copied almost verbatim from John Durand's _Life and Times of A. B. Durand_ and a few other sources. Her account is original only in its errors, among which is her notion that Durand did

not move to New York until after he had become a well-known
engraver but lived in Hoboken--of all places--all along![68]
Also, as a biographical study, we may note Julian Blanchard's
article on "The Durand Engraving Companies" (1950) in which he
unravels the tangle of commercial firms organized by Durand
and his brothers. Writing on a somewhat more serious plane
are those who have attempted to establish Durand's place in the
history of American culture. To Edgar P. Richardson (1944)
Durand belonged to the "romantic-realist"--a term devised by
Richardson--movement.[69] Thus: "The transparent romantic
realism of Asher B. Durand is filled with a fine objective
sentiment"[70]--a statement that seems to raise more questions
than it answers. Again, concerned with the same problem,
Alexander Eliot (1957), following Caffin's notion of the
nationalistic motive of the Hudson River School, characterizes
the work of Durand and his fellows as the product of "a new
pride in the American wilderness" created by the rise of "Jacksonian democracy."[71] Eliot does not explain what connection
there is between democracy--Jacksonian or any other--as a
political institution and the wilderness. While Jackson did
receive a part of his electoral support from the frontier,
Durand, who never went further West than central New York State,
did not turn to landscape painting until the end of Jackson's
term in office and did not begin to paint truly wilderness subjects until four years after Jackson's death in 1845.

The historians who have attempted to relate Durand's
style of landscape painting to European traditions have offered

a variety of answers. William James Stillman (1901) pio-
neered in this direction when he stated that Durand was "a
painter of real power in a manner quite his own, which borrowed, however, more from the Dutch than from the Italian
feeling, to which Cole inclined."[72]  Similarly, Wolfgang Born
(1948) found that Durand's paintings were reminiscent of
Jacob van Ruisdael,[73] and to him Kindred Spirits (Fig. 201)
recalled the work of the German Romantic, landscape painter
Caspar David Friedrich.[74]  E. P. Richardson (1956) also noted
the influence of the Dutch landscape painters in Durand's The
Old Oak of 1844 (Fig. 184).[75]  This search for sources and
affinities has, however, been carried much further by Frederick
Sweet (1945) and Barbara Novak (1962).  Frederick Sweet,[76] like
nearly everyone else, referred to the influence of Durand's
work as an engraver upon the method and style of his painting.[77]
Considering the fact that Durand's style as an engraver was
based upon English and Continental work in this medium, his
engraving may be regarded as one route of contact between his
painting and European artistic traditions--although Sweet does
not point this out explicitly.  Further, Sweet discovered that
paintings by and after Joseph Vernet and Salvator Rosa were
available to Durand for study in the early years of his
career,[78] although he does not contend that Durand was decisively influenced by them.  Of greater importance, according
to Sweet, were the English topographical lithographs and engravings, reflected in Durand's landscape painting up to the
time of his European tour in 1840-1841.[79]  In the work of the

next decade, Sweet, like Durand's contemporaries, discerned
the influence of Claude Lorrain, whose landscapes Durand
studied while abroad.[80] Finally, Sweet believed that after
about 1850 Durand cast off "the traditional Baroque formula
. . . in favor of a completely direct and realistic treatment."[81] As an afterthought, Sweet refers to an affinity between Durand's landscapes and the German Romantic landscapes
of shortly after 1800, but believed that "there was no possible
contact between" the two schools.[82] We shall, however, have
occasion to note what may have been a decisive encounter between Durand and later representatives of the German school at
the moment when he shifted to his later, "realistic" style.
Barbara Novak[83] has followed Sweet in recognizing the influence
of Claude on Durand's landscapes of the 1840's,[84] and she has
taken a step further by pointing to an affinity between certain
of Durand's outdoor studies of the 1850's and a landscape by
Courbet of the 1860's.[85] She does not, however, attempt to
trace any common source to account for this affinity. Beyond
these observations she attempts to relate two of Durand's
painted studies of the mid-1850's (Figs. 175 and 176) to the
work of Rubens which Durand had studied some fifteen years
earlier. More particularly, Miss Novak wishes to see a connection between the apparent freedom and spontaneity of these
studies and the oil sketches of Rubens.[86] Yet she is unable
to show that Durand, who did admire Rubens' highly finished
paintings, ever saw any of his oil sketches. Further, there
is no real need to look for the influence of Rubens in these

atypical studies when Durand was thoroughly familiar with the oil sketches of Thomas Cole, one of which he owned.[87] In the absense of any large and pervasive influence of Rubens on the work of Durand we may suppose that James Flexner was correct when he wrote that Rubens' "free and impulsive manner . . . was . . . far from his /Durand's7 own temperamental possibilities."[88]

Durand's stylistic development as a landscape painter has been explored with any degree of system only by Frederick Sweet (1945), who saw four major phases to Durand's style:

1. Before 1840 there is tightness, lack of robust color in general, and minute painting in the foreground. The yellow-green and golden brown of this period were borrowed from Thomas Cole.

2. In the 1840's "a more diffused light effect and better integrated color" appear. "The hardness of the engraver's technique" is replaced by a more solid and rich mode of painting. In the studio compositions of this period, natural scenes are suffused with a golden, glowing, atmospheric effect.

3. In the 1850's Durand's style becomes more "realistic" under the influence of his studies painted out-of-doors. "The yellow-green tonality gives way to rich blue-greens." The fussy inclusiveness of some of his earlier work gives way to clarity and selection. In this period the distance between

views or studies and studio compositions, which
in the earlier work had been notable, is diminished.

4. In the 1860's "his work tends to become hard and
very matter-of-fact."[89]

By and large, Sweet turned his first-hand knowledge of the paintings to good account and produced a very acceptable stylistic
summary.

There remains now only to look at the two writers who have
attempted to interpret Durand's landscapes in terms of his own
writing on the art. While Oliver Larkin quoted from Durand's
Letters on Landscape Painting to support his approbation, and
Virgil Barker did likewise to support his condemnation of Dur-
and's landscapes, only Barbara Novak (1962) and James Flexner
(1962) turned to the Letters objectively to discover what Dur-
and really thought. Miss Novak was primarily interested in
Durand's comments on light, color, and atmosphere and plucked
a few of these out of context in order to suggest that Durand's
theories anticipate those of the French Impressionists.[90]
Flexner has made more extensive use of the Letters. Flexner
notes Durand's objections to history-landscapes, his preference
for unadorned scenery, that bespeaks the glory of God rather
than man,[91] his demand that figures in a landscape should enhance but not supplant the significance of nature,[92] his distrust of color,[93] his insistence upon the superior beauty of
nature as compared with art,[94] his advice regarding the effect
of hue and value upon the expression of space,[95] and Durand's

belief that atmosphere carries the spectator into the picture.[96] As long as Flexner cites Durand's comments on mainly technical questions, he is on firm ground; but when he comes to the larger issues of Durand's Letters, he is vague and inaccurate. We are informed that the ideas expressed in the Letters "had backgrounds in European esthetic theory, and in the less formal aspects of American religious thought."[97] But we are left wondering what esthetic theory or what religious thought. In speaking of the significance that nature held for Durand, Flexner notes that the painter regarded natural phenomena as "'types of divine attributes.'"[98] But, he offers no suggestions as to which phenomena typified which of the attributes of God.[99] Again, trying to get at Durand's view of the religious significance of nature, Flexner states: "Nature, he /Durand/ wrote, 'in its wondrous structure and function that minister to our well-being is fraught with high and holy meaning, only surpassed by the light of Revelation.'"[100] But Flexner offers no clue as to the meaning of even the structure and functions. In speaking of the proper effect of a landscape painting upon the spectator, Flexner cites Durand's view that a painted landscape ought to evoke "'the same feelings and emotions which we experience in the presence of reality.'"[101] And in defining the emotions that the paintings do convey, Flexner speaks of "a sense of worship, as grave as religion and as grateful as a happy heart."[102] Now, is it possible that in his experience of the varied scenes of nature Durand felt only this? And, if he felt nothing more, how can we account for the existence of

at least three distinct types of landscape images among his
mature, studio compositions? How could Durand have expected
to convey the same emotion through mutually exclusive types
of visual images? Further, with respect to the proper appreciation of a painting, Flexner ascribes to Durand the belief that
a painting of nature, "instinct with divinity created a visual
sermon which would elevate all who examined it."[103]

Flexner attempts, also, a summary of Durand's comments on
imitation, interpretation, expression, and the ideal. Durand
did not believe that anything beyond the foreground could be
imitated in minute detail and must therefore be "summarized as
realistically as possible."[104] Furthermore, a painting should
provide an interpretation rather than a "photographic reproduction" of nature.[105] And the painter should select those
phenomena which most strongly excite his emotions in order
that the picture may carry "man closer to the divine."[106] But
also, the painter should select in order to produce perfect
tree forms. This latter act of selection, however, was not
like that of the Neo-classicists; for while they used their
"reasoning power to 'abstract' away" evil, Durand "regarded
what appeared to be evil as a superficial misconception and
distortion of creation's underlying goodness."[107] However, if
for Durand evil did not really exist somewhere, how could the
"superficial misconception" arise? Perhaps what Flexner is
trying to say, or ought to be trying to say, is that, where to
the Neo-classicist evil resided in the world, to Durand, and
the Romanticists generally, evil resided in man. But, still,

we have no answer to the most perplexing question of why the
artist should seek to create the perfect tree when his belief
that any tree is imprefect is but a "superficial misconception." Flexner answers this question by stating that for Dur-
and "selection meant in effect intuitive synthesis which revealed all characteristic forms in the high and noble manifestations which he believed were inherent in whatever was real."[108]
Is Flexner here talking about the act of selection that produced
the imperfect or the perfect trees which Durand painted?

In general, Flexner is most successful in summarizing that
portion of the _Letters_ that offers hints to young artists. The
value of his effort to treat the more subtle issues is vitiated
by both his failure to relate Durand's ideas to the broader
currents of early nineteenth century thought and to particular
paintings. Yet, no matter how unsuccessful Flexner's discussion
of Durand's theological, philosophical, and aesthetic views,
he deserves great credit as the first to have attempted a serious
discussion of these questions. If his answers are inadequate,
it is mainly because adequate ones could not be obtained within
the limits Flexner set for himself. It is to be hoped that
Flexner's treatment of "the esthetic of the Hudson River School"
will eventually be regarded more as the first than the last
word on the subject.

IV. The Problems That Remain.

Where do we stand now in the study of Durand? What remains to be done? The criticism of the first four decades of the twentieth century amply indicates that Durand like other members of the Hudson River School, in the words of S. G. W. Benjamin, "seldom arrested and enchained attention by the expression of daring technique or imaginative power, as the outcome of concerted influences exerted in one direction, . . . bounding into the arena and challenging the admiration of the world."[109] But perhaps it is not universally in the nature of art to be thus blatantly self-advertising. Perhaps it is not even universally in the nature of art to appeal to all men in every epoch. The fact that Durand's reputation has survived and excited criticism through the past century would suggest that something valid lurks within his engravings and paintings and character even though it has not always been immediately evident.

If we take up the study of his work again, we should do so in the character of the historian of art and of the theory of art. We should approach Durand as an artist of his times, we should approach his art as the art of his times, primarily in order to discover what sort of an artist and what sort of art those rude and treacherous times could produce. That is, we should try to advance the historical investigation that was initiated in the mid-1940's. With the historians of the past twenty years we should both take cognizance of Durand's work

as an engraver, portrait, and genre painter for the light that
this throws upon the development of his ideas, and recognize
his major achievement in his work as a landscape painter. Indeed, it is largely due to the obscurity of the connection
between Durand's landscape paintings and the ideas expressed
in his Letters on Landscape Painting that further study both
of his art and of the ideas by which it was governed seems
worthwhile.

Any effort to illuminate the connection between the Letters
and the landscapes is rendered difficult by the sentimentalism
of the former and the familiar look of the latter. If the
Letters are read apart from the religious and aesthetic ideas
of Durand's time, they are virtually meaningless. If the paintings are studied apart from an enlightened reading of the Letters,
they reduce themselves to so many, cluttered pictures evoking
forgotten places. If we acknowledge these difficulties, we
must come to recognize in the sentiment of the Letters and in
the familiar look of the paintings a kind of code used at once
to obscure and to reveal the artist's meanings and purposes.
When American painters realized in the 1820's that they could
not attract the attention of their contemporaries to the large
issues of morality and religion through epic and Biblical
history paintings, they sought a new language that would be
more palatable to the spectator, as an earlier generation had
used logic and a classical ordination of form to enforce its
highest insights. The need to sugar-coat the pill of civilization is one reason for the veil of sentiment and the familiar

that Durand threw over his writing and painting. The other reason consists in the fact that the moral and religious truths he sought to present were not generally acknowledged even by the more intelligent portion of the populace. To disguise the sectarian character of his aims, Durand used sentiment and familiarity as an esoteric symbolism had been used in an earlier period. In pursuit of a generally acceptable, new language Durand advanced through the several phases of his career--reproductive engraver, portrait, genre, and landscape painter--until in the 1840's and 1850's he spoke the dominant idiom of the Hudson River School. But a language, no matter how esoteric, must be so co-ordinated with the content it is to express that the content will be clearly apparent once the vocabulary and syntax of the language have been deciphered. Perhaps the best kind of visual language is that which works its proper effect upon the common spectator even though he does not experience its full effect.

In order to gain an intellectual comprehension of the meanings and feelings that Durand sought to express we must recover something of the moral, theological, and aesthetic realities of his intellectual environment. The affinity frequently cited by the older, as well as the more recent, writers between Durand's paintings and the poetry of William Cullen Bryant offers the main clue to the recovery of Durand's ethical, theological, and aesthetic beliefs. Starting from Bryant, we are lead to the Unitarianism of Channing, the aesthetics of Archibald Alison, and the Stoicism of Seneca.

Through a study of these authors we may, I believe, come into contact with the main content that lies behind the facade of Durand's sentiment and familiarity. Of course, there were other writers and artists--among the artists Thomas Cole is of primary importance--who helped to shape Durand's mature thought and work. Our principal task will be to see how far the significance of Durand's art is enhanced when it is studied in connection with the work of his contemporaries and the minds of the past with which there is reason to believe he had contact.

To develop a more complete understanding of Durand's art there are other problems that we must consider. To what degree was the style of his work affected by the pictorial traditions that happened to be fashionable or current? From what sources did he derive his ideas of what a work of art per se ought to be? How was his art affected by events in his personal life and the economic and political struggles of the nation? And how did Durand conceive of the function of a work of art apart from its capacity to communicate ideas and express emotions? What relationships exist between Durand's drawings and painted studies from nature and his studio compositions? These and other questions must receive our attention as we proceed. We should, quite frankly, shift our ground from cultural to bio-graphical to iconographical to iconological to stylistic prob-lems whenever by posing a different type of question we may hope to obtain the more interesting answer. If we are to obtain a well-rounded conception of Durand's art as a whole, we cannot limit ourselves to any single and exclusive line of enquiry.

In the body of the present study I have not provided either a regular biography or a chronological analysis of Durand's work as a whole. Rather I have attempted to isolate segments of Durand's career or clusters of mutually related works or ideas and to discuss the problems which they seem to pose. Thus in Chapter One I describe briefly the state of New York culture in the 1810's, review Durand's general education, and treat his training and early work as an engraver and painter. Special emphasis is placed upon those engravings and paintings in which he sought to express ideas which he had made his own. The main objective of this chapter is to map out the broad range of artistic, social, and religious factors that made up, as it were, the foundations of Durand's mind and art; hence the several topics discussed are related more to the man than to one another. Chapter Two deals with the second major segment of Durand's career--the period from 1830 to 1837--a period during which he attained notable success in his explorations of the fields of portraiture, the ideal figure, and genre in both engravings and paintings. This chapter is devoted mainly to the interpretation of the works belonging to a number of different types of picture. In these works we may observe Durand's wide search for a new language in which to express adequately the new ideas which he encountered in his transition from Neo-classicism to Romanticism. In Chapter Three we turn to a consideration of the ideas that made up the

basis of the Romanticism of Durand's work as a landscape
painter. The idea of recreation, the associational aesthetics
of Alison, and a mood of revery dominated Durand's landscapes
from 1837 to around 1847 but continued to affect his later
work as well. It is also in Durand's work from the late 1830's
that we find the first traces of a distinctly Stoic point of
view.

The first three chapters, then, trace the genesis and
development of Durand's art. The last four chapters deal with
his work as a mature landscape painter in the years after 1847.
Each of these chapters treat, not a segment of Durand's career,
but a single, large problem posed by his mature art. In Chapter
Four I have tried to describe and account for Durand's fascination with and study of nature. In Chapter Five I have attempted
to reconstruct the manner in which Durand might have intended
that the spectator experience the space of his paintings.
Chapter Six treats of the emotional qualities--how they may
get into the painting and how they may affect the spectator.
And Chapter Seven is an even more perilous search for theological symbolism in what appear to be realistic transcripts of
familiar nature.

In general, I have conceived of the present study somewhat
as a series of essays, each treating what appeared to be a
separate aspect of Durand's art or a discrete set of ideas
connected with his art. Were a study of Durand to be cast as
an examination of his ideas of God, Man, or Nature, it might
be written more briefly, with a greater degree of unity, and

less apparent repetition. But such an approach could lead only to a definition of Durand's views on questions to which he provides no really original answers. And, should we study Durand's philosophical ideas, as revealed in his work, for themselves, it is likely that we should lose sight of his art in the process. The character and value of Durand's art, I believe, transcends the character and value of his ideas. What mainly interests us is his art, and it is only worth while to study his ideas, insofar as such a study contributes to an understanding of his art. For example, the idea that a rural scene may excite memories of childhood is of little interest in comparison with the fact that certain of Durand's paintings were contrived so as to excite these memories. Hence, I have treated landscapes evoking childhood under one heading, while other aspects of Alison's associational aesthetic are introduced into the discussion of other phases of Durand's art. The reader, then, will repeatedly encounter ideas maintained by Alison and Bryant and Seneca as well as the problems of the relationships between God, Man, and Nature whenever these may be made to illustrate a different part of Durand's art or the theory by which that part was governed. While the type of analytic study I propose may necessarily entail a degree of apparent reiteration, I think that this approach will carry us closer to the significance of Durand's art than would a more synthetic and exclusive study governed by broader concepts more remote from the phenomena of the works of art themselves.

To the body of this study I have appended (I) an Itinerary of Durand's travels, (II) a Catalogue of Paintings, Other Than Oil Studies from Nature, (III) a Catalogue of Oil Studies from Nature, (IV) a Catalogue of Drawings, (V) and a list of the Portraits of Asher B. Durand, Other Than Self-Portraits, that have come to my attention.

As a warning to the reader, I should like to express my feeling that, if we are ever to discover the deeper significance of the American art of the three decades preceding the Civil War, we must adopt something of the attitude recommended by Nathaniel Hawthorne:

> A picture, however admirable the painter's art, and wonderful his power, requires of the spectator a surrender of himself, in due proportion with the miracle which has been wrought. Let the canvas glow as it may, you must look with the eye of faith, or its highest excellence escapes you. There is always the necessity of helping our resources of sensibility and imagination. Not that these qualities shall really add anything to what the master has effected; but they must be put so entirely under his control, and work along with him to such an extent, that in a different mood, when you are cold and critical, instead of sympathetic, you will be apt to fancy that the loftier merits of the picture were of your own dreaming, not of his creating.[110]

To this we need add that the cold and critical intellect may
not be so necessarily opposed to the eye of faith as Hawthorne
supposed. What a painting is--that is, how its component means
contribute to a particular end--can, probably, be grasped only
by an imaginative synthesis of all the relevant subordinate
elements that relegates each component to its proper level and
that recognizes the contribution of each to a single end. Yet
the analytic faculties serve a legitimate function when they
stabilize the ultimate illumination by differentiating and
defining the component means and the end of a painting and when
they redefine each when in the works of a later time its value
has shifted. It is to this analytic endeavor that we must
bring all of the relevant documentation at our disposal in order
to establish definitions that will yield more to the pressure
of additional evidence than to the predisposition of new spectators.

Finally, we should pause a moment over the problems posed
by the terms "Neo-classic," "Romantic," and "Realist." To my
knowledge each of these, as yet, lacks the widely agreed-upon
and precise meaning of such terms as "Impressionism" or
"Cubism." Historians of English literature designate as Neo-
classical the period of Alexander Pope that falls immediately
before the period to which some art historians apply the same
term. While the art historian Fritz Novotny distinguishes
sharply between "Classicism," beginning in the mid-eighteenth
century, and "Romanticism," beginning in the early nineteenth
century,[111] another art historian, H. W. Janson, finds that

"Neoclassicism . . . is no more than an aspect of Romanticism."[112] The multiple, and frequently contradictory meanings attached to the terms "Romanticism" or "Romantic" have so frequently been discussed that there is no need to review the discussion here.[113] In the search for a more precise vocabulary some art historians have resorted to the use of such composite terms as "Romantic-Classicism,"[114] "Classical-Idealism," "Romantic-Idealism," "Romantic-Realism," and "Objective-Realism,"[115] which may prove useful in the description of individual works of art, but are too specifically phenomenological in their reference to denote the style of particular periods.

In the present study I shall use the term "Neo-classic" to designate an art that is largely controlled by intellectual or "academic" rules. The term "Romantic" will be used when subjective feelings and/or trains of associations are the controlling factors. And the term "Realistic" will be employed when, in a painting, a multitude of present or probable natural phenomena are described as co-existing in harmony with one another. The term "classic" I reserve for works in which there is an evident effort to reconcile seemingly contradictory realities, such as vitality and repose, the "one" and the "many," or the Sublime and the Beautiful. Thus, in broad terms, Durand moves from Neo-classicism to Romanticism to Realism, but throughout his work a classic urge is discernible, which becomes most evident in the later and least Neo-classic landscapes of what I term the "composite" type.

If, however, we apply the terms Neo-classic, Romantic, and Realist to paintings in which the qualities of logic, feeling, and nature, respectively, are uppermost, we still lack terms of sufficient breadth to fully define the unique identity of the art of the periods 1760 to 1800, 1800 to 1848, and 1848 to 1870. Some paintings by Benjamin West evoke as much emotion and by similar means as certain paintings by Delacroix, and the work of each would need to be termed Romantic despite their having worked in different periods and under very different circumstances. Again, Constable's concern with the intellectually apprehended order of nature would make his art Neo-classical, while his evident concern with the description of particular, natural scenes would make him a Realist like Courbet. I do not believe that a Neo-classic, a Romantic, or a Realist movement can be identified on the basis of internal evidence alone. Thematically, morphologically, and structurally, the art of 1760 to 1800 all too often overlaps that of the period 1800 to 1848. And the continuity of certain interests and of the use of particular devices is what we should expect in the art of neighboring countries during a limited period of time. While we may be able to distinguish the art of places or epochs distantly separated in space or time on a purely phenomenological basis, when we are dealing with contiguous cultures, resort must be made to more external criteria; namely, to the question of the functions or human ends which the art of each culture was contrived to serve. Now, when we add to the study of themes, morphology, and structure the

study of the functions of a type of art, we are immediately
faced with a multitude of difficult problems which can only
be solved by reference to both the crises in the public and
personal affairs of the period and to the period's speculation
on the means that the artist may employ to meet these crises.
Such a study of the function of art would, of course, end in
the demonstration that particular works of art were, in fact,
informed by certain theories and addressed to the needs of an
unique age and condition of humanity. Despite its difficulty,
a study of this sort, if successful, would permit one to define
more fully the character of the art of a culture; and, of
greater importance, it would reveal more clearly the human
relevance, the humanistic values, of the art itself. It is an
elucidation of these that is too often lacking in the best
studies of both iconography and style narrowly conceived as
visual structure alone. The present study is primarily an
attempt to define the human purposes or needs which the style
and iconography of an individual artist's work are fitted to
serve. Only after the function of the art of other painters
active between 1760 and 1870 has been more adequately defined
will we begin, perhaps, to see Neo-classicism, Romanticism,
and Realism as discrete artistic movements to which intellect,
emotion, and nature are not, after all, central.

CHAPTER ONE.  DURAND'S EDUCATION AND EARLY WORK AS AN ENGRAVER
AND PAINTER.

I.  The Development of New York City as a Center of Wealth
and Culture.

At the close of the War of 1812 New York City displayed
few signs of its future prosperity.[1]  Having been occupied by
the British and largely burned in 1776, the city remained under
British military rule throughout the Revolution, and its population amounted to less than twenty-five thousand in 1783.[2]
As the seat of American government in 1789 and 1790 it had
enjoyed a period of limited growth which the conservatism of
its great landholders and their war with Jefferson's Democrats
had done little to augment.  Yet, despite the recurring epi-
demics of yellow feaver--1797, 1798, 1801, and 1803--the city
did expand in size until by 1807 it embraced some sixty thousand
persons.  During the years following the Revolution, the city
witnessed a rapid growth of trade, manufacturing, and population.  Steam navigation was introduced on the Hudson.  Two
decades before his death in a duel with his rival Aaron Burr,
Alexander Hamilton had drawn up the constitution of the Bank
of New York, the city's first such institution.  Newspapers
sprang up, until by 1807 there were nineteen.  The old King's
College, now Columbia University, provided higher education,
while the Society for Establishing a Free School organized

45

grammar schools. Institutions fostering a broader culture
included the New York Academy of Fine Arts, organized in 1801,[3]
and the New-York Historical Society (1804).[4]  Then in 1804,
what had seemed to be the dawn of a great maritime and commercial power faded when Jefferson's Embargo Act and the subsequent
war with England destroyed the trade upon which New York's
prosperity must depend.

The conclusion of hostilities in 1814 meant to New Yorkers,
as to Americans generally, the release from a seven-year submission to suffering, loss, and boredom.  Now the frustrations
of the past might be forgotten.  Ambition and energy again
turned to the calculations and the constructiveness that nourish
all phases of commerce, of theology and science, as well as
literature and the fine arts.  By 1823 the number of banks had
increased to thirteen.  In 1815 a committee undertook to lay
plans for the construction of a canal to connect the Great Lakes
with the harbor of New York, and the actual digging was begun
at Rome, New York on July 4, 1817.[5]  In 1819, having been refused
the use of any pulpit in the city, William Ellery Channing
introduced Unitarian Christianity to New Yorkers in a hall at
the Medical College, and the "Unitarian" First Congregational
Church (All Soul's) was organized.[6]  Scientific research
received new impetus in the post-war years from DeWitt Clinton,
Dr. Samuel L. Mitchell--who organized the Lyceum of Natural
History in 1817--Amos Eaton's popular lectures on a wide
variety of scientific topics, the botanical studies of Frederick
Pursh--who assisted Dr. David Hosack in the operation of the

latter's Elgin Botanic Garden (founded in 1801)--and William
Maclure's field work in geology.[7]  In literature, the work
of the older New York writers, Washington Irving (1783-1859)
and James K. Paulding (1778-1860),was supplemented by the
efforts of an enthusiastic group of younger men--Fitz-Greene
Halleck (1790-1867), Joseph Rodman Drake (1795-1820), Robert
Charles Sands (1799-1832), and McDonald Clarke (1798-1842) --
all of whom were at work in New York before James Fenimore
Cooper (1789-1851) published his first novel, Precaution, in
1820.  Again, the return of peace and visions of prosperity
set the stage for a new and now more vigorous effort to promote
an interest in the fine arts.  In October of 1816 DeWitt
Clinton and Cadwallader D. Colden, at that time deeply engrossed
in creating the Erie Canal, along with Dr. David Hosack,
John R. Murry, Charles Wilkes, and William Cutting revivified
the several-years-dormant American Academy of Fine Arts.  On
the twenty-third of that month Governor Clinton delivered what
Thomas S. Cummings described as "probably the first address
delivered before any academy of arts in the United States,"[8]
and two days later the first exhibition of the Academy was
opened.  After his discourse, Clinton resigned as President
in favor of John Trumbull (1756-1843), who had returned from
England earlier that same year.  But Trumbull was not the only
professional artist seeking patronage in New York between 1815
and 1820.  John Vanderlyn (1775-1852) had settled there after
his return from France in 1815, William Dunlap (1766-1839) was
painting portraits and religious subjects, while Charles C.

Ingham (1796-1863), recently arrived from Ireland, John W. Jarvis (1812-1868), Samuel L. Waldo (1783-1861), and William Jewett (1789/90-1874) were producing portraits of distinction. Although the Federal Government had removed from New York in 1790, by 1820 the city was well on the road to becoming the young Republic's principal center of trade and could begin to compete with Boston and Philadelphia as a center of intellect and culture.

## II. The Emergence of Asher B. Durand.

New York's flourishing economy in the post-war years must
have been among the factors that induced the engraver Peter
Maverick (1780-1831), then residing with his large family on
a farm near Newark, to send his young partner Asher B. Durand
to open the office of "Mess? P. Maverick-Durand Engravers"[9]
at the corner of Pine Street and Broadway in October, 1817.[10]
An ambitious, yet sensitive, young man, just turned twenty-one,
with a decided taste for art, poetry, and the beauty of nature,
Asher Durand did not come to New York totally unprepared to
participate in the larger sphere of activity that the city
afforded. Although his formal education had not extended beyond five or six years of intermittent attendance at a village
grammar school, during his five-year apprenticeship[11] to the
relatively cultured Peter Maverick and as a member of the
Bloomfield Forum he was able to extend the range of his ideas.
Something of the character of the Bloomfield Forum, a young
men's debating society, may be ascertained from letters written
to Durand by one of his New Jersey friends, James Gibbs, Jr.,
after Durand's move to New York.

> Our debating society still continues but the members
> feel the want of you. They however are not so much
> in the Spirit of it as formerly; rather too dull.
> This much I can say (and that is considerable) that
> the toung /sic/ of calumny is bridled for we here
> /sic/ no stories respecting Universalism, Atheism,

Armenians, and a catalogue of professions to /sic7
numerous here to innumerate /sic7 and too superfluous
for you or I to listen to.[12]

And on November 30 he informed Durand of a more recent intellectual effort in Bloomfield:

The Bloomfield _Forum_ discussed a very important topic
last evening (Saturday) which was "are the intellectual
faculties of women as strong as those of men"--I sir
had the pleasure to advocate the cause of the fairest
part of creation.[13]

But Durand's move to New York did not end his extra-business
interests. He found time to write verses and to read poetry--
particularly that by Thomson and Goldsmith.[14] And as he engraved
portraits or illustrations for American editions of Byron,
Scott, Shakespeare, Young, Cowper, Akenside, Milton, Beattie,
and Campbell,[15] he was aware of the work of other poets as
well. Further, in New York he was able to find new sources of
intellectual stimulation. By 1821 the forgotten, Byronic poet
and dietary reformer Sylvester Graham (1794-1851) had secured
Durand's election as an honorary member of a Newark debating
society, which was probably somewhat more sophisticated than
that in Bloomfield.[16] Somewhat later he became a member of
Cooper's "The Lunch" or "Bread-and-Cheese Club." At the meetings
of "The Lunch" he came into social contact with the foremost
lawyers, educators, poets, and painters in the city.[17] When
the Sketch Club, the ancestor of the Century Association, was
organized in 1829, Durand was among its founding members.[18] The

membership of the Sketch Club included the younger artists
Henry Inman (1801-1846), Thomas Cole (1801-1848), Robert W.
Weir (1803-1889), Thomas S. Cummings (1823-1859), and George
W. Hatch (1805-1867) and writers Robert C. Sands, Gulian
Verplanck (1786-1870), and William C. Bryant who produced the
first volume of the <u>Talisman</u>, a gift book, in 1828. Although
drawings were sometimes executed at meetings, the club's main
purpose was the "encouragement of social and friendly feelings
among the members."[19] In this, it must have been eminently
successful, since its membership, which by 1844 included a
good number of amateurs, continued to meet until 1869.[20]

Still, the new and varied interests of Durand's early
years in New York did not supplant his love of nature. The
meadows on the New Jersey side of the Hudson were accessible
and constituted a pleasant retreat from the filth and noise of
the city. That Durand availed himself of these advantages as
early as 1819 is indicated by a letter from James Gibbs dated
July 28 of that year:

> You inform me in your last . . . of your rambles at
> Hoboken. The various scenes of nature 'in her frowning
> and smiling aspect rocks and precipices--groves and
> fields arranged in all the verdant glories of exhila-
> rating summer.' pleasing scenes for the contemplative
> mind--and lastly you saw lovely women--those whom
> nature need not be asshamed /sic/ of--yes their /sic/
> are those whom nature need not be asshamed /sic/

off /sic/--but nature exhibits herself in smiling as
well as frowning aspects.[21]

The varied phenomena of nature must have more strongly affected
Durand's mind and feelings than any other single area of his
experience. From the forms, light, colors, and atmosphere of
nature he could derive a wide variety of ideas. A person of
Durand's native bashfulness could experience nature more intimately than human society; and, alone in nature or with a
chosen companion, he might give freer rein to his feelings than
he would have dared among the tradesmen of the city. Also,
because he lacked a sound humanistic education, the realm of
human personality, passion, and action must have remained
largely a mystery to him. His experience of nature, however,
he could understand in the light of the popular eighteenth
century, rural and nature poetry that was readily accessible.
By illuminating a large area of Durand's experience this poetry
must have induced him to attach especial importance to that
experience. Eventually, poetry descriptive of nature came to
serve as the model upon which he was able to articulate his
own experience of nature--at first in odes to South Orange and
Springfield, New Jersey, villages near the place of his birth.
Later, when he first attempted to express his experience of
nature in visual terms, James Thomson's Seasons inspired his
Musidora (Fig. 10), which combines the "smiling" aspects of
nature and the female figure--a lovely form rather than a
vessel of passion like Delacroix's Medea[22]--such as he must

have described in the letter which elicited the response from James Gibbes cited above.[23]

Gradually, through the study of literature, attendance at the theatre, participation in debates, conversation with intelligent men, and the experience of nature, Durand was able to compensate for his lack of formal education and to preserve his somewhat whimsical spirit amid the demands of a business career.

As he came to New York with some ideas on current issues and a desire to learn more, so, also, he arrived with considerable skill in engraving. As a boy he had been able to learn something of engraving in the workshop of his mechanically-inclined father. In an autobiographical fragment, Durand wrote of his childhood discovery of engraving:

My father and my two elder brothers were accustomed to engrave monograms and other devices on the various articles manufactured by them, and in this art I was early initiated. But I was not content with this, having shown some skill in drawing animals as well as the human figure, excited to do so by my admiration for the woodcuts in school books, and by the copper-plate engravings that fell in my way . . . On examining these with a strong magnifier, I could not refrain from trying to imitate their, to me, wonderful mechanism. Never shall I forget the joy I experienced on finding, after a few trials, that my efforts were, in a degree, successful. In these attempts I was not only obliged to make my own tools, but I had also to invent them, there being no one at hand to instruct me.[24]

Such talents as evinced in this work did not long remain unrecognized by those visitors to his father's shop who had taken upon themselves the burden of artistic taste. One gentleman, Enos Smith, an amateur miniature painter, took Asher to New York in 1811 in an effort to secure his apprenticeship to the engraver William S. Leney. But Leney's conditions--a thousand dollars plus expenses--were beyond the elder Durand's means. In the next year, however, Mr. Smith was able to place Durand with Peter Maverick, so that his five-year apprenticeship began in October, 1812.[25] During these years Durand learned more from the exercise of techniques already mastered and from the engravings which he copied[26] than from his master. The autobiographical fragment ends with a summary of his progress as an apprentice: "My progress was rapid. I soon surpassed my shopmates, and became the chief assistant of my master."[27] Immediately upon the termination of his apprenticeship, Durand became the sole partner of his former master.

Slight as the training received during his apprenticeship may have been, it was sufficient to secure to the firm of Maverick and Durand a large share of the New York engraving business during the three years of the partnership. Trade cards--"Theodore Clark Hat Maker" (S. 1008, Fig. 2),[28] "Thomas Ash Chair Manufacturer" (S. 1002), "John Johnson & Sons Hat Makers" (S. 1017), "West Point Foundry and Boring Mill" (S. 1039)--certificates--"New York Typographical Society"

(S. 913)--bank notes--for the Missouri Exchange Bank (S. 1231),
St. Louis Land Office (S. 1241), Jersey Bank (S. 1273), Sussex
/New Jersey7 Bank (S. 1375), and the Eagle Bank /Providence,
Rhode Island7 (S. 1586)--and, toward the end of the partnership,
an increasing number of book illustrations for American
publishers made up the large part of Durand's work while the
partner of Maverick. In copying the engraved illustrations in
English books for local publishers, Durand must have found
stimulation to explore the more elaborate forms of pictorial
engraving, upon which his reputation as an engraver primarily
rests. Of the partners it was Durand who executed most of the
literary illustrations. And it was from the study of English
engravings which he copied, as well as the larger, imported
engravings available in New York, that he acquired the technique
needed to do original, reproductive work.[29] It was this experience that led him to attempt, probably in 1819, an engraved
translation of Samuel Waldo's painting entitled Old Pat or A
Beggar with a Bone (Fig. 3), and Durand's success brought his
abilities to the attention of John Trumbull.[30]

III. Uncommissioned Engravings.

The engraving after Old Pat is the first clear sign of
Durand's will to transcend the limitations of engraving as a
mere craft or trade, catering to the demands of the business
world. Hitherto he had merely supplied the existing needs of
the community. Now he sought to create new needs by bringing
something novel and unsolicited into the world. The Old Pat
was merely the first of several projects for which Durand sought
the support of the public only after the work was accomplished.
Durand's next "original" engraving stands somewhere between a
commissioned and an uncommissioned work. Since 1818 John Trumbull had been seeking patronage for a folio engraving after
his Declaration of Independence (Fig. 4).[31] While the lack of
such an engraving might never be felt by the public, possibly a
certain number of people could be made to feel a need for the
work before its execution. By 1820 Trumbull had received sufficient encouragement that, impressed with Durand's Old Pat,
he offered him the commission at half the price--six thousand
dollars--demanded by the English engraver James Heath. When
Durand accepted the project without consulting Maverick, who
by agreement was to have first choice of all work offered to
the firm, the partnership was dissolved.[32]

Free at last to direct his own affairs, Durand was able
to undertake other engraving ventures of a speculative character.
At the time he received the commission from Trumbull, Durand was

already at work on a series of portraits of popular clergymen.
This venture he later described as

> the most humiliating work I ever did. I used to get
> them up in conjunction with the painter. The general
> public would not buy them, so we had to appeal to the
> ministers and the congregations; and hawking them about
> in this way, by personal appeals, I barely made a
> living by engraving them.[33]

If in the foregoing Durand intended to specify one painter, it
was probably Samuel L. Waldo. Durand's engraving after a portrait of James Milnor (Fig. 5) by Waldo and Waldo's partner in
painting, Jewett, is dated 1819 and bears the firm name
"P. Maverick. Durand & Co." Later portraits of clergymen
after paintings by Waldo and Jewett, signed by Durand alone,
include the Alexander McLeod, J. M. Matthews, Philip Milledoler,
J. B. Romeyn (Fig. 6, published in 1820), and John Summerfield
(published by Waldo, copyright December, 1822). The engravings
of Milner, Matthews, Milledoler, McLeod, and Romeyne were exhibited by Durand at the American Academy of Fine Arts in 1820,
the first year in which he exhibited at that institution.

If we are correct in supposing that it was Waldo with
whom Durand collaborated in producing these clerical portraits,
that painter assumes a rather more important role in Durand's
career than has hitherto been recognized. Waldo may have encouraged Durand to attempt original reproductive engraving and
suggested that he copy the Old Pat as an experiment. Once this

plate had been successfully completed, perhaps in the winter
of 1818-19, Waldo may have induced Durand to attempt the series
of portraits of clergymen. Moreover, it may not have been the
quality alone of the Old Pat engraving that brought Durand to
the attention of Trumbull. As a Director of the American
Academy, who also painted a portrait of Trumbull--probably in
the winter of 1819-20[34]--Waldo may have intervened personally
with Trumbull on Durand's behalf. It seems likely that we ought
to recognize in Waldo a source of the stimulus that moved Durand
to enter the higher branches of his craft.

The uncertain financial returns from the Declaration of
Independence[35]--uncertain for Trumbull, Durand received the
stipulated three thousand dollars--and the clerical portraits
did not deter Durand from further, ambitious projects. Most
important among these were the full length portrait of the
gymnasium proprietor William Fuller in fighting costume (Fig. 7),
after a painting by Charles Ingham, and the Musidora (Figs. 9
and 10), Durand's first work after a design of his own. The
William Fuller was published in 1823, the Musidora, in 1825.

As we shall have occasion to note, Durand was an assiduous
student of the Antique during his early years in New York. This
interest clearly reveals itself in the classical figures which
he designed and engraved as vignettes for bank-notes. And in
1825 he was commissioned to engrave the Apollo Belvedere (Fig. 8)
as an illustration to an address delivered by Robert Ray before
the American Academy of the Fine Arts. With greater or less
distinctness, both the Fuller and the Musidora may be regarded

as expressions of Durand's interest in the Classical tradition. The muscular, poised, and alert figure of the gymnasium proprietor is a modern equivalent to those Greek athletes whose perfect, natural forms had, according to Winckelmann and his followers, supplied the Greek sculptor's ideal of masculine form. This idea cannot have been unknown in New York for Dunlap later incorporated it in the introduction to his History of the Rise and Progress of the Arts of Design in the United States:

> The sculptors . . . of Greece are our teachers to this day, in form; and he most excels who assiduously studies the models they have left us. This seems to contradict the precept that bids the artist study nature alone. But it must be remembered that we speak only of that form, the perfection of which the ancients saw in nature, and embodied in their religion. That natural perfection which they saw under their bright skies, at the games instituted in honor of their gods, they combined in the statues of those gods . . . This appears to be the source from which the wonders of Praxiteles and Phidias sprung--the Jupiter, the Minerva, the Hercules, the Venus, the Apollo.[36]

In representing the modern athlete out-of-doors Ingham and Durand have been able to draw from nature a form equivalent to that which inspired the Greek sculptor. With the Fuller Ingham and Durand participate in that large current of enthusiasm for things specifically Greek, ancient and modern, which affected

Western European and American political thought and art in
the first decades of the nineteenth century. In America, Greek
forms were imitated primarily in architecture, while Greek
themes, as in the _Fuller_ and other engravings by Durand after
American paintings, were frequently treated in painting and
poetry.[37]

Unfortunately, when, two years later, Durand designed his
_Musidora_, no contemporary model offered herself--certainly he
was not able to select the best parts from New York's most beautiful young ladies. Now he was able to approximate the Antique
through the more direct method of borrowing the figure from a
particular statue. A maiden of sufficiently modest behavior
was discovered in an Antique Venus published in Bartolomeo
Cavaceppi's _Raccolta_ _d'antiche_ _statue_, _busti_, _bassirelievi_ _ed_
_altre_ _sculture_ (Fig. 11).[38] In using this figure, however,
Durand felt free to make certain changes. The amount of drapery
has been abbreviated, the length of the trunk shortened, the
arm at the left made to reach further from the body as the figure
now supports herself by leaning on a rock, and the leg at the
left has been withdrawn so that its entire, inner contour has
disappeared. Finally, one may note that the contours of the
right leg, clearly the _piece_ _de_ _resistance_ of the figure, were
invented by Durand with no small, though not entire, success.[39]

The Neo-classicism of these two engravings becomes even
more apparent if they are studied in connection with Benjamin
West's discussion of the ideal male and female figures. It
should be remembered that the shadow of Benjamin West continued

to fall over the New York School even after the founding of
the National Academy in 1826. As late as 1833 a copy of Galt's
_Life_, _Studies_, _and_ _Works_ _of_ _Benjamin_ _West_ was offered by the
Academy as the reward for the second best drawing by one of its
students,[40] and as early as 1820 Durand associated intimately
with three of West's pupils--Dunlap, Trumbull, and Samuel Waldo.
Of the three, Waldo, who had studied under West most recently
and proposed in 1818 that the American Academy commission Sir
Thomas Lawrence to paint a full-length portrait of West,[41] may
have introduced Durand to the second volume of Galt's _Life_
soon after its publication in 1820. And it is the second volume that contains abbreviations of West's Academic discourses.

In his Discourse of 1794 West insists that an artist's
work must be informed by a "philosophical spirit"[42] if it is
to possess any "merit beyond the productions of the ordinary
paper hanger."[43] In the early stages of the exercise of this
philosophical spirit the artist will learn to discriminate the
moral character pertaining to the male and female figures
respectively:

> . . . he will discover that the general construction
> of the human figure in the male indicates strength and
> activity; and that the form of the individual man, in
> proportion to the power of being active, is more or
> less perfect. In the male, the degree of beauty depends
> on the degree of activity with which all the parts of
> the body are capable of performing their respective
> and mutual functions . . .[44]

Here, then, is an account of masculine beauty that may have
inspired Durand's interest in Ingham's painting and may,
indeed, have suggested to Ingham the plan of painting the picture.  In the picture, Fuller's strength and activity are
stressed, and the figure is presented in an active stance,
permitting "all the parts of the body . . . ⸢to perform⸣ . . .
their respective and mutual functions."  As beauty in the male
figure depends upon the full and uninhibited functioning of a
mechanical organism, rather than its approximation to an average
or central form of the species such as Reynolds had described
in the third of his Discourses, a high degree of such beauty
is compatible with the particularity of a portrait.  It is this
kind of beauty, which West also discovered in the Apollo
Belvedere,[45] that Ingham and Durand sought to realize in the
portrait of Fuller.

The Musidora, on the other hand, appears to embody the
feminine ideal defined by West:

> . . . but the characteristics of perfection of form in
> the female are very different; delicacy of frame and
> modesty of demeanor, with less capability to be active,
> constitute the peculiar graces of woman.[46]

And in describing more fully the condition of the human organism
that denotes the perfect feminine character, he wrote:

> Were the young artist . . . to propose to himself
> a subject in which he would endeavor to represent the
> peculiar excellences of woman, would he not say, that
> these excellences consist in a virtuous mind, a modest

mien, a tranquil deportment, and a gracefulness in
motion? And, in embodying the combined beauty of
these qualities, would he not bestow on the figure
a general, smooth, and round fulness of form, to indicate the softness of character; bend the head gently
forward, in the common attitude of modesty; and awaken
our ideas of the slow and graceful movements peculiar
to the sex, by limbs free from that masculine and
sinewy expression which is the consequence of active
exercise?--and such is the Venus de Medici. It would
be utterly impossible to place a person so formed in
the attitude of the Apollo, without destroying all
those amiable and gentle associations of the mind which
are inspired by contemplating "the statue which enchants
the world."[47]

The final epitaph applied to the Venus de' Medici was borrowed
by West from the story of Musidora in Thomson's Seasons. After
bathing in a woodland brook Musidora discovers a note revealing
that her chaste but curious lover, Damon, had observed her
exercise. These lines describe the maiden's first reaction
upon her discovery of the note:

> With wild surprise,
>
> As if to marble struck, devoid of sense,
>
> A stupid moment motionless she stood:
>
> So stands the statue that enchants the world;
>
> So bending tries to veil the matchless boast,
>
> The mingled beauties of exulting GREECE.[48]

Employing a similar, Classical Venus, Durand has represented
Musidora as she is described at this moment in the story.
The moral character of the female figure is expressed in those
qualities of form and bodily organization which West had enumerated. Her movement is tranquil and graceful. "A general,
smooth, and round fullness of form" indicates "softness of
character." And in removing the drapery which appears about
the legs of Cavaceppi's Venus, Durand's is able to exhibit
"limbs free from that masculine and sinewy expression which is
the consequence of active exercise." Thus Durand has represented the figure at a moment in which the moral qualities that
constitute feminine beauty are expressed in the form and posture
of the figure.[49]

But, while the figure is in fact represented as of this
moment in the story, it is not this moment that Durand intended
to illustrate. He has moved the form described at a later point
in the story back to an earlier moment--that in which she has
just approached the brook and

> . . . . . .with timid eye around
>
> The banks surveying, stripp'd her beauteous limbs,
>
> To taste the lucid coolness of the flood.[50]

These lines appear on the plate. In making the shift, Durand
has suppressed any element of fright in favor of the tranquility
proper to the ideal female. Also in selecting the earlier
moment for illustration, Durand has represented Musidora while
Damon looked on and

. . . drew

Such madning draughts of beauty to the soul,

As for a while o'erwhelmed his raptured thought

With luxury too daring.

Being of different sizes, the Fuller (h. 19 3/4 x 13 1/2)
and the Musidora (h. 15 5/8 x w. 10 11/16) cannot have been
executed as a pair. Yet there are several ways in which the
two are closely related to one another. They both depict a
partly nude figure, and they both were inspired by Antique
models. Further, each represents a figure poised for athletic
and health-preserving recreation, for the Musidora incident is
introduced in the Seasons to exemplify Thomson's praise of
swimming, by which it is immediately preceded:

This is the purest exercise of health,

The kind refresher of the summer-heats;

. . .

Thus life redoubles . . .

. . .

. . . Hence the limbs

Knit into force . . .

. . .

Even from the body's purity, the mind

Receives a secret sympathetic aid.[52]

Finally, the two prints are related as defining the contrasting
perfection of the male and female human being.

Now, according to West, the ideal male figure may be sublime
and the female, beautiful.

When the student has settled in his own mind the general and primary characteristics, in either sex, of the human figure, the next step will enable him to reduce the peculiar character of his subject into its proper class, whether it rank under the sublime or the beautiful, the heroic or the graceful, the masculine or the feminine, or in any of its other softer or more spirited distinctions.[53]

If we turn from West to Edmund Burke's Philosophical Enquiry into the Origins of our Ideas of the Sublime and Beautiful, it may be demonstrated that, in all probability, with these two prints Durand sought to excite the feelings of the sublime and beautiful as these are defined by Burke. According to Burke, the sublime is productive of moral health as physical exercise is of bodily well-being:

Labour is not only requisite to preserve the coarser organs in a state fit for their functions; but it is equally necessary to these finer and more delicate organs, on which, and by which, the imagination and perhaps the other mental powers act.[54]

The sublime affords the necessary exercise of the finer and more delicate organs:

As common labour, which is a mode of pain, is the exercise of the grosser, a mode of terror is the exercise of the finer parts of the system . . . if the pain and terror are so modified as not to be actually noxious; if the pain is not carried to violence, and

the terror is not conversant about the present destruction of the person; as these emotions clear the parts,
whether fine or gross, of a dangerous and troublesome
encumbrance, they are capable of producing delight . . .[55]

Durand's figure of Fuller, while structured on the pattern of
the Apollo Belvedere as recommended by West,is more than just
an ideal male form. In addition, Fuller, even more than the
Apollo, threatens the spectator with his fists, and thereby is
introduced a modicum of pain or terror into the spectator's
experience of the image. Thus,the image of bodily exercise
functions to produce a health-preserving exercise of the spectator's finer organs.

Beauty, on the other hand, operates quite differently in
Burke's theory. Beauty is connected with and, indeed, is a
cause of man's willingness and fitness to live in society:

But man, who is a creature adapted to a greater variety
and intricacy of relation, connects with the general
passion /i.e., "the passion which belongs to generation"7, the idea of some social qualities, which direct
and heighten the appetite which he has in common with
all other animals; and as he is not designed like them
to live at large, it is fit that he should have something to create a preference, and fix his choice; and
this in general should be some sensible quality; . . .
The object therefore of this mixed passion, which we
call love, is the beauty of the sex. Men are carried
to the sex in general, as it is the sex; and by the

> common law of nature; but they are attached to parti-
> culars by personal <u>beauty</u>. I call beauty a social
> quality; for when women and men, and not only they,
> but when animals give us a sense of joy and pleasure
> in beholding them . . . , they inspire us with senti-
> ments of tenderness and affection towards their per-
> sons; . . .[56]

Thus, the beauty of Musidora, which so delighted her Damon, may
also afford pleasure to the spectator, may restrain his nomadic
propensities, and excite the social "sentiments of tenderness and
affection." The <u>Musidora</u> affords the beauty that is requisite
to the origin of society, and the <u>Fuller</u> contributes the sublimity that is requisite to the preservation of the moral health
of the individual in society.

These two engravings very suitably stand as a preface to
Durand's later work, for he continued to concern himself with
the sublime and the beautiful, the perfect or typical in form,
the moral health of the individual, and the sentiments upon
which the continuity of society depends. Durand's interpretation of these matters, however, was never static, and we shall
be largely concerned with the changing means that he employed to
achieve particular ends. The materialistic psychology of Burke,
Durand soon abandoned along with the academic forms of West.
In 1825 the <u>Musidora</u> was too distant from the public understanding
to be popular, and "as far as remuneration for his labour is
concerned, not enough was obtained by the sale of impressions
to pay for paper and printing."[57]

Such projects as the <u>William Fuller</u> and the <u>Musidora</u> served less as immediate sources of income and more to establish and maintain Durand's reputation as America's foremost line engraver. It was his reputation as a draughtsman and engraver, together with his brother Cyrus' mechanical ingenuity, that brought him and several firms with which he was associated a large portion of the current, bank-note business.[58] Where in 1821 the <u>Declaration of Independence</u> commission had permitted him to marry Lucy Baldwin,[59] it was the profits from his bank-note work that permitted Durand in 1827 to build the house in Amity Street,[60] which he retained until he retired and returned to New Jersey in 1869. It must, also, have been the degree of financial security afforded by the bank-note business that allowed Durand to undertake, in collaboration with William Cullen Bryant, his most speculative venture--the publication in 1830 of the first--and, unfortunately, the last--number of a periodical entitled <u>The American Landscape</u>. Probably the emphasis on the merely topographical and informative in both the six engravings after paintings or drawings by Cole, Weir, W. J. Bennett, and Durand, and Bryant's descriptive letterpress rendered the work unpopular. Aside from a certain romantic wildness in one of Cole's less romantic landscapes (Fig. 13) and Bryant's unelaborated characterization of the American wilderness as more immediately from the hand of God than European scenes and some reference to the history and legends associated with the places represented, it is rather a dull affair. Hence, the "undertaking proved a failure, accompanied with loss."[61]

The landscapes contributed by Durand--Catskill Mountains
(Fig. 15) and Delaware Water Gap (Fig. 14)--are mainly of
interest in so far as they foreshadow his later work as a landscape painter. The drawing (Fig. 17) from which the Catskill
Mountains was derived stands certainly among Durand's earliest
efforts at representing a particular locality. The drawing is
notable as a straight-forward account of a scene, the interest
of which has not been heightened by any element of drama other
than that depending upon the discontinuity of foreground and
middleground and upon the extensiveness of the view across a
valley. What drama there is results from the structure of the
earth's surface itself rather than from any adventitious
movement of atmosphere or reference to human action. One might
also note that, in the drawing, Durand has made no concession
to any Neo-classic concern with symmetry or the limitation of
the extension of space beyond the sides of the drawing. The
whole scene stands as a slice of the earth's surface portrayed
entirely for itself. This sort of refusal to embellish the
actual scene clearly points toward Durand's later oil studies
from nature. The present drawing, like the later paintings,
reflects a deep respect for nature and a sense of the suffi-
ciency of the interest excited by nature itself.

When Durand came to translate the drawing into an engraving,
he did succumb to an urge to embellish the scene by attempting
to confine the lateral extension of space through the introduction of a slender and highly improbable tree at the left and
by emphasizing the dark, wooded hill-side at the right. And

he sought to establish a bridge between the spectator and inanimate nature by introducing five cows into the foreground.
Still, his engraving is more naturalistic in spirit than either
of Thomas Cole's later views of the same scene (Figs. 18 and
19).[62]

Of Durand's work in the years around 1830, the landscape
engravings do not really foreshadow the direction that his art
was to take in the immediate future. Rather, it is the historical, genre, and fancy subjects engraved for the gift books
(Figs. 21-24)[63] as well as the engraved portraits of eminent
persons that prefigure the work of his early career as a
painter. With the completion of the Ariadne (Fig. 34 in 1835),
Durand was ready to abandon engraving. By this time he had
established his reputation as a portrait and history painter,
and it is to his preparations for this later career and to his
early achievements therein that we may now direct our attention.

IV. Durand's Academic Studies in New York.

As we have seen, Durand arrived in New York a fairly competent craftsman. Through no small effort to develop his skill and knowledge, he was able by 1825 to produce an original engraving of considerable merit. But this skill and his knowledge were not acquired altogether in the regular pursuit of an engraver's career. On the one hand, he was able to transcend the limits of commercial engraving. On the other, from his first year in the city he sought to acquire a broader knowledge of art which would eventually enable him to abandon engraving altogether.

New York around 1820 offered few opportunities for the study of art, but these few Durand grasped with an unusual eagerness. Soon after its resuscitation in 1816 the American Academy of Fine Arts permitted students to draw from its collection of casts after Antique statues. Dunlap gives a brief account of this first Antique school in New York:

> During some months of summer weather in 1817-1818, the
> gallery of the statues, or saloon of the antique, was
> regularly attended by the keeper . . . and irregularly
> attended by some few students, and one artist, (Mr. Durand) who then was an excellent draughtsman; as the casts
> were made part of the exhibitions, students could only
> be admitted early in the morning, and the whole business
> declined.[64]

In view of the fact that Dunlap himself was the keeper in attendance, his statement that Durand drew at the American Academy during this period is probably correct. But since Durand did not arrive in New York until the autumn of 1817, if the gallery was open to students only during the summer months, it must have been in 1818 that he began his studies. From the autumn of 1818 to that of 1824, the school remained in decline. Its failure was probably due as much to an insufficiency of students as to any hostility toward art instruction on the part of the Academy's president, John Trumbull.[65]

The American Academy made a second effort to provide a school in the autumn of 1824. This second school--again students drew from casts--lasted into the autumn of 1825, and it is probable that Durand again attended upon occasion. But at this period it is possible that he derived more benefit from the other resources of the Academy. John Durand describes four of his father's notebooks--two labeled Anatomical Notes collected while attending the Lectures of Dr. Post--1824, another containing studies of facial expression, and the fourth containing notes on Antique costume.[66] The anatomical notebooks must have recorded lectures delivered by Dr. Wright Post, an emminent New York surgeon, perhaps at the Medical College rather than at the Academy.[67] The other two may be notes on books belonging to the Academy library. Also, it is not impossible that Durand found Cavaceppi's Raccolta d'antiche statue, busti, bassirelievi ed altre sculture ristaurate in the Academy library while working on the Musidora.

The collection of casts, an occasional lecture, and a
small library might have satisfied the needs of art students
in 1817, but by 1824 and 1825 the number and ambition of students had increased considerably. Such young men as Thomas S.
Cummings (1804-1894), Frederick S. Agate (1807-1844), John W.
Paradise (1809-1862), Gherlando Marsiglia (1792-1850), George
W. Hatch (1805-1867), John L. Morton (1792-1871), Charles C.
Ingham (1796-1863), Thomas Cole (1801-1848), and the sculptor
John Frazee (1790-1852), all of whom were fully determined to
be professional artists, were not content with an Antique
academy to which they were admitted only at inconvenient hours
and only at the pleasure of an irascible custodian.[68] Realizing
that the American Academy was not and would not be a reliable
source of art instruction, a number of the younger artists
formed the New-York Drawing Association at a meeting on November
8, 1825, over which Durand presided.[69] An account of this
third school of art was printed in The Atheneum Magazine for
December, 1825:

> We close our remarks for this number, by adding
> the pleasing information given us by an artist, that
> an association of artists and students, under the sur-
> veillance of the President of the Academy, and under
> the direction of Mr. Morse as their immediate Presi-
> dent, regularly attend to drawing from the Antique,
> three evenings each week.[70]

The New-York Drawing Association lasted only as long as
there remained the possibility that the artists would be able

to gain control of the amateur-dominated American Academy. After negotiations to this end had failed, they created on January 24, 1826 the National Academy of Design to be controlled exclusively by professional artists.[71] From January, 1826 the new National Academy provided an opportunity to draw from casts after Antique statues. Indeed, Durand himself supplied some of the casts.[72] The immediate success of the National Academy in its effort to offer instruction received praise in The New-York Review for April, 1826:

> Nothing will tend more to make artists put forth their strength . . . than that union, blended with liberal competition, which has taken place, in the formation of the National Academy of Design. We have been present at one of their evening schools; we have seen, what is altogether new in this city, a numerous class of students from the antique, each with his lamp, his crayon, and paper, intent upon the casts of the Apollo, the Laocoon, the Hercules, or the Niobe; while many of our first artists were either intermingled with tyros, and teaching by example, or walking from desk to desk, and instructing by precept. We likewise heard from the professor of anatomy an elegant and instructive lecture.[73]

In the same article Durand is described as "an invaluable member of the school for the Arts of Design,"[74] and John Durand later wrote that his father had attended "the school of the National Academy of Design, in which he was both pupil and teacher. Not a moment was lost. None of his compeers, perhaps, pursued the study of art technically with more ardour and enthusiasm."[75]

But the program of instruction envisioned by the founding Academicians was broader than a mere Antique school. On March 22, 1830 Henry Inman promised that a life school would soon be opened.[76] This, however, does not appear to have materialized until the winter of 1834-1835.[77] A note in one of Durand's sketch books[78] indicates that he did participate in a life school at about this time.

Perhaps of greater importance to Durand's development as an artist than the actual practice of drawing, at a time when he was already a competent draughtsman, were the various lectures sponsored by the National Academy on topics related to art.[79] During the first two years of the Academy's existence lectures on anatomy and perspective were offered regularly. These were supplemented by lectures on mythology and ancient history by William Cullen Bryant (1828-1831), painting in general by Samuel F. B. Morse (1828-1838), sculpture by Horatio Greenough (1829?), historical composition by William Dunlap (1831), history by Gulian C. Verplanck (1831), and the chemistry of colors by John J. Mapes (1833 and 1836-1838). We may assume that Durand heard most of these lecturers at one time or another, and that those who touched upon topics relevant to his own art effectively directed his practice toward the realization of more clearly defined ends.

Aside from drawing schools and the various lectures, Durand had one other opportunity to expand his knowledge of the

higher branches of art. We should not discount the impact of
the continuing exhibition of paintings at the American Academy
upon a young artist during the years around 1820. Recalling
his own "habit of spending many hours a day in the rooms, and
frequently without being interrupted," Cummings described the
collection of pictures as "no insignificant exhibition for its
date, or the existing taste for Art."[80] It may be supposed
that Durand, who contributed engravings to the American Academy's exhibitions of 1820, 1823, 1824, 1825, and 1833, did
frequently avail himself of this opportunity to study good
original works of art and copies of the masterpieces of the
past. It should be noted that the student had easier access
to original paintings by or copies after the old masters in
New York at the exhibitions of the American Academy than did
students between the date of the demise of this institution
in 1841 and the foundation of the Metropolitan Museum in
1870.[81]

At the American Academy one could study paintings attributed to Baroque masters such as Albani, Annibale and Agostino
Carracci, Domenichino, Giordano, Guercino, Reni, Rosa, Rubens,
Ribera, Snyders, Teniers, and a large number of seventeenth
century Dutch landscape and genre painters. The authenticity
of the paintings exhibited under these names is not so important
as the fact that they must have provided art students with a
fair idea of the character and variety of Baroque painting.
The paintings loaned by the Count de Survilliers must have been
of more than mediocre quality.[82] Indeed, there is some evidence

to suggest that Durand's early efforts at figure painting were
inspired by works on exhibition at the American Academy. A
Samson and Delilah, after Rubens, appeared four years before
Durand first exhibited his Samson Shorn of his Locks by the
Philistines, While Asleep in the Lap of Delilah in 1827. A
Hagar, the Angel and Ishmael in the Desert by Francesco
Trevisani, from the Jumel Collection, exhibited in 1817, fore-
shadows Durand's composition of the same subject exhibited in
1829. A Magdalene, attributed to Titian, from the "Spanish
Collection from Seville," exhibited in 1825, may have suggested
the subject for Durand's Mary Magdalene at the Sepulchre, exhibited the following year. Finally, Durand's engraved Musidora,
representing the maiden as she disrobes to bathe in the stream,
may reflect the story of Susannah, treated in a painting by
Dunlap and in a fragment of a painting attributed to Van Dyck,
both exhibited in 1818. Trumbull's Susannah and the Elders,
painted in 1811, was not exhibited until 1833 but may have
been known to Durand at an earlier date. Also, the many Dutch
seventeenth century landscapes must have contributed to Dur-
and's ultimate conception of the degree of realism appropriate
to a work in this genre. In none of these cases, however, can
we be certain that the prior exhibition of a painting at the
American Academy of Fine Arts caused Durand to treat the same
or a similar subject at a later date, for many other paintings
were exhibited which Durand never sought to imitate.

In summary, we may observe that, during these early years
in New York, Durand fully participated in the city's post-war

spirit of optimism and enterprise. He quickly found a source
of mental stimulation and of new ideas in his association with
the city's most creative and erudite citizens. Although his
early training under Peter Maverick must have been somewhat
less then mediocre, by seizing such opportunities as the city
then afforded for the study of art he was soon able to divert
a part of his artistic energies from engraving. The only thing
lacking to his study in these years was a prolonged opportunity
to learn the technique of painting from a painter, yet it became increasingly evident that this was his ultimate objective.
Two years after undertaking the Declaration of Independence, the
first of his major engravings, Durand executed his first painting, a portrait of his mother--and this was followed in the later
1820's by other experiments in painting.

V. Unitarianism in New York and Durand's Religious Views.

The William Fuller and Musidora engravings are the first important works by Durand to be informed by academic concepts. As we have noted, these figures are primarily moral images presenting the perfect man and woman in such a way as to produce certain effects upon the spectator.  In neither is there any implication of supernatural agency or any suggestion of a concern with religious issues on the part of the artist.  His second group of works inspired by academic theories consists of three Biblical subjects exhibited at the National Academy in the late 1820's.  Now, it is, of course, possible that in painting these Durand was simply following the same path along which Benjamin West and Copley in London and Trumbull and Dunlap in New York had sought popular acclaim.  Before accepting this view, however, we should enquire whether Durand might have been motivated by a particular system of religious thought--whether he sought to treat not simply Biblical histories but the burning, religious issues of the period.  As we shall see, the paintings may be interpreted in the light of William Ellery Channing's Unitarianism.  But before turning to the paintings we should pause to note the status of the Unitarian movement in New York in the 1820's and the evidence pointing toward Durand's connection with it.

Although as a child Durand studied the orthodox Westminster Catechism,[83] before his arrival in New York he had already become acquainted with the Universalist and Arminian or Unitarian

doctrines in the debates of the Bloomfield Forum, as suggested
above by the letter Durand received from James Gibbs, Jr.
shortly after his removal to New York. The tone of Gibbs'
statement suggests that religious issues had been explored in
the Forum's debates but that neither he nor Durand had been
converted to any sectarian belief. Once in New York, Durand
must soon have become aware of the rapidly developing Unitarian
movement in the city. Within two years of Dr. Channing's New
York lecture of 1819, the Unitarians established a church in
Chambers Street,[84] and Edward Everett, whose portrait Durand
later painted, delivered the initial sermon. The Unitarian
Church of the Messiah was organized in 1825, and a building on
the corner of Prime and Mercer Streets erected in 1826. On
its completion Channing delivered the dedication sermon. The
movement was further supported by the establishment in 1821 of
the Unitarian Library and Tract Society of New York, by the
presence of the Sedgwick brothers, Henry and Robert, and the
occasional visits of Jared Sparks, editor of the Baltimore
Unitarian Miscellany and Christian Monitor.[85] In 1824 and
1825 Henry Sedgwick encouraged William Cullen Bryant, a Unitarian convert, to abandon the practice of law in Great
Barrington, Massachusetts and move to New York to pursue a
literary career. Both Henry and Robert Sedgwick used their
influence to introduce Bryant to prominent New Yorkers and to
secure for him the co-editorship of the New York Review and
Athenaeum Magazine in June, 1825. Also, we may note that in
1827 another prominent Unitarian, Lewis Tappan, the first

treasurer of the American Unitarian Association, founded in 1825, moved from Boston to New York, where he helped found the Journal of Commerce. In the same year, however, he withdrew from the American Unitarian Association, as it seemed to him insufficiently militant in matters of social reform.[86]

Unitarianism in New York was not unopposed. Writing of the years around 1820, Parke Godwin states that "the Unitarian sect, to which he (i.e., Bryant) belonged, was small in numbers, and not in good odor with its orthodox rivals."[87] When Channing visited New York in 1819, not a single clergyman was willing to lend him his pulpit; and Dr. John W. Francis, one of the doctors responsible for Channing's use of the Medical College, recorded the verbal lashing he received from the orthodox Rev. John M. Mason:

> "You are all equally guilty," cried the doctor, with enkindled warmth. "Do you know what you have done? You have advanced infidelity by complying with the request of these sceptics. . . . Belief; they have no belief; they believe in nothing, having nothing to believe. They are a paradox; you cannot fathom them. How can you fathom a thing that has no bottom?"[88]

In the preface to a collection of his writings published in 1830, Channing ascribes the controversial tone of certain pieces to his will to oppose "a revival of the spirit of intolerance and persecution." And he goes on to note that in the late 1810's and 1820's "penalties, as serious in this country as fine and imprisonment, were, if possible, to be attached to the

profession of liberal views of Christianity, the penalties
of general hatred and scorn; and that a degrading uniformity
of opinion was to be imposed by the severest persecution,
which the spirit of the age would allow."[89]  And Parke Godwin
suggests that some degree of hostility toward Bryant as a
Unitarian may have delayed his securing a position in New
York in 1825.[90]  Throughout the 1820's, while it gained in
number of adherents and in intellectual support, Unitarianism
remained a controversial issue.

Durand's own religious faith is something of a mystery.
Nowhere in his extant letters or journals does he identify
himself with a particular sect.  Although he was raised in
Calvinist orthodoxy, his association as a youth with Peter
Maverick must have tended to liberalize his views.  Maverick's
father, Peter Rushton Maverick, had been one of the prominent
Deists in New York in the 1790's.  With Philip Freneau and
John Lamb he had unsuccessfully tried to secure the City Hall
courtroom for a lecture by the Deist Elihu Palmer in 1797.
And later, in 1800, he was among the sponsors of the short-
lived, Deist weekly The Temple of Reason.[91]  His son Peter does
not appear to have actively advocated the cause of liberalism
in religion, but the fact that his first eight children were
not baptised until October 8, 1814 and that he is not listed
as a communicant of Trinity Church in Newark, to which he did
contribute financially,[92] suggest that he did not especially
concern himself with the mysteries of revealed religion.  From
an early period in his life Durand, also, did not find church

attendance essential to his spiritual well-being. This is
clearly indicated by a passage from the _Journal_ in which he
recorded his experience during his voyage to England in 1840:

Today again is Sunday. I have declined attendance on
church service, the better to indulge reflection unrestrained under the high canopy of heaven, amidst
the expanse of waters--fit place to worship God and
contemplate the wonders of his power. This mode of
passing the Sabbath became habitual with me in early
life midst other scenes than these, 'tis true, yet,
if more consonant with my feelings, (as the world of
the woods & plains & mountains ever is,) certainly
not less impressive. /A sentence is crossed out here,
probably by a later hand. The sentence reads: "The
voice of Nature is always . . . it is the voice of
God."7 The sounds of inanimate Nature, all partake
of mournful solemnity--"the rush of many waters" as
here on the mighty ocean--the roar, or the whisper of
winds through the shaddowy /sic7 forest--the ceaseless
murmur of the water fall--the pattering of the summer
shower, and, need I name the awful thunder?--all tend
to awaken thoughtful meditation and rational man in
the open walks of Nature needs no temple made with
hands, and the silent thought of praise or supplica-
tion, accompanied by that fitting voice asks no other
aid /several words crossed out7 to bear it to the
mercy-seat of Heaven.[93]

Like Channing and Bryant, Durand recognized the advantages of meditating out-of-doors in contrast to the organized, indoor worship of a particular sect. But also, like Channing and Bryant, he maintained a faith in the truth and redemptive power of Christianity. As late as 1855 in his _Letters_ on _Landscape_ _Painting_ he acknowledged the ultimate value of Christian Scripture as the highest source of truth.[94] While we cannot attach Durand to any particular religious sect, it is more than possible that he tended to interpret the Christian Scriptures in the light of an increasingly non-sectarian point of view, such as that of the writings of Channing. Although we have no positive evidence to prove that he ever read Channing, many aspects of Durand's work as a painter may appear most brightly illuminated in the light of these writings.

There is ample evidence to indicate that Durand closely associated with men who were Unitarians or sympathetic to Unitarian doctrines. As early as 1819 William Dunlap, who, in 1797 had recorded James Kent's remark that "men of information . . . /are/ . . . nearly as free from vulgar supersitition or the Christian religion as they were in ye time of Cicero from the pagan supersition--all . . . except the literary men among the Clergy,"[95] debated with himself over the truth of the Unitarian denial of Christ's equality with God. Possibly he had heard Channing's New York lecture in May, 1819 and did not find time to study the relevant theological and Biblical texts until his sojourn in Norfolk, Virginia in the autumn. In any case, on December 7, he wrote in his diary: "As far as I can yet see, the Unitarians are right."[96] And on December 11, he added: "As far as I have yet seen, Christ teaches Unitarianism."[97] Dunlap knew Durand at this time and wrote to him a few days later proposing that he engrave a portrait of the Rev. Richard C. Moore, Bishop of Virginia.[98] In addition to Dunlap, anytime after his arrival in New York in 1825, Bryant might have discussed Unitarian ideas with Durand. Finally, Durand certainly knew and conversed frequently with New York's two Unitarian clergymen--the Rev. Orville Dewey (1794-1882) and the Rev. Henry Whitney Bellows (1814-1882). Both were members of the Sketch Club by 1844,[99] and both were honorary members of the National Academy.

From conversations with any of these men--and Durand associated on terms of intimacy with each--Durand must have acquired a deeper comprehension of Unitarian beliefs regarding Man, God, and Nature as well as an understanding of Channing's theories about the social, moral, and religious functions of art. Channing' writings were widely disseminated, and Durand must have read some of them. But, we should always bear in mind that ideas are more readily transmuted into art after they have been warmed in conversation. The conversations, however, that went on in the studio, at clubs, and at the National Academy are not recorded. Hence, in an effort to recover the matter of these conversations we have no choice but to return to the cold written word itself. When particular passages are cited in the interpretation of particular paintings, I do not intend to imply that Durand painted with book in hand. Although some of the ideas with which we shall deal can only be rendered intelligible to the modern reader by elaborate illustration, they are, for the most part, ideas that could have become firmly seated in Durand's mind through his own interested reading and discussions with his Unitarian friends.

VI. <u>Historical</u> <u>Compositions</u> <u>Based</u> <u>upon</u> <u>Scripture</u>: <u>1826</u>-<u>1829</u>.

Durand's contributions to the exhibitions at the American Academy in 1820, 1823, 1824, and 1825 had been predominantly engravings. It must have seemed prudent to exhibit there the kind of work in which he was more skilled and for which he sought immediate public patronage. The dignity of the older institution did not suggest the exhibition of explorations into new realms. Hence, he exhibited but one painting, a <u>Portrait</u> <u>of</u> <u>One</u> <u>of</u> <u>the</u> <u>Artist's</u> <u>Children</u> (App. II, no. 2), in these years. With the foundation of the National Academy the situation was reversed. The new Academy's very lack of resources must have been a strong incentive to its members to produce something like the kind of painting that graced the walls of the older Academy. A new spirit of enterprise and self-reliance permeating the new Academy must have induced its more adventurous members to attempt the more difficult branches of art, even though the spectator might need to admire more the boldness of the effort than the quality of the result. The instability of the new Academy offered a rare opportunity to fail grandly in public, an opportunity which several, including William Dunlap of the older generation, eagerly seized.

After acquiring an appreciation of the Antique, a knowledge of anatomy, perspective, expression, and costume, the painter might then ask what subject he ought to treat. A painter seeking academic honors in New York in the mid-1820's would have been directed by precept and example to Biblical subjects. These

had the authority of both Reynolds and West, whose academic
discourses were well known. From the 1790's both West and
Copley, whose work was familiar through engravings to Americans who had never visited England, had turned their attention
primarily to Biblical subjects. Of West's students, Washington
Allston was especially prolific in Biblical painting. His
Belshazzar's Feast[100] was widely known by rumor, and his Rebecca
at the Well[101] was shown at the first National Academy exhibition. The American Academy exhibitions afforded many examples
of Baroque religious painting; and Trumbull appeared in New
York more as a painter of sentimental religious subjects[102]
than of the heroic deeds of modern times. The figure studies
for the large imitations of West's great Biblical paintings,
sent by Dunlap to the early National Academy exhibitions, were
well received.[103] So, also, we find that the more ambitious of
the younger New York painters--Thomas Cole,[104] William Sidney
Mount,[105] and Durand--were attracted to themes from Scripture.

Before 1830 Durand exhibited three compositions based upon
Biblical narrative--Mary Magdalene at the Sepulchre (exhibited
in 1826), Samson Shorn of His Locks by the Philistines While
Asleep in the Lap of Delilah (exhibited in 1827 and again in
the review exhibition of 1831), and Hagar and Ishmael in the
Wilderness (exhibited in 1829). Unfortunately none of these
paintings has been located, and it is most probable that they
were all destroyed by Durand, there being no evidence to suggest
that any one of them left his possession. The remaining visual

documents consist only of a drawing for the <u>Hagar</u> (Fig. 25)
and two fragments of an historical composition--a male and
probably a female head--which may be remnants of the <u>Samson</u>
(App. II, nos. 419 A-B).  Yet as these paintings seem to be
the product of a moment uncontaminated by a desire to paint
for the public, their subjects may be studied for some indication of Durand's deeper interests at this point in his
career.

A <u>Mary Magdalene at the Sepulchre</u> was the first Biblical
composition painted and exhibited by Durand.  From the Biblical
passage printed in the National Academy exhibition catalogue,
we learn that it represented the confrontation of the courtesan
and the risen Christ:

> Jesus saith unto her, Mary.  She turned herself, and
> said unto him, Robboni, which is to say, Master.  Jesus
> saith unto her, Touch me not:  for I am not yet ascended
> to my Father:  but go to my brethren, and say unto
> them, I ascend unto my Father and your Father, and
> <u>to</u> my God and your God.[106]

The painting probably followed the traditional arrangement of
this subject--a garden setting, the Magdalene in adoration,
and Christ standing near the tomb.

But for our purposes the text quoted is particularly
important in that it evokes several Unitarian doctrines.  Perhaps these doctrines may be most clearly indicated if we follow
somewhat the statement of Unitarian belief which makes up the
second part of Channing's "Discourse at the Ordination of the Rev.

Jared Sparks" delivered in 1819 in Baltimore. First, obviously, is the notion of God's unity:

> In the first place, we believe in the doctrine of
> God's unity, or that there is one God, and only
> one.[107]

This view is held in opposition to that according to which:

> . . . there are three infinite and equal persons,
> possessing supreme divinity, called the Father, Son,
> and the Holy Ghost. Each of these persons, as des-
> cribed by theologians, has his own particular con-
> sciousness, will, and perceptions. They love each
> other, converse with each other, and delight in each
> other's society.[108]

In the passage quoted by Durand from St. John, Jesus emphatically
distinguishes between himself and God--"I ascend unto my Father
and your Father, and to my God and your God." If Jesus were
the incarnate God of the Trinitarians, it should be impossible
for him to ascend to a Being existing in himself. In italici-
zing the word "to" Durand implies that a being existing in a
place other than that occupied by God must be a different
being. A Trinitarian would have italicized the word "unto"
in the phrase "I ascend unto my Father."

The second doctrine is that of the unity of Jesus:

> We believe that Jesus is one mind, one soul, one being,
> as truly one as we are, and equally distinct from the
> one God.[109]

This doctrine is held in opposition to that which asserts that:

> . . . Jesus Christ, instead of being one mind, one
> conscious intellectual principle, whom we can under-
> stand, consists of two souls, two minds; the one divine,
> the other human; the one weak, the other almighty; the
> one ignorant, the other omniscient. Now we maintain
> that this is to make Christ two beings.[110]

The notion of Christ's humanity, a mere corollary to that of
the unity of God, is reflected in that part of the passage from
St. John wherein Jesus implies his equality with mankind by
sending Mary "to my brethren." The same idea is suggested as
he acknowledges over himself and mankind the same God.

Channing next treats of the moral character of God:

> To give our views of God, in one word, we believe
> in his Parental character. We ascribe to him, not only
> the name, but the dispositions and principles of a
> father. We believe that he has a father's concern for
> his creatures, a father's desire for their improvement,
> a father's equity in proportioning his commands to
> their powers, a father's joy in their progress, a
> father's readiness to receive the penitent, and a
> father's justice for the incorrigible.[111]

Again, in the passage from St. John, Jesus three times applies
to God the name of Father.

The Unitarian "views of the mediation of Christ and of the
purposes of his mission" are the last topics that need concern
us. Regarding Christ's mission, Channing writes:

> We believe, that he was sent by the Father to effect
> a moral, or spiritual deliverance of mankind; that
> is, to rescue men from sin and its consequences, and
> bring them to a state of everlasting purity and happi-
> ness. We believe, too, that he accomplishes this sub-
> lime purpose by a variety of methods; . . . by his
> glorious discoveries of immortality; by his sufferings
> and death; by that signal event, the resurrection,
> which powerfully bore witness to his divine mission,
> and brought down to men's senses a future life . . .[112]

Here the resurrection serves as a proof to man's senses of the
reality of life beyond death. As Jesus was seen alive after
his death, the resurrection appearances, such as the one illustrated in Durand's painting, validate the doctrine of a future
life. As the appearance of Jesus to Mary "brought down to
men's senses a future life"--and it is this which he instructs
her to proclaim, so Durand's painting serves the same function.
That cannot be denied which one has seen--either in reality
or an image of reality. On the thorny problem of the mode of
operation of Christ's mediation Channing refuses to be dogmatic:

> We have no desire to conceal the fact, that a
> difference of opinion exists among us, in regard to
> an interesting part of Christ's mediation; I mean, in
> regard to the precise influence of his death, on our
> forgiveness. Many suppose that this event contributes
> to our pardon, as it was a principal means of con-
> firming his religion, and of giving it a power over

the mind; in other words, that it procures forgiveness
by leading to that repentence and virtue, which is the
great and only condition on which forgiveness is bestowed.[113]

The essence of this doctrine is that it presents Christ's sacrifice as the cause of a change in man.  This view is to be
understood in contrast to any doctrine which interprets Christ's
death as "an influence in making God placable or merciful, in
awakening his kindness toward's men" or which presents Christ
as a person of the Godhead who dies to atone for the infinite
crimes of man against an infinite Being.  In sum, Channing
would reject any view that

. . . leads men to think that Christ came to change
God's mind, rather than their own; that the highest
object of his mission, was to avert punishment, rather
than to communicate holiness; and that a large part
of religion consists in disparaging good works and
human virtues, for the purpose of magnifying the value
of Christ's vicarious sufferings.[114]

Hence, the death of Christ in no way alters God's relationship
to man, but that very act ought to alter man's relationship to
God.  As the death of Christ effected in the Magdalene "that
repentence and virtue, which is the great and only condition
on which forgiveness is bestowed,"[115] so ought a painting
implying his death and illustrating his resurrection to have
a similar effect upon the spectator.

In the text from St. John, Durand discovered a Biblical
passage which clearly suggests the Unitarian doctrines of
the unity of God, the unity of Christ, and the paternal character of God. It should now be observed that none of these
doctrines could have been "read" from the painting itself.
No one looking at a painting of Jesus and the Magdalene before
the sepulchre in the garden would have necessarily brought to
mind any of the ideas. The text, then serves as a sort of preface to the painting, adumbrating the theological context in
terms of which the picture is to be experienced. The painting
itself ought to perform the function ascribed by Channing to
the event represented. First, then, the painting, like the
resurrection itself, must function to substantiate the doctrine
of immortality. Second, in implying the death of Christ, the
painting must effect the same result as the event--that is,
it must lead to redemption through repentence and virtue.
From nearly the outset of his career as a painter, Durand
appears to conceive of painting as a means to assure the spectator that the doctrine of immortality is not an idle fantasy
and to transform the spectator in such a way as to render that
immortality accessible to him.

We may, of course, hesitate to believe that Durand would
consciously seek to affirm five doctrines in one painting.
Yet we must bear in mind that at this particular moment the
Unitarians were on the offensive in propagating the liberal
faith, and were quite willing to use poetry and painting in
doing so. Indeed, in the preceding year, the New York Uni-

tarians had used poetry to communicate the same set of ideas which Durand apparently intended to inculcate through his painting. George Bancroft--whose father, the Rev. Aaron Bancroft, was the first President of the American Unitarian Association--supplied Bryant with translations of two poems in which Unitarian doctrines appear. These, one by Goethe and the other attributed to the Greek poet Musasus, Bryant printed in the July, 1825 number of the <u>Athenaeum</u> <u>Magazine</u>.[116] The Greek poem, "The Hymn Sung by the Hierophant, at the Eleusinian Mysteries," is introduced as a poem "in which the <u>Unity</u> <u>of</u> <u>the</u> <u>Deity</u> is promulged /sic/." This doctrine is stated in the following epiphany:

> Behold! the One Supreme,
> Who rules the world, whose eye's far-piercing beam
> The Universe surveys;
> From whom all life and all creation spring.
> Lo! he exists alone,
> But by his glories and his mercies known.

The poem by Goethe, printed under the title "The Indian God and the Bayadeer," describes a visit of Siva to earth. He participates in human "desire, and joy, and sighs" and meets a Bayadeer--a Magdalene--by whom he is loved. He dies, she leaps upon his funeral pyre, and both ascend to heaven. The moral of the story is that

> Of the godhead, the smiles on the contrite are bent;
> Immortals will stoop to the souls that repent;
> Through flames to the skies the lost sinner may soar.

The story then, like Durand's painting and the verses attached
to it, illustrates God's paternal love for Man, the reality of
immortal life, and that immortality is accessible through
repentence. The two poems printed by Bryant around the time
when Durand began his composition might very well have inspired
him to undertake it. However, it is just as likely that the
painting grew out of conversations between Bryant and Durand
on the ideas expressed in the poems and the painting.[117]

Samson Shorn of His Locks by the Philistines While Asleep
in the Lap of Delilah and Hagar and Ishmael in the Wilderness
were exhibited without explanation at the National Academy in
1827 and 1829 respectively. The possibility that Durand executed
these merely as exercises in figure composition should not, of
course, be too quickly set aside. It is worth noting, however,
that the subjects of both paintings may be related to passages
in Channing's discourse entitled "Unitarian Christianity Most
Favorable to Piety," delivered in 1826 at the dedication of
the Second Congregational Unitarian Church in New York. Here
Channing describes the trinitarian theologians under the image
of Samson enslaved:

> . . . they seem to me to move in chains, and to fulfil
> poorly their high function of adding to the wealth of
> human intellect. In theological discussion, they re-
> mind me more of Samson grinding in the narrow mill of
> the Philistines, than of that undaunted champion
> achieving victories for God's people, and enlarging
> the bounds of their inheritance.[118]

The figure of Samson in Durand's painting might, by the initiated, have been regarded as a metaphor for the vanquished intellect which fails to fulfil its exalted destiny. But Durand represented Samson being enslaved rather than in slavery. In so doing he was able to indicate the agents by which the hero (or the mind) was overcome. The Philistines who treacherously attack Samson might be understood as a metaphor for the Trinitarian theology which Channing in the same paragraph characterizes as "a system which has a tendency to confine the mind . . ." Thus, as Samson lost his strength when he was shaved by the Philistines, so the mind of the theologian, which according to Channing ought to win victories for God among men, ceases to benefit humanity when it is ensnared in the doctrines of the Trinitarians. As Channing laments the "barrenness and feebleness" of, and the lack of "vitality" in, theological thought, so Durand represented only that attack of the Philistines which rendered Samson impotent and excluded any implication of the subsequent blinding.

Durand's third Biblical painting, Hagar and Ishmael in the Wilderness, may also have been inspired by a passage in the same discourse. In describing God's mercy Channing states

> . . . that the yearnings of the tenderest human parent towards a lost child, are but a faint image of God's deep and overflowing compassion towards erring man.[119]

The concern of the parent for her child forms a prominent part of the Biblical account of the sojourn of Hagar and Ishmael in the wilderness.

Then the water in the skin became exhausted, and
throwing the child under one of the bushes, she went
and sat down about a bowshot away; "For," said she,
"I cannot bear to see the child die!" so she sat down
some way off, and lifted up her voice in weeping.[120]

This concern was certainly implicit, and, very probably, actually
stressed in Durand's painting.  Hence, in selecting this subject
Durand may have intended to indicate God's compassion through
its earthly type.  But it should also be noted that in the
Biblical narrative Hagar's lamentation is immediately followed
by God's compassionate response--"God, however, heard the boy's
cry."[121]  And an angel reveals to Hagar a well of water from
which she may refresh her son.

While the Hagar and Ishmael was not exhibited until 1829,
Durand apparently began work upon it somewhat earlier.  Indeed,
the New-York Historical Society possesses a drawing of the subject inscribed at the lower left "Durand 1827" and at the lower
center "Hagar" (Fig. 25).  If the date given on the drawing is
correct, Durand must have begun work on the Hagar theme while
still at work on the Samson.  If this were the case, both works
would have been undertaken shortly after Channing's Discourse
of 1826 mentioned above.  In the drawing, Durand does not closely
follow the Biblical text.  According to the text the child
should be at some distance from the mother at the moment of
the angel's arrival.  Instead of this, Durand allows the angel
to appear while the mother and child are still united in a
single group expressive of parental tenderness.  This motif of

human tenderness at the left is balanced in the composition
by the angel, who is the agent of the divine compassion symbolized, according to Channing, by the compassion of the
human parent. It would thus seem at least possible that Dur-
and's deviations from the Biblical narrative were controlled
by his desire to express the terms of Channing's metaphor.
Yet, the fact remains that the picture could only have been
fully understood as representing a type of God's compassion
by a spectator who had previously been informed that such was
the painter's intention. Not forewarned, one would have seen
only the representation of a Biblical story involving a certain,
adventitious change of fortune. If we adopt this view, Durand's
deviations from the Biblical narrative might readily be explained as the result of his study of earlier treatments of the
story, for example Benjamin West's,[122] in which mother and child
are united in a tender group at the moment of the angel's
appearance.

In the Mary Magdalene, we can be fairly certain, Durand
did intend to illustrate Unitarian theological concepts. There
is less certainty about the other two paintings, both of which
could be simply attempts at pictorial dramas. Yet, if we find
Unitarian ideas expressed in the first painting, this in itself
would add support to a contention that the other two are expressions of Unitarian thought as well. Further, we may, at
least, doubt that Durand would have employed Biblical stories
in paintings of an exclusively dramatic character. Had he
intended no theological comment in the Samson and the Hagar,

he might better have chosen subjects from, say, Shakespeare
from which any religious implication would be lacking.
Finally, if in the _Samson_ Durand did intend an attack on the
more complacent of the orthodox clergy, he could only have
presented the idea in a way that should be meaningful exclusively to those who remembered Channing's words, if at the
same time he wished to avoid the enmity of the powerful clergy
against whom the painting was directed.[123]

.    .    .

During the period 1817 to 1830 Durand produced a number of
important engravings, which won for him the esteem of the
community and a moderate prosperity. But, viewed in connection
with his later career, this period still should be regarded as
part of his education. It was a period for Durand of exploration
of remarkably wide scope. He gained access to the ideas of the
intelligentsia of New York as well as to the ideas of artists
and men concerned with religious issues. In his studies at
the Academies he became acquainted with the vocabulary of forms
of Antique sculpture and the idioms of Baroque painting. As
his range of intellectual and artistic experience expanded, he
was able to move beyond the realm of commercial engraving to
express himself, albeit tentatively, on some of the large
humanistic and theological issues of the day. In the _Fuller_
and the _Musidora_ he concerned himself with the question of the
quality of humanity that ought to flourish in a republic. In
the Biblical pictures he dealt with Man's relationship to God.
But in handling both of these issues he sought not simply to

produce visual statements of abstract ideas, but, of more
importance, he tried to deal with these in such a way that
the visual image would assimilate the spectator to an ideal
state. Already in these works there is reflected the belief,
which Durand held to the end of his career, that a work of
art should be both useful to society and beautiful. The
utilitarian objective, indeed, dominates the primarily informative American Landscape engravings.

In this period Durand sought more to acquaint himself with
the established Neo-classical style than to develop a style of
his own. It was the eagerness of Durand and other young artists
to study Antique casts that precipitated the formation of the
National Academy. But once he had begun to master the Neo-
classical style, Durand almost immediately abandoned it in favor
of the newer Romantic styles imported by Allston, Thomas Cole,
and others from England. While the Neo-classical husk soon fell
from Durand's art, the ideas with which he concerned himself
in the 1820's continued to attract his attention. His concern
with the sublime and the beautiful, his concern with human
character and theological questions impelled him to seek new
expressive means. Despite their obvious weakness the American
Landscape engravings do announce the beginning of Durand's
search for a style more adequate than that fostered by the
Academy which five years earlier he had helped to form.

CHAPTER TWO: CLASSIC AND ROMANTIC CURRENTS, A PERIOD OF
TRANSITION, 1830-1837.

I. Personal and Public Crises Around 1830.

To the extent that success and happiness depend upon the
conscientious application of an individual's own talents, Dur-
and prospered in the 1820's. But everything is not given
merely to talent and diligence. In what lies beyond human
control, Durand in the late 1820's was less fortunate. His
second child died in 1827. Two years later his wife's health
failed. When her removal to New Jersey failed to produce a
definite recovery, she and Asher made a slow and painful mid-
winter journey to St. Augustine, Florida, where she died in
February, 1830.[1] The death of Durand's wife in 1830 might
well have appeared to him as the effect of Divine retribution,
for he himself had in the previous year brought a man to death
in vengeance.[2] If, indeed, this confluence of events left
Durand with a sense of personal guilt, it may be regarded as
a major factor contributing both to the spiritual crisis that
he appears to have endured in the early 1830's and to that
deep concern with the problems of innocence, guilt, and redemption which is reflected in many of his later paintings. The
following year he left the house in Amity Street, with its
painful memories of his wife, and began a sort of restless,

103

nomadic life. During the years 1831 to 1837 he lived successively at four different addresses in New York, made frequent trips to New Jersey, and travelled as far afield as Brunswick, Maine, in one direction and Montpelier, the Virginia estate of James Madison, in the other.

Professionally, during the period of his wife's illness his work as a commercial engraver became distasteful. The increasingly competitive, bank-note business came to depend less on the quality of the work executed and more on successful lobbying at Albany. This latter aspect of the business was conducted largely by Durand's partner Elias Wade, Jr., but must have been among the factors which induced Durand to gradually abandon his efforts in this direction. From the later part of 1829 to the middle of 1831, Durand accomplished very little either as an engraver or a painter. In 1830 he contributed nothing to the annual exhibition at the National Academy. And to the exhibition of 1831, a review exhibition, he sent three paintings previously shown in 1827 and one landscape (App. II, no. 10)--a painted version of the Catskill Mountains engraving published in The American Landscape. This landscape was probably the only painting completed during these two years. The lack of any major work from the years 1830-1831 is the measure of the severity of the misfortunes Durand suffered at this time. Finally, both Henry T. Tuckerman and John Durand[3] state that overwork and too close a confinement to the engraver's bench resulted in the failure of Durand's own health. Although neither gives the precise date of this disorder, it was probably sometime around 1830.

America, also, had become something quite different by 1830 from what it had been in 1817. Nearly coincident with the crises in Durand's personal life, the nation had experienced that revolution that brought Andrew Jackson to the Presidency in 1828. While it is possible that Durand, like Bryant, had supported the new President--Durand had engraved a large plate after Vanderlyn's full-length portrait of Jackson during the campaign of 1828[4]--it is also probable that he could not approve of all of the measures advocated since the election. Parke Godwin vividly summarized the national situation as seen by Bryant upon assuming the editorship of the _Evening Post_ in 1829:

> Unfortunately, he found himself, from the outset of his editorial career, in sharp conflict with a large and powerful force of public opinion. A mass of schemes growing out of the needs of a young and impatient material civilization . . . which not only proceeded upon theories of government the reverse of his own, but which threatened to swamp all rational notions of government in a deluge of selfish and avaricious clamors. These schemes were prosecuted by a great party, strong alike in numbers, intelligence, and wealth, and upheld by leaders distinguished for intellect and eloquence. One segment of this numerous body, comprising the bankers and merchants, endeavored to

control, by means of allied incorporations, the issues
of paper currencies which exercised all the functions
of money; another part, composed of the manufacturers,
demanded bounties in the shape of prohibitory and discriminating taxes against foreign rivals; and a third
raved for subsidies to enable them to construct local
roads and canals, and to clear out unnavigable harbors
and rivers in the name of local improvements.  They
all agreed in one thing--mercenary intentions against
the common treasury. . . . It was in this light, at
least, that Mr. Bryant saw these projects, and he set
himself against them with all his ardor and ability.[5]

As ambition and impatience began to become the ruling forces in
American life, more sensitive and serious men hoped to inculcate
the virtues and moral restraints so evidently needed by their
contemporaries.  Bryant had ample opportunity to speak through
the editorial column of the _Evening Post_.  Channing and other
Unitarian clergymen were particularly active in preaching a
social gospel.

The Reverend Orville Dewey--Channing's disciple and the
minister of the Second Congregational Unitarian Church in New
York, a close friend of Bryant, and a member of the Sketch
Club--has been described as the first New York clergyman to
apply the doctrines of Christianity "to the business of the
market and the street, to the offices of home and the pleasures
of society."[6]  In 1838 he published his _Moral Views of Commerce,
Society, and Politics, in Twelve Discourses_.  At a time when

those who attended a church preferred "to hear an exposition
of abstract doctrines, or a general discussion in morals, or
even an impressive and eloquent exhibition of some solemn
truth relative to the 'world that is to come,'"[7] Dewey's efforts
to bring religion down into the public and private affairs of
daily life was met with considerable hostility. Although the
voice of truth remained, as ever, feeble, it was amplified by
the paintings of a few artists, Durand among them, who in the
mid-1830's undertook to employ their art as an instrument to
improve the conscience of the age.

Durand's return to the heart of the city in 1831 marks the
beginning of a new phase of his career. In the years 1833 to
1835 he continued to work as an engraver, devoting himself
largely to the execution of nineteen plates for the National
Portrait Gallery of Distinguished Americans. But by 1835 he
had determined to abandon engraving. His large plate after
John Vanderlyn's Ariadne Asleep on the Island of Naxos, published
in this year, was his last major work in an art to which he had
devoted twenty years. By the time he abandoned engraving, he
had already established a firm reputation as a portrait painter
with the exhibition of five portraits at the National Academy
in 1833. Through the exhibition of 1837, portraits constituted
the largest single class of work exhibited by Durand in any
single year. In the mid-1830's, however, he exhibited one
history painting, two comic pictures, and a number of landscapes,
which indicate that he felt again his old eagerness to experi-

ment and suggest that, ultimately, he would not be satisfied
to remain a portrait painter.

In considering his work prior to 1830, we were able to
divide it into two large categories: one consisting of purely
commercial work done at the request of the public and the other
of work done on his own initiative and calculated to improve
or instruct the public conscience. His work from 1832 to 1837
may still be categorized as commissioned or uncommissioned.
But now, much of the work done at the request of the public
displays a concern with moral values and is, therefore, related
to his uncommissioned work of the 1820's. These works, painted
at the request of men who shared Durand and Bryant's concern
over the moral temper of the times, were calculated to correct
public attitudes and practices that seemed to lie within the
realm of human control. Although executed for various individuals, they were addressed primarily to the general public and
probably would not have been produced had Durand been unable
to exhibit them. These, then, may be regarded as his public
pictures.

In contrast to the public pictures, others reflect or were
calculated to relieve the personal anguish that had resulted
from events beyond human control--disappointed ambition, waiver-
ing faith in his own abilities, and the deaths of his child and
wife and, later, his patron, Luman Reed. These paintings were
addressed primarily to himself and, we may assume, would have
been created even had Durand had no opportunity to exhibit
them. In general, Durand did not intend that these should be

sold. As the direct products of his own emotional experience, they may be regarded as his private works.

With these distinctions in mind we may turn to an examination of the works belonging to the two categories.

II. Private Pictures:  Children and the Female Figure.

A. Portraits of Children.

In the 1820's and 1830's Durand appears to have been especially fascinated by children and to have regarded them as particularly suitable subjects for pictures. The first painting
that he exhibited publically was the Portrait of One of the
Artist's Children (App. II, no. 2) shown at the American Academy
in 1823. A Portrait of a Child (App. II, no. 3) was shown at the
first exhibition of the National Academy in 1826. An elaborate
drawing of his daughter Caroline dates from 1828 (Fig. 28). A
group portrait, the Children of the Artist (Fig. 29), painted in
the summer of 1832, was the first major work completed as he began to recover from the shock of his wife's death. This was
followed by other portraits of children--another portrait of
Caroline (App. II, no. 129), three of his daughter Lucy (App. II,
nos. 133-135), and one of his son John (App. II, no. 132). These
portraits, several of which were exhibited but not intended for
sale, must have been painted primarily for Durand's personal
gratification.

In painting the earliest of the group, Portrait of One of
the Artist's Children, Durand was not following a well-estab-
lished fashion in American painting, for it was not until the
mid-1830's that portraits of children, by artists such as Henry
Inman and William Dunlap, became popular. Durand, however,
was not the first to exhibit a portrait of a child in New York.
In 1818 Samuel Waldo and his partner William Jewett exhibited

a _Portrait_ _of_ _Master_ _McCoun_ and a _Portrait_ _of_ _the_ _Three_
_Children_ _of_ _Mr._ _J._ _K._ _Hamilton_ at the American Academy.  As
it was about this time that Durand "received advice and instruction . . . respecting portraiture" from Waldo,[8] the latter
may have had some effect in turning Durand's thoughts toward
the representation of children.  Other painters--Elias Metcalf,
Charles R. Leslie, John W. Jarvis, and John Trumbull--also exhibited portraits of children at the American Academy before
1820.

Of these several artists, Trumbull may have provided the
strongest impetus to Durand's interest in portraying children.
It was Trumbull who treated the theme of childhood within a
larger framework of ideas.  From the first exhibition of the
American Academy, he exhibited two Biblical paintings in which
children are the actors.  One, _The_ _Saviour_ _and_ _St._ _John_ _Playing_
_with_ _a_ _Lamb_ (Fig. 26), includes a visionary cross in the sky
toward  which the infant Jesus looks.  Memories of this painting
may have inspired Durand's later paintings in which the sportiveness of childhood is emphasized and sometimes combined with a
more serious state of meditation.[9]  Trumbull's other Biblical
painting, _Our_ _Saviour_ _with_ _Little_ _Children_ (Fig. 27), was
based on a passage in the Gospel according to St. Luke:

> And they brought unto him also infants, that he would
> touch them:  but when his disciples saw it, they re-
> buked them.  But Jesus called them unto him, and said,
> Suffer little children to come unto me, and forbid
> them not:  for of such is the kingdom of God.  Verily

> I say unto you, Whosoever shall not receive the king-
> dom of God as a little child, shall in no wise enter
> therein.[10]

Regarded from a theological point of view, the child is an ex-
emplar of Christian faith and the type of the redeemed. These
concepts may have inspired Durand's earliest portraits of
children exhibited in 1823 and 1826, which have not been located.

But the child's freedom from guilt is explicitly indicated
in the drawing of Caroline Durand of around 1828 (Fig. 28).*
Here, the child sits on the floor of the nursery. To the right
of the child is an overturned stool and a spoon; to her left,
an upset sewing basket containing a spool of thread and a pair
of scissors. The child is obviously deep in mischief among
the emblems of matronly virtue. Her abuse of these things suggests her exemption, as yet, from the sin that may in some
degree be overcome by the virtues which these things represent.
The idea of the girl's innocence is further affirmed by the
fact that she holds what appears to be the quarter of an
apple, which she, as the type of the redeemed, may eat with
impunity.

The Children of the Artist (Fig. 29), painted in the summer
of 1832, representing the three surviving children of Durand's
first marriage--John, Caroline, and Lucy, is his most elaborate
treatment of the theme of childhood. The three, very serious
children sit or stand, shaded by the foliage of a venerable tree,
at the corner of a brick house to the left-hand side of the
immediate foreground. At the right an open landscape vista--

* The theological interpretation of this drawing and the
Children of the Artist, discussed below, seems strained
(D.B.L. 1977).

water, meadows, and distant mountains--contrasts with the closed setting for the children. The general scheme of the composition--children in the foreground of an extensive landscape--is closely related to Gainsborough's Girls and Pigs (Fig. 30), exhibited at the Royal Academy in 1782, purchased by Sir Joshua Reynolds,and engraved by Richard Earlom in 1783.[11] Indeed, certain details relate the compositions by Gainsborough and Durand so closely as to suggest that Durand studied Earlom's engraving. John Durand and Gainsborough's girl sit on a stone wall at the corner of a vine-covered cottage. The girl displays a pensive seriousness quite like that of Durand's children. Durand has omitted the pigs but has introduced three chickens in their stead--and the position of two of these chickens, pecking at a worm, is similar to that of the two, eating pigs.

In commenting upon the children in Gainsborough's fancy-pictures, Reynolds speaks only of their "natural grace and elegance."[12] To him, the child was neither the exemplary Christian nor the type of the redeemed. And in Gainsborough's Girl and Pigs there are no theological overtones. Yet, in Durand's painting the Fall of Man is definitely evoked by the basket of fruit held by the seated girl and by the fact that John Durand peels an apple toward which the standing girl points. All of the children give their full attention to this apple, which, like Adam, John has clearly received from the little girl, a second Eve. By including this re-enactment of the once-disastrous events in the Garden of Eden did Durand

intend to characterize his own children as beings of evil?
Perhaps he agreed with

> those whose language respecting children, if it have
> any meaning, directly affirms their guilt and their
> desert of ruin. According to some, human nature is
> sinful, corrupt, depraved at birth. Infants are
> demons in human shape, objects of God's abhorrence,
> and, if treated according to their deserts, they would
> be plunged into hell.[13]

But this conception of childhood contradicts the idea of children
as the type of the inheritors of heaven. If the kingdom of God
is of such as these, they must be exempt, due to their faith,
from the fatal effects of the primal transgression. Paradoxi-
cally, the children remain innocent despite their toying with
the apple. The idea of the essential innocence of children was
especially advocated by Channing, who in the essay cited above,
asserts not only that children are without sin but also that
they possess charms to heal the troubled heart:

> I ask, then, if children were demons, fit for
> hell, would God have given them that attractive sweet-
> ness, that mild beauty, which renders them the most
> interesting objects on earth, and which compels us to
> shrink with horror from the thought of their ever-
> lasting ruin? . . . Who has not felt the turbulent
> passions of his nature calmed at the sight of child-
> hood? And is this winning child, whom God has adorned

with the charms most suited to engage the heart,

abhorred by God and fit only for the flames of Hell?[14]

Perhaps, in the time of distress following his wife's death,
the affective and healing powers of children were verified in
Durand's own experience.  In both the drawing of Caroline and
the painting of the three children, Durand does assert that
the child participates in fallen, human nature.  Indeed, the
sobriety of the three children, as compared with the gaiety
of Caroline, reflects the heightened awareness of guilt which
Durand had attained by 1832.  But, if the child is subject to
guilt, it is far more innocent than the adult, and therefore
it may, in large degree, typify the redeemed.  As the type of
the redeemed, the painted image of the child, precisely like
the Catholic image of a saint, may contribute to the redemption of the adult--may calm the turbulent passions.

The idea of the relevance to the adult of childhood or
the memory of childhood figures prominently in the poetry of
William Wordsworth, to which Durand must have been introduced
by Bryant if he did not discover it himself.  In the "Intimations of Immortality from Recollections of Early Childhood"
it is not so much the child that is important to the man, but
rather Wordsworth points out the endurance of the child in
the man.  The image of the child might serve to strengthen in
the man

> . . . those first affections
> Those shadowy recollections,
> Which, be they what they may,

Are yet the fountain light of all our day,

Are yet a master light of all our seeing;

Uphold us, cherish, and have power to make

Our noisy years seem moments in the being

Of the eternal Silence; truths that wake

To perish never;

Which neither listlessness, nor mad endeavor,

Nor Man nor Boy,

Nor all that is at enmity with joy,

Can utterly abolish or destroy![15]

Due to this endurance of the child in the man, he is able, not continually, but occasionally, to recover in adulthood something of the "vision splendid"[16] that attends the child. In Durand's painting the well-illumined children against a dark background are balanced by a shadowy landscape against a bright sky at the right. The group at the left reawakens the child in the man, and it is this "child," rather than the man, who is able to perceive the vision of varied forms, space, and light at the right. It is this child in the man that prevents the collapse of the world into a narrow and dark "prison" like that in which the children do enact the Fall. The idea of childlike faith as the "master light of all our seeing" is of course a distinctly Romantic idea and stands in contrast to the Neo-classicist's concept of proportion and the Antique as redeeming agents. And yet, the two points of view are closely related in that each entails the creation of an ordered universe--a cosmos--where none existed prior to the operation of the tran-

scendental factor. Where the Neo-classicist employs geometry
to create the world that God would have made had He been able,
Durand and Wordsworth, through the recovery of the child's
vision, rise to a vision of the world God did make--a world
He made for man's spiritual nourishment.

The three chickens also suggest that the right-hand side
of the painting refers more to Durand himself than to the
children. In including these Durand was inspired, not by the
Romantic poetry of Wordsworth, but, again, by the Gospels.
The birds would seem to be those referred to in the Gospel
according to Matthew:

> Behold the fowls of the air: for they sow not, neither
> do they reap, nor gather into barns; yet your heavenly
> Father feedeth them. Are ye not much better than they.[17]

As God provides for the birds, so He shall provide for man.[18]
Perhaps the prominent plants in the right-hand foreground of
Durand's painting were suggested by another illustration of
God's care for man:

> And why take ye thought for raiment? Consider the
> lilies of the field, how they grow; they toil not,
> neither do they spin: And yet I say unto you, That
> even Solomon in all his glory was not arrayed like one
> of these. Wherefore, if God so clothe the grass of
> the field, which to-day is, and to-morrow is cast into
> the oven, shall he not much more clothe you, O, ye of
> little faith?[19]

Illustrating a total reliance on God in worldly affairs, the
chickens and the plants, although they are not lilies, recall
the nourishment of Ishmael in the wilderness, as illustrated
in Durand's earlier painting,[20] and recommend the kind of
Christian faith that is exemplified, also, in the innocence
of the children. But the birds and plants stand in the painting as "sermons" addressed primarily to Durand himself rather
than to the children who are oblivious of them.

One other element in the painting also suggests that the
right-hand side was inspired by the sixth chapter of Matthew.
We have already suggested that Durand may have been influenced
by Wordsworth's notion of the endurance in the man of the
child's ecstatic vision. Certainly, the ideas and poetry of
Wordsworth were current in America in the 1830's, especially
in the circle of Bryant. But Durand might as well have been
influenced by the concept of the inner light of faith which
is adumbrated in Matthew:

> The light of the body is the eye: If therefore thine
> eye be single /pure, innocent?/, thy whole body shall
> be full of light: But if thine eye be evil, thy whole
> body shall be full of darkness. If therefore the
> light that is in thee be darkness, how great is that
> darkness![21]

If the birds and the plants, external things, refer to an inner
condition of willingness to rely on God, so might the external
light refer to the inner light of faith.[22]

This inner light of faith is functionally related to
Romantic concepts of imagination. For example, according to
Gulian Verplanck, the study of the "elegant arts"

> leads on its real votaries from the pleasure derived
> from the mechanical imitation of nature's ordinary
> appearances to the deeper delight afforded by the
> selection of whatever is grand or graceful in her
> forms, powerful or lovely in her expression. Then it
> is that new susceptibilities to some of the purest
> and most exquisite of mental pleasures awaken gradually
> in the breast, and we become conscious of sentiments
> and powers before dormant and unknown. We no longer
> gaze around with that gross, material sense to which
> nought but material objects can be present and visible.
> A keener mental sight opens within. To the eye of
> sense, the whole earth may be cold and blank; while to
> the eye of cultivated imagination, every part of
> creation beams with rays of light, and glory, and
> beauty.
>
> In such moments--for alas! they are only moments--
> the world loses its hold, base cares and bad passions
> flit away, and the mind, though not redeemed from the
> thraldom of vice of /or "or"/ the burden of sorrow, is
> for a time calmed and purified.[23]

Here Verplanck is not thinking specifically of the Wordsworthian
child's vision or of the Biblical vision of faith, but the vision
of Romantic imagination. However, to him, imagination, like

either of the other two kinds of vision, leads the self away from the world, vice, and passion. The difference between the Biblical light of faith and Wordsworth's "vision splendid" of childhood is that where the latter must diminish with the years and can only be fully restored temporarily by the grace of God, the former, like Verplanck's "cultivated imagination," may increase with the years. Wordsworth's diminishing light can best be lamented in a sort of elegiac verse, while the Biblical light of faith can more appropriately be treated in the visual image, where it can be seen and serve to strengthen the faith of the spectator. However, the difference between Wordsworth's "child-light" and the Biblical light is slight; for, in the adult, both may exist in different degrees from one individual to another. And the light of faith is "the fountain light of all our day" and "a master light of all our seeing," which contrasts as much with worldly seeing as "treasures in heaven" are opposed to "treasures upon earth." Indeed, Wordsworth's "Intimations of Immortality" might be regarded as a sort of Romantic commentary on Matthew 19:14 (children as the type of the redeemed) and Matthew 6:22-23 (the light of faith), but a commentary colored by his recognition of the frailty of faith in real life. In the painting of the children, based on these and related passages, Durand seems to have used the Biblical images in an effort to strengthen his own faith at a time of personal crisis.

B. Portraits of Ladies and Studies of the Female Figure.

1. The Frank Sisters.

In the mid-1830's Durand returned to the theme of the female figure in a landscape setting with which he had experimented in the Musidora engraving of 1825. The first of these later works is the double portrait of Mary Frank and her sister Jane Cordelia Frank (Fig. 31), painted in 1834. As Durand married Mary Frank in the same year, the painting may be regarded as a private picture and as one in which Durand would be free to interpret the girls as he pleased. But, if Durand sought to impose an ideal upon the Frank sisters, it clearly differs from that which informed the Musidora. The graceful movement of Musidora has here been supplanted by the static, seated pose. In the earlier work the anatomical structure of the body was exposed to reveal its delicacy and softness. In the later work the repose of the figures renders their anatomical organization as irrelevant as it is concealed. The sense of the physical vitality of a human machine in the Musidora has been replaced by a passive calm, a state of pure being. In approaching the problem of portraying the two girls, Durand has rejected the tradition of Reynolds, Lawrence, Sully, Jarvis, and Morse--a tradition in which the figure is frequently represented in an animated pose and sometimes actually in motion--in favor of the tradition of Gainsborough--a tradition from which any decided gesture or haste is excluded.

Perhaps, the closest parallel to Durand's Mary and Jane Cordelia Frank is Gainsborough's Elizabeth and Mary Linley

(Fig. 32). That is, the two paintings are related in their subject matter and interpretation of personality. While Gainsborough's subtle pencilings and his exquisite combinations of rose, blue-silvers, and browns were far beyond Durand's grasp, in both paintings the girls display a mood of tranquility, and in both they are placed in a natural setting unmodified by the hand of the gardener and unadorned even by a stray fragment of architecture.

A part of the interest that may be given to a portrait of two sisters,[24] beings almost as identical as nature can produce, is the discrimination of the unique character of each. Gainsborough has notably achieved this by having the nearer girl turn an interested and ingenuous face toward the spectator, while her sister turns a pensive gaze toward nothing, lost in her own dreaming meditation. In Durand's painting, Mary, in white, is the more pensive, and Jane the more alert. Mary has apparently been thinking about the object toward which she points, or pursuing thoughts suggested by that object, and continues to do so even after having recommended it to her sister's attention. Jane seems just to have looked toward it, and still she regards it as a new discovery. The object is nothing more than a stone bearing the girls' initials and the date of the painting. As a fragment of nature bearing their initials, the stone reflects the girls in the "corner stone" of nature. If the stone reflects the girls in a solid material, the pool of water reflects the girls-- the white dress of one, the black dress of the other--in a fluid

material. Hence, the reflections of both girls in the stone
and water suggest the idea of an analogy between nature and
the female. The same analogy is, of course, present in the
painting by Gainsborough. However, in the Gainsborough the
differentiated personalities of the girls are reflected in an
undifferentiated nature. Durand, on the other hand, has tried
to differentiate the personality of nature in such a way as
to reflect more exactly the diverse personalities of the girls.
The dark-clad Jane sits before the heavy dark foliage of short
trees that limit the space behind her. Mary, in her light
dress, sits at the foot of a tree that ascends beyond the edges
of the painting; she sits before an infinite vista, beneath the
most strongly illuminated portion of the sky. Jane, then,
might be regarded as a personification of those aspects of
nature that are dark, limited, and earth-bound. Mary is the
personification of the aspiring, of light, and the infinite
in nature. Both girls are feminine, and nature is feminine.
But, as the female personality may be polarized as passive and
active, spirtual and worldly, sacred and profane, so the feminine
personality of nature may be analyzed in similar terms.

But Durand married Mary Frank in the same year that he
painted the portrait. Surely his intention must have been fixed
at the time it was painted, and we should expect some reference
to the anticipated marriage. Perhaps he was inspired by Wordsworth's definition of the ideal wife in "She Was a Phantom of
Delight,"[25] which certainly parallels the painting in several
respects. In the painting as in the poem, the female is des-

cribed in terms of nature--eyes like stars, twilight hair, all else like spring and dawn. Wordsworth's list of domestic virtues, we may assume, Durand was willing to apply to his fiancée, although they are not explicitly referred to in the painting. But she is clearly "a being breathing thoughtful breath." Should we see in the center pool a "fountain of life" and in the tablet at the lower left a sort of rudimentary tombstone, Mary would, then, be "A Traveller between life and death." Her association with the more etherial aspects of nature--light and space and the ascending tree--identify her as "A lovely apparition" or "a Spirit still, and bright / With something of an angel light." In terms of Wordsworth's poem, Mary Frank approximates to the ideal of woman in a marital relationship to man. Durand's interest in this theme is indicated by a painting entitled The Bride (App. II, no. 400), exhibited at the National Academy in 1845; and in the following year he defined woman as a source of solace in the painting A Passage in the Life of Woman (App. II, no. 224), exhibited at the Academy with the verses by an unidentified poet:

When pain and anguish wring the brow;

A ministering angel thou!

Neither of these paintings, unfortunately, has been located.[26]

2. Ariadne Asleep on the Island of Naxos.

At some time in the early 1830's--probably 1831--Durand was able to purchase John Vanderlyn's large painting Ariadne Asleep on the Island of Naxos.[27] Painted in 1812 and inspired by the Vatican, Hellenistic statue believed to represent Ariadne, Vanderlyn's painting is a superb example of later Proto-Romantic, French Neo-classicism. The combination of an arbitrarily posed body with a rich and shadowy landscape setting relates it to contemporary works such as Prud'hon's <u>Portrait of Josephine Beauharnais</u> or Baron Gros' <u>Christine Boyer</u>.[28] The painting fascinated Durand, who copied it twice (Fig. 33) before he published the large, engraved reproduction in 1835 (Fig. 34). Moreover, its impact can be traced in both the <u>Children of the Artist</u> and the <u>Frank Sisters</u>. In all three paintings one or more figures are prominently placed in the foreground. In each a copse of trees limits space at one side, while a distant vista opens up at the other. In all three, darkness dominates one part of the background; light, the other; and the massive trunk of a tree appears immediately behind the figures. Finally, the quietude of the figures in each of Durand's portraits approximates to the sleep of Ariadne.

But, more particularly, Vanderlyn's painting seems to approach very closely to the concepts of the polarity of nature and of the composition of the <u>Frank Sisters</u>. The contrast of earth and water is suggested in the foreground of Vanderlyn's painting; but Durand's engraving gives it more emphasis by transforming what in the painting is only the bank of a pool into a brook running between two banks. The addition of the nearer bank of this brook is Durand's only significant modification of the painting. In the engraving, as in the <u>Frank Sisters</u>, Durand appears to indicate that the contrary elements of earth and water lie at the base of nature. The contrast between a dark, material, and confining and a light, airy, and infinite aspect of nature fills the background of the paintings by Durand and Vanderlyn. Just as Vanderlyn defined certain polar qualities in nature, so are polar qualities reflected in the arbitrary contrasts of pure frontality and the pure profile in the various parts of the figure. Thus, the contrasts within the single figure here correspond to the contrasting moods of the two figures in the Frank Sisters. In either picture, the female is the analogue of a dualistic nature. When Durand published his Ariadne engraving, he must have regarded it primarily as a restatement, in terms appropriate to the general public, of ideas which he had previously embodied in terms that were primarily appropriate to himself and his family.

Lastly, the Ariadne contains an element of pathos that is absent from the Frank Sisters. The former represents not simply a sleeping female, but one who, while she sleeps, is abandoned by her lover. In the engraving, as in Vanderlyn's painting, Theseus on the distant shore prepares to depart. Ariadne's loss may be interpreted as a metaphor for any of the losses that befall mankind--as a metaphor for the tragic element that is part of man's mature experience of life. As such, her loss recalls Wordsworth's "still, sad music of humanity," and the picture parallels that passage in "Lines, Composed a Few Miles Above Tintern Abbey" in which Wordsworth defines the influence of adult experience upon his vision of nature:

> For I have learned
>
> To look on nature, not as in the hour
> Of thoughtless youth; but hearing oftentimes
> The still, sad music of humanity,
> Nor harsh nor grating, though of ample power
> To chasten and subdue.  And I have felt
> A presence that disturbs me with the joy
> Of elevated thoughts; a sense sublime
> Of something far more deeply interfused,
> Whose dwelling is the light of setting suns,
> And the round ocean and the living air,
> And the blue sky, and in the mind of man:
> A motion and a spirit, that impels
> All thinking things, all objects of all thought,
> And rolls through all things.

Not only in its story does the painting evoke a certain chastening
sadness, but it also encompasses that range of phenomena which
Wordsworth specifies as being inhabited by a single "presence"--
"the light of setting suns," "the round ocean," "the living
air," "the blue sky," and "the mind of man."  It is certainly
possible that Vanderlyn himself had composed the painting with
Wordsworth's lines in mind.  He could have become familiar
with the poem through Coleridge, with whom he and Allston
associated in Rome in 1808.  Yet, whatever Vanderlyn's intention, Durand might have studied the picture from a Wordsworthian
point of view at a time when he appears to have been studying
the poet.  And if Durand interpreted the picture as an image of

nature as seen through an awareness of human sorrow, it becomes, in the words of the poet:

> The anchor of my purest thoughts, the nurse,
>
> The guide, the guardian of my heart, and soul
>
> Of all my moral being.[29]

3. Ideal Portraits.

Early in 1835, Durand paid a reverential visit to the friend
of Wordsworth and Coleridge, Washington Allston. Allston
praised his engraving after the Ariadne[30] and may have introduced
him to those of his ideal portraits which an anonymous critic
in the following year described as belonging "to a new class
of pictures." Of Allston's "ideal portraits," Beatrice, Rosalia,
and The Valentine,[31] the critic wrote:

> Unlike the single figures of any other artist, they are
>
> not created merely to be looked at and so remind us
>
> ideal beauty; but to be communed with as living beings
>
> whom we may love, and who love us; and who bid us rise,
>
> with them, into the heaven of poetry, in which their
>
> Creator dwells and they with him.[32]

In his Ideal Head (Fig. 35) of 1836, Durand sought to create
an elevating image in the tradition of Allston. Here, Durand
departs from his earlier interest in the analogy between the
female and nature. The half-length female figure sits before
a heavy curtain, that fills the entire background of the painting and effectively removes the figure from any particular,
wordly situation. The environment is "abstract." Even less

emphasis is placed upon the physical body of the figure than in the Frank Sisters. The body is in total repose. Where the Frank Sisters are aware of an object, the girl here is aware of no object. What she sees is something seen within the mind--a vision, a dream--which is so attractive that it arrests her gaze at the point where it chanced to turn at the moment of the vision's descent. The world of things and the physical life of the body have been suppressed in order to make of the figure a vessel containing nothing but the dream. As the painting was not exhibited during Durand's lifetime, clearly it belongs to the class of his works that were painted for his own purposes. In this case, perhaps, Durand was immediately inspired by the statement in the essay on Allston already cited:

> A father of a family could hardly give to his daughters
> a refining and elevating influence to compare with that
> of one of this class of pictures.[33]

A year or two later Durand produced another interpretation of the female spirit in a second portrait of his wife (Fig. 36). Again, she is seated out-of-doors before a wood. But now the wood closes behind her, a dark, mysterious background. Mary is seated against the trunk of a tree and immediately behind the picture plane--or even in front of it, as no object interposes between her and the spectator. The idea of the analogy between the female and nature seems to be absent here. Rather, she is one of those figures which Allston's critic described as "to be communed with as living beings whom we may love, and who love us; and who bid us rise . . ." As Durand's wife, she is

one whom he loved and by whom he was loved. Her position at
the front of the painting brings her nearly into the world of
"living beings"--real persons, rather than painted illusions.

Yet, if she is no longer the analogue of nature, why did
Durand employ nature as the setting? Most likely he was
inspired in this also by Allston's critic, who in a passage
that includes two quotations from Wordsworth's "She Was a
Phantom of Delight," a poem that parallels certain aspects of
Durand's earlier portrait of Mary Frank with her sister, wrote
of Allston's picture of Dante's Beatrice:

> We rejoice to think . . . that young beings may open
> their eyes upon the divine Beatrice, and even live in
> her presence; who, even from the canvas, may descend
> with power into the wandering wood, where is lost at
> midday, the youth, who, still true to his earliest
> love, may be led to the highest heaven by so fair a
> form.[34]

May we see in the background the wood of perdition from which
the female saves the lost wanderer--Durand himself? Unlike
the girl, lost in a dream, in the Ideal Head, Mary looks toward
the spectator, reassuring and sympathetic, her mind filled with
an awareness of his presence.

Durand's last important, ideal female portrait was painted
in Rome in 1841. The Il Pappagallo (Fig. 37) seems to define
most clearly a part of Durand's aim in the two  earlier, ideal
portraits. Here a single decollete, female figure offers two
cherries to a parrot perched on a ring. The background is

merely shadow. The painting is the culmination of Durand's
effort, nourished first by his study of the work of Allston
and later by his study of Titian, to achieve a Titianesque
style. The subtle modulation of light and shadow, the complicated pattern of light, the soft, dissolving contours of the
Ideal Head reappear here with greater refinement. In employing
a Titianesque style it would seem that Durand primarily sought
to bestow upon the figure the reality of a "living being"--
but a living being more pure and spiritual than those encountered
in real life. The figure, placed at or in front of the picture
plane, seems nearly to inhabit the spectator's world. By sup-
pressing line in favor of color, Durand may have borne in mind
an idea such as that expressed by Plutarch: "in pictures the
colours are more delightful to the eye than the lines, because
those give them a nearer resemblance to the persons they were
made for, and render them the more apt to deceive the beholder."[35]
The subject of Il Pappagallo recalls Zeuxis's painting of a
child carrying grapes, mentioned in Pliny:

> . . . Zeuxis having painted a child carrying grapes,
> the birds came to peck at them; upon which . . . he
> expressed himself vexed with his work, and exclaimed--
> "I have surely painted the grapes better than the
> child, for if I had fully succeeded in the last, the
> birds would have been in fear of it."[36]

The action in Durand's painting turns upon the bird's fear of
the girl. She gently offers the cherries, while the bird eyes
them suspiciously. That the bird does not immediately peck at

the cherries indicates that he accepts the girl as a reality.
If he ultimately pecks--and we may believe he will--his doing
so would also confirm the reality of the girl's gentle spirit.[37]
From 1836 in his ideal female portraits, Durand sought not
merely to imitate reality but to create realities on the canvas.
Later, we shall see that this aim also affected his work as a
landscape painter.

With the exception of the _Ariadne_ engraving, the works that
we have been considering, from the _Children of the Artist_
through _Il Pappagallo_, were created primarily to satisfy private
longings. They are the products of the artist's deep-seated
need for images that should communicate something of their
innocence and purity to the artist himself. Yet, within the
group as a whole, we may discern a certain development. The
_Children of the Artist_ and, to a lesser degree, the _Frank Sisters_
teach an unconcern with wordly affairs and an utter reliance on
God in all of the phases of life. But this condition of faith
also involves a spiritualized vision which transforms nature
and reveals its order. The vision of faith is adumbrated in
the illuminated vista in the _Children of the Artist_. In the
_Frank Sisters_ and _Ariadne_ nature is analyzed in terms of
spiritual and material aspects, both of which find their analogue
in the female figure or figures. In the later paintings, the
spiritual aspect of reality is at once symbolized by and located
in the ideal female form. The earliest of the paintings, heavy
with theological concepts, stands in contrast to the last,

wherein a pure spirituality--existing outside particular theological concepts--is embodied in "real" human forms.

The classical style with which Durand had struggled in
the 1820's has given way to something different in these works
of the 1830's. As the children in their immaturity deviate
from any canon of ideal form, so do the Frank sisters in their
individuality. While the Ariadne was, in fact, derived from
a Hellenistic statue, it was not one that displays the graceful movement and modest bearing, which West had recommended as
contributing to the ideal female, and which Durand had pursued
in the Musidora. The later paintings lack even the Antique
proportions of the Ariadne. Indeed, in these Durand's practice
conforms to that of Allston as described by the anonymous
critic. He, like the older painter,

> . . . takes the most ordinary nature as the urn from
> which he intends to overflow us with delight; and it
> seems to be a triumph he covets, to show that beauty
> may radiate from forms which are not according to
> classic rule, that is, which are deficient in those
> exact curves and that symmetry, which, in God's works,
> as we daily see, are not essential to a perfect and
> full effect.[38]

The beauty of the form in nature is not what the physical eye
beholds, but what the vision of faith, the vision of the child-
in-the-man, perceives through the form. Rather than construct
a perfect, material form in the classical sense, Durand seeks
to express through real forms, his vision of a spiritual

reality lying beyond the material--to reveal the infinite "angel light" within the finite form. In the process the material form may be somewhat generalized, may yield up some- thing of its particularity and hardness, but it is not per- fected as a form. In these paintings of the later 1830's, Durand breaks free both from the Neo-classical tradition of perfect form and from any specific concepts of Biblical theology, although something of the Neo-classical remains in his continuing concern with an ideal, and something of the Bible remains in his concern with the spiritual. His identifi- cation of the spiritual with the ideal and his discovery of both in the "real" place these later paintings squarely in the newer tradition of the Romanticism of Wordsworth, communicated to Durand through his works and by his American interpreters, among whom we can name Allston, Bryant, Channing, and the anony- mous author of the essay on Allston.

III.  Public Pictures:   Portraits of Heroes, Presidents, and Gentlemen.

We may draw a broad distinction between portraits designed to satisfy the requirements of a family and its descendants and those designed for the general public and posterity. Durand's portraits of members of his own family belong to the first category, while his early engraved portraits of clergymen were intended to appeal, at least, to the larger body of members of a particular religious sect. But portraits of a fully national significance may be divided between two categories--portraits of the ruler and portraits of national heroes. Portraits of the ruler imply that the state exists as an organized body under one head. Portraits of heroes, on the other hand, celebrate the dynamic aspect of the state, the active forces that bring it into existence and preserve it amid the turmoils of time. A ruler may, of course, be a hero, or a hero a ruler. But the two types are ideally separable, and often in practice--especially in countries the government of which rests upon a constitution. Generally, when the welfare of the state is regarded as resting with one person, as in a monarchy, images of the ruler will be the principal form of nationally significant portraiture. Where the welfare of the state is the product of the effort of many persons, as in a republic, portraits of heroes predominate.

While the full-length portrait of Brigadier-General Samuel Waldo--probably painted by Robert Feke in 1748--indicates that portraits of heroes were not unknown in America before the

Revolution, in both America and England, between the end of
the American Revolution and the beginning of the French, they
became a major genre. The Baroque type of portrait, exemplified by the Samuel Waldo[39] and celebrating at once the man
and his acts by placing the figure in front of a scene referring
to his career, was especially popular within this period. But
in the 1780's there appears a group of paintings in which the
distinction between the man and his act is abolished. John
Singleton Copley's Charles I Demanding the Arrest of the Five
Impeached Members of Parliament (1783-85), is probably the
first painting in which portraits of the actors are introduced
into the representation of a dramatic event involving a moral
decision. Trumbull adopted this idea in his serial history
of the American Revolution, as did Jacques Louis David in some
of his French Revolution paintings and Baron Gros in his records
of the Napoleonic campaigns. However, this mode, like the hero-
portrait in any form, tended to die out in England and America
after 1789. In 1792 Trumbull painted a full-length of Washington
standing before a battle scene, returning to the older tradition
of the separation of the man from his actions. But the citizens
of Charleston, South Carolina, for whom Trumbull painted this
portrait, which still identifies Washington as a hero, rejected
it in favor of one that should represent him in the civil
costume of his role as President.[40] When the spectacle of the
egalitarian Revolution in France and its repercussions elsewhere engendered in America a more conservative spirit among
the Federalists in the 1790's, the portrait of the ruler, with

its implications of a state definitively established, tended to supplant the portrait of the hero. Gilbert Stuart, especially, popularized the image of Washington the ruler in the Athenaeum (1796), Vaughan (1795) and Lansdowne (1796) portraits. And, later, in 1822 Stuart painted a uniform series of the four Presidents for a John Daggett. When this series, called the Daggett Presidents or the American Kings, was exhibited at the "Stuart Benefit Exhibition" at the Boston Athenaeum in 1828, it was described as "the only uniform series of the Presidents in existence,"[41] although Stuart had painted another set for Colonel George Gibbs of Newport, Rhode Island.[42]

A. Portraits of Presidents.

Stuart's two series of Presidential portraits anticipate two projects upon which Durand worked in the early 1830's. In 1832 George P. Morris, editor of the New-York Mirror, decided to publish an engraving embracing portraits of the seven, American Presidents. This large plate, (Fig. 39), completed within two years and published with the August 9, 1834, number of the Mirror[43] was the work of a group of artists. The engraving itself was executed by Durand's former pupil John W. Casilear; but the portraits and the design of the whole from which he worked were provided by others. Durand visited Boston in October, 1832, to copy the portrait of Washington by Stuart in the Athenaeum (App. II, no. 12). He employed the same austere, portrait bust when painting James Madison from life about a year later at Montpelier (Fig. 41). In copying Sully's full-length portrait of Jefferson[44] at West Point (App. II, no. 390), Durand omitted all but the head and shoulders, in order that this portrait might correspond to the others. The engravings of John Adams and John Quincy Adams were made from copies by David Claypoole Johnston (1799-1865)--after originals by Stuart. The James Monroe was engraved from a portrait-- "the last for which Mr. Monroe ever sat"--then owned by a Silas E. Burrows, painted by an unnamed artist. Finally, the engraving of Andrew Jackson was taken from a portrait painted by a "Major Earle, of the United States army, a relative of the General."[45] All are pure bust portraits, a type which, as we shall later see, was very frequently employed in male portraits of the 1830's.

Robert W. Weir's design of an emblematic setting for the portraits seems to offer some clue as to the significance attached to the Presidents at this period. In the text accompanying the plate, it is described as presenting "the lineaments of a succession of eminent men, whose lives, and actions, and characters, are identified with the history of our country."[46] While this would seem to direct the spectator's attention primarily to the lives and characters of the Presidents--briefly described in the text--it also suggests that the Presidents might symbolize the nation with whose history their lives are identified. And, in Weir's design, the Presidents are associated with symbols indicating the qualities and, hence, the reality of the nation, rather than symbols referring to the life of each individual. According to the text, the engraving as a whole represents

> . . . one end of a room in the capitol of the United
> States. In the center is a large mirror, reflecting
> a statue of the Goddess of Liberty from the opposite
> side, and surmounted by the American Eagle with
> banners.[47]

The Capitol building indicates the locus of the national government rather than anything proper to one of the Presidents. The symbols of liberty and power again characterize the nation rather than the individual Presidents. These symbols at the center of the composition are differentiated in respect to their tangibility. The eagle is a solid object at the top of the mirror and stands as the sign of physical energy and power. The Goddess of Liberty, the sign of an ideal concept, is merely reflected in the mirror. If the eagle and the Goddess symbolize two aspects of the state, we may regard the Presidential portraits as symbolizing the third aspect--the human agency by which the qualities of power and liberty are brought to bear on public life. If we consider the Presidents represented as symbols of one aspect of the national government, the whole would assert the reality of the government, possessing power which may be employed by the President for the preservation of liberty.

Seen in this light, the engraving would have been particularly relevant when it was conceived in 1832. As early as 1826 the debate in Congress over the right of the Federal govern-

ment to impose protective tariffs on foreign trade had led
John C. Calhoun in his Exposition and Protest to defend the
right of each state to nullify those Federal laws which it
considered unjust. In November, 1832, the Federal tariff acts
of 1828 and 1832 were declared void in South Carolina by a
convention of its citizens. Further, the convention threatened
secession if the government attempted to force the collection
of duties. It would seem to be this denial of the authority
of the Federal government that George P. Morris intended to
contradict when he conceived the Presidential engraving.

Shortly after the publication of the Mirror engraving,
Durand was commissioned to paint a complete set of Presidents.
Late in 1834, Luman Reed requested that Durand go to Washington
to paint a portrait of Andrew Jackson (Fig. 40),[48] which he did
in February and March of 1835.[49] Before he had completed this,
Reed decided that Durand should also secure portraits of all
of the other Presidents. This series was ultimately given to
the Museum and Library of the Navy Yard in Brooklyn,[50] wherein
it would be as accessible to the public as were the portraits
engraved for the Mirror. That Reed placed it in a Federal
building suggests that he regarded the portraits as a symbol
of the government. Later in the same year Durand was requested
by Reed to make replicas of this set of portraits for the
latter's gallery (Figs. 42-43). While this series may still
have suggested the reality of the Federal government, isolated
from any other sign or materialization of the government, it
could, equally, have been regarded merely as representative of

eminent men. And, of course, any of the portraits in all three series might have been regarded in this way, for in each the portrait remains that of an individual person and never approaches an abstract type.

B. Portraits of National Heroes.

Despite the popularity of Presidential portraits in the early nineteenth century, an interest in portraits of heroes did not altogether disappear. Charles Willson Peale's Philadelphia Museum, founded in 1786, eventually contained some two-hundred and forty portraits of Revolutionary heroes and other eminent men. This collection, begun during a period especially productive of hero-portraits, inspired Rembrandt Peale's smaller collection of national heroes in his Baltimore Museum, established in 1814. The War of 1812 added to the number of men whose portraits would be nationally significant, and such portraits were frequently produced for public places. Rembrandt Peale added portraits of distinguished veterans of this war to his collection, and in 1814 the City of New York commissioned John W. Jarvis, Vanderlyn, Samuel Waldo, and Sully to portray a group of men through whose efforts the nation had been preserved. In an address delivered before the American Academy of Fine Arts, October 23, 1816, De Witt Clinton, Mayor of New York when these paintings were commissioned, defined the value of such portraits and proposed that their number be increased:

> The portrait collection of this city, by comprising many of the principal heroes of the country, is entitled

to great praise in its tendency to stimulate to
noble deeds . . . and its merits would be greatly
enhanced if it were extended so as to embrace illus-
trious men who have done honor to the Arts and
Sciences, or who have distinguished themselves in
other respects as men of extraordinary talents or
virtues.[51]

The various classes of emninent men specified by Clinton had
already appeared in the Peale galleries and were to reappear
in a major project of the 1830's, to the success of which Dur-
and largely contributed.

1. The Dominance of the Bust Portrait.

The continuing popularity of the portrait of the hero--
military, civil, or cultural--is indicated by the public's
support of the National Portrait Gallery of Distinguished Americans, edited by James Herring and James Longacre, under the
supervision of the American Academy of Fine Arts. This work
was undertaken in 1832, and extended to four, quarto volumes
by 1840. The plan comprised engraved portraits as the front-
ispieces to the biographical and character sketch of individuals
who had contributed significantly to the foundation, preservation, or civilization of the American Republic. In the words
of the prefatory "Address" to volume one, the editors describe
the work as:

. . . an effort at once to preserve the features, and
to rescue, from the wasting hand of time, the memory

of those whose noble deeds, exalted fame, or eminent
virtues, have shed a lustre upon their age.

Combining a visual image and a narrative of the achievement of
each individual, the <u>National Portrait Gallery</u> clearly belongs
to the tradition of the Revolutionary paintings by Trumbull,
who presided over the Academy which sponsored the work. But
in contrast to Trumbull's paintings, a sharp separation is here
maintained between the portrait of the individual and the
account of his life. The man is presented in the engraved
portrait, and his "noble deeds" are described in the literary
text.

Durand engraved nineteen plates and painted three of the
portraits from which engravings were made. In the visual portion of the work, the editors were frequently compelled to
secure engravings after such portraits as were available. But
despite this limitation, they do appear to have sought an image
in which a maximum amount of attention is brought to bear on
a realistically rendered face, and a minimum of the spectator's
attention is diverted to the other parts of the body or to the
figure's environment. In all four volumes, there does not
appear a single full-length portrait--for example, in Durand's
engraving after Trumbull's full-length <u>Washington</u> and G. Parker's
engraving after Jarvis' <u>William Bainbridge</u> all of the figure
but the head and shoulders has been omitted.[52]

While the use of portraits from other times and painted
for other purposes renders the series less homogeneous than it
might have been, a portrait such as that of William Wirt (Fig.

45), drawn from life and engraved by James Longacre, one of
the editors, may be regarded as the central type to which
many of the others closely assimilate. In studying this portrait as a work of art, one is struck by the quality of completeness. The face, collar, and shirt-front form a central
passage of light, flanked by the dark masses of the coat.
The area around the head is in a grey tone, gradually growing
darker toward the sides and top of the picture so that the
relative darkness at the top resumes the stronger dark of the
coat at the bottom. That the organization of the picture produces a visual whole, precludes our dwelling on the fact that
the artist has represented only the head and shoulders of the
man. We do not think of the figure as being cut off by the
lower edge of the picture. In representing the bust alone,
the artist has excluded any implication of movement or effort
on the part of the figure. Even the tension of muscles--
implicit in a full-length, static figure--is absent. Further,
as the figure exerts no physical effort, he does not exist in
a physical environment upon which effort could be exerted.
Nor does any object accompany the man to bespeak his profession,
possessions, or the events of his life. Anything denoting
realities extrinsic to the man himself has been omitted.
Finally, as any physical act, so any mental act is absent.
He does nothing about which he might think, there is nothing
to stand as the object of his thought, and there is nothing
in the face to indicate that he pursues some train of thought
independent of acts or things. The picture represents the man

himself, the man in isolation from all experience of the
worlds of human action, things, and thoughts. Silently and
solemnly he inhabits the inviolable realm of his own existence.[53] Yet the figure itself is no abstraction. The artist
has not sought to impose a general form of ideal humanity upon
the individual; he exists as a highly praticularized form,
sharply differentiated from all other persons by the uniqueness
of his features.

Many of the portraits in the <u>National Portrait Gallery</u> are
treated in the same way. Durand's <u>Aaron Ogden</u> (Fig. 46), painted
and engraved by himself, is identical. His portrait of Edward
Everett, engraved by George Parker, is enriched by the presence
of the base of a column, which belongs still to an ideal world;
and at the base of the triangle formed by the shirt-front
there appears a single hand, poised in an involuntary gesture
undirected by the will. Durand's Presidential portraits,
either copies or originals, are of the same type as the <u>William
Wirt</u> with only an occasional slight deviation--the inclusion
of the back or arm of a chair or a bit of drapery behind the
figure. Finally, Durand employed exactly the same formula in
his portraits of men painted for the private individual. These
include, among others, the portraits of his pupil and partner
John Casilear, several of his patron Luman Reed (Fig. 47),
Joseph Hoxie (Fig. 48), John Fessenden (Fig. 49), and two portraits from a later period of his friend William Cullen Bryant
(Fig. 50).

A type of portraiture so simple in form and subtle in its
exclusions was not Durand's invention nor the invention of his

generation. The portrait bust, isolated from particular acts, things, and thoughts, is essentially the sculptor's form. Such isolated forms, displaying the unique physiognomy of the individual, were especially common in Republican Rome and persisted under the Empire. They were revived in the mid-fifteenth century in Italy and were produced in the later eighteenth century by such sculptors as Houdon, whose bust of Franklin was engraved by Edward Wellmore as a part of the engraved title-page to the second volume of the National Portrait Gallery. Again, sculptors such as Horatio Greenough, John Frazee, Robert E. Launitz, and Shobal V. Clevenger popularized the "Roman" portrait bust in America in the 1820's and 1830's. J. Gross' engraving after the bust of Nathaniel Bowditch by John Frazee appears in volume four of the National Portrait Gallery. But the realistic, sculptural bust merely parallels the character and appeals to the same taste as the graphic portrait bust. The modern, painted bust appears in Flanders and Italy in the fifteenth century. And the type achieved wide popularity among the French, seventeenth century, portrait engravers who were inspired by Philippe de Champaigne. The engraved frontispiece preserved the type through the eighteenth century, a period when painted portraits and engraved portraits sold independently became more elaborate in terms of action, thought, or setting. Reynolds occasionally painted portrait busts, but in the 1830's Durand painted only busts when portraying the male figure. Finally, the isolated, realistic, bust portrait was the normal image of the sitter employed in

eighteenth century miniatures. It was Gilbert Stuart who
revived the use of the bust in important, painted portraits
of eminent persons. Although bust portraits were also painted
by Charles Willson Peale, Trumbull, Dunlap, and Samuel L.
Waldo, it was Chester Harding who in the 1820's excluded any
element of drama in favor of the austerity of Stuart at his
purest. Harding's stark style, eliminating all but the man,
proved immensely popular in Boston in 1823, and he exhibited
one or two works annually at the National Academy from 1827
to 1829. These works, one of which Durand later engraved for
the National Portrait Gallery (i.e., Charles Carroll of
Carrollton), along with the work of Stuart, which Durand had
an opportunity to study closely in the early 1830's, served
as the source from which Durand and other New York painters
derived the form of portraiture which remained dominant up to
the 1860's and continued thereafter.[54]

2. Three Types of Bust Portraits.

Although all bust portraits represent the same portion of
the human frame, they do not all make the same statement about
the sitter, nor do they all hold the same significance for the
spectator. We have just noted the preference for the bust in
portraits of male sitters in the 1830's, and we have indicated
something of the older traditions from which these stem. But
now we must discriminate more particularly three types of the
bust portrait and the significance of each. The three normal
possibilities are the profile, the bust with head turned partly
toward the spectator, and the face that looks at the spectator.

While all bust portraits represent the individual as a being
that may be detached from a context of sub-human things without
losing any of its reality, the particular content of the bust
portrait varies in accordance with the position of the subject's
head in relation to the spectator.

First, the profile bust of antique coins and medallions
and mid-fifteenth century Italian paintings establishes the
existence and, in many cases, the identity of the subject by
presenting the form of the head. The profile, half-length
portrait was introduced to America by John Smibert in the
Berkeley Group[55] of 1729. The second male figure from the
right was probably borrowed from Titian's Pope Paul III and
his Grandsons.[56] But the profile bust obtained little currency
in America, until shortly after 1800 it was occasionally
employed by John Vanderlyn and Jacob Eichholtz in paintings,
James Sharples and Saint-Memin in pastels, and Giuseppe Vala-
perta and Johann Christian Rauschner in wax bas-reliefs. The
popularity of the profile portrait around 1800 was stimulated
as much by Antique precedent as by the Physionotrace, invented
by Gilles-Louis Chretien in 1786. After 1820 the profile bust
was limited almost exclusively to coins and medallions,
(cf. App. V, no. 8) and the paper silhouette. Only one profile
portrait by Durand, that of an unidentified young man, painted
in 1845 (App. II, no. 210), has come to my attention. This

portrait, very small in size, is hardly more than a miniature executed in oil.

A second type of bust portrait is that in which the head is turned more toward the front so that both of the subject's eyes are visible but do not meet the gaze of the spectator. This type was especially favored in the second half of the eighteenth century by several pupils of West. Matthew Pratt and Abraham Delanoy both portrayed West, and West portrayed Charles Willson Peale with averted gaze in the 1760's, although these are half-lengths.[57] The pure bust portrait with averted gaze was frequently employed by C. W. Peale and John Trumbull in their portraits of American Revolutionary heroes. In this type of portrait, the head assumes a distinctive form which establishes the existence and identity of the sitter. But to these qualities is added an indication of movement and, perhaps, of the play of inner forces of the personality. The form of the sitter is combined with an expression of his animating spirit, but he continues to occupy a world as remote from the spectator's as that inhabited by the profile bust.

Among Durand's portraits, this type appears in his copies of Stuart's John Adams (App. II, nos. 31-32) and James Madison (App. II, nos. 43-44) and in his own Andrew Jackson (Fig. 40), John Quincy Adams (Fig. 44) and Joseph Hoxie (Fig. 48).

In the third type of bust portrait the subject looks directly at the spectator. The earliest example of this type is probably Jan Van Eyck's Man in a Red Turban.[58] Half to full length figures that look at the spectator appear with great frequency in the work of Lely and Kneller, and this arrangement was adopted by the American painters John Smibert, Robert Feke, and Copley, who formed their conception of portraiture from English engravings.[60] But it was Gilbert Stuart, primarily, who popularized, in late eighteenth century America, the bust-length figure with eyes turned toward the spectator.

This is the type that Durand, directly influenced by the work of Stuart, most frequently employed. Examples include copies of the Atheneum Martha (App. II, no. 391) and George Washington (Fig. 42) and of Stuart's Thomas Jefferson (App. II, nos. 42 and 43) and James Monroe (App. II, nos. 46 and 47) as well as his original portraits: James Madison (Fig. 41), John Quincy Adams (Fig. 43), Aaron Ogden (Fig. 46), Luman Reed (Fig. 47), John Fessenden (Fig. 49), and William Cullen Bryant (Fig. 50).

The precise meaning of this type of portrait is rather difficult to define. Like the profile portrait and the portrait with eyes averted, it may present a thorough account of the form of the head. Like the portrait with eyes averted, it may record the personality of the sitter. But the portrait with eyes that meet the spectator's may possess qualities of veracity and of reality that transcend the limits of the profile or eyes-averted portraits. This third type of portrait probably originated as and retains the character of a mirror-image rendered permanent. To see oneself clearly in a mirror, one must focus his eyes somewhere within the silhouette of the reflected image. As long as the eyes are turned in this direction, they will meet

those of the spectator, should the image become permanent.
The mirror-image portrait carries with it a certain guarantee
of the likeness of its image to the subject portrayed. If
I look into a mirror, I see myself, and the image that I see,
I am confident, corresponds to what I am. If I look at a
painted mirror-image portrait of myself, I can verify the
truth of the portrait by comparing the painted mirror-image
with a real one. Of the three types of portraits, the veracity of the third alone can be verified by the sitter himself.
The subject of a profile, or an eyes-averted portrait has to
rely largely on the honesty of the painter, who simply tells
him that he looks thus. The verifiable mirror-image compels
belief in the truth of the portrait, even though the spectator
knows that the painted image has been idealized or otherwise
created independently of the artist's experience of the sitter.
For all of their abstractions, the mirror-image arrangement
bestows upon the portraits of Lely and Kneller a stamp of
truth, equivalent to or even exceeding that which could have
been obtained by the utmost discrimination of minute detail.

Secondly, while we merely look at the figure in the profile or the eyes-averted portrait, we encounter the figure in
the mirror-image portrait as a human being. If the person
portrayed is oneself, there exists an absolute and unique
harmony between oneself and the person in the portrait. The
Narcissus legend is an affirmation of the deep appeal of this
absolutely harmonious encounter. While all else that we encounter is, in greater or less degree, alien to us, in the

mirror we see ourselves, and at this point alone the disparity between subject and object collapses. This Narcissistic transcendence of alienation would seem to underlie the appeal of all mirror-image portraits that are addressed to the sitter. As a device to bridge the gulf between man and the world, the mirror-image portrait was utilized virtually to the exclusion of any other type by Smibert, Feke, and Copley. But when the mirror-image is employed in a portrait that is not addressed to the sitter, it ceases to be a device to bridge the gap between man and the world. Now the person encountered in the portrait is not the same as the spectator. The same disparity pertains as in any encounter between two human beings. As a disparity now exists between the person portrayed and the spectator, the latter must accommodate himself to the former, as a guest must accommodate himself to his host. If the person portrayed is the same sort of person as the spectator, the relation between sitter and spectator may be companionable. If the person portrayed possesses a moral superiority, the process of accommodation on the part of the spectator entails his moral elevation. The mirror-image portrait may, I believe, be described as guaranteeing its own veracity and presenting the subject as a person, whom we encounter as we encounter a real person. Therefore, it is a portrait potentially fitted to effect the moral elevation of the spectator.

With these theoretical distinctions in mind, we may, now, turn to a consideration of the theory and practice of portrait painting in America in the 1830's.

3. The Portrayal of the Soul.

Durand's contemporaries were consciously concerned with the veracity and affectiveness of portraits. As to truth, what was demanded in the 1830's was not so much a thorough account of facial features for their own sake, but a revelation of the unique mind or soul of the individual. Durand's friend Gulian C. Verplanck, scholar, literator, and politician, maintained the idea that the mind of a man is revealed in his facial features. In an address delivered before the American Academy in May, 1824, he stated that the portrait might express "the mind speaking in the features"[61] of an individual. It is precisely this effort to represent the mind or spirit or soul of the man that justifies the emphasis on the head in the bust portrait.

But this idea was something of a commonplace of the time. The anonymous author of the sketch of Gilbert Stuart in the National Portrait Gallery speaks of his ability, by conversing with his sitter, to draw "forth the inmost soul upon the surface of the countenance, while he fixed it /i.e., the soul/ on his canvas by the magic of his colors."[62] In the same place an unnamed "eminent artist," identified by Professor Egbert as Washington Allston, is quoted as stating that Stuart possessed the capacity to reject "'the conventional expression which arises from manners'" in favor of "'that more subtle indication of the individual mind.'" And the same writer goes on to praise Stuart's capacity

> . . . to animate his canvass—not with the appearance
> of mere general life, but with that peculiar distinc-
> tive life, which separates the humblest individual
> from his kind. He seemed to dive into the thoughts
> of men—for they were made to rise and speak on the
> surface . . . In his happier efforts, no one ever sur-
> passed him in embodying . . . those transient appari-
> tions of the soul.[63]

What the portrait painter in the tradition of Stuart represents
is not the man, but the mind or even the soul of the man revealed
in the features of his face. If this soul is but a "transient
apparition" in the man himself, it is something that the painter
can present as an essence. And it is by discriminating the
unique soul that the painter defines the individuality of each
sitter.

If the portrait painter's task is to define the unique
soul of the individual, it is much the same as what Plutarch
sought to accomplish in his **Lives**. In the prefatory remarks
to the "Life of Alexander," Plutarch draws a distinction between
history as the full account of an individual's action and a
life as the rendering of the man's "virtues or vices," his
"real character," his "peculiar turn of mind," or his "soul."
He states that it is not

> . . . always in the most distinguished achievements
> that the man's virtues or vices may best be discerned;
> but very often an action of small note, a short saying,
> or a jest, shall distinguish a person's character more

than the greatest sieges or the most important battles.
Therefore, as painters in their portraits labour the
likeness in the face, and particularly about the eyes,
in which the peculiar turn of mind most appears, and
run over the rest with a more careless hand; so we must
be permitted to strike off the features of the soul in
order to give a real likeness of these great men, and
leave to others the circumstantial detail of their
labors and achievements.[64]

The effort at once to grasp the spiritual essence of the man
and his uniqueness is a fundamentally Romantic aspiration and
stands in contrast to any Neo-classical effort to grasp the
perfect form and structure of Man.  Unconditioned by time, this
depth of being is akin to a Platonic idea.  But, as the unique
possession of the individual rather than something in which all
the members of a class participate, it is a thoroughly Romantic
and Christian reality.

In pursuit of this spiritual essence the painter may employ
the eyes-averted or the mirror-image arrangement, while the
profile is less suitable.  Both of the two former types appear
in the National Portrait Gallery.  And, as we have noted, Durand
normally employed either the eyes-averted or the mirror-image
busts both when he copied and when he painted from life.  In
the 1850's at the peak of his career, after he had abandoned
portrait painting, he could still ask:

Where is the portrait-painter, having a just sense of
his responsibilities, who has not often thrown down

> his brush in dispair, after many fruitless attempts
> to express the soul that beams at times through the
> eye of beauty, and so with the yet more mysterious
> power of lofty intellect?[65]

However, by the 1850's Durand had long since come to seek this
soul in nature rather than in the individual human being:

> And there is to be seen a corresponding soul and depth
> of expression in the beauty of landscape nature, which
> dignifies the art that embodies it, and improves and
> elevates the mind that loves to contemplate its pic-
> torial image.[66]

But, if Durand's aim were only to portray the soul, this aim,
while it would account for the presence of both the eyes-averted
and the mirror-image types among his portraits, does not account
for his apparent preference for the latter type.

4. Portraits as Models of Virtue.

Again, we must return to our initial distinction between
portraits produced primarily for the gratification of the person
portrayed and those addressed to the public at large. While
all of Durand's male sitters in the 1830's are represented in
much the same way, his engravings for the National Portrait
Gallery and the three series of Presidents were addressed
primarily to the public and thus belong to a category distinct
from that to which the portraits of Luman Reed, John Casilear,
or John Fessenden belong. All of the portraits present the
unique spirit of the man. But Durand's friend Verplanck re-

garded portraits of eminent persons as fitted also to inculcate virtue in the public mind.  In his Address on the Fine
Arts of 1824, he states that portrait painting becomes "public
and national" and teaches morality and the love of excellence
when it represents

> . . . those whose valour made us free, or by whose
> wisdom we may become wise; . . . Then it becomes,
> indeed a teacher of morality; it then assists in the
> education of our youth; it gives form and life to
> their abstract perceptions of duty or excellence; and,
> in a free state and a moral community, where the arts
> are thus made the handmaid of virtue, when the imagina-
> tion of the young patriot calls up the sacred image of
> his country, it comes surrounded with the venerable
> forms of the wisest and best of her sons.[67]

National heroes, men of genius, and some women--these are represented in the National Portrait Gallery,which was sponsored by
the American Academy before which Verplanck delivered his
Address.  Verplanck might have derived this conception of the
utility of portraits of eminent persons from Plutarch, who at
the beginning of his "Life of Paulus Aemilius" describes the
effect of "sublime images of the best and greatest men" upon
the conscience:

> Democritus has a position in his philosophy,
> utterly false indeed, and leading to endless super-
> stitions, that there are phantasms or images con-
> tinually floating in the air, some propitious, and

some unlucky, and advises us to pray that such may
strike upon our senses as are agreeable to and perfective of our nature, and not such as have a tendency to vice and error. For my part, instead of
this, I fill my mind with the sublime images of the
best and greatest men, by attention to history and
biography; and if I contract any blemish or ill
custom from other company, which I am unavoidably
engaged in, I correct and expel them, by calmly and
dispassionately turning my thoughts to these excellent examples.[68]

Whatever the merit of Democritus' position, Verplanck would have
been willing to regard the portrait of an eminent person as a
"phantasm . . . agreeable to and perfective of our nature," and
would agree with Plutarch that such portraits might serve to
restore to health a conscience blemished by ill custom or company.

The comments of Verplanck and Plutarch would allow any
honest portrait of an eminently virtuous person to be regarded
as morally elevating. But the predilection of Stuart and Durand
for the mirror-image in portraits of great men would suggest
that they believed or felt that this type would most fully
answer the purpose. Thus, in encountering the Madison (Fig. 41),
the John Quincy Adams (Fig. 43), the Aaron Ogden (Fig. 46), or
the William Cullen Bryant (Fig. 50), the spectator is obliged
to rise to the evidently superior, moral dignity of the man
he meets. In connection with these paintings, the reader may
recall the 1837 Portrait of Mrs. Durand (Fig. 36), in which

she looks kindly toward the spectator, and our suggestion
that it was conceived as an influence to raise the spectator
out of the dark-wood of despair. On the other hand, the <u>Ideal</u>
<u>Head</u> (Fig. 35) and the <u>Il Pappagallo</u> (Fig. 37), both of which
belong to the eyes-averted type, we have interpreted more as
portraits of a particular condition of spirit rather than
elevating agents.

Finally, we should note that all of Durand's portraits
of his friends and the members of his family, that have come
to my attention, belong to the mirror-image type. Examples
of these include the several portraits of Luman Reed (Fig. 47),
the very fine portrait of Durand's mother-in-law Mary B. Frank
(App. II, no. 405), the portrait of Eugene H. Durand as an
infant (App. II, no. 414C), the very charming pair of Mr. and
Mrs. Edmund B. Pease, presented to the sitters by the artist
(App. II, nos. 157 and 156), and the genial portrait of John W.
Casilear (App. II, no. 121). While the figures in these paintings retain a proper dignity, with the exception of Mrs. Frank
they are less austere and forbidding than the portraits of
great men. Here the relation between sitter and spectator tends
toward a kind of comradship.

5. Sublime Portraits.

One final observation. In the Langhorne and Langhorne
translation of Plutarch's <u>Lives</u>, especially popular in the
early nineteenth century, "images of the best and greatest men"
are termed "sublime."[69] That the portrait bust might be sublime

was affirmed by the "eminent artist" quoted in the life of
Gilbert Stuart in the National Portrait Gallery. Of the
Athenaeum Washington he wrote:

> And well is his ambition justified in the sublime head
> he has left us: a nobler personification of wisdom
> and goodness, reposing in the majesty of a serene
> conscience, is not to be found on canvas.[70]

Durand's last major effort in male portraiture was the series
of eight male, bearded heads painted in Rome in 1841 (Figs. 51-
52). These studies of the head alone--without a body and without any sort of setting, inhabiting its own special, visionary
world--recall in their bearded majesty such studies as Allston's
Isaac of York or his Head of a Jew.[71] The bare canvas surrounding the head recalls, also, Stuart's Athenaeum Washington.[72]

In these heads Durand abandoned the mirror-image portrait.
Here, the eyes of the figures avoid any contact with the spectator. While the sense of an inner soul and even of the eternity of that soul is not necessarily diminished, perhaps it
has lost something of its uniqueness. But of greater importance
is the fact that the spectator can no longer encounter the
painted figure as a person akin but superior to himself. The
process of encounter and accommodation, provoked by the mirror-
image portrait, is no longer possible. In contemplating a
"public or national," mirror-image portrait, the spectator may
ultimately inhabit the moral sphere of the subject. The spectator and subject become comrades in moral excellence. But
the Roman heads do not greet the spectator as a host greets

his guest. They do not invite the spectator to enter their sphere. Their sphere remains always inaccessible, as an ideal toward which one may always strive. The ideality of the Roman heads is marked by their unfinished state, which counteracts the quality of illusion. The figures are not men but ideas, while, as ideas, they become concrete and physically present. In the same way, but with a greater measure of abstraction, Picasso in 1911 transformed the figure into an idea, but then rendered the idea in the concrete terms of paint and canvas. The extenuation or universalization of Durand's ideal of human perfection is probably the result of his experience of Europe and especially of Italy. Where prior to his trip abroad his ideal of human character was limited to what individuals had achieved, his ideal now is the infinite excellence that man ought to pursue. But, still, as was the case with his Presidential portraits, his ideal is founded on retrospect. He described the men whom he painted in Rome as "old patriarchs that go about the streets here looking as tho' they belonged to a period at least 2000 years ago."[73] Such a retrospective, rather than dialectical, search for the ideal was characteristic of both Neo-classicism and Romanticism.

In the loftiness and inaccessibility of the ideal embodied in the Roman heads, they become especially sublime. Painted in a Titianesque, tonal manner they are closely related to Il Pappagallo, but at the same time their grandeur and almost fierce aloofness strongly distinguish them from the pensive gentleness of the girl. Il Pappagallo concludes Durand's effort to grasp the beauty of the female spirit in a "real" form. In the heads of the men whom Durand saw as possessing "the dignity of bearded majesty,"[74] he sought to express the sublimity of the primitive male character undefiled by modern conventions. The sublimity of the male character and the beauty of the female spirit display a polarity which, as we shall see, Durand was able to express through the forms of nature in his mature landscape painting. The Roman paintings of 1841 complete Durand's study of the sublime and the beautiful in human character which he had undertaken with the Fuller and Musidora engravings of the 1820's.

While Durand's interpretation of human character in the later works is remote from that in his earlier, we may trace two themes throughout the group. The male, or sublime, figures represent an ideal goal which one may strive to attain--whether it be simply the goal of physical well-being illustrated in the Fuller or the ideal of human perfection embodied in the Roman heads. The female or beautiful figures, on the other hand, stand as powers that sustain one in the pursuit of the goal--whether it be the vision of loveliness in the Musidora or the gentleness of the Il Pappagallo. As the embodiment of the ideal, the male figures become increasingly abstract. As the source of sustenance, the female figures become increasingly tangible, until the Il Pappagallo verges on trompe-l'oeil illusion.

IV.  Public Pictures:  Moral Issues in History and Genre
Paintings.

Pictures that deal explicitly with moral issues may be
divided between two categories.  One class of paintings describes vices; the other, virtues.  Of pictures that describe
vices, one class condemns the vice by demonstrating the disaster
to which it eventually leads; and another class condemns the
vice by ridicule.  The first method was that of Hogarth and
Goya; the second, that of Gavarni and Daumier.  In either case,
the vice is represented in order, at once, to recommend and
to validate an opposite line of conduct.  During the eighteenth
and early nineteenth centuries, this type of moralistic art
made use of incidents from common life, treated in a non-
classical, realistic style.  Pictures presenting examples of
virtue were not so much intended to validate a particular
line of conduct--the validity of the virtue being taken for
granted--as to celebrate an act in which that virtue became
operative in the conduct of a particular person.  While a
picture representing a moral act may encourage emulation on
the part of the spectator, the principal aim of such pictures
is more commemorative than didactic.  During the later eighteenth and early nineteenth centuries, this type of painting
treated particular historical events--either from ancient or
medieval or modern times--and presented the event in a classical style so that the "reason" in the order of the painting
might express the reason in the order of the event.  Paintings
such as West's three pictures of around 1770 celebrating heroic,

patriotic sacrifice--The Death of General Wolfe, The Death
of Epaminondas, and The Death of the Chevalier Bayard--mark
the beginning of this kind of painting in the eighteenth
century.

The wars, revolutions, new republics, and infant empires
of the half-century preceeding the fall of Napoleon afforded
many instances of heroic and virtuous acts for the painter to
memorialize. After the restoration of peace and with the con-
solidation of governments, the artist who, in the phrase of West,
regarded the arts "as the means of perpetuating all public
fame, all private honour"--the artist who stood as the "watch-
man who observes the great incidents of his time, and rescues
them from oblivion,"[75] would necessarily find fewer events
from which to choose. In a commercial center such as New York,
could the painter celebrate merely the honesty of the clerk
in his shop, the prudence of a cashier in his bank, the integrity
of the mayor in his office? We may doubt that Horatio Alger's
heroes were ever taken seriously by any but the most inexper-
ienced. Further, where in a time of peace could the artist
find examples of an absolute moral commitment comparable to
that of the hero who gave his life in battle or the rebel who
declared the independence of a nation at the risk of his neck.
In a commercial republic, the portrait rather than the history
painting was the main instrument by which to celebrate individual worth. But the portrait can represent the spirit of the
man more effectively than his moral acts. Finally, the
decisions that effected the destiny of the nation were, by

the 1830's, made by party-leaders and the voters rather than by the individual. Clearly, it would be difficult to represent a party casting its votes to select the better policy. In the Oath in the Tennis Court, of 1791, David carried commemorative history painting as far as possible in this direction, although the painting remained unfinished. Hence, we should not be surprised that history paintings celebrating particular examples of moral conduct should disappear under these conditions.

A. The Capture of Major André.

While Durand painted no subjects from contemporary history, he did paint one picture which, clearly, celebrates the moral decision of a particular individual. His Capture of Major André (Fig. 53) was painted for the New York frame-maker and gilder Lewis P. Clover.[76] Its date, however, is somewhat uncertain. John Durand states that it was painted in 1833. But Lewis P. Clover, Jr., who studied engraving under Durand, stated in a letter to Durand, November 15, 1879, that the picture "was painted while I was a pupil of yours--and that I had the honor to stand as model for the Major."[77] If we note that Clover was born on February 20, 1819, it would seem unlikely that he had become Durand's pupil by 1833. Among Durand's papers only one letter, from the summer of 1835, indicates a relationship between Durand and the young Clover. Clover might, more probably, have become Durand's pupil after his fifteenth birthday early in 1834 or his sixteenth in 1835. A date of late 1834 or early

1835 would account for the fact that Durand did not exhibit the painting at the National Academy until the latter year.

When the painting was exhibited, the following explanatory text appeared in the catalogue:

> Mr. Paulding looked at the papers, and said he was a spy.
>
> He said, if we would let him go, he would give us his horse, watch, any amount of money, and bring it to any place that we might pitch upon, so that we might get it. Mr. Paulding, answered, "No, if you would give us ten thousand guineas you shall not stir one step."

In the painting Paulding, the third figure from the left, holds the paper which has identified André as a spy, and at the same time scornfully rejects the offered wealth. However, this moment of the story is not that which Durand had first selected for representation. A pencil sketch (Fig. 54) reveals that Durand had first thought to treat the more exciting moment in which the document was discovered. That ultimately he rejected this early moment suggests that he was conscious of some superiority in the later.

The moment in which Paulding refused André's offer does afford two advantages. In the painting Durand has shifted the emphasis from André to Paulding. The drawing may be more properly termed The Capture of Major André, for here the emphasis is upon the revelation of his identity. He stands erect, while the patriots--kneeling, crouching, or registering surprise-- assume a secondary role. Here the historical fact--that André's

deceit was penetrated by the simple Americans--is the dominant
factor. The drawing displays the transitory movements and
emotions of real life. In the painting, the situation is quite
different. The moment of action and surprise is past. The
capture of André is already accomplished. Now it is Paulding,
as he rejects the proffered watch, who becomes the hero of the
piece. Strongly illuminated and with emphatic gesture he becomes the center of interest, while André, now a suppliant,
is de-emphasized in his dark coat that assimilates to the
shadows of the tree before which he stands. In this moment
of decisive refusal all ephemeral movement and feeling have
been eliminated. The three figures at the left stand as erectly
as the fourth sits and holds his rifle at the right. Frontal
and profile figures alternate across the picture plane, re-
placing the more varied figures of the drawing. The two central figures stand in an artificially contrived spot of light,
and Paulding assumes the eternal pose of the Apollo Belvedere--
an avenging God of truth. The minor elements of the composi-
tion--limbs, rifles, rocks, trees, horizon--assume a rigid geometric parallelism. As the narrative interest of the moment in
which André's identity is discovered gives way to the moral
interest of Paulding's refusal, so pictorial mobility is replaced
by an immutable formality. The order of the painted composition
bespeaks the finality of the moral decision.

The painting, then, embracing the moral order of the composition and that of the decision, may have been directed against

those economic vices that troubled the 1830's. Here, in an
image that was popularized through engravings, Durand has
implicitly asserted that the common citizen may and ought, like
Paulding, to scorn that wealth which can be gained only at the
expense of the welfare of the state. Perhaps Durand intended
nothing more than to recommend integrity in any financial
transaction involving the public welfare. But he may have
had a specific issue in mind. If we try to relate the painting
to a particular situation, three things should be borne in mind:
(1) that Durand's first thought, as indicated by the drawing,
included no reference to a financial transaction but embraced
only the arrest of the spy, (2) that the protagonists in both
the drawing and the painting belong to opposing parties, and
(3) in the painting, André seeks to corrupt his captors. As
no financial transaction was involved in Durand's first conception of the work, he cannot, at the beginning, have intended
to condemn the various schemes by which individuals sought to
enrich themselves at the expense of the nation. The situation
in the drawing is simply a victory of one party over another--
of the patriotic Paulding and his companions over the British
agent. In this light, it would be possible to regard the
drawing as an effort to celebrate the "victory" of the Whig
party in the New York Mayoralty election of April, 1834. This
election assumed unusual importance as the first major contest
between the Whig party, a combination of Federalists and
dissident Democrats, and the loyal Jackson Democrats of the
Tammany Society, whom the Whigs regarded as "Tories," too loyal

to "King Andrew." In his diary on November 23, 1834, William
Dunlap traced the usage of the labels Whig and Tory. His
summary closes with an account of their use in America:

> In America in 1776 Whig meant ye opposers of the pre-
> tensions of the English parliament & Tory the friends
> of the Ministry, now Tory is applied to the Jacksonmen
> or supporters of the pretensions of the president &
> Whig to their opponents, the same men (the rich and
> the commercial) who were ultra federalists & advocates
> of England against France.[78]

Clearly, in Durand's drawing, André, the king's agent, might
be understood as a metaphor for the Tory or Democratic party
of 1834; and Paulding and the other Americans, as a metaphor
for the Whig Party. The use of an episode from the Revolution
in support of the Whig cause would have been entirely in harmony with the policy of the party. After the election, thou-
sands of New York Whigs banqueted in Castle Garden. Over the
entrance hung a Revolutionary flag flanked by portraits of
Wahington and Lafayette.[79] Durand's first idea may have been
to use the Revolutionary incident in which the patriots (Whigs)
defeat the scheme of the English (Tories or Jacksonian Democrats) simply as a metaphor to celebrate the defeat of the
Democrats at the polls.

But in the finished painting, André actively tempts his
captors, and their refusal has become the main action. Now,
the Whig-Democrat contest of 1834 rested principally upon the
question of the recharter of the Bank of the United States. The

Whigs regarded the Bank as essential to a sound, national currency. Indeed, in the winter of 1833-34 Jackson's opposition to the Bank produced a moderate financial crisis which turned many New York merchants against his policies.[80] While Jackson himself opposed the Bank partly for personal reasons and partly out of fear of a money monopoly, his supporters were less disinterested. State banks in all parts of the country, hoping to be able to circulate quantities of inflationary paper money, were impatient with the restrictions imposed by the Bank of the United States. According to Robert W. July, "In New York State the local financiers and the Albany Regency /Jacksonian/ were closely connected, and each hoped to destroy the organization /i.e., Bank of the United States/ which was depriving New York of the country's financial leadership."[81] The Bank question was at the center of the mayoralty election of 1834, for the Whig candidate was Gulian C. Verplanck, who in 1832 lost his seat in the House of Representatives because of his refusal to approve Jackson's veto of resolutions in favor of the Bank's recharter passed in both Houses of Congress. The point at issue in the 1834 election was whether state banks should be allowed to create an inflationary economy or the Bank of the United States should continue to maintain a hard money policy.

Coming at a time when numbers of workers were without jobs and merchants bankrupt, the election excited intense animosity. Violence erupted on the first of the three days the polls were open. The Whig committee rooms in the Sixth Ward were sacked and the ballots destroyed by the Democrats, leaving several

Whigs critically injured. On the third day, the mayor, himself
wounded, declared the city to be in a state of insurrection.
When the votes were counted, Verplanck lost by one-hundred and
eighty votes. Whig candidates were, however, elected to all
of the seats on the City's Common Council. To the Whigs this
constituted a victory, a firm indication of popular disapproval
of an unregulated, state, banking system. As the people rejected the inflated and relatively worthless currency that
state banks could continue to circulate, as they rejected it
despite strong inducements from the Democrats, so Paulding--
the symbol of Whig patriotism--rejects the wealth offered by
the Tory André--the symbol of the Jacksonian state banking
interests. While this painting still celebrates the victory
of the Whigs over the Democrats, of truth--Paulding as Apollo--
over falsehood, at the same time it celebrates the triumph of
the economic policy of the victorious party.

B. Paintings for Luman Reed.

Our discussion of Durand's Presidential portraits has already acquainted us with his patron Luman Reed. Between the
years 1833 and 1836, Reed, a New York merchant who had amassed
a considerable fortune, was unquestionably the most serious
patron of art in America. By the later part of 1834, Dunlap
could speak of "the munificent patronage Mr. Reed . . . has
bestowed on the fine arts, and his friendship for our distinguished artists" and describe him "as standing among the
greatest benefactors to the fine arts, and the most purely

disinterested that our country can boast."[82]  Durand, Thomas
Cole, the landscape painter, and George W. Flagg (1816-1897)--
Washington Allston's nephew and pupil, portrait, genre, and
history painter--received the largest share of Reed's patronage.
William Sidney Mount, the painter of Long Island, rural life,
painted two pictures for Reed, who also offered commissions to
Henry Inman and Samuel F. B. Morse.[83]  Reed employed artists
on the kind of work in which each was interested and paid them
well.  But, also, he entered into the personal interests of
the artists, offering encouragement and advice, communicating
his own enthusiasm, and encouraging his business associates
to follow his example.  To exhibit his pictures, Reed devoted
the top story of his newly erected house in Greenwich Street
to the purposes of a gallery.[84]  This was probably the first,
private, art gallery in a New York home and was opened to the
public one day a week.[85]  Here the paintings could be displayed
adequately, and here Reed's friends could learn what it meant
to be an art patron.

At the beginning of his career as a patron Reed appears to
have left the choice of subject to the discretion of the individual artist.  Cole's series of five paintings, The Course of
Empire, was commissioned in September, 1833.  On the eighteenth
of this month Cole stated his plans for the series, which he
had conceived several years earlier.  At this time Cole had
received assurance of almost unlimited patronage, for, in the
same letter, he speaks not only of the five paintings of the
Course of Empire but of some twenty or more others, which would

fill an entire room in Reed's home.[86] Nowhere is there an
indication that Reed made any suggestion as to subjects. His
patronage of George W. Flagg was equally liberal. Flagg,
whose career commenced as a much petted, thirteen-year-old
prodigy in Boston in 1830--he was "allowed unlimited licence
in kissing"[87] his female sitters--came to Reed's attention
about 1833.[88] An arrangement was made whereby Flagg--still
only fifteen or sixteen--would receive an annual salary in
exchange for any fancy pictures he might paint. Portraits he
might continue to paint on his own.[89] Reed probably exercised
no control over the subjects of the eleven sentimental and
dramatic pictures, reminiscent of the Boydell Shakespear and
other English engravings from around 1800, which he acquired.[90]
However, by the time Reed first employed Durand, in 1835, he
had formed more definite ideas as to the kind of painting he
wanted. Clearly, it was he who decided that Durand should
produce the two sets of Presidential portraits. And the subjects of three other paintings--Durand's The Wrath of Peter
Stuyvesant (Fig. 60) and The Pedlar Displaying his Wares
(Fig. 56), and Mount's The Truant Gamblers (Fig. 58) may have
been selected, by Reed or the artists or both, to complement
the themes of certain other paintings completed or commissioned
for the gallery. As these three paintings are mutually related
in their themes, we must treat them in some detail.

The paintings belonging to the first phase of Reed's
patronage generally avoid moral questions. Flagg's Murder of
the Princes in the Tower (Fig. 55), exhibited at the National

Academy in 1834, and his <u>Lady Jane Grey Preparing for Execu-tion</u>, exhibited in 1835, may both be classified as dramatic paintings in that they excite the spectator's pity and thereby purge it. The character of Cole's <u>Course of Empire</u> cannot so easily be defined. According to his letter to Reed of September 18, 1833, he conceived of the series as an "epitome of Man," tracing the progress of man from barbarism, through the states of civilization, luxury, and viciousness, to his final ruin-- the changes of natural scenery would "give expression to each picture."[91] As a series of progressive states ending in ruin, the paintings approximate to the serial sermons of Hogarth. But unlike, say, Hogarth's <u>The Stages of Cruelty</u>, no vice is present in the first two states. Rather, Cole's series much more closely approximates the character of a Greek dream, which begins well and ends with ruin after a change of fortune. The personal hero of the drama, however, is displaced by the collective hero--Mankind. Like an Aristotelian drama, the series would, like the two paintings by Flagg mentioned above, serve to arouse feelings of fear and pity in the spectator. These feelings, once aroused, would be purged; thus restoring the spectator to a state of psychic health, which would save him from the condition of viciousness. But a dramatic reversal requires a tragic flaw or the operation of some moral cause that is capable of transforming prosperity into ruin. In his letter to Reed, Cole specifies only a general condition of viciousness as the cause of the destruction in the fourth paint-ing. But, by the time the series was completed in 1836, he

had formulated in the motto which he applied to the whole
series a somewhat more exact statement of the causes of
destruction:

>First freedom, and then glory, when that fails,
>
>Wealth, vice, corruption.

Of the three factors--wealth, vice, corruption--the first is expressed in the magnificent scene in the central painting, showing the city in its full prosperity. The other two factors
are nowhere distinctly evoked. But the letter of September,
1833, indicates that Cole planned to paint three other pictures,
smaller than those in the series, which would be hung above
the series itself in Reed's gallery. These would "be something
in character with those over which they hang."[92] As the series
alone took more time than Cole anticipated, he and Reed may
have decided that other artists might paint three pictures to
accompany the Course of Empire and to define more precisely
the nature of the forces by which it is destroyed. The three
paintings by Durand and Mount, painted in 1835, seem to complement the series in this way.

The theme of wealth or luxury is treated in Durand's Pedlar
Displaying his Wares (Fig. 56), finished early in 1836 and
exhibited at the National Academy the same year. Here, a shrewd
Yankee pedlar has descended upon the family of a plain but
prosperous farmer. The pedlar's beads and cloth especially
attract the attention of the farmer's two daughters. The elder
one at the right has already set aside a satin shawl and now
holds up a striped material from which she might make a new

apron. A string of beads has captured the fancy of her
younger sister who, with an expression and gesture eloquent
with childish pleading, secures from her father the requisite
funds. The budding love of luxury in the little girl is
clearly ridiculed, as her brother recommends her action to
his mother as an example of the absurd. In contrast to the
two girls, the mother holding an infant and the aged grandmother
seated at the left are immune to the glitter of "riches."
The grandmother does not even see what is happening, while
the mother looks on with calm disinterest. The contrast between the sobriety of the older women and the frivolity of
the girls as well as the ridicule of the boy serve to demonstrate that a taste for vanities is, indeed, wrong.

The contrast between the girls' luxuriousness and the
grandmother's evident pursuit of wisdom, as well as her ignorance
of the pedlar and his wares, may have been suggested to Durand by
the following passage from Plutarch's Of the Love of Wealth:

> The happiness riches pretend to is such that it
> depends upon spectators and witnesses; else it would
> signify nothing at all. But it is quite otherwise
> when we consider temperance or philosophy, or such
> knowledge of the Gods as is requisite, for these,
> though unknown to all other mortals, communicate a
> peculiar light and great splendor within the soul,
> and cause a joy that dwells with it as an inmate,
> whilst it enjoys the chieftest good, though neither
> Gods nor men may be privy to it. Such a thing is

truth, virtue, or the beauty of geometrical or astro-
logical sciences; and do riches, with their bravery
and necklaces and all that gaudery that pleases girls,
deserve to be compared with any of these? When nobody
observes and looks on, riches are truly blind and
deprived of light.[93]

But, in deciding that a condemnation of luxury would
constitute a suitable theme for a painting, Durand may have recalled the definition of the function of taste offered by Gulian
Verplanck in his Address on the Fine Arts:

> The beneficial effects of good taste are to be found,
> even where you would least suspect its presence. It
> everywhere silently excludes wanton superfluity, or
> useless expenditure in labour or ornament. It inculcates
> a wise and dignified economy.[94]

By contrasting an indifference to material riches with a childish
fascination with vanities, by ridiculing this fascination in the
figure of the boy, Durand has created a genre scene which condemns "wanton superfluity" and "useless expenditure in . . .
ornament," and inculcates that "wise and dignified economy"
which stands in contrast to the extravagance of the girls. The
lesson conveyed by the subject is precisely the same as that
conveyed by the painting as a painting--that is, as an object
of taste.

Without employing satire, William Sidney Mount in his The
Truant Gamblers (Fig. 58) of 1835 attacks a representative of
vice in general, which is the second of the causes specified

by Cole as contributing to the ruin of the empire. While
three of the boys are absorbed in their game, a fourth looks
up in time to see their stern parent approach, stick in hand,
to punish all four. Mount demonstrates that the game of the
boys is wrong by letting us know that they are to suffer for
it. Our participation in the fear of the one boy and our
anticipation of the pain they are soon to experience precludes
our questioning the justice of the father's intent. While the
boys' gambling exemplifies vice in general, it can also be
understood as a metaphor for the financial speculation rampant
in the American economy of the 1830's. As a businessman Reed
had had ample opportunity to observe the ruinous effects of
unrestrained speculation. While Durand's painting condemns
the luxurious tastes of his contemporaries, Mount condemns the
tendency to trust to luck in an effort to secure these luxuries
to oneself.

The third painting, Durand's Wrath of Peter Stuyvesant
on Learning of the Capture by Treachery of Fort Casimir (Fig. 60),
painted in 1835, illustrates the following passage from Washington Irving's Knickerbocker's History of New York:

> On receiving the direful tidings, the valiant Peter
> started from his seat--dashed the pipe he was smoking
> against the back of the chimney--thrust a prodigious
> quid of tobacco into his left cheek--pulled up his
> galligaskins, and strode up and down the room, humming,
> as was customary with him when in a passion, a hideous
> northwest ditty.[95]

The title of the painting evokes the idea of treachery or corruption--the third of the evils specified by Cole--and it is this corruption that is the cause of Stuyvesant's wrath. The painting itself, however, like the text which it illustrates, focuses primarily upon the emotion of anger. But anger--even anger caused by corruption--may be regarded as an evil, tending to destroy man's equilibrium and incapacitate his reason. Through the representation of anger, the spectator may be made to feel it, and ultimately be relieved of it.

Yet, we may discern another level upon which the picture operates. Irving's narrative, like the painting itself, possess a comic aspect. The contrast between the frightened, gangly messenger Dirk Schuiler and the stumpy, complacent trumpeter Anthony van Corlaer, forming a sort of visual equivalent to the contradictory and disproportionate feelings at work within Stuyvesant at the other side of the room, must create some mirth no matter how mild. The force of Stuyvesant's anger is mitigated by the humor of the piece. While the spectator may at a conscious level participate in Stuyvesant's wrath, at some deeper level of emotion he feels the absurdity of it all.

The painting may be seen from still another point of view. Anger is indeed present as well as humor; but the humor is directed at Reed and his circle. According to Daniel Huntington,[96] the figure of Stuyvesant is a caricature of Luman Reed; that of Anthony van Corlaer, a caricature of the miniature painter Gen. Thomas S. Cummings; and Dirk Schuiler, the messenger, is a caricature of Durand. Viewed in this light, Durand appears to satirize Reed's "wrath" over that civil corruption which he sought to counteract by commissioning these paintings for his gallery. Hence, the painting fills an exoteric function by condemning corruption and purging anger through the delineation of that passion in a comic situation. In addition, it has an esoteric function, in that it serves mildly to correct what cannot have been more than a mildly displayed but real vice in Luman Reed and others of his circle.

> First freedom, and then glory, when that fails
>
> Wealth, vice, corruption.

Exemplifying each of these evils, the paintings by Durand and Mount serve to define the causes of the empire's fall. Where Cole presents an epitome of man universally, these paintings treat particular evils in individual and personal terms, in limited human situations. Where Cole's series is primarily dramatic, these paintings are primarily ethical, demonstrating the quality of certain acts mainly through the use of contrasts and various kinds of humor. We have suggested that these pictures might have been planned to hang above Cole's five paintings, as a second series commenting upon the first.[97] All are nearly the same size--The Pedlar, 24 x 34; The Gamblers, 24 x 30; and Peter Stuyvesant, 24 x 30 inches--and all are smaller than the canvases of Cole's series. The first and last two of Cole's paintings are approximately 39 x 61 inches; the central canvas is 50 1/2 x 75 inches. Furthermore, if the three are arranged in the order in which Cole lists the evils--

wealth, vice, corruption--Durand's two indoor scenes would
flank Mount's outdoor scene, thereby closing the group at
either end and producing a kind of symmetry. Finally, if each
of the three were hung above the three central pictures in the
Course of Empire, certain correspondences would emerge between
the individual pictures of the two series.

Cole's second picture, The Arcadian, or Pastoral State,
represents that phase of civilization in which agriculture,
commerce, and religion flourish. Durand's Pedlar represents
a farmer and his family (agriculture), the pedlar (commerce),
and the grandmother reading what may be a Bible (religion).
The aged man drawing a mathematical figure in Cole's painting
(mechanics) may have suggested the grandfather's clock at the
left side of Durand's. But Cole also locates the origin of
the visual arts in this state of civilization by representing
a boy drawing a rude picture. We have noted that, when interpreted in relation to Verplanck's Address on the Fine Arts,
Durand's picture, as it condemns luxury in its subject matter,
accomplishes what Verplanck defined as the effect of a painting qua painting. Hence, in a variety of ways, Durand's painting is related to Cole's.

Cole's Consummation of Empire presents civilization in that
state of prosperity of which, in small, Mount's truant gamblers
dream. In the foreground of Cole's painting a group of small
boys indulge in their own dream of speculative commerce and
material grandeur as they sail toy boats in a pool. So late
as the 1830's, transoceanic commerce was more of a gamble than

a rational business due to the frequency of shipwreck. Turner
had earlier used the motif of boys sailing toy boats as an
emblem of vanity in the foreground of his Dido Building
Carthage,[98] and Cole must have borrowed the idea from this
source. Also, by introducing the triumphal procession of a
victorious army, Cole has indicated that the prosperity of
the empire rests on nothing more firm than chance and fortune.
In Mount's painting the just parent approaches to terminate
the boys' experiment with chance, to deflate their dreams of
easily gotten riches. In much the same way, the austerity of
Mount's painting contrasts radically with the gorgeous pile
of architecture in Cole's and tends to deflate any visionary
dream of grandeur that Cole's painting might stimulate. Mount's
picture stands to Cole's as the farmer stands to the boys.

Lastly, as a scene of violent movement, anger, even viciousness, Durand's Peter Stuyvesant corresponds to Cole's Destruction.
Stuyvesant's mind is filled with wrath and war as is Cole's
picture. By including caricatures of Reed, himself, and Cummings, Durand, perhaps, sought to eliminate from their hearts,
first of all, the emotions that involve the empire in its
final catastrophy.

As late as 1834 and 1835, Durand in the Capture of Major
André, like Cole in the Course of Empire, retained something of
the Neo-classical tradition in a work addressed primarily to the
general public. The rational composition and the Antique pose
in the Major André, like the architecture of Cole's series,
still evoke Antiquity. Further, as a celebration of the

virtuous act of one man, the Major Andre is related to paintings by West and David, Copley and Trumbull from the years prior
to 1800. But, if we consider the painting as a metaphor for
the victory of the Whig party, the Neo-classical hero splinters
into the anonymous, heroic humanity of that aspect of Romanticism celebrated by Goya in his Dos de Mayo (1814), by Rude in
La Marseillaise on the Arc de Triomphe, by Delacroix in Liberty
Leading the People, or by Daumier in The Uprising (L'Emeute).
Similarly, in Cole's Course of Empire the personal hero of the
Greek drama has been replaced by a totally anonymous, collective
humanity. Other Romantic painters treated the history of
civilization--Delacroix in the twenty paintings in the library
of the Palais Bourbon and Peter Cornelius in the frescoes in
the Ludwigskirche in Munich and the Campo Santo in Berlin. But
in Cole's series there is neither an Orpheus nor an Attila to
preside over the rise and fall of civilization--as there is in
Delacroix's paintings, nor is there any implication of divine
determination of human events, as in Cornelius'. Cole's
humanity, deprived of all superhuman or supernatural assistance,
is very much like the hero of the Greek drama who can only
unfold his own character and discover his fate through time.

Elements of Neo-classicism are far less discernible in
the three, later paintings by Durand and Mount. The continued
prominence of the figures, the lucid groupings, the limited
space, and the ordination of the figures and background plane
parallel to the picture plane in each still recall the Neo-
classical tradition. But the representation of evil, rather

than the celebration of virtue, and the various devices used
to define the evil as such--contrast and humor--are essentially
non-classical. In representing an interior, thoroughly
described, and a family group, each member of which is individ-
ualized, Durand's Pedlar recalls the pre-Neo-classical genre
and portrait traditions of seventeenth century Holland. The
gesture of the boy, who recommends to his mother the eagerness
of his sister as an example of the absurd, is one that occurs
in Dutch painting; for example, in Nicolas Maes' The Idle
Servant,[99] one servant with a gesture of her right hand directs
the attention of the spectator toward a slothful companion who
has fallen asleep over her work.

However, the vestigial Neo-classicism of the composition
of both of Durand's paintings and the use of caricature appear
to have been inspired more directly by the comic illustrations
of Thomas Rowlandson. Indeed, the Pedlar is, in several respects, fairly similar to Rowlandson's Doctor Syntax Turned
Nurse (Fig. 57), illustrating William Combe's The Third Tour
of Doctor Syntax in Search of a Wife, published in 1821. In
Rowlandson's print, the figures dominate the interior of a
small room, the rear wall of which parallels the picture plane.
In both pictures, from left to right appear a shelf, a clock,
a cradle, a man seated, a standing girl, and a chair. Rowlandson's Doctor Syntax, like Durand's pedlar, is seated on an
ample chair near the center of the picture, his body facing
the spectator, his head turned toward the spectator's left.
Durand's skinny, awkward, angular figure is very similar to

the Doctor. There are of course other figures and furnish-
ings in Durand's painting that were not inspired by Rowlandson. Yet, such additions as he did make are merely inserted
into the scheme provided by the print. They enrich without
destroying its basic order.

That Durand consulted the Doctor Syntax illustrations
while working on the two paintings for Reed is also suggested
by the similarity between the figures of Dirk Schuiler and
Anthony van Corlaer in the Peter Stuyvesant and Doctor Syntax
and the veterinarian Glanders, respectively, in Rowlandson's
Death of Punch (Fig. 61), appearing in the same volume as the
Doctor Syntax Turned Nurse. In both Peter Stuyvesant and the
Death of Punch, a tall, thin, awkward figure and a short, fat
figure are juxtaposed.[100] In both, the tall figure is in
contrapposto, the arms swinging in one direction, while the
head is turned back over the shoulder. Also, Durand's painting
is related thematically to Rowlandson's print, which illustrates
an incident in which Doctor Syntax grows angry--Syntax began
to fume and vapour--over Glanders' verdict that Syntax has
worked his horse to death.

C. Channing's Concept of Comic Art.

The fact that Durand borrowed certain pictorial ideas
from Rowlandson does not, however, explain his initial interest
in comic subjects. The idea of using comic situations for
moral purposes was probably suggested to Durand or Reed or
both by Channing's defense of humor in his "Remarks on the

Character and Writings of Fénelon" of 1829. Advocating a
rapprochement between literature and religion, in its most
comprehensive sense, he asserts that the "sportive and comic
forms of composition"

> have their root in the constitution which God has given
> to us, and ought not therefore to be indiscriminately
> condemned. . . . Man was made for relaxation as truly
> as for labor; and by a law of his nature, which has
> not received the attention it deserves, he finds no
> relaxation so restorative, as that in which he reverts
> to his childhood, seems to forget his wisdom, leaves
> the imagination to exhilarate itself by sportive in-
> ventions, talks of amusing incongruities in conduct
> and events, smiles at the innocent eccentricities,
> and odd mistakes of those whom he most esteems, alows
> /sic/ himself in arch allusions or kind-hearted satire,
> and transports himself into a world of ludicrous com-
> binations. We have said, that on these occasions, the
> mind seems to put off its wisdom; but the truth is,
> that in a pure mind, wisdom retreats, if we may say,
> to its centre, and there unseen, keeps guard over this
> transient folly, draws delicate lines which are never
> to be passed in the freest moments, and, like a judi-
> cious parent watching the sports of childhood, preserves
> a stainless innocence of soul in this very exuberance
> of gaiety. The combination of moral power with wit
> and humor, with comic conceptions and irrepressible

laughter, this union of mirth and virtue, belongs to
an advanced stage of character; and we believe, that
in proportion to the diffusion of an enlightened
religion, this action of the mind will increase, and
will overflow in compositions, which, joining innocence to sportiveness, will communicate unmixed delight. Religion is not at variance with occasional
mirth. In the same character, the solemn thought and
the sublime emotions of the improved Christian, may
be joined with the unanxious freedom, bouyancy and
gaiety of early years.[101]

If the three paintings by Durand and Mount are regarded simply
as comic pictures, they would provide that restorative relaxation of which Channing speaks. Of the comic situations enumerated, Durand's Pedlar exemplifies "amusing incongruities in
conduct," while in painting the Peter Stuyvesant, he "smiles
at the innocent eccentricities . . . of those whom he most
esteems," allowing "himself in arch allusions or kind-hearted
satire." But also, in looking at this painting, the spectator
is transported "into a world of ludicrous combinations."
Curiously, it was the Reverend Orville Dewey--Channing's
assistant in Boston and since November, 1835, the minister of
The Second Congregational Christian Church in New York--who
described Durand as a painter of "grotesque and common life."[102]
This comment, published early in 1836, must have been inspired
by the Peter Stuyvesant, which Dewey probably saw at the 1836
National Academy Exhibition.

Mount's <u>Truant Gamblers</u>, also, may be connected with a part of Channing's defense of humor. Channing likens the rational mind to "a judicious parent" who watches over "the sports of childhood," and holds folly within certain limits. Mount has represented an incident in which the excessive folly of the children is about to be restrained by the "judicious parent." From this point of view the painting is a metaphor for the mind itself. The mind consists, according to Channing, of a controlling reason (the "parent" in Mount's painting) and an erratic element (the boys)--imagination, wit, humor, mirth, sportiveness, freedom, bouyancy, gaiety--which is to be restrained but not suppressed. As a metaphor for the mind defined in terms of contrary elements, but capable of regulating itself, Mount's painting could justly hold the governing, central position in a group of paintings treating the dangers that confront a state controlled by no agency other than the minds of individual men.

The last paintings executed by Durand for Reed raise no moral issues but retain the element of humor recommended by Channing. Reed wished to have pictures painted oh the doors of his gallery, and they were provided by Flagg and Durand. Cole was to have had a hand in this project, but his work on the <u>Course of Empire</u> kept him at Catskill until after Reed's death. The door panels painted by Flagg have not been located, but four of Durand's are preserved in the New-York Historical Society. These represent children playing blind-man's bluff (Fig. 62), boys playing in a meadow after school (Fig. 63), boys playing marbles (this picture may not have been a door-panel) (Fig. 64), and a boy chasing a pig (Fig. 65). The subjects of two other panels by Durand--a Woman Churning in a Shed With a Child on the Floor and Farmers Eating Dinner Under a Tree--are mentioned in a letter, dated February 17, 1836, from Reed to Cole.[103] The panels representing the sports of children are closely related to the contemporary works of William Collins, William Mulready, and Thomas Webster which were popularized through engravings in English gift-books. Webster's Children on a Seesaw (Fig. 66) is very close in spirit and form to Durand's Blind-Man's Buff or Boy Chasing a Pig.

One of the panels, Farmers Eating Dinner under a Tree, differs in character from the other door panels and will be discussed in the following chapter. But the meaning of the others may be ascertained if they are studied in connection with Channing's defense of humor. The juxtaposition of an adult and a child in the Woman Churning in a Shed with a Child on the Floor recalls Mount's Truant Gamblers, and may also have been intended as a representation of Channing's metaphor for the dual aspects of the mind--"a judicious parent watching the sports of childhood." The three pictures of children's games and the Boy Chasing a Pig may be regarded as the products of that "union of mirth and virtue" in the artist's mind which, according to Channing, "will overflow in compositions . . . joining innocence /i.e., the children7 to sportiveness." And such compositions "will communicate unmixed delight." These later paintings of children stand in sharp contrast to the earlier Group of Children. In this, the innocence of the children is affirmed by their sober, almost ritualistic, peeling of the once-fatal apple. In the later paintings, Durand takes the quality of innocence as granted and is able, thereby, to set the children in motion in such a way that their sportiveness affords a restorative relaxation in addition to that soothing of the spirit that the child's innocence itself is able to effect.

Durand's three, major paintings of the mid-1830's--Major André, the Pedlar, and Peter Stuyvesant--are related to his work as a portrait painter in the same period. The Major Andre, as we have seen, celebrates the noble act of a particular man, Paulding, and his companions and apparently stands as a metaphor for the Whig victory in New York City in 1834. The portraits of eminent men may, also, be regarded as a celebration of individual virtue. But, we have noted that the portraits of eminent men were viewed as instruments capable of effecting the moral elevation of the spectator. The didactic factor appears in more explicit terms in the Pedlar and Peter Stuyvesant and in the whole group of paintings by Mount and Cole to which they are related. The door-panels, on the other hand, lack any quality of celebration or instruction. These appear primarily fitted to afford a certain type of pleasure. As we shall see, the element of pleasure tends to dominate Durand's work in the next decade. Under the impact of events to which we shall refer shortly, in the late 1830's and early

1840's instruction and celebration of virtue--the true and
the good--seemed less relevant to the nature of painting.
In this period Durand's painting came to be controlled primarily by that which gives pleasure--i.e., beauty. After
about 1848 the true and the good were restored to painting,
not as factors opposed to beauty, but as the source of higher
pleasures.

V. Public Calamities and the Decline of Art in New York.

As a patron during a period of three years, Luman Reed
successfully released the energies of New York art that had
been gathering strength since the establishment of the New York
Drawing Association in 1825. The skill that artists had acquired
in the schools of the National Academy he put to work. The
dreams that they had dreamed in the shadow of the American
Academy he helped them to realize. By encouraging the artists
to attack the real, social, economic, and political problems
of their time, he supplied a direction and purpose that had
previously been lacking. He eminently, and perhaps consciously,
supplied the deficiency which Gulian Verplanck had felt when
he spoke of the state of art in America in 1824:

> The natural talent is here; and, when conscious of its
> heaven-given strength, but ignorant or uncertain how
> to apply it, it heaves and pants in the young breast,
> and rises in vain aspirations after it knows not what,
> or wastes itself in idle and blind efforts, how little
> is wanting to unveil to it the secret of its own
> powers, to give to it a steady impulse and true direc-
> tion, and enable it to expand and dilate itself by its
> own energies, to the full stature and majestic propor-
> tions of Genius![104]

Reed's patronage had permitted Cole to realize his grandiose
conception of the Course of Empire, Flagg to study in Europe
and experiment with dramatic compositions that would nowhere

else in America have been purchased, and Mount to exercise
his talents as a genre painter. In the case of Durand, Reed
provided opportunities to learn more of painting from the
study and imitation of portraits by Stuart. And, once the
portraits were done, he encouraged him to renew his interest
in history, genre, and landscape painting.

His patronage was important in setting an example for his
contemporaries in the New York, business world. The professional
men and patricians who had founded the American Academy were,
after Reed's death, supplanted by members of the mercantile
class as the principal patrons of art. In effecting a _rappro-
chement_ between art and the real issues of life, Reed left a
form of art that could justly command the interest of the business world. It was a group of business men who contributed
the funds to purchase the Reed collection, and it was Reed's
partner Jonathan Sturges who carried on his work as a sympathetic
patron. In a letter dated February 21, 1837, Sturges wrote to
Thomas Cole:

> I am confident that the exhibition this year will be
> more than usually interesting--I feel a sort of Family
> pride that you and Durand should stand at the head
> this feeling _you_ will . . . appreciate. It is a feel-
> ing connected with the memory of Mr. Reed. [105]

If, by the time of Reed's death in June of 1836, talent had not
expanded and dilated itself "to the full stature and majestic
proportions of Genius," it was no longer due to frustrating
economic or spiritual circumstances.

For three years Luman Reed had created an atmosphere of excitement and hope among the artists--an atmosphere which might never have been born of the times unassisted. As we observed at the outset of this chapter, the earlier 1830's were permeated by an unremitting acquisitiveness which could discern value in little else but landshares, profitable "public" works, and protective tariffs. In this twilight time of the spirit, the irrelevance of most forms of art must have been felt with especial keenness by the artists themselves. If, however, Reed saved the artist from a despair engendered by this materialism, there were other calamities--natural, social, and economic--which his enthusiasm could not wholly obscure.

The period between 1815 and 1830 was one of relative calm and order in New York. While yellow fever did return to take its toll in 1819, 1822, and 1823, a general spirit of optimism and progress absorbed the energies of the people. A craving for excitement, which could become a source of danger in a city of 170,000, must in large part have been satisfied by the festivals arranged to celebrate the visit of Lafayette in 1824 and the completion of the Erie Canal in 1825. In this same period, however, the problems attendant upon any rapid growth of population began to make themselves felt. Between 1820 and 1829 the number of people arriving through the port of New York to make their home in America amounted to 90,077--slightly more than half the population of the city in 1825. In the following decade immigration amounted to 343,517--approxi-

mately twice the 1825 population. In the decade of the
1840's over half a million people arrived in the city. Of
course, all did not remain in New York itself, but the population of the city did increase rapidly. Simply considering
population, New York in 1830 was a vastly different city from
what it had been in 1820 or 1817. A lingering rural quality
soon gave way to denser building and an expansioñ of the area
of the city. Those who, unlike Durand, could not build homes
uptown around Washington Square, in many cases found themselves
herded together in teeming tenements around The Five Points.

It was this more densely populated city that bore the
brunt of the Asiatic cholera epidemic of 1832. The first case
was reported on June 25, 1832. Before the disease disappeared
in the early autumn, 2996 of the 5,835 people afflicted had
died. While the total number of dead was only one and one-half
per cent of the 200,000 population, the proportion of dead to
those actually living in the city was much greater, for all
who were able retired to the country. Of this plague, Parke
Godwin later wrote:

> It had broken out with great fury, and, being a new
> and almost unknown scourge, the terror created can
> scarcely be imagined at this day. I remember passing
> through New York at the time, . . . and it seemed to
> me like a town suffering siege. The streets were
> deserted, many shops and houses were closed, every
> face wore an expression of despondency and fear, and
> almost the only noises heard in the streets were the
> rattle of death-carts as they carried off the dead.[106]

Within the next few years the cholera plague must have come to appear merely as a harbinger of greater calamities. October, 1833, saw the beginning of the tremendously unpopular advocation of the abolition of slavery. The opposition of the New York mercantile class to agitation that threatened to alienate Southern markets caused people of all classes to resort to intimidation and violence. During an anti-slavery meeting in New York about 1834, one of the principal partici- pants was warned by a prominent merchant:

> We cannot afford to let you and your associates succeed
> in your endeavor to overthrow slavery. I have called
> to let you know, and to let your fellow-laborers know,
> that we do not mean to allow you to succeed. We mean
> to put you down, by fair means if we can, by foul means
> if we must.[107]

By fair means the merchant probably referred to legislative abridgment of civil liberties, by foul he meant mob violence such as the New York riots of October, 1833, and July, 1834. Both means were practiced with sufficient success, both in New York and elsewhere, to maintain slavery for another thirty years.

Later, in August, 1835, the city's stone cutters, angered over the use of State prisoners at Sing Sing to cut stone for the New York University Building, incited a riot, only quelled by the Twenty-Seventh Regiment. The last of the great riots of the 1830's occurred on February 10, 1837. During this winter the supply of flour and other goods became short, and

prices rose--flour from seven to twelve dollars per barrel.
However, it was rumored that the shortage was artificially
created by merchants attempting to extract higher prices.
This view was advocated at a mass meeting in the City Hall
Park, and the 53,000 barrels of flour in the warehouse of
Eli Hart cited as evidence. The mob stormed Hart's warehouse
and dumped five hundred barrels into the street before the
National Guard intervened.

But the temper of the populace and the interests of wealth
were not the only sources of danger. The night of December 16,
1835, a fire broke out. Thirteen acres, upon which stood 693
buildings valued at eighteen million dollars, were burned over
before the fire was extinguished three days later.

At the end of these years of disorder, the crowning disaster
fell on May 10, 1837. Early in 1837 the balance of trade turned
against the United States. One hundred and fifty million
dollars were demanded at a time when the country had no more
than seventy three million in specie. Hence, the nation was
faced with the alternative--suspension of payment or declaration of bankruptcy. On the tenth of May, all New York banks
stopped payment, soon followed by those throughout the country.
The paper-money economy, together with speculations in land
and industry, suddenly collapsed. In a moment, business had
ceased to exist. But New York State law specified that any
bank should lose its corporate status upon suspension of payment for more than one year. Under this necessity, James G.
King, of the New York banking firm of Prime, Ward, and King,
raised a loan of one million pounds sterling in England, which

was shipped to America in March, 1838.[108]  With this capital
the New York banks were able to resume payment by their dead-
line.  And they forced the Bank of the United States of
Philadelphia, the successor to the unrechartered Second Bank
of the United States, to resume at a time when it was entirely
unable to do so.  The Philadelphia Bank limped on for somewhat
over a year before closing permanently in October, 1839,
leaving the Southern banking system in chaos.[109]  With the
aid of English capital the New York bankers had achieved that
position of preëminence in the American economy which they
had envisioned when supporting Jackson's opposition to the
Bank of the United States in 1833 and 1834.

Through these years, 1832-1837, the several crises suffered
by the city and the nation must have provided the more thoughtful citizen with new insights into the fragility and vanity of
such "realities" as life, property, civil liberty, and wealth.
It was after the clear manifestations of the corruption of
the times, in the repeated rioting of 1834, that Reed came to
conceive of his gallery of paintings as an instrument of moral
reform.  Through art, Reed sought to improve the conscience of
his contemporaries.  But Utopia was, in fact, not around the
corner, and the country continued to dispute the expansion of
slavery, the annexation of Texas, the rights of workers:  all
with continued party spirit, suppression of opposition, hatred,
and violence.

If, briefly, Reed had created a mood of hopefulness among the artists, that mood was quickly dissipated by his death, soon after which Cole wrote to Durand:

> The tone of your letter induces me to urge again the necessity of your leaving the city for a time in order to renovate your strength and by that means your spirits--I have been and am much depressed--but I should be much more so if confined in the City--Nature may not cure but she will soothe--We have lost our friend, he who appreciated all our feelings all our efforts--but our place & duties as members of society still remain & we must exert ourselves to contribute to the well-being of that society--in producing works of excellence we cannot fail to do so.[110]

On the eighteenth of August, 1836, Cole wrote in his journal:

> I often think that the dark view of things is perhaps the true one. If such a view were always presented, I doubt whether we could long survive. But Heaven has granted us a sunshine of the heart, that warms all these barren cold realities of existence, and dazzles and deceives, perhaps that we may live.[111]

On the first of September, Durand wrote to Cole of his own state of depression:

> I have in hand a view of a country seat up the east river 4 feet long and 4 miles flat . . . The picture of my family is pretty far advanced but as yet I have but little satisfaction in it in short I am dissatis-

fied with myself and all my works and . . . will
trouble you no more at present with the subject.[112]

It was probably to this letter that Cole replied on September 12 with a more ample recommendation of rural life:

I am sorry that you are at times so much depressed in
spirits; you must come and live in the country. Nature
is a sovereign remedy. Your depression is the result
of debility & you require the pure air of heaven. You
sit (I know you do) day after day in a close air tight
room toiling & stagnating & breeding dissatisfaction
at all you do; when if you had the untainted breeze to
breathe your body would be invigorated, your spirits
bouyant & your pictures would charm even you. . . .
I could say much more on this subject but perhaps my
arguments will be of little weight unless I could give
you a better example in myself of the _effect_ _of_ _country_
_air_.[113]

Apparently Durand paid serious attention to this advice, for
later in the same month he visited Cole at Catskill and executed
several drawings at Trenton Falls.[114]

But Durand was not the only one who, in the years around
1836, felt a need to escape New York, even if only temporarily.
Cole had established a permanent residence at Catskill in
1833. Mount returned to Stony Brook, Long Island in 1836.[115]
When Flagg returned from Europe in 1834, he worked in Boston
and New Haven rather than New York. Among the artists who had
not worked for Reed, William Guy Wall returned to Ireland in

1837. C. R. Leslie, in 1834, had become disgusted with West Point, resigned his teaching position, and returned to England. Robert W. Weir replaced Leslie at West Point in the same year. Christian Mayr, a portrait and figure painter of promise, left for Boston in 1839. Of the older artists, Dunlap died in 1839 and Vanderlyn departed for Paris in 1837 to work on the Landing of Columbus for the Federal government. And in 1837 Trumbull followed his collection of paintings to New Haven. After 1837 Samuel F. B. Morse exhibited nothing at the National Academy, devoting his energies to the development of the telegraph. In the early part of 1837, however, he still retained sufficient interest in his career as a painter to be sorely disappointed when he was not requested to paint one of the historical compositions for the Capitol Rotunda. On February 21 of that year, Theodore Allen, formerly associated in business with Luman Reed, reported to Cole:

> You can not have heard of the appointment of painters
> to their sovereign majesty, the people of the United
> States. They are Messrs. Vanderlyn, Chapman! Inman!!
> & Weir!!! Our friend Morse is most sadly disappointed,
> I really feel sorry for him. He says, so I am told,
> that for 20 years he has had in contemplation the
> painting of one of these pictures. The hopes & ambi-
> tion of his life are lost. He speaks of giving up
> his profession, etc. etc.[116]

On the following twentieth of March, Morse wrote to Cole of his gloomy foreboding:

> Your letter found me of course in trouble on account
> of the decision at Washington . . . I do not now see
> any way of avoiding exile from New York.[117]

A commission given to Morse by his fellow artists to soothe his
disappointment, a commission that he finally abandoned, was
hardly an adequate substitute for the long-desired, Federal
patronage.

Painters were not alone in discovering a distaste for New
York and a longing to be gone. In 1836 William Cullen Bryant--
with a solid reputation as a poet and the editor of a successful, daily newspaper--dreamed of a simpler life in the West.
In September, 1836, he expressed his discontent and sought the
advice of his brother John in Illinois:

> I think of making some disposition of my interest
> in the Evening Post and moving out to the western
> country with a few thousand dollars to try my fortune.
> What do you think of such a plan? . . . I have not been
> much pleased since my return with New York. The entire
> thoughts of the inhabitants seem to be given to the
> acquisition of wealth; nothing else is talked of. The
> city is dirtier and noisier, and more uncomfortable,
> and dearer to live in, then it ever was before. I have
> had my fill of a town life, and begin to wish to pass
> a little time in the country.

But then he wavered:

> I hardly think I shall come to Illinois to live; but
> I can tell better after I have tried it. You are so

distant from all the large towns, and the means of
education are so difficult to come at, and there is
so little literary society, that I am afraid I might
wish to get back to the Atlantic coast.  I should
like, however, to try the experiment of a year at the
West.[118]

In the same letter, rumors of disease in the West led him
to offer his views on the value of medicine.

Mother in her letter to me--her first letter--
praised the healthfulness of the situation.  It seems
to me, however, from what I have learned in one way
and another, that bilious fevers are considerably prevalent among you, and this is rather a bad form of fever.
Whether your being without physicians is much disadvantage I doubt.  Nature is, I believe, a better physician
than most of the physicians whom we call in, in vain
reliance on what we suppose to be their superior knowledge.  The practice of physic is here undergoing a
considerable revolution.  Physicians begin to think
that a vast many patients have been drugged out of the
world within the past fifty years, and the let-alone
system is becoming fashionable.  I am so far a convert
to it that I distrust a physician who is inclined to
work with large quantities of medicine.[119]

Earlier in 1836 Cole had advised Durand "Nature may not cure
but she will soothe;" and, again, "Nature is a sovereign remedy.
Your depression is the result of debility & you require the

pure air of heaven." One might see in the drugs which Bryant
condemned something quite like the larger part of the paintings
commissioned by Reed. These paintings might be viewed as a
set of medicinal compounds--this calculated to soothe, that to
excite to virtue, this to purge, that to cure an infectious
love of wealth, a morbid anger, a pathological taste for speculation. Indeed, the three, comic, genre paintings by Durand
and Mount share something of the function of tragedy as it was
defined by Milton, following Aristotle:

> Tragedy, as it was anciently composed, hath been ever
> held the gravest, moralest, and most profitable of all
> other poems; therefore said by Aristotle to be of power,
> by raising pity and fear, or terror, to purge the mind
> of those and such like passions, that is, to temper and
> reduce them to just measure with a kind of delight,
> stirred up by reading or seeing those passions well-
> imitated. Nor is nature wanting in her own effects
> to make good his assertion: for so in physic, things
> of melancholic hue and quality are used against melan-
> choly, sour against sour, salt to remove salt humours.[120]

Or the love of luxury to cure a love of luxury, of gambling to
cure gambling, of anger to cure viciousness. Reed's gallery
had something of the character of an apothecary shop, filled
with remedies for the several, prevalent sicknesses of society.
Bryant's idea of nature as the better physician parallels
Cole's conception of nature as the sovereign remedy to physical
and moral ills. And, a kind of painting that might be termed

"medicinal" gives way in 1836 to the therapeutic images of
simple, country life and nature exemplified in several of
Durand's door-panel paintings.

Like Bryant, Durand did not permanently quit New York
during the troubles of the 1830's. But, soon after the death
of Luman Reed, he did abandon what must, by then, have become
a fairly profitable career as a portrait painter. If he did
not altogether abandon the city, he did cease to make its inhabitants the object of his art. The inception of his career
as a landscape painter may be established from the record of
paintings exhibited at the National Academy in 1837 and 1838.
In the earlier year Durand exhibited seven portraits, three
landscapes, and a Biblical composition. In 1838 he exhibited
two portraits, two literary subjects, with landscape settings,
and nine landscapes, seven of which were listed as being for
sale. Most of these landscapes must have been painted in the
later part of 1837. Hence, it is in this year, in the summer
of which he had accompanied Thomas Cole on a sketching tour
to Schroon Lake, that Durand first devoted himself primarily
to landscape painting.

While Durand may, during his tour to Trenton Falls in
September, 1836, have found some relief from anxiety and depression, he apparently was unwilling to attribute the full cure to
the restorative powers of nature. It seems not unlikely that
the Biblical composition--Healing the Possessed (App. II,
no. 77), exhibited by Durand at the National Academy in the
spring of 1837--was conceived as another acknowledgement of

the healing power of faith.  The painting illustrated a passage
in the Gospel according to Luke:

> And Jesus rebuked him, saying hold thy peace and come
> out of him, and when the devil had thrown him in the
> midst, he came out of him and hurt him not.[121]

According to John Durand, this painting--"an ambitious composition representing Christ casting out devils, in which the
principal figure is the maniac at the feet of the Saviour"[122]--
was later destroyed at his father's request.  We might regard
this painting as an autobiographical metaphor.  Where, amid
the personal misfortunes of the early 1830's, Durand had derived
consolation from the innocence of his children and from the
grace and intelligence of Mary Frank, now, amid the graver
public calamities of the later 1830's, he is consoled by nature
and religion; for "Nature may not cure but she will soothe."
Nature soothes, religion cures.  For the next ten years Durand
would produce a type of landscape painting well fitted to
soothe, but from which any implication of an ultimate redemption is absent.  Not until 1848 was he to discover the means
to unite the tranquilizing powers of nature with the redemptive
powers of religion.  In the meantime, to soothe was enough.

While there is not any direct indication of religious
faith in his early landscape paintings, we might suppose that
it was a religious faith which permitted Durand to abandon
his career as a portrait painter in order to paint landscapes
for which the market was so small.  And the prospect of sales
must have been all but negligible during the financial crisis

of 1837. After working to supply the expressed needs of the world--as an engraver and as a portrait painter--for twenty years, Durand finally determined to accept his own, inner needs as the imperative to a new course of action. By 1838 he must have felt sufficiently comfortable in his new career, for in this year he returned with his family to the house in Amity Street, which he had abandoned after the death of his first wife eight years earlier. There he built a studio in 1840, and there he lived for the remaining thirty-one years of his New York career.[123]

CHAPTER THREE. NEW WORLDS OF TIME, PLACE, AND MIND.

I. The Development of the Recreational Painting in America.

Of the several calamities of the 1830's, it was the financial panic of 1837 that most adversely affected the largest number of people. Although an increasingly evident materialism, uncontrolled speculation, and hostilities engendered by party spirit had, during Jackson's Administration, appeared to some as signs of danger, it was the collapse of the banking system that most fully illuminated the fragility and vanity of mundane aspirations. Political animosity and economic rapacity appeared to be essential and inextricable elements of an intrinsically corrupt world.

To people such as Durand, Mount, Bryant, and Luman Reed, who had grown up in rural peace and security and who had lived in the simpler New York of the 1820's, the circumstances of life in the 1830's must have seemed threatening indeed. In a society constantly being remolded by forces beyond the control of the individual, the individual who is a permanent part of that society must continually discover himself in situations differing from those which he has learned to handle through previous experience. As a society changes, the individual's past experience becomes relatively ineffectual as an instrument to control new situations. This disproportion between the

actual state of the world at any given time and the experience
of the individual must give rise to fears and anxieties, to a
tendency to regard the world as something with which one must
incessantly struggle, and to a tendency to look back at the
"simpler" past with nostalgia. The real pain engendered by
this disproportion may so weaken the individual that he must
escape from the conflicts of life, if he is to affirm by his
acts the myth of the value of life itself. This was the course
adopted by Thomas Cole in his retreat to Catskill. And in his
two sets of painting, the Departure and Return (1837) and the
Past and Present (1838), he used the image of a more stable
society in a past epoch in what may be regarded as metaphors
for his own awareness of the agonizing disproportion between
the hopefulness of the past and the sense of failure in the
present, or between the prosperity of the past and the ruin
of the present. In these paintings time strips man of what he
once possessed without bestowing any new armor in which to
confront the world in its new condition. Time reduces man to
that condition of naked helplessness in which his only resource
is flight--for example, a flight to the more secure, Gothic
world represented in the paintings. But escape was also the
course meditated by Bryant when he dreamed of moving to
Illinois. However, Bryant--who like Durand was keenly aware
of the pains--and other more vigorous spirits, believing that
man's proper place is in the world of real conflicts among men,
refused to abandon the struggle with life.

For those who stayed, would there be no respite from the
pressures of life?  Something very like this question must
have been debated in the mid-1830's in the circle of Luman
Reed, for in the year 1835 there suddenly appears in the work
of Durand, Mount, and Flagg a new kind of picture--a kind of
picture calculated to afford the spectator what we may term,
in Channing's phrase, a "restorative relaxation."  If the
struggle of life tended to weaken the individual, then the
individual stood in need of a certain nourishment.  On one
hand this nourishment might be something analogous to food
and something that could be expressed by the representation of
food.  This may be described as a sensuous pleasure that is
not only non-debilitating, but positively restorative or re-
creative--i.e., the spectator's enjoyment of imitations of
nature as well as of form and color.  On the other hand, the
nourishment afforded by the painting might effect the reaffirma-
tion of the spectator's identity, of his integrity as a moral
being.  The idea of the painting as affording a restorative
pleasure appears to precede the notion that the painting might
reaffirm the spectator's moral integrity, but the second idea
was a direct outgrowth of the first.  If we are to believe that
the first type of picture was conceived as a response to a
pain caused by the nature of the social structure, rather than
as the response merely to private misfortunes, we should be
able to demonstrate that a number of painters experimented
with it.  A consideration of several paintings by Durand, Mount,
and Flagg will suggest that this was the case.

A. Recreational Paintings by Durand, Mount, and Flagg.

In 1835 and 1836 these three painters executed a group of closely related pictures. The group comprises the following works:

1. Durand, <u>Farmers</u> <u>Eating</u> <u>Dinner</u> <u>under</u> <u>a</u> <u>Tree</u> (door-panel for Luman Reed's Gallery), Dec. 1835-Jan. 1836.

2. Mount, <u>Farmers</u> <u>Nooning</u>, 1836.

3. Mount, <u>Bargaining</u> <u>for</u> <u>a</u> <u>Horse</u>, 1835.

4. Flagg, <u>The</u> <u>Chess</u> <u>Players</u>--Check-Mate, 1835-1836.

Durand's <u>Farmers</u> <u>Eating</u> <u>Dinner</u> has not been located, but by the title we are assured that it represented a number of farmers relaxing, while they take, probably, their mid-day meal. This painting may have suggested the theme of Mount's <u>Farmers</u> <u>Nooning</u> (Fig. 67), painted for Luman Reed's partner Jonathan Sturges. Here, the farmers sit or sleep in the shade of a tree, but are not eating. Nevertheless, their rest in the shade on a warm day, like the meal of Durand's farmers, may be regarded as a form of relaxation that is at once pleasurable and restorative.

The other two paintings are of somewhat more complex character. Mount's <u>Bargaining</u> <u>for</u> <u>a</u> <u>Horse</u> (Fig. 68) illustrates the following passage from the installment of Jack Downing's <u>Journal</u>, published in the <u>New</u> <u>York</u> <u>Gazette</u> for October 28, 1835:

> Seth suspended for a moment the whittling his twig, and there seemed a crisis in the argument--a <u>silent</u> <u>pause</u>--when a shrill voice from the front gate adjoined the meeting instanter. It was the voice of Aunt Nabby herself, breathing authority and hospital-

ity: _Joshua, come to dinner, and bring the folks
along with you._[1]

In the painting, the two farmers and the horse stand before a
shed in the foreground. Seth has stopped his whittling, indicating the moment of crisis in the debate. But the tension
of the encounter suggested in the painting, is about to be
dissipated, for already we see Aunt Nabby at the front gate.
Her immanent invitation will interrupt the struggle for profit
that has, evidently, been going on for some time between the
two farmers.

Flagg's remarkably competent and, in some respects, elegant
composition Check-Mate (Fig. 69) is a transposition of the
dramatic situation of Mount's _Bargaining for a Horse_ to a higher
social plane. Here we have left behind the realm of labor or
the quest of profit. But the game between the lady and the
gentleman has reached no less critical an impasse than that
between the bargaining farmers. The lady in Flagg's painting
is clearly the victor, as she sits toying anxiously with her
necklace while waiting for the gentleman to concede defeat.
But, here again, although the situation is one of tension, it
is about to be relieved as the servant offers a decanter of
wine and two glasses on a tray, while casting a benign and
sympathetic glance toward the helpless gentleman.

All four paintings display certain common characteristics.
In each, something of the realities of life is indicated. In
the first two, the toil from which the farmers find a brief
respite is clearly implied. In the other two the conflict

between Seth and Joshua or between the lady and gentleman may
be understood as representative of the conflicts of will between people generally. In the first two paintings the farmers
are represented as enjoying a brief and restorative respite
from toil. In the other two, the tension of the present conflict will give way to a similar indulgence in restorative
relaxation. All four pictures are based upon a contrast between the pressures of real life and a period of relaxation
in which these pressures are or will be relieved. As the
pressures experienced by the figures in the painting will be
relieved by a temporary indulgence in sensuous gratification,
so the pressures experienced by the spectator in his own life
may be relieved by his delight in the visual image itself--his
delight in the imitation of things and feelings, his delight
in forms and colors.

Paintings that afford the spectator a "restorative relaxation"--diversion as well as nourishment--can suitably be classified under the heading "recreational." Such recreational
paintings hold a unique position, standing between ethical
paintings on one hand and escapist paintings on the other.
The three paintings executed by Durand and Mount as a gloss
on Cole's Course of Empire belong, as we have noted, to the
category of ethical paintings. As instruments intended to
alter the opinions and guide the conduct of the spectator,
these paintings may be regarded as forces operating within the
struggle of life itself. In contrast to these stand such of
Cole's later works as the Dream of Arcadia (1838, Fig. 70) and

the _Architect's_ _Dream_ (1840),[2] both of which clearly reflect
Cole's escapist attitude, indicated also by his early withdrawal from New York. In the escapist painting the artist
creates a world that is wholly cut off from the realities of
life, an image into which the spectator may flee from the pressures of the world, ultimately to become, perhaps, traped in
the dream. Also, the escapist painting demands that the
spectator divest himself of his role as an active participant
in the world of affairs. He must cease to be himself in becoming an Arcadian. In contrast to the ethical painting, the
recreational offers the spectator no advice--it does not attempt
to modify his opinions or conduct; in contrast to the escapist,
it does not totally withdraw the spectator from the real world,
nor does it demand that he abandon his role as a participant in
that world. Contemplating the recreational painting, the spectator is reminded that his place is in the world of affairs, but
he is allowed a moment's rest in which to restore his energies
for renewed combat.

Once the recreational type of painting had been established
in 1835 and 1836 in the circle of Luman Reed, both Mount and
Durand were able in later works to enrich and vary it. Mount's
later paintings of this type need not concern us now, but Dur-
and's require further discussion, because his manipulation of the
type is a fairly critical index of both his sensitivity to the
current social situation and of his continued reluctance to
confine himself within the limits of a single type of picture.

B. Escape and Recreation in Three Later Paintings by Durand, 1838-1839.

In 1838 Durand exhibited two paintings at the National Academy--Dance on the Battery in the Presence of Peter Stuyvesant and Rip Van Winkle's Introduction to the Crew of the Hendrick Hudson, in the Catskill Mountains--which were inspired by the writings of Washington Irving. Unlike his earlier Wrath of Peter Stuyvesant, neither of these implicitly or explicitly attacks any vice or teaches any lesson. Unlike his Pedlar Displaying his Wares, neither represents a real scene of contemporary life. In each painting the place represented is one that is remote from the locale of the practical labors of life. In both the persons represented have retired to places wherein they are no longer constrained to toil. Finally, the events represented' in each occur in a remote or legendary past.

The Dance on the Battery (Fig. 71) embraces a piper at the left, a group of New Amsterdam burghers clustered around the seated figure of Peter Stuyvesant at the center, and a pair of dancing figures at the right. The figures at the center and to the left sit or stand in a row before two massive tree-trunks, that recall the trunks in the Children of the Artist, the Frank Sisters, and Vanderlyn's Ariadne. Indeed, the background further recalls the setting in the Ariadne, an expanse of the water of New York harbour appearing in the distance at the right. As in the Frank Sisters, the two aspects of land-scape are again co-ordinated with the contrasting groups of figures--the more sedentary being associated with the more

massive, restricted, and dark part of nature, while the dancers
are associated with light, airiness, and infinite space. Again,
as in other genre paintings, Durand has placed the figures
prominently in the foreground in a row that parallels the picture plane. The idea of uniting figures and landscape in such
a way that both are of equal interest may have been suggested
to Durand by a painting such as C. R. Leslie's Gipsying Party
(Fig. 24)--also a recreational picture, which he had earlier
engraved. Durand may, however, have been more directly inspired by Rowlandson. A light-hearted scene of dancing out-of-
doors appears in The Tour of Doctor Syntax in Search of the
Picturesque, in which the figures are ranged across the immediate foreground (Fig. 72). While the figures in the Doctor
Syntax print are divided between spectators and dancers, it
differs from Durand's painting in representing a round dance
to the music of a fiddle. Durand has represented a jig performed by two figures to the music of the single piper, and
in this alone his figures recalls the rustic dancers that sometimes appear in the foregrounds of Claude's pastorals,[3] although
Claude's figures are always much smaller in proportion to the
landscape.

Durand's painting quite faithfully illustrates Irving's
description of an open-air dance:

> It would have done one's heart good, also, to have
> seen the valiant Peter, seated among the old burghers
> and their wives of a Saturday afternoon, under the great
> trees that spread their shade over the Battery, watching

the young men and women as they danced on the green.
Here he would smoke his pipe, crack his joke, and
forget the rugged toils of war in the sweet oblivious
festivities of peace. . . . Once, it is true, the harmony of the meeting was rather interrupted. A young
vrouw, of great figure in the gay world, and who, having
lately come from Holland, of course led the fashions
in the city, made her appearance in not more than half-
a-dozen petticoats, and these too of most alarming
shortness. A universal whisper ran through the assembly,
the old ladies all felt shocked in the extreme, the
young ladies blushed and felt excessively for the 'poor
thing,' and even the governor himself was observed to
be a little troubled in mind.[4]

The feelings registered in the face and gesture of several of
the spectators are in response to the "alarming shortness" of
the young woman's petticoats. The picture is based upon a comic
narrative and presents something of the comic due to the
introduction of varied figures, each of whom deviates from any
canon of the perfect human form.

As the painting represents a group of normally industrious
people at a time and in a place of relaxation, it belongs to
the recreational type of picture. However, it differs in several
significant respects from a painting such as Mount's Farmers
Nooning. In Mount's painting we are informed by the fact of
their being in the fields where they have recently been at work
that the farmers are only temporarily relaxing from toil. In

the <u>Dance</u>, on the other hand, the citizens of New Amsterdam
are at a much greater remove from both the time and the place
of toil. The world of reality and of relaxation are no longer
contiguous. In that the world of recreation has now become
an isolated realm, it is a place to which the citizens escape
from the realities of life. Similarly, as the painting represents a scene from an epoch remote from Durand's own, it demands
that the spectator depart from his own time, that he project
himself back into the epoch represented. The spectator, like
the figures represented, escapes from his own world.

While an escapist painting demands that the spectator
depart from his own time, it also demands that he divest himself of his role as an actor in his own times. Now, according
to Irving, Stuyvesant regarded these Saturday afternoon dances
as eminently fitted to disengage the thoughts of the citizens
from, especially, the political issues of the day:

> In fact, he /I.e., Peter Stuyvesant7 really believed,
> though I fear my more enlightened republican readers
> will consider it a proof of his ignorance and illiberal-
> ity, that in preventing the cup of social life from
> being dashed with the intoxicating ingredient of poli-
> tics he promoted the tranquility and happiness of the
> people--and by detaching their minds from subjects
> which they could not understand, and which only tended
> to inflame their passions, he enabled them to attend
> more faithfully and industriously to their proper call-

ings; becoming more useful citizens and more attentive to their families and fortunes.[5]

As Durand causes the spectator to forget the cares of his times as he withdraws to the world of ancient merry-making, the artist also introduces the spectator to a group of people who have been induced by the master of ceremonies, Stuyvesant, to forget the political issues of their time. Since Stuyvesant conceived of the dances as a means to distract the thoughts of the citizens from politics, we might assume that Durand intended that his painting of the dance should withdraw the spectator's attention from the political issues of the years 1837 and 1838.

According to Irving, Stuyvesant believed that once the attention of the people had been diverted from politics, thereafter they would be able to conduct their own personal affairs more efficiently. While the Saturday dances may not increase the powers of the individual, they do prevent his expending what energy he has on matters that do not concern him. Again, this benefit that the dances provide to the participant, the painting provides to the spectator. The spectator is withdrawn to a foreign time and compelled to forget the problems that belong to his own time; but in the foreign time the spectator is introduced to common citizens with whom he can identify himself. He is not required to abandon his own identity, nor is it necessary that he entirely forget his personal situation in order to experience the painting fully. Hence, he, like the dancers, can return to the world of real life, cleansed of anxieties over public issues and, thereby, prepared to pursue his own fortune with fewer distractions.

Durand's other painting based upon a story by Irving--<u>Rip</u> <u>Van</u> <u>Winkle's</u> <u>Introduction</u> <u>to</u> <u>the</u> <u>Crew</u> <u>of</u> <u>the</u> <u>Hendrick</u> <u>Hudson</u> <u>in</u> <u>the</u> <u>Catskill</u> <u>Mountains</u> (App. II, no. 87)--was more thoroughly escapist. Although the painting itself has not been located, the title alone indicates that the painting included the figure of Rip and the phantom forms of Hudson's crew in a mountain setting. Much later John Durand described the painting as representing "a ghostly assembly playing ninepins in a low, weird, supernatural light . . ."[6] From these slight indications it would seem probable that Durand illustrated that moment in the story when Rip, still burdened with a keg of liquor, first discovers the phantom Dutchmen playing ninepins:

> Passing through the ravine, they came to a hollow, like
> a small amphitheatre, surrounded by perpendicular
> precipices, over the brinks of which impending trees
> shot their branches, so that you caught only glimpses
> of the azure sky, and the bright evening cloud. . . .
> On entering the amphitheatre, new objects of wonder pre-
> sented themselves. On a level spot in the center was
> a company of odd-looking personages playing at ninepins.
> They were dressed in a quaint outlandish fashion: some
> wore short doublets, others jerkins, with long knives
> in their belts, and most of them had enormous breeches,
> of similar style with that of the guide's. Their visages,
> too, were peculiar . . . The whole group reminded Rip

of the figures in an old Flemish painting, in the

parlor of Dominie Van Schaick, the village parson,

and which had been brought over from Holland at the

time of the settlement.[7]

In Durand's painting, presumably, Rip has come into contact with
the supernatural inhabitants of a supernatural valley. He stands
in much the same situation as Cole's voyager, who enjoys a vision
of angels, at the end of the Voyage of Life series (1839).
Already acquainted with beings from another world, like the
voyager, he has not yet entered the realm of timelessness in
which these supernatural personnages dwell. It is in the next
moment of the story that Rip begins to imbibe the soporific
liquor:

He even ventured, when no eye was fixed upon him, to

taste the beverage, which he found had much of the

flavor of excellent Holland draught. One taste provoked

another, and he reiterated his visits to the flagon so

often that at length his senses were overpowered, his

eyes swam in his head, his head gradually declined, and

he fell into a deep sleep.[8]

Hence, in the painting, Rip stands on the threshold of temporary
oblivion, a qualified timelessness, from which he will awaken
in twenty years.

The painting focuses upon Rip's presence in a supernatural
place, among supernatural beings, at the entrance to a supernatural time. Rip exists not in this world but in another. His
presence in this other world is due precisely to his distaste

for the adversities of the real world. Earlier in the story
Irving describes "poor Rip" as

> . . . at last reduced almost to despair, and his only
> alternative to escape from the labor of the farm and
> the clamor of his wife was to take gun in hand and
> stroll away into the woods.[9]

In this painting Durand adopts a fully escapist point of view.
The world of the painting into which both Rip and the spectator
are introduced is non-contiguous to the world of toil. In no
sense can this world be regarded as a place of recreation.
Rather, it is a place of oblivion, of complete forgetfulness of
one's own time and place, one's active role therein, and of
one's self. It is this obliteration of the ego that renders
the painting more escapist than any other by Durand. It is
worth noting that this painting was begun in July, 1837, hardly
three months after the New York banks closed. Although he was
at work on both this and the Dance on the Battery as late as
February 7, 1838, the Rip Van Winkle was probably conceived
earlier and appears to reflect Durand's more immediate reaction
to the bank crisis. As a combination of the recreational and
the escapist types of painting, the Dance on the Battery would
seem to be the product of a slightly later and calmer moment.

In one other painting combining figures and an elaborate
landscape--Sunday Morning (1839, Fig. 73)--Durand returns to
the pure recreational mode. Although in this painting Durand
did not illustrate any particular literary text, it seems not
unlikely that he was in some way inspired by Joseph Addison's

comments on a rural, Sunday morning in The Spectator. In
1819 Addison's essay had served as the basis for what Charles
R. Leslie described, in a letter published in part by Dunlap,
as "The first original composition that made me known . . ."[10]
While it is unlikely that Durand ever saw this painting, it
may have been described to him by Leslie during his stay in
America, 1833-1834, or Durand may simply have noticed it mentioned in Dunlap. Whether or not Durand was inspired by Leslie's
earlier painting, Addison's comments do seem to illuminate the
character and value of Durand's painting. Addison's essay
begins:

> I am always very well pleased with a country Sun-
> day; and think, if keeping holy the seventh day were
> only a human institution, it would have been the best
> method that could have been thought of for the polishing
> and civilizing of mankind. It is certain the country-
> people would soon degenerate into a kind of savages and
> barbarians, were there not such frequent returns of a
> stated time, in which the whole village meet together
> with their best faces, and in their cleanliest habits,
> to converse with one another upon indifferent subjects,
> hear their duties explained to them, and join together
> in adoration of the Supreme Being. Sunday clears away
> the rust of the whole week, not only as it refreshes
> in their minds the notion of religion, but as it puts
> both the sexes upon appearing in their most agreeable

forms, and exerting all such qualities as are apt to give them a figure in the eye of the village.[11] Here Sunday morning is described as an especially designated time in which the country people are not only relieved of the labors of the week, but are also refreshed or recreated in their full human dignity. Once restored, they will return to their appointed tasks, which, even now, are not far away in some other world but near at hand in the adjacent fields to be pursued again on the morrow. The present moment is one of recreation within the world of real life.

In one respect the Sunday Morning stands in contrast to the Rip Van Winkle. In the Rip, one tormented man plunges into oblivion, while in the Sunday Morning the presence of representatives of the several ages of man and both sexes suggests that the restorative relaxation of a Sunday morning is accessible and relevant to humanity in general. The normal human collective supplants the pathological individual. In another respect the two paintings are more closely related. As Rip approached the supernatural through the wilderness (a place of exemption from labor), the country folk approach the supernatural (indicated by the church building) on Sunday morning (a time exempt from labor). Both paintings involve an approach to the supernatural along a path apart from the toils of ordinary life. But in Sunday Morning the path itself has been moved back into the world of reality. And the encounter with the supernatural is correspondingly less devastating. While the path pursued by Rip ends in the obliteration of the ego, the path pursued by

the country folk ends in the elevation of the ego. After
experimenting with the idea of escape, Durand returns to the
recreational picture. But now, the recreation involved is
no longer analogous to physical nourishment; it is no longer
merely a delight in imitation, form, and color. Rather, the
recreation entails an affirmation and an elevation of the
individual's identity. In contemplating the picture, the
spectator, like the figures therein, may idealize himself as
he temporarily eludes a degrading submission to the toil and
anxieties of real life. But, also, he may become conscious
of himself as himself, as a being possessing an unique identity
that is not the product of his struggle with the world.

C. Recreational Landscapes.

Landscape painting may be either escapist or recreational.
It is escapist if:

1. The world represented is relatively remote from the
world of the spectator's normal habitation.

2. The spectator must relinquish his own identity before
he can fully participate in the world represented.

3. If the world represented offers no distinct nourishment beyond that afforded by the mere fact of escape.

The landscapes of Claude and the arcadian tradition in painting
and poetry generally are escapist. Contemplating Cole's <u>Dream
of Arcadia</u>, we translate ourselves to a world that in reality
is inaccessible and transform ourselves into beings that do
not suffer, but we are not necessarily cured of our own suffer-

ing. Channing in his "Remarks on the Character and Writings of John Milton" described a similar flight to an untroubled realm:

> Still there are times, when the spirit, oppressed with pain, worn with toil, tired of tumult, sick at the sight of guilt, wounded in its love, baffled in its hopes, and trembling in its faith, almost longs for the "wings of a dove that it might fly away" and take refuge amidst the "shady bowers," the "vernal airs," the "roses without thorns," the quiet, the beautiful, the loveliness of Eden.[12]

In such an Eden we encounter no dangers, we are relieved but not cured of the sickness which sent us thither. This still awaits us upon our return. An escapist landscape stands, then, in contrast to a recreational, which may display the following characteristics:

1. The world represented is relatively close to that in which the spectator normally dwells.

2. The spectator need not relinquish his identity when entering the painted world.

3. The world represented offers a certain nourishment other than that afforded by the mere fact of escape.

This approach to nature is clearly indicated in the following lines from Bryant's "Inscription for the Entrance to a Wood:"

> Stranger, if thou hast learned a truth which needs
> No school of long experience, that the world
> Is full of guilt and misery, and hast seen

> Enough of all its sorrows, crimes, and cares,
> To tire thee of it, enter this wild wood
> And view the haunts of Nature. The calm shade
> Shall bring a kindred calm, and the sweet breeze
> That makes the green leaves dance, shall waft a balm
> To thy sick heart.[13]

The woods are fairly near at hand. The individual may go to them, not disguised as an Arcadian shepherd, but in his own person. Once there, he is calmed, cured of the sickness within his heart by the soothing influence of a gentle breeze.[14]

But, as we have seen, the recreational type of painting at first, in such works as Mount's Bargaining for a Horse, combined a motif representative of the realities of life with a motif of a period of temporary relief in which life itself is nourished by food. Now, there existed in America during the Romantic period a point of view from which nature was regarded as a source of nourishment for the spirit analogous to food or drink for the body. In expressing this analogy, nature was spoken of as a "banquet" or a "drink" or a "feast." As early as 1821, the banquet and drink metaphors were combined in a letter to Durand from his friend, the poet and dietician, Sylvester Graham:

> You seem to regret my dear fellow that you are
> obliged to forego the rural enjoyments of the country,
> and speak as though to me, there might be a continual
> banqueting on nature's wild, yet honest beverage of
> truth.[15]

About ten years later, the portrait painter Frederick W. Philip
wrote enviously to Durand:

> Oh if I had the tongues of millions I could not speak
> all I feel, that should be her /i.e., nature's7 due--
> her just her true reward--Do you know this friend?
> Oh yes I know that you do, 'tis Nature all glorious,
> ever beautiful.  Oh that I knew her so well--oh that
> I could converse with her with the freedom that you
> can--to taste her sweets, her nectarine juices as you
> must--what an enviable banquet.[16]

In these two uses of the metaphor of the banquet, an individual simply longs to partake of it for its own sake.  But, by
the mid-1830's the banquet of nature came to stand explicitly
in opposition to the cares of life.  In his "Essay on American
Scenery," Thomas Cole states that "Nature has spread for us a
rich and delightful banquet."[17]  But in the same essay he also
describes nature as "an unfailing fountain of intellectual
enjoyment, where all may drink, and be awakened to . . . a keener
perception of the beauty of our existence"--a perception that
is not accessible to "those whose days are all consumed in the
low pursuits of avarice, or the gaudy frivolities of fashion."[18]
And, at greater length, he describes the experience and the
value of a temporary retreat from the city in a statement that
defines with entire adequacy the recreation obtainable by one
who, in this case, "drinks from pleasure's purest cup:"

> He who looks on nature with a "loving eye," cannot
> move from his dwelling without the salutation of beauty;

even in the city the deep blue sky and the drifting
clouds appeal to him. And if to escape its turmoil--
if only to obtain a free horizon, land and water in
the play of light and shadow yields delight--let him
be transported to those favored regions, where the
features of the earth are more varied, or yet add the
sunset, that wreath of glory daily bound around the
world, and he, indeed, drinks from pleasure's purest
cup. The delight such a man experiences is not merely
sensual, or selfish, that passes with the occasion
leaving no trace behind; but in gazing on the pure
creations of the Almighty, he feels a calm religious
tone steal through his mind, and when he has turned to
mingle with his fellow men, the chords which have been
struck in that sweet communion cease not to vibrate.[19]

Here, the turmoil of the city is analogous to the haggling of
the farmers in Mount's painting. "Pleasure's purest cup" is
like the dinner to which Aunt Nabby summons the combatants.
The "calm religious tone" is, at once, the same as the calm
which Bryant described as induced by the experience of nature
and like the lasting benefit derived from a cool drink of water
on a warm day.

Much later, when in 1855 Durand wrote his Letters on
Landscape Painting, he was still willing to acknowledge the
validity of the analogy between the experience of nature and
a banquet. While Cole wrote of the experience of nature itself,

Durand speaks here of the spectator's experience of a landscape painting:

> But, suppose we look on a fine landscape simply
> as a thing of beauty--a source of innocent enjoyment
> in our leisure moments--a sensuous gratification with
> the least expenditure of thought or effort of the
> intellect. . . . How many of our men of fortune, whom
> nature and circumstances have well fitted for such
> enjoyment, surrender, as it were, their birthright,
> for a mess of pottage, by resorting to costly and need-
> less luxuries, which consume without satisfying--while
> Art invites to her feast of beauty, where enjoyment
> never cloys, and entails no penalty of self-reproach![20]

While Durand would not admit that a landscape painting should
provide only a sensuous gratification, he does regard the fact
that it provides a delight arising from imitation, forms, and
colors as among its potential values. The sensuous gratification afforded by the painting is not debilitating; and, as it
is like that afforded by a feast, it must provide some sort of
nourishment that continues to benefit the spectator after the
feast itself has been taken. As Durand wrote this at the peak
of his career and as it echoes the idea implicit in his own
Farmers Eating Dinner under a Tree of twenty years earlier, we
may accept it as applicable to any of his landscapes after the
mid-1830's.

Within the same period, another metaphor--that of the oasis
--was employed for the subjective processes of imagination or

for the experience of a landscape painting. In his "Essay on
American Scenery" Cole conceived of the realm of feeling,
sentiment, or imagination as an oasis in a world of mental
habits dominated by considerations of utility:

> In this age, when a meager utilitarianism seems
> ready to absorb every feeling and sentiment, and what
> is sometimes called improvement in its march makes us
> fear that the bright and tender flowers of the imagina-
> tion shall be crushed beneath its iron tramp, it would
> be well to cultivate the oasis that yet remains to us,
> and thus preserve the germs of a future and a purer
> system.[21]

To Cole, the oasis is merely one kind of subjective activity
which is threatened by a dominant utilitarianism.

When Durand used the same metaphor in his Letters on Landscape Painting, the oasis is the work of art regarded as providing
a restorative relief from the pressures of reality:

> To the rich merchant and capitalist, and to those
> whom even a competency has released from the great
> world-struggle, so far as to allow a little time to
> rest and reflect in, Landscape Art especially appeals--
> nor does it appeal in vain. There are some among "the
> innumerable caravan" that look to it as an oasis in
> the desert, and there are more who show signs of lively
> susceptibility to its refreshing influence.[22]

But, whether the oasis is the subjective state that informs a
work of art, or the work of art itself, it is a sphere both of

relief from a debilitating environment and of that refreshment which will permit one to continue the arduous toil across the desert of this world. Durand's conception of a landscape that affords a temporary recreative pause during a relatively harsh journey of life recalls to mind the motif of the rest on the flight into Egypt frequently introduced by Claude into his landscapes[23] as well as the Delectable Mountains and Land of Beulah which John Bunyan provided for the nourishment and temporary repose of his pilgrim.

From time to time Durand introduced into his landscapes groups of figures who derive either sustenance or relaxation from nature. In the foreground of his Landscape with Children (1837, Fig. 75), a girl gathers strawberries while a boy and another girl eat from a basket that has already been filled. The Dover Plains (1848, cf. Fig. 76) includes a similar group of children gathering strawberries. And a Pastoral Landscape (1849) was exhibited at the National Academy with the lines from Bryant's poem, "The Fountain":

Blue-eyed girls

Brought pails, and dipped them in the crystal pool;

And children, ruddy-cheeked and flaxen haired,

Gathered the glistening cowslip from the edge.

These motifs serve to enforce the idea of the experience of nature as a banquet or a restorative beverage.

The experience of nature as an oasis is indicated also in the Landscape, View of Rutland, Vermont (ca. 1840, Fig. 77), which, according to Edgar P. Richardson, was "painted on commission

as a portrait of the boyhood home of the original purchaser."[24]
Here two ladies and two gentlemen, who relax beneath three
trees at the left foreground, use nature as though it were an
oasis. It is worth noting that Durand later stated that nature
is regarded as an oasis by

> . . . those who trace their first enjoyment of exis-
> tence . . . to the country, to some pleasant landscape
> scenery; to such the instinct of nature thus briefly
> impressed, is seldom or never overcome . . . To him
> who preserves the susceptibility to this instinctive
> impulse, in spite of the discordant clamor and conflict
> of the crowded city, the true landscape becomes a thing
> of more than outward beauty.[25]

In the painting, of the four figures who do employ nature as
an oasis, one stands pointing across the meadows as though
recommending to the others the scenes of his boyhood.[26]

However, the temporary withdrawal to nature or the contemplation of the landscape painting might offer other forms of
nourishment aside from those that are analogous to the banquet
or oasis. In the Children of the Artist of 1832, which we discussed at length in the last chapter, Durand represented the
three children, fitted to calm the troubled heart, and the
pecking chickens and large-leafed plants as sermons preaching
an unreserved faith in God of which the innocence of childhood
is the emblem. In the Landscape with Children, Durand returned
to images of children which should tranquilize. And this may
also be the effect of the experience of nature itself, as Bryant

affirmed in the verses cited above. But, also, Durand has again
emphasized the plants that "toil not neither do they spin,"
and here, rather than chickens, it is the children themselves,
picking strawberries, that "sow not, neither do they reap, nor
gather into barns." As the children, so nature calms--"The
passions . . . shrink / And tremble and are still." The <u>Dover</u>
<u>Plains</u> of 1848 is closely related to the <u>Landscape</u> <u>with</u> <u>Children</u>.[27]
Here, again, three children appear in the foreground, two of
whom gather berries amid a profusion of prominent plants. Again,
the values of innocence, calm, and faith may be as well derived
from the children and the plants as from the larger landscape
scene itself. But here a third child, her back to the spectator,
stands upon a pile of boulders looking out over the spreading
valley. Presumably, she is experiencing something of that rapture
which Wordsworth had described as essential to the child's
experience of nature. Or, perhaps, she sees nature as Wordsworth's
disciple Bryant had taught his daughter to see:

> . . . . with delighted eye
> To gaze upon the mountains,--to behold
> With deep affection, the pure ample sky
> And clouds along its blue abysses rolled,
> To love the song of waters, and to hear
> The melody of winds with charmèd ear.[28]

Bryant's "Lines on Revisiting the Country," in which these verses
appear, was clearly inspired by Wordsworth's "Lines Composed a
Few Miles above Tintern Abbey, on Revisiting the Banks of the
Wye during a Tour." In both poems the speaker is accompanied

by a child, and in Wordsworth's poem the child's response to
nature aids the poet in the recovery of his own childhood
vision:

> . . . and in thy voice I catch
> The language of my former heart, and read
> My former pleasures in the shooting lights
> Of thy wild eyes. Oh! yet a little while
> May I behold in thee what I was once . . .[29]

The presence of the contemplative child in Durand's painting may
aid him, or the spectator, to recall his own early rapturous
vision.

But, according to Wordsworth, the more striking phenomena of
nature, especially sunsets, may effect this same recollection.[30]
In 1838, Durand painted what is probably his first landscape in
which a sunset is the principal motif (Fig. 78). In subject
matter Durand has here excluded any implication of human life,
presenting a place beyond, or other than, that in which man
dwells. Compositionally, he has molded nature to a near symmetry,
in which two dark masses of foreground flank a distant vista
dominated by horizontal lines. Individual forms are reduced to
comparatively simple shapes--such as the approximately rectangular
mass of foliage at the right--and described with a minimum of
attention to distracting detail. The more complex or multipartite
forms of nature have been omitted. Considering merely the forms
and their organization, Durand has divested nature of any element
of animation, has imposed an arresting stillness, an empty
silence. But this rigidity of things embraces and seems to

imprison the liquid symphony of a richly stained sunset-sky, charging with its color the middle-ground water and tinging tufts of foliage across the valley. The land is motionlessly transfigured by an abnormal radiance. Despite its somewhat naïve design, this is certainly among the most intensely emotional landscapes painted by Durand. The solitude and stillness of the place and the force of the light constitute a world perhaps more thoroughly opposed to the world of daily experience than even the supernatural realm envisioned in the Rip Van Winkle. The painting is far more austere in its forms, and the light itself receives more emphasis than is the case in Thomas Cole's Summer Sunset (Fig. 79), painted a few years earlier for Luman Reed, which Durand may have had in mind when he painted his sunset. While Cole's painting offers the spectator a sip from "Pleasure's purest cup," Durand seems to present that fleeting, brilliant, apparitional light that Wordsworth had regarded as a blessing from God, to

> . . . remind me of the light
> Full early lost, and fruitlessly deplored;
> Which, at this moment, on my waking sight
> Appears to shine, by miracle restored!
> My soul, though yet confined to earth,
> Rejoices in a second birth.[31]

Or, perhaps, we can equally regard the sunset brilliance as the external sign and nourishment of the inner light of faith. Here the special phase of nature strengthens the inner spiritual essence of the spectator: it affords a recreation that is a second birth.

Although as a landscape painter, Durand in no way limited himself to sunsets, they do form a conspicuous part of his work. The Sunset of 1838 was followed by many others, among which Lake Scene, Sunset (1843, App. II, no. 193) and a Sunset exhibited in 1848 attracted the high praise of his. contemporaries. Henry T. Tuckerman opened his chapter on Durand, as though viewing Durand's sunsets as his major achievement, with the following description of a sunset over an American lake in the wilderness:

> Whoever has sailed across one of our immense lakes-- the inland seas of this vast continent--at the close of a day when summer was verging into autumn, and the keen wind swept over the broad waters as they glowed with crimson or saffron in the magnificent sunset, cannot easily forget a scene unequalled in any part of the world. The expanse of water spreading to the horizon seems kindled into transparency by the warm and deepening hues as they flash unobstructed upon the waves; as twilight comes on, the view grows sublime, and when the vivid tints gradually vanish in darkness, a deep and almost sacred impression is left upon the mind. Durand gives, in one of his landscapes called a Lake Scene, a remarkably happy idea of a prospect like this.[32]

Clearly from Tuckerman's assertion that sunsets are fitted to produce "a deep and almost sacred impression . . . upon the mind" we may be assured that Durand's contemporaries saw in them something more than a beauty affording gratification only to the sense of sight.

Of the Sunset of 1848, representing also a lake scene, an unnamed critic in The New World stated that "More than any other production of his masterly pencil, this last picture by Mr. Durand places him on a level with Claude."[33]  And, of course, most of Durand's sunsets are very much in the tradition of Claude.  The arrangement of Durand's 1838 Sunset, like Cole's 1836 Summer Sunset, approximates, in no matter how simplified a way, the arrangement of a typical Claude pastoral.  The spectator looks directly into a warm, glowing evening light, which is reflected by a middle-ground body of still water, and filters through, tinging the thinner and silhouetting the heavier masses of foreground foliage.  Claude's Pastoral Landscape of 1644 in the National Gallery of Canada, Ottawa, is a good example of this type.  Or, Durand's lake scenes at sunset, such as the painting described by Tuckerman (cf. Fig. 188), in which the water approaches the foreground and the light plays upon its nearer waves and lappings against the shore, are clearly derived from Claude's port and embarkation scenes.  In an embarkation such as that of Carlo and Ubaldo of 1667, in the collection of The Lady Lucas, the water comes nearly to the lower edge of the painting, its waves shimmering in light reflected from the sunset-sky.[34]  In contemplating the sunset landscapes of both Claude and Durand, the spectator's eye is filled, his soul bathed, in a light other than that of ordinary day.  But between the sunsets of the two painters there is this difference: in the Claudes there is a fine balance between the interest of the forms of earth and the light of the sky, while in the Durands an imbalance is struck--the forms of the earth tending to be subordinated to the more radiant sky. In Claude there is an equilibrium between what might be termed the body and the soul of nature, while in Durand's sunsets, as in his ideal female portraits of the later 1830's, the soul of nature--the light, corresponding to the inner light of faith--is more prominently displayed. It is this heightened sensation of the spiritual that at once reveals the influence of Turner's visionary revision of Claude and stamps Durand's paintings as distinctly Romantic.

In summary, Durand avoided the purely escapist landscape such as Cole sometimes created. Instead of an opportunity to escape the ills of life, Durand provides a temporary relief, that entails some sort of restorative nourishment. This nourishment may be so simple as the sensuous pleasure derived from the experience of forms and colors, a pleasure like that of a feast or banquet. Or the landscape, like an oasis, may provide a moment of rest amid the ardours of life's pilgrimage. But the most exalted kind of nourishment is the recovery of innocence, faith, and the vision of childhood. If, in looking at the landscape the spectator is restored to a condition of which childhood is the emblem, this does not mean that he loses his own identity in the process. Rather, the spectator is able to recover an awareness of his essential self--the child that endures in the man, however much it becomes buried beneath the crusts deposited by anxieties stemming from the world-struggle in which the individual must of necessity participate. The reawakened awareness of the child in the man is the discovery of one's true identity apart from worldly contingencies, and it is the discovery of what one will be, for the child is still the type of the redeemed in eternity.

II.  Landscape and Associations.

The escapist landscape, as we have noted, presents the spectator with a world relatively remote from that which he normally inhabits and demands that he divest himself of his own identity and assume that of the figures in the painting. This kind of painting has the advantage that, once the spectator is withdrawn from his own world, he may participate in the labors, pipings, or dancing of the inhabitants of this other world.  The painting holds his attention insofar as he becomes a fascinated actor and experiences the world of the painting from within.  The recreational painting, on the other hand, while also presenting the spectator with a world other than that of his daily life, does not demand that he abandon his own identity.  In the hands of Durand the recreational painting is not so much an instrument to turn the spectator into someone else, but rather it is an instrument to awaken the spectator to a sense of his own true identity.  As the spectator does not exchange his own identity for that of one of the actors in the picture, it would seem that he could in no real way become an active participant in any event represented.  And, as he does not become an actor, it would seem that his interest in the painting would begin to fail as soon as he should grasp its message regarding his own personality.

Fortunately, Durand had access to a theory of the appreciation of art in terms of which the spectator might undertake a certain type of mental activity without identifying himself with any of the figures in the work of art under consideration. Cole and Bryant had studied the Essays on the Nature and Principles of Taste by Archibald Alison (1757-1839)[35] early in their careers,[36] and the influence of Alison's associational psychology can readily be traced in the work of each. As Alison's Essays were read by Durand's closest friends, there is no reason to believe that he did not also read them. And, as we shall soon have occasion to note, evidence from Durand's own paintings and his writings on art suggests very strongly that he did master Alison's ideas. Alison's account of the manner in which a work of art might release or excite a train of associations revealed to Durand the means to deeply engage the spectator's mind without requiring that he relinquish his own identity.

According to Alison, paintings or other objects of taste excite a train of thought, a series of associations in the mind of the spectator, and it is this, rather than the thing itself, which is the cause of delight or the emotion of taste:

> When any object, either of sublimity or beauty, is presented to the mind, I believe every man is conscious of a train of thought being immediately awakened in his imagination, analogous to the character or expression of the original object. The simple perception of the object, we frequently find, is insufficient to excite these emotions, unless it is accompanied with this operation of the mind, unless, according to common expression, our imagination is seized and our fancy

busied in the pursuit of all those trains of thought, which are allied to this character or expression.[37] Although this train of thought is controlled by a painting, poem, or a scene in nature, it has no issue in the world of practical affairs. Indeed, it conducts the mind further and further away from these into a sphere wholly its own. Thus, in contemplating any object of taste, we forget ourselves and the world and are drawn away into a controlled daydream:

> It is then, only, we feel the sublimity or beauty of
> their productions, when our imaginations are kindled
> by their power, when we lose ourselves amid the number
> of images that pass before our minds, and when we
> waken at last from this play of fancy, as from the
> charm of a romantic dream.[38]

Amid the images of the imagination engendered by an object of taste, the scenes of the world are forgotten.

That Durand, as late as 1855, accepted Alison's account of the operation of the imagination is suggested by the following passage from his Letters on Landscape Painting:

> Suppose such a one /i.e., a substantial merchant7, on
> his return home, after the completion of his daily task
> of drudgery--his dinner partaken, and himself disposed
> of in his favorite armchair, with one or more faithful
> landscapes before him, and making no greater effort
> than to look into the picture instead of on it, so as
> to perceive what it represents; in proportion as it is
> true and faithful, many a fair vision of forgotten days

will animate the canvas, and lead him through the
scene; pleasant remininscences and grateful emotions
will spring up at every step, and care and anxiety
will retire far behind him. If he possess aught of
imaginative tissue, and few such natures are without
it, he becomes absorbed in the picture--a gentle
breeze fans his forehead, and he hears a distant
rumbling; they come not from the canvas, but through
the open window casement. No matter, they fall purified on his sensorium, and that is far away in the
haunts of his boyhood.[39]

Durand here differs from Alison in only one important point.
Alison takes some pains to point out the normal incapacity of
the man of business to allow himself the kind of spontaneous
train of associations which the enjoyment of art requires.
Indeed, he states quite bluntly that in the mind of man of
business "the prospect of any beautiful scene in nature would
induce no other idea than that of its value."[40] Yet Durand
had found a number of business men to be as susceptible to the
pleasures of the imagination as the young person to whom,
according to Alison, these pleasures are especially reserved.

A. Paintings Evoking Ideas of Childhood.

By 1855 the associationist manner of enjoying art was not
a new idea to Durand. The enjoyment of the rural scenes of
childhood arises from what Alison classifies as accidental
associations,[41] which are due to education, individual habits

of thought, the particular profession in which one is engaged, and so on. Upon the feelings connected with the environment of childhood, Alison comments:

> There are few men who have not associations of this kind /i.e., accidental/ with particular Forms, from their being familiar to them from their infancy, and thus connected with the gay and pleasing imagery of that period of life; from their connection with scenes to which they look back with pleasure . . . and such Forms, from this accidental connection, are never seen, without being in some measure the signs of all those affecting and endearing recollections.[42]

It seems not impossible that this passage was known to Durand in 1845 when he painted the Old Man's Reminiscences (Fig. 80). Here, an old man is seated in the left foreground, gazing back into the painting toward the rural environment of his child-hood--a river, trees, meadows, a school house. But in this painting "many a fair vision of forgotten days" animate the canvas not only in the old man's (or spectator's) imagination. They are actually represented. And Durand has ranged the incidents of early life from foreground to distance as the incident pertains to an earlier moment in life. Hence, the eve of adulthood is expressed in the meeting of an amorous couple beneath giant trees at the left and in a farmer on a hay wagon at the right, indicating respectively the love and labor of early maturity. Beyond the river, we enter a purer realm of childhood--a child in a swing, boys running in a

field; and, at the extreme right, the school-house pours forth
its young occupants--an image recalling the major motif of one
of the door panels Durand painted for Luman Reed, as well as
Henry Inman's <u>Dismissal of School on an October Afternoon</u>
(Fig. 81).[43]

Several years later Durand painted the <u>Morning Ride</u> (1851,
Fig. 83) in much the same spirit. Here the old man, as the
spectator within the picture, has been replaced by a lady and
gentleman on horseback. They pause in the road near a brick
house, surrounded by a picket fence, and shaded by venerable
trees. Around the house are seen a host of sportive youths and
children--a girl in a swing, a boy playing with a dog, a boy
and girl teasing one another, a youth on horseback, a man with
a rake, a group of dancing people, a boy and girl by a fountain,[44]
and an infant and a grandmother seated at the foot of a tree.
Of all of these rustic figures, not one displays any awareness
of the presence of the lady and gentleman on horseback. Clearly
they belong to different worlds and to different times. The
sportive rustics about the house are no more than the "fair
vision of forgotten days" which return to the minds of the lady
and gentleman as they pause in their ride--rather, they are
the gentleman's memories, for he looks at the rustics, while
the lady only looks at him. As in the <u>Old Man's Reminiscences</u>,
the associations connected with the place are actually represented.

These two paintings recall <u>Rip Van Winkle</u> in that the old
man or the gentleman has withdrawn himself from the realm of

wordly contention and approaches a place where he rediscovers
the phantoms of the past. But, in Rip Van Winkle the encounter
with the past results in the obliteration of personal identity.
In either of the later paintings the encounter with the past
serves to restore the spectator in the painting to his own past
and to his own true self. The later paintings, also, differ
from the Sunday Morning of 1839. In contemplating this painting, the spectator is invited to identify himself with the
actors in the painting, to think as they think, to do as they
do. But the later paintings invite recollection rather than
participation, and therefore the spectator is able to retain
a larger measure of his own identity--especially in the case of
the Morning Ride--and he is able to add his own memories to
those of the spectator within the painting that are already
represented.

B. Paintings Evoking Ideas of People and Events.

There is still other evidence to indicate that Durand was
familiar with the theory of association at a much earlier date.
In 1830 Durand and Elias Wade, Jr., in collaboration with
William Cullen Bryant, prepared the first issue of The American
Landscape. Each of the six engraved views therein is accompanied by an explanatory text. The unnamed writer of the
description of the ruins of Fort Putnam, illustrated in Dur-
and's engraving after a painting by Robert W. Weir (Fig. 16),
sought to bestow an interest on the place by enumerating the
several ideas and events that it might bring to mind:

These ruins are rich with the most hallowed associations; for they are fraught with recollections of
heroism, liberty, and virtue. There Arnold plotted
the subjugation of his country, and, surrounded as he
was by an army and a militia, unpaid, unclothed, and
suffering, he could find none among them base enough
to receive his gold, and participate in his treason.
As we muse over this magnificent scene of great events,
the imagination insensibly kindles, and the plain below, and the forts, and rocks, become peopled again
with the soldiers and the chiefs of the revolution.
The majestic Washington, the young and gallant Hamilton, the veteran disciplinarian Steuben, the fearless
Putnam, the daring Willet, the cool and sagacious
Clinton, successively pass before us. In the hollow
recess of the bank beneath, the melancholy Kosciusko
was wont to mourn alone and without hope over the woes
and the wrongs of Poland. Upon the cliffs on the
right, the young and high-spirited LaFayette often sat
meditating lofty thoughts, good to America, to France,
to mankind, whilst bright and gorgeous visions of glory
and freedom floated before him.[45]

The place is rendered interesting because of its association
with certain virtues, its association with an event (Arnold's
treason), and its association with eminent men. These three
classes of association are among those which,according to Alison,
are fitted to give interest to a place or thing. Thus, ancient

relics excite ideas of the "gallantry, the heroism, the patriotism of antiquity."[46] Runnymead or the field of Agincourt bring to mind the events which passed in those places.[47] And again, "The scenes which have been distinguished by the residence of any person, whose memory we admire" evoke recollections which "give a kind of sanctity to the place where they dwelt" and convert "everything into beauty which appears to have been connected with them."[48]

It was Cole who most frequently exploited the interest of a place arising from its association with persons or events. In his "Essay on American Scenery" of 1836 he stated that

> . . . American scenes are not destitute of historical
> and legendary associations--the great struggle for
> freedom has sanctified many a spot, and many a mountain,
> stream, and rock, has its legend, worthy of poet's pen
> or the painter's pencil.[49]

In several of his early, American landscapes--such as the View near Ticonderoga or Mount Defiance of 1826[50] or the Chocorua's Curse of around 1827[51]--he introduced tragic legends pertaining to the scenery represented.[52] Later, in painting The Valley of the Vaucluse (Fig. 84) in 1841, Cole seems to have followed a suggestion in Alison: "The valley of Vaucluse is celebrated for its beauty, yet how much of it has been owing to its being the residence of Petrarch!"[53] Indeed, when Cole visited Avignon in May, 1831, he described the city and his response to its picturesqueness: "Avignon is surrounded by ancient walls; and crammed as it is with immense twisted towers overlooking the surrounding country, it has a grand effect." But his added comment--"When I remembered it was once the residence of those kings of the Romish church, the popes, and of Petrarch and Laura, feeling and imagination waked into busy play"[54]-- makes one feel that the city interested him more because of its associations than its actual appearance.

Durand, however, appears to have been less attracted to scenes interesting only because of the events or persons associated with them. After his return from Europe he did exhibit a View, Parish Church, at Stratford, on Avon, the Burial Place of Shakespeare, which must have been more interesting from the connection between the objects and the poet than from any degree of picturesqueness. But Durand preferred real or ideal scenes capable of giving rise to a more intangible or abstract set of associations. A consideration of two pairs of paintings-- the Morning of Life and the Evening of Life (1840) and the Farm Yard on the Hudson and the View of Oberweisal on the Rhine (1843) may illustrate this preference.

C. Paintings Evoking Ideas of Time.

The earlier two paintings were exhibited at the National Academy in 1840 under the titles: Landscape, Composition, Morning (Fig. 85) and Landscape, Composition, Evening (Fig. 86). From these titles we might suppose that Durand primarily intended to arrange the light, color, and forms of nature in such a way as to express the two times of the day. The task of organizing the elements of nature in order to express different

times of day was one set for the artist by Thomas Whately in
an extended passage in his Observations on Modern Gardening,
which is quoted by Alison:

> Some species and situations of objects are in them-
> selves adapted to receive or to make impressions which
> characterize the principal parts of the day:  their
> splendour, their sobriety, and other peculiarities
> recommend or prohibit them upon different occasions:
> the same considerations direct the choice also of their
> appendages:  and in consequence of a judicious assemblage
> and arrangement of such as are proper for the purpose,
> the Spirit of the Morning, the Excess of Noon, or the
> Temperance of evening, may be improved or corrected by
> the application of the scene to the season.[55]

Durand restricted himself to the splendour, spirit, or animation
of morning and the sobriety and temperance of evening.  Whately
then proceeds to offer some concrete suggestions as to the
imagery appropriate to each season.  Several of the elements
enumerated are incorporated into each of Durand's paintings;
although, if, as we assume, he paid attention to the text, he
did not follow it slavishly.

Among the motifs befitting morning are pure white buildings,
such as the temple introduced by Durand at the right side of
the first painting.  Such buildings may "face the eastern sun,"
as do Durand's, for "the freshness of the air allays the force
of the sun-beams, and their brightness is free from glare."[56]
Streams should be vivacious, as is that in the foreground; and

the lakes, transparent, as the larger body of water in the middle-ground at the left. Finally, Whately recommends an "open exposure" like that at both sides of Durand's painting. At evening "all splendour fades; no buildings glare, no water dazzles, the calmness of a lake suits the quiet of the time, the light hovers there, and prolongs the duration of the day."[57] All of these terms may be applied to the second painting. Although contrasts of light and shade should not appear, some diversity of "tints" should be preserved. This may be accomplished if an illuminated western facade of a building of "dusky hue" (Durand's cathedral) be played against the dark greens of trees "which by their situation are the first to be obscured."[58] Finally, dark lawns may be opposed, again as in the painting, to the still illuminated surface of a tranquil body of water. Hence, in arranging each of these ideal compositions, Durand has selected those elements that contribute to the expression of each season of the day, and in part his selection appears to have been guided by Alison's quotation from Whately.

Nevertheless, Durand was not content to exhibit simply a morning and an evening. While the two times of day are expressed, they are rendered emblematic of the passage of time and two phases in the life of Man. The idea of the passage of time is first expressed in the browsing goat at the left foreground of Morning. It is resumed in the ruined capital and column drum at the center foreground, and the solitary column and blasted tree at the right of Evening. Time is presented as outside the control of reason and as a reality that destroys both man and his works. The ideas of childhood and old age are, obviously, expressed in the figures present in each painting. According to Alison, "The peculiar forms of infancy are expressive to us of innocence, ignorance, feebleness, thoughtlessness, and vivacity."[59] I leave it to the reader's ingenuity to discover these several qualities expressed in the various groups of children in the first painting. The forms of old age are expressive "of decay, diminished strength, abated capacity, and approaching dissolution"--all of which may be heaped upon the solitary and infirm gentleman in the foreground of Evening. Considered merely from the associational point of view, the pair of paintings is fitted to release a train of ideas relative to the mutations of nature, the passage of time, and the ages of man--in short, the flux and instability of earthly things. From this point of view, the paintings are very closely related to Cole's two sets of pictures, Departure and Return (1837) and Past and Present (1838), both of which treat the theme of vanity.

Durand's Morning and Evening of Life are, however, related to the work of Cole in another way. The Grecian environment in Morning was inspired by Cole's Dream of Arcadia (1838). In both paintings we find a Greek temple and an avenue of trees which shelter a statue. Other motifs in Durand's painting were borrowed from Cole's Departure and Return of 1837. The goat as a symbol of devouring time appears in both of Cole's paintings. Cole and Durand used the contrast between flourishing and blasted trees to express the passage of time. And, finally, the Gothic cathedral in Durand's _Evening_ was suggested by the cathedral in Cole's _Return_. Clearly, in expressing the ideas of the passage and destructivnesss of time Durand relied heavily upon the very Romantic paintings of Cole.

But Durand's paintings are as closely related to another of Cole's series--the _Voyage of Life_, begun early in 1839 and completed early in 1840. Four paintings--_Childhood_, _Youth_, _Manhood_, and _Old Age_--comprise this series. In childhood the voyager experiences joyousness and wonder; in youth, romantic dreams and a castle in the air. Manhood is beset by the demon forms of suicide, intemperance, and murder, from which,and from the perils of the conflicting elements, the voyager is saved only by his religious faith indicated by his "upward and imploring look." In the final painting--

> The stream of life has now reached the Ocean to which all life is tending. The world to Old Age is destitute of interest. There is no longer any green thing upon it. The broken and drooping figures of the Boat show that time is nearly ended. The chains of corporeal existence are falling away; and already the mind has glimpses of Immortal life. The angelic Being, of whose presence, until now, the Voyager has been un-conscious, is revealed to him; and with a countenance beaming with joy, shows to his wondering gaze scenes such as the eye of mortal man has never beheld.[60]

Cole conducts his voyager through four of the stages of life in this world, and up to the point at which he stands upon the threshold of another.

Durand's paintings treat also of the ages of man, but he excludes the two central phases of life--youth and manhood and the false dreams and real grief that belong to these. He represents only those phases of life that are uncontaminated by worldly hopes and despair. Also, where Cole represented man progressing through four stages, each of which differs from the other, Durand represents two stages that closely assimilate to one another. To Durand, the characteristic occupation of both childhood and old age is worship. A religious edifice appears in both paintings, and the children bring offerings to a goddess as the old man meditates before a cathedral. The children practice a pagan religion of nature, while the old man practices a religion of faith. But the latter is merely a development of the former, and both pictures bespeak an attitude of devotion common at once to the beginning and the end of life. Man does not assume different characters in the different stages of life, but rather spiritualizes and deepens that which he was at first. Hence, the spectator is not led through a variety of human characters, but is recalled to an awareness of the one essential character of devotion that may be present in all the stages of life, as it is most clearly at the beginning and end. While, on the one hand, the paintings evoke ideas of the transitoriness of earthly things, they also evoke an awareness of a piety that begins in an infantile but

joyous nature worship and ends in a depth of faith that tri-
umphs over the decay of man and things. Where Cole's voyager
only becomes aware of the divine amid the cruel scenes of
manhood, Durand's hero is essentially pious from the cradle.
To Durand, while physical nature decays, man's spiritual nature
continually expands, nourished but not threatened by the world
during its earthly pilgrimage. Cole conducts the spectator to
another world, but Durand reminds him that he is such a being
as is fitted to dwell in that world.

The paintings of the second pair--Farm Yard on the Hudson
(Fig. 87) and View of Oberweisal on the Rhine (Fig. 88) of
1843--are not so closely related in visual terms as are the
Morning and Evening of Life. In the Oberweisal the figures
are dwarfed by an extensive landscape, while in the Farm Yard
they are more prominent and exist in a setting that is restricted
to the foreground. Indeed, the pictures belong to two different
categories of landscape painting. The Oberweisal is a topographical view, in the tradition of Thomas Girtin and the early
Turner, presenting the distinctive monuments of a place and
their natural and human context. The Farm Yard belongs to that
class of Durand's painting in which interest attaches equally
to the figures and the setting--one may compare the earlier
Dance on the Battery. In character, then, the two paintings
contrast with one another. Yet this is no reason to prevent
our regarding them as pendants. They were both painted for
the same patron, at the same time, and are of the same size. The
formal differences between the two merely indicate an opposition
in content--or the range of associations each is to evoke.

The range of associations, again abstract, rather than
of a particular person or event, is fairly limited, and appears
to be similar to that defined in the following passage from
Cole's "Essay on American Scenery" of 1836:

> But American associations are not so much of the past
> as of the present and the future. Seated on a pleasant
> knoll, look down into the bosom of that secluded
> valley . . . You see no ruined tower to tell of out-
> rage--no gorgeous temple to speak of ostentation; but
> freedom's offspring--peace, security, and happiness,
> dwell there, the spirits of the scene. On the margin
> of that gentle river the village girls may ramble un-
> molested--and the glad school boy, with hook and line,
> pass his bright holiday--those neat dwellings, unpre-
> tending to magnificence, are the abodes of plenty,
> virtue, and refinement.[61]

In the Oberweisal we see a cluster of ruined towers "to tell of
outrage" as well as two less dilapidated fortifications--also,
"a gorgeous temple to speak of ostentation." A toiling,
anonymous humanity seems to complete the criticism of European
life. In the American farm yard all bespeaks "peace, security,
and happiness"--"freedom's offspring." The most prominent
motif is not a grim fortification, but a romping group of
children with a lively, small dog. While Durand represents
the farm yard rather than the farm house, the former speaks
as well of "plenty," "virtue," and possibly some degree of
"refinement." Considered in the light of Cole's text, the

paintings evoke the contrasting sets of associations connected with European and American scenes respectively. The Romantic nationalism indicated in the more favorable presentation of the American scene is entirely in harmony with Durand's expressed love of his native land. From Switzerland during his tour of Europe in 1840 and 1841 he had written:

> I wish to continue in Europe as long as it shall be pleasant, for the benefits it will yield me as a landscape-painter--for that object no country in the world can equal it! But for purposes more important, of higher interest than can be found in this or any other country, give me our own dear native land! . . . I am free to confess that I shall enjoy a sight of the signboards in the streets of New York more than all the pictures in Europe; and for real and unalloyed enjoyment of scenery, the rocks, trees, and green meadows of Hoboken will have a charm that all Switzerland cannot boast; only let me see them in the presence of family and friends, and they in health and prosperity.[62]

Clearly, Durand valued American over European scenes due to the associations in his own mind between those and his friends and family.[63] This feeling is clearly reflected in the greater prominence and individual identity given to the figures in the Farm Yard on the Hudson. Durand's love of America is also reflected in his later recommendation that the American landscape painter limit himself to native scenes:

Go not abroad . . . in search of material for the exercise of your pencil, while the virgin charms of our
native land have claims on your deepest affections.
Many are the flowers in our untrodden wilds that have
blushed too long unseen, and their original freshness
will reward your research with a higher and purer
satisfaction, than appertains to the display of the
most brilliant exotic.[64]

While a painter such as Cole, who did not associate American
scenery with any deep human affections, continued to exhibit
European views throughout his career, Durand abandoned them
after exhibiting an _Italian_ _Cottage_, probably only a water
color, at the National Academy in 1844.

While European scenes disappear from Durand's later work,
his love of America continued to express itself in paintings
dealing with the American frontier. In 1839 he exhibited at
the National Academy a painting entitled _Landscape_, _Western_
_Emigrants_. This was followed in 1844 by an _Emigrant_ _Family_
and in 1847 by _Landscape_ _with_ _Covered_ _Wagon_ (Fig. 89). Of these
only the last has been located. This represents a covered
wagon drawn by horses and followed by a man and boy along a
wilderness road. The two earlier paintings were probably of
similar character. All three paintings, we may assume, were
fitted to withdraw the mind of the spectator from his own cares
in the city. But also these might carry the mind into the past
and the future. Nature itself bespeaks the past, but not merely
the past of a particular historical epoch such as the Medieval

period of European history suggested by the View of Oberweisal on the Rhine. Rather, the wilderness carries the mind back to the very beginning of the world. The imaginative painter or spectator, according to Durand,

> . . . reads the historic record which time has written on all things for our instruction, through all stages of their silent transition, since the period when this verdant earth was a lifeless, molten chaos, "void and without form."[65]

On the other hand, the motif of the emigrants carries the mind forward to thoughts of their future life and labors in the wilderness, and beyond that to the subsequent unfolding of the larger civilization of which the emigrants carry the first seeds. The notion that the wilderness may evoke ideas of the future was especially advocated by Thomas Cole. In the passage which we have cited as the program for Durand's Oberweisal and Farm Yard, Cole continues:

> And in looking over the yet uncultivated scene, the mind's eye may see far into futurity. Where the wolf roams, the plough shall glisten; on the gray crag shall rise temple and tower--mighty deeds shall be done in the now pathless wilderness; and poets yet unborn shall sanctify the soil.[66]

The intrusion of the settler into the wilderness defines the dividing line between all of that past time in which nature obeyed her own impulses and that future time in which nature will become the servant of man.

Two other paintings focus also upon the line of demarcation between the past and the future. In 1853 Durand exhibited his Landscape, Progress (cf. Fig. 90). Here, a wild foreground, inhabited by Indians--primaeval nature--gives way in the middle ground to a milder river-valley in which the beginnings of civilization--roads, houses, steamboats, the electric telegraph-- have already been made. The objects of the foreground bring to mind ideas of the most remote past, while ideas of the full development of civilization in the distant future are evoked by the middle-ground and distance. The First Harvest (Fig. 91), exhibited two years later, focuses even more precisely upon the critical line between past and future. The wildness of primitive nature is still dominant in a mountain-valley where a settler reaps the first harvest from his hardly cleared field. The associations with nature are of the past; those with civilization, of the future. But past and future meet so closely that both sets of associations may intermingle with one another.[67]

These last two paintings closely parallel Bryant's poem, "The Fountain," in which, after describing a woodland spring in some detail, the past and future of the place pass before his visionary eye. Indeed, this poem inspired several of Durand's paintings, and the First Harvest may have been suggested by the following lines:

> So centuries passed by, and still the woods
> Blossomed in spring, and reddened when the year
> Grew chill, and glistened in the frozen rains
> Of winter, till the white man swung the axe

Beside thee--signal of a mighty change.

Than all around was heard the crash of trees,

Trembling awhile and rushing to the ground,

The low of ox, and shouts of men who fired

The brushwood, or who tore the earth with ploughs;

The grain sprang thick and tall, and hid in green

The blackened hill-side; ranks of spiky maize

Rose like a host embattled . . .[68]

Also, the First Harvest is closely related to a group of paintings by Cole dating from the late 1820's--Daniel Boone and his
Cabin on the Great Osage Lake,[69] View Near Conway, New Hampshire,[70] and another View Near Conway, New Hampshire, engraved
in London in 1831 (Fig. 92).[71] All three of these paintings
represent the first phases of the settlement of the wilderness
and carry the origin of this type of picture back to the period
when the first of James Fenimore Cooper's Leatherstocking novels
popularized the theme of the frontier.

III. Landscape and Revery.

By stimulating thoughts of persons, events, or moral qualities, a painting might adequately reveal to the spectator a
level of consciousness uncontaminated by the problems of real
life. Yet, such paintings as the Old Man's Reminiscences and
the Morning and Evening of Life still evoke a restricted range
of fairly definite ideas. While opening a new level of consciousness, these paintings still impede the full and free life of
that level of consciousness. Possibly another kind of painting
might be discovered which should at once carry the mind away
from any thought of the realities of life and at the same time
allow the mind full and free activity. Now revery is just such
an undirected state of mind; and Alison, in comparing it with
an associative train of thought, described it as both withdrawing
the mind from the world and as not being subject to any restraining factor:

> There is a state of mind, also, which every man must
> have felt, when, without any particular object of medi-
> tation, the imagination seems to retire from the reali-
> ties of life, and to wander amid a creation of its own;
> when the most varied and discordant scenes rise as by
> enchantment before the mind; and when all other faculties
> of our nature seem gradually to be obscured, to give to
> this creation of Fancy a more radiant glow. With what
> delight such employments of imagination are attended,
> the young and romantic can tell, to whom they are often

more dear than all the real enjoyments of life; and
who, from the noise and tumult of vulgar joy, often
hasten to retire to solitude and silence, where they
may yield with security to these illusions of Imagination, and indulge again their visionary bliss.[72]

Here revery is presented as a purely subjective state of free
mental activity, not caused by "any particular object of meditation." But then he goes on to quote a long passage from Jean
Jacques Rousseau in which revery is contrasted to all of the
unpleasant efforts of thought demanded by the cares of the
world, and is described as arising in particular situations.
The following portions of the text seem to illuminate the function of a sizeable body of Durand's paintings:

> Quand le beau tems m'invitoit, j'allois me jetter
> seul dans un bateau que je conduisois au milieu du lac,
> quand l'eau étoit calme, et là, m'étendant tout de mon
> long dans le bateau, les yeux tournés vers le ciel,
> je me laissois aller et dériver lentement au gré de
> l'eau, quelquefois pendant plusieurs heures, plongés
> dans mille rêveries confuses, mais délicieuses, et qui
> sans avoir aucun objet bien déterminé ni constant, ne
> laissoient pas d'etre à mon gré cent fois préférable
> à tout ce que j'avois trouvé de plus doux dans ce
> qu'on apelle les plaisirs de la vie.
>
> . . .
>
> Tel est l'état où je me suis trouvé souvent à l'isle
> de St Pierre dans mes rêveries solitaires, soit couché

dans mon bateau que je laissois deriver au gré de
l'eau, soit assis sur les rives du lac agité, soit
ailleurs au bord d'une belle riviere, où d'un ruisseau
murmurant sur le gravier. . . . Quelquefois me rêveries
finissent par meditation, mais plus souvent me meditations finissent par la rêverie; et durant ces égaremens
mon ame erre et plâne dans l'univers sur les aîles
de l'imagination, dans des éxtases qui passent toute
autre jouissance.

Tant que je goutai celle-la dans toute sa pureté,
toute autre occupation me fut toujours insipide. Mais
quant une fois, jetté dans la carrière littéraire,
. . . je ne pus plus retrouver, que bien rarement, ces
cheres éxtases, qui durant cinquante ans m'avoient tenu
lieu de fortune et de gloire; et sans autre dépense que
celle du tems, m'avoient rendu dans l'oisieveté le plus
heureux des mortels.[73]

This totally unwordly state of mind consists of "mille rêveries
confuses, mais delicieuses" and having "aucun objet bien determine ni constant." Revery is differentiated from meditation
with its more definite ideas, and stands in contrast to the
wearisome labor of thought. So far Rousseau agrees entirely
with Alison in his remark quoted above. But Rousseau also
enumerates the circumstances in which one is particularly susceptible to revery. Four types of situations are specified:
lying in a drifting boat, seated on the shore of a lake,
wandering along the bank of a river, and or by a brook mur-
muring over pebbles.[74]

Durand frequently represented those situations which are conducive, according to Rousseau, to a state of revery. Indeed, scenes of boating, lake shores, the banks of rivers, and brooks make up a large category of his works as a landscape painter. If Durand never represented a figure actually recumbent in a drifting boat, the motif of boating for the sake of pleasure appears in a number of his paintings. In 1837 he exhibited a painting entitled The Embarkation, and in the following year, two landscapes, both entitled Landscape: Sailing Party. The Embarkation of 1837 may have been similar to the painting entitled Hudson River, dated 1847 (Fig. 93). In this painting a placid stretch of water dominates the right side of the composition, and a group of four people enter a small boat from a point of land in the middle-ground. There is no reason to believe that this is not a pleasure party, setting out to enjoy an hour on the water. Other boating motifs appear in the Franconia Notch of 1857 (Fig. 196), the River Scene of 1861 (Fig. 158), and the large View of Black Mountain from the Harbour Islands, Lake George of 1875 (Fig. 163).

In a Landscape of 1866 (Fig. 160) Durand represented a solitary figure lost in revery on the bank of a river. Also, there is a large number of paintings in which lakes or the banks of brooks and rivers are presented in such a way as to be immediately accessible to the consciousness of the spectator. Two late landscapes--the View of Black Mountain from the Harbour Islands, Lake George (1875, Fig. 163) and the Souvenir of the Adirondacks (1878, Fig. 164)--afford good examples of lake scenes. The <u>View</u> <u>in</u> <u>the</u> <u>Catskills</u> (1847, Fig. 150) or <u>Woodland</u> <u>Brook</u> (1859, Fig. 178) are among Durand's paintings in which a brook assumes a prominent position. And the <u>Summer</u> <u>Afternoon</u> (1865, Fig. 159) may exemplify a river scene. All of these "water-landscapes" may be regarded, not so much as exciting a train of definite associations, as merely providing the occasion for a period of revery. The painting tends to become somewhat unimportant for itself. It is important insofar as it is able to free the mind from all worldly anxieties. It is important to the extent that it allows the mind to turn in upon itself, allows consciousness to become conscious of itself till, at last, the spectator no longer sees, but dreams.

The motif of boating on a placid river occurs occasionally in the work of Claude, and was probably borrowed by Durand from this source. Indeed, the composition of Durand's <u>Hudson</u> <u>River</u> (1847, Fig. 93) was inspired by the composition of a landscape with boating party by Claude, now in the Metropolitan Museum (Fig. 94). As Claude's painting itself was, in 1847, quite inaccessible to Durand, it is most likely that he studied the folio engraving by Vivares executed in 1741, when the painting was in the collection of Dr. Mead.[75] Durand's paintings of 1837 appear to have been the first in which the boating motif is employed to suggest a Rousseauesque revery as the proper experience of nature. After 1837 the boating motif was frequently employed by American painters to set a mood of revery. George Caleb Bingham wrought the most intense expression of this mood in his <u>Fur</u> <u>Traders</u> <u>Descending</u> <u>the</u> <u>Missouri</u>[76]

and The Trappers' Return.[77] The logical extension of the combination of boating and revery is to paint the picture itself while "dreaming" in a drifting boat. This point was reached when Daubigny launched his studio-boat, "Le Botin," on the Oise in 1857[78] and, again, when Monet equipped his studio-boat in 1873.[79] In the work of Daubigny and Monet, a non-conceptual type of mental activity, like that of revery, displays itself increasingly in the non-plastic style of the paintings themselves.

The solitary figure lost in revery, seated on the bank of a river was used by Durand in the Landscape of 1866 and, perhaps, in earlier works, although none has, as yet, come to my attention.[80] The figure here recalls the pensive shephards in Claude's pastorals or the figure of Psyche in Landscape with Psyche and the Palace of Amor.[81] However, in all of Claude's paintings the figures no matter how pensive, belong in some way to the scene represented. Durand's pensive interloper is more exactly prefigured by Sir Brooke Boothby in Wright of Derby's Sir Brooke Boothby in a Landscape, with a Volume of Rousseau.[82] Here, the figure, obviously not a shepherd, reclines by the side of a brook in a grove. He has been reading Rousseau, but now puts the book down merely to dream. Perhaps, there is something of revery in certain of Gainsborough's portraits of ladies in landscape settings, but mere revery does not appear to have interested landscape painters in the Romantic Period. If Durand did not use the figure in revery before 1866, his Landscape would parallel such Post-Romantic paintings as Corot's Bohémienne rêveuse or his Orientale rêveuse,[84] Courbet's Girls on the Banks of the

<u>Seine</u> of 1856[85] and Monet's <u>The River</u> of 1868[86] in which a
solitary girl sits beneath a tree as she gazes across the sunny
water. If we consider either his use of the boating or the
solitary figure motif as an indication of the mood of revery,
Durand's attitude more closely approximates that of the Impres-
sionist than of the Romantic landscape painters.

But even should neither motif be present, the painting,
when it is a pure landscape containing no motif that would impel
the spectator's thoughts in a particular direction, may be regarded as permitting the spectator to indulge in dreams as he
looks upon it. The experience of real nature or of the pure
landscape permits one to forget the ills of life, while, at the
same time, he may pursue an utterly free train of thought.
Bryant shared Durand's awareness of the value of a temporary
escape from the cares of life to dream in nature. In the poem
"Green River" he describes such an excursion into the dream-land
of nature:

> Though forced to drudge for the dregs of men,
> And scrawl strange words with the barbarous pen,
> And mingle among the jostling crowd,
> Where the sons of strife are subtle and loud--
> I often come to this quiet place,
> To breath the airs that ruffle thy /the river's/ face,
> And gaze upon thee in silent dream . . .[87]

In this state of revery the individual loses his consciousness
of the world, his mental life ceases to be the product of
immediate sense perceptions. His own mind and its own opera-

tions become the sole objects of his attention. As he sinks
deeper and deeper into revery, he becomes increasingly aware
of the unique mind or soul within himself. While in his
Stuartesque portraits Durand had sought to reveal to the spectator the unique soul of the man portrayed, in the landscapes
of revery, he seeks to make the spectator aware of the unique
and free mind or soul within himself.

IV.  Disinterestedness.

After the crises of the 1830's, Durand devoted the large
amount of his professional efforts to the creation of images
which should relieve and restore the mind wearied by the pressures of business, politics, and society.  He did not, however,
entirely abandon his earlier interest in ethical paintings,
paintings which should indicate the duties of the individual
engaged in the struggle of life itself.  His recreational
paintings provide one solution to the problem of how the individual might preserve his integrity without actually fleeing the
stage of real life.  In the ethical ideal of disinterestedness,
Durand found another solution to this same problem.  The notion
that disinterested action might at once preserve the integrity
of the individual and contribute to the welfare of society
was clearly stated by Durand in a figure painting exhibited
both at the National Academy and at the Apollo Association in
1843.

The Last Interview between Harvey Birch and Washington
(Fig. 95), representing Birch as he refuses a bag of gold offered
by Washington in payment for his services as a spy, focuses upon
the moment of the following dialogue from James Fenimore Cooper's
The Spy:

> "I have told you that the characters of men who
> are much esteemed in life, depend upon your secrecy;
> what pledge can I give them of your fidelity?"

"Tell them," said Birch, advancing, and uncon-
sciously resting one boot on the bag, "tell them that
I would not take the gold."[88]

In a sense this painting may be viewed as a revision of Durand's
_Capture of Major André_, painted ten years earlier. Both paintings deal with a morally ambiguous incident of spying. The spy
himself is good or evil depending upon which side in the conflict
one favors. In the _Major André_, Paulding refuses to accept a
bribe that he could have received to the detriment of the young
Republic. Birch, on the other hand, refuses the money that he
might justly have accepted as a fair recompense for his service
to the Republic. That he does not do so establishes at once
his integrity and the nobility of his motive. The morality of
the painting is quite classical, as it is precisely what Plutarch
recommended in his _Discourse Concerning Socrates's Daemon_:

> So, continued Epaminondas, justice is exercise against
> covetousness and love of money; but . . . is not a mere
> cessation from stealing or robbing our neighbor. So
> he that doth not betray his country or friends for gold
> doth not exercise against covetousness, for the law
> perhaps deters, and fear restrains him; but he that
> refuseth just gain and such as the law allows, volun-
> tarily exercises, and secures himself from being bribed
> or receiving any unlawful present . . . he that will
> not lay himself open to the favors of friends and the
> gifts of kings, but refuseth even what Fortune proffers
> . . . is never disturbed or tempted to unlawful actions,

but hath great and brave thoughts, and hath command
over himself, being conscious of none but generous
designs.[89]

The <u>Harvey</u> <u>Birch</u> is unique among Durand's later paintings
as it inculcates a particular virtue--disinterestedness. Now
it is precisely this virtue which Durand came to recognize as
that to be displayed especially by the artist. The artist,
like the priest ought not to be motivated by ambitions of wealth
and social prestige. Durand expressed his views on this subject
only in his <u>Letters</u> <u>on</u> <u>Landscape</u> <u>Painting</u> of 1855:

> It is better to make shoes, or dig potatoes, or
> follow any other honest calling to secure a livelihood,
> than seek the pursuit of art for the sake of gain. For
> whoever presumes to embrace her with the predominant
> motive of pecuniary reward, or any mere worldly distinc-
> tions, will assuredly find but a bundle of reeds in
> his arms. The great law that provides for the sustenance
> of the soul through the ministry of spiritual things,
> has fixed an immovable barrier between its own pursuits
> and those which supply our physical wants. For this
> reason, we cannot serve God and Mammon, however specious
> our garb of hypocrisy; and I would sooner look for figs
> on thistles than for the higher attributes of Art from
> one whose ruling motive in its pursuit is money.[90]

However, having painted the <u>Harvey</u> <u>Birch</u> more than a decade
earlier, it is likely that he had already reached these con-
clusions in the years around 1840. Also, Durand's views are

very similar to those expressed by Cole in his _Journal_ on August 3, 1840:

> This abnegation of themselves, this un egotistical spirit possessed by the Gothic artists, foreign to our own times, has been, I believe, the true source of excellence in the fine arts, in every age; and as there has been more or less of that chaste devotion, so have the arts risen or sunk. In the art of Greece this lofty feeling can also be traced: parts, for instance, of the Parthenon, which the Athenian multitude never gazed upon, ruin has revealed to modern eyes, sculptured into forms as elaborate and exquisite as any of the parts most exposed: the work was to Minerva, and not to man.
>
> Every great artist works to God, forgetful of the caprices, the prejudices and even the desires of men: he labours to gratify his soul's devotion to the beautiful and true which are centered in God.
>
> When artists descend to labour merely as a means of obtaining reputation and emolument, they abandon the path that leads to highest excellence, and are found forever grovelling with the sordid spirits of this world.[91]

Durand's objection to the profit motive was evidently inspired by his meditation on the sixth chapter of Matthew:

> No man can serve two masters: for either he will hate the one, and love the other; or else he will hold to

one and despise the other. Ye cannot serve God and
Mammon.[92]

which, as we have noted, he studied when painting the group
portrait of his children in 1832. Cole's criticism of the
profit motive, from a more aesthetic point of view, was probably
inspired by his contact with the Nazarene tradition in Rome.
Like the Nazarenes he appeals to the authority of both Gothic
and Greek artists. But both Durand and Cole agree that the
artist, like Harvey Birch, can only successfully fulfill his
role if he possesses that disinterestedness which permits him
to scorn the wealth and honor of the world. While in the 1820's
Durand had sought to correct and instruct the world through
paintings for which he could hardly have expected to find a
purchaser, in 1855 he was able to inform the public that it
ought to buy no paintings but those which had been conceived
without reference to a potential sale. By 1855, painting in
America had become a liberal art--an art freely created by the
artist and serving to liberate the spectator.

## v. Durand's Stoicism.

In the 1830's and 1840's Durand was influenced by various artists both of his own and earlier times. Gainsborough and Stuart stand behind his portraiture. His ideal female figures derive in some degree from Allston and Titian. Rowlandson and the Dutch seventeenth century inspired his genre work. Cole and Claude influenced his landscape painting. His work is shadowed by many artists, none of whom were able to affect his art as a whole. Derived from various traditions, his art was founded elsewhere than in any one. We have noted affinities between his work and the writings of Channing, Bryant, Alison, Wordsworth, Rousseau, and Plutarch, as well as the Bible; and in several cases Durand appears to have been directly inspired by a particular text. Yet, none of these writers affected the totality of his work. We must not neglect to observe that, in a significant measure, Durand's art, like that of any Romantic, was grounded in his own self and his own experience. At the same time, however, there is one framework of thought--the Stoicism of Seneca--which might be regarded as the medium through which his own experience became articulate. It is in the Essays and Letters of Seneca that we find, not simply a foreshadowing of single aspects of his art, but a set of ideas by which it is comprehensively illuminated. In the following, I shall attempt to illustrate the affinity between the more important of the ideas that guided Durand's art and certain aspects of Seneca's unsystematic philosophy.

A. The Instability of Fortune.

We have noted that Durand began his career as a portrait painter in the years immediately following the death of his wife. This, as well as other personal losses--of one child, of his health for a time, and of close friends, gave to Durand a clear awareness of the transience of those things that seem most to redeem man's situation. It is not unlikely that,during the period of his grief over his wife's death, someone, possibly Bryant, loaned Durand a translation of Seneca's "Of Consolation," in which he would have encountered the following, very adequate description of his own experience:

> My Marcia, all these adventitious circumstances
> which glitter around us, such as children, office in
> the state, wealth, large halls, vestibules crowded with
> clients, seeking vainly for admittance, a noble name,
> a well-born or beautiful wife, and every other thing
> which depends entirely upon uncertain and changeful
> fortune, are but furniture which is not our own, but
> entrusted to us on loan.[93]

The group portrait of his children, the first major work completed by Durand after the loss of his wife,might have been inspired by the following from the same chapter of the "Of Consolation":

> Whatever gift Fortune bestows upon a man, let him
> think while he enjoys it, that it will prove as fickle
> as the goddess from whom it came. Snatch what pleasure
> you can from your children, allow your children in

their turn to take pleasure in your society, and drain
every pleasure to the dregs without any delay.

The painting would continue to afford that pleasure,that may be
derived from one's children,beyond the term of their own lives.
Seneca continues:

> We cannot reckon on to-night, nay, I have allowed too
> long a delay, we cannot reckon on this hour: we must
> make haste: the enemy presses on behind us: soon that
> society of yours will be broken up, that pleasant
> company will be taken by assault and dispersed. Pillage
> is the universal law: unhappy creatures, know you not
> that life is but a flight?

Durand's several portraits of members of his family and his
closest friends--the Frank sisters, Casilear, Reed, Cole, and
Bryant appear to be so many attempts to forestall the attacks
of Fortune upon his most intimate associates.[94] The idea that
adversities are the work of Fortune has,of course,one advantage; namely, it relieves the sufferer from the feeling that
his misfortune is the just punishment of his own evil nature,
for Fortune is not just:

> We have come under the dominion of Fortune, and a harsh
> and unconquerable dominion it is: at her caprice we
> must suffer all things whether we deserve them or not.[95]

If adversity is not the just retribution of a just god, it is
not something sacred to be humbly accepted. Rather, the sufferer
is entirely justified in rebelling against an amoral Fortune in
order to break her sovereignty if he can.

B. Retirement.

Although Seneca suggests that one may prove his fortitude
by courting ill-fortune, for the most part he recommends that
the philosopher retire from the strife of the world. In the
essay "On Tranquility of Mind" he quotes Athenodorus:

> But since human ambition is unscrupulous and many
> detractors stand ready to twist right into wrong, since
> ingenuousness is defenseless and will always be more
> likely to be tripped than to succeed, it is best to
> withdraw from the forum and public life.[96]

Retirement, however, does not mean that the individual must cease
to serve mankind. Seneca continues to quote Athenodorus in the
following:

> But retirement should be of such a nature that, however
> insulated a man keep his leisure, he must still be
> willing to be of service to individuals and to mankind
> by his intelligence, his voice, his counsel. The man
> who brings candidates forward, defends the accused,
> votes on war and peace, is not the only one who serves
> the state; he who exhorts the youth, who, when good
> preceptors are so rare, imbues their minds with virtue,
> who seizes them as they race for money and holds them
> back, slowing them down, at least, if nothing else--
> he, too, is working for the community, albeit in a
> private station.[97]

Cole retired from the city, but he still could remind Durand of
"our place and duties as members of society," and, this being

the case, "we must exert ourselves to contribute to the well-being of that society--in producing works of excellence . . ."[98]

C. The Liberal Arts.

While Durand did not permanently withdraw from the city until 1869, at a much earlier date, in order to guarantee the integrity of his motives as a painter, he did seek to withdraw himself from any participation in the dominant ambitions of the city. Durand's belief that the painter ought not to be inspired by the desire for wealth is in complete accord with Seneca's evaluation of the liberal arts:

> You can't rest till you know my opinion of the liberal accomplishments? I respect none, I rank none with manifestations of good if cash is its upshot.[99]

And, regarding painters and other artisans as serving merely an enfeebling love of luxury, Seneca condemns all of the plastic arts:

> The fact is I refuse to admit painters into the precinct of the liberal accomplishments, marble-masons, and other servants of sumptuousness.[100]

If a painter were, necessarily, only a servant of sumptuousness, Durand would have acknowledged the justice of Seneca's exclusion.

But the facts that painting has sometimes been practiced for gain and has sometimes served a taste for luxury do not prove that it may not be a liberal art. According to Seneca, a liberal art is one which is both practiced by a free man and one that liberates the person to whom it is addressed:

Why they're called liberal accomplishments you know--
because they're worthy of the _homo liber_--the free man.
Yet only the accomplishment which liberates is liberal
in the true sense--philosophy, the sublime, the forcible,
the magnanimous. All the rest are petty and childish.[101]
The painter becomes a _homo liber_ when he abjures the profit
motive. His art becomes one that liberates when it withdraws
the attention of the spectator from the struggle of life or,
indeed, from the bonds of life and the enslavement to Fortune.

To distinguish more in detail the liberal from the non-
liberal arts, Seneca borrowed the following hierarchy from
Posidonius:

> Posidonius says there are four kinds of arts--the
> workaday--mercenary, the scenic, the pupillary, and the
> liberal. The workaday are those of the artisan, manual
> crafts engaged in catering for life and making no pre-
> tense of any aesthetic or moral ideals. The scenic are
> those which aim at diversion of eye and ear. Among
> their professors you may count the engineers who invent
> automatically rising platforms, stages that noiselessly
> sprout upwards story upon story, and various other
> surprises--solid floors that yawn, great chasms myste-
> riously closing, tall structures slowly telescoped.
> It is by these devices that the uneducated, who wonder
> at anything sudden because they don't know its cause,
> are dazzled. The pupillary (which aren't altogether
> unlike the really liberal) are those arts which the

Greeks call ἐγκυκλίους—encyclic—and our own writers
liberal. But the only liberal arts, or rather, to
speak more truly, arts of liberty, are those which
concern themselves with virtue.[102]

Most of Durand's work as an engraver belongs to the category
of the "workaday--mercenary" arts. The scenic arts would embrace
the Gothic novels of the late eighteenth century as well as
those paintings by Benjamin West, John Martin, Francis Danby,
Turner, P. F. Poole, Delacroix, Allston, Rembrandt Peale,
Dunlap, and Thomas Cole which employ the various devices of
the sublime as defined by Burke--the obscure, confused, uncertain, vast, infinite--to excite astonishment, a mindless wonder
and pleasant terror, as they dazzle the eye. This kind of
painting Durand avoided on all but one occasion. In 1852 he
exhibited God's Judgment Upon Gog (App. II, no. 287), a painting
very much in the Burke tradition. Durand's mature work may
largely be divided between the last two--the pupillary and the
liberal--of Posidonius' four categories.

As they concern themselves with virtue, his ethical figure
paintings, inspired by history and literature--Major André,
The Pedlar, The Wrath of Peter Stuyvesant, and Harvey Birch,
actually set the spectator free as they point out to him the
proper course of conduct. Even his portraits of heroes and
rulers may be regarded as serving to liberate the spectator, as
they present to his mind the images of men eminent for their
virtues. Yet Durand must have realized that literature is

better fitted to define and inculcate specific virtues, and
that the task of painting lies elsewhere.

After the mid-1830's most of Durand's paintings belong to
the third of Posidonius' categories. The pupillary or encyclic
arts are what are normally termed the liberal arts. In defining
the function of these Seneca wrote:

> As what the ancients called prima litteratura--the novitiate
> in letters--the stage in which children are taught to
> read, doesn't teach the liberal arts but prepares a place
> for their acquisition, so the liberal arts don't carry
> the spirit all the way to virtue, but set it in trim for
> the journey.[103]

But what kind of art would it be that sets the spirit in trim
for the journey toward virtue? Dramatic paintings suited to
purge the mind of pity and fear, might answer to this end. But
a drama requires an element of time which is, at least, difficult to express in a single picture. Hence, the purgation of
drama might better be accomplished by poetry. The other kind
of picture that might set the spirit in trim for its journey
is that which we have termed recreational--the escapist painting,
of course, would divert the traveler from the journey itself.
As we have seen, Durand, Mount, and Flagg began to paint
recreational pictures in 1835. And, it seems not unlikely that
they were directly inspired by the following passage from the
last chapter of Seneca's essay "On Tranquility":

> The intellect must not be kept at consistent
> tension, but diverted by pastimes. Socrates was not

ashamed to play with little boys, Cato took wine to
relax his mind when it was fatigued with official
responsibilities, and Scipio's soldierly and triumph-
crowned person trod the paces of the dance, . . .
The mind must have relaxation and will rise stronger
and keener after recreation. Just as fertile fields
must not be forced (without fallow periods their
richness is soon exhausted), so incessant labor will
crush the mind's elan. A little respite and relaxation restores the mind's energy, but unrelieved mental
exertion begets dullness and languor.

Sport and amusement would not exert so strong an
attraction if the pleasure they gave were not inherently
natural, but frequent resort to them will rob the mind
of all weight and energy. . . . There is a great difference between slackening and letting go. Our founding fathers established holidays upon which men must
foregather for jollity on the ground that such respites
are an essential ingredient for labor. . . .

We ought to take outdoor walks, to refresh and
raise our spirits by deep breathing in the open air.
Sometimes energy will be refreshed by a carriage drive
. . . and a more generous wine. Drink washes cares
away, stirs the mind from its lowest depths, and is a
specific for sadness as for certain maladies. Bacchus,
who invented wine, is surnamed Liber, not because of
the license wine gives the tongue, but because it

liberates the mind from its bondage to care and
emancipates it and animates and gives it greater
boldness for any enterprise. But in liberty modera-
tion is wholesome, and so it is in wine. . . . We
ought not to indulge too often, for fear the mind
contract a bad habit, yet it is right to draw it
toward elation and release and to banish dull sobriety
for a little.[104]

Here we find not only an assertion of the restorative value of
temporary periods of relaxation. but also the ultimate source
of inspiration for Durand's recreational paintings. As Scipio,
so that later "soldierly and triumph-crowned person" Peter
Stuyvesant was not adverse to enjoyment of the dance illustrated
in Durand's Dance on the Battery. Like the holidays of the
ancient Romans, so the Saturday afternoon dances in old New
Amsterdam, and the Sunday morning foregathering at church--
illustrated in Durand's Sunday Morning (1839 and 1860)--both
provide that respite from labor that is essential to its
resumption. The liberating effect of wine is illustrated in
Durand's Rip Van Winkle, who tastes among the phantom crew
the beverage that frees him from all of the troubles of the
world. But the magic liquor carries Rip too far from reality.
Hence, Durand came to regard nature as the draught (banquet or
oasis) that "liberates the mind from its bondage to care and
emancipates it and animates it and gives it greater balance for
any enterprise." As we have noted, any landscape not encumbered
with a contradictory meaning, but especially sunsets, may afford

a nourishing intoxication. In Durand's work after 1836, there is a large concern, not with the inculcation of particular virtues, but with the preparation of the mind of the spectator for the subsequent realization of any virtue.

D. Proper Concerns.

By introducing into the landscape motifs fitted to release certain trains of associations, Durand increased its power to liberate the spectator's mind from the cares of the world. In the largest number of his associational landscapes, the spectator is explicitly invited to turn his thoughts to the several periods of time--past and future and sometimes present. Now, according to Seneca, time is one of the objects, along with the universe and the soul, to which the philosopher will prefer to direct his thoughts:

> Philosophy is something great and spacious: it needs room: there are lessons to learn about heaven and earth, about past and future, about perishable and eternal, about time. Consider what a host of questions time alone involves. First whether it exists independently; second . . .[105]

Durand's Morning and Evening of Life bring to mind questions of the "perishable and eternal." This pair and the Old Man's Reminiscences deal with the past and future of the individual. The Morning Ride of 1851 deals with the present and past of the individual. The pair of paintings View of Oberweisal on the Rhine and Farm Yard on the Hudson, deals with past and

future times in terms of two different countries. And _Progress_
and _First Harvest_ carry the mind to past and future times in
America. All of these paintings merely raise the questions of
heaven and earth and time without attempting a philosophical
disquisition on any of the topics. The paintings merely induce
the spectator to meditate upon the topics without directing
the course of his meditation.

But the meditation is not an end in itself; rather it serves
to overcome man's sense of the brevity of human existence. The
busy man is aware only of the transient present. According to
Seneca:

> The present is fleeting, to the degree that it seems
> non-existent. It is always in motion, it flows on
> headlong; it ceases to be before it has come, and will
> no more brook delay than the firmament or the stars,
> whose incessant drive never allows them to remain
> stationary. It is only with the present that busy men
> are concerned, and the present is so transitory that
> it cannot be grasped; but because their attention is
> distracted in many directions they are deprived of even
> this little.[106]

On the other hand:

> The philosopher's life is . . . spacious; he is not
> hemmed in and constricted like the others. He alone
> is exempt from the limitations of humanity; all ages
> are at his service as at a god's. Has time gone by?
> He holds it fast in recollection. Is time now pre-

sent? He utilizes it. Is it still to come? He
anticipates it. The amalgamation of all time into
one makes his life long.[107]

In contemplating the Morning and Evening of Life the spectator
utilizes the present to recollect the past and anticipate the
future. All time comes together in the self, or the self expands to inhabit all time. In either case the self ceases to
be merely the product of the immediate sensations of the moment
and comes to define itself in terms of all time, i.e., eternity.
It is thus that any picture serving to carry the spectator's
attention away into the past and/or future times may be said
to introduce him, not to his material nature that is embedded
in the moment, but to his spiritual nature, or soul, whose
proper abode is eternity or the realm of the timeless. This
was clearly the view of Cole, who wrote:

> Poetry and painting sublime and purify thought,
> by grasping the past, the present, and the future--
> they give the mind a foretaste of its immortality, and
> thus prepare it for performing an exalted part amid
> the realities of life.[108]

Cole's Course of Empire, finished the year he wrote this, presents the spectator with the image of all earthly time. When
the time of the paintings ends in the fifth with Desolation--
"Yet still here am I" the spectator may murmur, aware of the
endurance of his ego beyond time.

The meditation on time ends in a meditation on the self,
on the soul, and the soul is the other topic toward which,
scorning petty issues, the philosopher will turn his thoughts.

There are countless questions about the spirit alone; where it comes from, what are its qualities, when it begins to exist, how long it exists; whether it passes on from place to place and changes its habitations, thrust into a series of creature-shapes successively or is but once a slave and is then set free to roam the universe; whether it's corporeal or incorporeal; what it will do when it ceases to act through us, how it will use its freedom when it has escaped this present cage; whether it forgets its past and begins to know itself at the moment when it is parted from the body and moves away into the sublime.[109]

If the meditation on time brings one to an awareness of one's soul, revery reveals to one the very life and activity of that soul. In the solitude of nature, forgetful of the world, the soul lives its own life in dreams. Again, this state of pure self-consciousness in solitude was recommended by Seneca:

It is important to withdraw into one's self. Association with a different sort of people unsettles ideas made orderly, reawakens passions, and aggravates mental cankers not yet thoroughly healed. But the two ought to be combined and alternated, some solitude, some society. Solitude will give us an appetite for people, society for ourselves, and the one is a cure for the other. Solitude will allay loathing of the crowd, and the crowd the ennui of solitude.[110]

Solitude, the withdrawal into one's self, like relaxation,
is to be a temporary state. The existence of the painting
that induces revery permits the spectator to maintain a balance between an absorption in the self that breeds sloth in
utter solitude and an absorption in the crowd that ends in
the loss of one's own identity.

E. Eclecticism.

On one hand Durand in no way regarded himself as an original
genius, pouring forth the uniqueness of his own being into works
displaying no knowledge of past or current intellectual and
pictorial traditions. On the other hand, his work in the 1830's
and 1840's reveals clearly that he was not the mere imitator
of a single master or school. In his Letters on Landscape
Painting he advises the student to "go first to Nature to learn
to paint landscape," but he does not omit to point out that,
once the student has learned to imitate nature, he

> . . . may then study the pictures of great artists with
> benefit. They will aid you in the acquirement of the
> knowledge requisite to apply to the best advantage the
> skill you possess--to select, combine, and set off
> the varied beauty of nature by means of what, in
> artistic language, is called treatment, management,
> &c., &c.[111]

In addition to the study of pictures--

> . . . books and the casual intercourse with artists,
> accessible to every young student, will furnish you
> with all the essential mechanism of the art.[112]

Although Durand states that he himself had never received any formal instruction as a painter, he does admit that "many an useful lesson has been taught me by intercourse with professional brethren--even often from the student and the tyro."[113]

Durand's willingness to adopt good methods when he encountered them, the number of copies after Renaissance and Baroque masters which he made in Italy, his evident effort to explore a variety of intellectual and pictorial traditions clearly reveal him as an adherent to the kind of eclecticism advocated by Seneca:

> We, too, ought to imitate the bees and sort out the different things we've amassed from a diversity of reading (for they keep better apart), and afterwards by concentrating the powers of our intelligence attentively upon them, blend these varied pilferings into a single flower; so that even if the sources are evident, it shall be evident also that the resultant whole is something different from the sources.[114]

To Seneca, eclecticism is not simply the borrowing of a thing for the sake of itself, but the borrowing of a thing because it may, by an act of reason, be made part of a whole that differs in character from any of its constituent parts. Durand's eclecticism is perhaps most clearly revealed in the Morning and Evening of Life. Here, he borrowed ideas from Alison, Whatley, perhaps even Wordsworth, and visual images from the work of Cole. While all of these sources remain quite evident, they have been reworked by an act of reason in such a way that

the paintings truly possess their own unique character and one
that is not anticipated in any of the sources.

In conclusion, we should note that both Durand and Seneca
would have the reason "blend these varied pilferings" into
flowers, not monsters. To both, reason ceases to be reason when
it no longer conforms to nature. That which reason contrives
of the material it has gleaned from many sources must still
conform to nature--to the order of internal human nature
and/or the order of external landscape nature. Nature, in
both senses--and the two are really the same, the idea of
order being the common denominator--sets the limit beyond which
the workings of the human mind become nothing but so many public
opinions and painful errors.

The problem of the degree of coincidence between Stoicism
and Romanticism is beyond the scope of this essay. We shall,
however, continue to note such parallels as seem pertinent
between Durand's art and theory of art and the philosophy of
Seneca.

# CHAPTER FOUR: THE STUDY OF NATURE.

During the years from 1837 to 1847 Durand was a Romantic landscape painter. In his work of these years emotion, associations, escapism, revery, and an effort to unite the opposite ends of life take precedence over the description of landscape phenomena. Durand presents us with abstract, often conventionalized, pastoral landscapes. The scene is rigorously controlled in its forms and their organization by the artist's purpose. After 1847 Durand was a Realist, shifting his point of view quite as early as painters such as Gustave Courbet in France and the Pre-Raphaelites in England. This shift in style did not necessarily entail a slackening of interest in emotion, association, escapism, revery, and other abstract concerns, for these continue to be at issue. The difference lies rather in a new prominence of description. In his paintings from 1848 onwards, the individual phenomenon possesses a reality of its own which permits it to co-exist in harmony with other phenomena. Forms and sometimes their organization are now controlled less by the artist's purpose than by nature itself. In the present chapter we may trace the development of Durand's mature, realistic style and attempt to define its origins, sources, and meanings. In the last three chapters, we may turn from the style itself, which must be regarded as a means, to those ends for which Durand employed it.

Durand's _Letters on Landscape Painting_ were published in 1855 at the peak of his career and at a time when he could speak with the authority of the President of the National Academy, which office he held from 1845 to 1861. While the _Letters_ do contain ideas especially relative to the proper effect of a landscape upon the spectator, which are applicable to his Romantic period, the extensive discussion of style must be studied in connection with his later realistic period. The concept of style expressed in the _Letters_ is founded upon a radical distinction between art--the achieved works of the past-- and nature--the phenomena making up landscape-nature and the laws by which they are governed. We may best preface a study of the development of Durand's realism with an examination of his conception of the relative value to the landscape painter of nature, on the one hand, and the traditions of art, on the other.

I. The Primacy of Nature.

According to Durand, the student is to "go first to Nature to learn to paint landscape."[1] And, "If he is imbued with the true spirit to appreciate and enjoy the contemplation of her loveliness, he will approach her with veneration, and find in the conscientious study of her beauties all the great first principles of art."[2] Nature is the foundation of the landscape painter's art, and contributes the first principles of that art. More than this, Nature embraces all that is valid in art and extends beyond the limits of the highest art:

> There is not a tint of color, nor phase of light and dark, force or delicacy, gradation or contrast, or any charm that the most inventive imagination ever employed or conceived worthy to be regarded as beautiful or for any other quality, fitting to the aim of Art, that is not to be seen in Nature, more beautiful and more fitting than Art has ever realized or ever can; and there is no acknowledged excellence in any picture extant, which justly commands our admiration, which has not been transcribed, more or less faithfully, from her glorious volume.[3]

Elsewhere Durand states that "the most successful transcripts /of nature/ that Art is able to produce must appear but abortions in her presence, and only tolerable when withdrawn and examined in the seclusion of the painting room."[4]

From the beginning of his career as a landscape painter, Durand had been keenly aware of the inadequacy of art as an instrument to grasp the plenitude of nature. As early as 1838 he wrote to Thomas Cole:

> The Glorious Spring appears advancing and waking at every step the delightful anticipations of renewed excursions among the unapproachable charms of this beautiful creation. I mean unapproachable by our feeble efforts of imitation. Still the prospect is enchanting and the hope of snatching some one of her innumerable graces, drives us on, and if it be but an "ignus fatuus" still it leads thro' pleasant walks and compensates in its course, for all the toil and difficulty.[5]

The painter is a sort of Apollo, who pursues not a half-seen vision in the mind but a Daphne, quite apparent to the eye. But unlike Apollo, who expects to overtake Daphne, the painter pursues nature knowing he can never fully grasp it. Again, unlike Apollo, who either will or will not overtake Daphne, the painter is able to apprehend in paint a portion of nature. His work will be valuable precisely in proportion to the quantity and quality of natural phenomena that he is able to record.

If the landscape painter's art is derived from nature and seeks to embrace nature, it follows that the value of a particular work may be judged in terms of its fidelity or "truth" to nature. In his Letters Durand does define a variety of

values that a landscape painting may possess, but his sense
of the significance of nature itself caused him, like other
mid-nineteenth century writers, to speak as though fidelity
to nature were the only value pertinent to landscape painting:

> I have maintained throughout these letters, the
> distinction between the mere pleasing picture and that
> of the true representation of Nature. . . . All that
> has made Claude pre-eminent, is truthfulness of repre-
> sentation in his light and atmosphere, and moving
> waters--if other portions of his work were equally
> true, he would be still greater. And why have the
> nobler compositions of Gaspar Poussin only given him
> an inferior rank, but because they lack in correspond-
> ing truthfulness. I might instance hundreds of others,
> ancient and modern, who owe their reputation to the
> degree of representative and imitative truth which
> distinguishes their works. Closing the list with the
> name of Turner, who has gathered from the previously
> unexplored sky alone, transcripts of Nature, whose
> mingled beauty of form and chiaroscuro have immortalized
> him, for the sole reason that he has therein approached
> nearer to the representation of the infinity of Nature
> than all who have gone before him.[6]

In summary, from the study of nature, the artist derives
the foundation of his style. The study of nature is also one
form of the pursuit of the infinite. And the value of a painting is to be judged in terms of its truth.

The position of primacy which,in Durand's theory,nature
holds as the object to be imitated, his insistence that true
art may never violate nature, parallels the fundamental Stoic
imperative to follow nature if one would lead a moral life:

> To express shortly what I mean, the medium in
> which good finds expression is sometimes repugnant to
> nature, but good itself never, for good never exists
> apart from reason, and reason follows nature. "Then
> what is reason?" The copying of nature. "What is
> the sovereign good of man?" Conduct according to
> nature's intention.[7]

The idea that morality is consistent with nature, that a moral
being follows, imitates, or lives in harmony with nature, is
probably the fundamental reason for Durand's insistence upon
the imitation of nature in art. Indeed, he states quite clearly
in his __Letters__ that the study of nature brings the painter into
a desirable moral harmony with nature:

> There is yet another motive for referring you to
> the study of Nature early--its influence on the mind
> and heart . . . we insensibly, as it were, in our daily
> contemplations,
>
> To the beautiful order of his works
> Learn to conform the order of our lives.[8]

The verses quoted form the last two lines of Bryant's "A Forest
Hymn":

> Be it ours to meditate,
> In these calm shades, thy milder majesty,

And to the beautiful order of thy works
Learn to conform the order of our lives.[9]

It is to the order of nature, or what to the Stoics is the reason in the universe, rather than to unpredicated nature that the individual is to conform.

The ideas that one ought to conform to nature and that one ought to live in harmony with nature controlled the use of the human figure in Durand's mature landscapes. In discussing the use of figures Durand first notes in his Letters that the figures and the setting ought not to be unrelated:.

> A landscape with figures, introduced merely for pictorial effect, without enhancing the meaning, may render the picture more beautiful and artistic, and yet amount to little more than a sort of human cattle piece.[10]

On the other hand, the figures should not assume an importance which isolates them from the landscape:

> And whenever the human figure becomes paramount, and gives to the picture a significance independent of, and superseding the sentiment of the landscape, it is no longer a legitimate landscape, and falls under some of the departments of figure subjects.[11]

The only other alternative is that which Durand recommends; namely, that the figures should harmonize with or enhance the significance of nature:

> . . . when the human form exerts an influence in unison with the sentiment of inanimate nature, increasing its

significance without supplanting it, the representative character of the landscape is not affected;
and whatever imaginative force may attach to the
figure itself, the value of representative truth is
not lessened.[12]

Normally, Durand's figures pursue an activity or experience a
particular psychic condition that is the product of the impingement of nature upon a self-aware mind. When his figures are
not meditating upon nature (Figs. 148 and 189), they either
relax--as in the Hudson River (Fig. 93)--or act upon nature--
as in Forenoon (Fig. 110). Rarely do Durand's figures merely
walk about in the workaday paths of country people. Always
they display a mental consciousness of nature as they are
"improved" by or "improve" it in turn. Durand insists upon
illustrating an exchange between the mind of man and the moral
order of nature. Hence, these figures display the same consciousness of nature that the painter is to feel, and,
occasionally, a painter in person appears in the landscape
(Figs. 122 and 156).[13]

    The landscape painter, then, is to base his art upon the
study of nature because of the moral law and model for human
conduct embedded in nature. Durand was convinced that the
actions and attitudes of the individual must be shaped by a
law promulgated from a trans-human source. But the law was
not to be founded upon the logic of the eighteenth century
philosophers any more than in the faith of orthodox theologians. In his own experience of American politics and his

study of Channing's criticism of orthodox Christianity, Durand
had ample opportunity to observe the inadequacies of both
philosophical reason and the orthodox faith.  Hence,in nature
he found a law and order of primal purity, uncorrupted by the
will to power of party or sect.  Thus, in his _Letters_ he could
write:

> Childlike affection and religious reverence for the
> beauty that nature presents before us, form a basis
> of reliance which the conflicts of opinion can never
> disturb.[14]

The spiritual certainty which Durand sought in the study of
nature closely parallels the Christian fundamentalist's
absolute faith in the text of the Bible.

II. The Subordination of Artistic Traditions.

Despite his insistence on truth to nature, Durand was entirely willing to admit the utility of the study of paintings by the masters of the past. Indeed, as we have seen, at the beginning of his career as a painter, he eagerly studied the work of earlier artists, copying from Stuart, Sully, and Vanderlyn in America and from Rembrandt, Titian and others in Italy. Up until 1840 he was willing to borrow figures and motifs from contemporary and older paintings and prints. And in 1855, remembering his own study of works of art, he acknowledged, as we have noted, that the "study of the pictures of great artists" will aid the student "in the acquirement of the knowledge requisite . . . to select, combine, and set off the varied beauty of nature by means of what, in artistic language, is called treatment, management, &c., &c."[15] The art of the past does not supply the content of a painting, but it may suggest the most effective means by which material gleaned from nature may be organized.

But the study of works of art, in one respect useful, in several others is fraught with danger. The dangers against which Durand warns are four:

1. that a painter might be tempted to imitate the style of another.

2. that the painter may represent only a conventional rather than real nature.

3. that the painter may be tempted to give undue
prominence to the sensual qualities of art.

4. that he may overemphasize the technique of art at
the expense of the real content of the picture.

We may review Durand's comments on each of these topics.

A. The Preservation of the Artist's Integrity.

According to Durand, "every true artist has his own manner,
i.e., certain peculiarities of execution, &c., the result of
his organization."[16] These idiosyncracies of manner obtrude
themselves first upon the student's attention, so that if he
form his own style upon the works of another, he runs a grave
risk of imitating merely what is the result of the artist's
physiological make-up. To form one's style on the art of
another would entail the loss of one's own identity. The same
danger is likely to befall the painter who learns his art from
a particular master. At the very outset of his Letters, Durand
depreciates the value of a period of study under the supervision
of an established master. While a period of studio training
may permit the student to acquire a knowledge of the techniques
of art in a fairly short time, it leaves him "in danger of
losing his own identity and from the habit of seeing with the
eyes and following in the tracks of his master become /ing7
in the end what is most degrading in the mind of every true
artist, a mere imitator, a mannerist."[17] The only way to
preserve one's identity is to go, not to pictures or to a
teacher, but to what Durand terms "the studio of Nature."

Durand's insistence upon the importance of that integrity
that displays itself in a personal style may seem strange coming
from one whose mature works seem so impersonal. His paintings
certainly display none of that autographic bravura which the
later nineteenth century, under the influence of Velazquez
and Frans Hals, came to recognize as especially controlled by
the artist's unique temperament. Rather than impose a single
mode of execution in painting the diverse phenomena of nature--
as Gainsborough, for example, had done in his landscapes and
as Monet was to do later--Durand tends to differentiate his
touch according to the texture of and atmosphere affecting
things. In the study of an earth-bank with rocks and trees
(Fig. 118), one may note the shaggy paint indicating the bark
of trees, the smooth surfaces of rocks, a sort of stippling
for earth and mosses, and a delicately feathery touch in the
more distant foliage. This object-controlled technique is
related to the diversified linear patterns which Durand had
employed as an engraver in order to describe the varied surfaces of things in line and black and white exclusively. Yet,
the object-controlled technique is not uniquely that of the
engraver, but goes back to the descriptive, painted portraits
which, as an engraver, Durand frequently had to reproduce.
Particularly, in portraits by Gilbert Stuart and his followers
there is a definite diversity of touch as the artist seeks to
describe face, hair, neck-cloth, drapery, and background. It
was from these portraits that Durand learned to paint, and it

is quite natural that his landscapes should also display the object-controlled technique of the portrait painter.

How can we see this apparently impersonal, object-controlled technique as an expression of the self? Any answer to this very crucial question depends upon our definition of what constitutes the self. Broadly, we may think of the self as being either that which makes me unique or that which is most enduring in and essential to me. The first concept may be regarded as Plutarchian, and as that which Durand held when, as a portrait painter, he sought to define the unique human spirit through the thorough description of the individual face. The second concept was defined by Seneca when he wrote:

> Praise in him /a man/ what can neither be removed nor bestowed, what's inseparable from his humanity. And what, you ask, is that? His spirit, and reason per- fected in that spirit. For man's a creature of reason. So his good is consummated if he fulfills the end he's born to. And what does this reason demand of him? A very easy thing--to live in accord with his own nature.[18]

Here, the self is that reason which is truly possessed by the individual, but may be shared by other individuals. While the unique, Plutarchian self may, in accord with its particular law, express itself in any act from the most fierce to the most gentle; the Stoic self, by its law, is confined to a far narrower range of acts. Any impulse that contradicts reason must be suppressed in order that a rational self-mastery may

express itself. In Durand's object-controlled manner of painting, we may discern the rational self in the very act of dis-
entangling itself from all conventional gestures and irrational
impulses. As the Calvinist seeks to divest himself of pride,
so the Stoic seeks to suppress those of his propensities that
contradict reason. But, as the rational is also that which
is in harmony with nature; so, when the painter is in full
possession of his reason, every irrational and, therefore unnatural, element will be eliminated from his painting. The
rational and the natural painting will, then, be the highest
verification of the self. It will not be the product of that
humble, self-abnegation that John Ruskin, influenced by
Calvinist theology, recommended. Durand's Stoic rationalism
is more closely related to the scientific rationalism of the
theory of Benjamin West and George Seurat, for all three
artists would agree that the self is born and matures in proportion to its capacity to discipline itself in such a way as
to discover the correspondence between the rational mind and
the rational order of matter.

B. The Conventional Versus the Natural Painting.

If the imitation of an artist's style results in a loss of
the painter's identity, the imitation of the conventions of
art result in the loss of the true image of nature. Conventionalism means "the substitution of an easily expressed falsehood
for a difficult truth."[19] The ease with which conventionalities
may be imitated results in their proliferation--

> To obtain truthfulness is so much more difficult
> than to obtain the power of telling facile false-
> hoods, that one need not wonder that some delusive
> substitute occupies the place which Nature should
> hold in the artist's mind.[20]

The effect of "the poisons of conventionalism" upon the spectator "will be the corruption of veneration for, and faith in,
the simple truths of Nature, which constitute the true Religion
of Art, and the only safeguard against the inroads of heretical
conventionalism."[21]  Durand specifies several of the conventions
which the landscape painter is too likely to embrace:

> The fresh green of summer must be muddled with brown;
> the pure blue of the clear sky, and the palpitating
> azure of distant mountains, deadened with lifeless
> grey, while the grey unsheltered rocks must be warmed
> up and clothed with the lichens of their forest
> brethren--tricks of impasto, or transparency without
> character--vacant breadth, and unmitigated darkness--
> fine qualities of color without local meaning.[22]

In contrast to the conventional painter stands, of course,
the natural painter:

> If it be true--and it appears to be demonstrated, so
> far as English scenery is concerned--that Constable
> was correct when he affirmed that there was yet room
> for a natural landscape painter, it is more especially
> true in reference to our own scenery . . . The "lone
> and tranquil" lakes embosomed in ancient forests, that

abound in our wild districts, the unshorn mountains
surrounding them with their richly-textured covering,
the ocean prairies of the West, and many other forms
of Nature yet spared from the pollutions of civilization, afford a guarantee for a reputation of originality that you may elsewhere long seek and find not.[23]

The accessibility of virgin material to the "natural landscape
painter" not only offered the painter an opportunity to avoid
the conventions and to display his originality, but was the
basis upon which Durand could anticipate the growth of a
national school of art, which should, collectively, abjure the
conventions of the past:

I desire not to limit the universality of the Art,
or require that the artist shall sacrifice aught to
patriotism; but, untrammelled as he is, and free from
academic or other restraints by virtue of his position,
why should not the American landscape painter, in
accordance with the principle of self-government,
boldly originate a high and independent style, based
on his native resources?[24]

Durand's conception of the opposition between the natural
and the conventional painters was borrowed directly from John
Constable. Constable's statement regarding the need for a
natural painter appears in a letter, dated May 29, 1802, an
excerpt from which was printed in Leslie's _Life of Constable_:

I shall return to Bergholt, where I shall endeavor to
get a pure and unaffected manner of representing the

scenes that may employ me. There is little or nothing in the exhibition worth looking up to. <u>There</u>
<u>is</u> <u>room</u> <u>enough</u> <u>for</u> <u>a</u> <u>natural</u> <u>painter</u> . . . truth in
all things only will last, and can only have just
claims on posterity.[25]

Presumably, the pictures in the exhibition represented to
Constable little more than the extended elaboration of the
conventions. The opposition between art and nature, however,
he defined more fully in the "Preface" to his <u>English</u> <u>Land-</u>
<u>scape</u>, published in 1830 to 1832. But the relevant passage
from the "Preface" was quoted by Leslie:

> In art, there are two modes by which men aim at distinc-
> tion. In the one, by a careful application to what
> others have accomplished, the artist imitates their
> works, or selects and combines their various beauties;
> in the other, he seeks excellence at its primitive
> source, nature. In the first, he forms a style upon
> the study of pictures, and produces either imitative
> or eclectic art; in the second, by a close observation
> of nature, he discovers qualities existing in her
> which have never been portrayed before, and thus forms
> a style which is original. The results of the one are
> soon recognized and estimated, while the advances of
> the artist in a new path must necessarily be slow, for
> few are able to judge of that which deviates from the
> usual course, or are qualified to appreciate original
> studies.[26]

There can be no doubt that Durand drew his ideas regarding conventionalism, the imitation of nature, and originality directly from Constable's statements in Leslie's _Life_, if not from conversations with Leslie himself regarding Constable's ideas.[27]

Again we may note a degree of agreement between the view of conventionalism held by Constable and Durand and Seneca's demand that the philosopher think for himself rather than repeat old truths only:

> . . . there'll be no new discoveries if the old ones content us. Besides, he who follows another discovers nothing, in fact doesn't even investigate. And what follows? Shan't I tread in the footsteps of my fore-runners? Why yes, I shall use the old highway, but if I find a shorter cut over less broken ground I shall metal that. The pioneers are our guides, not our governors. Truth's open to everyone, and the claims aren't all staked yet. A great deal of it's left for explorers to come.[28]

Neither Durand nor Constable would have insisted that the landscape painter be ignorant of the art of the past, but both agree with Seneca that much truth about nature remains to be discovered by the natural painter, who shares with the scientist and the theologian a thirst for infinite experience, which is, probably, a different thirst from that of the mystic for the infinite.

C.  The Sensual Versus the Spiritual in Art.

To the more sensuous aspects of art Durand objects in
terms as strong as those in which he spoke of the conventions.
His criticism of sensuousness is coupled with his condemnation
of the artist whose primary motive is wealth and worldly distinction.  The pursuit of money

> is one of the principal causes operating to the degrada-
> tion of Art, perverting it to the servility of a mere
> trade; and next to this, is its prostitution by means
> of excess in color, strong effects and skillful manipula-
> tion, solely for the sensuous gratification of the
> eye.  Through such motives the Art becomes debased,
> and a picture so painted, be its subject landscape or
> figure, may well be considered but an empty decoration.[29]

Durand's criticism of both the profit motive and of sensuousness
reflects the puritan tradition in western civilization.  More
particularly, he appears to have been directly inspired by
Channing's "Remarks on the Character and Writings of John
Milton."  Here Channing states:

> That there is a wisdom, against which poetry wars, the
> wisdom of the senses, which makes physical comfort and
> gratification the supreme good, and wealth the chief
> interest of life, we do not deny; nor do we deem it
> the least service which poetry renders to mankind, that
> it redeems them from the thraldom of this earthborn
> prudence.[30]

Channing, like Durand, couples the criticism of wealth with that of sensuous gratification and sees in poetry a force antagonistic to both. Sensual gratifications--and the pursuit of wealth--belong to man as a citizen exclusively of the world.

In contrast to a commercial and/or sensual art stands an art that is the product of and appeals to man's spiritual nature. According to Durand that artist holds the highest rank "who has kept in due subordination the more sensuous qualities with which material beauty is invested, thereby constituting his representation the clear exponent of that intuition by which every earnest spirit enjoys the assurance of our spiritual nature, and scorns the subtlety and logic of positive philosophy."[31] Again Durand appears to have derived the notions that the painting should address man's spiritual nature from Channing. According to Channing, poetry is the

> divinest of all arts; for it is the breathing or expression of that principle or sentiment, which is deepest and sublimest in human nature; we mean, of that thirst or aspiration, to which no mind is wholly a stranger, for something purer and lovelier, something more powerful, lofty, and thrilling than ordinary and real life affords.[32]

As the poet, so the painter may feel this thirst, and it is a quest of the spirit which must be impatient of any sensuality that would contradict the basic motive to art by strengthening the bonds of the artist to ordinary and real life. As poetry

originates in this immortal thirst, so the poem is addressed
to the reader's spirit:

> It is the glorious prerogative of this art, that it
> "makes all things new" for the gratification of a
> divine instinct.[33]

Of the function of the best poetry Channing states:

> In its legitimate and highest efforts, it has the
> same tendency and aim with Christianity; that is, to
> spiritualize our nature.[34]

To Durand the painting may assure the spectator of his spiritual
nature. To Channing the poem may cause the reader to become
more spiritual. If there is any difference between the two
views, it is mainly the result of the different circumstances
in which each wrote.

At present we need only observe that, while pleasing to the
eye, Durand's paintings do display a definite subordination of
any positive sensuality. Form, light, and space speak more
clearly than color, and there are no overwrought qualities of
paint to interfere with our apprehension of the natural
phenomena represented. Spiritual qualities of a more positive
sort we shall encounter in our discussion of the significance
of space, of emotion, and symbolism in Durand's paintings.
Here, we may only add that Durand's paintings did not achieve
their maximum spirituality until he had effected a rapprochement between painting and poetry.

D.  Rhetoric Versus Significance.

The study of the art of the past is likely to lead the
painter into one other path of error.  Durand objects at some
length to the display of technical mastery for its own sake:

> All the best artists have shown that the greatest
> achievement in the producing of fine color, is the con-
> cealment of pigments, and not the parade of them; and
> we may say the same of execution.  The less apparent
> the means and manner of the artist, the more directly
> his work will appeal to the understanding and the
> feelings.  I shall never forget the reply of Allston
> to some friends who were praising a very young student
> in Art for great cleverness, especially in the _freedom_
> of his execution.  "Ah," said he, "that is what we
> are trying all our lives to get rid of."  With that
> he opened a closet, and brought out a study of a head
> that he had painted from life, when a young man, at
> one sitting, and placed it beside a finished work on
> his easel, at which we had been looking:  "There,"
> said he, "that is freely painted."  No other comment
> was required; in the one, paint and brush attracted
> the attention, in the other neither was visible, no-
> thing but the glow of light and color which told its
> truth to Nature--and thus it is with the works of all
> the greatest colorists.  Their skill is perceived in
> the concealment of the means by which the desired effect
> is attained, consequently their productions defy the

utmost sagacity of the critical examiner to detect any
specific mixture or compound by which their characteristic excellence has been attained. It is neither
warmth nor coolness that elicits admiration; force nor
delicacy; high key nor low key; but always harmony and
entire subordination of means. Now, we are not to
suppose that this subordination has been especially
aimed at by the artist, but that it is the consequence
of the process by which higher aims have been reached.[35]

Durand must have been aware of the need to subordinate the
technique of art to a higher end from nearly the beginning of
his career as a painter, for Allston's comments must have been
delivered during the period of Durand's only acquaintance with
him in 1835. If Allston's demonstration made Durand suspicious
of technique, the following passage from Alison's Essays on
Taste must have confirmed his doubts:

For an error /the "prevalence of Expression of
Design, over the Expression of the Composition in which
it was employed"7, which so immediately arises from
the nature, and from the practice of these Arts themselves, it is difficult, perhaps impossible, to find a
remedy. . . . But I humbly conceive, that there is no
rule of Criticism more important in itself, or more
fitted to preserve the Taste of the Individual, or of
the Public, than to consider every composition as
faulty and defective, in which the Expression of the
Art is more striking than the Expression of the subject,

or in which the Beauty of Design prevails over the
Beauty of Character or Expression.[36]

That both Durand and Alison regard the prominence of technique
as indicative of a deficiency in the expression of character
in a work of art suggests that Durand consulted Alison's text
while writing his Letters. Alison's idea that the tendency
toward an overemphasis on technique "arises from the nature,
and from the practice of these Arts themselves" is reflected
in Durand's statement that the danger "is a condition incidental
to, and inseparable from, the very Nature of Art."[37]

In his Letters on Landscape Painting Durand identifies the
technicalities of painting with the rhetoric of literature:

> All the technicalities above named are but the language
> and the rhetoric which expresses and enforces the
> doctrine--not to be unworthily employed to embellish
> falsehood, or ascribe meaning to vacuity.[38]

Durand's insistence upon an honest and lean technique is related
to Seneca's demand that the philosopher speak plainly.

> Language which aims at truth should be plain and un-
> adorned; there's nothing true at all in the rhetoric
> that makes a popular appeal. Its object is to sway
> a crowd and carry thoughtless hearers with it by sheer
> dash: it baffles scrutiny and is gone. Now, how can
> the uncontrollable control? Again surely language
> designed to resolve the soul's health must sink deeply
> into us. Remedies are useless if only momentary.
> And then too there's a great deal of the empty and

unprofitable about popular rhetoric--more sound than
sinew. My bugbears must be made less frightening, my
temptations subdued, my illusions dispelled, my self
indulgence curbed, my avarice reprimanded, but which
of these ends can be achieved in a hurry? Does any
doctor treat his patient as he passes the door?[39]

. . .

The realist artist, according to Durand, is to study nature
and therein find the key to his own human nature. The study of
the art of the past is admissable as long as it serves to assist
the painter in organizing data collected from nature. On the
other hand the study of the art of the past becomes a positive
evil when the personality of another is substituted for one's
own, when the conventional usurps the place of the natural,
when the spiritual is overwhelmed by the sensual, when significance gives way to a display of technical facility. In formu-
lating his theory of realism, Durand was aware of the ideas of
a number of modern writers--Constable, Bryant, Channing, Alison,
and even Reynolds. But the foundation of Durand's theory of
realism is the Stoic philosophy of Seneca, which is not so
much concerned with the pursuit of truth as with the curing of
man's moral maladies. We may suggest that, as a realist,
Durand regarded painting less the sister of poetry and more
in the light of a mute philosophy--although, as noted above,
he was not unwilling to accept what aid poetry offered. As the
philosophical objectives of Durand's art depend entirely upon

its realism, we may turn now from theory to a consideration
of the development of realism in Durand's practice.

III.  Studies from Nature.

As we have seen, Durand's theory of landscape painting
was based on a concept, like that of the Stoics, according to
which one ought to follow or imitate the order of nature.  If
the painter is to abjure the conventions of his art and grasp
something of the order of nature, it is essential that he
learn to see nature and that he discover the technical devices
which will permit him to reproduce its forms and effects.
These two aims may be regarded as reciprocally dependent, the
one upon the other.  As the artist attempts to represent nature
his vision may become more acute.  As his vision becomes more
acute, he will be able to render a more complete account of
nature.  If, as did Durand, the artist seeks to establish an
identity among the three factors--nature, the mental idea of
nature, and the pictorial image of nature--he will necessarily
need to draw or paint in the presence of nature itself.  This
Durand had begun to do some years before his decision to devote
his full energies to landscape painting.  That he continued to
draw and paint from nature throughout his career as a landscape
painter was owing to a variety of factors which we shall discover in the course of our consideration of his outdoor studies.

A.  Drawings from Nature.

Durand's outdoor studies consist of both drawings and
paintings.  The quantity of both is impressive.  A brief consideration of the drawings will serve as a convenient introduction to the more complex problems posed by the paintings

from nature. Durand's landscape drawings fall easily into three categories. One group comprises studies of trees; another, panoramic and confined scenes; the third, and very much smaller, group is made up of studies of foreground earthbanks, boulders, and fallen trees.

Trees fascinated Durand as they did Thomas Cole and other Romantic landscape painters. Indeed, one of Durand's earliest studies of a tree (1837, Fig. 96), in its rhythmic curves and contorted system of leafless branches, assimilates closely to Cole's early drawings of anthropomorphic trees.[40] The influence of Cole's example on this early drawing was quite direct, for, in all probability it was executed when Durand worked with Cole at Schoon Lake in 1837.

The leafless tree in the 1837 drawing, although drawn from nature, seems exaggerated and overly dramatic in its boldly stated, rhythmic curves. In the mid-1840's we find trees of a more restrained and classical character. The exclusive interest in the writhing trunk gives way to a more harmonious, balanced interest in trunk, branches, and masses of foliage (Figs. 97 and 98). But, while all parts of the trees are equally prominent, at the same time they are all subordinated to the play of light which creates a pattern of light and shade indiscriminately over trunks, branches and foliage. Ultimately, this pattern of light is of greater importance than the representation of particular forms and textures.

In the late 1840's nearly all phases of Durand's art undergo a major reorientation. We must analyse the shift at a later point, but its existence is clearly reflected in the notable differences between the drawings in Figures 98 and 99. The unifying pattern of light of the earlier drawing has given way to a more scrupulous study of forms and textures seen close at hand. It is as though a veil had been withdrawn, and all the particularities of things that formerly had been hidden by light now reveal themselves. We have arrived, as it were, at the inner sanctuary of nature's forms. This same emphasis on the more solid form of trees and a corresponding de-emphasis on the less tangible masses of foliage is notable in other drawings of the same period (Figs. 187, 189A, and 200).

The Realist co-ordination of the maximum number of factors is fully achieved in drawings (e.g., Fig. 100) of the mid-1850's. Now, neither anthropomorphic drama nor a unified pattern of light is allowed to dominate the image, although both factors are present. In addition to the gesticulation of limbs and the play of chiaroscuro, the form and textures of roots, trunks, and branches and the less solid clusters of foliage all harmoniously co-exist. The knowledge gained in the close-up studies of around 1850 has been applied to the creation of a complete tree and of its environment of light and atmosphere. The same Realist synthesis is carried on in the 1860's, with an accentuated linear rhythm that recalls the overt drama of the 1837 drawing, but which now achieves a far greater lyricism and subtlety (Figs. 101 and 102).

The panoramic and confined landscape drawings develop in a somewhat different way. Confined scenes appear earlier. In the charming Rural Scene (Fig. 103) of 1827, such relatively intangible factors as irregular masses of foliage and the pattern of light are dominant. Two drawings of the mid-1830's (Figs. 103A and 146) display a similar lack of concern with the discrimination of particular forms and textures. These early drawings are, then, closely related, in their amorphousness, to the tree drawings of the mid-1840's. In the early panoramic drawings, however, there is a different emphasis (Fig. 17). The chiaroscuro of the confined views is almost totally displaced by line which defines the silhouette of the distant mountains and the contours of nearer objects. The greater measure of abstractness in the panoramic drawings is indicative of their function as sources of information about the disposition of land at a particular geographical location. Line is, also, the main descriptive means used in the drawings of Swiss and Italian scenes of 1840 and 1841 (Figs. 103B and 103C), and their abstractness is very apparent in Durand's insertion in the drawing of such phrases as "green grass" to indicate texture and color. By the mid-1840's even confined scenes are more dominantly linear (e.g., Fig. 103D), while in the 1850's line becomes more minutely descriptive of the inner and outer contours of land masses (Figs. 103E and 152). The erratic masses of foliage that remained in confined views of the 1840's (Fig. 103D) are increasingly regularized and subordinated in the 1850's and 1860's. Even the symmetrical foliage of the 1860's (Fig. 103F) is excluded in Durand's last panoramic drawings (e.g., Fig. 103G), where nearly every-

thing that is transitory in nature has been omitted in favor
of the large, simple relationships of earth, water, and sky--
the earth, losing any real interest in itself, as it serves
mainly to articulate the more etherial elements.

The third category of subject matter--foreground boulders
and earth-banks--Durand treated mainly in painted studies.
In either media the appearance of foreground studies coincides
with the effort to get beyond light and shadow to the substantial
forms and textures of nature, that appears in Durand's art around
1850. The drawing in Figure 103H illustrates the early phase
of this endeavor, while Figures 103I and 103J illustrate its
maturity in the 1860's and 1870's.

In summary, we may observe that the more enduring aspects
of nature--land formations--are consistently rendered with a
maximum of attention to form; and foliage, as a more ephemeral
thing, is treated with the greatest attention to chiaroscuro.
Durand did not draw individual leaves. Between these two extremes fall the rock and tree-trunk studies, wherein--especially
after 1850--one finds the combination of form and chiaroscuro
that produces texture and a sense of substance. In terms of
development, Durand's drawings shift from the Romantic emphasis
on special qualities--the drama of writhing branches or the
play of light and shade--to a more comprehensive, Realist
co-ordination of multiple qualities--drama, light, particular
form, texture, atmosphere, and so on. This more encyclopaedic
approach to nature first appears in full force around 1850,
but was anticipated by the panoramic, and therefore comprehensive,

drawings of the 1830's and 1840's--that is, the encyclopaedic rendering of phenomena was anticipated by the encyclopaedic rendering of things. In the 1850's Durand produced what might be termed maximal images--images in which a large number of things and of phenomena are expressed. In the later drawings, there is a tendency to reduce the number of things and phenomena, not in favor of a return to the dramatic and sensual qualities stressed in the early drawings, but in favor of a highly intellectual and linear austerity.

The painted studies from nature follow much the same pattern of development as may be traced in the drawings. Having encountered certain qualities of form and certain shifts in style in this brief survey of the drawings, we may now turn to the painted studies to observe more closely the development of Durand's concept of form and the factors by which it was affected.

B.  Painting from Nature.

By 1855 Durand had come to regard outdoor painting as an essential part of the landscape painter's art.[41] Without any qualification he could urge "on any young student in landscape painting, the importance of painting direct from Nature as soon as he shall have acquired the first rudiments of Art."[42] But Durand did not consider outdoor painting to be relevant only to the student. Of his own enduring fascination with painting from nature he wrote:

> in the advanced state of practice in which I find my-
> self, and at an age when early attractions might be

> supposed to lose some portion of their freshness,
> I feel no abatement in the interest of these pur-
> suits, and no amount of toil and fatigue can over-
> balance the benefits, either in consideration of
> utility or enjoyment.[43]

And, landscapes painted from nature form a very large segment
of Durand's mature work. Despite the high degree of finish
attained in most of these, they always retain the character of
studies or exercises in seeing and imitating nature. They do
not attain what Durand regarded as the highest aims of the art
of landscape painting. Their incompleteness as landscape
paintings sets them in contrast to the outdoor paintings of
the Impressionists and relates them to earlier traditions of
painted studies.

The practice of painting studies out-of-doors, from nature,
originated in the seventeenth century. According to Joachim
von Sandrart, Claude Lorrain would go into the fields and there
set his palette while looking at the scene he planned to paint
when back in the studio. Then, sometime after 1628, Sandrart
himself introduced Claude to a different method of working:

> /That/ hard and burdensome way of learning he pursued
> for many years walking daily into the fields and the
> long way back again, until he finally met me, with
> brush in my hands, in Tivoli, in the wild rocks at
> the famous cascade, where he found me painting from
> life and saw that I painted many works from nature
> itself, making nothing from imagination; this pleased

him so much that he applied himself eagerly to adop-
ting the same method.[44]

Sandrart goes on to state that,while he painted studies of the
rocks, trunks, trees, cascades, buildings, and ruins to use
as "fillers" in history paintings, Claude "only painted, on a
small scale, the view from the middle to the greatest distance,
fading away towards the horizon and the sky, a type in which
he was a master."[45] Elsewhere, Sandrart, speaking more
generally, says that Claude painted mountains, grottoes, valleys,
large trees, cascades, and other things from nature.[46]

During most of the eighteenth century the practice seems
to have died out, only to be revived around 1800 by, among others,
Pierre Henri de Valenciennes (1750-1819)[47] and Georges Mich-
allon[48] in Fran e and by John Constable and Joseph M. W.
Turner[49] in England. Camille Corot painted out-of-doors about
1822 and Théodore Rousseau five years later.[50]

Durand was the first American landscape painter to paint
studies in oil out-of-doors. At least, this was the belief of
two of his early biographers. In the Memorial Address of 1887,
Daniel Huntington stated:

> Durand had been a pioneer in engraving: he was
> now a pioneer in another very important branch of
> study, viz., that of painting carefully finished studies
> directly from nature out-of-doors. . . .
>
> Durand went directly to the fountain-head, and
> began the practice of faithful transcripts of "bits"
> for use in his studio, and the indefatigable patience

and the sustained ardor with which he painted these
studies not only told on his elaborate works, but
proved a contagious influence, since followed by
most of our artists, to the inestimable advantage
of the great landscape school of our country.[51]

John Durand was of the same opinion as to the priority of his
father's oil studies: "as far as I can learn, he was the first
artist in this country that painted directly from nature."[52]
However, none of Durand's biographers state exactly when or
why he first painted out-of-doors. Because of the crucial
role of studies from nature in Durand's art, it would be worthwhile to review the available evidence relative to the origin
and development of this interest.

C.  The Development of Durand's Interest in Painted Studies
from Nature.

1.  Durand's First Outdoor Studies:  1832-1837.

Two small paintings of trees owned by the New-York Historical
Society are the earliest extant pictures by Durand that were
executed out-of-doors (Figs. 104 and 105).  In each, trees in
heavy summer foliage, close to and paralleling the picture plane,
fill the large part of the canvas.  Both are painted in a looser
and more painterly manner than any of Durand's other outdoor
pictures and might better be termed sketches than studies.  In
each, brushwork, a sense of the pigment, and a strong contrast
of light and shadow take precedence over the description of
natural forms.  The boldness with which Durand here indicates

the play of light and color contrasts strongly with the detailed statement of form in his engraved work. In painting such free sketches as these, Durand must have discovered a joy in spontaneity and freedom which the discipline of engraving precluded.

But when were these sketches executed? According to records of the New-York Historical Society, based on family tradition, they were painted at Hoboken before 1834. They were given to the Society in 1903 by John Durand, who in the biography of his father, states that Durand carried his palette, already set, to Hoboken to paint and to find relief from the toil and confinement of the city.[53] Now, Durand began these excursions to the meadows on the New Jersey side of the Hudson--a popular place of recreation--soon after his arrival in New York in 1817.[54] But the sketches certainly do not date from the 1810's or 1820's.

The only piece of contemporary evidence for Durand's early interest in painting from nature is to be found in a letter, dated July 16, 1832, from his one-time partner Elias Wade, Jr. In this letter Wade invites Durand to visit him at Minquito Cove, Long Island, and adds:

> I forgot to state as an inducement for you to come here,
> that this section of the country presents numerous
> locust groves more beautiful than anything of the kind
> I ever saw. If you come out I think you should bring
> not only your sketch book but your palette, colors,
> canvass, &tc. I am quite sure you would find much that
> you would greatly admire. There is, of course, no

bold scenery, but there is foliage & effects in these side hill groves that could not fail to charm the lover of nature.[55]

Clearly Durand had painted out-of-doors before receiving Wade's invitation. Whether he visited Minquito Cove in 1832 is not known. However, it is just as likely that the trees in the two sketches are those to which Wade directed Durand's attention, as it is that they are trees he discovered for himself at Hoboken.

The only contemporary evidence indicating that Durand drew or painted at Hoboken in the 1830's is afforded by a letter, dated September 5, 1837, from Durand to Thomas Cole:

> I am still willing to confess myself a trespasser on your grounds, tho' I trust not a poacher, Landscape still occupies my attention, well, if the public don't wish me to take their heads, I will, like a free horse take my own, and "'ope the expanding nostril to the breeze." This miserable little pen, enclosing 250,000 human animals or more, should no longer hold me to swell the number; the vast range of this beautiful creation should be my dwelling place, the only portion of which I can at present avail myself being the neighborhood of Hoboken, which I am permitted to strip of its trees and meadows two or three times a week, and for which I am indeed thankful.[56]

Durand's excursions to Hoboken in 1837 were during his "leisure hours," and these may have been the visits John Durand had in

mind when commenting on his father's early studies from nature.
If the two sketches in the New-York Historical Society were
painted before 1834, they may have been painted at Minquito
Cove in 1832. If they were painted near Hoboken, they might
date from 1837. On the basis of subject matter it is impossible
to decide anything in favor of one date or the other. Durand
could have painted trees at Minquito Cove in 1832 and did paint
(or draw?) trees near Hoboken in 1837. All that is certain
is that he did work out-of-doors in 1832 and in 1837.

2. Outdoor Painting at Schroon Lake: 1837.

In describing his own visits to Hoboken in 1837, Durand
does not explicitly state that he painted there. But from a
slightly earlier exchange of letters between Durand and Cole it
is apparent that they both anticipated painting out-of-doors
in the summer of 1837. Prior to their joint expedition to
Schroon Lake in June and July of 1837, Cole requested that Durand
secure certain painting materials:

> You said you wished me to give you a list of colors.
> I scarcely know what can be got in bladders, but I
> think of the following. White, Roman Ocher Lena
> Siena Raw & Burnt, Burnt Umber, Chrome Yellow, Naples
> Yellow, Antwerp Blue, Madder Lake, Vandyke Brown,
> Light Red, Indian Red, A little Oil, & Some Copal
> varnish in a vial as a drier. Vermillion & even
> Crome Yellow we may carry unprepared . . . Camp stool
> I think you ought to have. Camp Umbrella if you can

get one I will join you in it if you like. It will
be well to get two sets of colours one for you & one
for me of course the bladders must be small the white
in greatest quantity. Rover or Dechaux must charge
to me.[57]

To this Durand replied:

I am a little at a loss to judge of the quanty /sic/
of colour necessary it appears to me for the most of
it we shall want more than what they call "small
bladders" which you know come at 8 cents each, of
course they must be small--their next size is usually
at 35 cts. each would that be too much? I have spoken
to Rover for you and shall procure of Dechaux for
myself & then see what is the difference. Dechaux is
going to get made an umbrella for me, there being none
already. I hope he will succeed. he has the camp
stool with easel attached that will do. I think you
said 1/2 dozen paste boards for each of us would be
the thing, by the by you have not mentioned yellow
ochre in your list, and will we not want some . . .
(?) or bone brown or asphaltum?[58]

Apparently prepared colors in some sort of skin containers were
a novelty at this time. Portable pigments, while not essential,
would, indeed, have facilitated outdoor painting.[59] The paste
boards which Cole recommended may have been used by Durand on
this occasion, but were rejected in favor of stretched canvas
for most of his later studies. That Durand, in 1837, had to

secure an umbrella, camp stool, and portable easel suggests
that he had not previously attempted a serious outdoor painting expedition.  Finally, one should note that it was Cole
who suggested that Durand procure the materials necessary for
outdoor painting.  Although paintings from nature do not form
a significant part of Cole's work, he should be given some
credit for encouraging a practice that Durand made an essentail
part of American landscape painting.[60]

3.  Reasons for Durand's Painting Out-of-Doors.

What evidence there is indicates that Durand first painted
out-of-doors in 1832 and resumed the practice in 1837.  After
1837 we hear nothing more of outdoor painting until 1844.  How
can we account for his interest in painting from nature in the
1830's?  Perhaps Durand was inspired by William Sidney Mount,
who as early as 1830 had painted the landscape setting of his
Boys Quarreling after School out-of-doors.  Later Mount built
a portable studio and painted finished genre pictures--for
example The Truant Gamblers and Bargaining for a Horse for
Luman Reed in 1836--from nature.[61]  While there is no evidence
suggesting that Durand was influenced by Mount in 1832, it is
entirely possible that, during the time both painters worked
for Luman Reed, Mount may have encouraged Durand, by precept
or example, to renew his effort to paint from nature.

What seems most likely is that in 1832 Durand's outdoor
paintings were inspired primarily by his own love of the beauty
of nature.  In his attempt to induce Durand to visit Minquito
Cove, Elias Wade, Jr., states that the locust groves are the

most beautiful he had ever seen and "could not fail to charm the lover of nature." The same love of the beauty of nature was expressed by Durand himself during the same summer:

> The luxury of Nature is so fascinating to my senses
> that I feel no disposition for anything but attempting
> to imitate her beauties, not by any actual view, but
> by catching some lovely feature.[62]

But, whatever painting from nature Durand did in 1832 does not mark the beginning of his career as a landscape painter. Between 1832 and 1837 portrait engraving and painting, as well as genre and historical painting, still occupied the large amount of his time. The letter to Cole of September 5, 1837, still indicates a fascination with the beauty of nature, but now this motive is combined with others. A lack of portrait commissions encouraged him to abandon the effort to place his art at the public's disposal. Rather than seek to accumulate the goods that society might bestow, Durand will now seek to develop the good within himself. Durand's simile of the "free horse" recalls Seneca's use of the lion in the wilderness as a metaphor for "the soul whose lustre proceeds from the good that's in it and no other."

> When the lion with a gilded mane is released from his
> cage--a manhandled beast, bullied into a meek accep-
> tance of his finery--isn't it a different thing from
> the enlargement of his unbroken brother of the wilds?
> The latter is a bounding fury, as nature intended
> him to be, a thing of rugged beauty seen only to be

feared, which is his glory. The other cowed creature of gold-leaf is contemptible beside him.[63]
Further, in the vein of Seneca, Durand contrasts the confinement
of the city--"the miserable pen"--to the "vast range of this
beautiful creation" and expresses a desire to dwell in the
latter. Seneca affirms that the individual ought not to make
his home in a single city but in the whole of Creation:

> Tell people rather how natural it is for man to let
> his mind range abroad over infinity. There's a great-
> ness, an aristocracy in the soul of man. It will
> suffer the setting of no limit but such as it shares
> with God. Firstly, it disdains a lowly home--an
> Ephesus, an Alexandria or other patch of earth, if
> there be such, yet more thickly populated and more
> architecturally blest. Its home's a realm whose
> frontiers circle the universal and supreme. It's
> all yonder vault within which lie sea and land, with-
> in which the air forms at once a link and a barrier
> between human and divine, in which countless sentinel
> luminaries are posted, moving sleeplessly upon their
> rounds.[64]

Clearly, by 1837 Durand was drawn to nature by moral concepts
as well as an aesthetic appreciation of her loveliness.

While in 1832 Durand had turned briefly to nature as a
source of consolation for his personal losses, in 1837 the
public crisis induced him to turn to the study of nature as a
profession. We may, then, suppose that the paintings from

nature of 1837 were executed, also, in preparation for a career as a landscape painter. His studies of this year may be regarded as "student" work, and may have been inspired as much by the example of Mount as by the following advice of Reynolds:

But while I mention the port-crayon as the student's constant companion, he must still remember, that the pencil is the instrument by which he must hope to obtain eminence. What, therefore, I wish to impress upon you is, that whenever an opportunity offers, you paint your studies instead of drawing them. This will give you such a facility in using colours, that in time they will arrange themselves under the pencil, even without the attention of the hand that conducts it. If one act excluded the other, this advice could not with any propriety be given. But if Painting comprises both drawing and colouring, and if by a short struggle of resolute industry, the same expedition is attainable in painting as in drawing on paper, I cannot see what objection can justly be made to the practice; or why that should be done by parts which may be done all together.[65]

According to Reynolds, the Venetians and Flemings painted their studies--in contrast to the Florentines and Romans who worked from drawings. When we recall that Durand's ideal female portraits of the later 1830's, inspired by Allston, do approximate to a Venetian tonality, we may be more willing to believe that Reynolds' advice might have attracted Durand's attention.

If Durand did paint from nature in 1837, there is no evidence to indicate that he continued to do so in the next few years. Perhaps, setting Reynolds' advice aside temporarily, he recognized the futility of painting before he had mastered the forms of nature with the pencil.[66] That the student of landscape painting--and in the late 1830's Durand was still a student--ought to draw rather than paint, Durand asserted in his Letters of 1855:

> Form is the first subject to engage your attention. Take pencil and paper, not the palette and brushes, and draw with scrupulous fidelity the outline or contour of such objects as you shall select . . . By this course you will also obtain the knowledge of that natural variety of form, so essential to protect you against frequent repetition and monotony. A moment's reflection will convince you of the vital importance of drawing, and the continual demand for its exercise in the practice of outline, before you begin to paint.[67]

D. Constable, Gilpin, and Durand's Outdoor Studies of the Mid-1840's.

Until 1844 Durand's studies from nature were mostly executed in pencil. With the pencil he could at once explore the variety of natural forms and seek a high degree of exactitude in the description of the form of a thing or of a place. In 1844, however, his interest in oil studies revived, and in the following year he sent three oil studies--Study in Jacob's Valley, near Kingston; Study near Marbletown; and Study from Nature--to

the American Art Union.[68] Two letters, one from Lucy Durand
to her father, dated August 20, 1844, and the other from Durand
to the painter Francis W. Edmunds, September 17, 1844,[69] indicate
that Durand worked at Kingston and Marbletown in the late
summer of 1844, and there is no evidence to suggest that he
returned in 1845. Hence, at least two of the studies exhibited
in 1845 must have been painted in the previous year.

These studies, I believe, derive at once from the example
of Constable and the writing of William Gilpin. During his
stay in London in 1840, Durand had renewed his acquaintance
with Charles R. Leslie, who had taught briefly at West Point
in the early 1830's. Through Leslie, Durand became aware of
Constable's plein-air oil sketches. In his Journal Durand wrote:

> In the evening in company with Rossiter paid a
> second visit to Leslie to make our acknowledgments
> for his kindness and bid him adieu. He showed us
> several sketches by his deceased friend Constable in
> water-colour, pencil, and other modes exhibiting great
> attention to Nature under her changing aspects, but
> all from home scenes and common familiar objects;
> among others a port-folio of oil studies from clouds
> and general skies, with notes on the backs stating
> the hour of the day, direction of the wind, and kind
> of weather. All his sketches were very slight, but
> indicating much naturalness and beauty of effect.[70]

These sketches had no immediate effect upon Durand's practice,
but he must have recalled them when reading Leslie's Memoir of

John Constable, which in all probability came to his attention
soon after its publication in 1843. Here, Leslie cited a
letter to Miss Bicknell, dated September 18, 1814, in which
Constable wrote: "This charming season, as you will guess,
occupies me entirely in the fields; and I believe I have made
some landscapes that are better than usual, at least that is
the opinion of all here."[71] And in explanation of this passage
Leslie adds:

> Among the landscapes mentioned in this letter, was one
> which I have heard him say he painted entirely in the
> open air. It was exhibited the following year at the
> Academy, with the title of "Boat-building." In the
> midst of a meadow at Flatford, a barge is seen on the
> stocks, while just beyond it the river Stour glitters
> in the still sunshine of a hot summer's day.[72]

This painting, sufficiently finished to be exhibited at the
Academy, must have been a more fully realized study than the
oil sketches of clouds which Durand had seen in London. And,
as a more finished study from nature, it more closely approximates the type of painting that Durand painted out-of-doors
in the summer of 1844.

Three studies, closely related thematically and stylistically, now in the New-York Historical Society, date from about
1844. Trees by the Brookside, Kingston, N.Y. (Fig. 109), from
which Durand derived forms for his Forenoon (Fig. 110), exhibited in 1847, might have been painted during Durand's visits
to Kingston in the summers of 1844 and 1846. Landscape with

a Beach Tree (Fig. 107) must have been painted in 1844 as
Durand borrowed forms from it for The Beeches (Fig. 108),
exhibited at the National Academy in 1845. As this study is
less elaborate than the former, it probably is the earlier,
so that the Trees by the Brookside would date from 1846. The
third, Study at Marbletown, N. Y. (Fig. 106),is not reflected
in any of Durand's known compositions, but displays a simplicity
that would relate it in date to Landscape with a Beech Tree.

Thematically all three are closely related, as each represents trees that are seen so near at hand that their trunks
assume a special prominence. In each, Durand has emphasized
the solid bulk of the trunks at the expense of the sunlit
foliage that largely attracted his attention in the studies
of the early 1830's. Stylistically, the varied textures of
the different barks of the nearest trees are described with a
remarkable richness. Durand has succeeded in avoiding facile,
flowing lines in defining the contours of trunks and branches.
For the nearest trees, foliage is suggested by dabs of paint
that go far toward implying the presence of a multitude of
individual leaves. In each, there is a three-step gradation
of clarity as the trees are more distant. Like the tree
drawings of the mid- and later 1840's, in the earlier of these
studies light and shadow tend to obscure detail while in the
later a somewhat greater emphasis on form is apparent. This
shift was accompanied by a drier manner in the study of
1846 (Fig. 109).

Durand's direct and indirect knowledge of Constable's
outdoor studies must have served to reassure him that painting
from nature was a necessary part of the landscape painter's
task.  However, his experiments of the mid-1840's seem to have been
more particularly directed by the writings of William Gilpin.
To indicate this connection we must pause to consider in some
detail Durand's composition The Beeches (Fig. 108) of 1845,
which was based upon one of the oil studies of 1844 (Fig. 107).
The composition is unusual due to the prominent placement of
two massive tree-trunks immediately in the foreground.  Also,
unusual is the fact that much of the foliage of these two
trees is cut off by the upper left and top edge of the picture.
Massive trees, truncated by the upper edge or one side of the
picture had already appeared in earlier works by Durand--for
example, Musidora, The Frank Sisters, Children of the Artist,
and Dance on the Battery.  But in the earlier works the form
of the tree or trees was quite unnatural, and they had merely
served as background for one or more figures.  Durand, in
fact, employed this type of tree again in An Old Man's Reminiscences (Fig. 80) of 1845.  But in The Beeches of the same
year the truncated, massive trees assume a new importance,
dominating the foreground, displaying a fascinating quantity
of natural detail, and thereby becoming the principal actors
in the piece.

The novelty of this composition was noted by Durand's
contemporaries.  In his Memorial Address of 1887, Daniel Hunting-

ton recorded the interest aroused by the painting when it was
shown at the National Academy:

> In 1846 /For 1845/ he won great applause by his exhibit
> of a large upright view from the edge of a wood . . .
> I remember well how the groups of artists gathered in
> front of it on varnishing day at the Academy, warmly
> discussing its merits and expressing their admiration.[73]

Earlier an anonymous writer in The Crayon had commented upon
the novelty of the work:

> Durand has one picture in this collection /that of
> A. M. Cozzens/ which . . . stamps his progress as an
> artist. It is, we believe, the first of his series
> of upright pictures, in which large trunks of trees
> are made prominent objects . . .[74]

And finally, John Durand described the painting as:

> . . . a large upright composition, the main interest
> of which is a vista beyond the massive trunk of a tree
> characteristic of local forest scenery. Novel and
> original in treatment, this work proved popular, and
> was followed in after years by others of the same
> order.[75]

While there is no evidence to prove beyond a doubt that
Durand studied Gilpin's books at all, it seems possible that the
novel use of foreground tree-trunks might have been suggested by
Gilpin's Forest Scenery. In discussing the beech tree (the
beech is the tree at the left in Durand's painting) Gilpin
praises its trunk and condemns the ramification of its branches:

> Its trunk, we allow, is often highly picturesque.
> It is studded with bold knobs and projections . . .
> It has another peculiarity also, which is sometimes
> pleasing; that of a number of stems arising from the
> root.[76]

This may have inspired Durand to admit the beech trunk into his
composition. He may have been the more willing to omit the
branch structure of the beech after reading Gilpin's criticism:

> But having praised the trunk, we can praise no other
> part of the skeleton. The branches are fantastically
> wreathed, and disproportionate; turning awkwardly
> among each other; and running often into long unvaried
> lines, without any of that strength and firmness,
> which we admire in the oak; or of that easy simplicity
> which pleases in the ash: in short, we rarely see a
> beech well ramified. In full leaf it is equally un-
> pleasing; it has the appearance of an overgrown bush.[77]

Gilpin also comments upon the texture of the beech's trunk:

> The bark too wears often a pleasant hue. It is naturally
> of a dingy olive; but it is always overspread, in patches,
> with a variety of mosses and lychens . . . Its smoothness
> also contrasts agreeably with these rougher appendages.[78]

Patches of moss or lichens appear not on Durand's beech but on
the trunk of its companion, identified by Tuckerman[79] as a
linden. Our conviction that the beech tree was introduced on
the authority of Gilpin would be strengthened if we were able

to discern other Gilpinesque forms, effects, or arrangements
in the painting.

Only the foreground knoll with its two trees was modelled
upon the painted study from nature. Except for the two trees
at the left of the middle-ground, which do appear in the study,
but in a different position, the remainder of the composition
appears to have been "made up." And it appears to have been
"made up" out of ideas suggested by Gilpin. Possibly the
three slender trees at the right of the middle-ground were
inspired by the following:

> Contrary to the general nature of trees, the beech
> is most pleasing in its juvenil state; as it has not
> yet acquired that heaviness, which is its most faulty
> distinction. A light, airy, young beech, with its
> spiry branches, hanging, as I have just described them,
> in easy forms, is often beautiful.[80]

Further, according to Gilpin, the exposure of a tree's roots
"is a circumstance on which /Its/ . . . beauty greatly depends."[81]
In the foreground and at the right middle-ground of Durand's
painting roots appear with a sort of programmatic insistence.
Of his paintings that have come to my attention, this is the
earliest in which roots appear. Again, the use of atmosphere
or haze in The Beeches appears to reflect Gilpin's comments on
this subject:

> The calm, overcast, soft, day, such as these cli-
> mates often produce in the beginning of autumn, hazy,
> mild, and undisturbed, affords a beautiful medium,

spreading over the woods a sweet, grey, tint, which
is especially favourable to their distant appearances.
The internal parts of the forest receive little advantage from this hazy medium: but the various tuftings
of distant woods, are wonderfully sweetened by it; and
many a form, and many a hue, which in the full glare of
sunshine would be harsh, and discordant, are softened,
and melted together in harmony.[82]

So much of the passage is an entirely adequate description of
the more distant part of Durand's painting. But Gilpin continues:

We often see the effects of this mode of atmosphere in
various species of landscape; but it has no where a
better effect, than on the woods of the forest. Nothing
appears through mist more beautiful, than trees a little
removed from the eye, when they are opposed to trees
at hand; for as the foliage of a tree consists of a
great number of parts, the contrast is very pleasing
between the varied surface of the tree at hand, and
the dead, unvaried appearance of the removed one.[83]

In earlier paintings such as the Morning and Evening of Life
Durand had used the change of value arising from the greater
amount of atmosphere interposing between the more distant object and the eye to establish the spatial position of the
former. But the more distant foliage is distinguished from the
nearer only by a change in value. In The Beeches he seems
quite consciously to have varied both clarity and value as
the foliage of the fore- and middle-ground is more distant. The

foliage of the nearest tree is represented leaf by leaf.
Leaves of the second tree are individually suggested. Of the
next, they are implied, while the foliage at the end of the
middle-ground is seen only as a feathery mass. The fact that
so complete a scale of clarity is so prominently present in
this painting, would suggest that the scale was executed as
an exercise in the kind of gradation described by Gilpin. A
three-step scale, as we noted, appears in all three of the tree
studies painted in the mid-1840's.

Another aspect of the painting seems to have been inspired
by Gilpin. From the density of trees at the left, it is clear
that Durand intended that the painting should represent the
edge of a woods or forest. Such a forest scene is described
by Gilpin in the following:

> The great beauty of these _close scenes_ arise from the
> openings and recesses, which we find among them.
>
> By these I do not mean the _lawns_, and _pasturage_,
> which I mentioned as one of the great divisions of
> forest-scenery; but merely those little openings among
> the trees, which are produced by various circumstances.
> A sandy bank, or a piece of rocky ground may prevent
> the contiguity of trees, and so make an opening; . . .
> or, what is the happiest of all circumstances, a wind-
> ing road may run along the wood. --The simple idea,
> which is varied through all these little recesses, is
> the exhibition of a few trees, just seen behind others.
> The varieties of this mode of scenery, simple as it
> is, are infinite.[84]

In the foreground of Durand's painting there is a bank which
is somewhat rocky. This much is found in the study. But the
winding road running along the wood is entirely Durand's in-
vention--inspired, it would seem, by Gilpin's text. Gilpin adds
that a forest scene might also be embellished by a reflecting
pool--

> A pool of water too is a lucky incident. When it
> is shrouded with trees, and reflects from its deep,
> black mirror the mossy branches of an oak, or other
> objects in its neighborhood, which have received a
> strong touch of sunshine.[85]

Instead of pools, Durand has introduced a reflecting brook and
river.

All of the significant elements of the composition appear,
thus, to have been suggested by Gilpin. The emphasis on "highly
picturesque" trunks, the exclusion of much of the branch
structure, the introduction of young trees, the brooks, winding
road, the forest interior theme, and the conceptualized atmospheric scale all suggest that Durand intended the picture to be
an exercise in Gilpinesque effects. That the composition did
not belong to a landscape tradition familiar to Durand's contemporaries is suggested by the surprise registered upon its
exhibition. That the arrangement of things in the composition
was not merely copied from nature is clearly indicated by the
deviations of the finished work from the study. Not derived
from either art or nature, we may be willing to believe it was
inspired principally by theory.

To this conclusion the very existence of the study painted
from nature adds support. In his discussion of woodland
recesses, Gilpin states that the forms of nature herself are
infinitely more varied than those the painter can invent:

> Nature is wonderfully fertile. The invention of the
> painter may form a <u>composition</u> more agreeable to the
> rules of his art, than nature commonly produces: but
> no invention can reach the varieties of <u>particular</u>
> <u>objects</u>.[86]

In his later <u>Letters</u> <u>on</u> <u>Landscape</u> <u>Painting</u>, Durand recommended
that the student and the professional landscape painter draw and
paint from nature in order to become familiar with her infinite
variety. But this study and recording of the particular forms
of forest scenery is precisely what, according to Gilpin, certain earlier landscape painters had done. Gilpin continues:

> Swanewelt, and Waterloo delighted in these <u>close</u>
> <u>forest-scenes</u>. They penetrated their retreats; and
> when they found a little opening, or recess, that
> pleased them, they fixed it on the spot. They studied
> its various forms--how the bold protuberances of an
> old trunk received the light and shade--how easily the
> large boughs parted; and how negligently the smaller
> ones were interwoven--how elegantly the foliage hung;
> and what varied shapes its little tuftings exhibited.
> All these things they observed, and copied with exact
> attention. Their landscape, bare of objects, and of
> the simplest composition, had little to recommend it,

but the observance of the minutiae of nature. These
they characterized with truth; and these alone have
given value to their works. This praise, however, is
chiefly Waterloo's.[87]

The studies painted by Durand in the mid-1840's are closer in
character to the work of Swanevelt and Waterloo, as described
by Gilpin, than to any of the studies by Constable that Durand
could have seen or read about. Like them, Durand penetrated
the forest, found a recess that pleased him and fixed it on the
spot. All of the forms of things Durand "observed and copied
with exact attention," and his studies have little to recommend
them "but the observance of the minutiae of nature." But Durand
would not be satisfied with so restricted a value. Gilpin does not
say that the painter ought to limit himself to the simple
imitation of particular forms. The area in which the painter
may most profitably exercise his inventiveness is not in the
creation of individual forms, but in their organization--"The
invention of the painter may form a composition more agreeable
to the rules of his art, than nature commonly produces . . ."
By deploying the forms of nature in his own composition Durand,
in The Beeches, was able to combine the merits of Waterloo with
those of Claude, Poussin, and Salvator, whose "extensive
scenes"--and The Beeches is an "extensive scene" for all of its
"forest-interiorness"--"depend more on composition, and general
effect, than on the exact resemblance of particular objects."[88]

Although individual forms were studied directly from nature,
their transference to the composition entailed certain notable

modifications. In the composition the textures of the main
trees have been simplified and regularized. Both trees were
lengthened--so that one gains an extra growth of lichen.
Also, in the process of attenuation, both trees have become
more slender in proportion and more elegant in pose. This
same tendency toward an abstract elegance may be observed in
a comparison of the tender shoot growing in front of the tree
to the right. This same effort to simplify and regularize the
forms of nature is displayed in the rendering of the second
pair of trees, behind and to the left of the first. These,
also, were modelled upon forms in the oil study, where they
appear behind and to the right of the major pair. In the
composition, the angular tree in the study has assumed a long
continuous curve to the right which serves to counter-balance
the leftward thrust of the foreground trees. The other trees
in the middle-ground of the study display almost consistently
the uninterrupted curves that the mind alone is able to conceive. Here, Durand has derived from the oil study an expanded
vocabulary of forms and textures, but the rhythms and organization of this material are supplied by the mind.

These natural forms, reformed, stand in strong contrast to
the highly conventional forms of an earlier landscape composition. In the Landscape with Children (1837, Fig. 37) there is
hardly a single form that might not have been conceived in the
artist's mind. The five foreground trees are only slightly
sinuous and relatively smooth stalks supporting a single mass
of fluffy material suggesting foliage. Other collections of

rather more woolly stalks may be seen at various points in the middle-ground. Of the foreground plants only the large-leaved growth immediately beneath the two seated children gives the effect of something not "made-up." A similar plant, probably studied from nature, appears in a drawing of 1837 (App. IV, no. 19. Cf. also no. 22). An even more schematic rendering of tree forms may be seen in the landscape setting to the Dance on the Battery of 1838 (Fig. 71).

The receipt for combining the ideal and the real, which Durand discovered in Gilpin, was followed in creating other compositions of the later 1840's. The Forenoon (Fig. 110), exhibited in 1847, was, as we have noted, based upon a tree study of 1846 (Fig. 109). As we shall see later, the Kindred Spirits (Fig. 201), exhibited in 1849, also combines real forms in a highly arbitrary composition. Both of these vertical compositions, in which massive trees, cut off at the top of the picture, appear in the foreground and in which a considerable vista is seen beyond, combine the forest interior idea with an extended space.

E. Mature Studies: 1848-1860.

In the late 1840's Durand intensified his effort to grasp the real forms of nature. At this time wilderness scenes such as the Landscape of 1849 (Fig. 188)--into which Durand introduced trees drawn from nature at Pine Orchard, New York, in September, 1848 (Fig. 187)--appear more frequently among his compositions, supplementing the cultivated scenes, which hitherto had exclusively attracted his attention. Also, in 1848 he began to exhibit painted studies from nature at the National Academy over which he now presided. In the years following, studies appeared almost annually--four in 1849, and two per year in 1850, 1851, 1853, and 1857. That in 1848 he stopped sending them to the popular Art-Union and exhibited them only at the more serious Academy suggests that by this time he had come to attach a higher significance to them.

Beginning in 1848 his summer excursions to the country were more completely devoted to painting from nature. His fascination with painting from nature is reflected in his letters of the years around 1850. In addition to the paintings themselves, the following excerpts from Durand's letters clearly indicate the degree of his interest in making oil studies of wild scenes at this period.

Elizabethtown, New York, June 22, 1848.

> We find so much to do in this place that we shall probably
> remain two or three weeks longer. . . . The mountain
> scenery is beautiful, superior to any I have met with
> in this country, but I have not yet done much at it,
> having commenced on a waterfall similar to that at
> Cornwall, also a study of rocks and another creek scene
> & now have a mountain in hand, but I have not pleased
> myself very well altho /sic/ among the four canvases
> covered there is some good material. I have begun
> with easier subjects first in order to get my hand in

and am just getting fairly in the traces so I feel
full of courage and good spirits. . . .[89]

Elizabethtown, July 2, 1848.

Since my last the weather has been very unfavourable
to our operation, having accomplished but one study
during the past week, but that is one of a most difficult order, & has been rendered more imperfect by
the bad weather, so that, altho' a useful study it is
not much as a picture.  It is a near view of a large
mountain, most difficult under the most favourable
circumstances.[90]

Elizabethtown, July 14, 1848.

I have covered some 9 or 10 canvases with /?/ not to
much care /?/ & we hope every day for better times.[91]

Palensville, New York, September 24, 1848.

The Clove where we now are is rich in beautiful wilderness, beyond all we have met with heretofore, altho'
extremely difficult of access.[92]

Palensville, October 2, 1848.

With the exception of two days, the weather has been
so cold that we have worked in our overcoats & over-
shoes, and in addition, have been obliged to keep up
a constant fire along side for an occasional warming.

I shall have done 3 studies here including one
begun on Saturday, which if I can have but two days
more, I think will be one of my best--and should we
have the uphoped for good luck of the remainder of

this week fair, I may get another of some sort for there is plenty of fine material at hand.[93]

Tannersville, New York, September 28, 1849.

The weather is so fine that I am unwilling to quit without one more study which if obtained will make six, as the fifth will be finished tomorrow.[94]

Tannersville, September 18, 1850.

I have finished two studies and commenced a third, one of them pretty good for me.[95]

Tannersville, October 9, 1850.

I suppose our time is now reduced to a brief space, so that, probably in a week more we shall retreat towards home.

I have completed 5 oil studies and am now on the 6th so my time has been pretty well spent, and if I shall be able to get one more & perhaps a drawing or two I shall be content.[96]

From Durand's letters of these years it is evident that he sought contact with a more natural kind of nature in the areas of primitive wilderness that remained in New York State. The strength of his will to grasp fragments of nature is reflected in his endurance of bad weather and the cold of autumn as long as a successful study might still be produced. Finally, it is only in these three years that he writes so frequently of his success or failure in painting oil studies. In later years, he continued to paint studies from nature, but no longer with so great a sense of struggle and accomplishment.[97]

1.  The Realism of Durand's Mature Studies from Nature.

The new realism of Durand's work around 1850 is well exemplified in three studies (Figs. 112-114), all of which
probably date from that year.  All three display significant
differences from the Landscape with a Beech Tree (Fig. 107)
study of 1844.  In the earlier study the two pairs of large
trees are the dominant forms.  Strongly lighted from the right
side, and thus strongly three-dimensional, these trees stand
out as the most important among all forms in the picture.  The
rocks, stumps, logs, branches, and plants scattered across the
foreground are decidedly subordinated due to the inferior degree
of plastic realization with which they are described.  In the
later studies, on the other hand, the tree forms have become
more slender, so that they no longer dominate the whole, but
exist as one type of form among others, that are described with
as much or more plasticity.  The emphasis on a major form,
thoroughly described, situated in an environment of subordinate
forms, gives way to an equal emphasis upon all things.  In
order to achieve this equality among the forms, Durand has
rejected the extended plain of his earlier studies in favor of
rocky banks.  Now the forms of nature no longer escape into
the distance but remain close to the artist's eye and subject
to minute study.  In these studies Durand successfully pursues
the infinite variety of form within a finite sphere.  And this
infinity of form is thrust upon the spectator in such a way
that it is inescapable.

Technically, the studies of 1850 differ from those of the
mid-1840's. The early looseness of handling gives way to a
new economy in the application of paint. The paint itself is
less obtrusive and clings more consistently to the surfaces
of things. Where before, paint was used to suggest the show
of actual light and shadow, Durand's vision now seems to penetrate to the hard surfaces of the things themselves. The
strong side-lighting of the early studies is dissolved--so as
to a play over all surfaces in greater or less degree, revealing
the infinitely varied, multiple facets which define a host of
discrete objects. In the earlier studies light played so
strong a role in the total scene as to obscure. Now light is
reinterpreted in such a way that it reveals. This new light
may be interpreted more as an intellectual light, emanating
from the knowing mind of the artist than a physical light
descending from the sun. Under the rays of this new light the
casual sparkle of sunlight disappears, and the life of forms
is arrested in its clasp. Under the impact of this visionary
light, the forms of one segment of nature detach themselves
from the fluidity of the whole. A bit of nature is transfigured and elevated to a higher plane insofar as it is fused
with the mind. The feeling of unity and coherence in these
studies does not arise from the character of the objective
forms represented but from the unity of the subjective light
in which they are studied. In the mid-1840's the act of painting from nature was primarily an attempt to reveal outward
appearances. The mind entered the creative process only when,

in the studio, Durand rearranged the objective data in a composition. By 1850 the mind has come to enter into the creative process at the very moment of the encounter with nature itself.

At this point, Durand, with Wordsworth, could have described himself as

> still
>
> A lover of the meadows and the woods,
> And mountains, and of all that we behold
> From this green earth; of all the mighty world
> Of eye and ear, both what they half create,
> And what perceive . . .[98]

In his Letters on Landscape Painting Durand insists that the mind ought to play an active role when the artist is painting from nature:

> the study of foreground objects is worthy whole years of labor; the process will improve your judgment, and develop your skill--and perception, thought, and ingenuity will be in constant exercise.[99]

Only through the exercise of mental judgment will the artist obtain a true imitation of nature, only thereby can he be "sure the work represents the model--not that it merely resembles it."[100] A landscape that merely resembles its object must be one in which the artist has primarily sought to record the appearances of nature. A landscape that imitates its object is the product of the combined operation of eye and mind, and their combined operation effects the transposition of appearance

to the realm of a more ideal reality. The plastic lucidity
of this ideal reality is what Durand sought in his later
studies.[101]

Perhaps Durand's new interest in wilderness landscape may
owe its impetus to no more remote a cause than the death of
Thomas Cole in February, 1848. When not composing allegories,
Cole had specialized in wilderness scenes. After Cole's death,
Durand would have been free to add the wilderness to his own
repertoire without trespassing upon his friend's ground. Indeed, Kindred Spirits (Fig. 201), a memorial to Cole exhibited
in 1849, was among Durand's first elaborate wilderness compositions. But, in this and another composed landscape of 1849
(Fig. 188), although tree forms studied from nature are introduced, the rock forms remain quite conventional and very much
subject to the accidental fall of natural light.

Judging from the studies that have been located, the new
interpretation of nature--the equality of all things and the
plastic realization of things illuminated by the light of the
artist's vision--does not appear earlier than the three studies
of 1850. By this time Durand had had opportunities to acquaint
himself with contemporary German landscape painting. In 1849
John G. Boker opened the Düsseldorf Gallery in New York, which
afforded a variety of extraordinarily realistic genre and
landscape paintings. Hans Friedrich Gude's Landscape--Nor-
wegian Scenery,[102] a realistic representation of a rocky,
mountain valley in the wilderness, is remarkably close in style
and spirit to Durand's wilderness studies of around 1850.[103]

At the same period a number of German landscape painters arrived in America. Among them was Joseph Vollmering (1810-1887). Vollmering, born in Anholt, Germany, had studied at the Amsterdam Academy before becoming a pupil of the Dutch landscape painter Barend Cornelis Koekkoek, with whom he remained from 1835 to 1844. As Vollmering arrived in America in 1847, he was probably the Mr. Vollmerre who exhibited three paintings--Cloister on Mt. Milobokus in Germany; Landscape; and Landscape, Composition--at the National Academy in 1848. A degree of relationship between the work of Vollmering and Durand is indicated by the fact that the largest painting exhibited by the former at the American Art-Union in 1849 was a Catskill Falls, described in the catalogue as "A rocky gorge through which the river is dashing; a party of spectators in the foreground." This picture, exhibited in the autumn of 1849, probably was painted in emulation of Durand's Kindred Spirits, incorporating the same elements and exhibited in the spring of the same year. Both were vertical compositions and were about the same size (Vollmering, 42 x 33; Durand, 44 x 36 inches ). Perhaps, Vollmering's painting was the product of an even closer association between the two men, for in a letter, dated Tannersville, September 28, 1849, Durand wrote: "Beside Casilear & Kensett we have Mr. Vollmering the German, with us or at least next door."[104] As Durand did not write "a Mr. Vollmering," we may assume that the German painter was already known to himself and his family. An additional point of contact between the two lies in the fact that in the

mid-1850's Durand's patrons Peter and William Kemble each purchased a painting from Vollmering.[105]

From the descriptions of the paintings exhibited by Vollmering in 1849 and 1850 at the American Art Union, we might
assume that he approached nature and described its forms in
much the same spirit as did Durand. Further, there is the
remarkable similarity between Durand's work in the 1840's and
early 1850's and the contemporary paintings by Vollmering's
teacher Koekkoek. The latter's Way-Side Shrine (Fig. 185) of
1837 came to America sometime in the nineteenth century and
is closely related to Durand's The Old Oak (Fig. 184) of 1844.
The spectator may "walk into" both paintings and stand beneath
the twisting boughs of a venerable tree which is silhouetted
before the strong light of a setting sun. In each, tiny birds
hover in the evening sky. The handling of the tree-trunk,
light, and foliage is so similar in the two paintings that it
is difficult to believe that Durand's was not immediately
inspired by the Dutch picture. Durand's View Toward the
Hudson Valley of 1851 (Fig. 189) is at least similar in character
to Koekkoek's Small Town on a River of 1840 (Fig. 190) in the
Gemeente Musea, Amsterdam. The river in Koekkoek's painting is
probably the Moselle, along which he and Vollmering and Durand
worked in 1840[106]--one wonders whether Durand encountered the
Dutch and German painters then.[107] Durand's View Toward the
Hudson and Koekkoek's Small Town on a River both reflect the
more Italianate pole of Dutch, seventeenth century landscape
painting--especially the work of Jan Both, whose landscapes

Durand studied closely in England and in Holland.[108]  Finally,
Koekkoek's work also embraces woodland scenes--e.g., Woodland
Scenery with Water on a Normal Day (Fig. 165),[109] inspired by
Hobbema--which parallel Durand's forest interiors only in
theme, for Durand's arrangement of trees is quite different
from anything in the Dutch tradition.  If Vollmering's paintings
reflected the work of his master, he must, upon his arrival in
America, have worked in a style very similar to that which Dur-
and had developed out of some of the same traditions from which
Koekkoek had drawn.

Of three paintings at the New-York Historical Society
attributed to Vollmering, two are oil sketches (Fig. 116) in
which he has suggested the most physical sort of light in a
very generalized manner.  The third (Fig. 115) is a close study
of the forms of a rocky brook with a range of hills beyond.
None of these is either signed or dated.  Assuming that all
three are by Vollmering, which type was he painting in the late
1840's?  Or, did he work in both manners throughout his career?
These questions we cannot answer.  All that is possible is to
suggest that he might at first have worked in the style of
Koekkoek and have shared the enthusiasm for the close study of
natural forms that is evident in his master's work.  Possibly,
at a later period, he manufactured sketchy reminiscences of
European scenes at a time when these were popular and the
interest in detailed transcripts of particular American scenes
had begun to decline among American patrons.  If the study of
the rocky brook represents Vollmering's style of the late

1840's, his work might have inspired Durand's study of rocky
brooks, painted in the year following his residence next door
to Vollmering at Tannersville in the Catskills.  In Vollmering's
study one may note an effort to make the paint adhere to the
various planes of particular rock forms.  Also, like Durand in
his 1850 studies, the German painter seeks to define the position
of the receding as well as the frontal planes of rocks.  In
the work of both, passages of impasto are used to suggest the
textured surfaces that are illuminated and these passages stand
in contrast to the smoother painting of less well-illuminated
or smoother surfaces.  Both artists seek to define the skeletons
of trees but elaborate the description of foliage at the same
time.  In the trees of each, we find little flakes of highlights
on trunks and leaves, while for the most part the trees and
foliage remain dark.  A tendency toward equal emphasis on all
forms is discernible, and in Vollmering's study plastic realization is carried to the background hills that close the scene.
Finally, in Vollmering as in Durand's studies we feel the effect
of the artist's mental vision upon the forms of nature, a vision
that defines, clarifies, and heightens the reality of natural
phenomena while at the same time it serves to detach the total
fragment from its context in nature as a whole.

A paucity of evidence precludes our reaching any final
decision about the influence of Vollmering upon Durand at the
time he developed a more realistic style.  However, if we recall that Durand had committed himself to the faithful imitation
of particular forms as early as 1844 with the painted forest

studies inspired by Gilpin, we may suppose that the decisive
change in style around 1850 was the result more of pictorial
than of literary influences. Durand probably read the first
volume of Ruskin's Modern Painters soon after its publication
in May, 1843.[110] Ruskin's demand that the landscape painter
truthfully imitate particular phenomena would only have confirmed Durand's own established aspirations. While Ruskin may
have confirmed Durand's objectives, while Gilpin provided him
with a practical method for the study of particular forms of
nature, it is very likely that Durand's experience of German
paintings most directly inspired the realistic style of his
maturity.

2. Foreground studies.

The three studies which we have just been considering are
typical in their subject matter of one sizeable category of
Durand's painted studies from nature. In the paintings of this
group, he closely examined and sought to represent the infinitely
varied and intricate complexities of a very limited area of
foreground earth-bank. The numerous foreground studies which
Durand painted in the years after 1850 had little direct connection with his compositions. Of the compositions that have come
to my attention, only one, Chappel Brook, dated 1872 (Fig. 122),
incorporates forms drawn directly from a foreground study
(Fig. 123). Otherwise, foreground studies appear to have been
executed primarily as exercises to increase the artist's knowledge. And this is the value which Durand assigns to them in

his <u>Letters</u>: "every <u>truthful</u> study of near and simple objects will qualify you for the more difficult and complex . . ."[111] And, at greater length in another "Letter" he wrote:

I have already advised you to aim at direct imitation, as far as possible, in your studies of foreground objects. You will be most successful in the more simple and solid materials, such as rocks and tree trunks, and the coarse kinds of grass, with mingling roots and plants, the larger leaves of which can be expressed with even botanical truthfulness; and they should be so rendered, but when you attempt masses of foliage or running water, anything like an equal degree of imitation becomes impracticable.

It should be your endeavor to attain as minute portraiture as possible of these objects, for although it may be impossible to produce an absolute imitation of them, the determined effort to do so will lead you to a knowledge of their subtlest truths and characteristics, and thus knowing thoroughly that which you paint, you are able the more readily to give all the facts essential to their <u>representation</u>. So this excessively minute painting is valuable, not so much for itself, as for the knowledge and facility it leads to.[112]

Among these studies fluctuations of style, most likely reflecting Durand's mood at a particular moment, may be noted. Throughout the series one is aware of the operation of the artist's mind in an effort to define and clarify the forms of

things.  But the rather even lighting which reveals a maximum
number of surfaces, seen in the studies around 1850 (e.g.,
Fig. 112), gives way to stronger contrasts of light that accen-
tuate certain planes in a group of studies dating from the mid-
1850's (Figs. 117-120).  Perhaps, in these studies Durand found
it necessary to polarize the light in order to embrace a richer
tangle of earth, rocks, trees, and plants.  Or, in a period
when his position seemed secure, he may merely have relaxed the
mental effort that is so apparent in the earlier studies.  In
their richness, these studies are among Durand's most magnificent.  However, they fail to display that anguished groping
after form that we find in studies of other periods--for example
from the early 1860's.  In the Bish-Bash Falls of about 1861
(Fig. 121), foliage and the softer mounds of earth have been
subordinated to an elaboration of the brittle surfaces of a
rocky scarp.  Here, again, the eye is sent by the mind to the
receeding and advancing planes of the whole system with equal
intensity.  The eye of the spectator finds no relief from solidity
in undifferentiated passages of obscurity.  The rocks are flung
at the spectator relentlessly, brutally (cf. Fig. 122).

In a study of ten years later (Fig. 123), this crystalline
harshness has disappeared.  If the effort of the artist's eye is
undiminished, his hand, as he approached his seventy-fifth
birthday, seems enfeebled.  A softness of execution corresponds
to the softness of the forms represented.  Asperities of surface
have been washed away by centuries of running water, have been
overgrown by a thick coat of moss, or have simply not been

observed by the artist's tired eye. The earlier, vital, wild
tumble of roots and earth, of trees and rocks has now become
a languorous decay of object and artist alike. Where in his
earlier foreground studies Durand had emphasized the outgrowing
of new life from old, here all of the prominent forms slowly
release their hold on whatever gave them form, as they dissolve
into the central pool of stagnant, elemental water. Nature
stands in a state of silent collapse. Whatever ideas and feelings
Durand put into this final foreground study must have held
especial importance for him, for, as already noted, it was
probably the only such study that he elaborated into a large
studio painting.

Like the studies of tree-trunks undertaken in the mid-1840's,
Durand's foreground studies may also be regarded as an innova-
tion--certainly in respect to the development of landscape painting in America. While some pictorial stimulation may be necessary
to effect a change in style, an interest in a new class of subject matter may easily be excited by literature. As the tree-
trunk studies reflect the influence of Gilpin, the foreground
studies were, in all probability, inspired by Ruskin. Ruskin
devoted a chapter of the first volume of Modern Painters to
foregrounds, and his stress on the study of rocks must have
affected Durand, in all of whose foreground studies, rocks hold
a prominent position. Indeed, Durand's earliest foreground
studies (e.g., Figs. 112 and 113) seem virtually to illustrate
the following passage from Ruskin:

The massive limestones separate generally into
irregular blocks, tending to the form of cubes or
parallelopipeds, and terminated by tolerably smooth
planes. The weather, acting on the edges of these
blocks, rounds them off; but the frost, which, while
it cannot penetrate nor split the body of the stone,
acts energetically on the angles, splits off the
rounded fragments, and supplies sharp, fresh, and
complicated edges. . . . Thus, as a general principle,
if a rock have a character anywhere, it will be on
the angle, and however even and smooth its great planes
may be, it will usually break into variety when it
turns a corner.[113]

Although the naturalistic character of Ruskin's observations
always leaves one in doubt as to whether an artist studied a
particular phenomenon at his suggestion or independently, in
this case, Ruskin's emphasis on the study of rocks in his
chapter "Of the Foreground" would account for the prominence
of rocks rather than weeds in Durand's foreground studies.
Given Durand's eclecticism, we may suppose that Durand could
incorporate a suggestion from Ruskin into the sprawling edifice
of his art without becoming a Ruskinian painter.

We have already noted that Durand's foreground studies
were conceived primarily as exercises in the imitation of nature,
and normally were not incorporated into his compositions. This
notion of the role of foreground studies may also reflect the
influence of Ruskin, who wrote in the same chapter:

Now, if there be any part of landscape in which nature
develops her principles of light and shade more clearly
than in another, it is rock; for the dark sides of
fractured stone receive brilliant reflexes from the
light surfaces, on which the shadows are marked with the
most exquisite precision, especially because, owing to
the parallelism of cleavage, the surfaces lie usually
in directions nearly parallel.[114]

The rock studies of the mid-1850's are Durand's most elaborate
studies of light and shade, but they do not display any marked
concern with the reflexes of light between parallel walls of
stone.

3. Tree Studies and Compositions.

While the foreground studies were undertaken primarily in
order to reach a more thorough knowledge of nature and played
an insignificant role in shaping any of Durand's compositions,
his tree studies of the 1850's were frequently reworked into
larger pictures executed in the studio. In the 1840's a single
tree or group of trees might be drawn or painted from nature
and later introduced into the foreground of a landscape composed
in the studio. In the 1850's Durand painted from nature studies
of groups of trees which were later merely revised in the studio
without the addition of a studio-composed setting. The major
trees, their setting and relationship, of his In the Woods of
1855 (Fig. 169) were directly borrowed from a smaller oil study
of a forest interior (Fig. 168). In the composition some of

the data of the study has been omitted, some trees assume more resilient curves, and a sort of triadic grouping of trees was introduced. But the forms of the land and trees--standing or fallen--have largely been preserved.

Probably related in purpose to the oil study for the In the Woods are three other, rather unusual paintings, dating from the 1850's (Figs. 175-177). These differ from the normal oil studies in that they are on canvases as large as those used for compositions, and they are painted only in sepia oil. From Durand's Letters on Landscape Painting, written during the period when he made these sepia paintings, it is clear that, for the purposes of study, the forms of nature could be adequately recorded in light and shade alone. In discussing the dangers of an excessive interest in color, he wrote:

> If you have a predilection for color, you will be most likely, in your early stage of practice, to give it undue importance, to an extent that may impede your progress--that is, sacrifice higher qualities to its fascination. I know no better safeguard to this liability, than to remind you that a fine engraving gives us all the greatest essentials of a fine picture, and often a higher suggestiveness than the original it represents . . . because the imagination fills in the rest, according to our own ideas of truth in its completeness. But, for the present I would especially direct attention to the light and dark, which make up the effect of the engraving . . . it lacks nothing but

color, which, though mighty in its power, is nothing
more than the eloquence of Nature employed for the
fullest enforcement of her Truth--the great ideas are
antecedent. . . . Study then, the light and dark of
objects in connection with color . . . and as I have
recommended first, the practice of outline with the
pencil, so I would also enjoin the study of light and
shade with pencil, sepia, or even charcoal--any material
you can best manage for this end.[115]

From this passage it is quite evident that Durand, still very
much in the Neo-classical tradition, accepted the forms behind
the play of color as the fundamental object of the painter's
attention. He was as willing to see nature in sepia as earlier
he had been willing to see the human form as a plaster statue
stripped of the colors of life. The three sepia studies of the
1850's record the "great ideas" of nature that exist beneath,
"antecedent" to, the colors that strike the eye.

But aside from the metaphysical advantages of the sepia
study, it possessed a more practical value. In transferring the
study for In the Woods to the large canvas, Durand must have
realized that the natural forms and their relationships would
necessarily be distorted in the process. At this time it must
have occurred to him that a smaller degree of distortion would
result if the study were as large as a studio composition.
But to finish a large canvas out of doors would require so much
time as to unduly reduce the amount of time available for other
outdoor studies. The sepia studies that record only the essen-

tial forms of things solved this problem. Of the three large
studies, only one is known to have been used as the model for
a studio composition. Nearly all of the forms of the sepia
study Trees and Brook (Fig. 177) reappear in the Woodland Brook
(Fig. 178) of 1859, which is, in fact, slightly smaller than
the study. In composing the Woodland Brook, Durand has eliminated
some and clarified other of the forms appearing in the study.
The effort to render the forms of the study more graceful
appears to have been relaxed, and hardly anything except some
hills and smaller trees in the distance appears in the painting that is not at least suggested in the study.

It is in such paintings as In the Woods, Woodland Brook,
or The Catskills (Fig. 180) of 1859 that Durand reaches the
culmination of his effort toward realism. The Catskills, considered by itself, is certainly among his most aggressively
realistic paintings. None of the richly varied, foreground
material impresses one as having been conceived by the mind
alone. Everything deviates from the regularity, simplicity, or
symmetry of a pure mental gesture. Everything denies a merely
mental genesis. And, indeed, the forms in this landscape were
taken from at least two oil studies and one drawing. The form
and richly textured surface of the more distant tree-trunk at
the right foreground derive from one oil study (Fig. 179).
The shelving rocks at center may derive, although reversed,
from one of Durand's most spectacular oil studies--a very large
(h. 40 x w. 32 1/2 inches) and fully finished painting
(Fig. 181)--if it was in fact painted out-of-doors.[116] Finally,

the river, which meanders across a distant plain, is related to
that in a drawing dated 1859 (Fig. 182)--although this unusual
drawing may have been executed in the studio. The trees,
rocks, and their landscape setting seem each to have been
studied from nature. And yet, as in the other compositions,
it is evident that the activity of mind, which in the production
of a study operated to half create the essential forms of things,
has been directed here toward the creation of a just and lucid
relationship of each thing to each other and of all to the
whole.

Among all of Durand's studies from nature, be they in pencil
or oil, studies of trees form the largest single group. As a
landscape painter, trees held for Durand a position comparable to
the centrality of the human figure for the history painter. As
the history painter might study the human figure and insert it
in a landscape setting, so Durand studied a tree or group of
trees for subsequent insertion into a landscape setting. But
the analogy between the practice of the history painter and
Durand's as a landscape painter may be carried further. In
his studies of the figure, the history painter, working in the
Neo-classical tradition, will seek to grasp an ideal or perfect
human form. The Neo-classicist's belief in the validity of
such ideal forms is predicated upon his faith in an order or
governing "reason" existing behind appearances. Similarly,
Durand believed that a governing "reason" in the universe impels
each tree toward an ideal form of its species, and that it is

the landscape painter's duty to seek this ideal among the
individual members of the species.

If the artist is to grasp the ideal form of a particular
species of tree, he must approach nature critically and selec-
tively. This Durand advised the student to begin to do in the
early phases of his studies. Addressing the student, Durand
wrote:

> Take pencil and paper . . . and draw with scrupulous
> fidelity the outline or contour of such objects as you
> shall select, and, so far as your judgment goes, choose
> the most beautiful or characteristic of its kind. If
> your subject be a tree, observe particularly wherein
> it differs from those of other species: in the first
> place, the termination of its foliage, best seen when
> relieved against the sky, whether pointed or rounded,
> drooping or springing upward, &c., &c.; next mark the
> character of its trunk and branches, the manner in
> which the latter shoot off from the parent stem, their
> direction, curves, angles. Every kind of tree has its
> traits of individuality . . . with careful attention
> these peculiarities are easily learned, and so, in a
> greater or lesser degree, with all other objects.[117]

John Durand states that his father did not copy nature indiscriminately but rather, "Finding trees in groups, he selected
one that seemed to him in age, colour or form, to be the most
characteristic of its species, or, in other words, the most
beautiful."[118] It is true that many of the trees in Durand's

painted studies are far from perfect specimens of the species
to which they belong. Also, many of the tree studies in oil
represent the trunk alone. We might suppose that in these
imperfect and truncated trees Durand was more interested in
studying the textures, lights, and shadows than in the perfect
form of the kind of tree. It is more often among his drawings
that we find studies of perfect trees in their entirety
(Figs. 98 and 102). It must have been primarily in these that
Durand exercised the selectivity of which his son speaks.

In discussing idealism, Durand speaks more at large of the
landscape painter's pursuit of perfect forms:

What then is Idealism? According to the interpretation commonly received, that picture is ideal whose
component parts are representative of the utmost perfection of Nature, whether with respect to beauty or
other considerations of fitness in the objects represented, according to their respective kinds. . . . The
extreme of this ideal asserts that this required perfection is not to be found or rarely found in single
examples of natural objects . . . In order to compose
the ideal picture, then, the artist must know what
constitutes the perfection of every object employed,
according to its kind, and its circumstances, so as
to be able to gather from individuals the collective
idea. This view of Idealism does not propose any
deviation from the truth, but on the contrary, demands

the most rigid adherence to the law of its highest
development.

. . . .

Every step of progress towards truthful representation of Nature will be so much gained of the knowledge
indispensible to the attainment of the ideal, for all
the generic elements of natural objects, by which one
kind is distinguished from another, are the same in the
imperfect as in the perfect specimen. The difference
lies in the disposition of them; so when you shall have
learned all that characterizes oak as oak, you will be
prepared to apply those characteristics according to
the requirements of ideal beauty, to the production of
the ideal oak. And this process continued through all
forms and combinations, defines the creative power of
Art, not in producing new things for its special purpose, but in supplying from Nature's general fullness,
all particular deficiencies in whatsoever things she
has furnished for its use. Thus far the meaning of
Idealism is limited to the perfection of beauty with
generic character and fitness in combinations.[119]

In its essentials Durand's theory of the ideal form of each
species of tree does not differ from Sir Joshua Reynolds' academic
concept of the ideal form as derived by the artist from a careful
comparison of individual members of a species. According to
Reynolds, by comparing one form with another, the painter

acquires a just idea of beautiful forms; he corrects
Nature by herself, her imperfect state by her more
perfect. His eye being enabled to distinguish the
accidental deficiencies, excrescences, and deformi-
ties of things, from their general figures, he makes
out an abstract idea of their forms more perfect
than any one original; and what may seem a paradox,
he learns to design naturally by drawing his figures
unlike to any one object. This idea of the perfect
state of Nature, which the Artist calls the Ideal
beauty, is the great leading principle by which works
of genius are conducted.[120]

Elsewhere Reynolds states "that the idea of beauty in each species
of beings is an invariable one," and that

perfect beauty in any species must combine all the
characters which are beautiful in that species. It
cannot consist in any one to the exclusion of the rest;
no one, therefore, must be predominant, that no one
may be deficient.[122]

From the latter passage it is quite apparent that Reynolds would
allow this concept of the ideal form of a species to be applied
to beings other than the human figure. Indeed, in the "Fourth
Discourse" he states that the landscapes of Claude are "founded
upon the same principle as that by which the History Painter
acquires perfect form."[123]

Given the availability of Reynolds' theory of specific
form and Durand's early training in the Neo-classical tradition,

there is little reason to believe that his concept of form
was materially affected by John Ruskin's reiteration of the
theory of specific beauty in the mid-nineteenth century.  In
such a passage as the following, Ruskin seems merely to echo
Reynolds:

> The true ideal of landscape is precisely the same as
> that of the human form; it is the expression of the
> specific--not the individual but the specific--characters
> of every object, in their perfection; there is an ideal
> form of every herb, flower, and tree:  it is that form
> to which every individual of the species has a tendency
> to arrive, freed from the influence of accident or
> disease.[124]

It seems more likely that Durand's adherence to the theory of
specific beauty, as defined by Reynolds, was the result of its
harmony with the Stoic philosophy.  According to Seneca, the
"good" of trees and plants lies in "What's in harmony with the
nature of each species."[125]  Durand's concern with specific
beauty may, then, be regarded as another aspect of his effort
to apprehend and project the moral order of nature.

Durand's enduring concern with ideal tree forms indicates
his interest in an element of order in nature.  Rocks, meadows,
hills, mountains, and bodies of water do not seem to approximate
any central form.  Clouds, in which Constable was able to discover approximations to ideal forms according to their species,
did not interest Durand in any marked degree.  For him, in the
tree the order of nature revealed itself to the eye.  And it

was for this reason, he took so intense an interest in them.
Perfect tree forms are prominent in the pastoral landscapes
which he produced from the late 1830's to the end of his career
as a landscape painter. The trees in Sunday Morning (Fig. 73)
of 1839 are as ideal as those in Summer Afternoon (Fig. 159) of
1865. But these pastoral landscapes, in the tradition of Claude,
also most clearly reveal a geometric order in their compositional
structure. The order of the ideal tree form, which bespeaks a
governing reason in nature, exists in the geometric context of
the compositional structure, which bespeaks a governing reason
in the artist. In these compositions, that which indicates a
reason in nature co-exists with that which indicates a reason
in man. The simultaneous but separate expression of the divine
and the human minds in these paintings reflects the Stoic concept of the divine and human minds as being akin to one another,
while each remains autonomous. As we shall see shortly, at the
end of his career, Durand discovered a means to fuse the order
of nature with the order of the composition in a way that expresses the union of the human with the divine mind.

4. Landscape Studies and Open Scenes.

As in the tree-trunk or forest-interior compositions, so,in
his more open landscapes of the late 1840's and 1850's, Durand
incorporated a greater amount of data derived from the direct
study of nature. This new interest is evident in the Landscape
of 1849 (Fig. 188). Both this painting and the more pastoral
View Toward the Hudson Valley of 1851 (Fig. 189) contain tree

forms that follow quite closely the trees in two drawings from nature. The left-hand foreground trees of the earlier painting were hardly more than transplanted from a drawing dated "Pine Orchard / Sept. 1848" (Fig. 187). The drawing is a study of trees without any setting. The two taller trees in the painting plus some of the smaller, attendant shoots appear in the drawing. But, while the trees in the painting are copied in some detail from the drawing, Durand still invested them with a greater clarity and sinuous elegance. The stubbornly straight lines in the drawing assume softer, more yielding curves in the painting. In the View Toward the Hudson the two slender trees to the right in the foreground and something of the bushy tree in the center were inspired by a drawing from nature (Fig. 189A)-- again, one representing trees in isolation. Much of the data of the rich and really magnificent drawing is repeated in the painting. But in the transplanting, the forms of the drawing become somewhat impoverished. The plenitude of nature is reduced to a simpler pattern, capable of appealing more directly to the mind's sense of rhythm and clarity in parts and of proportion in the intervals between one part and another.

The Beeches of 1845, the Landscape of 1849, the View Toward the Hudson of 1851 have something of the character of tree-portraits with a landscape setting, the latter, apparently, invented in the studio. Up to the early 1850's Durand's normal practice seems to have been to study tree forms from nature and then combine them with a middle-ground and distance largely conceived in the studio. From at least as early as 1852 Durand produced compositions that are more consistently inspired by the study of nature. A composition of that year (Fig. 151), representing scenery near Manchester, Vermont, is based upon two drawings. One, dated "Manchester, Aug. 27th 1851" (Fig. 152), represents the middle-ground and distance employed in the painting, while another drawing (Fig. 153) includes the three tall trees reappearing at the right-hand side of the painting. The forms of earth, as well as those of trees, are now much less controlled by the mind of the painter and much more dependent upon the forms of nature. While the forms displayed in the composition have, to some degree, been affected by the clarifying and organizing powers of the artist's mind, they are far from being forms that the mind could conceive unaided by the study of nature.

One may also compare the Franconia Notch (Fig. 196) of 1857 with the oil study (Fig. 195) from which its middle-ground and distance were derived. Despite the many modifications that appear in the composition--the addition of a rich foreground with tall trees, two trees planted at the center, a heap of wood and rocks at the right, a grove planted on a point of land at the right edge, a decrease in the width of the meadow at the beginning of the distance in the center, and the increased elevation of the most distant range of mountains--the fundamental forms and relationships of the study do reappear in the painting. Durand here does not exceed the limits of invention which in the ninth of his Letters on Landscape Painting, written two years earlier, he allowed the painter of views:

In requiring adherence to truthful representation,
I wish not to be understood as insisting on literal
portraiture, even in cases of actual view painting,
that is, with regard to the entire details of any
given scene. There can be no scene worthy of being
painted, that does not possess certain characteristic
features which constitute its interest. These features
are obvious at a glance, and must be preserved invio-
late; there are others more or less subordinate, such
should receive attention according to their relative
importance; and there are still others of no importance
at all . . . He may displace a tree, for instance, if
disagreeable, or render it a more perfect one of its
kind if retained, but the elevations and depressions
of the earth's surface composing the middle-ground and
distance, the magnitude of objects, and extent of the
space presented in the view, characteristic outline,
undulating or angular, of all the great divisions, may
not be changed in the least perceptible degree, most
especially the mountain and hill forms. On these God
has set his signet, and Art may not remove it when the
picture professes to represent the scene.[126]

It should, of course, be noted that Durand does not recommend
that every landscape be a view of a particular place. But, if
the painting is to portray a place, the forms of Nature, rather
than the conceptions of the artist, constitute the material
which he is to add to, subtract from, or arrange.

F. The Late Studies and the Order of Nature: 1860-1878.

After 1860, Durand continued to paint studies of rocky
earth-banks, of tree-trunks, and broader vistas. But from 1862
a new subject appears in his studies--lake and mountain scenery.
From the year 1862 to 1878 he often spent the summer on Lake
George, these trips becoming especially frequent in the 1870's.
In the summers of his old age, when he was no longer under
pressure to execute compositions for the annual exhibition,
when he had come to feel sufficiently acquainted with the
individual forms of nature, and when perhaps his hand could no
longer so clearly pick out the details of a tree's bark or a
mossy rock, Durand more frequently turned to the study of the
broader and simpler masses and planes of mountains and water.

Perhaps, still in the 1860's he painted the study of Lake
George (Fig. 132) with a rocky foreground, treated with the
meticulous attention to detail characteristic of his earlier
studies, but here combined with the lake in the middle-ground
and a range of mountains in the distance. In this Lake George
study we may note something new. His earlier studies display
no articulation with reference to the shape and proportions of
the picture plane itself. In foregrounds, trees, and vistas,
Durand had simply covered the canvas with imagery until there
was no more area to be covered. Indeed, sometimes he was so
indifferent to the picture plane that he stopped short of its
limits. To recreate a fragment of nature was the exclusive
purpose of the study. In studies such as those in Figures 117
and 179 the imagery is so dense and varied  that the eye can

pause nowhere long enough to undertake an exploration of the proportions of intervals between things or between things and the edges of the canvas. In the studies, the order of nature is not modified. In the compositions, on the other hand, the arrangement of the imagery is controlled by a pre-determined geometric pattern (Figs. 133-135). This geometric pattern we may term "the order of the painting" to distinguish it from that of nature.[127] Now, in the Lake George studies, Durand discovered in nature itself the long horizontal line below the horizon upon which the eye can rest. And once the eye pauses, the painter has the opportunity to explain the relationship of the position of this line to the position of other points within, and to the edges of the picture. Once the horizontal line has migrated from the compositions to the studies, the artist is able to control its position by a geometric order of the picture, which stands over and above the natural order of the imagery itself. In the study Lake George, New York, of about 1862, the total arrangement appears to be controlled by a geometric scheme; and, if we measure the intervals carefully (Fig. 132), it becomes evident that Durand made a regular division of the picture plane, which controls the position of the major terminations of the several large bodies of which the picture consists.

The Lake George, New York, study of about 1862 still contains a tremendous amount of concrete detail in the foreground. Although the right-hand end of the large block of stone at the left falls on a line that is distant from the left side of the

painting by three-fifths of its height, the facets and fragments of foreground rock are in no way controlled by the geometric order of the painting. Ten years later, in the study
entitled Harbor Island, Lake George (Figs. 136-137), a foreground
collection of rocks remains but is radically subordinated to
forms that are controlled more fully by the geometry of the
painting. Finally, in two late studies (Figs. 138-141), one of
which is dated 1878, the interest in recreating the minutiae of
particular natural forms has completely disappeared. Nearly
every aspect of nature that participates in an order independent
of the order of the painting has been excluded. In these last
studies, Durand has reached the critical point at which the
order of nature and the transcendental order of the painting
meet. Any greater stress on the order of nature would disrupt
the order of the picture, and any greater stress on the order
of the picture would shatter nature. The same critical balance
is maintained in Durand's last major composition--View of Black
Mountain from the Harbor Islands, Lake George (1875, Fig. 142),
based on at least three drawings and one oil study--and in his
last composition, Souvenir of the Adirondacks of 1878 (Fig. 143).

In addition to the order of the picture, which by the 1870's
coincides with the order of nature, there is another kind of
order in Durand's landscapes. Where the geometric order of the
picture controls the arrangement of imagery on the picture plane,
the order of atmosphere controls the position of objects in
space. Durand's landscapes of the 1830's certainly reflect an
interest in the problems of defining space by atmospheric grada-

tions.  But it was probably not until he painted <u>The</u> <u>Beeches</u>
in 1844 or 1845 that, under the influence of Gilpin, he came
to regard atmospheric perspective as subject to proportion.
An insistence upon proportionate gradation is apparent in Dur-
and's comments on atmosphere in the <u>Letters</u> <u>on</u> <u>Landscape</u> <u>Painting</u>:

> First direct your attention to the <u>dark</u> portions of the
> scene, the shaded sides of objects, and the shadows
> cast by them on the ground and on each other.  In the
> first place you will find these darks have lost some-
> thing in strength, and not only are they weaker but
> less distinctly marked with details, and more negative
> in color, as if by the infusion of a bluish gray,
> scarcely perceptible at first, but more obvious further
> on.  This invariably takes place at the first remove
> from the foreground, and must be carefully expressed,
> whether the eye discerns it or not, for it is a prin-
> ciple, (I have reference to objects seen in a clear
> day, all under the same conditions).  At every remove,
> then, the darks become weaker and weaker, and their
> details or markings within them fainter and fainter.
>
> I call your attention first to the darks, because
> their variations are more palpable and thorough, (espe-
> cially in color) than those of the lights, but the
> latter also undergo material changes, gradually losing
> their details, becoming softer in texture, and weaker,
> though not so essentially changed, in color; till at
> length, when individual form is no longer distinguish-

able, the mingling light and dark are resolved into
one mass of comparatively uniform color, as in the far
distant mountain. The sum of all this is simply the
natural gradation from darker to lighter, stronger to
weaker, on a principle as fixed as the chromatic scale
in music; and the practiced eye of the artist will
detect the slightest discord in the one, as will the
sensitive ear in the other.[128]

As, in the studies, a mental act of clarification takes precedence
over the recording of pure, physical sensations of light, so, in
the representation of space, the gradation of atmosphere should
be controlled by reason rather than empirical vision. This
regulative act of the mind may affect the atmosphere of both
the studies and the compositions.

G.  Classification of Images.

In the light of the foregoing discussion of Durand's oil
studies, we may suggest the use of the terms "empirical,"
"conceptual," and "synthetic" to denote three different kinds
of images:

1.  An empirical image would be one in which the indivi-
    dual forms, their arrangement on the picture plane,
    and their order in space are all determined primarily
    by the experience of the eye alone.

2.  A conceptual image would be one in which the forms
    and their spatial order are determined primarily by
    the mind.

3.  A synthetic image would be one in which the eye
    and the mind co-operate in the realization of
    forms and their planar-spatial ordination.

Using these terms we may summarize the broad development of Dur-
and's work as a landscape painter as follows:

STUDIES FROM NATURE          COMPOSITIONS

1830-1843

Form, empirical.

Order of picture plane,
   empirical.

Order of space, empirical.

(E.g., Fig. 104).

Form, conceptual.

Order of picture plane, conceptual.

Order of space, conceptual.

(E.g., Fig. 75).

1844-1847

As above.

(E.g., Fig. 106).

Forms, empirical, but corrected
   in the studio.

Order of picture plane, conceptual.

Order of space, conceptual (more
   thoroughly rationalized than
   in the 1830's).

(E.g., Fig. 108).

1848-1860

Form, synthetic.

Order of picture plane,
   empirical.

Order of space, synthetic.

(E.g., Fig. 131).

Form, synthetic.

Order of picture plane:
   a. forest-interiors, synthetic
   b. others, conceptual

Order of space:
   a. forest-interiors, synthetic
   b. others, conceptual

(E.g., Figs. 169 and 151).

1861-1870

| | |
|---|---|
| Form, synthetic. | Same as 1848-1860. |
| Order of picture plane, synthetic. | (E.g., Figs. 183 and 197). |
| Order of space, synthetic. | |
| (E.g., Fig. 132) | |

1870-1879

| | |
|---|---|
| Same as 1861-1870, but with a suppression of minute detail within the contours of things. | Form, synthetic. |
| | Order of the picture plane, synthetic. |
| (E.g., Fig. 138). | Order of space, synthetic. |
| | (E.g., Fig. 163). |

From this summary it is apparent that Durand's late studies and his last compositions are as pervasively the products of the mind as were his first compositions of the 1830's. In the late works, however, he succeeds in welding together the order of the human mind and a deep and immediate experience of natural phenomena. In the late works we may discover an adequate expression of the Stoic notion of the essential participation of the human reason in the Reason that creates and sustains the cosmos. Where, in the earlier works, Durand expressed the identity between the human and Cosmic Reason metaphorically, through the imposition of an arbitrary order in the compositions, in the late works he was able to discern in nature itself an order that approximated the kind of order he had previously imposed upon nature. The discovery of Lake George in the 1860's, we may suppose, saved Durand from the Naturalist's surrender to the

order of the manifold, a point of view which he closely skirted
in the forest-interiors. The discovery of Lake George permitted him to preserve a transcendental geometric order without
violation of the data generated in his synthetic contemplation
of actual scenery. In the most general terms, the evolution
of Durand's style parallels that of Paul Cézanne, who also moved
from a conceptual (1860's) to an empirical (1870's) and ultimately
(1880's and following) to a synthetic style that, like Durand's,
continues to incorporate the experience of nature.

IV.  Preparatory Versus Scientific Studies.

As a postscript to a discussion of Durand's studies from nature, we may, I believe, draw a distinction between preparatory studies and those studies, which for want of a better word, I shall call "scientific." When, in the late 1830's, Durand was at work on his figure compositions The Dance on the Battery and The Pedlar, he made a number of drawings of single figures and groups which reappear in the paintings. In making these drawings Durand was primarily concerned with working out the requisite gestures, postures, movements, and relationships of figures. They were not undertaken as a means to acquire a more thorough knowledge of the human figure as such. At an earlier date, in drawing from the plaster casts at the American and the National Academies, his aim was mainly to increase his knowledge of the ideal human figure. These "scientific" studies aided the artist in the acquisition of a complete mental image or knowledge of the object.

Durand's painted landscape studies may also be regarded as "scientific," rather than preparatory, studies. Often, it is true, he did introduce motifs from a study into a studio composition. When he did so, the borrowed motif is always transformed, never merely transferred. But, also, we should note that many of the painted studies were never directly exploited in the studio. The oil studies and the landscape drawings stand as a body of work akin to a student's accumulation of exercises. Dur-

and's real preparatory drawings for the landscape compositions
must have been made exclusively on the canvas itself.

As long as the human mind was regarded as a sort of slate
upon which sensory experience automatically inscribes itself,
an artist might at the beginning of his career, as a student,
store up a variety of forms by intensely studying casts and
the living model for a restricted period of time. Hence, in
the late eighteenth and early nineteenth centuries the <u>student</u>
was advised to imitate scrupulously the form set before him.
In his "First Discourse," Sir Joshua Reynolds complained that
in all of the academies he had ever visited "the students never
draw exactly from the living models which they have before
them. It is not, indeed, their intention, nor are they directed
to do it."[129] And, in the same place, Reynolds states:

> He who endeavors to copy nicely the figure before
> him, not only acquires a habit of exactness and pre-
> cision, but is continually advancing in his knowledge
> of the human figure; and though he seems to superficial
> observers to make slower progress, he will be found
> at last capable of adding (without running into capri-
> cious wildness) that grace and beauty which is necessary
> to be given to his more finished works, and which
> cannot be got by the moderns, as it was not acquired
> by the ancients, but by an attentive and well compared
> study of the human form.[130]

Benjamin West described the task of the student in similar
terms:

In your progress through that mechanical part of
your professional education, which is directed to the
acquisition of a perfect knowledge of the human figure,
I recommend to you a scrupulous exactness in imitating
what is immediately before you, in order that you may
acquire the habit of observing with precision every
object that presents itself to your sight. Accustom
yourself to draw all the deviations of the figure, till
you are as much acquainted with them as with the alphabet of your own language, and can make them with as
much facility as your letters; for they are indeed the
letters and alphabet of your profession, whether it be
painting or sculpture.[131]

As late as the 1820's, West's pupil Samuel F. B. Morse could
inform the students at the National Academy that:

Correctness is the first great requisite in Drawing.
Your great object should be to imitate the model before
you precisely as it appears, with all of its apparent
blemishes, too, if any part of it should seem defective
to you.[132]

And an anonymous author in the United States Review and Literary
Gazette for 1827 warned the National Academy's students of the
dangers of approximate sketches:

young artists . . . should be the least forward to exhibit pen and ink or pencil sketches . . . The pen and
ink or pencil sketch is only interesting from the hand
of a master, who, from long practice and perfect know-

ledge, can give a meaning to a single dash, can embody a thought in a single line, which must necessarily baffle the attempts of a less experienced hand,
and which the stripling student should, least of all,
essay to produce. Real facility of sketching is
acquired only by patient industry and persevering
toil, and no careless scratching and flourishing of
the pencil will ever pass as valuable with the discriminating connoisseur. . . . One carefully finished
object,--if it be but an apple,--where attention has
been paid to its drawing, its light and shade, and its
color, is of more real benefit to the young artist,
and more certainly indicative of talent, than fifty
careless, idle scratches.[133]

Until such time as "by patient industry and perserving toil" the
student has attained a "perfect knowledge" he is to abjure general
sketches in favor of highly finished, complete studies. But the
master, who "can give meaning to a simple dash," is no longer
expected to restrict himself to scrupulous study.

By the time Durand wrote his Letters on Landscape Painting,
the idea that the artist ought to master particular forms was
no novelty. What is new in Durand's mature practice is that
he intensified, rather than diminished, his study of the particular forms of nature. In drawing and painting from nature,
Durand carried on to the end of his career a practice which,in
an earlier period,had been regarded as exclusively appropriate
to the student. Durand's enduring concern with the scrupulous

study of nature was the effect of at least three separate causes. We have already touched upon each.

1. The concept of nature as something infinite, which the artist may pursue but never grasp. Each study is the path to knowledge of a new aspect of nature.

2. The idea that knowledge is not automatically inscribed on the tablet of the mind, but is created by an act of the mind itself. As a knowledge of nature depends in part upon the mind, it may be deepened with each successive mental act. What to the eighteenth century seemed attainable by a short period of arduous toil, becomes ultimately unattainable to the Romantic and Realist.

3. The concept of the representation of nature as an act in harmony with nature. As the act is a value in itself, it yields its unique value in degree at each occurrence of the act. As a spiritual exercise, it can lead to that harmony between the self and nature that is a form of redemption.

# CHAPTER FIVE: THE REALITY OF THE PAINTED WORLD.

Durand's mature work as a landscape painter rests firmly upon the concept that the painting should be primarily determined, not by a special set of laws governing picture-making, but by something completely foreign to art--that is, by the artist's sophisticated experience of nature. Yet, if this were the only concept governing his art, his paintings would amount to nothing more than scientific illustrations, lacking any of those fascinating and moving qualities which they do, indeed, possess. The fact that the studio compositions insistently deviate from any of the known studies of nature--either drawings or paintings--clearly indicates that they are controlled by objectives other than the mere effort to imitate the forms and effects of a particular segment of nature. These additional objectives amount, I believe, to three of major importance:

1.  The effort to arrange the imagery of the painting in such a way that the spectator may accept the painted world as a "real" world in which he may wander.

2.  The effort to arrange the imagery of the painting in such a way that the emotions of the spectator will be moved.

3.  The effort to arrange the painting in such a way as to excite in the spectator an awareness of his proximity to God.

These three objectives we may examine in this and the following two chapters.

.   .   .

While the landscape gardener may assemble and arrange the real objects of nature in such a way that the spectator can walk among them, the landscape painter cannot. The painted world of the picture must lack the magnitude, the life, and the material substance of the real world of nature. Lacking these qualities it cannot, obviously, possess the absolute reality of nature itself. If the forms in a painting, however, cannot be real, they may be selected and managed in such a way as to seem real in a greater or less degree. There are innumerable devices which the painter might apply to increase the apparent reality of the world in the picture. The following are those which Durand most commonly employed:

1.  The selection of phenomena that are normally accepted as real upon the evidence of the sense of sight.

2.  The presentation of forms in such a way that the spectator is induced to believe that he might touch them should he wish to do so.

3.  The presentation of forms in such a way that they may constitute the spectator's environment.

Each of these factors plays a more or less significant role in Durand's work as a landscape painter. Each contributed to the high degree of reality that he was able to bestow upon the painted scene.

I. The Selection of Visible Phenomena.

In daily experience we infer the reality of phenomena from their effect upon our sense of sight, touch, and/or hearing. In many cases we acknowledge the reality of phenomena when they affect only one sense. A sound may be regarded as real because it is heard even though it can be neither touched nor seen. We become aware of the existence of air when, in violent motion, it affects the sense of touch or hearing, although the air itself is not seen. Light and atmosphere can be seen but neither touched nor heard. Only objects normally affect two senses--sight and touch; but, rightly or not, we are usually willing to acquiesce in the fact of an object's existence when it immediately affects but one sense. We deny the reality neither of an object felt in the dark nor of one seen at a distance. In our experience of objects, their reality is confirmed rather than suggested when they affect both sight and touch. However, this level of certainty is rarely sought, since our experience of other phenomena leads us into the habit of accepting as real that which affects one sense alone.

The fact that we normally allow the evidence of a single sense to serve as evidence for the reality of phenomena is probably the basic condition upon which the "reality" of a painted image depends. Typically, Durand's landscape paintings embrace those phenomena alone which do affect the sense of sight--light, atmosphere, and objects. Sun-set light holds an important place in many of Durand's landscapes, while the more diffused light of forenoon or afternoon pervades others. With few exceptions, his landscapes display a definite presence of light, to the exclusion of passages of obscurity. Illuminated by sunlight, water vapors assume distinct form in clouds and hover over the earth in a pervasive haze without form. Light and atmosphere are, in our daily experience, perceived only by the sense of sight. And, we should have no more reason to question their reality when seen in the painting than when seen in nature. That we acknowledge the "reality" of the light and atmosphere in the painting from the evidence of a single sense must predispose us to acknowledge the reality of other visible phenomena upon the same criterion. Because earth forms, trees, buildings, and figures are seen, we may be willing to believe that they are real things. This sense of their reality must be heightened as they are seen from a distance so that their reality is not immediately accessible to the test of touch. Hence, the phenomena in the painting may be described as "real" for the same reason that we acknowledge the reality of similar phenomena in nature.

It is notable that Durand generally excluded one aspect of nature to which other landscape painters had devoted especial attention--that is, the movement of objects by the movement of air. Wind is implied in Cole's Expulsion from the Garden of Eden of 1828 (Fig. 202) and is the major motif in his Tornado in the Wilderness of 1836 (Fig. 144). And in London, Durand had seen some of Constable's oil studies of the effect of movements of air upon masses of water vapor. The implication

of wind entails a particular disadvantage which may have
deterred Durand from attempting it:  namely, wind being invisible can be indicated only be representing its effect upon
something else.  Cole showed its effect upon trees, and Constable sought to record its effect upon clouds.  In either case
the existence of the phenomena, in the pictures, can be inferred
only from its effect upon something else.  Hence, the spectator
cannot become aware of its "presence" until he has undertaken
a line of critical thought, which if applied also to his experience of the objects represented must immediately lead to an
awareness of their unreality.  Whether consciously or not, Dur-
and did avoid any reference to phenomena that could excite a
critical attitude toward the reality of other phenomena.

## II. Trompe-l'oeil.

Thus far, in discussing the "reality" of the painted forms, we have assumed that they cannot be touched. When we see a tree represented, we can touch the painting but not the "tree." If the painted "tree" were accessible to the sense of touch, the spectator might accept it as being as real as a tree in the forest. Such a painted tree would differ from a real tree in that it possesses less material substance and does not participate in the rhythmic growth and decay of the vegetable world. But, obviously, a tangible tree could not exist on the flat surface of a canvas. It is possible, however, for an artist to represent an object in such a way that the spectator may be induced to believe that he _might_ touch it. The illusion of tangibility may be created if an object is represented in a position from which the spectator might remove it without physically violating the space of the painting. Normally, the imagery of a realistic painting is protected by a "glass" before the whole. Were we able to extend a hand into a realistic painting, the difference in scale between our hand and the forms represented would immediately render the whole situation ridiculous. But, if the objects, realistically represented, adhere to a plane parallel to and nearly coincident with the picture plane and retain their normal size, the spectator might then become convinced of their tangibility and try to pluck them off. These, it seems to me, are the minimum conditions under which the illusion of _trompe-l'oeil_ is produced. The

illusion of trompe-l'oeil may be vastly increased if there is
something about the object represented that strongly moves the
spectator's desire to pick it up. Thus, the trompe-l'oeil
representation of a fifty-dollar bill will at once suggest to
the spectator that he can pick it up and at the same time offer
a strong incentive that he do so.

Among Durand's works of the 1830's there are several that
display an effort toward trompe-l'oeil representation. The
earliest of these, a work supervised if not actually executed
by Durand, is the engraved floral and leaf border to the study
of rocks and trees on the cover of The American Landscape
(Fig. 145), published in December of 1830.[1] Here, the objects
are represented against a background parallel to and coincident
with the picture plane. The leaves and flowers are in no way
attached to this background, upon which they cast shadows.[2]
Conventional as these botanical forms are, they are represented
in such a way that the spectator is invited to accept them
momentarily as real objects. While, in the border, the forms
created by art tend to become "nature," in the picture which
the border frames, nature--a mass of rock called Mambrino's
Helmet--tends to become an object created by art. Hence, in
frame and picture there is a kind of rapprochement between
nature and art.

Seven years later, Durand's thoughts returned to the possibilities of trompe-l'oeil representation. On June 22, 1837,
Durand and his wife set out with Thomas and Mrs. Cole to explore
the scenery around Schroon Lake.[3] A drawing, inscribed "June 19th,

1837 Procured this book" (Fig. 146), must have formed part of a sketchbook purchased by Durand for use on this trip. Since the inscription recording the date of purchase appears upon this page, it is not unlikely that it was the first in the book. This idea is substantiated by the fact that Durand has made it into a title-page. At the top center appears the word "sketch" and at the bottom center, the letters "A," "N," and "D" and the inscription "New York / 1837." The total inscription would probably read "Sketch / Book / Asher B. Durand / New York / 1837" were it not that several of the words are entirely or in great part "covered" by three landscape drawings represented en trompe-l'oeil. In this case the spectator is especially invited to pick up the fake pages in order to see the drawings on the second two sheets and to read the inscription beneath all three. It is particularly interesting that Durand should have made this excursion into trompe-l'oeil at the very outset of his career as a serious landscape painter and during one of his first journeys into the country to collect material for landscape paintings.

That Durand, in 1837, did wish to create landscape paintings possessing the reality of trompe-l'oeil still-life is curiously suggested by a dream he described to Thomas Cole in a letter, dated December 25, 1837:

> I have dreamed of you, I think more than once, but parti-
> cularly last night. Among other things I thought myself
> at your place, and being in great haste as usual, lest
> the steam boat should leave me, I felt extreme impatience
> to see some of your works but you were very tardy & only

gratified me after all, with a sight of what you introduced as a new style of painting, which consisted of a
folding screen painted in part and the rest covered
with actual leaves & flowers, profusely interspersed
with a variety of doll babies & so much of attraction
did it possess, that I could hardly get a view in consequence of the crowd of Ladies that were visiting you
and expressing their admiration, and withal, the Dolls
and Ladies were so mixed together, that I could scarcely
tell which were the living ones.  I thought to myself,
that I would rather see your composition of Schroon
Mountains which you have cut in two, but some how or
other, you were not disposed to show it to me and so it
ended now the only interpretation that I shall offer to
said dream is that you have not been out of my thoughts,
if I have defered writing.[4]

On January 4, 1838, Cole replied:

Your dream of doll babies &c. may admit of fuller interpretation than merely that I have been in your thoughts.[5]

Durand's dream seems to throw considerable light upon his motives
and objectives.  First of all, Durand appears to wish to evade
Cole.  He has "defered writing" to him; and when, in his dream,
he visited Cole, he felt anxiety over the possibility of his
being left behind by the boat.  Further, in the dream he was
impatient to see paintings by Cole which Cole was reluctant to
show.  Possibly Durand's impatience and Cole's reluctance
stemmed from Durand's desire that Cole should show paintings

of a kind Durand preferred, rather than those which Cole actually
did paint. This is borne out by the fact that the painting Cole
finally showed to Durand was quite like one which Durand painted
in 1837--the Landscape with Children (Fig. 75). Here is a
scene "painted . . . with leaves & flowers . . . interspersed
with a variety of doll babies." But the leaves, flowers, and
doll babies in the dream are no longer merely trompe-l'oeil
representations. They are thrust out into the spectator's space
and become thoroughly tangible forms, as real as any other forms
in the world of daily life. The spectators are described as a
very eager and appreciative group of ladies who eventually are
absorbed into the reality of the painting--becoming Musidoras,
Ariadnes, or the Frank sisters.

However we may ultimately interpret Durand's dream, it is
clear that he dreamed of paintings in which the representation
of objects should give way to the presentation of objects them-
selves--objects possessing both a visual and tangible reality.
That Cole did not paint such pictures appears to have somewhat
disturbed Durand. A certain distaste for Cole's painting is
suggested by Durand's dream desire to see the former's "composition of Schroon Mountains . . . cut in two." And indeed,
despite superficial visual similarities, it is difficult to
imagine two directions in art more divergent in motive than
Durand's and Cole's. At the same time that Durand dreamed of
an art of realities, Cole was experimenting with non-objective
color notations that should stir the emotions, like the tones
of music, independently of any reference to the forms of

nature.[6] As early as November 8, 1834, Cole had conceived of
a "color piano" based upon the idea of the "music of colours."
On that day he wrote in his journal:

> I believe that colours are capable of affecting the
> mind, by combinations, degree, and arrangement, like
> sound. . . . It is evident that there is an analogy
> between colour and sound; and with study and experiment
> it might be traced through all of its ramifications.
> I am not aiming to prove the analogy, but to show that
> there is plausibility in the theory that an instrument
> might be constructed by which colour could be played,
> and which would give to those, who had cultivated their
> taste in the art, a pleasure like that given by music.
>
> If I attempted to make an instrument, I should try
> the experiment with six colours and their semitints.
> . . . The instrument might be played by means of keys,
> like those of a piano, except, that instead of their
> moving hammers to strike strings, they might lift,
> when struck, dark or black screens from before coloured
> compartments. Transparent compartments, with either
> sunlight or artificial light behind, would perhaps
> produce the most brilliant effect.[7]

This was written on the eve of Cole's return to New York for
the winter, and did not immediately lead to the construction of
a machine. Possibly, his thoughts returned to this problem at
the end of 1837. For in the letter, already mentioned, written
to Durand on January 4, 1838, he states that he has been "making

a new kind of musical instrument, which if _it_ shall ever play,
and _I_ shall ever play, you shall hear, when you come to Catskill."[8] In the same letter he mentions the birth of a son on
New Year's Day. Soon the problems presented by the infant
usurped his concern with the musical instrument, for on February
12, he wrote to Durand: "I find that there is little need of
inventing musical instruments, when there are so many of Adam's
patent. I find I have a pretty loud toned one of that sort."[9]
Whether or not the musical instrument upon which Cole worked
early in 1838 was a "color piano," it is clear that in 1834 he
had conceived of an instrument which should excite emotion by
the presentation of varied colors alone. His interest in the
expressiveness of color was one of the factors which made Cole
adhere to the conception of a painting as something to appeal to
the eye--a vision--rather than to the sense of touch. If, when
Durand made his _trompe-l'oeil_ drawing in 1837 during his excursion to Schroon Lake with Cole, they had discussed the problem
of the degree to which the forms of a painting might or ought
to become visual-tactile realities, Cole politely settled the
issue when in a letter to Durand of March 20, 1838, he wrote:
"Pleasant things are dreams, unpleasant ones realities."[10]
Durand, however, did not accept the verdict and continued to
seek some way in which the forms in a painting might be invested
with the reality of things encountered in daily experience--or,
short of that, with the reality of the forms of a _trompe-l'oeil_
still-life.

III.  The Painted World as the Spectator's Environment.

Certainly, it would be impossible to paint trompe-l'oeil
landscapes.  As long as objects are represented within the space
of the painting, the spectator is unable to extend his hand
toward the fictional object.  But, although a "pane of glass"
protects the space of the painting from physical violation, the
images of a landscape painting may be so managed that the spectator may be induced to imagine that he possess a sort of small
body which may enter into the fictional scene.  By observing
the hand in proximity to a wide variety of objects, we develop
a rather definite idea of its magnitude, but of the magnitude
of the body as a whole we have no such fixed notion.  Hence,
while we cannot conceive of extending the hand into the space of
a small painting, we may believe that the whole body might easily
enter.  Or, perhaps, the entry of the spectator into the space
of the painting is made possible by the detachability of the
consciousness from the body.  While standing in the heat of the
sun and looking at a cool valley in the distance, we may "experience" the sensations which we should feel were we there.  The
spectator will more readily enter into a painted scene in proportion to its representation of pleasing rather than terrifying
incidents or objects.  Moreover, the spectator may enter the
painting, still able to walk and receive visual as well as
tactile sensations, in proportion as an accessible and adequate
plane upon which he may stand is provided and as the varied forms
of the painting are presented with a high degree of clarity.

There can be no doubt that Durand wished the spectator to enter the world of the painting. In his <u>Letters</u> <u>on</u> <u>Landscape</u> <u>Painting</u> he specified that as "a fine picture which at once takes possession of you--draws you into it--you traverse it--breathe its atmosphere--feel its sunshine, and you repose in its shade. . . ."[11] Elsewhere in the <u>Letters</u> Durand speaks of the spectator:

> . . . his dinner partaken, and himself disposed of in
> his favorite arm-chair, with one or more faithful land-
> scapes before him, and making no greater effort than
> to look into the picture instead of on it, so as to
> perceive what it represents; in proportion as it is true
> and faithful, many a fair vision of forgotten days will
> animate the canvas, and lead him through the scene:
> pleasant reminiscences and grateful emotions will spring
> up at every step, and care and anxiety will retire far
> behind him. If he possess aught of imaginative tissue
> . . . he becomes absorbed in the picture--a gentle
> breeze fans his forehead, and he hears a distant rum-
> bling; they come not from the canvas, but through the
> open window casement. No matter, they fall purified
> on his sensorium, and <u>that</u> is far away.[12]

The spectator may enter the painting. He may move about over the painted ground, breathe, be warmed by the sun, relax in the shade, feel breezes, hear sounds--in short live as he would in the world of daily life. Durand's use of the term "sensorium" suggests that he believed the spectator's entry into the painting is due to the detachability of consciousness from the physical body.

In order to induce the spectator to enter the painting, Durand employed several devices, certain of which can already be seen in one of the illusionistic door panels--Boys Playing Marbles (Fig. 64)--painted in 1836 for Luman Reed's Gallery. First, the front edge of the ground-plane meets the lower edge of the painting. Second, there is no obstacle to prevent the spectator's simply "stepping" into the painting, as he might step through opened French windows onto a terrace. And third, there is nothing to prevent the spectator from traversing the entire extent of the ground-plane to its most distant point. All three devices reappear in landscapes throughout Durand's career--Sunday Morning (1839, Fig. 73), Farm Yard on the Hudson (1843, Fig. 87), The Old Man's Lesson (1845, Fig. 82), View in the Catskills (1847, Fig. 150), Thanatopsis (1850, Fig. 204), High Point, Shandaken Mountains (1853, Fig. 154), In the Woods (1855, Fig. 169), and Summer Afternoon (1865, Fig. 159). In the Boys Playing Marbles the invitation to enter the painting becomes more insistent as none of the figures confront the spectator with a direct and forbidding gaze; as a figure stands looking into the painting's space with her back to the spectator; and another figure points into the distance, directing her gaze and ours. The motif of a figure pointing or looking into the picture reappears in other paintings. Pointing figures are seen in the Sunday Morning (1839, Fig. 73), Landscape, View of Rutland

Vermont (1840, Fig. 77), and The Morning of Life (note the
statue, 1840, Fig. 85). Figures merely looking into the distance may be noted in The Evening of Life (1840, Fig. 86) and
An Old Man's Reminiscences (Fig. 80). In viewing the paintings
just ennumerated, the spectator is able to imagine himself stepping into the painted world and rambling about on foot at will.
The painting stands as a kind of park into which the spectator
can, in imagination, escape and find relief from the anxieties
of the world without tiring the physical body, which he leaves
behind.

In addition to these devices, Durand regarded the influence
of atmosphere as the decisive factor, serving to draw the spectator's consciousness into the space of the painting. The function
of atmosphere he described in his Letters on Landscape Painting
in the following terms, addressing the student:

> When you shall have acquired some proficiency in fore-
> ground material, your next step should be the study of
> the influence of atmosphere . . . an intangible agent,
> visible, yet without that material substance which be-
> longs to imitable objects, in fact, an absolute nothing,
> yet of mighty influence. It is that which above all
> other agencies, carries us into the picture, instead
> of allowing us to be detained in front of it; not the
> door-keeper but the grand usher and master of ceremonies,
> and conducting us through all the vestibules, chambers
> and secret recesses of the great mansion, explaining on

the way, the meaning and purposes of all that is
visible, and satisfying us that all is in its proper
place.[13]

According to Durand, atmosphere is "the power which defines and
measures space."[14] As that which defines space, atmosphere
establishes between near and more distant objects the intervals
through which the spectator may amble.

An analysis of Durand's _Landscape, Sunday Morning_ (Fig. 148)
in terms of the literary text by which it was inspired will
permit us to discover something of the subtlety with which Durand
was able to use the device of rendering the painted world accessible to the spectator. When the painting was exhibited at the
National Academy in 1850, Durand printed two verses from Bryant's
short poem--"A Scene on the Banks of the Hudson"--in the exhibition catalogue:

And o'er the clear water swells
The music of the Sabbath bells--[15]

In composing the painting Durand followed the imagery of the
entire poem quite closely. The foreground enjoys a certain shade,
the Hudson lies largely unrippled, save for the gentle lapping of
water at the left. A church spire across the river suggests
"the music of Sabbath bells." And the solitary figure stands on
a "little nook of land, circled with trees." But for the point
of land and the distant "line of hills," all is water or sky--the
former reflecting the latter. Hence, the contemplative figure
gazes "into the airy deep."

So far, the painting is merely a visual translation of the
poem.  But, now, we must note that the spectator who only looks
at the painting sees nothing of the loveliness described by the
speaker in the poem.  The speaker sees little but the void of
sky and the sky-reflecting water.  The spectator, however, sees
a very different scene.  In his eye the massive trees dominate
the scene.  It is only by ceasing to look at the painting, it
is only by entering the painting and identifying himself with
the figure in the painting, that the spectator may share the
vision of the speaker, that is, the figure represented.

Finally, the poet insists that beauty is ephemeral and more
beautiful for that reason.  Had Durand simply represented the
vision of sky and water, he would have bestowed a permanence
upon it which should destroy much of its beauty.  But, since
this beauty beyond the trees is only to be glimpsed as the spectator makes the effort to project himself into the painting, the
vision is necessarily lost when that effort is relaxed.  Thus,
even in the enduring visual representation, the vision retains
that increment of beauty derived from its transience.

In other paintings a figure or group is placed upon a foreground knoll, from which the middle-ground of the landscape is
inaccessible.  The foreground figure looking or pointing off to
the distance may be seen in the View Toward the Hudson Valley
(Fig. 189), Dover Plains (1848), Kindred Spirits (1849, Fig. 201),
Progress (1853, cf. Fig. 90), and Hudson River, View of the
Fishkill Mountains (1856, Fig. 194).  Closely related to this
group is another in which we find the same type of ground-plane--

i.e., a foreground knoll or precipice, onto which the spectator may "step," beyond which lies an inaccessible valley--as
seen in the <u>View Toward the Hudson Valley</u>--but without any
foreground figures. This group includes the <u>Franconia Notch</u>
(1857, Fig. 196), <u>The Catskills</u> (1859, Fig. 180), and the
<u>Catskill Clove</u> (1866, Fig. 197).

Finally, there is a late group of paintings in which the
ground-plane is inaccessible to the spectator, as its front edge
falls below the lower edge of the painting. In order to "walk
into" these paintings--<u>Landscape</u> (1866, Fig. 160), <u>Scene Among
the Berkshire Hills</u> (1872, Fig. 162), <u>Lake George, View of
Black Mountain from the Harbor Islands, Lake George</u> (1875,
Fig. 163), and <u>Souvenir of the Adirondacks</u> (1878, Fig. 164)--
the spectator would have to step or jump down from the lower
edge of the painting in order to gain access to the ground-plane.
This last group of paintings is closely related to the <u>View
Toward the Hudson Valley</u>, but lacks the <u>répoussoir</u> knoll or
precipice.

In looking back over the several different treatments of
the ground-plane, a certain development may be noted in Durand's
work. Normally, in his earlier paintings--1836 to 1847--the
spectator may "walk into" the painting and traverse its whole
extent "on foot." These paintings permit the spectator to leave
the weight of his real body behind, as he rambles about without
fatigue in the painted world. While this first type continues
to appear up to the end of his career, from 1848 to 1856 Durand
painted a number of pictures in which contemplative figures

occupy a foreground knoll, precipice, or point of land beyond
which they cannot proceed, being barred from the middle-ground
and distance by a radical discontinuity of ground or by a body
of water. In viewing these paintings the spectator is able to
identify himself with the contemplative figure, but he is unable
to "walk" beyond the station of that figure. These paintings
were followed by another group in which an uninhabited foreground
height, accessible to the spectator, precedes an inaccessible
valley. In viewing these the spectator is able to "enter" upon
the precipice but go no farther. In the last group of paintings--
1866 to 1878--the landscape becomes entirely inaccessible to
the spectator. While this account of Durand's treatment of the
ground-plane fairly well fits the compositions that are known,
some revision or qualification may become necessary when more
of his paintings have been located.

In looking at the early type of landscape with its continuous ground-plane, the spectator sees a single scene. As he
"walks" into the picture the scene constantly changes as his
relationship to things changes. In these paintings the spectator may encounter hundreds of views within the initial scene.
The second and third types of pictures--those in which there
is a radical discontinuity of ground--offer only two major views.
In looking at the Landscape, Sunday Morning (Fig. 148), the
spectator first sees a group of trees and a broad river. But
once he has "walked" across the foreground plane to the nearer
bank of the river, he encounters a scene of a totally different
character. The opposing elements of the first view give way to

the calm harmony of the second. But the world of this second
picture may not be traversed on foot. The multitude of views
accessible to the spectator in the landscape with continuous
ground-plane is not accessible to the spectator who looks into
the picture within the Landscape, Sunday Morning. This spectator is brought to a halt and can only look at the single view
before him--at least, he can only look at the single view as
long as he regards himself as a being that can traverse nothing
but firm ground. The late paintings, lacking any accessible
foreground plane, would seem entirely to share the limitation
of the picture within the picture of the landscapes with a discontinuity of ground. In looking at View of Black Mountain
from the Harbour Islands, Lake George (Fig. 163), we can set
foot nowhere; we must remain outside the painting, gazing with
longing at the inaccessible world seen through the window that
is the picture's frame. That is, again, the scene remains
inaccessible as long as we remain subject to the limitations
of our physical nature.

But we are now faced with a problem. If, after 1847, Durand
frequently created ground-planes which the spectator can only
traverse to a limited degree, or not at all, how can we reconcile
this aspect of his painting with his statement of 1855 that
"That is a fine picture which at once takes possession of you--
draws you into it--you traverse it--breathe its atmosphere--feel
its sunshine, and you repose in its shade"?[16] In viewing such
paintings as the View Toward the Hudson Valley (1851), The
Catskills (1859, Fig. 180), or the Catskill Clove (1866, Fig. 197),

the spectator can, indeed, enter the painting, but he can
"walk" only over the more ragged and unpleasant foreground
knoll or ledge. What lies beyond he can only contemplate.
But what really happens when the spectator "walks into" a
painting to contemplate a more distant view? In "entering"
the painting or in identifying with the figure represented in
the painting, the spectator leaves behind his physical body.
He retains consciousness, receives sensations, but is no longer
subject to the laws governing the movement of his body. He
enters the painting as a human consciousness alone. If he can
forget that he has a physical body of a certain magnitude and
weight long enough to get into the painting at all, he may also
realize that, without a body, he can move about without a solid
ground upon which to tread. Thus, if a discontinuity of the
ground-plane prevents his "walking" over the entire landscape,
there is no reason why he cannot spread the wings of the soul
and fly whither he will. The flight of the soul differs from
mere contemplation, for in contemplation the self retains a
fixed position while looking at something. The soul in flight
carries all that is essentially the self to the distant form.
In paintings such as the View Toward the Hudson Valley or
Catskill Clove the foreground knoll or precipice serves merely
as a take-off point for the flight of the soul. In the earlier
painting, the figures represented appear as the locust's shell
that still clings to the bough after the animal itself has
flown. In the later, a foreground platform implies this intermediate stage. From the last paintings, such as Souvenir of

the _Adirondacks_ (1878, Fig. 164), the intermediate stage has
been excluded altogether--the whole painting becoming the
visionary space in which the soul is free to fly at will.[17]

IV.  Landscape Painting and the Liberation of the Soul.

As the painted world gains in "reality," becoming at last
the spectator's environment, the spectator loses his material
nature, becoming a liberated spirit.  At first glance this must
seem to be a fairly extreme interpretation of Durand's realism.
If, however, we accept the idea that Durand turned initially
to landscape painting as a means to escape the vanities of a
commercial culture, it seems less improbable that he should
ultimately seek to liberate the soul from its material prison.
The kind of landscape which the spectator may traverse entirely
"on foot"--occuring throughout Durand's career as a landscape
painter--is closely related to the paintings from around 1838--
Rip Van Winkle, The Dance on the Battery, and Sunday Morning--
in which the idea of escape from the cares of ordinary life is
explicit in the theme.  The next step toward the type of painting requiring that the soul wing itself may be discerned in
paintings such as the Hudson River (Fig. 93).  Here, the spectator may walk into the picture up to the bank of the river.
From there he can only proceed by a different mode of transpor-
tation.  There he enters the boat, but in so doing he enters
the realm of a new sort of consciousness.  The cares of finding
one's way amid the objects of solid earth give way to that state
of revery, carelessness of mind, which boating is fitted to
induce.  But, the paintings from 1848 onward that display a
discontinuous ground or the lack of a foreground plane require
more of the spectator than a state of passive revery.  As the

spectator's spirit is launched into the space of the painting,
it experiences not the tranquilizing monotony of bobbing on a
sheet of water, but the fullness of mental activity, while it
encounters the plenitude of the infinite. Also, it enjoys not
a limited release from the bonds of life, but a full freedom
to effortlessly move where it will in the whole of space.

The "Platonic" notion of the soul's thirst for release from
its confinement in the material body was adopted by Seneca:

> Well, for my part I do give the preference in interest
> and study to those matters which bring the spirit peace:
> I examine first myself and then the universe. . . .
> all these subjects . . . do upraise and relieve the
> spirit yearning under its heavy load for expansion and
> a return to that from which it's sprung. For this body
> of ours is the spirit's burden and scourge: beneath
> its pressure the spirit travails in bondage, unless
> philosophy draws near and bids it breathe more freely
> in the contemplation of nature, and lets it pass from
> the earthly to the divine. This is its freedom, this
> its truancy: now and again it steals from the prison
> that confines it and refreshes itself with a glimpse of
> the heavens . . . the spirit, penned in this dim and
> dismal dwelling-place, seeks the open whenever it can,
> and finds repose in contemplating nature. The adept
> or the votary of philosophy doesn't part company with
> the body, it's true; but the best part of him is far
> away, and his thoughts projected into the sublime.[18]

The soul is the prisoner of the body and seeks freedom. In the experience of nature, the soul enjoys a certain sense of liberation. And, while the experience of nature is not sufficient to effect the full release of the soul, even according to Seneca, something of the self does temporarily escape.

In the nineteenth century, Romantic painters and writers frequently treated this longing of the soul for freedom. Washington Allston's St Peter Released from Prison by the Angel[19] of 1812 implies the idea of the release of the soul from the bonds of matter. In his "Remarks on the Character and Writings of John Milton," Channing noted that poetry is born as the soul, within the body, seeks relief from its constraint "in imaginings of unseen and ideal being."[20] The two ideas in Channing's statement--one, that the soul seeks relief from its constraint, and two, that it does so "in imaginings of unseen and ideal beings"--were later portioned out, the latter to the poets, the former to the painters. Thus, in "The Poetic Principle," Edgar Allan Poe points out "that loveliness whose very elements, perhaps, appertain to eternity alone," and regards the poetic effort as the result of the poet's striving to "grasp now wholly, here on earth, at once and forever, those divine and rapturous joys, of which through the poem . . . we attain to but brief and indeterminate glimpses."[21] To Poe, the poet is moved less by the repulsion of the earth than the attraction of heaven.

The landscape painter, limited to the images of temporal realities, might concern himself, not as Cole had done, with the image of Paradise (e.g., Old Age, from the Voyage of Life), but with the creation of a situation in the experience of which the soul of the spectator might find relief from its earthly constraint. This view was adopted by Durand's friend and patron, the Reverend Elias L. Magoon. In 1852, Magoon published in The Home Book of the Picturesque--a book dedicated to Durand by its publisher George P. Putnam--an essay entitled "Scenery and Mind." Among the more coherent parts of this rather obscure essay Magoon describes the conditions necessary to the liberation of the soul:

> The human soul, thirsting after immensity, immutability, and unbounded duration, needs some tangible object from which to take its flight--some point whence to soar from the present into the future, from the limited to the infinite. . . . Mere space, contemplated under the dome of heaven, prostrates, rather than sustains, the mind; but Alpine heights, seen at a glance where earth and sky mingle, constitute the quickening and fortifying regions where mundane understanding and celestial imagination most happily blend in the suggestion of thoughts such as common language never expressed. Deep caverns, contracted lakes, projecting crags, impending avalanches, and glittering pinnacles, which rise in serene majesty till they are lost in mist and cloud, rolling over their summits like the waves of an ocean, realize prospects which seem to conduct the contemplation from this to another world.[22]

Here, the emphasis is primarily upon the escape from terrestrial
confinement. And it is precisely "some point whence to soar
. . . from the limited to the infinite" which Durand began to
multiply in those of his paintings that display an elevated
foreground and a distant valley. It is the occasion and means
of escape that Durand provides, not the indistinct visions that
are to be fitfully apprehended in a spiritual realm. Freed from
the bonds of the earth, the spectator is free to pursue his own
"thoughts such as common language never expressed."

While Magoon's text seems adequately to describe and to
define the value of the structure of space in certain of Durand's
paintings, it is possible that both Magoon and Durand were inspired by a broader current of thought that emerged around 1850.
It is likely that Durand was aware of and interested in the
manifestations of the spiritual world that became especially
numerous in the late 1840's. While there is no positive evidence
to indicate that Durand gave any credence to any of the varied
displays of spiritual agency, there is ample evidence to indicate
that his closest friends did so. William Cullen Bryant attended
seances around 1850--both those of the Fox sisters and those
of Daniel D. Home[23]--and later confessed his belief in the
spiritual world:

> Holding to the doctrine that there is a world of the
> spirit as well as a world of matter, I am not prepared
> to say that there cannot be a direct action of the
> mind upon the mind without the interposition of a
> bodily presence.[24]

Further, the wife of Durand's friend, the sculptor Henry Kirke Brown,[25] was a medium. According to William James Stillman, who with Durand's son published The Crayon in the mid-1850's,

> Mrs. Brown explained the possession of her occult powers by a voice in the manner of Socrates' demon, which, she said, was always present with her, and which she recognized as entirely foreign to her. . . . When she asked who was speaking to her, she received only the reply, "We are spirit."[26]

Also, on one occasion Bryant told Stillman that Mrs. Brown "had recounted to him events in his past life not known to any living person except himself."[27] And Stillman himself maintained a faith in spiritualism to the end of his life:

> Two conclusions I draw from my investigations as immovably established, so far as I am concerned. The first is that there are about us, and with certain facilities for making themselves understood by us, spiritual individualities; and, second, that the human being possesses spiritual senses, parallel with the physical, by which it sees what the physical sense cannot see, and hears what is inaudible to the physical ear. And my general and, I think, logical conclusion is that the spiritual senses appertain to a spiritual body which survives the death of the physical.[28]

Amid so many spiritualist enthusiasts, it would seem at least possible that Durand was affected by the new movement.[29]

In the summer of 1847 Alexander Jackson Davis published his monumental _Principles of Nature, Her Divine Revelations, and a Voice to Mankind_, which since November, 1845, he had, during a succession of trances, dictated to a Dr. S. S. Lyon and the Reverend William Fishbrough.[30] Despite its nearly eight-hundred pages, the book was immensely popular and ran to thirty-four editions in thirty years. Expanding on the Neo-Platonic tradition, especially as interpreted by Emmanuel Swedenborg, Davis not only asserted the reality of a spiritual world but claimed to be a direct contact with it. Slightly before Durand invited the spirit to wander through the space of his paintings, Davis habitually allowed his spirit to escape into higher realms. While dictating the _Principles of Nature_, Davis on one occasion requested a pause and said,

> I perceive that I shall now have to be absent (that is, from the body) about six or seven moments, during which time the scribe and others of you may relieve your muscles by taking exercise.[31]

The editor here adds:

> He then assumed his usual inclined position, and re-mained rigid and statue-like, breathing very slightly, for about seven minutes, at the end of which period he returned with rather unusual muscular convulsions, and under mental emotions which he could not entirely suppress.[32]

And elsewhere, Davis described in detail the mechanism of his withdrawal from the earthly to a higher sphere:

The transition of my being from the outer to the inner
world is produced by the action of forces contained in
another body, upon the similar forces contained in my
own material form. The process is that of destroying
the sensation of the outer, or rather of changing it to
the sensation of the spirit--at which time the medium
that connects my body with another is sustained by a
mingling of the forces of the two bodies, while the
actual sensation leaves the body and becomes the Form
of my spirit. This Form, then, is the body which I
possess while occupying higher positions in material
existence. Inasmuch, then, as the body is thus deserted,
I am enabled, by causes unrelated to behold the possessions of the Second Sphere, and to commune with the knowledge there existing, together with that of earth.
This elevation assists me to penetrate with spiritual
perception the whole arcana of the various earths in
the Universe.[33]

As Davis's spirit was withdrawn from the body "by the action
of forces contained in another body," so the painting might serve
as the other "body" in respect to a person less clairvoyant by
nature. In looking at the painting, the spectator loses his
awareness of it as a physical object hanging on the wall, he loses
his awareness of himself as a physical entity standing before it.
It is then that he may desert the body and "behold the possessions
of the Second Sphere" in the Form of his spirit. It is notable
that the scene beyond the foreground ledge in Durand's paintings

is, in fact, quite literally a "Second Sphere", totally different in character from the foreground.

To Davis, unlike Channing or Poe, the scenes of this Second Sphere are not phantasies unanticipated by earthly things:

> I behold the _spiritual_ Sphere as containing all the
> beauties of the natural Sphere combined and perfected.
> And in every natural Sphere these beauties are repre-
> sented, though in the first and rudimental degree; so
> that every earth is of itself an index and an intro-
> duction to the beauty and grandeur that are existing
> in the Second Sphere.  For from the natural the spir-
> itual is unfolded, or made manifest.[34]

The scenery of the second sphere consists of the same types of phenomena as may be seen on earth--plains with rich vegetation, regular and gentle undulations of land, flowers, trees, groves, rivers,[35] but none of the more terrible mountains and deserts of the earth.  It is just that imagery which fills the distance of such paintings by Durand as the View Toward the Hudson Valley (1851), the Hudson River, View of the Fishkill Mountains (1856), or the Catskill Clove (1866).  But, further, in Durand's paint-ings,this distant material is rendered more spiritual as it is strongly transfigured by the effect of atmosphere and often the light of a setting sun.  Finally, we should not neglect to note that, according to Davis, "a holy quietness pervades the whole spirit world," and a similarly absolute silence pervades virtually the whole of Durand's mature work.

Thus, the spectator, having deserted the natural body is able "to behold the possessions of the Second Sphere . . . to commune with the knowledge there existing together with that of the earth."[36] It would be, perhaps, rash to insist too closely on an interpretation of Durand's paintings in the light of Davis's spiritual adventures. However, insofar as we can do so, we may say that the painting affords the spectator delight as it releases the spirit from its material bonds and that it provides instruction as it introduces him, no matter how feebly, to a knowledge of a spiritual world corresponding to, but distinguishable from, the natural.

The element of instruction afforded by Durand's painting may be regarded in another light and set in relation to the work of his fellow landscape-painters. According to Channing, man's love of knowledge is a token of the immortality of the soul, and whatever satisfies in degree this love is a source of great pleasure.

> In the inexhaustible love of knowledge which animates the human understanding, we have a bright indication of the reality of a future existence. God has given to man a spirit which is evidently designed to expand through the universe, which disdains the confinement of space, and which, although for ages it has been making progress in the knowledge of nature, still thirsts for more extended information . . . he delights in discoveries which have no relation to his existence on this planet, he calls to his aid the arts, not merely to

render life comfortable, but to assist him in the most
remote researches. . . . The human mind has an intense
delight in what is vast and unexplored. Does such a
mind carry with it no proof that it is destined to wider
spheres of experience than earth affords--that it is
designed to improve for ever in the knowledge of God's
wonderful world?[37]

Insofar as Durand's paintings introduce the spectator to the
Second Sphere, or a second sphere, they in that degree satisfy
the soul's longing for a more extensive knowledge. Durand, at
least, introduces the spectator to a "wider sphere of experience
than earth affords"--but does so through the presentation of
common scenes transformed by distance, atmosphere, and light.
In contrast to the work of Durand stand the paintings of the
explorer artists--Frederick Church and Albert Bierstadt. The
South American scenes of Church and Bierstadt's Western landscapes of the 1850's and 1860's present not "wider spheres of
experience than earth affords," but serve to excite "an intense
delight in what is vast and unexplored." Where Durand painted
scenes the may be regarded as adumbrations of a world beyond
this, Church and Bierstadt, both influenced by German thought,
present scenes from the extreme boundaries of the "real"
world.[38] It is notable that the exotic scenes of Church and
Bierstadt fail to display anything like the forms which according to Davis are to be seen in the Second Sphere. In the work
of all three, however, we find an equal degree of what, for
want of a better word, we may term "the beyond." Durand freely

selected the forms he wished to include and dissolved these in distance, light, and atmosphere. Church and Bierstadt travelled to remote regions to grasp the forms characteristic of those regions. Both traditions were carried on by later artists; the spiritualized landscapes of George Inness being the full development of Durand's point of view; while Thomas Moran followed in the steps of the explorers Church and Bierstadt.

CHAPTER SIX: LANDSCAPE AND EMOTION.

I. Pragmatic and Expressive Theories of Art.

In his brilliant essay on Romantic literary theory and criticism, The Mirror and the Lamp, M. H. Abrams isolates four factors which have engaged the attention of art critics and theorists. These are:

1. The relationship between the work of art and the universe, i.e., a non-personal reality existing apart from the work of art.

2. The relationship of the work of art to the artist.

3. And to the spectator or audience.

4. The work of art itself.

Using the terms "the universe," "the artist," "the audience," and "the work of art itself" as differentia, Abrams is able to categorize diverse theories of art as being dominantly Mimetic, Expressive, Pragmatic, or Objective. We may study the emotional element in Durand's landscapes in connection with both expressive and pragmatic concepts of art.

According to Abrams, the pragmatic critic regards "the work of art chiefly as a means to an end, an instrument for getting something done, and tends to judge its value according to its success in achieving that aim."[1] Dominating the later eighteenth century, the pragmatic point of view owed much to the

Classical rhetoricians and to Horace's concept of the poet's
task as "to profit or to please, or to blend in one the delightful and the useful." The pragmatic idea is as much evident in
Samuel Johnson's statement that "The end of writing is to
instruct; the end of poetry is to instruct by pleasing," as it
is in Edmund Burke's notion that the sublime contributes to the
health of the nervous system as physical labor contributes to
the fitness of the muscles. Even at the end of the century
Archibald Alison believed that a work of art possesses value
only insofar as it serves to excite a train of associations in
the mind of the perceiver--the associations, in turn, exciting
emotion.

Abrams provides the following account of the expressive
theory of art:

> In general terms, the central tendency of the ex-
> pressive theory may be summarized in this way: A work
> of art is essentially the internal made external, re-
> sulting from a creative process operating under the
> impulse of feeling, and embodying the combined product
> of the poet's perceptions, thoughts, and feelings. The
> primary source and subject matter of a poem therefore,
> are the attributes and actions of the poet's own mind;
> or if the aspects of the external world, then these
> only as they are converted from fact to poetry by the
> feelings and operations of the poet's mind. . . . The
> paramount cause of poetry is not, as in Aristotle, a
> formal cause, determined primarily by the human actions

and qualities imitated; nor, as in neo-classic criticism, a final cause, the effect intended upon the
audience; but instead an efficient cause--the impulse
within the poet of feelings and desires seeking expression, or the compulsion of the "creative" imagination
which, like God the creator, has its internal source
of motion."[2]

Abrams traces dim foreshadowings of an expressive theory of art
in "Longinus' discussion of the sublime style as having its main
sources in the thought and emotions of the speaker; and . . .
in Bacon's brief analysis of poetry as pertaining to the imagination and accommodating the shows of things to the desires of the
mind."[3] The expressive theory reaches its first maturity in
Wordsworth's conception of poetry as "the spontaneous overflow
of powerful feelings."[4] And it reaches its full maturity in
John Stuart Mill's distinction between poetry and eloquence.
While there is no evidence that Durand studied any of Mill's
essays, they do provide so clear and succinct a statement of
the Romantic concept of the role of feeling in art that it will
be worthwhile to study Durand's paintings in relation to Mill's
definitions.

In his essay, "Thoughts on Poetry and its Varieties,"
published in 1833, Mill draws a fast line between poetry as the
articulation of emotion and eloquence as an endeavor to affect
an audience in some way:

Poetry and eloquence are both alike the expression
or utterance of feeling. But if we may be excused the

antithesis, we should say that eloquence is <u>heard</u>,
poetry is <u>overheard</u>.  Eloquence supposes an audience;
the peculiarity of poetry appears to us to lie in the
poet's utter unconsciousness of a listener.  Poetry is
feeling confessing itself to itself, in moments of solitude, and embodying itself in symbols which are the
nearest possible representations of the feeling in the
exact shape in which it exists in the poet's mind.
Eloquence is feeling pouring itself out to other minds,
courting their sympathy, or endeavoring to influence
their belief or move them to passion or action.

All poetry is of the nature of soliloquy.  It may be
said that poetry which is printed on hot-pressed paper
and sold at a bookseller's shop, is a soliloquy in full
dress, and on the stage.  It is so, but there is nothing
absurd in the idea of such a mode of soliloquizing.
What we have said to ourselves, we may tell to others
afterwards; what we have said or done in solitude, we
may voluntarily reproduce when we know that other eyes
are upon us.  But no trace of consciousness that any
eyes are upon us must be visible in the work itself.
But when he /the poet/ turns round and addresses himself to another person; when the act of utterance is
not itself the end, but a means to an end,--**viz.**, by
the feelings he himself expresses, to work upon the
feelings or upon the belief, or the will, of another--
when the expression of his emotions, or of his thoughts

tinged by his emotions, is tinged also by that purpose, by that desire of making an impression upon another mind, then it ceases to be poetry, and becomes eloquence.[5] Poetry is,then,a purely expressive and private art, while eloquence is a pragmatic and public art. Eloquence, however, does not necessarily lose in value by not being poetry; as, one might suppose, what eloquence lacks in purity it makes up in utility. The two are merely different.

Mill's characterizations of expressive poetry and pragmatic eloquence would seem to correspond rather closely to the character, respectively, of Durand's studies from nature and studio compositions. According to Mill the same distinction applies to painting and poetry:

> Whatever in painting or sculpture expresses human feeling--or character, which is only a certain state of feeling grown habitual--may be called, according to circumstances, the poetry or eloquence, of the painter's or the sculptor's art: the poetry, if the feeling declares itself by such signs as escape from us when we are unconscious of being seen: the oratory, if the signs are those we use for the purpose of voluntary communication.[6]

In the studies Durand confesses his feeling "in moments of solitude" and embodies it "in symbols which are the nearest possible representations of the feeling in the exact shape in which it exists in the poet's mind." The studies are "of the nature of soliloquy." They were not painted to be sold, and, if they did occasionally appear in exhibitions, they remained "soliloquy in full dress"--reiterations in the public eye of what was said in private. The compositions, on the other hand, certainly presuppose a spectator. While feeling may still be present, it is "feeling pouring itself out to other minds, courting their sympathy, or endeavoring to influence their belief or move them to passion or action." The compositions seem to be pragmatic in character, for in these, "the act of utterance is not itself the end, but a means to an end,--viz., by the feelings he himself expresses, to work upon the feelings or upon the belief, or the will, or another." Both the studies and the compositions might be imbued with feeling, but the studies would be like upright vessels in which feeling is stored up, while the compositions would be overturned vessels from which it pours out to nourish the spectator.

## II.  Emotion in Durand's Paintings.

But, we must now pause to ask whether Durand was at all
concerned with emotion in any way at all.[7]  His advice to the
young, and even mature, painter regarding the faithful imitation and representation of natural forms and phenomena would
suggest that Durand's theory of art ought more properly to be
classified as mimetic.  Beyond his insistence on the imitation
of nature, Durand further maintained that the artist's reputation for originality depends, not on his investing old subjects
with emotions, but on his representation of hitherto unrecorded
scenery:

> The "lone and tranquil" lakes embosomed in ancient for-
> ests, that abound in our wild districts, the unshorn
> mountains surrounding them with their richly-textured
> covering, the ocean prairies of the West, and many other
> forms of Nature yet spared from the pollutions of civili-
> zation, afford a guarantee for a reputation of original-
> ity that you may elsewhere long seek and find not.[8]

Here, Durand had most immediately in mind the example of Thomas
Cole--mentioned in the same paragraph--who had established his
reputation with scenes of the Catskill wilderness, one of which
Durand himself had purchased in 1825.  A strong mimetic element
cannot be denied in Durand's theory and practice of art.  The
mimetic element, however, need not exclude either pragmatic or
expressive aims.

In his <u>Letters</u> <u>on</u> <u>Landscape</u> <u>Painting</u>, Durand frequently touches upon the role of feeling in art.  A landscape ought to be addressed to and excite the emotions of the spectator.  With respect to the spectator a landscape

> becomes companionable, holding silent converse with the feelings, playful or pensive--and, at times, touching a chord that vibrates to the inmost recesses of the heart, yet with no unhealthy excitement, but soothing and strengthening to his best faculties.[9]

As such a painting is addressed to the spectator, it may be classified as a species of eloquence.  As it is calculated to affect and improve the spectator, it clearly belongs to a pragmatic type of art.

The same pragmatism is evident when Durand defines the range of emotion which the landscape painter may hope to make the spectator feel:

> I maintain that all Art is unworthy and vicious which is at variance with Truth, and that only is worthy and elevated which impresses us with the same feelings that we experience in the presence of the Reality.[10]

In the eight "Letter," Durand restates the same definition:

> Let us . . . be thankful in the assurance that it is by reverent attention to the realized forms of Nature alone, that Art is enabled by its delegated power to reproduce some measure of the profound and elevated emotions which the contemplation of the visible works of God awaken.[11]

The actual work of art is regarded simply as an instrument
fitted to excite in the spectator, at home, the same emotions
felt by the artist in nature. But we must especially notice
that, in these passages, the faithful imitation of nature is
not presented as the highest value a landscape may possess.
The imitation of nature is merely a means to the achievement
of a higher end. Or, perhaps, we might say that the capacity
of a painting to excite the proper emotions in the spectator
becomes the measure of the painting's fidelity to nature. A
detailed representation of various natural objects, no matter
how faithfully rendered, might be regarded as not being true
to nature, should it fail to excite those emotions which are
experienced in the presence of nature. Conversely, a landscape
might excite in the spectator the proper feelings without displaying the minute description of natural forms that we find
in Durand's paintings.

Not only does imitation turn out to be subservient to the
affectiveness of the painting, but also the study of other works
of art may contribute to the painter's achievement of a properly
affective work:

> I would see you /i.e., the student/ impressed, imbued to
> the full with her /i.e., nature's/ principles and prac-
> tice, and after that develope the principles and practice
> of Art; in other words the application of those phenomena
> most expressive of the requisite sentiment or feeling.[12]

The study of paintings by the masters of the past will permit
one to intelligently select and arrange the forms and effects

which will contribute to the emotion to be experienced by the spectator. In discussing Idealism, Durand enlarges somewhat upon the necessity of selection for the sake of the affectiveness of the work:

> Thus far the meaning of Idealism is limited to the perfection of beauty with generic character and fitness in combinations. But the ideal of Landscape Art does not end here; it embraces, and with even higher meaning, the application of these perfections to the expression of a particular sentiment in the subject of the picture,--whether it be the representation of the repose and serenity of Nature in quiet and familiar scenes, or of her sterner majesty in the untrodden wilderness, as well as of her passional action in the whirlwind and storm--each has its own distinctive ideality. In this direction we come to the action of the imaginative faculty, which perfects the high Ideal.[13]

From the passages cited thus far from Durand's _Letters_ we may gather up the following aspects of his theory of expression:

1. That a painting ought to move the spectator.

2. That a landscape painting ought to excite in the spectator, at home, those emotions which the artist felt in the presence of nature.

3. That the representation of the phenomena of nature is adequate to excite the proper emotions.

4. That the artist must select the proper phenomena from nature if the painting is to excite the proper emotions.

5.  That a painting may be termed ideal and imaginative
    when it most adequately expresses an emotion.

The notion that it is the landscape painter's task to select
and combine those phenomena fitted to excite a particular emotion,
Durand must ultimately have derived from Archibald Alison.  In
the following, Alison describes just such a creative encounter
with nature:

> Amid a great extent of landscape, however, there are few
> spots in which we are sensible of any beauty . . . and
> wherever such spots occur, they are always distinguished
> by some prominent character; the character of Greatness,
> Wildness, Gaiety, Tranquility, or Melancholy.  As soon
> as this impression is made, as soon as we feel the ex-
> pression of the scene, we immediately become sensible
> that the different Forms which compose it are suited to
> this Character; we perceive, and very often we imagine
> a correspondence among these parts, and we say, accord-
> ingly, that there is a relation, a harmony among them,
> and that Nature has been kind, in combining different
> circumstances with so much propriety, for the production
> of one effect.  We amuse ourselves, also, in imagining
> improvements to the scene, either in throwing out some
> circumstances which do not correspond, or in introducing
> new ones, by which the general character may be more
> effectually supported.  All this beauty of Composition,
> however, would have been unheeded, if the scene itself
> had not some determinate character; and all that we

intend, by these imaginary improvements, either in the
preservation of greater Uniformity, or in the introduction of greater Variety, is to establish a more perfect relation among the different parts to this peculiar
character.[14]

While most scenes display forms of mutually contradictory character,
some scenes possess sufficient harmony of form that some single
feeling or idea is strongly impressed upon the spectator. In the
presence of so unified a scene, one may recognize that its unity
of expression might be heightened by certain nice adjustments.
These may be made by the gardener or landscape painter, but he
is only to alter nature in such a way as to heighten _its_ expression. He is not to impose an expression foreign to that which
the scene initially possessed. From Durand's statements and
from his practice, we may believe that he acknowledged the justness
of Alison's observations and would further agree that:

> The superiority of the productions of Sculpture and
> Painting to their originals in Nature, altogether con-
> sists in the power which the Artists have to correct
> these accidental defects, in keeping out every circum-
> stance which can interrupt the general Expression of
> the subject or the Form, and in presenting, pure and
> unmixed, the Character which we have associated with
> the objects in real Nature.[15]

An image so arranged that it excites particular emotions
in the spectator could be described as merely pragmatic, as long
as it is not directly controlled by the artist's own feelings. It

is entirely possible that, in a totally dispassionate frame of
mind, an artist might assemble those motifs known to be capable
of moving the spectator. But when Durand comes to discuss the
value of the traditional devices and rules of art, he focuses
upon the controlling role of the artist's feelings. When he
states that a knowledge of the principles of art cannot "create
the feeling, which overrules all principles, and gives the
impress of true greatness,"[16] clearly it is the feeling of the
artist that he has in mind. More specifically, Durand wrote:

> All that I would advise is this--let materials be few
> and simple at first; as you advance you will add what
> your feeling calls for. . . . those who can appreciate
> the higher attributes which make a picture a noble work
> of Art, will tell you that all the above-named requisites
> may be very imperfectly employed, and yet the picture
> may be truly fine, and even great; they will tell you
> that the difference consists in that which distinguishes
> the versifier from the poet, and this is all it is
> essential to know.[17]

The "poet" is, then, one who works from his own feeling, while
the "versifier" would be one who, in a mechanical way applies
those forms which are believed capable of eliciting certain
responses from the spectator.

If the painting, that is calculated to excite in the spectator those emotions that one might feel in the presence of nature,
is, in fact, controlled by the painter's personal emotion, it
should be classified not as mere pragmatism but as eloquence,
following Mill's definition. The selectivity exercised by Durand

in his compositions clearly indicates that they were intended
to elicit particular responses from the spectator. Hence, they
are pragmatic. Because they are, also, expressions of the
painter's emotion, they become eloquence. If, on the other
hand, while still controlled by the painter's personal emotion,
the painting is not consciously arranged so as to excite a
special emotion in the spectator, it must then be what Mill
would acknowledge as poetry. The relative lack of selectivity
in the oil studies from nature indicates that, in painting
these, Durand was less immediately concerned with affecting
a spectator. There is no reason, however, why they might not
have been as much controlled by Durand's personal feelings as
the compositions. Indeed, in the _Letters_ he states that the
study from nature _may_ become, in the hands of a skillful artist,
an expression of feeling:

> There is yet another motive for referring you to
> the study of Nature early--its influence on the mind
> and heart . . . _/In rightly contemplating7_ the objects
> of your study, the intellect and feelings become ele-
> vated and purified, and in proportion as you acquire
> executive skill, your productions will, unawares, be
> imbued with that undefineable quality recognized as
> sentiment or expression which distinguishes the true
> landscape from the mere sensual and striking picture.[18]

It is precisely as the study is colored by an emotion of which
the artist himself is not consciously aware, that it becomes
preëminently poetic--that it is poetry rather than eloquence.

In an earlier chapter we described Durand's mature studies
as records of the artist's mental recreation of his empirical
experience of nature. As the mind contributes somewhat to the
formation of the image of nature, it is almost necessary that
the act of mental formation should be affected by the emotional
disturbance wrought in the artist by his encounter with nature.
Hence, while the continued study of nature introduces the artist
to its infinite variety and demands a constantly renewed act
of mental formation, it also permits the artist to express in
private terms and in their primal purity those emotions which
he may later make public in a studio composition. Only occasionally do Durand's studies display the signs of a strong
emotion (see Figs. 128 and 129). More typically they embody a
mood of brooding calm. But, according to Mill, a mood of calm
may still be regarded as emotion:

> We shall not pause to ask whether it be not a misunder-
> standing of the nature of passionate feeling to imagine
> that it is inconsistent with calmness; whether they who
> so deem of it, do not mistake passion in the militant
> or antagonistic state, for the type of passion univer-
> sally; do not confound passion struggling towards an
> outward object, with passion brooding over itself.[19]

And, of the effect of this emotion of calm upon the mind in its
pursuit of truth, Mill adds:

> But without entering into this deeper investiga-
> tion; that capacity of strong feeling, which is supposed
> necessarily to disturbe the judgment, is also the mate-

rial out of which all motives are made; the motives, consequently, which lead human beings to the pursuit of truth.[20]

From this point of view, the emotion excited by the experience of nature is the cause of the mental act by which the mind carries out that re-formation of sense impressions which is a transmutation of empirical experience into Truth.

Due to the private character of the emotions expressed in the studies, any further effort to translate them into words would prove relatively unrewarding. The situation is different in the case of the compositions. That Durand did continue to paint compositions bespeaks his enduring faith in the utility of art to the general public and his allegiance to the Academic and Neo-classic traditions according to which a work of the highest art ought to be addressed to mankind generally rather than exclusively to oneself. Insofar as he conceived these as instruments to arouse certain feelings in the spectator, it is at least possible that he may have relied in some degree upon the use of an expressive vocabulary, consisting of terms regarded as fitted to arouse certain emotions. Indeed, the greater his concern with moving the public, the more he would be likely to employ terms the affectiveness of which could be verified by theory and experience. In the remainder of this chapter we shall attempt to prove that, to a significant degree, Durand's mature compositions were controlled by the concepts of the sublime and beautiful maintained by several writers, but especially by Archibald Alison.

III.  The Sublime and The Beautiful.

A.  Durand's use of the terms.

In our study of Durand's early work as an engraver and portrait painter, we have observed the degree to which he sought to
bestow a distinct and contrary character upon the male and the
female figures.  His early engravings Portrait of William Fuller
and the Musidora, in a programmatic manner, conform to Benjamin
West's characterizations of the perfect male and female:

> It would be utterly impossible to place a person so
> formed in the attitude of the Apollo, without destroying
> all those amiable and gentle associations of the mind
> which are inspired by contemplating "the statue which
> enchants the world."[21]

In the 1830's Durand continued to explore the opposition between
male and female characters in a number of portraits.  This
direction reaches its culmination in the contrast between Il
Pappagallo and the series of Roman patriarchs painted in 1841.
In these portraits and figure studies, the male figures come
to embody an ethical ideal and moral admonition, while the female
figures afford a sustaining tenderness.

By the time Durand visited Europe, he was far more interested
in landscape painting than in the problems of character in human
beings.  The Journal of his tour of England and the Continent
indicates that he had by this time transferred the notion of
polar characters from human to natural phenomena.  The following
excerpts from the Journal[22] reveal Durand's concern with the

polarization of nature, his application of the terms "sublime" and "beautiful" to contrary phenomena, and something of what is proper to each class.

> June 4, 1840 /At sea7 Winds increase . . . and the vast ocean presents to view some of its features of sublimity.
>
> June 5 /At sea7 Beautiful morning, mild south wind.

Presumbaly, the mildness of the wind left the sea less turbulent than on the preceeding day.

> June 14 /Of Virginia Water in Windsor Park7 . . . a kind of circular artificial lake a mile or two in extent bordered with meadows and low wood, little surpassing in beauty some of our American mill ponds . . . but the ride to it thro' the immense park of magnificent oaks and beeches was all that I could desire of the beautiful in that class of scenery . . .

The lake, however insufficiently superior to certain American ponds, does display some beauty. The oaks and beeches display a "magnificence" which relates them to things sublime rather than beautiful. The concluding phrase, here, clearly indicates that Durand tended to classify his experiences of nature--that he did not look upon scenery as an undifferentiated entity.

> August 26 /Godesberg, Rhineland7 The scenery here presents many points of great beauty, but it possesses more of historical & legendary interest, than any great extent of the picturesque.

The distinction between the beauty and the historical-legendary interest of a scene anticipates Durand's mature view of landscape

painting as properly representing pure nature--the work of
God--rather than architecture--the work of man.[23]

> September 11 /Travelling from Zurich to Lucerne, Durand
> passed/ thro' one of the most delightful districts of
> this enchanting country, rich in the humbler beauties
> of cultivated nature, the picturesque cottage and velvet
> textured meadows with a profusion of fruit & forest
> trees . . .

At the same time he also wrote of

> . . . the grandeur & magnificence of mountain heights,
> which . . . presented their giant peaks in all the
> majesty of form /?/ & beauty of atmospheric colouring
> peculiar to a bright and tranquil summer day.
> September 17 /At Lucerne/ Made a tour of the Lake by
> steam boat . . . have enjoyed much of the beauty and
> grandeur of its magnificent scenery. The southern ex-
> tremity . . . possesses more of the characteristics of
> sublimity, than any scene I have yet witnessed.
> September 23. One is here in the full presence of Mt.
> Blanc and his surrounding guards, the various Aguilles,
> the latter more extraordinary & sublime than himself.
> September 24 /On the road to St. Martin/ Another fine
> day . . . Left Chamony . . . passing the Glacier Bossons
> & that of Faconey, stretching down to the very level
> of green fields & gardens, a singular contrast. Full
> view of Mt. Blanc on leaving the valley . . . purple
> and gold tints, in the fleecy clouds. Fair weather

afforded a complete view of the sublimity and beauty
of the scenery.

October 1 /At Thun7 . . . the sky cleared and exhibited
this lovely scene in all its beauty . . . walked several
miles over hill & dale, wood & meadow, all day long
feasting on the prospects afforded in this beautiful
region.

October 2 /At Thun7 . . . the lake & distant Alps were
seen at intervals, tinged with rose & purple, tranquil
and beautiful in the last rays of setting sun.

In the period of his full maturity as a landscape painter--
in the 1850's--Durand continued to separate his experiences of
nature between the categories of the sublime and the beautiful.
In a letter, dated August 20, 1855, published in The Crayon, he
wrote that among the White Mountains are to be found "passages
of the sublime and beautiful."

. . . for those who have the physical strength and mental
energy to confront the /sublime7 . . . among the deep
chasms and frowning precipices, I doubt not it would be
difficult to exaggerate, and the simple truth would be
sufficient to convey the full idea of "boundless power
and inaccessible majesty," represented by such scenes.[24]

And, of the beautiful, he continues:

But to one like myself, unqualified to penetrate the
"untrodden ways" of the latter /i.e., sublime scenes7,
the beautiful aspect of the White Mountain scenery is
by far the predominant feature. . . . subordinate

> mountains . . . descend to the fertile plain that
> borders the Saco, stretching many miles southward,
> rich in varying tints of green fields and meadows,
> and beautifully interspersed with groves and scattered
> trees of graceful form and deepest verdure.[25]

In addition to this application of the terms to scenery that
Durand actually visited and amid which he painted in the 1850's,
the Letters on Landscape Painting of the same year afford a
number of more general references to the two types of landscape
phenomena.

In "Letter II" he speaks of the "inexpressible beauty and
grandeur" of nature as objective qualities thereof.[26] As the
landscape painter receives "impressions of beauty and sublimity,"[27]
it is evident that the two terms may also be employed to describe
the subjective experience of nature.

The aim of the artist should be to select those scenes in
which the sublimity or beauty of nature is most fully displayed:

> I do not say that simple naturalness necessarily
> makes a picture great, but that none can be great without
> it; for Nature herself is unequal, in the eye of Art.
> It is the province of Art, then, and all the license
> that the artist can claim or desire, is to choose the
> time and place where she displays her chief perfections,
> whether of beauty or majesty, repose or action. Let
> her settings be thus controlled, and the artist will
> have no occasion to idealize the portrait, no need to

shape her features on his classic model--or eke out an
expression that he does not see . . .[28]

In this passage Durand restricts the painter to the portrait of
particular scenes in which the sublime or the beautiful predominate. But he himself often exercised a greater measure of
creativeness. His own practice is more adequately described in
the discussion of the ideal of expression, which we have already
cited:

> But the ideal of Landscape Art . . . embraces, and with
> even higher meaning the application of these perfections
> /of individual forms/ to the expression of a particular
> sentiment in the subject of the picture--whether it be
> the representation of the repose and serenity of Nature
> in quiet and familiar scenes, or of her sterner majesty
> in the untrodden wilderness, as well as of her passional
> action in the whirlwind and storm--each has its own
> distinctive ideality.[29]

Here, it would seem, the painter is allowed a larger measure of
freedom to recreate nature in the image of sublimity or beauty.

In the Letters Durand does not provide exhaustive catalogues
of sublime or beautiful phenomena. Perhaps, by 1855, he did
not feel obliged to inform the reader that meadows are beautiful
and mountains sublime. Rather, he limits himself to a few comments
on three aspects of nature--clouds, the color green, and sunlight.
Durand speaks of the "beauty and sublimity of the glorious sky,"[30]
and enumerates more specifically

The long processions of the quiet cirri, in their robes
of purity skirting the gorgeous thrones of majestic
cumuli; and the dark rain-clouds, agitated and convulsed
with awful threatenings, like a revolutionary tumult,

> ". . . with fear of change
>
> Perplexing monarchs!"[31]

Of the color green, Durand wrote:

Who will assert that the fresh green of summer is not
beautiful, ever grateful to the sight, and soothing to
the mind--the poet delights to revel in it, and the
dusty eyes of the tired citizen regards /sic/ it as a
Godsend whenever permitted to enjoy it![32]

In its capacity to tranquilize, the green of the summer landscape
is clearly an affective phenomena, not simply a quality of nature.

In "Letter VI" Durand discusses sunlight at some length.
First, he speaks of sunlight as an expression of joy, as a
creative power, and as strongly affecting the spectator:

Sunshine is the joyous expression of Nature, the
lovely smile that lights up all her beauty, so changing
and adorning all it rests upon, as to seem itself
creative. . . . Who does not feel that existence is a
blessing and the world beautiful, when, after tedious
days of sullen cloud and storm, and worse monotonous
drizzle, suddenly the sun breaks forth in noon-day
splendour? So gladdening is his presence, that we
forget at once the long gloom of his absence.[33]

Later in the same "Letter," Durand treats more specifically of
the effect of sunlight when represented in a painting:

> We are not liable to over-estimate the value of sunshine
> to the landscape. By it all beauty is rendered more
> beautiful, and the ungainly made attractive. . . . it
> imparts a cheerful sentiment to the picture that all
> observers feel and enjoy; even the fearful darkness of
> storm and tempest is palliated and becomes agreeable,
> if but a gleam of sunshine enliven some corner of the
> scene; and, as it glides through the woven arches of
> the solemn forest, touching here and there some mossy
> trunk and pendant bough, and chequering the rich mould
> beneath with variegated gems, it cheers the silent
> gloom, and surprises us with the sudden presence of
> unlooked-for beauty.[34]

While Durand's own writings contain no complete theory of
the sublime and beautiful, there is sufficient evidence to
indicate that he continued to polarize his experience of nature.
The aspects, types, and phenomena of scenery which in his unsystematic writings, he identifies as sublime and beautiful may
be listed as follows:

| 1840 | SUBLIME | BEAUTIFUL |
|---|---|---|
| | The stormy sea | The calm sea |
| | Mature oaks and beeches | Meadows |
| | Mountain peaks | Cultivated nature |

| Glaciers | Atmosphere intervening between the spectator and distant mountains |
| | Fleecy clouds |
| | The colors of the sunset sky |

| 1855 | SUBLIME | BEAUTIFUL |
| | Deep chasms | Quiet and familiar scenes |
| | Frowning precipices | Repose |
| | Untrodden wilderness | Cirri clouds |
| | Action | The greeness of summer |
| | Whirlwind and storm | Sunlight |
| | Cumuli clouds | |
| | Rain clouds | |

There is no reason to believe that in 1855 Durand would have excluded from the categories of the sublime and beautiful any of the phenomena upon which he commented in 1840. The later list, however, differs in some slight degree from the earlier. In the first list, we find only phenomena that are directly obvious to the eye. In the second list, clouds cease to be merely "fleecy" and are divided among three types that can only be differentiated by an act of mental judgment rather than of simple vision. While on one hand this shift must be the product of Durand's reading of John Ruskin's discussion of clouds,[35] on the other hand it reflects the same general shift from an empirical to a more critical approach to nature that we have already noted as having occurred in Durand's work around 1850.

One other slight relocation of emphasis should be noted in the second list. In 1840 Durand, as a Romantic, could be struck by the spectacular beauties of sunlight, but in all of the European _Journal_ he says nothing of the light of common day. In the _Letters_ the longest discussion of beauty is devoted to the effects of ordinary sunlight on things and on the human consciousness. This fascination with ordinary light, anticipated by John Constable, relates Durand's thinking to that of European mid-century landscape painters--to Courbet, Monet, and Renoir in France and to the Macchiaiuoli in Italy. However, an awareness of the "creative" power of ordinary sunlight tended to distract the attention of the major European landscape painters from sunsets, which Durand continued to paint to the end of his career.

Aside from Durand's more conscious concern with clouds and sunlight in the 1850's, his notion of what is sublime and what is beautiful does not appear to have materially changed with the passage of time. Certainly, throughout these years, he maintained a dualistic view of nature. Yet, the range of imagery in Durand's mature work exceeds the phenomena which, in the occasional comments that are preserved, he specifies as being sublime or beautiful. Lacking a systematic account of the sublime and beautiful from Durand's own pen, we may turn to the writings of William Cullen Bryant and the philosopher Archibald Alison, both of whom certainly influenced Durand's work. We have already presented reasons for believing that certain of Durand's paintings in the 1840's were decisively affected by Alison's associationalist aesthetic. Around 1850 Durand frequently produced paintings illustrating verses from Bryant's poetry. In studying the concrete imagery of the poet and the more conceptual system of the philosopher, we may build up a more complete catalogue of the phenomena belonging to each category. If the categories of Bryant and Alison do not contradict Durand's, and if they embrace phenomena that do, in fact, appear in Durand's painting, we may, with all due caution, use them as tools to interpret Durand's poetic vocabulary.

B. Bryant and Alison on the Sublime and the Beautiful.

1. Forest Scenery.

In an early essay, William Cullen Bryant described a forest:

. . . its countless varieties of colour, its full masses of foliage, and the deep repose of its interior, should afford an idea of extent and sublimity; while the humbler family of flowers should convey a pleasant conviction that, throughout the wonderful economy of creation, beauty and sweetness are found accompanying and adorning strength, and lavishing the charm of their attractions upon the rude and the rough.[36]

The colors, the masses of foliage, and the repose of a forest are sublime, while flowers are beautiful. The same distinction between arboreal sublimity and floral beauty appears in his "A Forest Hymn." Exemplifying grandeur and strength is--

This mighty oak--

By whose immovable stem I stand and seem

Almost annihilated . . .[37]

While

        Nestled at his root

     is beauty, such as blooms not in the glare

     Of the broad sun.  That delicate forest flower,

     With scented breath and look so like a smile.[38]

In ascribing sublimity to mature trees and beauty to tender plants
Bryant agrees entirely with Alison.  In his very short chapter
"Of the Sublimity of Forms," Alison wrote:

> The Forms that in general distinguish bodies of great
> duration, and which of consequence express to us great
> Power or Strength, are in most cases Sublime.  In the
> Vegetable Kingdom, the Forms of Trees are Sublime, prin-
> cipally in proportion to their expression of this
> quality.[39]

Although frequently displaying the straight lines in angular
relationships, which according to Alison are normally not beautiful, plants become beautiful when viewed in another light:

> In the Vegetable World, although it is generally
> true that winding Forms are those that are assumed by
> the young, or feeble, or delicate plants, yet this rule
> is far from being uniform, and there are many instances
> of similar productions being distinguished by Forms of
> an angular kind.  There are accordingly many cases,
> where this Form is considered as beautiful, because it
> is then expressive of the same qualities which are
> generally expressed by Forms of the other kind . . .
> The known delicacy, however, and tenderness of the Vege-

table, at least in this climate prevails over the general expression of the Form, and gives it the same Beauty which we generally find in Forms of a contrary kind.[40]

2. Rocks and Mountain Summits.

In the first line of his "Monument Mountain" Bryant sets up a polarity of "the lovely and the wild," which I take to be equivalent to the polarity of the beautiful and sublime. In the fifth line he substitutes the terms "beauty" and "majesty."[41] If "the wild," "the majestic," and "the sublime" are not strictly synonymous they are, in Bryant's verse, interchangeable. In the following lines Bryant describes the emotion of the sublime and ennumerates many of the aspects of nature that give rise to it:

> There, as thou stand'st,
> The haunts of men below thee, and around
> The mountain-summits, thy expanding heart
> Shall feel a kindred with that loftier world
> To which thou art translated, and partake
> The enlargement of thy vision. Thou shalt look
> Upon the green and rolling forest-tops,
> And down into the secrets of the glens,
> And streams that with their bordering thickets strive
> To hide their windings. Thou shalt gaze, at once,
> Here on white villages, and tilth, and herds,
> And swarming roads, and there on solitudes
> That only hear the torrent, and the wind

And eagle's shriek.  There is a precipice
That seems a fragment of some mighty wall,
Built by the hand that fashioned the old world,
To separate its nations, and thrown down
When the flood drowned them.  To the north, a path
Conducts you up the narrow battlement.
Steep is the western side, shaggy and wild
With mossy trees, and pinnacles of flint,
And many a hanging crag.  But to the east,
Sheer to the vale go down the bare old cliffs--
Huge pillars, that in middle heaven upbear
Their weather-beaten capitals, here dark
With moss, the growth of centuries, and there
Of chalky whiteness where the thunderbolt
Has splintered them.  It is a fearful thing
To stand upon the beetling verge, and see
Where storm and lightning, from that huge gray wall,
Have tumbled down vast blocks, and at the base
Dashed them in fragments, and to lay thine ear
Over the dizzy depth, and hear the sound
Of winds, that struggle with the woods below,
Come up like ocean murmurs.[42]

Curiously, Bryant has here introduced some reference to all of
the things which Alison specifies as being sublime due to the
ideas of duration, strength, and power which they excite.  Bryant's
"Mossy trees" would be, as noted above, acknowledged as sublime
by Alison.  The various forms of rock would be sublime:

Nothing is more sublime than the Form of Rocks, which
seem to be coeval with Creation, and which all the
convulsions of Nature have not been able to destroy.[43]

Further, according to Alison,

The sublimest of all the Mechanical Arts is Architecture,
principally from the durableness of its productions;
and these productions are sublime in proportion to their
Antiquity, or the extent of their Duration.[44]

From this point of view, Bryant's "mountain-architecture"

Huge pillars, that in middle heaven upbear

Their weather-beaten capitals, here dark

With moss, the growth of centuries . . .

would be preeminently sublime. Finally, Alison wrote of military
architecture:

The Gothic Castle is still more sublime than all, because,
besides the desolation of Time, it seems also to have
withstood the assaults of War.[45]

Hence, a part of Bryant's mountain takes the form of an ante-
deluvian fortification.

In addition to the idea of duration Bryant's description
encompasses other ideas which to Alison are sources of the sublime. According to Alison magnitude of height, depth, and length
may be sources of the sublime:

Magnitude of Height, is expressive to us of Elevation, and Magnanimity. . . .

Magnitude of depth is expressive to us of Danger or
Terror, and from our constant experience, of images of
Horror . . .

Magnitude of Length, is expressive to us of Vastness, and when apparently unbounded, of divinity; that
being naturally imagined to be without end, to which
we can discern none. It is impossible to see a vast
plain, and above all the ocean, without this impression.
In spite of the knowledge we have of the immense space
between us and the fixed stars, and of the comparatively
trifling distance between any two points on this globe,
yet the former is not nearly so sublime as the view
of the ocean without shore, or even a great plain without bounds.[46]

In Bryant's poem the spectator's heart expands because of the
height on which he stands. The distance to the ground below--
depth--is a source of fear:

It is a fearful thing

To stand upon the beetling verge . . .

. . . and to lay thine ear

Over the dizzy depth . . .

And he directs our attention to what may be seen in the plain
below (magnitude of length). We need not contend that Bryant
consciously composed his description as an exercise in the
Alisonian sublime. It does, however, seem clear that both
writers held identical views as to the causes and character of
the emotion of the sublime.

So far we have noted that both Bryant and Alison ascribe
sublimity to forms associated with the ideas of Duration and
Magnitude. Duration may include ideas of strength and power,

and Magnitude may include ideas of elevation, magninimity, danger, terror, horror, and vastness, according to Alison. To complete our view of Alison's conception of the sublime, we may note that objects associated with ideas of splendour, or magnificence (objects relating to sovereignty and victory), of awe or solemnity (objects relating to religion and the burial of the dead), and of stability (due to magnitude in breadth) belong to this category.

3. The Scenery of Plains.

We have observed that Bryant and Alison agree as to the beauty of the smaller and more tender plants. In Bryant's poems other forms appear as beautiful--especially things located in a valley through which a river winds. While in the "Monument Mountain" the summit is sublime, beneath extends a realm of beauty--

> But the scene
> Is lovely round; a beautiful river there
> Wanders amid the fresh and fertile meads,
> The paradise he made unto himself,
> Mining the soil for ages. On each side
> The fields swell upward to the hills; beyond,
> Above the hills, in the blue distance, rise
> The mountain-columns with which earth props heaven.[47]

Winding river, fertile meadows, swelling fields, hills and distant mountains are all beautiful. A very similar scene is described in his "After a Tempest"--

I stood upon the upland slope, and cast

Mine eye upon a broad and beauteous scene,

Where the vast plain lay girt by mountains vast,

And hills o'er hills lifted their heads of green,

With pleasant vales scooped out and villages between.[48]

And, again, in "Green River"--

Yet fair as thou art, thou shunnest to glide,

Beautiful stream! by the village side;

But windest away from haunts of men,

To quiet valley and shaded glen;

And forest, and meadow, and slope of hill,

Around thee, are lonely, lovely, and still.[49]

In "A Walk at Sunset" he insists upon the beauty of sunlight--

Oh, sun! that o'er the western mountains now

Go'st down in glory! ever beautiful

And blessed is thy radiance, whether thou

Colorest the eastern heaven and night-mist cool,

Till the bright-star vanish, or on high

Climbest and streamest thy white splendors from mid-sky.

Yet, loveliest are thy setting smiles, and fair,

Fairest of all that earth beholds; the hues

That live among the clouds, and flush the air,

Lingering and deepening at the hour of dews.[50]

And in "To a Cloud"--

Beautiful cloud! with folds so soft and fair,

Swimming in the pure quiet air!

> Thy fleeces bathed in sunlight, while below
>
> Thy shadow o'er the vale moves slow.[51]

The sky--

> Ay! gloriously thou standest there,
>
> Beautiful, boundless firmament![52]

Flowers, the things of valleys, sunlight, clouds, the pure blue sky largely exhaust the range of phenomena to which Bryant explicitly attributes beauty.

Alison approaches the question of beauty from a rather different point of view. He is not so much concerned with enumerating the objects that give rise to those ideas that are the source of the emotion of beauty, but takes a more abstract view and directs our attention to the lines which define things. He distinguishes four different types of line--the straight line (cf. the letter "I"), angular ("z"), curved ("c"), and serpentine ("s")--all but the first of which may define the silhouette of a form.[53] Alison then goes on to note the qualities and some of the objects with which each type of line may be connected in nature. These connections may be summarized in the following table:[54]

| SUBLIME | | BEAUTIFUL | |
|---|---|---|---|
| Angular | Straight | Curved | Serpentine |
| Hardness | Softness | Weakness | Same ideas as |
| Strength | Smoothness | Fragility | those associated |
| Durability | | Delicacy | with curved |
| | | | lines plus: |
| | | | Ease |
| (Rocks, metals, | | (Smaller plants, | Volition |
| large trees, | | feeble animals) | Freedom from |
| powerful ani- | | | force or |
| mals) | | | constraint |

Maturity                          Infancy
Vigor                             Tenderness


(Mature plants                    (Young plants           (River, vine)
and animals)                      and animals)


Roughness                         Softness
Sharpness                         Smoothness
Harshness                         Fineness
Constraint
Force

Alison also distinguishes between the qualities connected with
heavy and fine lines:[55]

      HEAVY LINES                    FINE LINES

(when perpendicular)              Smoothness
    Strength                      Fineness
    Stability                     Delicacy

(when horizontal or
  oblique)
    Harshness
    Roughness

Considering the direction of a line together with its character
of boldness or fineness, Alison offers the following suggestions
as to the relative beauty of lines:

1. Heavy and straight lines express strength and smoothness and are beautiful to some degree.

2. Fine and straight lines express delicacy and smoothness
   and are more beautiful.

3. Heavy and angular lines express strength and harshness
   and are seldom beautiful.

4. Fine and angular lines express delicacy and roughness
   and are beautiful only when the expression of
   delicacy prevails over that of roughness.

5. Heavy and curved (or serpentine) lines express the contradictory ideas of strength and gentleness and are therefore indifferent.

6. Fine and curved (or serpentine) lines express delicacy and ease and are very beautiful.[56]

Although Alison does not identify it as such, I believe that we may assume that the least beautiful line--the heavy and angular-- is the most sublime, as such a line is characterized as being expressive of those qualities of strength and harshness which are among the causes of the emotion of the sublime. Fine and curved lines are the most beautiful.

Now it may be noted that the natural forms which Bryant considered beautiful--plants, winding rivers, swelling ground, hills, distant mountains, masses of foliage, and clouds--generally display the curved or serpentine lines which according to Alison are connected usually with those ideas of weakness, fragility, delicacy, tenderness, softness, smoothness, or fineness that are normally the cause of the emotion of beauty. Most of the natural forms termed beautiful by Bryant are referred to when Alison introduces the evidence of common language to support his theory of beauty:

> In describing the beautiful forms of Ground, we speak
> of gentle declivities, and gentle swells. In describing
> the beautiful forms of Water, we speak of a mild Current,
> gentle Falls, soft windings, a tranquil Stream. In
> describing Forms of the vegetable kingdom, we use similar
> language. The delicacy of Flowers, of Foliage, of the

young shoots of Trees and Shrubs, are expressions everywhere to be heard, and which everywhere convey the belief of the beauty in these Forms.[57]

The major point of difference between the two lists of beautiful
phenomena is Bryant's Romantic appreciation of the beauty of
sunlight, sky, and clouds. An appreciation of these he shared
with Durand, who had especially studied the skies and light in
the landscapes of Claude and Turner.

4. Summary.

Aside from Alison's lack of interest in light and the sky,
he and Bryant so far agree in their views of sublimity and beauty
that we might draw up a single table of the sublime and beautiful
objects and lines and the ideas connected with these objects
and lines specified by both writers. Such a table would serve
as a sort of key permitting one to decode the imagery of any
painter who was demonstrably influenced by the writing of Bryant
or Alison on the topic of the sublimity or beauty of form. A
table of this kind may be formulated as follows:

| SUBLIME OBJECTS | BEAUTIFUL OBJECTS |
|---|---|
| Large plants (trees) | Small plants |
| Strong Animals | Feeble animals |
| Mature plants and animals | Young plants and animals |
| Instruments of war | Winding rivers |
| Rocks | Swelling ground |
| Ancient buildings | Hills |
| Fortifications | Distant mountains |
| Instruments of sovereignty | Foliage of trees |
| Buildings and instruments | Clouds (in blue sky) (Bryant) |
|   of religion | The blue sky (Bryant) |
| Things relating to the burial | Sunlight and sunset (Bryant) |
|   of the dead | |
| An abyss | |
| The ocean | |
| An extensive plain | |
| Mountains near at hand | |

| SUBLIME LINES | BEAUTIFUL LINES |
|---|---|
| Angular | Curved |
| Heavy, straight lines | Serpentine |
| whether vertical, | Straight |
| horizontal or oblique | Fine |

| SUBLIME QUALITIES | BEAUTIFUL QUALITIES |
|---|---|
| Danger | Weakness |
| Power | Fragility |
| Duration | Delicacy |
| Strength | Infancy |
| Splendour | Tenderness |
| Magnificence | Softness |
| Awe | Smoothness |
| Solemnity | Fineness |
| Magnitude of height | Ease |
| Magnitude of depth | Freedom |
| Magnitude of length | |
| Terror | |
| Horror | |
| Vastness | |
| Infinity | |
| Hardness | |
| Durability | |
| Maturity | |
| Vigor | |
| Roughness | |
| Sharpness | |
| Harshness | |
| Constraint | |
| Force | |

There can be, I think, no doubt but that both Bryant and Durand read Alison attentively, and that each sought to apply the associationist aesthetic to his particular art. To this generalization it might be objected, however, that Bryant transformed Alison's aesthetic into poetry, and Durand translated Bryant's poetry into painting. A number of Durand's paintings-- The Fountain (1848, App. II, no. 244), Pastoral Landscape (1849, App. II, no. 256), Landscape, Sunday Morning (1850, Fig. 148),

Thanatopsis (1850, Fig. 204), Primeval Forest (1854, App. II,
no. 315), and In the Woods (1855, Fig. 169)--illustrate particular passages from Bryant's poetry; and numerous paintings,
not inspired by a particular text, display strong affinities
of topography and mood to scenes described by Bryant.  Such an
affinity between the work of the painter and poet was recognized
by their contemporaries.  In 1847 Henry T. Tuckerman set Durand's
The Beeches alongside certain verses by Bryant and declared that
"in spirit they are identical."[58]  And the critic George Sheldon
wrote:"The mention of Mr. Bryant's name suggests the fact of a
resemblance between the aims and the methods of Mr. Durand and
those of the author of 'Thanatopsis' . . . Mr. Durand's 'In the
Woods' . . . and his 'Primeval Forest' . . . are 'Forest
Hymns.'"[59]  But while it is certain that Bryant wrote Alisonian
poems before Durand painted Alisonian pictures, and while Durand
did, around 1850, paint pictures inspired by Bryant's poems, we
are not for these reasons constrained to believe that Durand
did not study Alison independently and apply his ideas in ex-
ecuting original "poetic" compositions.  Earlier in his career,
Durand painted Alisonian compositions--for instance, The Morning
and Evening of Life (1840, Figs. 85 and 86) and the Old Man's
Reminiscences (1845, Fig. 80)--which are not paralleled in
Bryant's poems.  Hence, we may simply suggest that Durand's
paintings and the poetry of Bryant were both inspired by the
aesthetics of Alison; while in the years around 1850, in an
effort to expand the emotional range of his paintings and to
render it more concrete and more accessible to the spectator,
Durand produced a number of works illustrating Bryant's verses.

IV. The Dominance of the Beautiful in Paintings by Durand.

On the basis of the table formulated above, we may define three large categories of Durand's paintings. In the paintings of one group beautiful forms dominate; in another, sublime; and in the third, extensive passages of the sublime and of the beautiful are combined. To the first category clearly belong the Landscape with Children (1837, Fig. 75), Sunday Morning (1839, Fig. 73), Evening (1845, cf. Fig. 149), View in the Catskills (1847, Fig. 150), Vermont Scenery (1852, Fig. 151), High Point, Shandaken Mountains (1853, Fig. 154), A Glimpse in New Hampshire (1857, cf. Fig. 155), Landscape, Artist Sketching (1858, Fig. 156), The Pedestrian (1858, Fig. 158), Summer Afternoon (1865, Fig. 159), the Scene Among the Berkshire Hills (1872, Fig. 162), and the View of the Black Mountains from the Harbor Islands, Lake George (1875, Fig. 163).

A painting such as the View in the Catskills (1847) is fully dominated by curved or serpentine lines defining young trees, the course of a brook, swelling ground, masses of foliage, and billowing clouds. The herd of idle cows merely reinforces the idea of gentleness. Other of Durand's later paintings--Summer Afternoon (1865) and Landscape (1866, no. 371)--are closely related to the idyllic images of the 1840's. Trees grow from a grassy plain extending to a distant range of low hills on the horizon. A large part of the ground--about one-half--is given over to the mirror-like surface of a tranquil river. The sun floats low in the western sky but has not yet exploded into the

colors of sunset. The tree forms, as is normal in Durand's
"beautiful" landscapes, are at once characteristic of their
species, and perfect (i.e., complete) in form. As elsewhere,
the massive strength of the trunks is obscured by foliage growing nearly to the ground.

In the early 1850's Durand painted several landscapes in
which a hilly plain prefaces a distant range of mountains.
Both the Vermont Scenery (1852) and the High Point: Shandaken
Mountains (1853) display forms defined by curved or fine lines--
stones, hills, a brook, the regular and rounded masses of foliage
of trees. The trunks of trees that might suggest strength are
rather slender and tend to be obscured by delicate leafage.
Undulations of the earth's surface in the foreground or middle-
ground which might become rough or harsh are softened as they
are clad in meadow grass or woods. The distant mountains, which
seen from a nearer point would be sublime, are softened by
atmosphere and defined largely by the fine curved lines of their
silhouette. None of the forms, either animate or inanimate,
is marked by signs of the operation of external force or re-
straint. Trees display the curves of unimpeded growth. Hills
and mountains swell easily from the plain.

The beauties of sunset and the peace of evening dominate
a group of landscapes executed throughout Durand's career--
Landscape - Sunset (1838, Fig. 78), The Pedestrian (1858), and
the Souvenir of the Adirondacks (1878), his last painting. In
each of these the transitory radiance of light, reflected from
a body of water of absolute stillness, transfigures rounded

forms of foliage and distant mountains. In these, the interest
in the earth and of its vegetation is duly subordinated to the
interest in the pervasive light. The earth becomes merely the
theater in which a fragile drama of light is played.

Within the limits of the beautiful, Durand was able to create
three types of landscape. In the 1840's and 60's he appears to
have been especially interested in the "plain-water-tree" type
of landscape. The "plain-and mountain type" appears in the early
1850's, while the "sunset-over-a-valley" type appears from the
beginning to the end of his career as a landscape painter.

V.  The Dominance of the Sublime.

Given a definite predilection for the various types of
beautiful landscape, one might not expect that Durand should
show much interest in sublimity.  And, it is true, with only
one or two exceptions he did not undertake the highly dramatic
scenes frequently projected by Thomas Cole.  Storms, a wild
welter of rocks, yawning abysses, and obscurities Durand avoided.
No enthusiasm for the dangerous-sublime of Edmund Burke touched
him.  However, Durand did execute a series of forest interiors
which, when studied in connection with Bryant and Alison's
definitions of the sublime, may be recognized as such.

If we are correct in assuming that Durand intended The
Beeches (Fig. 108) of 1845 to be a woodland scene, it would
stand as the first of his forest-interiors, in which the trunks
of trees, studied from nature, hold a prominent position in the
foreground of the painting.  In the Forenoon (Fig. 110) and
In the Woods (Fig. 111), both painted in 1847, Durand presented
full-length portraits of tree-trunks and employed canvases with
the dominant vertical axes, which he used repeatedly for such
works.  These tree portraits of the 1840's, however, should be
distinguished from the forest interiors of the 1850's and the
1860's.  In the earlier paintings the individual, foreground tree
forms are invested with a certain sinuosity which allows their
sublimity to assimilate to the beauty of the extensive, atmospheric distances beyond.  In these pictures we stand near the
edge of the woods looking out over meadows or a valley.  In the

later paintings, on the other hand, we discover ourselves deep in the recesses of the forest itself and have lost touch with freely receding distances. The earlier paintings belong to the class of landscapes in which elements of sublimity and beauty are combined. The forest scenes, painted between 1850 and 1870 are Durand's most important works in which the sublime is. dominant.

The painting entitled In the Woods (1855, Fig. 169) is typical of the later forest-interiors. Enlarged with only slight modifications from an oil study, the finished painting displays fewer of the rhythmic sinuosities that give the earlier pictures a somewhat ambiguous character. Here, the massiveness of some trees, the youth of others, their dense and irregular arrangement, the broken stumps, the littered forest floor, a pervasive obscurity heightened by scattered flakes of light contribute to a forest that is sublimely primeval and silent but does not provoke fear. As an adequate evocation of the forest, Durand's painting is related at once to the forests of Jacob van Ruysdael and Meindert Hobbema and to their mid-nineteenth century imitators--B. C. Kockkoek (Fig. 165), Narcisse Diaz,[60] Théodore Rousseau,[61] and Gustave Courbet, whose Deer in Covert by the Stream of Plaisir-Fontaine[62] transcends the Dutch tradition. In America a number of artists, following Durand's lead, painted forest-interiors. Durand's pupil Josephine Walters (Fig. 166) and possibly his friend E. D. Nelson[63] painted forest-interiors under Durand's immediate supervision. Other artists, such as William T. Richards,[64] Worthington Whittredge,[65] James Hart

(Fig. 167), and Albert Bierstadt[66] carried on and modified the type at a greater distance from Durand. One should note a Forest Scenery near Frankfort Germany exhibited by Joseph Vollmering at the National Academy in 1856, which he may have painted prior to his arrival in America. William James Stillman's Camp of the Adirondack Club, Tollanshee Lake, 1857[67] and A. F. Bellows, Forest Life, Encampment on the Penobscott,[68] like Courbet's The Quarry,[69] define the forest as a place for viril recreation.

The idea of nature as a place of recreation, common to all of Durand's landscapes, is certainly relevant to In the Woods; for this painting is clearly an illustration to Bryant's "Inscription for the Entrance to a Wood." The poem begins with an invitation to the reader, weary of the "guilt and misery, the sorrows, crimes, and cares" of the world, to enter the "haunts of Nature."[70] The experience of the forest, the poet promises, will cure the visitor:

> The Calm shade
> Shall bring a kindred calm, and the sweet breeze
> That makes the green leaves dance, shall waft a balm
> To thy sick heart.[71]

A large part of the remainder of the poem is merely descriptive of the forest, and Durand has closely imitated Bryant's imagery. His painting includes

> . . . birds, that sing and
> In wantonness of spirit . . .
> The squirrel . . .
>
> . . . .

. . . the sun from the blue sky

Looks in and sheds a blessing on the scene.

. . . .

And the old and ponderous trunks of prostrate trees

That lead from knoll to knoll a causey rude

Or bridge the sunken brook, and their dark roots,

With all their earth upon them, twisting high,

Breathe fixed tranquility.[72]

Durand stressed the twisting roots, but they are not those of fallen trees.[73]

On one hand, then, the forest affords a healing balm to the "sick heart." But this is the office of nature generally. If the forest is sublime, it must affect the spectator in a more particular way. According to Seneca, the forest is fitted to excite an awareness of God:

Have you ever come upon a grove thick with venerable trees which tower above the ordinary height and by their layers of intertwined branches dim the light of heaven? The height of the forest, its quiet seclusion, the marvel of thick and unbroken shade in untrammeled space, will impart a conviction of diety.[74]

Durand must have been familiar with this passage, for it was quoted in English by the Reverend Elias L. Magoon in his essay "Scenery and Mind," published in The Home Book of the Picturesque in 1852.[75] In Seneca's view, the qualities of height, solitude, and obscurity--all of which to Alison are sublime--"infuse into the breast the notion of a divinity," in Magoon's translation.[76]

Even in Seneca's text these qualities do not symbolize diety or any of its attributes, but produce only an emotional awareness. Hence, while the forest may be a place in which to find relief from the ills of the world, it may also be a place in which the prevailing sublimity may cause one to "feel" the existence of God. As a place of refuge and cure in which one may experience God, the forest is also a sort of temple or cathedral.

In the later eighteenth and nineteenth centuries the forest was frequently identified as the place of worship of primitive man. According to William Gilpin, who regarded the forest as distinguished by the qualities of "grandeur and dignity" rather than "beauty,"[77]

> in the days of nature, before art had introduced a kind of combination against her, man had no idea of worshipping God in a temple made with hands. The templum nemorale was the only temple he knew.
>
> In the resounding wood
> All vocal beings hymned their equal God.[78]

Later, Friedrich von Schlegel, possibly following Tacitus' statement that the Germanic people worshipped their Gods beneath the trees,[79] wrote that

> The ancient Germans had no temples for the worship of their Gods; they kindled fires upon the lofty mountains, and brought their offerings to the lonely shore, or the deep recesses of the forest, and the shade of their sacred oaks.[80]

As late as 1870,the idea was illustrated in an engraving by
James R. Rice, <u>The</u> <u>First</u> <u>Temples</u> (Fig. 171),after a painting
by the Philadelphia artist Joseph Johns. This engraving was
published in the Reverend Doctor Daniel March's <u>Our</u> <u>Father's</u>
<u>House</u>, <u>or</u> <u>the</u> <u>Unwritten</u> <u>Word</u>. Unlike the earlier writers,
March could regard the forest as a fitting place for modern
man again to worship:

> The time has not yet wholly past when devout men go out
> into the solemn woods and bow down beneath the shade of
> ancient trees to hear the voice of God . . . /Trees7
> still offer the sacred retreat and solemn shade where
> men may meet with angels.[81]

The ideas that the forest was the place in which primitive
man worshipped and in which modern man may worship are also
united in Bryant's early poem, "A Forest Hymn":

> The groves were God's first temples, Ere man learned
> To hew the shaft, and lay the architrave,
> And spread the roof above them--ere he framed
> The lofty vault, to gather and roll back
> The sound of anthems; in the darkling wood,
> Amid the cool and silence, he knelt down,
> And offered to the Mightiest solemn thanks
> And supplication. For his simple heart
> Might not resist the sacred influences
> Which from the stilly twilight of the place,
> And from the gray old trunks that high in heaven
> Mingled their mossy boughs, and from the sound

Of the invisible breath that swayed at once

All their green tops, stole over him, and bowed

His spirit with the thought of boundless power

And inaccessible majesty. Ah, why

Should we, in the world's riper years, neglect

God's ancient sanctuaries and adore

Only among the crowd and under roofs

That our frail hands have raised? Let me, at least,

Here, in the shadow of this aged wood,

Offer one hymn--thrice happy, if it find

Acceptance in His ear.[82]

As to Seneca, so to Bryant the forest may impress its "sacred influences" upon the heart, and as it does so is a fitting place for worship. The forest moves the spectator to an awareness of God and also calls from him a positive act of adoration. There is no reason to believe that Durand did not expect that his forest-interiors would humble the spectator's "spirit with the thought of boundless power / And inaccessible majesty,"[83] ideas eminently productive of the emotion of the sublime.[84]

By the mid-nineteenth century, the forest was regarded not only as the primitive man's place of worship but also as the model from which architectural houses of worship were derived. Chateaubriand believed that all temples, Pagan and Christian, were inspired by the forest,[85] but more commonly it was the Gothic cathedral alone that was supposed to have been invented in imitation of the forest. In his _Forest Scenery_, William Gilpin mentions the supposed derivation of the forms of Gothic temples or cathedrals from forests.[86] Given the notion of the derivation of the Cathedral from the forest, the poet or painter is able to define or heighten the emotional impact of either by describing it in terms of the other. Thus, the cathedral at Cologne was described by the German voyager and scientist Georg Forster (1759-1794) somewhat as though it were a forest:

> Whenever I visit Cologne I always go into this magnificent temple in order to feel the thrill of the sublime . . . The splendour of the heavenward arching choir has a majestic simplicity that transcends all imagination. Extended to an enormous length the groups of slender piers stand like the trees of a primeval forest; only at their highest tips are they split into a crown of branches that bends with its neighbor in pointed arches . . .[87]

Of the exterior of the same cathedral, Durand wrote in the _Journal_ of his European tour in 1840--perhaps copying from a guide book:

> . . . its double range of stupendous flying buttresses and intervening piers, bristled with a forest of . . . pinacles /sic/, /which/ strike the beholder with awe & astonishment.[88]

Conversely one might describe a forest in terms of the cathedral. This Bryant does in his "Forest Hymn":

> Father, thy hand
> Hath reared these venerable columns, thou
> Dids't weave this verdant roof.
>
> . . .

These dim vaults,

These winding aisles, of human pomp or pride

Report not.[89]

The last three of the verses by Bryant just cited served as the
text for Durand's Primeval Forest, exhibited at the National
Academy in 1854. While the painting itself has not come to
light, we may confidently assume that it belonged to the series
of forest-interiors, of which series it was the first. In all
probability, it displayed a density of imagery, a naturalness
in the delineation of individual forms, and a certain obscurity
such as we find in In the Woods of the following year. To the
forest-image, the verses printed in the exhibition catalogue add
both the idea of the forest as a refuge from that "pomp and
pride" which may render civil life unpleasant and the conflation
of the forest with temple or cathedral--"These dim vaults /
These winding aisles."

This tendency to describe the forest in terms of a cathedral
was not without effect on the organization of Durand's forest
interiors. Nearly all of these display a nave-and-aisle plan
and pointed arches in the "vaulting." Assuming both the form
and significance of the cathedral, Durand's paintings are more
closely akin to the seventeenth century Dutch church interiors,
such as those by Pieter Jansz Saenredam,[90] than to the forest
interiors of Ruysdael and Hobbema, which appear to be devoid of
any religious significance.[91] The specification of the forest
and of nature generally as a fitting place for the religious
meditations or anyone except holy-hermits does not occur before

the nineteenth century. In John Constable's <u>Salisbury</u> <u>Cathedral</u>
<u>from</u> <u>the</u> <u>Bishop's</u> <u>Grounds</u> (Fig. 172), nature is clearly identi-
fied as a place for religious experience, as the trees are arranged,
similar to Durand's, on the aisle-nave plan with pointed rib-
vaults just as in the cathedral seen beyond. An alternative
method of indicating the appropriateness of nature as a place
for worship was invented by Caspar David Friedrich. In his
<u>Cloister</u> <u>Graveyard</u> <u>in</u> <u>the</u> <u>Snow</u> (Fig. 173 and cf. Fig. 174), trees
and a church appear, as in the Constable, but here the church
has fallen into ruin. Although a trinitarian concept of God,
expressed in the three remaining, whole windows of the ruined
choir, and the mystery of resurrection, expressed in the graveyard
crosses, persist, the church as an institution has been displaced
by nature. In all probability, Durand was totally unaware of the
work of Friedrich. Yet, he must have seen a painting, <u>Red Rock</u>,
<u>Eherbergh</u>, <u>Germany</u>, exhibited by Joseph Vollmering at the Ameri-
can Art-Union in 1849. In the tradition of Friedrich, Vollmering
illustrated the idea of the church, as an institution, supplanted
by nature; for this painting was described in the Art-Union
catalogue as representing

> A church-yard, with the ruins of a church in the fore-
> ground. Behind rise precipitous rocks of a reddish
> color; a dark storm cloud is rising at the right.

Durand's forest-interiors are related both to Constable's
<u>Salisbury Cathedral</u> and to the paintings of Friedrich and Voll-
mering--but more essentially to the latter. The aisle, nave,
and vaults of Constable's painting do reappear in Durand's. But,

unlike Durand, Constable makes nature a mere preface to the institutionalized Christianity indicated by the cathedral itself. Constable's painting is more closely related to Durand's early Sunday Morning of 1839 (Fig. 73) than it is to his forest-interiors.[92] Durand's forest-pictures are more closely related to the paintings of Friedrich and Vollmering in which the church, as an institution, is supplanted by nature. While the German painters introduced the ruined church building in order to indicate that the religious experience that once took place in and through the church may now occur in nature, Durand achieves the same end simply by imposing something of the cathedral form upon the forest. Durand's solution closely relates his forest-interiors to one other painting by Joseph Vollmering. The latter's Landscape (Fig. 115) is not a forest scene, but displays trees arbitrarily bent in a way that suggests the rib-vaulting of a cathedral. We look through the arch into the receeding "nave" of the temple of nature as a whole. But this painting, possibly a study from nature, lacks any of the sublimity and, therefore, any of the expressiveness of Durand's forest-scenes.

In painting the forest-interiors, Durand must have recalled his own experience of cathedral-interiors. While in London in 1840, Durand had attended Sunday services in both Whitehall Banqueting Hall and Westminster Abbey. Of the service at Whitehall, he wrote:

There is a fine organ here, the performance on which was the best part of the service, the sermon being a common

place effort and dryly read, and but for the contemplation of the architecture, of the room & the paintings
by Rubens . . . /I/ should esteem attendance here as
lost time.[93]

The service at Westminster impressed him far differently:

The service there may justly be call'd divine, never
have I witnessed so solemn & impressive a performance.
Surely the Gothic style of architecture is of all
others the most suitable for exercises of devotion or
religious ceremony. The sensations, inspired on entering this venerable mausoleum of Kings, heroes & sages,
peculiarly fit the mind & heart for solemn reflection
and devout emotions which are more & more expanded &
elevated . . . I was moved even to tears as the full
soft notes of the majestic organ, mingled with the
sound of many voices chanting the appropriate service,
reverberated through the lofty arches and mysterious
recesses of this mouldering pile.[94]

At Rouen Durand again was deeply moved by the Gothic churches
he visited there. In the Cathedral he

. . . spent an hour or more in contemplating the wonders
of its interior . . . It would be vain to attempt a
description of this ancient edifice, or to express the
sensations that came over me as I lingered under the
lofty arches, and gazed with surprise and admiration
on the beautiful & complicated tracery of its ornamental
altars & chapels and more especially the exquisite rich-

ness & splendor of the many coloured windows of stained
glass, thro' which the tinted rays of the morning light
streamed across the long, misty aisles, and fell on the
. . . columns . . . as if the very light of heaven was
not permitted to enter . . . without undergoing a regen-
erating influence.[95]

Also, at Rouen he visited St. Ouen, the interior of which he
described as "presenting a tout ensemble, the most captivating
and enchanting," and lamented that he had not more time "to
indulge in the visionary emotions excited by the surrounding
presence of this consecrated temple."[96] Durand must have expected that his forest interiors would excite the same "visionary
emotions" in the spectator. The painting might as well excite
forest-emotions away from the forest as cathedral-emotions away
from the cathedral. In either case, the church, as an institution to coerce or direct the feelings of the worshipper, has
been eliminated and, as in the Protestant tradition, no priest--
except the painter--intervenes between man and God.

Finally, it should be noted that in these paintings, especially, Durand sought to keep his own intervention at a minimum.
As we have noted in Chapter Four, the forest paintings were
normally based on oil studies--in color or sepia--that contain
all the important data of the studio compositions. In the case
of In the Woods, the finished painting is mainly an enlargement
of an oil study. The later Woodland Brook is a copy in color
of a large sepia study. In adhering more closely to the forms
of nature in these compositions than in any other class of his

work, Durand expressed that emotion of humility which, according
to Bryant in the "Forest Hymn," the sublimity of trees, the
mysterious agency of solemn trunks, and over-arching boughs
through which a dim, colored light filters, are fitted to produce. Hence, the paintings of the forest as a place of refuge,
a place designed to arouse religious emotions, a temple that
belongs to no sect and harbors no priest, were carried out in
such a way that

> No fantastic carvings show
> The boast of our vain race to change the form
> Of thy fair works.

VI. The Combination of the Sublime and the Beautiful.

So far we have considered those paintings that are dominated by qualities of beauty or sublimity in some purity. In addition to these there is a large group of paintings in which phases of beauty and sublimity appear in approximately equal portions. In creating what seems to have been his first forest-picture, The Beeches, Durand was rather reluctant to part with the forms of the beautiful. The sublimity of this painting is marred by too obvious a penchant for curved and serpentine lines, for tender plants, smooth water, and limpid light. As late as 1847 a tendency to elaborate arbitrary curves may still be seen in the forms of the trees, along with a continuing fascination with wreathing vines, plants, and a winding river in the distance.

While in these paintings the expression of curved lines tends to weaken the effect of the massive trees, Durand seems at the same time to have sought a way to encompass both the sublime and the beautiful without destroying the power of either. His earliest solution to this problem,[97] among the paintings that come to my attention, is to be found in the painting or drawing executed to serve as the model for an engraved illustration (Fig. 186) of the line "My own green forest-land"--that is, America--for an edition of the poems of Fitz-Greene Halleck published by D. Appleton and Company in 1847. The illustration is panoramic in character, and we might suppose that Durand intended something like an encyclopaedic account of the American landscape. That the picture includes mountains, rocks, trees, waterfall, plain, river, and tilled fields--an unusually complete repertoire of motifs--lends some support to this conjecture. Indeed, if Durand's intention was to produce a comprehensive view of native scenery, his thoughts might have recurred to what he had written in the "Prospectus" to his ill-fated periodical The American Landscape in 1830: "Nature is not less liberal of the characteristics of beauty and sublimity in the new world, than in the old." If, sixteen years later, he still held this view, we should expect a comprehensive view to contain qualities belonging to each category. And, indeed, in a picture that recalls the descriptive part of Bryant's "Monument Mountain," this appears to be the case. The foreground mountains, trees, rocks, and waterfall are sublime. In the distance, as in Bryant's poem, sublimity gives way to an extensive plain of beauty terminated by the undulating line of distant mountains and the light of a setting sun. In a sense, the painting presents two pictures--a scene of sublimity making up the foreground and scene of beauty in the distance.

The same method of combining the sublime and the beautiful was employed in later paintings. The Thanatopsis (1850, Fig. 204) is probably Durand's most successful synthesis of a sublime foreground and a beautiful distance. In many other paintings he has merely superimposed a sublime foreground upon a beautiful distance. This group of paintings includes Dover Plains (1848, cf. Fig. 76), Kindred Spirits (1849, Fig. 201), Landscape (1849, Fig. 188), Landscape, Sunday Morning (1850, Fig. 148), View Toward the Hudson Valley (1851, Fig. 189), Progress (1853, cf. Fig. 90), Landscape (1855, Fig. 192), Franconia Notch (1857, Fig. 196), Catskill Clove (1866, Fig. 197), and others.

In a rather literal sense one may regard these as "double" paintings; that is, the two scenes may be viewed separately. This phenomenon is especially well demonstrated by the Landscape, Sunday Morning, which was discussed in Chapter Five above. Here, the strong oblique lines of the foreground point of land and the massive trees growing therefrom give to this portion of the picture a decidedly sublime character. According to Bryant in "A Scene on the Banks of the Hudson," from which the imagery of the painting was derived, the still water and sky and the soft forms of the distant bank all make up a scene of beauty. The spectator, looking at the painting, can only fully experience the beauty the poet describes when he projects himself into the painting and identifies himself with the figure represented therein. But in merely looking at the painting, without entering into it, the spectator is presented with a vision in which the sublime is dominant. The same arrangement is discernible in other paintings. If, in looking at the Kindred Spirits, the spectator should post himself where stand the two figures in the painting, then much of the foreground sublimity no longer meets his gaze. The two figures on the foreground knoll in the View Toward the Hudson Valley (1851) only look out over the tranquil valley. Or, finally, if one stands at the brink of the precipice in the Catskill Clove, one sees only the curved and rounded wooded hills and a fading plain stretching on.

But did the painting affect the spectator only after his entry into its space, it is likely that he would not pause before it long enough to consider undertaking this enterprise. Obviously the painting must also affect the spectator as he looks <u>at</u> it. As viewed from without, such pictures as the <u>View Toward the Hudson Valley</u> present a combination of sublime and beautiful imagery. According to Channing, the effect of the sublime is heightened when it is combined with the beautiful:

> No sublimity is so real as that which makes itself deeply felt in union with beauty; just as the highest moral greatness is that which, whilst it awes by unshaken constancy of principle, at the same time attracts us by the greatness of love. Wild scenes, where power is manifested in desolation, act at first with great force on the mind, especially on the least refined; but power and goodness are congenial, and the highest manifestations of power are benignant. The power which reveals itself solemnly amidst beauty, by this very circumstance shows its grandeur, and acquires a more enduring sway over the soul.[98]

In an earlier painting, <u>The Beeches</u>, Durand tended to invest the forms of sublime trees with that beauty which belongs to the curved lines by which these forms were defined. In the later paintings, sublime forms continue to dominate the picture as they appear in the foreground. But in these, the beauty that enhances sublimity is relegated to its own domain in the distance.

We seem, now, to be faced with a certain difficulty. Does not this combination of the sublime and the beautiful destroy that unity of expression in the whole which, as we have seen, Alison demanded? If we turn to Alison's chapter, "Of the Composition of Forms," it will be found that the answer to our question is "no." Here, Alison observes that most forms display not one kind of line--curved or angular--but both together.[99] The same is true of most combinations of forms in nature. That is,

> Simple Forms are distinguished to the Eye, by the uniformity or similarity of the Line by which they are described. Complex Forms are distinguished by the mixture of similarity and dissimilarity in these Lines, or, in other words, by their Uniformity and Variety.[100]

Alison then sets forth two rules governing the composition of dissimilar lines:

> 1. I conceive it will be found, that the union of such qualities /i.e., the qualities expressed by different lines/ is felt as beautiful, only in those cases where the object itself has some determinate Expression; and that in objects where no such general Expression is found, no Beauty is expected in their Composition.[101]

That is, a composition might consist of heavy, fine, curved, straight, and angular lines and remain beautiful as long as all of the lines contribute to a single total expression.

> 2. I believe it will be found, that different proportions of Uniformity and Variety, are required in Forms of differ-

ent characters; and that the principle from which we determine the Beauty of such proportion, is from its correspondence to the nature of the peculiar emotion which the Form itself is fitted to excite. Everyone knows that some Emotions require a greater degree of uniformity and others a greater degree of variety in their objects; and perhaps, in general, all strong or powerful Emotions, and all Emotions which border upon pain demand uniformity or sameness, and all weak Emotions, and all Emotions which belong to positive pleasure, Demand variety or novelty, in the object of them.[102]

The proportion of uniformity and variety will vary according to the kind and intensity of the emotion to be aroused.

If Durand paid any attention to these rules in composing pictures belonging to the three different categories of his work-- (1) beautiful compositions, (2) sublime, and (3) sublime and beautiful--we should expect to find a single dominant expression in any painting, and we should expect the proportion of uniformity and variety to vary in accordance with the kind and intensity of emotion expressed in each. In looking at those paintings in which the beautiful forms are predominant, we may be impressed with a feeling of tranquility and that in a fairly strong degree. In looking at those paintings in which sublime forms dominate, one may be strongly impressed with a feeling of awe, and, perhaps, of humility. But what of the paintings combining passages of the sublime and beautiful? According to

Alison such synthetic paintings ought to produce weak emotions
or "Emotions which belong to positive pleasure." I would suggest that Durand aimed at the latter instead of the former
kind of emotion; and, further, that the emotion he sought to
stimulate was very similar in character to the second of two
kinds of peace described by Channing:

> There is a twofold peace. The first is negative.
> It is relief from disquiet and corroding care. . . .
> But there is another and a higher peace, to which this
> is but the prelude, "a peace of God which passeth all
> understanding," and properly called "the kingdom of
> heaven within us." It is the highest and most strenuous
> action of the soul, but an entirely harmonious action,
> in which all our powers and affections are blended in
> a beautiful proportion, and sustain and perfect one
> another . . . Has the reader never known a season, when,
> in the fullest flow of thought and feeling, in the uni-
> versal action of the soul, an inward calm, profound as
> midnight silence, yet bright as the still summer noon,
> full of joy, but unbroken by one throb of tumultuous
> passion, has been breathed through his spirit, and given
> him a glimpse and presage of the serenity of a happier
> world? Of this character is the peace of religion. It
> is a conscious harmony with God and the creation, an
> alliance of love with all beings, a sympathy with all
> that is pure and happy, a surrender of every separate
> will and interest, a participation of the spirit and

life of the universe, an entire concord of purpose with
its Infinite Original.[103]

The fact that the landscape represents an extramundane realm
affords the first kind of peace--"relief from disquiet and
corroding care." The fact that it represents passages of the
sublime and the beautiful in harmonious proportion renders it
comparable to those antique statues in which, according to
Channing, was embodied something of the "peace of God" and from
the contemplation of which the spectator might discover this
peace within himself:

> We even think, that we trace this apprehension in the
> works of ancient art which time has spared to us, in
> which the sculptor, aiming to embody his deepest
> thoughts of human perfection, has joined with the ful-
> ness of life and strength, a repose, which breathes
> into the spectator an admiration as calm as it is ex-
> alted.[104]

In Durand's composite paintings the elements of the sublime
operate as the strength, while the elements of beauty operate
as the repose of ancient sculpture. From this point of view
his mature landscapes assimilate to the classical forms which
he had studied so avidly in his youth from casts at the American
and the National Academies. The composite paintings do seem to
stir "Emotions which belong to positive pleasure," as Alison
said that such combinations might, but the positive pleasure
to be felt may be regarded as something akin to beatitude.

Although we may distinguish between those landscapes in which elements of the beautiful are dominant and those in which elements of the sublime dominate, we must observe that Durand but rarely attempted a composition in which one element excludes the other entirely. Nearly all of his landscapes may be placed somewhere _between_ the poles of the beautiful and the sublime-- nearly all approximate in some measure the composite type in which the two expressions are harmoniously balanced. Some sublimity lurks within his most beautiful compositions; some beauty within his most sublime. Perhaps the ultimate value of Durand's art lies in the fact that it includes a center at which the contradictory realities of experience and mutually opposed forces within the self may be harmonized. No matter how far the expression of an individual picture is drawn from this center, there remains some implication of the opposite pole which constantly tends to draw the consciousness of the spectator back to the center point of equilibrium and of humanity.

. . . .

As a postscript to this discussion of the harmony that Durand sought through the combination of sublime and beautiful forms, we should notice his views on the contribution of color and light to that harmony. Durand, despite his interest in forms, was not insensitive to the charms of lights and color. The sixth of his _Letters_ _on_ _Landscape_ _Painting_ is devoted to the representation of sunlight and the green of summer scenes.

These factors are also treated in a part of the seventh
"Letter," and from his comments here it is apparent that Dur-
and regarded green and gray as contributing to the harmony of
a painting.

Green is potentially the mean between contrasting warm and
cool hues:

> Green, it is true, is a cool color, but in sunshine it
> becomes warm green, by a marked addition of yellow.
> If this be still cool in comparison with other warm
> colors, it is not cold nor chilly, but of an agreeable
> temperature between the two extremes.[105]

If the medium green remains a local color, gray serves more pervasively to harmonize the cool and warm tones.

> In some degree, gray is almost always present; at times
> so delicately seen as scarcely to be perceptible, at
> others more visible, yet liable to be overlooked unless
> sought for, and at all times so quiet and unobtrusive,
> it seems to admonish the artist that if he would secure
> the benefits of its presence, he must never give it
> undue prominence--it is the summer breeze that chastens
> the heat of all warm colors, and tempers the cold ones
> into an harmonious union with them . . .[106]

Durand's conception of green and gray as functioning to
reconcile opposites of warm and cool color is certainly related
to the theory of the "middle tint" maintained by William Page.
During a conversation in Rome in 1856, Page

pointed out that black and white were day and night

to the artist, sun and shadow, lightness and darkness,

and the perfect equilibrium of these opposites was to

be found in the middle tint. In this middle value was

resolved the contrast of the great opposites of chia-

roscuro.[107]

George Inness, Jr., also described Page's theory:

Now, the middle tone was Page's idea. He claimed that

the horizon should be a middle tone: that is, it should

be half-way between the lightest light and the greatest

dark in the picture. Father /i.e., Inness/ agreed with

him on that point, but what they could not agree upon

was just what a middle tone really was.[108]

Apparently, Page would have agreed with Durand that contrary

qualities of color ought to be present, but that they ought at

some point to arrive at an equilibrium. However, there are two

points of difference between their respective theories. To

Page the contraries are light and dark. To Durand they are warm

and cool hues. Perhaps it was this point of difference that

gave rise to the disagreement between Page and Inness noted by

the latter's son. Inness may have agreed with Durand, that

warmth and coolness were to be reconciled, while Page maintained

it was light and shade. Secondly, Page seems to have believed

that the middle tint should occupy only a portion of the picture,.

the rest being dominated by contrasts of light and shade. Such

contrasts are apparent in the Portrait of Mrs. Page.[109] Durand,

on the other hand, believed that, while the mediating influence of green might be localized, the mediating influence of gray should pervade the total painting.  Durand's concept and use of a pervasive mediating tone more precisely anticipates the practice of the American tonalists such as Inness, J. Francis Murphy, Dwight Tryon, and George Fuller than does Page's "middle tint" theory.[110]

If in his theory and practice Durand anticipates the tonalists, he by no means went all of the way in this direction.  He explicitly warns of the monotony into which the tonalists were apt to fall:

> In consequence of the prevalence of green in our summer landscape, the presence of sunlight  becomes indispensable as the best means to counteract monotony.  For, Nature, indeed, abhors monotony as she does a vacuum, and perhaps it is to this feature above all others that we may ascribe the unpleasantness of a dull, cloudy day.  I am inclined to believe that sleep would ensue from the contemplation of a surrounding mass of unvaried color, as soon as from the most somnorific monotony of sound or motion.  In form, light and dark, and especially in color, it is repulsive, and only admissable in the picture when necessary to the expression of a particular sentiment.[111]

Normally, Durand would maintain a certain degree of contrast in light and color; just, as we have seen, he usually maintains some degree of contrast between sublime and beautiful forms.  If, however, the emotional significance of the painting calls for a

smaller degree of contrast, he would admit a certain monotony;
just as there is a certain monotony of form in his forest-
interiors and his pastoral landscapes.  In matters of light
and color, as in form, Durand pursued harmony, but not a harmony
gained by the suppression of all opposition within the painting.

CHAPTER SEVEN:  THE RELIGION OF NATURE.

In the 1830's Durand's most positive motive in the study of
nature appears to have been a profound love of natural beauty.
Even before he commenced his career as a serious landscape
painter, he wrote:

> The luxury of Nature is so fascinating to my senses that
> I feel no disposition for any thing but attempting to
> imitate her beauties, not by any actual view, but by
> catching some lovely feature.[1]

And in 1838, shortly after he had ceased to be interested in any
species of art but landscape painting, he wrote to Thomas Cole:

> The Glorious Spring appears advancing and waking
> at every step the delightful anticipations of renewed
> excursions among the unapproachable charms of this
> beautiful creation.  I mean unapproachable by our feeble
> efforts of imitation.  Still the prospect is enchanting
> and the hope of snatching some one of her innumerable
> graces, drives us on, and if it be but an _ignus_ _fatuus_
> still it leads thro' pleasant walks and compensates in
> its course, for all the toil and difficulty.  For myself
> I cannot but too often yield to the melancholy reflect-
> ion, that tho' among the most passionate I fear to find
> myself at last a discarded lover of lovely nature and

that I shall descend into the vale of years without
ever realizing even in a modest /?/ degree, the deli-
cious reveries of my youthful days and soothing hopes
that have beguiled my onward steps.[2]

A pure love of nature's "innumerable graces" displays itself in
such early landscapes as the <u>Landscape with Children</u> (1837,
Fig. 75), the <u>Landscape-Sunset</u> (1838, Fig. 78), and the <u>Sunday
Morning</u> (1839, Fig. 73). As late as the mid-1840's Durand
labored almost exclusively to grasp those aspects of nature that
delight the eye.

From nearly the beginning of his professional life in 1817,
however, he must have been aware of an object, transcending any
merely material beauty, to be apprehended amid the scenes of
nature. By the mid-1830's both Bryant and Thomas Cole had
affirmed that nature bespeaks something beyond itself--its
Creator. In a very early essay Bryant had argued that, while
nature does not reveal the fullness of God's nature, its qualified testimony is not to be ignored:

. . . while <u>nature</u> holds an instructive volume, while
she publishes to the heart <u>her</u> religion, a voice is
heard from every moving sphere: it addresses itself
to the reason of man--it is the voice of divine truth!
It commands him to compare the religion of <u>nature</u> with
that higher and holier system revealed, in beneficent
goodness, from heaven to "Moses and the prophets."

And, on making the comparison, can no difference
be discovered? Yes; the natural religion is but an

evidence of the power, the illimitable dominion of God;
and, as such, is entitled to the reverence of man; the
revealed contains the sacred precepts of His grace, His
mercy, and His love![3]

Nature points to God, but His power and dominion alone are revealed therein. The light of divine grace fails to shine through
the veil of material things. Later, in his "Preface" to Durand's
The American Landscape of 1830, Bryant enumerated the tokens of
a Creative Being especially to be discerned in the American
Wilderness:

> Foreigners who have visited our country, particularly
> the mountainous parts, have spoken of a far-spread
> wildness, a look as if the new world was fresher from
> the hand of him who made it, the rocks and the very
> hillocks wearing the shape in which he fashioned them,
> the waters flowing where he marked their channels, the
> forests, enriched with a new creation of trees, stand-
> ing where he planted them, in short, of something
> which, more than any scenery to which they had been
> accustomed, suggested the idea of unity and immensity,
> and abstracting the mind from the association of human
> agency, carried it up to the idea of a mightier power,
> and to the great mystery of the origin of things.[4]

Six years later Cole in similar language wrote:

> . . . the most distinctive, and perhaps the most impres-
> sive, characteristic of American scenery is its wildness.

It is the most distinctive, because in civilized
Europe the primitive features of scenery have long since
been destroyed or modified. . . .

And to this cultivated state our western world is
fast approaching; but nature is still predominant, and
there are those who regret that with the improvements
of cultivation the sublimity of the wilderness should
pass away: for these scenes of solitude from which the
hand of nature has never been lifted, affect the mind
with a more deep toned emotion than aught which the
hand of man has touched. Amid them the consequent
associations are of God the creator--they are his undefiled works, and the mind is cast into the contemplation of eternal things.[5]

According to Bryant nature reveals "the power, the illimitable
dominion of God," and according to both Bryant and Cole, the
American, primeval wilderness carries the mind up to thoughts
of God in his role as creator. But at this time, Durand was
more especially interested in the beauties of nature, that only
feebly, if at all, bespeak the power and dominion of God. In
his early years as a landscape painter, he generally avoided
scenes of wilderness in favor of the more gentle, cultivated
pastures, the expansion of which Cole lamented. To Bryant and
Cole, nature reveals only a limited notion of God's character,
and this fragmentary revelation is transmitted through those
wilder aspects of nature which did not attract Durand's attention.

I. The Revelation of God in Nature in Durand's Landscapes.

Early in his career, Durand had treated religious issues
in such paintings as Mary Magdalene at the Sepulchre of 1826.
We might expect that, as a landscape painter, he should eventually resume his effort to combine art and religion. What
seems to be his earliest painting in which divine agency is
presented as the cause of a "natural" event is an historical
rather than a landscape painting. To the 1844 exhibition at
the American Art-Union, Durand contributed a small picture
representing the escape of General Putnam from a band of hostile
Indians (Fig. 198). The painting must have been inspired by the
account of the event in Colonel David Humphreys' The Life and
Heroic Exploits of Israel Putnam,[6] written in 1788 for the
Society of the Cincinnati of Connecticut. According to Humphreys, Putnam and a party of five men were, in 1758, attacked by
Indians above the rapids of the Hudson. In this circumstance
they saw no alternative to death at the hands of the Indians
but flight down the river--a course that entailed "an almost
absolute certainty of being drowned." Yet, this plan Putnam
adopted, and "trusting himself to a good Providence, whose
kindness he had often experienced, rather than to men, whose
tenderest mercies are cruelty, /he/ was now seen to place himself sedately at the helm, and afford an astonishing spectacle
of serenity." The narrative continues:

> His companions, with a mixture of terror, admiration,
> and wonder, saw him incessantly changing the course,

to avoid the jaws of ruin that seemed expanded to swallow
the whirling boat. Twice he turned it fairly round to
shun the rifts or rocks. Amidst these eddies, in which
was the greatest danger of its floundering, at one
moment the sides were exposed to the fury of the waves;
then the stern, and next the bow, glanced obliquely onward, with inconceivable velocity. With not less amaze-
ment the savages beheld him sometimes mounting the
billows, then plunging abruptly down, at other times
skillfully veering from the rocks, and shooting through
the only narrow passage; until, at last, they viewed the
boat safely gliding on the smooth surface of the stream
below.[7]

In Durand's painting, the Indians' reaction to the escape is
emphasized rather than the escape itself. A party of warriors
stands prominently in the foreground. Humphreys' account concludes with the statement that the Indians regarded the escape
as having been effected with the aid of the "Great Spirit:"

At this sight, it is asserted, that these rude sons
of nature were affected with the same kind of supersti-
tious veneration which the Europeans, in their dark ages,
entertained for some of their valorous champions. They
deemed the man involnerable, whom their balls, on his
pushing from shore, could not touch; and whom they had
seen steering in safety down the rapids that had never
before been passed. They conceived it would be an
affront against the Great Spirit to attempt to kill this

favoured mortal with powder and ball, if they should
ever see and know him again.[8]
The Indian at the left, restraining the fire of the one at the
center and pointing toward the sky, is, obviously, communicating
to the latter his sudden awareness of the operation of providence.
The power and illimitable dominion of God is manifest through
a human event rather than through the wilder aspects of nature.
That God rules nature and events is a truth of natural religion
and is here recognized by "natural" man.

The next painting in which Durand sought to express a
connection between nature and God appeared at the American Art-
Union in 1847. Closely related in its personae and theme to
the Escape of General Putnam, The Indian Vespers (1847, App. II,
no. 233) was prefaced by the following verses, by an unnamed
poet, which were printed in the catalogue:

Lo! the poor Indian, whose untutored mind

Sees God in clouds, and hears him in the winds.
Although the present location of the painting remains unknown,
we might assume that it represented one or more Indians wrapt
in the contemplation of nature. While in the earlier painting
the Indians ("natural" man) had recognized the operation of
divine providence in a human event, here they discern the presence of God in natural phenomena. But the Indians discover
only God and not the mighty. or creative or sustaining personality revealed earlier through nature to Bryant and Cole. Dur-
and's conception is still uncomplicated by any effort to discern
a diversity of divine attributes in the forms of nature.

If we would understand his mature view of the relationship between nature and God, we must examine his own writings as well as the theological literature to which he had access. In the Letters on Landscape Painting, Durand speaks not only of the beauty and sublimity but also of the "beauty and significance" of nature.[9] In the latter phrase Durand suggests a distinction not between two categories of visible qualities but between visible qualities and invisible meanings. Nature signifies something, is symbolic. First, the creation signifies a creator, and it is, according to Durand, the proper task of the landscape painter to focus upon those phenomena that are the work of God. Landscape paintings in which the work of man mingles too prominently with that of God fail to attain the true end of this genre. A landscape painting

> will be great in proportion as it declares the glory of God, by a representation of his works and not the works of man.[10]

Similarly, any human action ought to be emphatically subordinated:

> . . . the true province of Landscape Art is the representation of the work of God in the visible creation, independent of man, or not dependent on human action, further than as an accessory or auxiliary.[11]

In these statements Durand may have intended a criticism of the architectural luxuriance and the human drama which Thomas Cole had frequently introduced into his landscapes. Representing primarily natural phenomena, the landscape painting would confront the spectator with nature's testimony to the existence and glory of God.

Nature's significance does not end with the mere indication of God's existence. Beyond this, nature also reveals the personality or attributes of God:

> The external appearance of this our dwelling-place, apart from its wondrous structure and functions that minister to our well-being, is frought with lessons of high and holy meaning, only surpassed by the light of Revelation. It is impossible to contemplate with right-minded, reverent feeling, its inexpressible beauty and grandeur, for ever assuming new forms of impressiveness under the varying phases of cloud and sunshine, time and season, without arriving at the conviction
>
>     . . . That all which we behold
>
>     Is full of blessings . . .
>
> that the Great Designer of these glorious pictures has placed them before us as types of the Divine attributes . . .[12]

Unfortunately Durand provides no account of the divine attributes nor of their types in nature.

How did Durand conceive of God, and how did nature symbolize His personality? To answer these questions we must demonstrate that a theology in which nature does reveal the character of God was immediately accessible to Durand and that the terms of this theology do illuminate the imagery of Durand's mature paintings. The theology of William Ellery Channing appears to meet both of these requirements. And at precisely the moment with which we are now concerned--1848--the figure of Channing appeared in a picture by Durand. In 1849 Anne C. Lynch (Mrs. Botta) published a collection of her poems (copyright, 1848) which included one entitled "To the Memory of Channing." From this poem the following lines were embellished by an engraving after a drawing by Durand (Fig. 199):

> Great Teachers formed thy youth,
>
> As thou didst stand upon thy native shore,
>
> In the calm sunshine, in the ocean's roar;
>
> Nature and God spoke with thee. . . .[13]

In the engraving, Channing stands upon a cliff, his back to the spectator, looking out over the sea toward the light of a setting sun. Channing is not simply a witness to the glory of God, but through nature is in direct communication with Him. Given that in 1848 Durand was aware of Channing, and that he was aware of Channing's conception of the revelation of God in nature, we might not err too far should we at least attempt to apply certain of his ideas to the interpretation of paintings by Durand dating after 1848.

In his discourses and sermons, Channing had commented frequently upon the relationship between God and nature. As a Christian he, of course, held that revealed religion contained a more just and complete view of God and of human destiny than was to be obtained from natural religion. Natural religion, indeed, he viewed as defective in that it failed to announce the unity of God, the goodness of God, and the immortality of

the human soul.[14]  Yet, once these truths had been revealed
in Scripture, Channing was able to discern intimations of God's
unity and goodness and of man's immortality throughout nature.
Of the three ideas--God's unity, His goodness, and man's
immortality--the second and third are particularly relevant to
an interpretation of Durand's later paintings, and must be discussed here in some detail.

To Channing, the character of God is purely benevolent.
God is unqualified Good.  This goodness, nevertheless, sometimes
expresses itself in what may properly be termed justice--as long
as it is understood that justice and goodness are reconcilable.
The character of God was discussed with some clarity in a sermon
of October, 1814:

> Far be it from me to obscure the lustre of Divine good-
> ness, or to set before you that Being who *is* Love itself
> in any other light than that of the brightest benignity.
> I would have you penetrated with the conviction that
> God is most just; but I would have you hold this truth
> in consistency with that most interesting of all truths,
> that God delights to do good, and that all his operations
> are directed by benevolence.  Benevolence and justice
> are harmonious attributes of God, to which all others may
> be reduced; and the true idea of justice is, that it is
> a branch or mode of exercise of benevolence. . . .
>
> Divine justice is, in fact, an exercise of enlarged
> benevolence, enjoining and enforcing by rewards and
> punishments those dispositions and actions on which the

peace, order, improvement, and felicity of rational
beings depend. I repeat it, <u>the principle of justice
is benevolence</u>.[15]

Divine justice is distinct from divine goodness only as a sort
of inferior goodness which must operate before the higher goodness may fully realize its ends. Divine justice chastens and
improves man in such a way that he becomes the fit recipient of
the fullness of divine goodness. The operation of justice is
prior to and preparatory for the display of goodness:

> God's justice, then, is a wise benevolence, employing
> rewards and punishments to exalt intelligent creatures
> to the most perfect and happy character, to a participa-
> tion of /for "in"?/ that love or moral goodness which
> forms his own felicity.[16]

While God is in essence goodness, when He is regarded in His
relationship to man, and when He is regarded as a factor in the
scheme of human redemption, His goodness sometimes displays
itself as justice. In this limited sense His justice may be
distinguished in operation from His goodness.

Now, if justice and goodness are operationally distinct
attributes of God, and if, once they are known from revelation,
their reflections may be discerned in nature, then we may say
that nature reflects that duality of the Divine character which
appears when He is regarded as a factor in the order of human
salvation. I find but one passage in the <u>Memoir</u> where Channing
describes contrary aspects of nature as bespeaking the justice

and goodness of God. Of a storm at sea, seen from a distance, he wrote in his journal that

> . . . we might contemplate it as a solemn minister of Divine justice and witness of God's power to a thought-less world . . . [17]

And of a calm at sea,

> It was hard to connect what I now saw with my last view of the ocean, to feel that I was looking on the same element. The irregular, broken, wildly tossing, tumul-tuous billows had vanished, and lengthened, continuous, slowly advancing swells followed one another, not as in pursuit, but as if finding pleasure in gentle motion.
>
> Instead of bursting into foam, or being tossed into infinite inequalities by the sweeping, hurrying winds, their polished molten surface, whilst varied by soft flowing lines, was unruffled by a single breath. They seemed, as they rolled in regular intervals towards us, like the gentle heaving of a sleeping infant's breast. I did not feel as if the ocean was exhausted by its late efforts, but as if, having accomplished its mani-festations of awe-inspiring might, it was now executing a more benignant ministry, speaking of the mercy and the blissful rest of God. [18]

The storm--that is, a phase of nature that is sublime--is the emblem of God's justice. The calm--that is, a phase of nature that is beautiful--is an emblem of God's mercy or goodness. The sublime gives warning and chastens and corrects "a thoughtless world." The beautiful brings peace--"I looked and was at peace."[19] The sublime and the beautiful together would then provide an adequate emblem of the full character of God--the God who corrects through His justice and receives the humble in His mercy.

Now let us suppose that a landscape painter should create an image in which a passage of the sublime in nature is combined with a passage of the beautiful. As the beautiful is an emblem of Divine love, and the sublime is an emblem of Divine justice, the two together would constitute an emblem of the divine character as it displays itself in relation to man. It is worthy of note that between his description of the sublime storm and the beautiful calm at sea, quoted above, Channing interposed certain observations on the manner in which the sublime and the beautiful in nature often appear in combination:

> There is a great beauty joined with this majesty
> /i.e., that of the storm/ as through all nature. We
> seldom see more /for "mere"?/ power. The awful mountain
> top delights to bathe its grandeur in the richest,
> softest beams of the rising or setting sun; sweet flowers
> wave and smile in the chasms of the precipice; and so
> the mountain billow often breaks into sparkling spray,
> and the transparent arch beneath shines with an emerald
> brightness, which has hardly a rival in the richest
> hues of the vegetable creation.[20]

We may recall that in a group of paintings, the earliest of which dates from about the time of his illustration to Anne C. Lynch's

"To the Memory of Channing," Durand did combine passages of the sublime and the beautiful in the same painting. Paintings, such as Dover Plains (1848, cf. Fig. 76) and View Toward the Hudson Valley (1851, Fig. 189) are typical of this composite type of landscape. While we cannot definitely state that Durand created this type of picture under the influence of the passages just quoted, it would seem at least possible that in these Durand intended that the sublime portion should stand as an emblem of divine justice, and the beautiful, of divine love.[21]

If the sublime and the beautiful were presented as equivalent, they would suggest that justice and love are equally essential attributes of God. This, as we have noted, was not Channing's view. According to Channing, God's justice is a mode in which divine love temporarily operates to prepare man for the reception of divine grace. Hence, the operation of justice precedes grace and eventually gives way to it. The prior operation of God's justice in respect to man is the condition of man's salvation. It would seem that, in his composite paintings, Durand sought not only to combine emblems of divine justice and love, but also to arrange them in that order in which they must be experienced by man if he is to be redeemed. Hence, the sublime passage appears in the foreground; the beautiful, in the distance. As the spectator encounters first the warning of the sublime and secondly the beatification of the beautiful, he would in a sense experience the mystery of his own salvation. He enters into the warning purgatory of the foreground sublimity as a soul that still must walk. But, at the further limit of this, there remains nothing but the heaven of the beautiful over which the purified soul may wing its way in freedom.

If we apply the same ideas to the forest-interior paintings, we may, I believe, recognize in their arboreal sublimity "a solemn minister of Divine justice and a witness of God's power to a thoughtless world." Emblematic especially of divine justice and power, the forest remains a "cathedral" in which religious emotions may be stirred. But the forest-cathedral is more closely related to the Protestant than to the Catholic church building, in that it stands more as a place of exhortation and conversion than as the earthly image of the Heavenly Jerusalem. Yet, even in the forest there is some sign of the divine love that operates subsequent to the operation of justice, for tender plants and filtered sunlight mitigate the sublimity of the trees.

Finally, what of the pastoral landscapes that display primarily natural forms and effects that are beautiful? In terms of the present set of ideas, these would be emblematic of God's love. But if love is ultimately the sole and essential attribute of God, then these landscapes would represent him most simply. However, these landscapes might also be regarded in the light of another statement of Channing. In his "Remarks on the Character and Writings of Fénelon," Channing noted

> that our love of nature has an affinity with the love
> of God, and was meant as a preparation for it; for the
> harmonies of nature are only his wisdom made visible;
> the heavens, so sublime, are a revelation of his

515

immensity; and the beauty of creation images to us his
overflowing love and blessedness.[22]

The harmonies of nature, the heavens, and the beauty of nature
are fully represented in these paintings, in which Durand consciously perfected and organized the various aspects of nature.
Even if these paintings are regarded as emblematic of the more
differentiated attributes--wisdom, immensity, and love--they
would still represent the single person of God who possesses
these diverse qualities. Viewed in either way, the pastoral
landscapes tend more to reveal God than to convert the spectator (forest-interiors) or to provide a foretaste of redemption
(composite landscapes).

That Durand regarded nature as symbolic of the attributes
of God we know from his own statement. Yet, is it really possible
that the forest-interiors and the composite landscapes were regarded by Durand as instrumental to the spectator's redemption?
Amid the realistic imagery of the normal composite picture,
there is, of course, nothing that guarantees the certainty of
such an interpretation. We could hardly expect so refined an
explanation from Durand himself. There are, however, several
thematic paintings that, when studied closely in connection
with their sources, do seem to point to the relevance of the
notions of a redeemer and redemption to an understanding of the
two types of landscape.

II. <u>Kindred</u> <u>Spirits</u>.

Judging from the frequency with which it has been shown in recent exhibitions and reproduced in every type of publication from the popular magazine to the scholarly journal, it is apparent that Durand's <u>Kindred</u> <u>Spirits</u> (Fig. 201) is his most appealing painting. In a sense it has come to hold the position for the present generation of <u>the</u> Hudson River School painting.[23] A polished yet virile technique, clarity of form, variety of natural phenomena, an elegance in the twining trees, harmonious colors softened by atmosphere make up the interest of the painting to the eye. But when we notice that William Cullen Bryant and Thomas Cole--their names are inscribed on a tree at the left foreground--have been introduced into the picture in some sort of conversation upon the features of nature, we are also invited to think of that love of nature shared by poet and painter alike. But, no matter how long we look at the painting, we see nothing more than what first meets the eye: a rocky, wooded clove--albeit, of a rather artificial and pieced-together character--in which stand the poet and the painter. Several writers have recently compared the poetry of Bryant with the painting of Cole[24] and discovered sufficient similarity of theme and imagery to justify Durand's application of the title <u>Kindred</u> <u>Spirits</u> to them. Nature and nature's poets--perhaps that is all that Durand intended.

Nevertheless, if we attempt to recover the circumstances in which the painting was executed, we may be able to discover other levels of meaning. On February 6, 1848, Thomas Cole was stricken with a severe inflammation of the lungs, and within a few days, on February 11, he died at his home in Catskill, New York.[25] A week later, during a special meeting of the National Academy, its president, Durand, offered the following comments upon the career of his friend and colleague:

> It was ever his great aim to elevate the standard
> of landscape art, and he has been eminently successful.
> He has advanced it far beyond the point at which he
> found it among us, and more than this, he has demon-
> strated its high moral capabilities which, hitherto,
> had been at best, but incidentally and capriciously
> exerted, and hence, he is richly entitled to the name
> of Benefactor.[26]

About three weeks later--May 4, 1848--Bryant delivered his full-length "Funeral Oration" before the National Academy. Shortly thereafter a retrospective exhibition of Cole's paintings opened at the Gallery of the American Art-Union. The painting <u>Kindred Spirits</u> was commissioned by Durand's faithful patron Jonathan Sturges and presented by him to Bryant. In presenting the painting, Sturges gave the following account of the considerations which had induced him to have Durand paint it:

> Soon after you [i.e., Bryant] delivered your oration
> on the life and death of our lamented friend Cole, I
> requested Mr. Durand to paint a picture in which he
> should associate our departed friend and yourself as
> kindred spirits. I think the design, as well as the

execution, will meet your approbation, and I hope that
you will accept the picture from me as a token of
gratitude for the labor of love performed on that
occasion.[27]

The painting was exhibited at the National Academy in 1849 with
no explanation as to its meaning.

A. Kindred Spirits and Bryant's "Funeral Oration."

Because the painting was intended as a token of appreciation
of the "Funeral Oration," we might expect to find therein a passage
that could have suggested the idea of uniting poet and painter
in the contemplation of nature.  In fact, the following contains
ideas and images which may have suggested the subject:

There are few, I suppose, who do not recollect the lines
of Walter Scott, beginning thus:

Call it not vain; they do not err

Who say, that when the poet dies,

Mute nature mourns her worshipper,

And celebrates his obsequies.

This is said of the poet; but the landscape painter is
admitted to a closer familiarity with nature than the
poet.  He studies her aspect more minutely and watches
with a more affectionate attention its varied expressions . . . All her boundless variety of outlines and
shades become almost a part of his being and are blended
with his mind.[28]

Here, the study of nature by poet and painter is compared to the advantage of the latter. This may have suggested the introduction of the two figures in the painting. But also, it may have suggested the animated gestures of the painter as the fonder devotee. From this point of view, the painting might be regarded a memorial of Cole's deep love for and knowledge of the varied aspects of nature.

The painting assumes a deeper significance in the light of another thought in the "Oration":

> Let me say, however, that we feel that much is taken
> away from the charms of nature when such a man departs.
> To us who remain, the region of the Catskills, where
> he wandered and studied and sketched, and wrought his
> sketches into such glorious creations, is saddened by
> a certain desolate feeling when we behold it or think
> of it. The mind that we knew was abroad in those scenes
> of grandeur and beauty, and which gave them a higher
> interest in our eyes, has passed from the earth, and
> we see that something of the power and greatness is
> withdrawn from the sublime mountain tops and the broad
> forest and the rushing waterfalls.[29]

In the painting Cole is "restored" to his old haunts, and they cease to be so desolate as when he was absent. By restoring the painter, Durand reinvests mountain, forest, and waterfall with something of their old power and greatness. Seeing Cole again among the scenes they both had loved might have afforded Bryant a measure of consolation. But if the significance of

the painting ended here, it would hardly display "the high moral
capabilities" which, according to Durand, Cole has shown that
landscape painting might possess. If there is a key to a higher
level of meaning, it must be sought elsewhere.

B. Keats's Seventh "Sonnet."

The title itself affords, perhaps, the best clue. In composing
the painting, Durand bore in mind a sonnet by John Keats. The
seventh "Sonnet" in the collection published in 1817 is something
like a program for the imagery of the painting:

> O Solitude! if I must with thee dwell,
>
> Let it not be among the jumbled heap
>
> Of murky buildings; climb with me to the steep,--
>
> Nature's observatory--whence the dell,
>
> Its flowery slopes, its river's crystal swell,
>
> May seem a span; let me thy vigils keep
>
> 'Mongst boughs pavillion'd, where the deer's swift leap
>
> Startles the wild bee from the fox-glove bell.
>
> But though I'll gladly trace these scenes with thee,
>
> Yet the sweet converse of an innocent mind,
>
> Whose words are images of thoughts refined,
>
> Is my soul's pleasure; and it sure must be
>
> Almost the highest bliss of human kind,
>
> When to thy haunts two kindred spirits flee.[30]

Several aspects of the scene in the painting are mentioned in
the poem--a height from which one might view a "dell" through
which a river (in Durand's painting merely a brook)runs. In

the poem the speaker expresses the wish to contemplate nature
"'Mongst boughs pavillion'd." This phrase inspired the especially elegant limb arching over the figures in the painting.
That Durand devoted considerable thought to this limb is indicated by the existence of a preparatory drawing--probably made
from nature--of the limb alone (Fig. 200). Furthermore, the
poem contains reference to two distinct persons--the speaker,
Solitude's companion, and the wished-for "innocent mind." We
might wonder whether Durand intended that each of these persons
be identified with one of the figures in the painting. The
speaker may be connected with Cole. It was he who permanently
withdrew from the city to reside amid the scenes of nature at
Catskill. Also, in many periods of his life, he was the chosen
companion of Solitude. Bryant, then, could be identified with
the longed-for friend "Whose words /as a poet/ are images of
thoughts refined." Hence the two are the "kindred spirits" of
Keats's "Sonnet."

Now, if Cole and Bryant are Keats's "kindred spirits," we
might assume that they presently enjoy "Almost the highest bliss
of human kind," which in the poem is not yet attained by the
speaker. In the contemplation of and the conversation upon
nature, Cole and Bryant experience a qualified beatitude. But
if the "Sonnet" permits us to identify their experience as a
qualified beatitude, does it not also permit us to associate
with the painting the idea of an unqualified beatitude--that is,
the idea of immortality? From Durand's Christian point of view

immortality was certainly "the highest bliss of human kind."
But, of course, we must ask whether there is anything about the
painting itself that could suggest the idea of man's redemption.

C. Cole's _Expulsion_ _from_ _Eden_.

The more one studies Durand's landscape, the more one is
struck by the utter arbitrariness of its composition. Into what
soil do the four trees at the left send their roots? To what
mass of land is the rock upon which Cole and Bryant stand attached?
How did one of the Hudson's palisades--the cliff at the right--
find its way amid these wooded hills? Throughout, the landscape
bears unmistakeable signs of having been "made up" in the studio.
But, it was not "made up" purely out of imagination. In fact,
it is clearly a consciously contrived modification of the landscape at the left side of Cole's early _Expulsion_ _from_ _Eden_ (Fig.
202). This picture, executed in 1828, was included in the
memorial exhibition at the American Art-Union in 1848. There
can be no doubt that Durand saw it there, and he may have later
borrowed it while working on the _Kindred_ _Spirits_. In a letter
to Durand, dated June 4, 1849, his son John states: "Mr. Cole's
picture I have not sent to-day because Conely is not here to
attend to the boxing of it up. I will send it tomorrow by the
Superior."[31] Unfortunately he does not mention the title of the
painting in question. Whether or not Durand had Cole's painting
in his studio while working on the _Kindred_ _Spirits_, the various
elements--twisting and broken trees, rocky ledge, cliffs, waterfall, and distant mountains--of Cole's thoroughly sublime scene

do reappear, chastened and subdued, in Durand's painting.
Indeed, Cole and Bryant stand in the Kindred Spirits in much
the same situation as Adam and Eve in the Expulsion. In Cole's
painting the world of nature is a sort of hell in which Man
is punished for his sin. There is nothing in the world into
which Adam and Eve are driven that bespeaks anything but the
savagery of nature--that is, the wrath of God. In Durand's
painting the same world has assumed a kindlier aspect. Yet,
Durand's landscape is not the fictional, tropical Paradise
glimpsed at the right in Cole's painting. Where Cole represented
man in the moment of being cast out of Eden, it might seem that,
in revising Cole's composition, Durand sought to represent man
in the process of returning--not to Eden, for the physical
bridge no longer exists--but to an immortal life in a purely
spiritual Paradise. Cole's Adam and Eve experience almost the
highest evil of human kind, for they have not yet encountered
the full brutality of their new world. Perhaps Durand's kindred
spirits experience "Almost the highest bliss of human kind,"
because they approach, but have not attained, redemption.

D. Other Paintings by Cole.

The idea that painting might lead the soul to the gates of
Paradise would not have seemed strange to one familiar with the
work of Cole. In his early series, The Voyage of Life (1839),
the voyager passes through the evils of the world, saved by his
faith,[32] and in the fourth picture enters the sea of eternity
over which the veil draws back to reveal a supernal light and

angelic beings. In the last year of his life, Cole returned to
the same theme in his unfinished series The Cross and the World.
The last picture of this series was described as follows in
The Literary World, April 15, 1848:

> In the fourth picture the Pilgrim of the Cross has
> reached the end of his pilgrimage. He stands upon life's
> remotest verge, and sees the boundless and infinite open
> before his astonished gaze. The clouds that so long have
> enveloped his path are torn away, and through the vista
> he sees a vision of transcendent glory, of boundless
> immensity. Innumerable angels seem to hover about the
> bright clouds that seem like steps and approaches to
> the cross, which, now fully revealed, pours its effulgence
> over the scene; angels "trailing clouds of glory" and
> bearing the palm and crown of immortality, advance to
> meet him. The world beneath his feet, with its trials
> and temptations, is forgotten.[33]

If Durand intended to represent his kindred spirits as experiencing
almost the highest bliss of human kind, and if we may even define
this experience as an arrival upon the threshold of redemption,
then he sought to accomplish no more than what Cole had undertaken
in the later part of his career. Through his modification of
Cole's Expulsion, Durand has displaced the pessimism of Cole's
early painting by an optimism paralleling that which Cole himself
expressed in his later work. Where, in the Expulsion, man is
driven from the presence of God, in the Cross and the World
and in Kindred Spirits, man returns to God. The journey of

return through nature to God, of course, Cole had already completed at the time <u>Kindred</u> <u>Spirits</u> was painted.

The species of imagery employed in the <u>Cross</u> <u>and</u> <u>the</u> <u>World</u>
differs radically from that employed in <u>Kindred</u> <u>Spirits</u>. Cole,
in the last painting of his series, indicates the supernatural
realm through the use of such conventional symbols as the Cross,
palm, crown, and celestial light--all borne or accompanied by
angels. Durand has dispensed with all of this in favor of the
real forms, light, and colors of nature itself. For, according
to Channing, these forms do reveal the reality of immortal life
to the discerning spirit:

> The proof of immortality, which is suited to all under-
> standing, is found in the Gospel, sealed by the blood
> and confirmed by the resurrection of Christ. But this,
> I think, is made more impressive, by a demonstration
> of its harmony with the teachings of nature. To me,
> nature and revelation speak with one voice on the great
> theme of man's future being. Let not this joint witness
> be unheard . . . But when . . . I look round on the
> creation, and see there the marks of an omnipotent
> goodness, to which nothing is impossible, and from which
> everything may be hoped . . . I can and do admit the al-
> most overpowering thought of the everlasting life,
> growth, felicity of the human soul.[34]

Here, at last, the revelation of nature ceases to be inferior to
that of Scripture. Both announce the goodness of God and the
reality of human redemption.

From the foregoing it would seem apparent that Durand in the _Kindred Spirits_ did not intend simply to comment on certain parallels between the painting of Cole and the poetry of Bryant. He did not intend simply to define the relative depth of the painter's and the poet's study of nature. He did not intend simply to console Bryant by "restoring" Cole to his old haunts. Rather, it seems more than likely that he intended to assert that man may approach immortal life through the contemplation of nature. Or, more specifically, he intended to suggest that Cole had achieved redemption through his assiduous pursuit of this path. Nature may lead man back to God--Nature had led Cole, lately deceased, back to God. Such, it would seem, is the message of the painting. Some argument in favor of Cole's attainment of salvation would, of course, be an appropriate element in a memorial painting. And, if Durand did in fact intend such a reference, it would parallel Bryant's use in the "Funeral Oration" of the fact that Cole had died in full possession of his mental faculties as an argument for the reality of eternal life. Hence, the relationships noted between Durand's painting, Keats's "Sonnet," Cole's _Expulsion_, and Bryant's "Funeral Oration" all lend support to the hypothesis that Durand sought to connect the idea of man's redemption with landscape painting. And, since _Kindred Spirits_ is a composite landscape, it seems not impossible that the idea of redemption might be connected with the other works in this group as well.

E. The Redeemer.

But we have yet to find in the imagery of Kindred Spirits
any reference to God in the character of redeemer. In terms of
Sturges' letter to Bryant and Keats's "Sonnet" it is clear that
Cole and Bryant, as represented in the painting, are the "kindred
spirits" referred to by its title. If, however, we turn to
Channing we discover another pair of spirits which are kindred:

> It is plain, too, that likeness to God is the true
> and only preparation for the enjoyment of the universe.
> In proportion as we approach and resemble the mind of
> God, we are brought into harmony with the creation; for,
> in that proportion, we possess the principles from
> which the universe sprung; we carry within ourselves
> the perfections of which its beauty, magnificence, order,
> benevolent adaptations, and boundless purposes, are the
> results and manifestations. God unfolds himself in his
> works to a kindred mind . . . every reflecting man will
> feel, that likeness to God must be a principle of
> sympathy or accordance with his creation; for the creation
> is a birth and a shining forth of the Divine Mind, a
> work through which his spirit breathes. In proportion
> as we receive this spirit, we possess within ourselves
> the explanation of what we see. We discern more and
> more of God in everything, from the frail flower to the
> everlasting stars.[35]

Further, according to Channing, the enlightened human mind discerns in nature not only God, but also His attributes:

> The universe, I know, is full of God.  The heavens and
> earth declare his glory.  In other words, the effects
> and signs of power, wisdom, and goodness, are apparent
> through the whole creation.  But apparent to what?
> Not to the outward eye; not to the acutest organs of
> sense; but to a kindred mind, which interprets the
> universe by itself.[36]

The human mind, as it becomes spiritually illuminated, approaches
to a state of kinship with God.  But also, as the individual
human spirit is so illuminated, it will experience a love of
those natural forms which reveal, to the enlightened, the fullness of the divine character, his power, wisdom, and goodness.
From this point of view, the clove contemplated by Cole and
Bryant not only affords intimations of immortality, but also
brings them into communication with the divine mind which reveals itself in nature to an enlightened, and therefore kindred,
human mind.

Now, if God reveals the differentiations of his character
to a kindred spirit through nature, then nature, as the medium
of communication, must be multiform rather than uniform.  A
multiform landscape does in fact appear in Kindred Spirits.
The twisted tree trunks and ragged rocks of the foreground
clearly stand in contrast to the harmonious lines and colors
of the distant hills.  If these forms represent diverse aspects
of the divine character, the foreground must bespeak God's
power, wisdom, and/or justice, while the more gentle distance
would indicate his goodness and mercy.  The different voices

with which God speaks to man in these contrasting aspects of
nature might be coördinated with the fact that, in the painting, Bryant's gaze is confined within the foreground sublimity,
while Cole points with his cane to the distant beauty as he
turns to address Bryant.  At the time the picture was painted,
Bryant was, of course, still alive.  To him the chastening
effect of the sublime, emblematic of God's power, wisdom, and
justice, was most relevant to his eventual redemption.  However,
Cole was deceased at the time the picture was painted.  As he
already, we may assume, dwelt among the blessed, a full participant in divine goodness, the chastening effect of God's justice
is no longer relevant to his spiritual progress.  Hence, he is
represented in the painting as being aware exclusively of the
divine goodness revealed in the beautiful hills toward which
he directs Bryant's attention.[37]  The whole painting would seem
to represent the contrary characters that God appears to display
in the role of redeemer.  But when the spectator so far forgets
his own material nature, when he identifies himself with the
nearer figure in the painting (as Durand clearly intended that
Bryant should do), when he heeds the advice of his companion,
and when he looks beyond the sublimity of the foreground, his
gaze is met by a pure vision of the divine goodness in which
the redeemed soul exclusively participates.

III. _Thanatopsis_.

As we have noted, the artificial landscape in _Kindred Spirits_ was inspired by Cole's early _Expulsion from the Garden of Eden_. If our interpretation of _Kindred Spirits_ be correct, it would seem that Durand quite consciously intended to controvert the pessimism of the earlier work. About a year later Durand painted _Thanatopsis_ (Fig. 204), an elaborate composition, the imagery of which was inspired by Bryant's early poem. The following verses from the poem were printed in the catalogues of the National Academy and the American Art-Union when the painting was exhibited at each institution in 1850:

> The hills,
>
> Rock-ribbed and ancient as the sun--the vales
>
> Stretching in pensive quietness between;
>
> The venerable woods--rivers that move
>
> In majesty, and the complaining brooks
>
> That make the meadows green; and poured round all
>
> Old Ocean's gray and melancholy waste,--
>
> Are but the solemn decorations all
>
> Of the great tomb of man.[38]

This passage suggested a part of the imagery of the painting. Durand's hills are "rock-ribbed and ancient as the sun." To the left extends a quiet valley. The woods in the foreground are especially "venerable," and across the plain a river moves "in majesty" along green meadows. Finally, in the extreme distance is "old ocean" which may or may not be a "gray and melancholy

waste." But other and more subtle images in the poem reappear
in the painting. In introducing the idea of death the poet
speaks of

> . . . sad images
>
> Of the stern agony, and the shroud, and pall,
>
> And breathless darkness, and the narrow house . . .

images that are comparable to the fragments of funereal monuments,
Egyptian, Classical, and Medieval, scattered in chronological
order from left to right across the foreground. Durand's setting
sun seems to encompass the image and idea of

> Yet a few days, and thee
>
> The all-beholding sun shall see no more
>
> In all his course . . .

In death

> . . . shalt thou go
>
> To mix forever with the elements,
>
> To be a brother to the insensible rock
>
> And to the sluggish clod, which the rude swain
>
> Turns with his share, and treads upon.

In the painting such a "rude swain" appears on the hillside toward
the left. Further,

> The oak
>
> Shall send his roots abroad, and pierce thy mould.

This particular attack upon human remains is clearly exhibited
in the roots of a tree which clasp a skull at the right-hand
foreground. This tree and the distant plowman define the limits
within which the distinct signs of death are confined. The

castle and the cathedral suggest the people of the remote past--
"kings, the powerful of the earth . . . hoary seers"--whose
companions we shall be in death. Finally, the burial party seen
beneath the trees at the right, reflects the lines:

> As the long train
>
> Of ages glide away, the sons of men,
>
> The youth in life's green spring, and he who goes
>
> In the full strength of years, matron and maid,
>
> The speechless babe, and the gray-headed man
>
> Shall one by one be gathered to thy side,
>
> By those, who in their turn shall follow them.

No significant image appears in the painting that is not related
to an image or idea in the poem.

But, in painting the picture did Durand simply intend to
reaffirm the ideas expressed in the poem? In the poem itself
Bryant claims only to present "Nature's teaching" in regard to
death. And, at the time it was written, nature taught him only
that life is brief, that the dead are reabsorbed into the
material world, that in all places and times man has perished
and shall perish. The concluding stanza, added as an afterthought, invites the reader to conduct his life in such a way
that the final act, which none may escape, may be executed
with equanimity. Nowhere is there the least reference to an
immortal life beyond the grave. It may be observed that, in
a certain sense, Bryant's poem is similar to Cole's Expulsion.
In both works nature is presented simply as a realm of death
which neither reveals a redeemer nor indicates man's redemption.

If Durand in 1849-1850 intended to reaffirm Bryant's early understanding of "Nature's teaching," our interpretation of Durand's <u>Kindred</u> <u>Spirits</u> must be entirely wrong. If, on the other hand, our interpretation of <u>Kindred</u> <u>Spirits</u> is correct, then Durand must have intended to revise in his <u>Thanatopsis</u> the lesson inculcated in Bryant's.

By what means might Durand have sought to accomplish this revision? If we re-examine that portion of the poem quoted by Durand in the exhibition catalogues, it may be noted that the natural phenomena ennumerated are neither described in detail nor arranged in a particular spatial order. In his early poem Bryant, like Cole in his <u>Expulsion</u>, emphasizes the expression rather than the forms or structure of nature. In translating the poem into a visual image, Durand has retained something of the diverse expressions, but also he has described the phenomena in much greater detail and arranged them in a certain order. It is this last factor that is of greatest importance. Durand has made a landscape out of Bryant's list of the elements of landscape. And in so doing he appears to have carefully separated the sublime from the beautiful. The former--emblems of death, venerable woods, cathedral, castle, and mountains--is limited to the foreground and right middle-ground. The beautiful-- winding river, meadows, ocean, and setting sun--occurs in the left middle-ground and the distance. The sublime precedes, parallels, and finally gives way to the beautiful. In the differentiations of the landscape, as Durand has organized it, we might be willing to see emblems of the diverse aspects of the divine character. The purely sublime foreground might be regarded as emblematic of divine justice; the mixed middle-ground, of divine power and mercy; and the distance, of divine love. Or, in terms of the scheme of man's redemption, the three distances might be regarded as denoting Hell, Purgatory, and Paradise respectively.

But is there really anything in the painting that points to the relevance of a concept of the divine character to its interpretation? Possibly the cathedral and its relationship to the burial grove provide the answer to this question. Neither of these motifs was directly derived from the imagery of the poem. At most they were merely suggested. Now, since the grove is represented as a place of burial, an act connected with a religious rite, and as it is intimately connected with a cathedral, we may identify the grove with the templum memorale of Bryant's later poem "A Forest Hymn."[39] According to Bryant, the first effect of the forest upon its visitor is to bow

His spirit with the thought of boundless power

And inaccessible majesty.

The proliferation of symbols of death in the foreground of Durand's painting must reinforce the humbling effect of the grove itself. But once the spectator has attained this state of reverent humility, he is able to discern the presence of God in nature:

Grandeur, strength, and grace

Are here to speak of thee.

Forms expressive of these qualities Durand has reserved for the
second phase of his landscape--i.e., the middle-ground. There
can be no question but that the mountains display grandeur, the
castle strength, and the plain with its winding river, grace.
Finally, in the "delicate forest flower" Bryant's forest-worshipper may discover

> An emanation of the indwelling Life,
>
> A visible token of the upholding Love,
>
> That are the soul of this great universe.

In the beauty of the sea and sunset-light of the distance Durand
may also have sought to adumbrate God's upholding love or the
soul of the universe.  Hence, the order--humility, awareness of
the manifold character of God, and awareness of the undifferentiated essence of God--of the progressive religious experience
of the forest-worshipper, would appear to have governed the
order in which Durand spatially distributed the motifs enumerated
in Bryant's "Thanatopsis."  Arranged as they are in Durand's
painting, the natural phenomena specified in a poem in which
God is not even mentioned are made to awaken in the spectator
a consciousness of God, whose essence is progressively revealed.

In Bryant's "A Forest Hymn" nature does not merely reveal
the character and essence of God; it also conveys the concept of
immortality, and the following lines might almost be read as a
conscious correction of the hopelessness of his earlier poem:

> Life mocks the idle hate
>
> Of his arch-enemy Death--yea, seats himself
>
> Upon the tyrant's throne--the sepulchre,

> And of the triumphs of his ghostly foe
>
> Makes his own nourishment. For he $\underline{/}$i.e., Life$\underline{/}$ came forth
>
> From thine $\underline{/}$i.e., God's$\underline{/}$ own bosom, and shall have no end.

Bryant had in mind here only the fact that vegetable life eternally nourishes itself upon its own decay. In his painting, however, Durand has represented life as nourished by death in the tree which sends its roots amid human decay in the right foreground. While human decay is not represented as directly nourishing the immortal life of man, perhaps Durand intended to express the idea that a full awareness of the reality of death induces that humility in the living individual which is the foundation of human salvation, or eternal life. As in the vegetable world "eternal" life is nourished by death, so in the moral world eternal life is nourished by a humble submission to the fact of death. In contemplating Durand's painting the spectator's pride is destroyed both by the sublimity of the forest-temple and by the numerous images of death. Then, once the spectator has been purified by his experience of the foreground, he is able to escape the prison of his material being and fly away, as a pure spirit, over the symbols of the middle-ground and distance which afford that revelation of the Being of God which is reserved for the redeemed alone.[40]

When Durand's _Thanatopsis_ is interpreted in the light of Bryant's later poem, it would appear that here again he has corrected an early work in terms of a later. While in Bryant's "Thanatopsis" the fact of death stands only as an imperative to moral conduct in this world, in Durand's painting the fact of death is presented as a cause of man's redemption and as a prelude to a vision of God. Through a calculated manipulation of symbols Durand is able to conduct the spectator out of the world of matter and into the presence of the supreme spiritual reality.

IV. <u>Other</u> <u>Paintings</u> <u>Dealing</u> <u>with</u> <u>the</u> <u>Theme</u> <u>of</u> <u>Immortality</u>.

If, in fact, <u>Kindred</u> <u>Spirits</u> does embody symbols of the
character of God, in his role as redeemer, and of the scheme of
man's redemption, we might expect to find similar ideas expressed in other paintings. We have already discussed the
religious emotions that the forest-interior paintings may arouse.
Viewed as a "temple" the forest becomes a place of worship, it
excites the feelings appropriate to a place of worship, and it
supplants the institutionalized, and therefore sectarian, church.
But it is also most likely that Durand intended that his forests
possess the same meaning that Bryant, in a section of the "Forest
Hymn" partially cited above, ascribed to the forest itself.
According to Bryant, animate things die and decay but are ever
born again:

> My heart is awed within me when I think
> Of the great miracle that still goes on,
> In silence round me--the perpetual work
> Of thy creation, finished, yet renewed
> Forever. Written on thy works I read
> The lesson of thy own eternity.
> Lo! all grow old and die--but see again,
> How on the faltering footsteps of decay
> Youth presses--ever gay and beautiful youth
> In all its beautiful forms. These lofty trees
> Wave not less proudly that their ancestors
> Moulder beneath them. Oh, there is not lost

One of earth's charms:  upon her bosom yet,

After the flight of untold centuries,

The freshness of her far beginning lies

And yet shall lie.  Life mocks the idle hate

Of his arch-enemy Death--yea, seats himself

Upon the tyrant's throne--the sepulchre,

And of the triumph of his ghastly foe

Makes his own nourishment.  For he came forth

From thine own bosom and shall have no end.

Life, then, participates in the eternity of God.  Death, in nature, is but a transition between one form of life and another.  Curiously, Bryant does not explicitly employ the resurrection of nature as an argument for the resurrection of man.  This latter view, however, is set forth by Gilpin:

How does everything around us bring its lesson to our minds!  Nature is the great book of God.  In every page is instruction to those who read.  Mortality must claim its due.  Death in various shapes hovers around us--Thus far went the heathen moralist.  He had learned no other knowledge from these perishing forms of nature, but that men, like trees, are subject to death.

. . . Ita

Debemur morti nos, nostraque . . .

Better instructed, learn then a nobler lesson.  Learn, that that God, who with the blast of winter shrivels the tree, and with the breezes of spring restores it, offers it to thee as an emblem of thy hopes.  The same God pre-

sides over the natural, and moral world. His works
are uniform. The truths, which _nature_ teaches, as
far as they go, are the truths of _revelation_ also.
It is written in both these books, that, that power,
which revives the tree, will revive thee also, like
it, with increasing perfection.[41]

The cycle of death and resurrection in nature, which promises
resurrection for man as well, is expressed in Durand's forest-
interiors by the prominently displayed fallen trees, which in
their decay nourish the living. His paintings, in this respect,
are closer to Bryant than to Gilpin. Gilpin's notion that it
is the death of nature in winter that assures mankind of the
fact of resurrection is illustrated in Caspar David Friedrich's
Cloister Graveyard in the Snow of 1810 (Fig. 173). Friedrich's
painting, as we have noted, displays a ruined abbey indicating
the displacement of institutionalized religion by nature. But
it also contains a funeral party and the graves that enclose
the dead whose resurrection is promised by the incipient re-
vivication of nature, now moribund beneath its blanket of snow.
The fundamental difference between Durand's paintings and that
by Friedrich is that Friedrich's offers no present and visible
tokens of the character of God in his role as redeemer, while
Durand's sublime forest, indicative of power, majesty, and
justice, displays also signs of divine mercy in the frail forest
plants and the sunlight that filters through the foliage.

If any doubt remains that Durand intended his forest-interiors as emblems of the fact of resurrection, we need only

turn to his <u>Letters</u>. The following passage, inspired by Bryant's
"Forest Hymn" may be applied to the forest interiors, as it was
in these that Durand exercised the least degree of selectivity:

> However subordinate the department of view-paint-
> ing may be considered in its general sense, it rises
> at times to the level of the highest creations of Art,
> so far as the expression of its elements is concerned.
> Many an actual picture of this description may be found
> amongst the primitive wilds of Nature, where
>
>> Upon her bosom yet
>> After the lapse of untold centuries,
>> The freshness of her far-beginning lies.
>
> The reverent imagination ceases to exalt in its
> own conscious power to change and recreate, while it
> contemplates the great miracle of God's creation,
> "which still goes on in silence"--where all deficiency
> in picturesqueness is more than supplied by that "fresh-
> ness of the far-beginning" of things which connects us
> with the past, and symbolizes our immortality.[42]

Durand, like Bryant and Gilpin, regarded the forest as a temple
or place of worship. As such and due to the character of its
forms it may be considered sublime. Its sublimity is fitted to
induce a sense of humility, humility uncontaminated by any idea
of man's arrogant effort to effect his own salvation by reform-
ing the things of nature to temporal ends. In experiencing
the forest-temple, the spectator is affected not only by the
expression of power and majesty, but he also contemplates death,

emblematically indicated by the fallen and decaying trees. Having become acquainted with the fact of death, there are also redeeming intimations of God's love and of a rebirth, of immortality, in which the spectator too might share.

Although the church as a sectarian institution is visually absent in Durand's later landscapes, we should not suppose that he had rejected the New Testament as an adequate account of the mechanism of man's salvation in favor of a pantheistic notion of redemption through a mere awareness of an identity between self and nature. In his search for a supra-sectarian religious faith, Durand did not abandon the Bible, which he continued to regard as the source of the highest "lessons":

> The external appearance of this our dwelling-place, apart from its wondrous structure and functions that minister to our well-being, is frought with lessons of high and holy meaning, only surpassed by the light of Revelation.[43]

With Channing and Gilpin, Durand shared the belief that once the "higher" truths are apprehended from revelation, they may be traced in the dealings of nature.

This idea unmistakably underlies Durand's God's Judgment upon Gog (App. II, no. 287), exhibited at the National Academy in 1852. This elaborate composition, formerly in the Metropolitan Museum in New York, but at present unlocated, was unique among Durand's work, in that here he adopted the "dangerous-sublime" of Edmund Burke, which Thomas Cole had especially appropriated. The painting was described in 1856 as:

. . . a wild supernatural scene, totally unlike any of
his other pictures, and one over which, of course, the
critics differed widely. This was a commission, the
subject being assigned.[44]

Like Kindred Spirits and Thanatopsis, the painting illustrated a
literary text. In the National Academy's exhibition catalogue,
the spectator was referred to Ezekiel, chapter 39, verse 17,
"and context." The seventeenth verse was printed in the catalogue:

And, thou son of man, thus saith the Lord God;
speak unto every feathered fowl, and to every beast of
the field, Assemble yourselves, and come; gather yourselves on every side to my sacrifice, that I do sacrifice for you, even a great sacrifice upon the mountains
of Israel, that ye may eat flesh, and drink blood.

This eating of flesh and drinking of blood is not what we normally
associate with a Hudson River School landscape. But, I think,
it must be evident that, in this passage, Durand or his patron
found a means to naturalize the Eucharist and thereby to symbolize, no matter how darkly, the self-sacrifice that a beneficent
Deity has made in order to open up a path of salvation for man.
When we note that it was Jonathan Sturges who assigned this subject, in which an identification of the religion of nature with
Christianity is explicit, and when we recall that it was also
Sturges who commissioned the painting Kindred Spirits, Durand's
first major work in which the identification is implicit, we
gain some insight into the depth of sympathy between painter

and patron and a clearer notion of the patron's real awareness of meanings that have become totally esoteric to the modern viewer.

V. Love Through All.

An adequate interpretation of Kindred Spirits and Thanatopsis appears to depend upon an acceptance of the sublime as a
symbol of divine justice and the beautiful as a symbol of divine
love. We may recall that, according to Channing, justice and
goodness are ultimately reconcilable--justice being but "a branch
or mode of exercise of benevolence."[45] Love is all but displays
itself sometimes as what is properly called justice. The difference between the two is operational rather than essential. If
justice is a branch of goodness, then the sublime may be considered a branch or mode of the beautiful. Both the sublime and
the beautiful should announce God's love. That all of the forms
of nature reveal a single and consistent divine love is insisted
upon by Channing in the following passage from a sermon of 1805:

> The Christian possesses a great advantage in the
> contemplation of nature. He beholds unity in the midst
> of variety. He looks round on the changing scenery,
> and in every leaf of the forest, every blade of grass,
> every hill, every valley, and every cloud of heaven, he
> discovers the traces of Divine benevolence. Creation
> is but a field spread before him for an infinitely
> varied display of love. This is the harmonizing prin-
> ciple which reduces to unity and simplicity the vast
> diversity of nature,--this is the perfection of the
> universe. It clothes in moral glory every object we
> contemplate. The Christian truly may be said to hear

the music of the spheres. He hears suns and planets
joining their melody in praise to their benignant
Creator. His ear, and his alone, is tuned to this
heavenly harmony. His soul is love.[46]

In his _Letters_, Durand clearly acknowledged the operation
of creative love in the universe. In speaking of the beauty of
the color green in nature, Durand described it as "the first
witness of organic life in the creation" and "the universal sign
of unimpeded and healthy action," but goes on to designate it
as "above all, the chosen color of creative Love for the earth's
chief decoration."[47] Channing's notion of love as a pervasive
and unifying force in nature is identical in its universality to
what Durand later described as the soul of nature or "the
spiritual beauty with which nature is animate." This "soul"
Durand attempted to describe in the following:

Every experienced artist knows that it is difficult
to see nature truly; that for this end long practice is
necessary. We see, yet perceive not, and it becomes
necessary to cultivate our perception so as to comprehend
the essence of the object seen. The poet sees in nature
more than mere matter of fact, yet he does not see more
than what is there, nor what another may not see when
he points it out. His is only a more perfect exercise
of perception, just as the drapery of a fine statue is
seen by the common eye, and pronounced beautiful, and
the enlightened observer also pronounces it beautiful;
but the one ascribes it to the graceful folding, the

other to its expression of the figure beneath, but neither sees more nor less in quantity than the other, but with unequal degrees of completeness in perception. Now, the highest beauty of this drapery consists in the perfection of its disposition, so as to best indicate the beautiful form it clothes, not possessing of itself too much attractiveness, nor lose its value by too strongly defining the figure. And so should we look on external nature.

Why have the creations of Raphael conferred on him the title of _divine_? Because he saw through the sensuous veil, and embodied the spiritual beauty with which nature is animate, and in whose presence the baser "passions shrink and tremble, and are still." . . . Childlike affection and religious reverence for the beauty that nature presents before us, form a basis of reliance which the conflicts of opinion can never disturb. . . . Where is the portrait-painter, having a just sense of his responsibilities, who has not often thrown down his brush in despair, after many fruitless attempts to express the soul that beams at times through the eye of beauty, and so with the yet more mysterious power of lofty intellect? And there is to be seen a corresponding soul and depth of expression in the beauty of landscape nature, which dignifies the art that embodies it, and improves and elevates the mind that loves to contemplate its pictorial image.[48]

Here Durand is attempting to define the ultimate object of representation for the painter. It is not the painter's task to represent something other than what may be seen in nature. He does not _invent_ fantasies of his own. But, as he cultivates his perceptions, as he looks upon nature with the eye of faith, he perceives something more than the crude material facts of nature, that alone are accessible to the vulgar eye. What the painter sees and seeks to represent is an indwelling spirit, a soul, that reveals itself in the outward form of things. The spirit itself is similar to that described by Wordsworth--

> . . . And I have felt
>
> A presence that disturbs me with the joy
>
> Of elevated thoughts; a sense sublime
>
> Of something far more deeply interfused,
>
> Whose dwelling is the light of setting suns,
>
> And the round ocean and the living air,
>
> And the blue sky and in the mind of man:
>
> A motion and a spirit, that impels
>
> All thinking things, all objects of all thought,
>
> And rolls through all things.[49]

But Wordsworth does not identify this "something . . . deeply interfused" with Divine Love, and, unlike Durand and Channing, he locates its presence more particularly in the etherial aspects of nature than in all things indiscriminately.

If the spirit described by Durand is related to that described by Wordsworth, it is also noteworthy that the passage in which Durand defines this spirit appears to have been in-

spired by a passage wherein Channing seeks to characterize the
ultimate object represented in Wordsworth's poetry:

> The great poet of our times, Wordsworth, one of the few
> men who are to live, has gone to common life, to the
> feelings of our universal nature, to the obscure and
> neglected portions of society, for beautiful and touching
> themes. Nor ought it to be said, that he has shed over
> these the charms of his genius; as if in themselves they
> had nothing grand or lovely. Genius is not a creator,
> in the sense of fancying or feigning what does not exist.
> Its distinction is, to discern more of the truth than
> common minds. It sees under disguises and humble forms
> everlasting beauty. This it is the prerogative of Words-
> worth to discern and reveal in the ordinary walks of
> life, in the common human heart. He has revealed the
> loveliness of the primitive feelings, of the universal
> affections of the human soul. The grand truth which
> pervades his poetry is, that the beautiful is not con-
> fined to the rare, the new, the distant, to scenery and
> modes of life open only to the few, but that it is poured
> forth profusely in the common earth and sky, that it
> gleams from the loneliest flower, that it lights up the
> humblest sphere, that the sweetest affections lodge in
> lowly hearts, that there is a sacredness, dignity, and
> loveliness in lives which few eyes rest on . . .[50]

As Durand did later, so here, Channing asserts that it is not
the office of the poet to invent fantasies, but rather to see

more in nature than meets the common eye. Channing's statement that genius sees "everlasting beauty" under "disguises and humble forms" is reflected in Durand's image of the statue and its drapery. Furthermore, what, according to Channing, Wordsworth sees in simple circumstances is the "loveliness of primitive feelings . . . the universal affections of the human soul"; that is, the universal spirit of love (affection) as it displays itself in mankind. This soul of mankind is clearly something quite similar to the "soul that beams at times through the eye of beauty" which, according to Durand, the portrait painter seeks, often in vain, to represent. And, following Wordsworth's "Tintern Abbey," from which he quotes in the Letters, Durand discerns a similar "soul and depth of expression in the beauty of landscape nature."

Is such an omnipresent expression of divine love really present in Durand's landscapes? If, in the composite pictures, he sought to indicate the justice and love which pertain to God as the redeemer, is it even logically possible that the expression of a single essence could coexist with this duality? Despite the disparity of expression, there are, I believe, two factors which serve to reunite the sublime and the beautiful into a single expression of an all-pervading divine love. First, all of the forms participate in a single, breathless stillness. The sublime is purely dependent upon immobile forms from which any implication of clamor has been eliminated. Second, all of the forms of nature are trapped in an intricate web of line. The larger forms in the distance are defined with the same precision as the smaller forms in the foreground. As a portrait painter in the 1830's, Durand had sought to describe the spiritual character of the man by a scrupulously detailed description of the outer form of the face, which he regarded as strictly controlled by that spiritual character. This concept of portraiture persists in his portrait of William Cullen Bryant, painted in 1854, one year before his comment on the identical aim of the portrait and landscape painter. The "portrait-realism" of his mature landscapes would seem to be less the product of his early experience as an engraver than of his experience as a portrait painter. In landscapes as in portraits, matter clothes spirit with that economy which denotes the unimpeded, plastic influence of the latter upon the former.

But Durand's landscapes represent more than just the hard forms of the earth and its vegetation. Light and atmosphere also play an important part, but they are described with so much control as to seem as measureable in their infinitude as the finite forms of matter. All things, tangible and intangible, are the visible utterance of an indwelling creative love. In the work of other painters—an Inness or Monet—light is elevated to the rank of sole, visible creative force, transfiguring nature by impingement. And Durand himself was not insensitive to the powers of light, to which he devoted the whole of the sixth of his _Letters_.

> Sunshine is the joyous expression of Nature, the
> lovely smile that lights up all her beauty, so changing
> and adoring all it rests upon, as to seem itself crea-

tive.  Mingling with the fitful humors of the atmosphere, it develops the full power of color, and evolves
the interminable variety of light and shade which constitutes the magic of chiaroscuro . . . I have more
respect for the devout heathen who worships the sun as
the visible Divinity, than for the artist whose pictures
betray insensibility to the charm of sunlight.[51]

Here, sunlight almost becomes a creative and divine power in its
own right--but not, in fact.  Rather, sunlight remains only
another utterance--"the lovely smile"--of the indwelling love,
and those who worship the sun are still heathen.  Sunlight is
but one phenomenon among others; and, despite all of the selectivity of his compositions, they continue to display a classic
reconciliation of the one and the manifold.  The consistency
with which Durand defines the manifold phenomena of nature in
the painting is merely an affirmation of his faith that these
are defined eternally by an indwelling spirit, coextensive with
the universe.  His mature paintings are not so much copies of
what has been created in the universe as they are assertions
that the universe is being created by an eternally present God
that is love.  Ultimately, to childlike affection and reverence,
nature reveals not merely types of the divine character, but
an all-pervasive God in the silence and forms of light, air,
and all of the things of the earth.  Conversely, when the painting itself is regarded as the work of the painter, it stands as an
affirmation of the conformity of human reason to the Stoic,

universal order and of the kinship between the mind of the
painter and the essence of God that is love.

CONCLUSION.

Although an all-pervasive creative love may be the ultimate
object of Durand's mature landscapes, its affirmation was not
his exclusive purpose.  Throughout his career he sought to construct images which should affect and spiritually elevate the
spectator.  His art is ever humanistic in character, in that
its principal end is to transform the animal-man into the infinite human being.

But to humanize is impossible without an ideal of the human,
and this Durand derived from his own participation in the lingering
classicism of America in the 1820's and 1830's, from the writings
of Channing and his disciples, and from the Stoicism of Seneca.
In the 1820's, Durand defined a materialistic ideal of physical
well-being in his engraving of the gymnasium proprietor William
Fuller.  In the 1830's, he found a higher ideal in the calm and
benign countenances of those men who had shaped the American
nation.  In Rome in 1841, he discovered in the aloof grandeur
of bearded patriarchs an ideal that assumes universality in its
primitive, uncorrupted naturalness.  These heads represent Dur-
and's mature conception of the ideal at its inception, and this
ideal he only restated in portraying the bearded, impassive
Bryant (Fig. 50) in the mid-1850's.

In the 1850's Durand exhibited a landscape which more explicitly indicates his concept of the ideal human character.  To

554

the 1856 exhibition at the National Academy, he sent A Symbol
(App. II, no. 324) based upon the following lines from Goldsmith's
"The Deserted Village":

> The service past, around the pious man /I.e., the parson7,
>
> With steady zeal each honest rustic ran;
>
> E'en children follow'd, with endearing wile,
>
> And pluck'd his gown to share the good man's smile.
>
> His ready smile a parent's warmth exprest;
>
> Their welfare pleased him and their cares distrest:
>
> To them his heart, his love, his griefs were given,
>
> But all his serious thoughts had rest in heaven:
>
> As some tall cliff that lifts its awful form,
>
> Swells from the vale, and midway leaves the storm,
>
> Though round its breast the rolling clouds are spread,
>
> Eternal sunshine settles on its head.

The last four lines were printed in the exhibition catalogue. In
the painting the "tall cliff" has become a mountain, the sunlit
peak of which breaks through the heavy and turbulent clouds of
a storm over a valley, which contains foreground rocks and trees
and a church building at a greater distance. The storm-lashed
valley and the things therein--including the church as a symbol
of institutionalized, sectarian religion--clearly express the
worldly tribulations to which man is heir. And yet the mountain,
standing amid these cares, also rises above them into a more
secure region of eternal being. Durand did not propose to relieve
the worldly sufferer by denying the existence of pain, but by
recommending fortitude and supplying grounds for hope.

If the proximate source for A Symbol was Goldsmith's poem, its ultimate source may have been the following passage from Seneca:

> So, if you see a man undismayed by dangers, untroubled by desires, happy in adversity, calm in the midst of storm, eyeing mankind from above and the gods on their own plane, won't you be touched with awe before him? Won't you say, "Here's a thing too great and sublime for any credible comparison between it and the puny body in which it dwells? Into that body a divine force has descended. The splendid and disciplined soul which leaves the little world unheeded and smiles at the objects of all our hopes and fears, draws its driving power from heaven. So great a creation can't stand without divinity for its stay. Hence more than half its substance dwells in the being from which it descends. Sunbeams it's true touch the earth, yet belong to the body that emits them. Thus a spirit, great and holy, sent down to give us a nearer knowledge of the divine, lives among us but cleaves to the fountain of its existence: from this it is pendent, on this its gaze is fixed, thither it strives, and moves among our concerns as a superior.[1]

Interpreted in the light of Seneca, Durand's sunlight-capped mountain is at once representative of the ideal and, as always the case with his work, is fitted to affect the spectator in such a way as to draw him toward participation in that ideal.

But there is one difference between Seneca's hero and Goldsmith's clergyman, a difference that accounts for Durand's use of Goldsmith. Where Seneca's hero scorns the world and dwells in sublime isolation, the clergyman is a Christian and animated by a God that descends in love to relieve and console a less exulted humanity. Where the hero, like a god, lives apart from humanity, the clergyman is bound by love to inferior, yet struggling souls. In the same way, Durand's Roman patriarchs, as examples exclusively of ideal character, are aloof; but in the late portrait, the bearded Bryant turns his benign gaze, expressive of a sympathy and love similar to that displayed by Durand's female portraits of the 1830's, toward the spectator, as though he were inviting the spectator to enter that more exulted realm which he already occupies. Combining primitive and spiritual grandeur with sympathetic love, the poet, like Durand himself, the painter, places his own spiritual attainment in the service of mankind.

Having begun his career as a commercial engraver, a participant in the world's wild race for wealth, Durand ultimately becomes nature's priest, the hierophant presiding over an Orphic cult, hymning God and "that _intuition_ by which every earnest spirit enjoys the assurance of our spiritual nature, and scorns the subtlety and logic of positive philosophy."[2] The aggressive, bright, clean-shaven Durand of Trumbull's 1826 portrait (App. V, no. 2) gives way to the serene and benign, priestly figure in Daniel Huntington's portrait of 1857 (Fig. 205 and cf. Fig. 206). In the latter painting Durand is seated before his easel,

palette and brushes in hand, in the "studio of nature." Wearing
a simple black coat he turns his head, framed by the silvery
locks of hair and beard, to regard the spectator with a look
of passionless calm. The landscape in which he sits is of the
type that appears in his own composite landscapes. At the right-
hand foreground is a part of the trunk of a massive tree, emblematic of that divine power and justice that serve to subdue
the rebellious character of man. But in the case of Durand at
sixty-one years of age, the sublime has already accomplished
its good offices. Hence, the tree stands behind the figure and
is subordinate to the extended vista of valley and distant hills
shrouded in softening mists. The beauty of the land and sky
indicates the divine love in which Durand already so clearly
participates and stands also as that realm of space in which the
soul may begin its expanding flight prior to its ultimate
severance from the body. The painting on the easel, added to
the portrait by Durand himself, is a replica of a composite
landscape, Franconia Notch (Fig. 196), of the same year. Clearly
this landscape is here a symbol of the artist's capacity to
arrange, to see, nature in such a way that the painting will
provide him, as another, with a foretaste of his redemption.[3]
Sublime in his uncorrupted natural dignity, beautiful in his
tender sympathy, Durand has attained the ideal which in his
work he sought to adumbrate.

We cannot hope to understand the art of Asher Durand if we
search his work for pure plastic values. He did not conceive
of a painting as first of all an arrangement of lines, shapes,

and colors on a flat surface. His art is not controlled by an
effort to gratify the eye. Rather, his art can only be understood when it is regarded as instrumental to the rescue of the
human soul from vice, fragmentation, and bondage to the temporal
and the physical. In his portraits and figure paintings he
revealed man and woman first in their physical, then in their
moral, and finally in their spiritual perfection. In his history
and genre paintings he briefly competed with the theologian
and the philosopher in their effort to illuminate the dealings
of God and man with man. But it was not until he became a landscape painter in the late 1830's that he began to discover the
proper ends for his art. As these changed, and their diversity
is impressive, so his means changed. Healing refreshment, the
reintegration of the ego, the withdrawal of the spectator's
mind into a state of autonomous self-awareness, the liberation
of the soul from its earthly prison, excitement to a state of
emotional equanimity, the vision of a redeemer--all of these
things Durand was gradually able to accomplish through the image
of nature increasingly transfigured by his brooding passion and
reverence. If Durand does not introduce the spectator either
to Seraphic color or ethereal geometry, he does uproot the
consciousness from the mire of Democracy, and he does so in
such a way that his methods seem to be verified by the real
scenes accessible in the world to the common man to whom his
paintings were addressed.

If in its style Durand's art does not anticipate any major
current in Western art since Impressionism, his art does draw

the spectator into that state of spiritual freedom which has
been essential to the genesis of modern art. But also we may
note that the recreational aspect of his landscapes is related
to the aims of Gauguin and Matisse; his effort to awaken within
the spectator slumbering psychic realities is related to the
aims of the Surrealists; his awareness of the contribution of
mind and emotion to the creation of form anticipates aspects
of Cubism; his probable concern with Spiritualism anticipates
the influence of Theosophy on Kandinsky; and his awareness of
an animating energy in nature anticipates the cosmic energies
exposed in the later work of Monet and Van Gogh as well as in
the work of the German Expressionists. As Durand's drive toward
concreteness was impelled by his sense of the absurdity of the
unredeemed life and his experience of a series of deflationary,
public and private crises, so, in the twentieth-century, collage
and assemblage have flourished in moments of the most acute
doubt--pre-World War I France, post-World War I Germany, post-
World War II America.

At the risk of suggesting connections that are too tenuous
to be practical, we may, perhaps, find a certain anticipation of
Action Painting in Durand's notion of painting from nature as
an act, of ultimate worth, in harmony with nature. According to
Harold Rosenberg, in the development of American art,

> At a certain moment the canvas began to appear to one
> American painter after another as an arena in which to
> act . . . What was to go on the canvas was not a picture
> but an event . . . A painting that is an act is insep-

arable from the biography of the artist . . . The act-
painting is of the same metaphysical substance as the
artist's existence. The new painting has broken down
every distinction between art and life.[4]

Where to Durand, in painting his oil studies, his act--the product
of mental and emotional decisions interfused--was conditioned
and qualified by landscape nature, in the case of such Action
Painters as Pollack and deKooning the act is conditioned and
qualified by the nature of the pigment and canvas. The physics
of the encounter between paint and canvas disfigure any direct
and purely psychic gesture quite as decisively in the case of
the latter as did the outward appearance of nature in the case
of Durand. Of Pollack and deKooning, Sam Hunter has written:

For these two artists the revelation on canvas of the
dynamics of the painting process assumes the character
of a significant and vital action; the painting becomes
a denuded, structural exposure in time and space of
the artistic self engaged in a series of critical
esthetic episodes, choices and decisions. Because
these decisions must be made under the stress of immediate feeling and have been divorced both from traditional artistic values of representation and from reliance on external nature, the artist is driven into a
deeper communion with himself as the source of choice
and action. It is not too farfetched to say that the
renunciation of naturalist illusion and the development of pictorial quality alone as the real content of

the work of art have taken on the character of a profound spiritual commitment. The tensions of renunciation have opened up new modes of self-inquiry, wherein passion, disquiet and the individual's sense of existence are identified with the "act" of painting itself.[5] Durand's oil studies certainly expose the "self engaged in a series of critical esthetic episodes, choices and decisions." These decisions were made "under the stress of immediate feeling" and "have been divorced . . . from traditional artistic values of representation." If they still relie on external nature, we may admit that paint and canvas play the part of external nature for the more recent painters. In the forest we must suppose that Durand, too, was "driven into a deeper communion with himself as the source of choice and action." And his "sense of existence" must, in no small measure, have been "identified with the 'act' of painting itself." In Sir Roger L'Estrange's rendering of Seneca, virtue "consists in the action, and not in the things we do: in the choice itself, and not in the subject matter of it."[6] In painting the studies Durand made the choices and acted the free man. In his studio compositions he stooped to extend this freedom to his contemporaries and to ourselves.

If we attempt at this point a critical estimate of Durand's work, we may, I believe, persist in applying to him the stricture that S. G. W. Benjamin pronounced upon the Hudson River School generally—that the men of this School "seldom arrested and enchained attention by the expression of daring technique or imaginative power, as the outcome of concerted influences exerted in one direction, . . . bounding into the arena and challenging the admiration of the world."[7] Although a deficiency of concentration on matters of technique and imagination may exclude Durand's paintings from even the higher ranks of Western art, such virtues as his works do display have assured them a prominent position in the history of American art--and much of American art is at least as little comparable to that of Europe as is the art of Rome to that of Greece. But when all is said against the art of Durand that may justly be said, we must then ask whether daring technique and what Benjamin meant by imaginative power were not so foreign to Durand's art as to have destroyed it had they been present. To Durand, art was something other than the display of technique or pictorial fancies; and, also, it was something more than the expression of the sentiment which the critics of the later nineteenth-century discovered in his work and more than the mere representation that the early twentieth century formalist critics have seen.

While on one hand we cannot evaluate Durand's art from any other standpoint than his own theoretical point of view, on the other hand the fact that his art was informed by theory does not of itself necessarily add anything to its stature. We can no more condemn Durand for not having approached nature with the unique vision of Corot than we can admire him solely for having approached nature with a set of ideas. An estimate of Durand must first establish the value of his ideas and then judge the adequacy with which they are realized in an actual

painting. If his concepts were valueless, his paintings fall;
if his concepts were valuable but find an inadequate expression
in his paintings, the paintings again fall, and Durand turns
out to have been a very minor and derivative aesthetician.

The most serious charge that may be brought against Dur-
and's paintings--especially his landscapes--is their manifest
lack of that pictorial intensity that is "the outcome of concerted influences exerted in one direction." In the later work
of Corot we find paintings that appear to be the result of such
a focusing of energies upon the production of a lyrical essence,
all other aims being excluded. Durand's landscapes, even his
oil studies, have a number of distinct aims. In the studies
he sought to see nature, to create nature, to express his own
emotion, and to act in conformity with Nature. Such multidirectional and multi-level paintings find their analogue more
in the epic than in the lyric. But, if we admit that the epic
may be multidirectional, we must also admit that the best epics
display a high intensity at every point--that in whatever
direction the spectator is carried, he is firmly carried and
his attention rivetted to the work itself. Now, the creation
of this kind of epic demands that the artist regard the work
itself with an intense and almost blindly committed seriousness.
Such intense seriousness seems to inform the best Italian painting of the fifteenth century and finds its fullest expression
in the marvellous and often appalling frigidity of Florentine
Mannerism. In Durand's art, however, there is but little of
this.

Despite the fact that certain critics have discovered a detailed precision and hard sharpness in Durand's landscapes, I believe that these qualities are present relatively more than actually. Durand in no way approaches the brittle intensity of, say, Mantegna's landscape settings. Rather, in Durand's forms there is something soft, vague, dissolving, withdrawing, bland and, at times, insipid. He refuses to insist, to demand, to attach too great a significance to things. Indeed, there is a sort of irony in his forms which seem to be so clear and yet, once they have attracted the spectator's attention, willingly relinquish it. This irony is best illustrated in Durand's The Catskills of 1859 (Fig. 180), in which the natural forms, wrought with an unusual intensity, dissolve with as unusual a suddenness beyond the brink of the precipice. While he thrusts these trees so suddenly upon the spectator, he withdraws them as quickly. This same refusal to attach final significance to the painting itself may be discerned in the ancient Roman Odyssey Landscapes; in the Baroque painting of Caravaggio and his school; and in a part of the work of Benjamin West or Turner. In these, the adumbrations, dreams, shadowy evocations, reveries, and chains of poetic associations generated in the consciousness of the spectator count for more than the configuration of the image itself, although the image itself may approach at times a brutal assertiveness. In modern times this kind of art originated in the fear of idolatry on the part of both Protestants and Counter-Reformation Catholics in the sixteenth century, and the highest achievements of

the Protestant and Catholic phases of this art are to be found
in the work of Rembrandt and Guido Reni--paintings that are
musical insofar as they both attract and relinquish the spectator's attention. But just as we cannot compare the work of
Rembrandt to that of a pre-Reformation painter such as Raphael,
so Durand cannot be judged in comparison with a painter working
prior to the egalitarian and philosophical revolutions of the
eighteenth and nineteenth centuries. While Durand did study
Rembrandt, as Rembrandt had studied Raphael, by the 1840's and
1850's the American democratic atmosphere militated against
Durand's regarding himself as seriously as Rembrandt had regarded himself, and Durand's Stoicism militated against his
diverting too much attention from himself to his painting.

Durand, as we have seen, proposed to release the spectator
temporarily from the bondage of the world and compel him to
return to the world with a diminished sense of its value.
Thereby he hoped to rescue, at least, a remnant of humanity--
that is, of humanness--from the dehumanizing forces of the
times. His mature landscapes do, I believe, in large measure
satisfy this end; and were any greater degree of pictorial intensity introduced, they should do so less well. Before one
can evaluate Durand's paintings and establish their rank in
the history of American or Western art, one must find an answer
to the question, is a painting important for what it is or what
it does?

NOTES.

INTRODUCTION.

1. A. B. Durand, "Autobiographical Fragment," in John Durand, The Life and Times of A. B. Durand, New York, 1894, pp. 18-19. John Durand's biography of his father will hereafter be cited as John Durand, Life.

2. Ibid., pp. 19-20.

3. Julian Blanchard, "The Durand Engraving Companies," The Essay Proof Journal, vol. 7, no. 2, p. 81.

4. The partners in this firm were Asher and Cyrus Durand, Joseph Perkins (1788-1842), and Cyrus' brother-in-law Elias Wade, Jr. See ibid, vol. 7, no. 2, p. 81 and vol. 7, no. 3, p. 147.

5. The Grolier Club, Catalogue of the Engraved Work of Asher B. Durand, New York, 1895. Hereafter cited as Grolier Club.

6. Blanchard, op. cit., vol. 7, no. 3, p. 149, describes a vignette inscribed: Drawn & Eng. by A. B. Durand 1839.

7. For all works cited as having been exhibited at the American Academy of the Fine Arts, at the National Academy of Design, or at the American Art-Union see Mary Bartlett Cowdrey, American Academy of Fine Arts and American Art-Union, 2 vols., New-York, 1953, vol. 2, and National Academy of Design Exhibition Record, 1826-1860, 2 vols., New York, 1943.

567

8. In an unsigned article, "An Aged Artist," The Studio, vol. 2, nos. 31-34, August, 1883, p. 60, Durand is quoted as having said:

> But, alas! my working days are over. The same desire lives within me, the same love of my art fills my breast, but my eyes are dim and my hands, as you see, are very unruly and will not obey my commands, for they are always trembling. The outward and real beauties of nature . . . no longer impress themselves on my brain. The glories of the sunset and the dawn are lost to me now. But here (tapping his forehead) I can still call up beautiful sylvan scenes, pictures of the mountains and streams, and the faces of friends. My last study I produced in 1878. It is a picture characteristic of the Adirondack Scenery.

And in the same article, p. 61, Charles Lanman reports that Durand last used the brush to fill in the foregrounds of two studies in 1880. John Durand, Life, p. 200, states that Durand quit painting upon completion of the Souvenir of the Adirondacks in 1879. However, this painting appears to be dated 1878 and is probably the painting referred to above. See also App. II, no. 387.

9. According to the Greenwood Cemetery records Durand died of "Coma Cere Congestion" on September 17, 1886, at Maplewood, South Orange, New Jersey. The undertaker employed was Theodore T. Freeman. Durand was buried on September 21, 1886, in lot no. 1053, section 60 at Greenwood. According to John

Durand, Life, p. 209, the Rev. Dr. Lewis P. Clover, Jr.,
Durand's one-time pupil in engraving, officiated at the
funeral ceremony. Brief obituaries appear in the New-York
Daily Tribune, Sept. 18, 1886, p. 5, column 5, and Harper's
Weekly, vol. 30, no. 1553, Sept., 1886, p. 619.

10. William Dunlap, History of the Rise and Progress of the Arts
of Design in the United States, 2 vols., New York, 1834,
vol. 2, pp. 285-289.

11. Henry T. Tuckerman, Artist-Life, New York, 1847, pp. 79-88.

12. Henry T. Tuckerman, Book of the Artists. American Artist
Life, New York, 1867, pp. 187-196.

13. E. Anna Lewis, "Art and Artists of America, Asher Brown
Durand," Graham's Magazine, vol. 45, no. 4, October, 1854,
p. 322.

14. A. B. Durand Papers, NYPL.

15. Thomas Charles Ferrer, "A Few Questions Answered. An Essay
Read before the Society /for the Advancement of Truth in
Art7, Tuesday, March 31, 1863," The New Path, vol. 1, no. 2,
June, 1863, pp. 14-15. The Society for the Advancement of
Truth in Art's distaste for Durand's landscapes is also
indicated in the following from a New Path review of Albert
Bierstadt's Rocky Mountains:

> So great a charm have mere grandeur of landscape
> . . . and the word "the West"--to the mass of our
> people . . . that this picture must inevitably have
> been run after and praised, even if, instead of
> being a reasonably good piece of work, as it is,

it had been as bad as one of Cole's or Durand's
masterpieces. ("Notices of Recent Pictures.
Bierstadt's Rocky Mountains," The New Path, vol. 1,
no. 12, April, 1864, p. 161.)

The writer is not named.

16. James Jackson Jarves, The Art-Idea, Benjamin Rowland, Jr.,
    ed., Cambridge, Mass., 1960, pp. 188-189.

17. Eugene Benson, "A. B. Durand--Our Veteran Landscape Painter,"
    Appleton's Journal, vol. 3, no. 58, May 7, 1870, p. 520.

18. G. W. Sheldon, American Painters, New York, 1879, p. 129.

19. Loc. cit.

20. S. G. W. Benjamin, Art in America, A Critical and Historical
    Sketch, New York, 1880, p. 63. Benjamin's comments on
    Durand appeared first in Harper's New Monthly Magazine,
    vol. 59, no. 350, July, 1879, pp. 254-255.

21. Sadakichi Hartmann, A History of American Art, 2 vols.,
    Boston, 1902, vol. 1, p. 54.

22. Eugene Benson, op. cit., p. 520.

23. S. G. W. Benjamin, op. cit., pp. 66-69.

24. Ibid., p. 60.

25. S. Hartmann, op. cit., vol. 1, p. 54.

26. Ibid., p. 55.

27. William James Stillman, The Autobiography of a Journalist,
    2 vols., Boston, New York, and London, 1901, vol. 1, p. 95.

28. Daniel Huntington, Asher B. Durand: A Memorial Address,
    New York, 1887, p. 46.

29. C. H. Hart, "Asher B. Durand," in Grolier Club, pp. 6-7.

30. Ibid., p. 7.

31. Samuel Isham, The History of American Painting, new edition
    with supplemental chapters by Royal Cortissoz, New York,
    1927, p. 229.  Isham's History was first published in 1905.

32. Ibid., pp. 230-231.

33. Charles H. Caffin, The Story of American Painting, de luxe
    edition, Garden City, New York, 1937, pp. 77-78.  Caffin's
    Story was first published in 1907.

34. Ibid., p. 75.

35. Ibid., p. 71.

36. Ibid., p. 72.

37. Ibid., p. 82.

38. Ruel P. Tolman, "Asher Brown Durand," Art in America, vol. 11,
    no. 4, June, 1923, p. 198.

39. Ibid., p. 199.

40. Frank Jewett Mather, Jr. in F. J. Mather, Jr., C. R. Morey,
    and W. J. Henderson, The American Spirit in Art, New Haven,
    1927.  Mather erroneously states, p. 23, that Durand en-
    graved only eleven, rather than nineteen, portraits for
    The National Portrait Gallery, and, p. 235, that the Musidora
    engraving of 1825 was published with the Ariadne in 1835.

41. Ibid., p. 42.

42. Ibid., p. 23.

43. Ibid., pp. 234 and 280.

44. Ibid., p. 235.

45. Ibid., p. 26.

46. Frederic Fairchild Sherman, "Asher B. Durand as a Portrait Painter," Art in America, vol. 18, no. 6, October, 1930, p. 315.

47. Ibid., pp. 310-315.

48. Alan Burroughs, Limners and Likenesses, Three Centuries of American Painting, Cambridge, Mass., 1936, p. 126.

49. Lloyd Goodrich, "A Century of American Landscape Painting," The Carnegie Magazine, vol. 13, no. 1, April, 1939, p. 5.

50. Ibid., pp. 5-6.

51. For other exhibitions that included paintings by Durand, see App. II.

52. Virgil Barker, American Painting: History and Interpretation, New York, 1950. There are a number of errors in Barker's account of Durand: that the Musidora was engraved from a painting rather than a drawing (p. 349); that Longacre and Herring's National Portrait Gallery was an augmented re-issue of an earlier work (p. 511); that this work contains line engravings by John Durand (loc. cit.); and that Kensett, Rossiter, and Casilear accompanied Durand to Europe in 1840 as pupils rather than companions.

53. Ibid., p. 343.

54. John W. McCoubrey, American Tradition in Painting, New York, 1963, p. 28.

55. Oliver W. Larkin, Art and Life in America, revised and enlarged edition, New York, 1960. Larkin's book was first published in 1949. Larkin erroneously states that the First Harvest (Fig. 91) was painted in 1858 rather than 1855.

56. Ibid., p. 143.

57. Ibid., p. 192.

58. Ibid., p. 204.

59. Loc. cit.

60. Ibid., p. 220.

61. Edgar P. Richardson, Painting in America, The Story of 450 Years, New York, 1956. Two factual errors may be noted in Richardson's account of Durand: that Durand served his apprenticeship to Maverick in New York rather than on Maverick's farm near Newark, and that Durand engraved illustrations for James Fenimore Cooper's novel The Spy and Washington Allston's Spalatro and the Bloody Hand. Durand did base a painting on The Spy (Fig. 95). Allston's Spalatro's Vision of the Bloody Hand is or was a painting not a literary work--see E. P. Richardson, Washington Allston, A Study of the Romantic Artist in America, Chicago, 1948, p. 210. Apparently Allston wished to have Durand engrave the painting (John Durand, Life, pp. 111-112), but no engraving of the painting was included in the Grolier Club exhibition of Durand's engraved work.

62. E. P. Richardson, Painting in America, pp. 169-170.

63. Ibid., p. 170.

64. Ibid., pp. 169-170.

65. Ibid., p. 170.

66. Daniel M. Mendelowitz, A History of American Art, New York, 1960, p. 301.

67. Ibid., p. 300.

68. Clara Endicott Sears, Highlights Among the Hudson River Artists, Boston, 1947, pp. 37 and 43.

69. For a fuller account of Richardson's concept of Romantic Realism see his The Way of Western Art, 1776-1914, Cambridge, Mass., 1949, pp. 71-102.

70. Edgar P. Richardson, American Romantic Painting, Robert Freund, ed., New York, 1944, p. 15.

71. Alexander Eliot, Three Hundred Years of American Painting, New York, 1957, p. 70.

72. W. J. Stillman, op. cit., vol. 1, p. 94.

73. Wolfgang Born, American Landscape Painting, New Haven, 1948, p. 40.

74. Ibid., p. 42.

75. E. P. Richardson, Painting in America, p. 170.

76. Frederick Sweet, "Asher B. Durand, Pioneer American Landscape Painter," The Art Quarterly, vol. 8, no. 2, Spring, 1945, pp. 141-160. There are, however, some factual errors in Sweet's article: Durand did not remain in partnership with his brother Cyrus until 1833 (p. 143). The partnership dissolved in 1831. Durand did not engrave illustrations for Cooper's The Spy or Mrs. Radcliffe's The Italian (loc. cit.). Durand did not teach engraving at the National Academy of Design (p. 144). Durand was probably not the first American painter to work out-of-doors (loc. cit.). The View in the Catskills in the Museum of Fine Arts, Boston, is dated 1847 not 1844 (p. 154). See App. II, no. 234. A biographical sketch of Durand by Sweet appears

in his <u>The</u> <u>Hudson</u> <u>River</u> <u>School</u> <u>and</u> <u>the</u> <u>Early</u> <u>American</u>
<u>Landscape</u> <u>Tradition</u>, Chicago and New York, 1945, pp. 43-48.

77. Sweet, "Asher B. Durand," p. 146.

78. <u>Ibid</u>., pp. 148-149.

79. <u>Ibid</u>., pp. 149-150.

80. <u>Ibid</u>., p. 154.

81. <u>Ibid</u>., p. 156.

82. <u>Ibid</u>., p. 160.

83. Barbara Novak, "Asher B. Durand and European Art," <u>The</u> <u>Art</u>
<u>Journal</u>, vol. 21, no. 4, Summer, 1962, pp. 250-254. There
is one major bibliographical error in Miss Novak's article.
Durand's <u>Letters</u> <u>on</u> <u>Landscape</u> <u>Painting</u> were published not
in eight installments in <u>The</u> <u>Crayon</u> (p. 252) but in nine.
Presumably, Miss Novak did not find the last letter. Dur-
and's <u>Letters</u> <u>on</u> <u>Landscape</u> <u>Painting</u> were published in 1855
in <u>The</u> <u>Crayon</u>, an art journal edited and owned by John
Durand and William J. Stillman, as follows:

"Letter I," vol. 1, no. 1, Jan. 3, 1855, pp. 1-2.

"Letter II," vol. 1, no. 3, Jan. 17, 1855, pp. 34-35.

"Letter III," vol. 1, no. 5, Jan. 31, 1855, pp. 66-67.

"Letter IV," vol. 1, no. 7, Feb. 14, 1855, pp. 97-98.

"Letter V," vol. 1, no. 10, March 7, 1855, pp. 145-146.

"Letter VI," vol. 1, no. 14, April 4, 1855, pp. 209-211.

"Letter VII," vol. 1, no. 18, May 2, 1855, pp. 273-275.

"Letter VIII," vol. 1, no. 23, June 6, 1855, pp. 354-
355.

"Letter IX," vol. 2, no. 2, July 11, 1855, pp. 16-17.

The individual letters will hereafter be cited as:A. B. Durand, "Letter I-IX."

84. Novak, op. cit., pp. 252-253.

85. Ibid., p. 251.

86. Ibid., p. 254.

87. The sketch, now in the New-York Historical Society, for the 1838 Dream of Arcadia (Fig. 147).

88. James Thomas Flexner, That Wilder Image, Boston and Toronto, 1962, pp. 66-67.

89. Sweet, "Asher B. Durand," pp. 153-156.

90. Novak, op. cit., p. 252.

91. Flexner, op. cit., p. 67.

92. Ibid., p. 68.

93. Loc. cit.

94. Loc. cit.

95. Ibid., pp. 68 and 70.

96. Ibid., p. 70.

97. Ibid., p. 72.

98. Ibid., p. 73, where, presumably, Flexner is quoting from "Letter III," p. 34, where Durand wrote:   "Types of the Divine Attributes."

99. Novak, op. cit., p. 252, was also aware of the fact that Durand saw divine attributes typified in nature, and states that sunlight was "to him . . . a type of the divine attribute"--as though the deity had but one.  To my knowledge, Durand nowhere identifies sunlight as such.

100. Flexner, op. cit., pp. 72-73. Durand's statement, as quoted, has come to mean just the opposite of what he wrote: "The external appearance of this our dwelling-place, apart from its wondrous structure and functions that minister to our well-being, is frought with lessons of high and holy meaning, only surpassed by the light of Revelation." ("Letter II," p. 34.)

101. Flexner, op. cit., p. 73.

102. Ibid., p. 71.

103. Ibid., p. 73.

104. Loc. cit.

105. Ibid., p. 74. Here, also, one should note that the sentence from Durand's fourth "Letter," p. 98, which Flexner reads: "The artist as a poet will have seen more than the mere matter of fact, but no more than is there and that another may see if it is pointed out to him" should read: "The poet sees in nature more than mere matter of fact, yet he does not see more than is there, nor what another may not see when he points it out."

106. Flexner, op. cit., p. 74.

107. Loc. cit.

108. Ibid., pp. 74-75.

109. S. G. W. Benjamin, op. cit., p. 69.

110. Nathaniel Hawthorne, The Marble Faun, or The Romance of Monte Beni, in The Complete Works of Nathaniel Hawthorne, 13 vols., Boston and New York: Houghton Mifflin Co., n. d., vol. 6, p. 282.

111. Fritz Novotny, _Painting and Sculpture in Europe, 1780 to 1880_, Baltimore, 1960.

112. H. W. Janson and Dora Jane Janson, _History of Art: A Survey of the Major Visual Arts from the Dawn of History to the Present Day_, New York, n.d., p. 454.

113. See, for example, Arthur O. Lovejoy, "On the Discrimination of Romanticisms," in _Essays in the History of Ideas_, New York: G. P. Putnam's Sons, Capricorn Books, pp. 228-253, and Jacques Barzun, _Classic, Romantic, and Modern_, Garden City, N. Y.: Doubleday and Company, Anchor Books, 1961, _passim_, and pp. 155-168.

114. The Jansons, _op. cit._, p. 453, suggest and reject this term.

115. These terms were used by E. P. Richardson in _The Way of Western Art_.

CHAPTER ONE.

1. On the history of New York City see especially Mary L. Booth, *History of the City of New York, from its Earliest Settlement to the Present Time*, New York, 1866; Martha J. Lamb, *History of the City of New York: its Origin, Rise and Progress*, 2 vols., New York and Chicago, 1877-1880; Benson J. Lossing, *History of New York*, New York, 1884; and James G. Wilson, ed., *Memorial History of the City of New York*, 4 vols, New York, 1892-1893.

2. Cadwallader D. Colden, *Memoir, Prepared at the Request of a Committee of the Common Council of the City of New York, and Presented to the Mayor of the City, at the Celebration of the Completion of the New York Canals*, Printed by order of the Corporation of New York, 1825, p. 77.

3. On the history of this organization see Theodore Sizer, "The American Academy of the Fine Arts," in Mary B. Cowdrey, *American Academy of Fine Arts and American Art-Union*, vol. 1, pp. 3-93.

4. R. W. G. Vail, *Knickerbocker Birthday: A Sesquicentennial History of the New-York Historical Society, 1804-1954*, New York, 1954.

5. Colden, *op. cit., passim*.

6. George W. Cooke, <u>Unitarianism</u> <u>in</u> <u>America</u>: <u>a</u> <u>History</u> <u>of</u> <u>its</u> <u>Origin</u> <u>and</u> <u>Development</u>, Boston, 1902, p. 119.

7. D. R. Fox, "The Rise of Scientific Interests in New York," in <u>Mind</u> <u>and</u> <u>Spirit</u>, vol. 9 of the <u>History</u> <u>of</u> <u>the</u> <u>State</u> <u>of</u> <u>New</u> <u>York</u>, New York, 1937, pp. 99-103.

8. Thomas S. Cummings, <u>Historic</u> <u>Annals</u> <u>of</u> <u>the</u> <u>National</u> <u>Academy</u> <u>of</u> <u>Design</u>, Philadelphia, 1865, p. 7.

9. Address on a letter from Maverick to Durand, October 30, 1817, A. B. Durand Papers, NYPL. Stephen DeWitt Stephens, <u>The</u> <u>Mavericks</u>, <u>American</u> <u>Engravers</u>, New Brunswick, N. J., 1950, p. 51, states that there were two phases to the Maverick-Durand company: the first involving only Maverick and Durand and the second including in addition Cyrus and, possibly, John Durand, Asher's brothers. The latter group worked, according to Stephens, under the firm name "Maverick Durand & Co." from sometime in 1818. While Cyrus and John Durand may have assisted Maverick and Durand, Blanchard, <u>op</u>. <u>cit</u>., vol. 7, no. 2, p. 81, does not specify either as a regular member of the firm at any time.

10. Stephen DeWitt Stephens, <u>op</u>. <u>cit</u>., pp. 51-57, and John Durand, <u>Life</u>, p. 25.

11. Stephens, <u>op</u>. <u>cit</u>., pp. 48-51, and John Durand, <u>Life</u>, pp. 22-25.

12. Letter from James Gibbs, Jr., to Durand, November 10, 1817. A. B. Durand Papers, NYPL.

13. Letter from James Gibbs, Jr., to Durand, November 30, 1817. A. B. Durand Papers, NYPL.

14. John Durand, <u>Life</u>, p. 38. A few verses from this period by Durand are quoted <u>ibid</u>., p. 33.

15. <u>Grolier Club</u>, pp. 70 ff.

16. John Durand, <u>Life</u>, p. 38.

17. Parke Godwin, <u>A Biography of William Cullen Bryant</u>, 2 vols., New York, 1883, vol. 1. p. 208, lists the following as members of The Lunch Club about 1825: Lawyers: James Kent, Thomas Addis Emmet, Edward D. Griffin. Professors: Duer, McVickar, Anthon, Moore. Poets: Percival, Hillhouse, Halleck, Sands, Bryant. Artists: John Vanderlyn, Samuel F. B. Morse, John W. Jarvis, William Dunlap. John Durand, <u>Life</u>, p. 80, copied Godwin's list but omitted Percival and the professors. Dr. John W. Francis, <u>Old New York; or Reminiscences of the Past Sixty Years</u>, New York, 1858, pp. 291-292, mentions the poet Halleck, the naturalist De Kay, the lawyers William and John Duer, the philosopher Renwick, the writers Verplanck and King, and the merchants Charles H. Davis and Philip Hone as members of the Club. He also states that "The meetings of the Club (or Lunch) were often swelled to quite a formidable assembly by Members of Congress, senators, and representatives, and in this array were often found Webster and Storrs, W. B. Lawrence, and the French minister Hyde de Neuville."

A note, dated Dec. 10, 1825, from Anthony Bleeker notifying Durand of his membership in the club is in the A. B. Durand Papers, NYPL.

18. John Durand, *Prehistoric Notes of the Century Club*, New York, 1882, pp. 8 and 21.

19. J. Durand, *ibid.*, p. 9, quotes a statement of the purposes of the Club from an early book of minutes: "1st. The encouragement of social and friendly feelings among the members by occasional meetings; 2d. Mutual improvement in the art which is chiefly to be practiced at these meetings; 3d. The production of an Annual." The New York Sketch Club must have been modeled upon the club founded in the early years of the nineteenth century by Thomas Girtin in London. The members of Girtin's club

> . . . met alternately at each other's houses. The subject was generally taken from an English poet, and was treated by each in his own way. The member at whose house they met supplied stained paper, colours, and pencils, and all the sketches of the evening became his property. (Walter Thornbury, *The Life of J. M. W. Turner, R. A.*, a new edition revised and mostly rewritten, London, 1877, p. 66.)

According to Thornbury, *loc. cit.*, Girtin's "society was the model, no doubt, for the celebrated one at whose meetings Chalons, Leslie, and Landseer, long after, spent so many happy hours."

For some drawings executed at meetings of the New York Sketch Club, see App. IV, nos. 344-347.

20. John Durand, *Prehistoric Notes*, *passim*. The membership of the Club is listed on pp. 21-22.

21. Letter from James Gibbs, Jr., to Durand, July 28, 1819. A. B. Durand Papers, NYPL.

22. Exhibited 1838. Musée de Lille.

23. Durand, of course, was not the only young man of lower middle class background to discover in eighteenth century nature poetry the key to an understanding of a major area of his own experience. In England, John Constable greatly admired Thomson's Seasons (see C. R. Leslie, Memoirs of the Life of John Constable, London: Phaidon Press, 1951, pp. 176, 198, and 328), as did Turner, and translations of this work or imitations of it may have inspired Romantic painters of the paysage intime such as Théodore Rousseau in France and Karl Blechen in Germany.

24. In John Durand, Life, pp. 20-22.

25. Asher B. Durand, "Autobiographical Fragment," in John Durand, Life, pp. 22-24.

26. John Durand, Life, p. 25: "During this apprenticeship his principal employment consisted in making copies for New York publishers of English engravings, illustrative of editions of Shakespeare and other poets, vignette designs for bank-notes, which then began to circulate freely, encyclopaedia plates, diplomas, and other miscellaneous productions. I find no example or record of original work done by him during his apprenticeship, which terminated in 1817, on becoming the partner of Maverick." For examples of Durand's work as an apprentice see especially Grolier Club, nos. 122-138.

27. A. B. Durand, "Autobiographical Fragment," in John Durand, *Life*, p. 24.

28. The engraved work of the Maverick-Durand firm is catalogued in Stephen DeWitt Stephens, *op. cit.* Stephens' catalogue numbers are used here. Some work signed by the firm is listed in the Grolier Club catalogue of Durand's engravings.

29. Charles H. Hart, *op. cit.*, p. 6, states that "Bervic's Louis XVI., Morghen's Moncado, commonly called the white-horse, Strange's Charles I., in his robes, and Titian's Venus, Sharp's John Hunter and Doctors of the Church, were a few of his constant companions and guides." John Durand, *Life*, p. 46, states that his father "procured the best examples of the works of eminent European engravers Bervic, Raphael Morghen, Willè, Sharp, Audouin, Strange, and the rest--and studied these closely."

30. John Durand, *Life*, p. 25, quotes a passage from Daniel Huntington's *Asher B. Durand; A Memorial Address*, in which Huntington records Trumbull's interest in the *Old Pat* engraving.

31. Theodore Sizer, ed., *The Autobiography of Colonel John Trumbull, Patriot-Artist, 1756-1843*, New Haven, 1953, pp. 320-322, traces the history of Trumbull's efforts to have the *Declaration of Independence* engraved.

32. John Durand, *Life*, pp. 25-26.

33. Barnet Phillips, "Asher Brown Durand," *New York Times*, date unknown, quoted in John Durand, *Life*, pp. 55-56.

34. Exhibited by Waldo and Jewett at the American Academy of the Fine Arts in 1820.

35. John Durand, *Life*, p. 55, states that the "engraving was too large . . . to suit the popular purse. During the progress of the work, Colonel Trumbull personally solicited subscriptions; he was obliged also to mortage the plate while in my father's hands, and never, probably, was fully remunerated by the sale of its impressions."

36. Dunlap, *op. cit.*, vol. 1, p. 10.

37. On the imitation of Greek forms by American architects, see Talbot Hamlin, *Greek Revival Architecture in America*, London, New York, and Toronto, 1944. From paintings by Robert W. Weir, Durand engraved the following modern Greek subjects as embellishments for gift books: *The Dying Greek* (1829, *Grolier Club*, no. 214), *Greek Boy* (*Grolier Club*, no. 215), and *Greek Lovers* (1825, *Grolier Club*, no. 216).

38. Bartolomeo Cavaceppi, *Raccolta d'antiche statue, busti, bassorelievi ed altre sculture ristaurate*, Rome, 3 vols., 1768-1772, vol. 3, pl. 16.

39. An engraving of Musidora kneeling to read Damon's letter (Fig. 12), probably copied from an English illustration, was published in James Thomson, *The Seasons*, New-York: R. and W. A. Bartow, and Richmond, Va.: W. A. Bartow, 1820. This engraving is signed "P. Maverick, Durand & Co." and was probably executed by Durand himself. (Two other engravings for this work are given to Durand in *Grolier Club*, no. 150, and Stevens, *op. cit.*, p. 149, nos. 754-

759, states that they are probably all by Durand. Stevens, no. 758, mistakenly states that the print in question is not signed and that Musidora holds a book rather than a letter.)

40. Cummings, op. cit., p. 131.

41. Dunlap, op. cit., vol. 2, pp. 207-208.

42. Quoted in John Galt, The Life of Benjamin West, Gainesville, Florida: Scholars' Facsimiles & Reprints, 2 vols. in one, 1960, vol. 2, p. 96.

43. Quoted loc. cit.

44. Quoted ibid., vol. 2, pp. 97-98.

45. The following passage from West's Royal Academy "Discourse" of 1794 appears ibid., vol. 2, pp. 99-101:

> The Apollo is represented by the mythologists as a perfect man, in the vigour of life. . . . His activity was shown in dancing, running, and the manly exercises of the quoit, the sling, and the bow. . . . were a sculptor to think of forming the statue of such a character, would he not determine that his body, strong and vigorous from constant exercise, should be nobly erect; . . . that his thighs, as the source of movement in his legs, should have the appearance of enlarged vigor and solidity . . . While his arms, firm and nervous by the exercise of the quoit, the sling, and the bow, should participate in the general vigor and

> agility of the other members;--and would not this
> be the Apollo Belvidere?

46. Quoted *ibid.*, vol. 2, p. 98.

47. Quoted *ibid.*, vol. 2, pp. 101-102.

48. James Thomson, "Summer," in *The Seasons, Poetical Works,*
2 vols., London: George Bell and Sons, 1897, vol. 1, p. 85,
lines 1344-1349. In the last three lines quoted, Thomson,
of course, refers specifically to the *Venus de Medici*, and
this reference is made explicit in a footnote in the Bartow
edition for which Durand engraved illustrations. But to
Thomson the statue embodies no significant psychological
or moral content: "A stupid moment motionless she stood:
/ So stands the statue . . ." It was only because West
restored a meaning to the statue that Durand could employ
the pose of an Antique Venus for his expressive Musidora.

 Stephen A. Larrabee, *English Bards and Grecian Marbles,*
New York, 1943, p. 77, comments on Thomson's use of the
*Venus de Medici* in the verses quoted and suggests, pp. 158-
159, that Lord Byron may have been in part inspired by
this passage when he wrote his description of the *Venus* in
*Childe Harold*, Canto IV, stanzas 49-53, in 1818. Byron
of course did not see the statue as the paragon of feminine
virtue that West described, but he did invest it with far
more life than did Thomson.

49. Durand's earlier *Musidora* (Fig. 12) illustrates a third
moment:

> But, when her Damon's well known hand she saw,
>
> Her terror vanished . . .
>
> (Lines 1353-1354 /for 1352 on plate7.)

The emotions of innocence and modesty felt by Musidora at this moment and described in the next few lines, are expressed in the engraving in a figure borrowed from the Baroque tradition of repentant Magdalenes. Thus, the non-classical pose is used to express a modesty that is merely a transitory feeling, while in the large engraving the Antique form is used to express a modesty regarded as essential to the female character.

50. Thomson, op. cit., vol. 1, p. 84, lines 1301-1303.

51. Ibid., vol. 1, p. 85, lines 1331-1334.

52. Ibid., vol. 1, p. 83, lines 1257-1268.

53. West, "Discourse" of 1794 in Galt, op. cit., vol. 2, p. 98.

54. Edmund Burke, A Philosophical Enquiry into the Origin of our Ideas of the Sublime and Beautiful, London:  F. C. and J. Rivington and others, 1812, p. 255.

55. Ibid., pp. 256-257.

56. Ibid., pp. 66-67.

57. John Durand, Life, pp. 75-76, where it is also stated that the plate was borrowed by the printer and destroyed in a fire.

58. According to Blanchard, op. cit., vol. 7, no. 2, p. 81, Asher Durand was a partner in the firm "A. B. & C. Durand, Wright & Co." which included Durand, his brother Cyrus, and Charles C. Wright from 1824 to 1827.  Blanchard states,

p. 88, that this firm was "supplied with exceptional talent,
and judging from the relative number of their proof notes
in the New-York Historical Society collection and from the
number of issued notes that are available to collectors,
they did a substantial business. At that time, this was
certainly one of the leading banknote firms in the country."
From 1828 through 1831 Durand was associated with the firm
"Durand, Perkins & Co." which included Durand, Cyrus,
Joseph Perkins, and Elias Wade, Jr. Blanchard states,
vol. 7, no. 3, p. 147, that Joseph Perkins (1788-1842), a
graduate of Williams College, was the script engraver and
that Elias Wade, Jr., Cyrus Durand's brother-in-law, was
probably the plate printer. In all the bank-note work,
Asher designed and engraved the vignettes (Grolier Club,
nos. 178-210, and an album of vignette drawings by Durand in
the New York Public Library--App. IV, no. 348). He did
this work even in the periods 1821-1823 and 1832-1839 when
he was not connected with an engraving firm (Blanchard,
vol. 7, no. 2, p. 86 and vol. 7, no. 3, p. 149). Cyrus
used a lathe of his own invention to produce the intricate
scroll-work that was intended to discourage counterfeiters.
On the Durand engraving firms see also: G. C. Groce and
D. H. Wallace, The New-York Historical Society's Dictionary
of Artists in America, 1564-1860, New Haven and London,
1957, pp. 196-198, and Foster Wild Rice, "Antecedents of
the American Bank Note Company of 1858," The Essay-Proof
Journal, vol. 18, nos. 71-72, 1961.

59. John Durand, _Life_, p. 35.

60. _Ibid._, p. 78.

61. _Ibid._, p. 73.

62. In both paintings by Cole the gap between the spectator and inanimate nature is destroyed: in the one (Fig. 18) he has introduced a contemplative wood-man; and in the other, a totally fortuitous mother and child. In the latter of Cole's paintings (Fig. 19), especially, nature becomes the setting for a tender human activity, while even in Durand's engraving, nature remains something alien to man. In 1831 Durand exhibited a painting of the Catskill Mountains at the National Academy of Design, and this may, perhaps, be identified with a somewhat hesitant, but large Catskill scene (Fig. 20), recently on the art market. The painting differs from Durand's drawing and engraving and from both paintings by Cole. Hence, it is not a mere amateur's copy of any of these. If it were painted by Durand, he must have felt a need to invest an exhibition piece with a higher formal and human significance than the engraving demanded. The landscape has become more symmetrical and closed. The scene is now populated by a boatman and reveals a tiny farm-house in the middle distance. The distance between the naturalism of the drawing and the humanism of the painting is approximately equal to that which will lie between his later painted studies and the compositions intended for academic exhibition.

63. _Grolier Club_, nos. 211-226.

64. Dunlap, _op. cit._, vol. 2, p. 279.

65. Cummings, op. cit., p. 18, states that at the time of his election in June, 1817, Trumbull "opposed the opening of the schools." He gives no evidence to support this statement and goes on to report that the collection of casts was made available to students in the summer following Trumbull's election.

66. John Durand, Life, p. 81.

67. Dr. John W. Francis, op. cit., p. 278, states that he was appointed professor of "The Anatomy of Painting" at the American Academy, so Dr. Post's lectures must have been delivered elsewhere.

68. The Antique academy was opened from six to nine in the morning, according to Dunlap, op. cit., vol. 2, p. 279. Dunlap and Cummings, op. cit., p. 204, both recount an incident in which Cummings and Frederick S. Agate were not admitted, and Trumbull expressed his hostility toward the students in no uncertain terms.

69. On the organization of the New-York Drawing Association see: Cummings, op. cit., pp. 21 ff.; John Durand, Prehistoric Notes, p. 7; Edward L. Morse, Samuel F. B. Morse, His Letters and Journals, 2 vols., Boston and New York, 1914, vol. 1, pp. 276-277; and Eliot C. Clark, History of the National Academy of Design, 1825-1953, New York, 1954, pp. 10-12 and 33.

70. "A Review of the Gallery of the American Academy of Fine Arts . . . ," The Atheneum Magazine, vol. 2, Dec., 1825, pp. 77-78. News of art and artists appearing in the

<u>Atheneum</u> <u>Magazine</u> and <u>The</u> <u>New-York</u> <u>Review</u> was probably
supplied by William Cullen Bryant during the years of his
editorship. See Godwin, <u>op</u>. <u>cit</u>., vol. 1, p. 227.

71. On the foundation of the National Academy, see Cummings,
<u>op</u>. <u>cit</u>., pp. 25 ff.; Edward L. Morse, <u>op</u>. <u>cit</u>., pp. 277-
281; and Eliot C. Clark, <u>op</u>. <u>cit</u>., pp. 12-15.

72. Cummings, <u>op</u>. <u>cit</u>., p. 23.

73. "Fine Arts," <u>The</u> <u>New-York</u> <u>Review</u>, vol. 2, April, 1826, p. 368.

74. <u>Ibid</u>., p. 370.

75. John Durand, <u>Life</u>, p. 82.

76. Cummings, <u>op</u>. <u>cit</u>., p. 117.

77. <u>Ibid</u>., pp. 134-135.

78. See App. IV, no. 10, folio 1.

79. During the Academy's first ten years, lectures were delivered
by the following professors and lecturers:

<u>1826</u> <u>and</u> <u>1827</u>. Professors: Dr. G. F. King, Anatomy; Charles
Shaw, Perspective.

<u>1828</u>. Professors: S. F. B. Morse, Painting; Doctors King
and John G. Goodman, Anatomy; Charles Shaw and John Neilson, Perspective; William Cullen Bryant, Mythology and
Ancient History.

<u>1829</u> <u>and</u> <u>1830</u>. Professors: Morse, Painting; Dr. King,
Anatomy. Horatio Greenough is listed in this and the
following years as the Professor of Sculpture, but his
residence abroad from 1829 to 1851 made his title merely
honorary. Dr. John Neilson, Jr., Perspective; Bryant,
Mythology and Ancient History.

<u>1831</u>. Professors: Morse, Painting; Greenough, Sculpture; Dr. J. Neilson, Jr., Anatomy; Bryant, Mythology. Lecturers: William Dunlap, Historical Composition; A. J. Mason, Wood Engraving; T. S. Cummings, Miniature Painting; Dr. Bushe, Anatomy; G. C. Verplanck, History; R. W. Weir, Perspective; C. C. Wright, Ancient Coins and Medals.

<u>1832</u>. All of the lecturers listed in 1831 are now listed as professors with the exceptions that Dr. Morton replaced Dr. Neilson, Jr. as Professor of Anatomy and C. C. Wright is no longer listed as Professor of Ancient Coins.

<u>1833</u>. Same as 1832 with the addition of the following **volunteer** lecturers: Charles Edwards, Antique Statues; William Emerson, Literature; John Inman, History; John J. Mapes, Chemistry of Colors.

<u>1834</u> and <u>1835</u>. Same as 1832.

<u>1836</u>. Same as 1832 plus two professors: Charles Edwards, Antique Statues; J. J. Mapes, Chemistry of Colors. Those serving in 1836 continued to serve in 1837 and 1838, after which no lectures of any kind appear to have been offered until in 1845, when Durand became president, Dr. Robert Watts was appointed Professor of Anatomy and William Bayless Professor of Perspective. These gentlemen served until 1852, after which time no more are listed in the Aca-annual exhibition catalogues, the source of the foregoing list. See, also, Cummings, <u>op</u>. <u>cit</u>., <u>passim</u>.

80. Cummings, op. cit., p. 18.

81. Perhaps a part of the cause of the failure of the American
Academy lay in the fact that the character of its organization and rather permanent exhibition was more that of a
museum than of an academy calculated to provide a body of
artists with opportunities to study and to exhibit. The
American Academy attempted to present a permanent exhibition in a period when the public could only be attracted to
art as a novelty and as a pretext for social intercourse.
The National Academy from its outset, through temporary
exhibitions of new works and through preview receptions,
established that alliance between art, novelty, and socia-
bility that has continued to characterize the New York
art world. Somewhat later the American Art-Union created
an even broader interest in art by associating it with
novelty's younger sister, chance.

82. These included: Agnostino Carracci, Martydom of St. Sebas-
tian, exh. 1826; François Gerard, Portrait of Napoleon I,
1825; Luca Giordano, Neptune and Amphitrite, 1825-26; Giov.
Pannini, View of the Ruins of Rome, 1825-26; Ribera, Head
of St. Peter, 1826-27; Hubert Robert, View of the Ruins in
Rome and Architectural Ruins, 1825-26; Salvator Rosa, two
landscapes, 1825-28; Rubens, Lions in a Trap, 1825-27;
Snyders, Boys at Play with a Lamb, with Fruit and Flowers,
1825-28; Schidoni, Charity, 1825-27; Snyders, Stag Hunt,
1825-27; Teniers, two landscapes with figures, 1825-26;
Van Huysum, two paintings of fruit, 1826-27; Carle Van Loo,

Rosamond, 1825-26; Joseph Vernet, <u>Landscape</u> <u>with</u> <u>Figures</u> <u>Bathing</u>, 1825-26.

83. A. B. Durand, "Autobiographical Fragment," in John Durand, <u>Life</u>, p. 20, states that "At seven years of age I was sent to the village public school where I was instructed in . . . the whole of the Westminster Catechism." In speaking of his father's boyhood home, John Durand, <u>Life</u>, p. 9, notes that "theological rancour and disputes caused no disturbance in the Durand household, and because, probably, the heads of it gave them no countenance. My grandfather and grandmother, both of equable temper, were averse to any heated manifestation of feeling or opinion."

84. George W. Cooke, <u>op</u>. <u>cit</u>., p. 119, states that this congregation was organized as early as 1819.

85. Cooke, <u>op</u>. <u>cit</u>., p. 111. Parke Godwin, <u>op</u>. <u>cit</u>., vol. 1, p. 189. states that Jared Sparks sometimes visited New York in the 1820's.

86. Cooke, <u>op</u>. <u>cit</u>., p. 137.

87. Godwin, <u>op</u>. <u>cit</u>., vol. 1, p. 211.

88. Francis, <u>op</u>. <u>cit</u>., p. 154. The story is quoted in Godwin, <u>op</u>. <u>cit</u>., vol. 1, p. 211 note.

89. W. E. Channing, <u>Discourses</u>, <u>Reviews</u> <u>and</u> <u>Miscellanies</u>, Boston, 1830, p. vii.

90. Godwin, <u>op</u>. <u>cit</u>., vol. 1, p. 211.

91. Stephens, <u>op</u>. <u>cit</u>., p. 28.

92. <u>Ibid</u>., pp. 46-47.

93. A. B. Durand, manuscript _Journal_ of his European tour, June 14, 1840. A. B. Durand Papers, NYPL. John Durand, _Life_, pp. 145-146, quotes parts of this passage in modified form and completely omits the part in which Durand denies the utility of institutionalized religion.

94. In "Letter II," p. 34, Durand states that "The external appearance of this our dwelling-place apart from its wondrous structure and functions that minister to our well-being, is frought with lessons of high and holy meaning, only surpassed by the light of Revelation."

95. William Dunlap, _Diary_, Dorothy C. Barck ed., 3 vols, New York, 1931, vol. 1, p. 151.

96. _Ibid._, vol. 3, p. 498.

97. _Ibid._, vol. 3, p. 499.

98. _Ibid._, vol. 3, pp. 503 and 508.

99. John Durand, _Prehistoric Notes_, p. 22.

100. 1817-1843. Dana Collection, Cambridge, Mass.

101. 1816. Dana Collection, Cambridge, Mass.

102. Trumbull's _The Saviour and St. John Playing with a Lamb_ (Fig. 26, 1801, Yale University Art Gallery), _The Woman Taken in Adultery_ (1808-1812, Yale University Art Gallery), and _Our Saviour with Little Children_ (Fig. 27, 1812, Yale University Art Gallery) appeared at the exhibitions of the American Academy in the late 1810's and 1820's. In 1827 Trumbull exhibited five religious subjects--_Holy Trinity_ (date and present location unknown), _The Bearing of the Cross_ (1826, Yale University Art Gallery), a _Dead Christ_

Christ (1827, Yale University Art Gallery), and a St.
John and the Lamb (1800, Yale University Art Gallery) at
the American Academy but no paintings of modern heroism.

103. At the American Academy Dunlap exhibited the following
subjects: Mary Magdalen, Christ on the Mount of Olives,
A Holy Family (all 1817), and Susanna at the Bath (1818).
At the National Academy he exhibited: five studies for
Christ on Mount Calvary (1826); a study for Death on the
Pale Horse, a study for Christ on Mount Calvary, and Our
Saviour and Mary Magdalene in the Garden (1827); two more
studies for the Calvary (1828); The Calvary, or the Moment
before the Crucifixion (1830); the Calvary, two studies
for it, and a study for Christ Rejected appeared in the
review exhibition of 1831.

104. Cole contributed the following Biblical subjects to the
early exhibitions at the National Academy: Landscape Composition, St. John in the Wilderness (1827); Garden of Eden,
a Composition and Expulsion from the Garden of Eden
(Fig. 202) (1828); The Subsiding of the Waters of the Deluge
(1829); and the Subsiding and the Garden of Eden again in
the review exhibition of 1831.

105. William Sidney Mount painted a Christ Raising the Daughter
of Jairus and a Saul and the Witch of Endor in 1828. See
Bartlett Cowdrey and Hermann W. Williams, Jr., William
Sidney Mount, 1807-1868, An American Painter, New York,
1944, pp. 13-14.

106. The Gospel according to John, ch. 20, verses 16-17.

107. W. E. Channing, "Discourse at the Ordination of the Rev. Jared Sparks, Baltimore, 1819," in Discourses, Reviews, and Miscellanies, p. 299.

108. Loc. cit.

109. Ibid., pp. 303-305.

110. Ibid., p. 315.

111. Ibid., p. 314.

112. Ibid., p. 317.

113. Ibid., pp. 317-318.

114. Ibid., p. 321.

115. Ibid., p. 318.

116. The translations are signed only with the initial "B." I attribute them to Bancroft on the basis of Godwin's statement, op. cit., vol. 1, pp. 226-227: "Mr George Bancroft, since eminent as an historian, aspired to poetry then, and translated for it /i.e., the New-York Review and Atheneum Magazine/ from Goethe and Schiller." Neither poem appears among the translations printed in Bancroft's Literary and Historical Miscellanies, New York, 1855, pp. 206-246.

117. Bryant must have known of this painting prior to its exhibition at the National Academy in May, 1826, for in the April, 1826, number of Bryant's New-York Review there appears a paragraph on the preparations of the painters for the first National Academy exhibition. Here it is stated that "Mr. Durand, so distinguished as an engraver, has found time to devote to painting, and with a success which might have been anticipated by those who have seen his draw-

ings." ("Fine Arts," The New-York Review, vol. 2, April, 1826, p. 370.) As Durand exhibited only two paintings in 1826--the Magdalene and a Portrait of a Child--whoever wrote the above, probably Bryant, must have been thinking of the Magdalene. The published statement could very well have been the encouraging words of a confederate.

118. W. E. Channing, "Unitarian Christianity Most Favorable to Piety. Discourse at the Dedication of the Second Congregational Unitarian Church. New York, 1826," in Works, seventh edition, 6 vols., Boston, 1847, vol. 3, p. 188.

119. Ibid., vol. 3, p. 192.

120. Genesis, ch. 21, verses 15-16.

121. Ibid., ch. 21, verse 17.

122. 1776, repainted in 1803. Metropolitan Museum of Art. The painting was engraved by John Young sometime after 1803.

123. In a review in The United States Review and Literary Gazette, of which Bryant was co-editor, Durand's Samson was described as "strictly dramatic; we are interested more in the expression of passions in the characters than in the event . . ." ("Review: The Exhibition of the National Academy of Design, 1827," The United States Review and Literary Gazette, vol. 2, no. 4, July, 1827, p. 247.) Again, we may say that, perhaps, this was all that Durand intended. On the other hand it is possible that the reviewer, who may have been Bryant himself, was careful to describe Durand's painting as purely dramatic in order to reassure those whose suspicion had been aroused by rumor.

CHAPTER TWO.

1. John Durand, _Life_, p. 82.

2. The details of Durand's revenge are obscure, but from John
   Durand's _Life_ and the A. B. Durand Papers it appears to
   have occured in the following manner.  In 1823 Durand's
   youngest sister, Elizabeth, married an Englishman named
   Joseph Manners, who at the time posed as a Methodist clergyman.  Manners, however, had already deserted one wife in
   England and soon left Elizabeth.  On December 8, 1823, Dur-
   and published "for the benefit of the community" a portrait
   "to identify the person with the true character of one of
   the BASEST OF MEN."  The portrait bore the following history
   of

> Joseph Mountjoy Manners, a native of England,
> was educated a preacher in the Methodist connexion,
> from which he was expelled for his crimes; afterwards
> he became an outlawed swindler, fled from England,
> leaving a wife and children, and came to the United
> States, where he soon married again into a respec-
> table family, and is extensively known as a lec-
> turer.  He is classically educated and, in appear-
> ance, a gentleman, but in fact a most accomplished

600

hypocrite. A volunteer in falsehood, none can be
too base for his purpose. He abandoned his second
wife without cause of complaint which has led to
the discovery of his real character and history,
has swindled his best friends, violated the most
sacred bonds of Honour and Affection, and, in short,
is not only an Infidel in Religion but in every
moral principle of society. (J. Durand, Life, p. 83.
An impression of the engraving is listed in Grolier
Club, no. 65. The impression at the New York Public
Library lacks the characterization.)

At a later date, probably in 1829, Durand learned from the
culprit himself of the effect of the print:

Your revenge is complete. Hunted from Boston
to New Orleans, . . . by your persecution, I now--
imbecile in mind and in body, little better than a
skeleton, fit only for an hospital where I may be
killed or cured--call upon you to be my friend.
. . . The fate of an immortal being is in your hands.
Decide as you please. I am prepared for pardon or
revenge. . . . Imitate the God who made us both, or
be the devil of men's imagination. The bearer will
bring you to me. (Quoted in John Durand, Life,
p. 84. The letter is not in the A. B. Durand Papers,
NYPL.)

John Durand sought to give the impression that Durand remained ignorant of Manners' fate--"My father was absent, and

as nothing more was heard from the offender, it is pre-
sumed that he died in Bellevue Hospital." (<u>Loc</u>. <u>cit</u>.)
However, Durand's partner Elias Wade, Jr., did try to find
Manners:

> . . . nor have I been able to learn anything more
> of Manners, although I have made diligent inquiry
> for him. He is not at the Hospital. He may
> possibly still be somewhere in Town watching your
> return, though I think it is a more probable sup-
> position that he has either jumped off the dock
> or has gone in search of more comfortable quarters
> than this City afforded him. (Letter from Elias
> Wade, Jr., to Durand, dated New York, September 12,
> 1829--A. B. Durand Papers, NYPL.)

Finally, contrary to John Durand, Asher did know for certain
that Manners died, for less than a month after receiving the
letter from Wade, he wrote on October 9, 1829, to the offended
Elizabeth (now Mrs. Tillon): "Everybody is glad to hear
of the Death of Mr. Joseph /Manners/." (Letter in the A. B.
Durand Papers, NYPL.) Hence, in 1830 Durand could have regarded his wife's death as God's vengeance for the murder
he himself had committed.

3. Tuckerman, <u>Book</u> <u>of</u> <u>the</u> <u>Artists</u>, p. 192, and John Durand,
   <u>Life</u>, p. 82.

4. <u>Grolier</u> <u>Club</u>, no. 54. After a painting by John Vanderlyn.

5. Parke Godwin, <u>op</u>. <u>cit</u>., vol. 1, pp. 256-257.

6.   Henry W. Bellows, The Unitarian Traditions of New York,
     New York, 1879, p. 37.

7.   Review of Orville Dewey's Moral Views of Commerce, Society,
     and Politics, in Twelve Discourses, in The New York Review,
     vol. 3, no. 6, October, 1838, p. 445.

8.   Dunlap, op. cit., vol. 2, p. 286.

9.   In the pair of paintings The Morning of Life and The Evening
     of Life (1840), the sportiveness of childhood appears in
     the first and the theme of an old man's solemn meditation
     in the second.  In An Old Man's Reminiscences (1845),
     children's games fill the background while the meditative
     old man sits in the foreground.  In the Dover Plains (1848),
     sportiveness and contemplation distinguish the attitudes of
     individual children.

10.  Gospel according to Luke, ch. 18, verses 15-17.

11.  The engraving is reproduced and the picture described in
     Chauncey B. Tinker, Painter and Poet, Cambridge, Mass.,
     1938, pp. 90-93.  The painting is reproduced in Ellis K.
     Waterhouse, Gainsborough, London, 1958, pl. 245.

12.  Reynolds, "Discourse Fourteen.  Delivered to the Students
     of the Royal Academy, on the Distribution of the Prizes,
     December 10, 1790," Discourses on Art, New York:  Collier
     Books, 1961, p. 223.

13.  W. E. Channing, "On the Sinfulness of Infants," Christian
     Disciple, vol. 2, no. 8, August, 1814, p. 245, quoted in
     Memoir, 3 vols., London, John Chapman, 1848, vol. 1, p. 379.

14.  Loc. cit.

15. Wordsworth, "Intimations of Immortality from Recollections of Early Childhood," in The Poetical Works, Boston: Phillips, Sampson, and Company, 1859, p. 488.

16. Ibid., p. 486.

17. Gospel according to Matthew, ch. 6, verse 26.

18. There is some precedent for the presence of barn-yard fowl in portraits of children: Reynolds, Lady Catherine Pelham-Clinton (as a child), 1781, reproduced in E. K. Waterhouse, Reynolds, London, 1941, pl. 226; and Pieter Vanderlyn (?), Cornelius D. Wynkoop, ca. 1740, reproduced in W. P. Belknap, American Colonial Painting, Cambridge, Mass., 1959, pl. LXIX, fig. 2. In the Reynolds the girl feeds a family of chickens, while in the Vanderlyn a single chicken pecks at something on the ground.

19. Gospel according to Matthew, ch. 6, verses 28-30.

20. Corot's Hagar in the Wilderness (1835, Metropolitan Museum of Art) offers an instructive contrast to Durand's Children of the Artist. Rejecting the iconographical tradition adopted for the Hagar story by Benjamin West and Durand, Corot places more emphasis on the wilderness than on the figures it contains. He brings first to our attention the fact that the figures are in a waste-land that affords no nourishment for man. Only secondarily do we discover the angel approaching to reveal the saving water to the an-guished mother. The picture would thus stand as a metaphor for the idea that nature provides no physical--that is, spiritual--nourishment except through the intervention of

a "transcendental" factor. Hence, to Corot, as to Durand
and to Wordsworth, a transcendental agency must affect
man before nature contributes to his spiritual life.
Opposed, however, to the views of Durand and Wordsworth
is the implication in the Corot that the purpose of the
transcendental agency is achieved directly without the inter-
mediary creation of an orderly world or cosmos. Hence, in
Corot's painting the cosmos of his earlier work gradually
gives way to the direct expression of valuable, psychic
conditions. The movement of Durand's development is in the
opposite direction. Because of the significance he attached
to the cosmos, as that which the eye of faith sees, the
large, single figures of his early work--for example, _Musidora_
--at each point of pressure splinter to yield finally the
highly differentiated aggregates of particulars that are
coördinated in his mature landscapes.

21. Gospel according to Matthew, ch. 6, verses 22-23.

22. Cf. Hawthorne's later use of the image of the lamp of faith:

> He fears not to tread the dreary path before him, be-
> cause his lantern, which was kindled at the fireside
> of his home, will light him back to that same fire-
> side again. And thus we, night wanderers through
> a stormy and dismal world, if we bear the lamp of
> Faith, enkindled at a celestial fire, it will surely
> lead us home to that heaven whence its radiance was
> borrowed. (Nathaniel Hawthorne, "Night Sketches"

(1851), in Twice-Told Tales, op. cit., vol. 1,
p. 484.)

23. Gulian Verplanck, "An Address Delivered at the Opening of
the Tenth Exhibition of the American Academy of the Fine
Arts," in Discourses and Addresses, New York, 1833, p. 149.

24. Double portraits of sisters were common in the later eighteenth century and early nineteenth century. E.g. Greuze,
Friendship; or, The Sisters (Musée du Louvre); Allston, The
Sisters, ca. 1818, (Mrs. Algernon Coolidge, Boston); Henry
Inman, The Sisters, engraved by Durand, Grolier Club,
no. 221 (Fig. 21. The engraving represents two of the six
figures in Inman's The Livingston Children, 1828, in the
collection of James Ricau. Hence, Durand's engraving is a
double portrait, but Inman's painting is not.); Samuel F. B.
Morse, Sisters, engraved by Durand, Grolier Club, no. 213
(Fig. 22).

25. The text of the poem runs as follows:

> She was a Phantom of Delight
> When first she gleamed upon my sight;
> A lovely Apparition, sent
> To be a moment's ornament;
> Her eyes as stars of Twilight fair;
> Like Twilight's, too, her dusky hair;
> But all things else about her drawn
> From May-time and the cheerful Dawn;
> A dancing Shape, an Image gay,
> To haunt, to startle, and waylay.

I saw her upon nearer view,

A Spirit, yet a Woman, too!

Her household motions light and free,

And steps of virgin liberty;

A countenance in which did meet

Sweet records, promises as sweet;

A Creature, not too bright or good

For human nature's daily food;

For transient sorrows, simple wiles,

Praise, blame, love, kisses, tears, and smiles.


And now I see with eye serene

The very pulse of the machine;

A Being breathing thoughtful breath,

A Traveller between life and death;

The reason firm, the temperate will,

Endurance, foresight, strength, and skill.

A perfect Woman, nobly planned,

To warn, to comfort, and command;

And yet a Spirit still, and bright

With something of an angel light.

(From The Poetical Works, Boston:  Phillips, Samson,

and Company, 1859, pp. 444-445.)

26.  In Samuel F. B. Morse's The Wife, engraved by Durand,
Grolier Club, no. 212 (Fig. 23) conjugal companionship is
stressed.

27. Henry Hawley, Neo-Classicism, Style and Motif, The Cleveland Museum of Art, 1964, no. 185, states that Durand purchased the painting from Vanderlyn in 1831.

28. Josephine Beaumarchais, 1805, Musée du Louvre. Christine Boyer, ca. 1800, Musée du Louvre.

29. Wordsworth, "Lines, Composed a Few Miles above Tintern Abbey, on Revisiting the Banks of the Wye during a Tour. July 13, 1798," in The Poetical Works, New York: John Wurtele Lovell, 1880, pp. 188-189.

30. Letter from Durand, Boston June 14, 1834, to John Casilear (A. B. Durand Papers, NYPL): "He [i.e., Allston] expressed a great desire to see my print of Ariadne and having brought an impression with me, I was enabled to gratify him, and if I had not become in some measure insensible to the tickling of praise on that print, I should feel fully satisfied with the high compliments which he bestowed on it."

31. The Valentine, 1809-1811, Estate of Miss Rose L. Dexter, Boston; Beatrice, 1819, Miss Ellen Bullard, Boston; Rosalie, 1835, Society for the Preservation of New England Antiquities. Allston painted numerous pictures similar in subject and mood. Rosalie and The Evening Hymn, of 1835, indicate Allston's interest in this kind of painting at the moment when Durand visited him.

32. "Allston the Painter," The American Monthly Magazine, new series, vol. 1, May, 1836, p. 444.

33. Loc. cit.

34. Ibid., p. 443.

35. Plutarch, "How a Young Man Ought to Hear Poems," Simon Ford trans., in _Miscellanies and Essays. Comprising all his Works Collected under the Title of "Morals,"_ translated by several hands, corrected and revised by W. W. Goodwin, 5 vols., Boston, 1871, vol. 2, p. 46.

36. Pliny, _Natural History_, J. Bostock and H. T. Riley trans., London: H. Bohn, 1857, XXV, 36.

37. The parrot was frequently introduced into portraits and fancy pictures of women in the late eighteenth and early nineteenth centuries. In George W. Flagg's _Lady and Parrot_ (Fig. 38) the equipoise between bird and woman, as in Durand's painting, guarantees the gentle heart of the latter.

38. "Allston the Painter," p. 445.

39. Ca. 1748. The Bowdoin College Museum of Fine Arts, Brunswick, Maine.

40. John Hill Morgan, _Paintings by John Trumbull at Yale University_, New Haven, 1926, pp. 68-69.

41. Mabel M. Swan, _The Athenaeum Gallery, 1827-1873; The Boston Athenaeum as an Early Patron of Art_, Boston, 1940, p. 69.

42. George C. Mason, _The Life and Works of Gilbert Stuart_, New York, 1879, pp. 111-112.

43. See the _New-York Mirror_, vol. 12, no. 6, Aug. 9, 1834, front.

44. 1822. See Edward Biddle and Mantle Fielding, _The Life and Works of Thomas Sully_, Philadelphia, 1921, no. 916.

45. _New-York Mirror_, vol. 12, no. 6, Aug. 9, 1834, p. 41.

46. _Loc. cit._

47. Loc. cit.

48. John Durand, Life, pp. 107-108.

49. Loc. cit. and A. B. Durand Papers, NYPL.

50. John Durand, Life, p. 114.

51. In Cummings, op. cit., p. 13.

52. The abbreviation of a half- or full-length portrait to a bust in an engraved reproduction was the common practice of French portrait engravers of the seventeenth century. See T. H. Thomas, French Portrait Engraving of the XVIIth and XVIIIth Centuries, London, 1910, p. 8.

53. The effort of Durand and his contemporaries to define the individual apart from all accessories--pioneered by Gilbert Stuart, Charles Willson Peale, and other painters of the early Republic--anticipates Walt Whitman's self-identification:

> Trippers and askers surround me,
> People I meet, the effect upon me of my early life
> or the ward and city I live in, or the nation,
> The latest dates, discoveries, inventions, societies,
> authors old and new,
> My dinners, dress, associates, looks, compliments,
> dues,
> The real or fancied indifference of some man or
> woman I love,
> The sickness of one of my folks or of myself, or ill-
> doing or loss or lack of money or depressions or
> exaltations,

Battles, the horrors of fratricidal war, the fever

of doubtful news, the fitful events;

These come to me days and nights and go from me again,

But they are not the Me myself.

("Song of Myself" /1855/ in Leaves of Grass, in

Leaves of Grass and Selected Prose, John Kouenhoven

ed., New York: The Modern Library, 1950, p. 26.)

According to R. W. B. Lewis, in this passage:

There is Emerson's individual, the "infinitely re-

pellent orb." There is also the heroic product of

romanticism, exposing behind the mass of what were

regarded as inherited or external or imposed and

hence superficial and accidental qualities the true

indestructible secret core of personality. There is

the man who contends that "nothing, not God, is

greater than one's self."

There, in fact, is the new Adam.

(R. W. B. Lewis, The American Adam; Innocence, Tragedy,

and Tradition in the Nineteenth Century, Chicago:

The University of Chicago Press, Phoenix Books,

n. d., p. 47.)

Lewis, I believe, in his study of the effort of Whitman,
Emerson, Thoreau,and others to recover an awareness of the
essential self in its perfection has treated this endeavor
as too specifically an American phenomenon, and has too
much ignored the European traditions of puritanism, monas-
ticism, and millenarianism which lie behind it.  A Whitman-

esque isolation of the essential self from all traditions and material contingencies was certainly fundamental to the beliefs and practices of the fifteenth century Bohemian Adamites:

> They held that God dwelt in the Saints of the Last Days, that is, in themselves; and that that made them superior to Christ, who by dying had shown himself to be merely human. They accordingly dispensed with the Bible, the Creed and all book-learning, contenting themselves with a prayer which ran: "Our Father who art in us, illumine us, thy will be done . . ." . . . On the strength of Christ's remark about harlots and publicans, the Adamites declared that the chaste were unworthy to enter their messianic Kingdom . . . The sect was much given to naked ritual dances held around a fire and accompanied by much hymn-singing. Indeed, these people spent much of their time naked, ignoring heat and cold and claiming to be in the state of innocence enjoyed by Adam and Eve before the Fall. . . . The Adamites, who had no possessions of their own, seized everything they could lay hands on. At the same time they set the villages on fire and cut down or burnt alive every man, woman and child whom they could find. . .
>
> (Norman Cohn, The Pursuit of the Millennium, second edition, New York: Harper Torchbooks, 1961 /7/,

pp. 233-234. See also chapters 7 and 8 and
Appendix.)

While it is doubtful that the American Adamites were aware of
the Late Medieval precedent, it seems highly likely that they
were influenced by Seneca's notion that the essential self,
"reason," or the good of man lies behind all of the adventitious decorations of social conventions:

> . . . we are imposed upon because we never estimate
> a man by what he is but add his trappings on. If
> you wish to arrive at a true estimate of a man and
> understand his quality, look at him naked. Make
> him lay aside his inheritance, his titles, Fortune's
> other specious trimmings; make him lay even his
> body aside and look at his soul to ascertain its
> quality and size and whether its greatness is its
> own or detachable.
>
> (Seneca, Letters, in The Stoic Philosophy of Seneca,
> Moses Hadas trans., Garden City, N. Y.: Doubleday
> & Company, 1958, "Letter LXXVI," p. 214.)

The image of man stripped of all non-essentials, except
decent clothing, has been normally adopted in photographic
portraits of middle-class subjects down to the present time.
Of course, in the earlier Neo-classical Age Canova and
Horatio Greenough had been willing to exclude all, or most,
of the clothing.

54. Durand's bust portraits of the 1830's may be contrasted with
the portraits of clergymen which he engraved after paintings

by Waldo and Jewett around 1820. Of these, for example, the Rev. James Milnor (1819, Fig. 5) and the Rev. J. B. Romeyn (1820, Fig. 6) are half-lengths, which include one hand in a decided gesture and a curtain or pilaster in the background. In both, the man looks out at the spectator.

55. 1729. Yale University Art Gallery.

56. 1546. National Museum, Naples.

57. Matthew Pratt's Portrait of West is in the Pennsylvania Academy; Delanoy's West and West's C. W. Peale are in the New-York Historical Society.

58. 1433. National Gallery, London.

59. See the numerous comparative illustrations in Waldron Phoenix Belknap, Jr., op. cit., pls. XI-XLIX.

60. In the late 1820's Durand collaborated with Verplanck, Robert Sands, and William Cullen Bryant in the production of The Talisman, a gift-book published annually in 1828, 1829, and 1830. Durand also knew Verplanck as a member of the Sketch Club in the early 1830's.

61. Verplanck, "An Address Delivered at the Opening of the Tenth Exhibition of the American Academy of the Fine Arts," p. 140.

62. National Portrait Gallery of Distinguished Americans, vol. 1, n. p.

63. Loc. cit.

64. Plutarch, "Life of Alexander," in Lives, J. Langhorne and W. Langhorne trans., 4 vols., New York: Harper and Brothers, 1846, vol. 3, p. 241. John Galt, op. cit., vol. 1, pp. 86-

87, states that Plutarch had been eminently successful in portraying the soul or "moral vigor":

> Plutarch, like the sculptors of antiquity, has
> selected only the great and elegant traits of
> character; and hence his lives, like those statues
> which are the models of art, possess, with all that
> is graceful and noble in human nature, the parti-
> cular features of individuals. He had no taste
> for the blemishes of mankind. His mind delighted
> in the contemplation of moral vigor; and he seems
> justly to have thought that it was nearly allied
> to virtue: hence many of those characters whose
> portraiture in his works furnish   the youthful
> mind with inspiring examples of true greatness,
> more authentic historians represent in a light far
> different.

To Galt and, I believe, to Plutarch the portrayal of the soul could be something quite different from the presenta-tion of an individual as a morally good person. If, as we shall suggest shortly, the portrait of the good man might excite a love of virtue in the spectator, the portrait of a vigorous spirit might excite the "moral vigor" of the spectator. In the same place Galt also says of Plutarch:

> In his peculiar class, Plutarch still stands alone,
> at least no author in any of the living languages
> appears to be yet truly sensible of the secret cause
> by which his sketches give that direct impulse to

the elements of genius, by which the vague and
wandering feelings of unappropriated strength are
converted into an uniform energy, endowed with
productive action.

As late as 1880 S. G. W. Benjamin, op. cit., pp. 50-51,
could state that Gilbert Stuart and Charles L. Elliott had
been especially successful in probing into and grasping a
depth of soul or character--the immortal part of man--
which, he believed, photography cannot approach.

65. A. B. Durand, "Letter IV," p. 98.

66. Loc. cit.

67. Verplanck, "An Address delivered at the Opening of the
Tenth Exhibition of the American Academy of the Fine Arts,"
p. 140.

68. Plutarch, "Life of Paulus Aemilius," in Lives, J. Langhorne
and W. Langhorne trans., vol. 2, p. 37.

69. Loc. cit.

70. "Gilbert Stuart," National Portrait Gallery of Distinguished
Americans, vol. 1, n. p.

71. Both painted in London, 1817. Isaac of York, The Boston
Athenaeum. Head of a Jew, Museum of Fine Arts, Boston.

72. Both of the Allston studies cited are unfinished in the sense
that the figure is not carried to the lower edge of the
picture plane.

73. Letter from Durand to his wife, Rome, Jan. 15, 1841.
A. B. Durand Papers, NYPL.

74. In the letter just cited (Rome, Jan. 15, 1841) Durand
    mentions a letter to his son John, written about December
    25, 1840, in which he describes his plans for painting in
    Rome. It was probably from this letter that John Durand
    quoted, Life, p. 163: "I am making arrangements for doing
    some studies from the old 'codgers' who walk the streets
    here in all the dignity of bearded majesty, old patriarchs
    who go about looking as if they belonged to a period two
    thousand years ago."

75. Benjamin West, "First Discourse to the Students of the
    Royal Academy. December 10, 1792," in Galt, op. cit.,
    vol. 2, p. 89.

76. John Durand, Life, p. 120. The circumstances in which this
    picture originated are discussed in three letters published
    under the heading "Durand's Picture of the Capture of Major
    Andre," in the Magazine of American History, vol. 24, no. 4,
    October, 1890, pp. 321-322. These letters were probably
    published by the Rev. Dr. Lewis P. Clover, Jr. In the first
    (John Durand to Clover, 1876), John Durand states that his
    father "thinks that he painted it independent of any
    commission, and that he probably sold it to him /i.e., the
    elder Clover/." In the second letter (John Durand to Clover,
    1878), John reports that his father recalls going to Tarry-
    town to make drawings of the locality of the arrest, but
    "he can recall no circumstance connected with the picture
    at the time he painted it . . ." The third letter (Clover,
    Senior, to his son, Dec. 14, 1878) contains the statement

that the picture was painted for the elder Clover and that
he accompanied Durand to Tarrytown. The memory of one of
the old men must have been weak. See also App. II, no. 24,
below.

77. Letter in the A. B. Durand Papers, NYPL.

78. William Dunlap, Diary, vol. 3, p. 840.

79. Robert W. July, The Essential New Yorker: Gulian Verplanck,
Durham, North Carolina, 1951, p. 195.

80. Ibid., pp. 185-186.

81. Ibid., p. 167.

82. Dunlap, History, vol. 2, p. 367.

83. Ibid., vol. 2, p. 450, note.

84. Loc. cit.

85. John Durand, Life, pp. 121-122.

86. Letter from Cole to Reed, Sept. 18, 1833, in Louis L. Noble,
The Course of Empire, the Voyage of Life, and Other Pictures
of Thomas Cole, N. A., New York, 1853, pp. 176-179.

87. Henry W. French, Art and Artists in Connecticut, Boston,
1879, p. 91.

88. French states, loc. cit., that Nathaniel Jocelyn and Thomas
Cole secured the patronage of Luman Reed for Flagg.

89. Loc. cit.

90. The following paintings by George W. Flagg, originally in
the collection of Luman Reed, are owned by the New-York
Historical Society: The Chess Players--Check Mate; Falstaff
Enacting Henry IV; Sleeping Female; The Little Savoyard;
Rebecca; The Woodchopper's Boy; The Match-Girl (London);

Lady and Parrot; The Nun; Lady Jane Grey Preparing for Execution; Mother, Child and Butterfly; Murder of the Princes. See Catalogue of the Gallery of Art of The New-York Historical Society, New York, 1915, pp. 3-9.

91. Letter from Cole to Reed, Sept. 18, 1833 in Noble, op. cit., pp. 170-177.

92. Ibid., p. 178.

93. Plutarch, "Of the Love of Wealth," Mr. Patrick trans., in Miscellanies and Essays, vol. 2, pp. 304-305.

94. Verplanck, "An Address Delivered at the Opening of the Tenth Exhibition of the American Academy of the Fine Arts," p. 125.

95. Washington Irving, Knickerbocker History of New York, in Works, New York and London: The Co-operative Publication Society, n. d., vol. 4, p. 252.

96. Huntington, op. cit., p. 26.

97. The eight paintings were never hung in this way, because Cole's were not completed until after the death of Reed. The frames on Cole's paintings today do not match those on the other three pictures.

98. Exhibited 1815. National Gallery, London.

99. National Gallery, London.

100. A short, fat figure and a tall, thin figure are also contrasted in Flagg's Falstaff Enacting Henry IV, completed before Durand undertook his picture, exhibited at the National Academy in 1834, and inspired by Thew's engraving, published by the Boydells, after Robert Smirke's paint-

ing. The pose and proximity of Durand's figures are, however, more closely related to the Rowlandson print.

101. W. E. Channing, "Remarks on the Character and Writings of
Fénelon," in *Discourses, Reviews, and Miscellanies*, pp. 210-
211.

102. Orville Dewey, *The Old World and The New*, 2 vols., New York,
1836, vol. 2, pp. 191-192. The entire statement reads:
"In Mount and Durand, as painters of grotesque and common
life, we have artists that enable us to look at the works
of Teniers and Wilkie without despair or discouragement."
None of Mount's paintings can be classified as "grotesque,"
nor can any of Durand's, except the *Peter Stuyvesant*.

103. Thomas Cole Papers, E. P. Lesley, Jr., ed., NYHS.

104. Verplanck, "An Address Delivered at the Opening of the
Tenth Exhibition of the American Academy of the Fine Arts,"
p. 147.

105. Thomas Cole Papers, E. P. Lesley, Jr., ed., NYHS.

106. Godwin, *op. cit.*, vol. 1, p. 283.

107. W. C. Bryant, ed. *Popular History of the United States*,
4 vols., New York, 1883, vol. 4, p. 334.

108. Martha J. Lamb, *op. cit.*, vol. 2, p. 733.

109. James G. Wilson, ed., *op. cit.*, vol. 3, pp. 351-354. On
the bank crisis of 1837 see R. C. McGrane, *The Panic of
1837*, Chicago and London: The University of Chicago Press,
Phoenix Books, 1965.

110. Letter from Cole to Durand, June 23, 1836. Thomas Cole
Papers, E. P. Lesley, Jr., ed., NYHS.

111. Quoted in Noble, op. cit., p. 221.

112. Letter from Durand to Cole, September 1, 1836. A. B. Durand Papers, NYPL.

113. Letter from Cole to Durand, September 12, 1836. Thomas Cole Papers, E. P. Lesley, Jr., ed., NYHS.

114. See letter from Theodore Allen to Cole, New York, September 22, 1836, Thomas Cole Papers, E. P. Lesley, Jr., ed., NYHS: "Durand and Casilear, I am told left here to visit you on Monday." And see App. IV, nos. 10, fol. 12 v. and 11, fols. 27 v., 29, 36, 37, 39, 40, and 43 v.

115. Cowdrey and Williams, op. cit., p. 5.

116. Letter from Theodore Allen to Cole, Feb. 21, 1837. Thomas Cole Papers, E. P. Lesley, Jr., ed., NYHS.

117. Letter from Morse to Cole, March 20, 1837. Thomas Cole Papers, E. P. Lesley, Jr., ed., NYHS.

118. Godwin, op. cit., vol. 1, p. 322. In the early 1820's Bryant had rebuked the desire to escape the ills of life in society by flight to the wilderness:

> Is not man, notwithstanding the claims which society has upon him, justifiable in seeking his own individual interest and happiness? Is he bound to associate with the world if he has been wronged by it? May he not act justly in choosing his place of abode, even if in so doing he separate himself from all busy intercourse with his kindred and with mankind? In fine, may he not banish himself from

the engagements of humanity and from the active
duties of life, if he believes that he shall find
in retirement and peace, that security from the
daggers of ingratitude and faithlessness, which
fate denies him amid the throng and press of the
world? . . . Should he retire in disgust from the
busy haunts of men "to the peace and seclusion of
some mountain solitude," to such scenes as those
around the beautiful Lake George, his sphere of
benevolence might be contracted--his sympathies
might run to waste--he might often shudder with the
consciousness of cowardly ingratitude towards his
Creator, in thus deserting the duties assigned to
him--yet self--self, that dearest object of man's
study, would be consulted, and he who the world
could never bless should be happy in loneliness
. . . and all of nature's wonderful evidences of
Omnipotence should there call forth his adoration;
should soothe his spirit during his earthly existence, and should point his hopes to that calm blue
sky, . . . Thus in solitude he might be virtuous
even to sanctity--thus might he learn wisdom, thus
enjoying the sweets of almost the days of innocence
when the first man was alone in the midst. of creation, he might live happily--thus die with resigna-
tion, undisturbed by the presence of those who had

deceived him, untempted by the look that won his affections, but to rob him of his peace.

But this is all nonsense! --It is an easy matter for a man to find fault with the world and to wail at fortune, when he could not even _imagine_ a world more admirably adapted to his happiness, and when his miseries and his disappointments are often the retributive results of his own follies, the natural consequence of the wildness of his plans, the instability of his hopes, and the merry use which he makes of his reason.--And should all whose insatiable minds would grasp at impossibilities, and who whine and mourn because their romantic desires are frustrated, be advised to seek retirement upon the picturesque shores of the secluded Lake George; rational apprehensions might be entertained whether those picturesque shores are sufficiently extensive to contain them--half the world might emigrate, and the other half left to push out new colonies each succeeding year!

("Lake George," New-York Mirror, vol. 1, no. 21, Dec. 20, 1823, pp. 164-165.)

119. Godwin, op. cit., vol. 1, p. 323.
120. John Milton, "Of that sort of Dramatic Poem which is Called Tragedy," prefaced to Samson Agonistes in The Poetical Works of John Milton, New York: American Book Exchange, 1880, p. 348.

121. Gospel according Luke, ch. 4, verse 35. Printed in the National Academy Catalogue.
122. John Durand, _Life_, p. 132.
123. _Ibid._, p. 142.

CHAPTER THREE.

1. Jack Downing, "Journal," New York Gazette, October 28, 1835.
   The passage is cited in the Catalogue of the Gallery of the
   New-York Historical Society, New York, 1915, p. 10.

2. The Toledo Museum of Art.

3. Cf. Landscape with Dancing Figures, 1648/49, reproduced in
   M. Röthlisberger, Claude Lorrain, the Paintings, New Haven,
   1961, vol. 2, fig. 197. This painting was frequently engraved in the late eighteenth and early nineteenth cen-
   turies--ibid., vol. 1, p. 283.

4. Washington Irving, Knickerbocker's History of New York,
   Book 7, chapter 1, in Works, New York and London: The
   Co-operative Publication Society, n. d., vol. 4, pp. 305-306.

5. Ibid., p. 305.

6. John Durand, Life, p. 132.

7. Washington Irving, "Rip Van Winkle," in Works, vol. 1, p. 86.

8. Ibid., vol. 1, p. 87.

9. Ibid., vol. 1, p. 84.

10. Dunlap, op. cit., vol. 2, p. 245.

11. Joseph Addison, The Spectator, 2 vols., Philadelphia:
    J. J. Woodward, 1832, vol. 1, no. 112, p. 172.

12. W. E. Channing, "Remarks on the Character and Writings
    of John Milton, 1826," in Discourses, Reviews and Miscel-
    lanies, p. 18.

13. W. C. Bryant, "Inscription for the Entrance to a Wood,"
    (1815) in The Poetical Works, 2 vols., New York:
    D. Appleton and Company, 1883, vol. 1, p. 23.

14. In "A Forest Hymn" (1825) Bryant describes the periodic
    retreat to nature as both strengthening the individual's
    sense of his own goodness and calming his distraught
    passions:

> But let me often to these solitudes
> Retire, and in thy presence reassure
> My feeble virtue. Here its enemies,
> The passions, at thy plainer footsteps shrink
> And tremble and are still.
>
> (The Poetical Works, 1883, vol. 1, pp. 133-134.)

As we have noted in Chapter Two, Thomas Cole believed that
the experience of nature would relieve the physical and
moral ailments arising from urban life: "Nature may not
cure, but she will soothe." (Cole to Durand, June 23, 1836.
Thomas Cole Papers, E. P. Lesley, Jr., ed., NYHS.) "Nature
is a sovereign remedy . . . provided you could consistently
leave the city you would be better in health and spirits
. . ." (Cole to Durand, Sept. 12, 1836. Thomas Cole Papers,
E. P. Lesley, Jr., ed., NYHS.) In the early 1850's Henry
T. Tuckerman defined the healing and refreshment that results from an instinctual sympathy between man and nature:

> There is an affinity between man and nature
> which conventional habits keep in abeyance but do
> not extinguish. It is manifested in the prevalent

taste for scenery, and the favor so readily bestowed upon its graphic delineation in art or
literature; but in addition to the poetic love of
nature, as addressed to the sense of beauty, or
that ardent curiosity to explore its laws and phenomena which finds expression in natural science,
there is an instinct that leads to a keen relish of
nature in her primeval state, and a facility in embracing the life she offers in wild and solitary
haunts; a feeling that seems to have survived the
influences of civilization and developes, when encouraged, by the inevitable law of animal instinct.
It is not uncommon to meet with this passion for
nature among those whose lives have been devoted
to objects apparently alien to its existence;
sportsmen, pedestrians, and citizens of rural propensities, indicate its modified action, while it
is more emphatically exhibited by the volunteers
who join caravans to the Rocky Mountains, the
deserts of the East and the forests of central and
South America, with no ostensible purpose but the
gratification arising from intimate contact with
nature in her luxuriant or barren solitudes.

To one having but an inkling of this sympathy,
with a nervous organization and an observant mind
there is, indeed, no restoration of the frame or
sweet diversion to the mind like a day in the

woods. . . . There is a certain tranquility, and
balm in the forest that heals and calms the ferverd
spirit and quickens the languid pulses of the weary
and disheartened with the breath of hope.  Its
influence on the animal spirits is remarkable; and
the senses, released from the din and monotonous
limits of streets and houses, luxuriate in the
breadth of vision and the rich variety of form, hue,
and odor which only scenes like these afford.
("Over the Mountains, or the Western Pioneer," in
The Home Book of the Picturesque, New York, 1852,
pp. 132-133.)

15. Letter from Sylvester Graham to Durand, June 27, 18/21/.
A. B. Durand Papers, NYPL.

16. Letter from Frederick W. Philip to Durand, September 17,
1832.  A. B. Durand Papers, NYPL.

17. Thomas Cole, "Essay on American Scenery," American Monthly
Magazine, new series, vol. 1, Jan., 1836, p. 12.

18. Ibid., pp. 1-2.

19. Ibid., p. 3.

20. A. B. Durand, "Letter IV," p. 98.

21. Thomas Cole, "Essay on American Scenery," p. 3.  Elsewhere
in the same essay, p. 12, Cole describes rural nature as
exciting an oasis-like condition in the soul of the spectator:  "May we at times turn from the ordinary pursuits of
life to the pure enjoyment of rural nature; which is in the

soul like a fountain of cool waters to the wayworn traveller."

22. A. B. Durand, "Letter IV," p. 98. In the same place Durand
states that a landscape may become "companionable, holding
silent converse with the feelings, playful or pensive--
and, at times, touching a chord that vibrates to the inmost
recesses of the heart, yet with no unhealthy excitement,
but soothing and strengthening to his best faculties."
This "soothing and strengthening" of the spectator's "best
faculties" is eminently characteristic of the recreational
paintings.

23. Cf. Landscape with the Rest on the Flight into Egypt, 1645,
Richard Cavendish Collection.

24. E. P. Richardson, American Romantic Painting, p. 31.

25. A. B. Durand, "Letter IV," p. 98.

26. For Durand's friend in the 1850's, Elias L. Magoon, nature
is an oasis because of the memories of "the sunny days of
childhood" it evokes: "hills, valleys, brooks, trees--our
first and fondest friends beyond the domestic hearth--are
never forgotten. Memory recalls the sunny days of childhood and youth; and, like the green spot in the desert, in
which the weary traveller lingers with delight, his toils
and privations half forgotten, we love to ramble again
amidst the scenes of earliest emotion and purest thought
. . ."
("Scenery and Mind," in The Home Book of the Picturesque,
pp. 3-4.)

27. A painting exhibited at the National Academy in 1854 under the title Strawberrying (App. II, no. 309) must have been related in character to these two earlier works.

28. W. C. Bryant, "Lines on Revisiting the Country," (1825) in The Poetical Works, 1883, vol. 1, p. 151.

29. Tuckerman states quite directly in Book of the Artists, p. 189, that Durand's "affinity with nature is akin to that of Wordsworth and Bryant."

30. See Wordsworth, "Evening Ode, Composed upon an Evening of Extraordinary Splendor and Beauty," in The Poetical Works, Boston: Phillips, Sampson, and Co., 1859, pp. 428-431.

31. Ibid., p. 431.

32. Tuckerman, Book of the Artists, p. 187.

33. "Dottings on Art and Artists, No. IV," The New World, March 11, 1848, p. 307.

34. In Florence in the later part of 1840 Durand noted his reactions to the landscapes of Claude in an undated draft of a letter to Thomas Cole:

> I hear you ask me what I think of them, of all, & of Claude in particular well the first picture which I saw of his, disappointed me. The second, third, fourth, fifth, sixth, & seventh, did not meet my expectations. Those were all, strictly speaking Landscapes. But when I came to his sea ports the embarkation of St. Ursula and that of the Queen of Sheba I could realize his greatness in the glowing

atmosphere & moving water.

(A. B. Durand Papers, NYPL.)

35. Archibald Alison, Essays on the Nature and Principles of
Taste, 2 vols., Edinburgh, 2nd ed., 1811. Alison's Essays
were frequently printed in America before 1860. The following editions have come to my attention:

Boston: Cummings and Hillard, 1812.

Hartford: Printed by G. Goodwin and Sons, 1821.

New York: G. and C. and H. Carvill, 1830.

New York: Harper and Brothers, 1844, 1846, 1852,
1856, and 1858.

36. In his journal on December 12, 1829, Cole wrote: "I think
there is in Alison's work on taste a passage in which he
attributes the decline of the fine arts to the circumstance
of painters having forsaken the main object of art for the
sake of its technicalities." (Quoted by Noble, op. cit.,
p. 116.) Alison's influence on Bryant is discussed by
Donald A. Ringe in two articles: "Horatio Greenough,
Archibald Alison and the Functionalist Theory of Art,"
College Art Journal, vol. 19, no. 4, Summer, 1960, p. 315,
and "Kindred Spirits: Bryant and Cole," American Quarterly,
vol. 6, 1954, pp. 234-236.

37. Alison, op. cit., vol. 1, pp. 4-5.

38. Ibid., vol. 1, p. 6.

39. A. B. Durand, "Letter IV," p. 98.

40. Alison, op. cit., vol. 1, p. 21.

41. Ibid., vol. 2, p. 192.

42. Ibid., vol. 2, pp. 192-193. Cf.: "The view of the house where one was born, of the school where one was educated, and where the gay years of infancy were passed, is indifferent to no man. They recall so many images of past happiness and past affections, they are connected with so many strong or valued emotions, and lead altogether to so long a train of feelings and recollections, that there is hardly any scene which one ever beholds with so much rapture." (Ibid., vol. 1, pp. 23-24.)

43. 1845. M. & M. Karolik Collection, Museum of Fine Arts, Boston.

44. In 1849 Durand exhibited a Pastoral Landscape at the National Academy (App. II, no. 256) to which he appended the following lines by Bryant:

> Blue-eyed girls
> Brought pails and dipped them in thy crystal pool;
> And children, ruddy-cheeked and flaxen haired,
> Gathered the glistening cowslip from thy edge.
> ("The Fountain," (1839) in The Poetical Works, 1883, vol. 1, p. 285.)

Both the verses and the painting are related to Bryant's much earlier recommendation to the poet of real and present life in place of fictional and remote, Pagan deities:

> . . . For my part I cannot but think that human beings, placed among the things of this earth, with their affections and sympathies, their joys and sorrows, and the accidents of fortune to which they

are liable, are infinitely a better subject for
poetry than any imaginary race of creatures whatever. Let the fountain tell me of the flocks that
have drank at it; of the village girl that has
gathered spring flowers on its margin; the traveller
that has slaked his thirst there in the hot noon,
and blessed its waters; the school-boy that has
pulled the nuts from the hazels that hang over it
as it leaps and sparkles in its cool basin; let it
speak of youth and health and purity and gladness,
and I care not for the naiad that pours it out.
("On Poetry in its Relation to our Age and Country,"
in Prose Writings of William Cullen Bryant, 2 vols.,
New York, 1889, vol. 1, p. 29.)

45. The American Landscape, no. 1, New York, 1830, p. 12.

46. Alison, op. cit., vol. 1, p. 39.

47. Ibid., vol. 1, pp. 25-26.

48. Ibid., vol. 1, pp. 24-25.

49. Thomas Cole, "Essay on American Scenery," p. 11.

50. Fort Ticonderoga Association, Inc.

51. Present location unknown. Engraved for The Token, New York,
1830.

52. These paintings are closely related to a passage from Thomas
Whately's Observations on Modern Gardening, which Alison,
vol. 1, pp. 27-29, quotes with strong approbation. Whately
describes a fairly desolate bit of nature and then, according
to Alison, heightens the effect of sublimity by mentioning

the suicide of a young woman and a skeleton found in a
cave--the suicide and the skeleton both belonging to the
place described.

53. Alison, op. cit., vol. 1, p. 25.

54. Cole's Journal, May 22, 1831, quoted in Noble, op. cit.,
p. 127. When Cole visited the Vaucluse on October 29, 1841,
he again referred in his account of the visit to Petrarch,
but devoted more of his comments to the appearance of the
place itself--possibly because he specifically anticipated
a painting when making his visit. (See Noble, op. cit.,
pp. 308-310.) In his "Essay on American Scenery" Cole
lamented the lack of associations connected with the American
landscape comparable to those which European scenes bring
to mind:

> I will now venture a few remarks on what has
> been considered a grand defect in American scenery--
> the want of associations, such as arise amid the
> scenes of the old world.
>
> We have many a spot as umbrageous as Vallom-
> brosa, and as picturesque as the solitudes of
> Vaucluse; but Milton and Petrarch have not hallowed
> them by their footsteps and immortal verse. He
> who stands on Mont Albano and looks down on ancient
> Rome, has his mind peopled with the gigantic asso-
> ciations of the storied past; he who stands on the
> mounds of the West, the most venerable remains of
> American antiquity, **may** experience the emotion of

the sublime, but it is the sublimity of a shore-
less ocean un-islanded by the recorded deeds of
man.

("Essay on American Scenery," p. 11.)

Cole adds, however, that memories of the Revolution and
thoughts of the present and future may be excited by the
American landscape:

Yet American scenes are not destitute of historical and legendary associations--the great struggle
for freedom has sanctified many a spot, and many a
mountain, stream, and rock, has its legend, worthy
of poet's pen or the painter's pencil. But American
associations are not so much of the past as of the
present and the future.

(Loc. cit.)

Cole's views on American associations were probably derived
largely from his reading of John Galt's biography of Benjamin West. Galt, op. cit., vol. 1, pp. 78-81, notes the
general lack of American associations but mentions the events
of the Revolution, although with less enthusiasm than does
Cole. Also, Galt, vol. 2, pp. 92-94, has the ruins of Rome,
rather than the American wilderness, excite ideas in the
mind of West of the future greatness of America. This latter
passage far more clearly anticipates Cole's Course of Empire
series than does Volney's Ruines, ou méditations sur les
révolutions des empires (1791), which Oliver Larkin, op.

cit., p. 202, and E. P. Richardson, *Painting in America*,
p. 167, have regarded as Cole's literary source.

55. Thomas Whately, *Observations on Modern Gardening*, quoted in
Alison, *op. cit.*, vol. 2, p. 42.

56. Whately, *op. cit.*, quoted in Alison, *op. cit.*, vol. 2,
pp. 42-43.

57. Whately, *op. cit.*, quoted in Alison, *op. cit.*, vol. 2,
pp. 45-46.

58. Whately, *op. cit.*, quoted in Alison, *op. cit.*, vol. 2, p. 46.

59. Alison, *op. cit.*, vol. 2, p. 325.

60. Cole's description of the *Voyage of Life* in Noble, *op. cit.*,
pp. 287-289.

61. Thomas Cole, "Essay on American Scenery," pp. 11-12.

62. Quoted in John Durand, *Life*, pp. 164-165. Cf. the following
from a letter from Durand to his wife, Milan, May 4, 1841
(A. B. Durand Papers, NYPL): "I need not tell you, that the
green meadows of Jersey, have to my mind, of this moment
more of beauty and loveliness, than all the boasted scenery
of this far-famed & too-much admired Italy." In the same
letter Durand expresses his desire to be reunited with his
family and friends in America.

63. Cole acknowledged the value of the social and domestic associations of a cultivated landscape: "In what has been said
I have alluded to wild and uncultivated scenery; but the
cultivated must not be forgotten, for it is still more important to man in his social capacity--necessarily bringing
him in contact with the cultured; it encompasses our homes,

and, though devoid of the stern sublimity of the wild, its
quieter spirit steals tenderly into our bosoms mingled with
a thousand domestic affections and heart-warming associa-
tions--human hands have wrought, and human deeds hallowed
all around."

("Essay on American Scenery," p. 3.)

64. A. B. Durand, "Letter II," pp. 34-35.

65. A. B. Durand, "Letter IX," p. 17.

66. Cole, "Essay on American Scenery," p. 12.

67. The First Harvest (Fig. 91) was described as follows in The
Crayon, vol. 3, no. 1, January, 1856, p. 30:

> The scene represented is a wild country in the midst
> of forests and mountains, with a clearing, where,
> in the middle distance, a settler's log-house stands
> by the side of a primitive road. The foreground is
> made up of a stream, with stony banks, bordered with
> isolated and half-felled trees, stumps, and logs,
> and upon it a rude bridge, over which the road passes
> by the side of a forest into the picture. Beyond
> are mountains confining the horizon. By the side
> of the road, and opposite the house, is a field of
> grain, with the settler engaged in reaping his crop,
> and upon this field alone, being the main light of
> the picture, the sunlight streams down from a
> heavily-clouded sky. The light so confined to the
> grain fields typifies encouragement to agricultural
> labor, as well as hope for the pioneer.

The wilderness would, then, typify the past; the grain-field, the present; the sunlight, hope and the future.

68. W. C. Bryant, "The Fountain," (1839) in The Poetical Works, 1883, vol. 1, p. 285.

69. Ca. 1826. Amherst College, Amherst, Mass.

70. Ca. 1828. Collection of Mr. and Mrs. Henry Farmer, New York.

71. The first two of these are reproduced in E. I. Seaver, op. cit., pls. II and XVI. Miss Seaver erroneously states, p. 49, that the engraved view near Conway was based upon the painting in the Farmer collection. But, this painting and the engraving are quite different.

72. Alison, op. cit., vol. 1, p. 165.

73. Rousseau, Les Rêveries du Promeneur Solitaire, quoted in Alison, op. cit., vol. 1, pp. 165-169.

74. The motifs of escape from the cares of the world, refreshment in the experience of nature, boating, relaxation on a river bank, and a dreamy mood of utter tranquility are all present in the verses Thomas Doughty printed in the catalogue of the 1836 exhibition of the Boston Athenaeum to explain his Landscape, Indian Summer (no. 69):

> Pause!--holy quietness pervades the scene:
> The very air is slumbering and still;
> The silvery haze, that far, the boughs between,
> With filmy curtain shrouds the distant hill
> No gentlest zephyr stirs. Hark! from the rill
> Stills on the ear, soft, murmuring melody!

And oh, how does the longing spirit will

    Prone in yon tiny boat, at ease to lie,

As with its snow white sail, it skims the forest by.

      .  .  .

Peace breathes around! The sportsman here hath come,

    And thrown him, languid, on the bank to rest;

Content in such a spot, no more to roam,

    Joy stirs within him and he feels him blest.

And I would come, with anxious cares opprest,

    Apart from all the vanities of life,

And pausing here--by nature's hand carest,--

    Gazing on all around with beauty rife,

Muse--with the world forgot--its sorrows and its strife.

75. Marcel Röthlisberger, op. cit., vol. 1, p. 109. The engraving was in reverse, but Durand must have reversed it once again.

76. 1845. Metropolitan Museum of Art, New York.

77. 1851. The Detroit Institute of Arts.

78. Robert L. Herbert, Barbizon Revisited, New York, 1962, p. 80.

79. William C. Seitz, Claude Monet, Seasons and Moments, New York, 1960, p. 56.

80. In earlier paintings such as the Kindred Spirits (1849), Sunday Morning (1850), or the View Toward the Hudson Valley (1851), figures meditate upon the vision of God afforded by nature, but this experience differs from revery.

81. 1664. C. L. Loyd Collection, Wantage.

82. 1781. National Gallery, London.

83. 1860-65. Metropolitan Museum of Art, New York.

84. Collection of Mr. and Mrs. J. Watson Webb.

85. Petit-Palais, Paris.

86. The Art Institute of Chicago.

87. W. C. Bryant, "Green River," (1819) The Poetical Works, 1883, vol. 1, p. 33. Cf. also the fourth stanza of Bryant's "Lines on Revisiting the Country," (1825), ibid., vol. 1, p. 152, and the first sixteen verses of "A Winter Piece," (1820), ibid., vol. 1, p. 34.

88. James Fenimore Cooper, The Spy, A Tale of the Neutral Ground, New York: Charles Scribner's Sons, 1931, p. 496. The dialogue in question comes almost at the end of the novel, and is shortly followed by Washington's statement that the conduct and character of Birch presage an exulted destiny for the infant nation.

89. Plutarch, "A Discourse Concerning Socrates' Daemon," Mr. Creech trans., in Miscellanies and Essays, vol. 2, pp. 397-398.

90. A. B. Durand, "Letter IV," p. 97.

91. Thomas Cole, Journal, August 3, 1840, quoted in Noble, op. cit., p. 286.

92. The Gospel according to Matthew, ch. 6, verse 24.

93. Seneca, "Of Consolation," XI, in Minor Dialogues, A. Stewart trans., London, 1889. Durand, of course, read neither Greek nor Latin. If he read Seneca, he must have used Sir Roger L'Estrange's Seneca's Morals. By way of Abstract, which was frequently printed in England and America in the late eighteenth and early nineteenth centuries. As I am inter-

ested more in demonstrating a parallel between Durand's
ideas and the philosophy of Seneca than in demonstrating
a direct influence of Seneca himself--although this, too,
I believe does exist--I have employed the more modern
translations of E. Phillips Barker, Aubrey Stewart, and
Moses Hadas in order to present Seneca's ideas undistorted
by the seventeenth century paraphrase.

94. William Rimmer's _Flight and Pursuit_ (1872, Museum of Fine
Arts, Boston) may have been inspired by the idea "that life
is but a flight." Winslow Homer in _The Gulf Stream_ (1899,
Metropolitan Museum, New York) illustrates the idea that
"pillage is the universal law."

95. Seneca, "Of Consolation," XI, in _Minor Dialogues_, A. Stewart
trans., London, 1889.

96. Seneca, "On Tranquility," III, in _The Stoic Philosophy of
Seneca_, Moses Hadas trans.

97. _Loc. cit._

98. Letter from Cole to Durand, June 23, 1836. Thomas Cole
Papers, E. P. Lesley, Jr., ed., NYHS.

99. Seneca, _Letters_, E. Barker trans., Oxford, 1932, "Letter
LXXXVIII," 1.

100. _Ibid._, 18.

101. _Ibid._, 2.

102. _Ibid._, 21-23.

103. _Ibid._, 20.

104. Seneca, "On Tranquility," XVII, in _The Stoic Philosophy of
Seneca_, Moses Hadas trans.

105. Seneca, Letters, E. P. Barker trans., "Letter LXXXVIII,"
     33.

106. Seneca, "On the Shortness of Life," X, in The Stoic
     Philosophy of Seneca, Moses Hadas trans.

107. Ibid., XV.

108. Thomas Cole, "Essay on American Scenery," p. 1.

109. Seneca, Letters, E. P. Barker trans., "Letter LXXXVIII," 34.

110. Seneca, "On Tranquility," XVII, in The Stoic Philosophy of
     Seneca, Moses Hadas trans.

111. A. B. Durand, "Letter I," p. 2.

112. Loc. cit.

113. Loc. cit.

114. Seneca, Letters, E. P. Barker trans., "Letter LXXXIV," 5-6.
     Cf. Benjamin West, "Discourse before the Students of the
     Royal Academy. December 10, 1811," in Galt, op. cit.,
     vol. 2, p. 173:

> But Gentlemen, if you aspire to excellence in your
> profession, you must not rest your future studies
> on the excellence of any individual, however exalted
> his name or genius; but, like the industrious bee,
> survey the whole face of nature, and sip the sweets
> from every flower. When thus enriched, lay up your
> acquisitions for future use; and with that enrich-
> ment from Nature's inexhaustible source, examine
> the great works of art to animate your feelings, and
> to excite your emulation. When you are thus mentally
> enriched, and your hand practiced to obey the powers

of your will, you will find your pencils, or your chisels, as magic wands, calling into view creations of your own, to adorn your name and your country.

CHAPTER FOUR.

1. A. B. Durand, "Letter I," p. 2.
2. Loc. cit.
3. A. B. Durand, "Letter VII," p. 275.
4. A. B. Durand, "Letter I," p. 2.
5. Letter from Durand to Thomas Cole, March 30, 1838. A. B. Durand Papers, NYPL.
6. A. B. Durand, "Letter VII," pp. 274-275.
7. Seneca, Letters, E. P. Barker trans., "Letter LXVI," 39.
8. A. B. Durand, "Letter II," p. 34.
9. W. C. Bryant, "A Forest Hymn" (1825), The Poetical Works, 1883, vol. 1, p. 134.
10. A. B. Durand, "Letter VIII," p. 354.
11. Loc. cit.
12. Loc. cit.
13. The figures in the landscapes of, for example, Meindert Hobbema and seventeenth century painters generally, fail to display an awareness of nature. They assume the role neither of the spectator nor the demiurgos. The critical realism of the nineteenth century depends upon the artist's assumption of one or both of these roles.
14. A. B. Durand, "Letter IV," p. 98.

15. A. B. Durand, "Letter I," p. 2.  Cf. also Durand's statement that the student

> . . . will find in the works of great masters all that could be desired of executive and constructive merit, and occasionally, perhaps, of examples of as great a degree of representative and imitative truth as art can ever attain, and with adequate perception and enlightened judgment to discern and appreciate these qualities, he may, indeed, profit by the study; . . . It is not the manner that you are to study, but to confine your examination of pictures to the discovery of the less obvious means employed, and the capacity of the materials of Art toward the representation of Nature, especially in all that indicates the treatment or disposition of the respective parts, so as to give the greatest prominence to the most essential characteristics.
> ("Letter VII," p. 275.)

16. A. B. Durand, "Letter VII," p. 275.

17. A. B. Durand, "Letter I," p. 2.

18. Seneca, Letters, E. P. Barker trans., "LetterXL," 8-9.

19. A. B. Durand, "Letter I," p. 2.

20. Loc. cit.

21. Loc. cit.

22. Loc. cit.

23. A. B. Durand, "Letter II," pp. 34-35.

24. Ibid., p. 35.

25. Letter from John Constable to John Dunthorne, May 29, 1802,
    in C. R. Leslie, Memoirs of the Life of John Constable,
    London: The Phaidon Press, 1951, p. 15. According to
    Jonathan Mayne, Constable wrote "natural painture" rather
    than "Natural painter," referring to style rather than the
    artist. (Ibid., p. 15 note.)

26. Ibid., p. 179.

27. The following criticism of a painting, Mountain Lake in an
    Autumnal Twilight, by Robert W. Weir, indicates that the
    distinction between the natural and the conventional paint-
    ing was available to an American as early as 1835:

> This is a painting about which opinions are divided,
> some crying it up to the stars as unrivalled, others
> somewhat doubtful of its exceeding merit. We con-
> fess that we incline to the latter. There is poetry,
> sentiment, effect, and meaning in the landscape,
> but, unless we be mistaken, there is not nature;
> and in stating this, we have stated, we conceive,
> the general fault of Mr. Weir's style--he constantly
> sacrifices truth to the altar of effect. So he can
> cloth his scene in a rich garb of mellow light,
> pour over his forests a flood of crimson sunshine,
> or steep them in the deep shadows of twilight, he
> cares not whether his trees resemble the stumps of
> birch brooms, or cauliflowers, or anything under
> heaven but that loveliest of natural things, a
> waving, wind-rocked tree. The present picture is

bold, and dazzling in its contrasts--a deep flush
upon the horizon, fading above into a darkness of
the skies that is not merely incipient--a dusk and
shadowy hill, rising like a black wall against the
lingering radiance--sky and hill reflected in mellow
colors on the mountain lake, and a foreground as
black as midnight!--This is all vastly fine, and
very effective--but, like the Chancellor Elden, we
doubt!--Often we have seen the lingering glow of the
west, and mountain towering against it, flat and
wall-like--often the reflection of both in the dead
pool or gentle river--but never such a foreground
with such a distance.  Oh with his talents, why will
not Mr. Weir be content with imitating, and lay
aside the bootless effort of improving upon nature?
We fear that all the advantage derived from an
Italian abode and study is counterbalanced by the
tendency it seems to give our artists of falsifying
effects.  The climates of our country and of Italy,
their atmosphere, their sunlights, their effects
are as wide as the antipodes; and we hesitate not
to say, that it is the accuracy of these very points
of atmospheric and aerial effect, that lend the
greatest attraction to landscape painting.  Yet we
are constantly annoyed with rich Italian sunsets,
which would suit well enough over the scorched
Campagna or the hot Abruzzi, but which are wholly

> false and out of place among our forests, deep and
> luxuriant, steamy with their excess of moisture,
> and our lakes veiled, like modest beauties, full
> half their time in delicate and vapory mistwreaths.
> Mr. Weir would be supreme, would he but condescend
> to be natural.
> ("Review: National Academy Exhibition, 1835," The
> American Monthly Magazine, vol. 5, no. 5, July,
> 1835, pp. 393-394.)

28. Seneca, Letters, E. P. Barker trans., "Letter XXXIII," 10-11.

29. A. B. Durand, "Letter IV," p. 97.

30. W. E. Channing, "Remarks on the Character and Writings of John Milton," Works, vol. 1, p. 10.

31. A. B. Durand, "Letter IV," p. 98.

32. W. E. Channing, "Remarks on the Character and Writings of John Milton," Works, vol. 1, p. 7.

33. Ibid., p. 8.

34. Ibid., p. 9.

35. A. B. Durand, "Letter VII," p. 274.

36. Alison, op. cit., vol. 2, pp. 116-117.

37. A. B. Durand, "Letter VII," p. 275. Cf. the following from Reynolds' "First Discourse," op. cit., p. 22:

> The Directors ought more particularly to watch
> over the genius of those Students, who, being more
> advanced, are arrived at that critical period of
> study, on the nice management of which their future
> turn of taste depends. At that age it is natural

for them to be more captivated with what is brilliant, than with what is solid, and to prefer splendid negligence to painful and humiliating exactness.

A facility in composing,--a lively, and what is called a masterly, handling of the chalk or pencil, are, it must be confessed, captivating qualities to young minds, and become of course the objects of their ambition. They endeavour to imitate these dazzling excellences, which they will find no great labour in attaining. After much time spent in these frivolous pursuits, the difficulty will be to retreat; but it will be then too late; and there is scarce an instance of return to scrupulous labour, after the mind has been debauched and deceived by this fallacious mastery.

By this useless industry they are excluded from all power of advancing in real excellence. Whilst boys, they are arrived at their utmost perfection; they have taken the shadow for the substance; and make the mechanical felicity, the chief excellence of the art, which is only an ornament, and of the merit of which few but painters themselves are judges.

38. A. B. Durand, "Letter III," p. 66.

39. Seneca, Letters, E. P. Barker trans., "Letter XL," 4-5.

40. Cf. Cole's <u>Study</u> <u>of</u> <u>Trees</u>, 1820's, illustrated in E. I. Seaver, <u>op</u>. <u>cit</u>., pl. 3, no. 67.

41. In an unsigned article, "An Aged Artist," <u>The</u> <u>Studio</u>, vol. 2, nos. 31-34, August, 1883, p. 61, Charles Lanman is quoted as saying of Durand's practice of painting out-of-doors that "He generally devoted a part of two days to each picture, limiting himself to the morning or afternoon of each day, according to the effects resulting from sun and shadow."

42. A. B. Durand, "Letter I," p. 2.

43. A. B. Durand, "Letter III," p. 67.

44. Joachim von Sandrart, <u>Der</u> <u>Teutschen</u> <u>Academie</u>, trans. by and quoted in Röthlisberger, <u>op</u>. <u>cit</u>., vol. 1, p. 48.

45. <u>Loc</u>. <u>cit</u>.

46. <u>Ibid</u>., vol. 1, p. 51.

47. In 1956-1957 one hundred oil studies from nature by Valenciennes--all but two of which belong to the Musée du Louvre--were exhibited at the Musée Paul-Dupuy, Toulouse. See the illustrated exhibition catalogue.

48. R. L. Herbert, <u>op</u>. <u>cit</u>., p. 19.

49. Walter Thornbury, <u>op</u>. <u>cit</u>., pp. 120-121, records the statement of the eldest son of the Rev. Mr. Trimmer, rector of Heston, near Brentford, that Turner

> . . . had a boat at Richmond, but we never went farther than the water's edge, as my father had insured his life. . . . From his boat he painted on a large canvas direct from Nature. Till you

> have seen these sketches, you know nothing of
> Turner's powers. There are about two score of
> these large subjects, rolled up, and now national
> property. . . . no retouching, everything firmly
> in its place.

And, pp. 152-153, Thornbury quotes Sir Charles Eastlake's account of the circumstances in which Turner made some oil sketches on prepared paper about 1814 at Plymouth. Turner, thus, did paint in oil out-of-doors from nature, but he does not appear to have done so regularly.

There is no need to unduly multiply examples of painters having painted out-of-doors. We may, however, mention one other British artist who painted out-of-doors earlier than Constable or Turner; viz., Henry Howard (1769-1847). According to Mr. Trimmer, quoted in Thornbury, p. 258, Howard made "oil sketches from Nature in the environs of Rome, full of taste and talent," and, according to Richard and Samuel Redgrave, A Century of British Painters, a new edition, London: Phaidon Press, 1947, p. 271, Howard was in Rome from 1791-1794.

50. R. L. Herbert, op. cit., p. 20.

51. Huntington, op. cit., pp. 28-29.

52. John Durand, Life, p. 81.

53. According to John Durand, ibid., pp. 80-81, his father's "Leisure hours were devoted to drawing or painting from Nature on his Hoboken rambles. For this latter purpose he set his palette before leaving his house in the city,

and carried it, with a home-made easel and camp-stool, to his favorite sketching-ground." Unfortunately, John Durand gives no date for these excursions.

54. Letter from James Gibbs to Durand, July 28, 1819. A. B. Durand Papers, NYPL.

55. Letter from Elias Wade, Jr., to Durand, July 16, 1832. A. B. Durand Papers, NYPL.

56. Letter from Durand to Thomas Cole, September 5, 1837. A. B. Durand Papers, NYPL. A part of this letter is quoted in John Durand, Life, pp. 140-141.

57. Letter from Cole to Durand, June 9, 1837. A. B. Durand Papers, NYPL.

58. Letter from Durand to Cole, June 13, 1837. A. B. Durand Papers, NYPL.

59. According to Groce and Wallace, Dictionary of Artists in America, p. 523, John Goffe Rand (1801-1873), a New Hampshire-born, portrait painter, developed a "screw-top compressible paint tube" while in London in the 1830's. While it is not known that Rand had anything to do with the "bladders" available in New York paint shops in 1837, it is clear that by 1840 prepared pigments were available in easily transportable containers. Durand knew Rand and visited him in London on July 17, 1840. (See Durand's Journal of his European tour, Durand Papers—NYPL.) In 1865 a number of New York painters expressed their appreciation of Rand's invention in the following testimonial and petition:

Testimonial to John G. Rand, Esq. / Inventor of the
Collapsible tube for Artist's colors.

We have always known Mr. J. G. Rand, the artist, as
the inventor of the Collapsible Tube used for Colors.
N. Y., Feb. 8th, 1865--E. Dechaux, Artists' Colorman.
653 B'way.

> W. Schaus, Artists' Colorman,
> 749 B'way.

> M. Knoedler, 772 B'way (Late
> Goupil & Co.)

The undersigned, desirous of presenting to Mr. J. G.
Rand, the inventor of the "Collapsible Tube," now
advanced in years and in poor health, some testimonial of their esteem for his character and valuable
services to Artists, subscribe for the above purpose,
the sum set opposite their names, payable to either
of the gentlemen named below who have consented to
act as a Committee:

> D. Huntington

> J. W. Casilear

Central Committee
of New York

> J. F. Kensett, Chairman

> S. P. Avery, Treasurer

> Vincent Colyer, Sec'y.

(A. B. Durand Papers, NYPL.)

60. The minuscule artist at work in the center foreground of
Cole's _The Oxbow_ (1836, The Metropolitan Museum of Art),
wields a brush loaded with paint.

61. Cowdrey and Williams, op. cit., pp. 14 and 16. The Country
    Lad on a Fence (1831), Long Island Farmer Husking Corn
    (1833), The Studious Boy (1834) and others were also painted
    out-of-doors. (Ibid., pp. 15-16 and p. 11.) Apparently
    Alvan Fisher (1792-1863) attempted to paint from nature at
    an earlier date. A sketchbook, dated 1817, contains a wash
    drawing inscribed: "Experiment but from Nature" and another
    inscribed: "Miserable but from Nature." While these were
    still only drawings, at some time Fisher exhibited a Mount
    Monadnoc--Painted Directly from Nature, which was probably
    in oil. On Fisher's outdoor work, see Alan Burroughs,
    "A Letter from Alvan Fisher, Reprinted with Notes," Art in
    America, vol. 32, no. 3, July, 1944, pp. 121-123.

62. Letter from Durand to John Casilear, dated Camptown, New
    Jersey, August 2, 1832. A. B. Durand Papers, NYPL.

63. Seneca, Letters, E. P. Barker trans., "Letter XLI," 6.

64. Ibid., "Letter CII," 21. Compare also the following on man's
    need to escape confinement for a life of mobility and change:

> I find some writers who declare that a man has a
> natural itch for change of abode and alteration of
> domicile: for the mind of man is wandering and un-
> quiet; it never stands still, but spreads itself
> abroad and sends forth its thoughts into all regions,
> known or unknown; being nomadic, impatient of repose,
> and loving novelty beyond everything else. You need
> not be surprised at this, if you reflect upon its
> original source: it is not formed from the same

elements as the heavy and earthly body, but from
heavenly spirit: now heavenly things are by their
nature always in motion, speeding along and flying
with the greatest swiftness. . . . Be not surprised, then, if the human mind, which is formed
from the same seeds as the heavenly bodies, delights
in change and wandering, since the divine nature
itself either takes pleasure in constant and exceeding swift motion or perhaps even preserves its
existence thereby.

(Seneca, "Consolation to Helvia," VI, in _Minor_
_Dialogues_, A. Stewart trans., London, 1889.)

65. Reynolds, "Discourse Two. Delivered to the Students of the
Royal Academy on the Distribution of the Prizes, December
11, 1769," _op_. _cit_., pp. 36-37.

66. Numerous studies in pencil of individual natural forms remain from the years 1835 to 1841. Plants and trees especially interested Durand before his trip to Europe in 1840.

67. A. B. Durand, "Letter II," p. 34.

68. That Durand turned again to painting from nature at this
time may indicate the influence of Regis Gignoux, who, after
his arrival from France in 1840, devoted a year to making
oil studies and pencil drawings from nature in the Catskill
and Allegheny Mountains. (See Lanman, "Our Landscape
Painters," _Southern_ _Literary_ _Messenger_, vol. 16, no. 5,
May, 1850, p. 274.) Gignoux exhibited more than eight

"Sketches from Nature" at the National Academy in 1843, and some, if not all, of these must have been in oil.

69. Both in the A. B. Durand Papers, NYPL.

70. Durand's Journal, July 29, 1840, A. B. Durand Papers, NYPL. Quoted in John Durand, Life, p. 151, with minor changes.

71. C. R. Leslie, op. cit., p. 49.

72. Loc. cit.

73. Huntington, op. cit., p. 33.

74. "Our Private Collections. No. III," The Crayon, vol. 3, no. 3, April, 1856, p. 123.

75. John Durand, Life, p. 173.

76. William Gilpin, Remarks on Forest Scenery, and Other Woodland Views, London, 1791, vol. 1, p. 43.

77. Ibid., vol. 1, p. 44.

78. Ibid., vol. 1, pp. 43-44.

79. H. T. Tuckerman, Book of the Artists, p. 193.

80. Gilpin, Forest Scenery, vol. 1, pp. 45-46.

81. Ibid., vol. 1, p. 19.

82. Ibid., vol. 1, pp. 234-235.

83. Ibid., vol. 1, p. 235.

84. Ibid., vol. k, pp. 213-214.

85. Ibid., vol. 1, pp. 215-216.

86. Ibid., vol. 1, p. 214.

87. Ibid., vol. 1, pp. 214-215.

88. Ibid., vol. 1, p. 215.

89. To John Durand. A. B. Durand Papers, NYPL.

90. To John Durand. A. B. Durand Papers, NYPL.

91. To John Durand. A. B. Durand Papers, NYPL.

92. To John Durand. A. B. Durand Papers, NYPL.

93. To John Durand. A. B. Durand Papers, NYPL.

94. To Caroline Durand. A. B. Durand Papers, NYPL.

95. To Caroline Durand. A. B. Durand Papers, NYPL.

96. To John Durand. A. B. Durand Papers, NYPL.

97. However, Durand did not pursue his later studies complacently. From Geneseo, N. Y., in 1859 he wrote: "With all my troubles I believe I have learned more of the management of colours in the painting of tones than by all my previous practice, although I have never produced so little in the same space of time, having made only four studies in five weeks." (Letter, quoted in John Durand, _Life_, pp. 186-187.) According to John Durand, _ibid._, p. 187, the studies here referred to showed "minute drawing, unsurpassed in those made in other places."

98. Wordsworth, "Lines, Composed a Few Miles above Tintern Abbey, on Revisiting the Banks of the Wye, during a Tour, July 13, 1798," _The Poetical Works_, New York: John Wurtele Lovell, 1880, p. 189.

99. A. B. Durand, "Letter III," p. 66. Wordsworth's notion that the mind performs a creative act in the process of perception is closely related to Lucretius' account of perception in the following:

> You must have noticed how even our eyes, when they set out to look at inconspicuous objects, make an effort and prepare themselves; otherwise it is not

possible for us to perceive distinctly. And even
when you are dealing with visible objects, you will
find that, unless you direct your mind towards them,
they have about them all the time an air of detach-
ment and remoteness.

(On the Nature of the Universe, Ronald Latham trans.,
London:  Penguin Books, 1951, Book IV, p. 155.)
Wordsworth, however, was more directly influenced by the
German idealist movement of the late eighteenth century--in
particular, Kant's notion that, in the words of R. W. B.
Lewis, "the mind 'thought order into' the sensuous mass
outside it instead of detecting an order externally existing."
(R. W. B. Lewis, The American Adam:  Innocence, Tragedy, and
Tradition in the Nineteenth Century, Chicago:  The University
Press, Phoenix Books, n. d., p. 51.) Lewis argues that
Walt Whitman adapted this "principle to artistic creativity
with a vigor and enthusiasm unknown before James Joyce and
his associates in the twentieth century." (Loc. cit.)
According to Wordsworth, Lucretius, Kant, and Whitman, in
the process of perception one does not so much discover an
order in phenomena but, rather, adds an order to phenomena.

Opposed to this view is that which holds that perception
is the processes of discovering a reality that exists independently of the act of perception.  From a Platonic point
of view Jonathan Richardson wrote:  "it is a certain maxim,
no man sees what things are, that knows not what they
ought to be." (Theory of Painting, Strawberry Hill edition,

1792, p. 60.) Here the idea of what a thing is precedes the recognition of it in perception. A somewhat more Aristotelian view was adopted by John Constable when in the third of his lectures on "The History of Landscape Painting," he quoted the verses:

> It is the Soul that sees; the outward eyes
> Present the object, but the mind descries.

and added, "We see nothing truly till we understand it." (Quoted in C. R. Leslie, op. cit., p. 318.) Here the act of perception does not create reality but understands a reality existing prior to the act of perception. This idea--that the artist seeks to understand nature as it exists independently of himself--is the ground from which Ruskin poured his praise on the work of Turner.

Durand, I believe, would have maintained both the idea that nature is "half created" in perception, and that what is perceived does correspond to a reality existing independently of the self. (Compare the discussion of Durand's painting The Children of the Artist of 1832 in Chapter Two.) Durand could have reconciled these two views on the basis of the Stoic concept of the kinship between the human mind that perceives and the divine mind that creates. (See the discussion of Kindred Spirits in Chapter Seven.)

100. A. B. Durand, "Letter III," p. 66.
101. In his oil studies Durand, like the more emotional landscapists of the later nineteenth century and the more recent Abstract Expressionists and Impressionists, records the re-

sult of his encounter with a realm of reality untrammeled by the conventions of urban society. Like them he presents an image fitted to release primitive or childlike instincts that exist prior to experience. In so doing he relieves the spectator of the burden of an exclusively intellectual existence. But,unlike the later artists,Durand, in the wake of Kant, believed that the organizing faculty of the mind also exists prior to experience. Hence, there is no contradiction in the fact that it is employed to organize the experience of nature. In a period between Neo-classicism and Naturalism, Durand was able to create a classic style in which the instincts and the intellect are equally affirmed. Something of this classic synthesis, the aim of Romanticism and Realism--note the manner in which the values of country and city are reconciled in the landscape Courbet paints in the Interior of My Studio, a Real Allegory Summing Up Seven Years of My Life as an Artist (1845-1855, Musée du Louvre)-- was regained in the Cubism of Picasso and Braque and the Surrealism of Dali.

102. Illustrated in J. T. Flexner, op. cit., p. 122.

103. Other Düsseldorf paintings were available to Durand for study in New York by 1850. On Feb. 11, 1850, Ogden Haggerty wrote to Durand: "The three little Düsseldorf pictures-- which if you do not see them at Williams & Stevens--will be found at my home, are at your service if you want them." (Letter to Durand, A. B. Durand Papers, NYPL.) Also, by 1856 John Wolfe, who possessed two paintings by Durand

(App. II, nos. 416 and 417), owned landscapes by the follow-
ing central European painters: B. C. Koekkoek (2 paintings),
Andrew Schelfhout, F. G. Waldmüller, H. F. Gude, and
A. Calame. And C. M. Leupp, another of Durand's patrons,
had a copy by L.-M.-D.-R. Robbe after Koekkoek ("Our Private
Collections, No. 1, John Wolfe," The Crayon, vol. 3, no. 1,
Jan., 1856, p. 27 and "Our Private Collections, No. 4,
C. M. Leupp," ibid., no. 6, p. 186).

104. Letter to Caroline Durand, A. B. Durand Papers, NYPL.

105. Vollmering was among a group of artists who attended a picnic
at Durand's home on June 8, 1872, according to G. W. Sheldon,
op. cit., p. 130.

106. Cf. Koekkoek's View on the Moselle River, signed and dated
1840, in the New-York Historical Society.

107. No such encounter is mentioned in Durand's European Journal,
A. B. Durand Papers, NYPL. However, Koekkoek's paintings
were known in New York and known to Durand by 1850. On Feb.
13, 1850, Durand's friend, the collector Rollin Sanford,
invited Durand to see paintings by Koekkoek and by J. B.
Klombeck, a pupil of Koekkoek. (A. B. Durand Papers, NYPL.)

108. Cf. Jan Both's Italian Coast Scene, in the London National
Gallery, with its foreground trees cut off at top and left
side, which is closer in its actual disposition and proportion of things to the Durand than to the Koekkoek.

109. 1849. Gemeente Musea, Amsterdam.

110. In a letter to his father of August 22, 1844 (A. B. Durand
Papers, NYPL), John Durand wrote: "I have _____ /bought?/

for you at Wiley & Putnam's the work on 'Turner,' price
$3 1/2. a new edition much enlarged . . . Mr. Edmonds
wishing to read it, I have lent it to him--as far as he
has read he 'can't go' Turner . . ." As no other book on
Turner published in 1843 or 1844 is owned by the British
Museum, we may suppose that it was the second edition
(London: Smith, Elder, and Company, 1844) of volume one
of Ruskin's Modern Painters that failed to excite Durand's
close friend, the genre painter and banker, Francis W.
Edmonds. Durand owned copies of the following works by
Ruskin: Modern Painters, 5 vols., London, 1846-1860, volumes 2-5 in the first edition; Stones of Venice, 3 vols.,
London, 1851-1853, first edition; The Seven Lamps of Architecture, London, 1855, second edition; Harbours of England,
London, 1856. These books were included in Durand's execu-
tors' sale at Ortgies and Company, April 13-14, 1887. This
sale also included a sizeable collection of engravings after
and books illustrated by Turner, which Durand must have
studied with Ruskin's help. But nowhere is Ruskin mentioned
in Durand's Letters on Landscape Painting. John Durand,
Life, p. 194, later mentioned the influence of Ruskin's
writing upon the American public mind and noted that Ruskin
had given "an immense impetus to the popularity of the
French School" due to his admiration for the work of Edouard
Frère, but does not suggest that Ruskin's writings had
affected the work of Asher Durand. Samuel Isham, op. cit.,
p. 244, believed that the American painters and public

lacked the background essential to an understanding of Ruskin's criticism: "Material, however, was entirely lacking with which to construct the curious mixture of mysticism, toryism, high church, and pastiche of fifteenth-century Italy. The best the painter could do was to go out and copy nature leaf by leaf, with a loving fidelity, and that was what the other painters had been doing for a generation with no impulse from Ruskin." Acknowledging his indebtedness, James Flexner, op. cit., pp. 128-130, adopted Isham's thought and much of his phrase. David H. Dickason, The Daring Young Men, The Story of the American Pre-Raphaelites, Bloomington, Ind., 1953, does not mention any sort of influence of Ruskin on the work of Durand. Finally, Roger B. Stein in Art, Nature, and Morality: John Ruskin and Aesthetic Controversy in America, unpublished doctoral dissertation in the History of American Civilization, Harvard University, 1960, p. 322, states that "the ideas of the best American landscape painters of the period /ī.e., the 1850's7 Durand, Kensett, and others, grew out of the American Wordsworthian tradition, quite independently of the /Pre-Raphaelite7 Brotherhood. They read Ruskin later and he corroborated and reinforced already existent ideas rather than showing them a new path." An explanation of the lack of any decisive influence of Ruskin on Durand is beyond the scope of the present work.

111. A. B. Durand, "Letter III," p. 66.

112. A. B. Durand, "Letter V," p. 145.

113. John Ruskin, _Modern Painters_, 5 vols., New York:  John Wiley and Sons, 1878-1879, vol. 1, pp. 309-310.

114. _Ibid._, vol. 1, p. 311.

115. A. B. Durand, "Letter III," pp. 66-67.

116. It is, of course, possible that the rock forms in _The Catskills_ and those in the large "study" both derive from a lost drawing or oil study.

117. A. B. Durand, "Letter II," p. 34.

118. John Durand, _Life_, p. 188.

119. A. B. Durand, "Letter VIII," p. 354.

120. Reynolds, "Discourse Three. Delivered to the Students of the Royal Academy, on the Distribution of the Prizes, December 14, 1770," _op. cit._, p. 46.

121. _Ibid._, p. 47.

122. _Ibid._, p. 48.

123. Reynolds, "Discourse Four. Delivered to the Students of the Royal Academy on the Distribution of the Prizes, December 10, 1771," _op. cit._, p. 66.

124. Ruskin, _op. cit._, vol. 1, p. xxviii.

125. Seneca, _Letters_, E. P. Barker trans., "Letter CXXIV," 13.

126. A. B. Durand, "Letter IX," p. 16.

127. I have not seen any painting by Durand upon which geometric compositional lines are discernible. It is possible that he made very faint lines or lines in an insubstantial medium such as chalk which have been obliterated by the layer of paint. In this connection, we should recall that Durand's work as a reproductive engraver must have involved the use

of a geometric grid in the transfer of the design of a painting to the plate, but no such lines are discernible in the finished print. We may, however, admit the possibility that he projected no lines at all, that what seem, after the fact, to be clear geometric divisions of the picture plane were not consciously planned. But even were this demonstrably the case, it remains true that long lines within the composition generate a set of proportional relationships among themselves and the edges of the painting. Whether these proportions were determined by geometry or the eye, they are, in fact, in the painting and so constitute an order that is _necessarily_ different from that of nature-- at least, insofar as the lines of nature do not relate to four lines terminating the scene. The degree to which the order of the picture is independent of that of nature certainly exceeds this minimal limit in the case of compositions such as that in Figure 134 where the trees at the right foreground were added to the scene by Durand.

According to Marcel Röthlisberger, _op_. _cit_., vol. 1, p. 31 and _passim_., Claude consistently allowed a proportional division of the picture plane to control the pattern of the composition. There is no reason, however, to suppose that Durand derived from Claude a practice that must have been current in New York studios.

128. A. B. Durand, "Letter V," p. 146.

129. Reynolds, "Discourse One.  Delivered at the Opening of the
     Royal Academy, January 2, 1769," op. cit., p. 24.

130. Loc. cit.

131. West, "Discourse to the Academy in 1797," in Galt, op. cit.,
     vol. 2, p. 108.

132. Quoted in Cummings, op. cit., pp. 44-45.

133. "Review; The Exhibition of the National Academy of Design,
     1827," The United States Review and Literary Gazette,
     vol. 2, no. 4, July, 1827, p. 258.

CHAPTER FIVE.

1. The landscape at the center of the cover was engraved by
   James Smillie after a "Sketch from Nature" by Durand. There
   is nothing to indicate whether Smillie or Durand designed
   and engraved the floral border.

2. Except for the symmetry and non-fragmented character of the
   border, it recalls borders such as Simon Bening's in the
   early sixteenth century. Cf. a page from Hortulus Animae,
   reproduced in D. Bergstrom, Dutch Still Life Painting in
   the Seventeenth Century, New York, 1956, p. 31, fig. 28.

3. Noble, op. cit., pp. 238-242.

4. A. B. Durand Papers, NYPL.

5. Typescript of the letter in the A. B. Durand Papers, NYPL.

6. The idea of an analogy between the effect of color and of
   sound was frequently cited in the eighteenth century. A
   Father Castel experimented with a color-clavichord as early
   as 1725, and by 1734 had completed a model constructed to
   "make sound visible and interpret it in terms of color."
   (See Irving Babbitt, The New Laokoon, London, Boston, and
   New York, 1910, pp. 53-58. For later references to seeing
   sound and hearing color, what Babbitt called "color audi-
   tion," see ibid., pp. 172-185.)

7. Quoted in Noble, op. cit., pp. 191-192.

8.  Quoted _ibid._, p. 247.

9.  Quoted _ibid._, p. 252.

10. Thomas Cole Papers, E. P. Lesley, Jr., ed., NYHS.

11. A. B. Durand, "Letter III," p. 66.

12. A. B. Durand, "Letter IV," p. 98.

13. A. B. Durand, "Letter V," p. 146.

14. _Loc._ _cit._

15. The entire poem reads as follows:

> Cool shades and dews round my way,
> And silence of the early day;
> Mid the dark rocks that watch his bed,
> Glitters the mighty Hudson spread,
> Unrippled, save by drops that fall
> From shrubs that fringe his mountain wall;
> And o'er the clear still water swells
> The music of the Sabbath bells.
>
> All, save this little nook of land,
> Circled with trees, on which I stand;
> All, save the line of hills which lie
> Suspended in the mimic sky--
> Seems a blue void, above, below,
> Through which the white clouds come and go;
> And from the green world's farthest steep
> I gaze into the airy deep.
>
> Loveliest of lovely things are they,
> On earth, that soonest pass away.

The rose that lives its little hour

Is prized beyond the sculptured flower.

Even love, long tried and cherished long,

Becomes more tender and more strong

At thought of that insatiate grave

From which its yearnings cannot save.

River!  in this still hour thou hast

Too much of heaven on earth to last;

Nor long may thy still waters lie,

An image of the glorious sky.

Thy fate and mine are not repose,

And ere another evening close

Thou to thy tides shalt turn again,

And I to seek the crowd of men.

(W. C. Bryant, "A Scene on the Banks of the Hudson,"

/1827/ in The Poetical Works, 1883, vol. 1, pp. 193-

194.)

16.  A. B. Durand, "Letter III," p. 66.

17.  Regis Gignoux's The Indian Pass in the Adirondack Mountains
(exh. Apollo Association, 1843; American Art-Union, 1845;
NAD, 1848; and perhaps American Art-Union, 1849--probably
four different versions) was fitted, according to Charles
Lanman, a landscape painter and friend of Durand, to permit
the spectator's "fancy" to fly off into space:

Immediately in the foreground of the picture, (which

is an upright,) are a mass of rocks, and a combina-

tion of trees, which form a kind of framework to
the picture, through which the eye passes, first
along the almost perpendicular side of a mountain,
and then far away and down into a sea of atmosphere,
hemmed in with the mighty bulwarks of the land.

. . . as he /the spectator/ fixes his vision upon
the distant mountain peak, he forgets himself and
allows his fancy to join the eagle, as he swoops
away into the upper air.

(Op. cit., p. 275.)

Gignoux's Mountain Pass in America (h.62 x w.40 inches), exhibited at the American Art-Union in 1849 and probably also
representing the Indian Pass, was described in the catalogue
as follows:

On the left a bold mountain with cliffs of naked
rock. Below, on the right and in the distance, a
broad river with many windings seen in the bright
sunshine; the whole landscape, however, softened
by misty vapor.

The great abyss of space must have provided an opportunity
for the spectator's spiritual flight. These Indian Pass
paintings by Gignoux foreshadow what we will later term the
composite landscape, combining the sublime and the beautiful
in such a way that they are experienced temporally, the
beautiful superseding the sublime. See Chapter Six,
Section VI.

18. Seneca, Letters, E. P. Barker trans., "Letter LXV," 15-18.

19. Museum of Fine Arts, Boston.

20. Channing, "Remarks on the Character and Writings of John Milton," in Works, vol. 1, p. 7.

21. Edgar Allan Poe, "The Poetic Principle," in Complete Works, 10 vols., New York: Fred de Fau and Company, 1902, vol. 1, p. 174.

22. Elias L. Magoon, "Scenery and Mind," in The Home Book of the Picturesque, p. 36.

23. Frank Podmore, Mediums of the 19th Century, 2 vols., New York: University Books, 1963, vol. 1, p. 191, and vol. 2, p. 225.

24. Godwin, op. cit., vol. 2, p. 387.

25. Huntington, op. cit., p. 34.

26. William J. Stillman, The Autobiography of a Journalist, vol. 1, p. 155.

27. Ibid., p. 154.

28. Ibid., p. 166.

29. In the mid-1850's William Sidney Mount "developed a lively interest in spiritualism." (Cowdrey and Williams, op. cit., pp. 7-9.) A Letter from "Rembrandt to his friend Wm Mount" is printed ibid., pp. 8-9, and a "spiritualist manuscript" by Mount is owned by John Davis Hatch, Jr. (Ibid., p. 7, n. 44.) William Page shared Mrs. Robert Browning's faith in spiritualism and also left a number of spiritualist notes. (Joshua Taylor, William Page, The American Titian, Chicago, 1957, pp. 132-135.)

30. Podmore, op. cit., vol. 1, pp. 158-159.

31. Alexander Jackson Davis, The Principles of Nature, Her Divine Revelations and a Voice to Mankind, 3rd ed., New York: S. S. Lyon and William Fishbrough, 1847, p. 637 note.

32. Loc. cit.

33. Ibid., p. 646.

34. Ibid., p. 653.

35. Ibid., et seq.

36. Ibid., p. 646.

37. W. E. Channing, Memoir, vol. 2, pp. 39-40.

38. Much of Joseph Turner's work records novel scenery. Thomas Cole's Sicilian landscapes (e.g., Mount Etna from Taormina, ca. 1844, Wadsworth Athenaeum, Hartford, Conn.) may have been inspired by the Sicilian landscapes of Karl Rottmann. Church was influenced not only by his mentor, Cole, but, in all probability, by Baron Alexander von Humboldt's Kosmos. (Tuckerman, op. cit., p. 372; Flexner, op. cit., p. 160; and Albert Ten Eyck Gardner, "Scientific Sources of the Full-Length Landscape: 1850," Metropolitan Museum Bulletin, vol. 4, 1945, pp. 59-65.) James Fenimore Cooper believed that a longing to view foreign parts is intrinsic to human nature:

> Every intellectual being has a longing to see distant lands. We desire to ascertain, by actual observation, the peculiarities of nations, the differences which exist between the stranger and ourselves, and as it might be all that lies beyond our daily experience. This feeling seems implanted in

our nature, and few who possess the means of doing
so fail to gratify it. . . . Those, however, who
are forbidden by circumstances to extend their
personal observations beyond the limits of their
own homes, must be content to derive their information on such subjects from the pen, the pencil, and
the graver.

("American and European Scenery Compared," in The
Home Book of the Picturesque, p. 51.)

Durand, however, believed that the landscape painter might
better limit himself to familiar, home scenes.

CHAPTER SIX.

1. M. H. Abrams, *The Mirror and the Lamp*: *Romantic Theory and the Critical Tradition*, New York: W. W. Norton and Co., 1958, p. 15.

2. *Ibid.*, p. 22.

3. *Loc. cit.*

4. *Ibid.*, p. 21.

5. John Stuart Mill, "Thoughts on Poetry and its Varieties," in *Dissertations and Discussion*, *Political*, *Philosophical*, *and Historical*, 2 vols., London: John W. Parker and Son, 1859, vol. 1, pp. 71-72. Mill's essay originally appeared in the *Monthly Repository*, Jan. and Oct., 1833.

6. *Ibid.*, p. 75.

7. Charles Lanman, like other of Durand's contemporaries, regarded his landscapes as expressive:

> We think him /Durand7 destitute of what is generally termed the imaginative faculty; but he has a passion for the poetic and more beautiful sentiment of the external world. . . . with Claude he would wander amid the more charming scenes of the country, like a timid but affectionate lover, portraying only those features in the sky, and upon the earth, which fill the heart with peace. . . . He is a true poet, but

one who loves the shady woodlawns of a cultivated
country, more than the beetling crag and deep
caverns of a mountain land.
(Lanman, _op. cit._, p. 272.)

8.  A. B. Durand, "Letter II," p. 35.

9.  A. B. Durand, "Letter IV," p. 98.

10. A. B. Durand, "Letter I," p. 2.

11. A. B. Durand, "Letter VIII," p. 355.

12. A. B. Durand, "Letter I," p. 2.

13. A. B. Durand, "Letter VIII," p. 354.

14. Alison, _op. cit._, vol. 2, pp. 9-10.

15. _Ibid._, vol. 2, p. 17.

16. A. B. Durand, "Letter III," p. 66.

17. _Loc. cit._

18. A. B. Durand, "Letter II," p. 34.

19. Mill, _op. cit._, p. 92.

20. _Loc. cit._

21. Benjamin West, "Discourse to the Royal Academy, 1794," in
    Galt, _op. cit._, vol. 2, pp. 101-102.

22. Durand's manuscript _Journal_ of his European tour begins with
    his embarkation at New York, June 1, 1840, and ends with his
    crossing the Alps into Italy, October 11, 1840. The _Journal_
    is, as previously noted, among the A. B. Durand Papers in
    the New York Public Library.

23. "It /i.e., landscape painting7 will be great in porportion as
    it declares the glory of God, by a representation of his
    works, and not the works of man. I appeal with due respect

from the judgment of those who have yielded their noblest
energies to the fascinations of the picturesque, giving
preference to scenes in which man supplants his Creator,
whether in the gorgeous city of domes and palaces, or in
the mouldering ruins that testify of his 'ever fading
glory,' beautiful indeed, and not without their moral,
but do they not belong more to the service of the tourist
and historian than to that of the true landscape artist?"
("Letter III," p. 66.)

24. A. B. Durand, "Letter to the Editor, North Conway, August 20, 1855," The Crayon, vol. 2, no. 9, Aug. 29, 1855, p. 133.

25. Loc. cit.

26. A. B. Durand, "Letter II," p. 34.

27. Loc. cit.

28. A. B. Durand, "Letter VII," p. 275.

29. A. B. Durand, "Letter VIII," p. 354.

30. Ibid., p. 355.

31. Loc. cit.

32. A. B. Durand, "Letter VI," p. 211.

33. Ibid., pp. 209-210.

34. Ibid., p. 210.

35. John Ruskin, op. cit., vol. 1, pp. 204-209. Ruskin, like Durand, speaks of cirri, cumuli, and rain clouds, and employs no other categorical terms for clouds.

36. New York Mirror, vol. 1, no. 5, Aug. 30, 1823, p. 34.

37. W. C. Bryant, "A Forest Hymn," (1825) in The Poetical Works, 1883, vol. 1, p. 132.

38. Loc. cit.

39. Alison, op. cit., vol. 1, pp. 321-322.

40. Ibid., vol. 1, pp. 359-360.

41. W. C. Bryant, "Monument Mountain," (1824), in The Poetical Works, 1883, vol. 1, p. 102.

42. Ibid., vol. 1, pp. 102-103.

43. Alison, op. cit., vol. 1, p. 322.

44. Loc. cit.

45. Loc. cit.

46. Ibid., vol. 1, pp. 325-326.

47. W. C. Bryant, "Monument Mountain," (1824) in The Poetical Works, 1883, vol. 1, pp. 103-104.

48. W. C. Bryant, "After a Tempest," (1824) ibid., vol. 1, p. 108.

49. W. C. Bryant, "Green River," (1819) ibid., vol. 1, p. 32.

50. W. C. Bryant, "A Walk at Sunset," (1821), ibid., vol. 1, p. 43.

51. W. C. Bryant, "To a Cloud," (1824) ibid., vol. 1, p. 118.

52. W. C. Bryant, "The Firmament," (1825) ibid., vol. 1, p. 148.

53. Alison, op. cit., vol. 1, p. 329.

54. Ibid., vol. 1, pp. 330-334.

55. Ibid., vol. 1, pp. 336-337.

56. Ibid., vol. 1, p. 338.

57. Ibid., vol. 1, p. 342.

58. Tuckerman, Artist-Life, p. 87.

59. George W. Sheldon, op. cit., pp. 129-130.

60. Woodland Interior, ca. 1867, Washington University, St. Louis.

61. The Forest at Fontainbleau, Bas-Bréau, 1836-67, Musee du Louvre.

62. 1866, Musée du Louvre.

63. See the review of the National Academy's 1869 exhibition in *Appleton's Journal*, vol. 1, no. 10, June 5, 1869, p. 309: "Is Mr. E. D. Nelson a pupil or an imitator of Mr. Durand? The latter's specialty for tree-trunks appears to be invaded in no. 231. A 'Scene on the Bronx River.' Tree-trunks are good in their way; but they may be disproportioned to foliage." Nelson's painting was probably more a simple tree-trunk picture rather than a true forest-interior.

64. *Germantown Woods*, 1864, Stewart Collection, The New York Public Library, on loan to the New-York Historical Society.

65. *Trout Pool*, no date, Metropolitan Museum of Art.

66. *Giant Redwood Trees of California*, no date, The Berkshire Museum, Pittsfield, Mass.

67. 1858, Concord Free Public Library.

68. 1860, Stewart Collection, The New York Public Library, on loan to the New-York Historical Society.

69. 1857, Museum of Fine Arts, Boston.

70. W. C. Bryant, "Inscription for the Entrance to a Wood," (1815) in *The Poetical Works*, 1883, vol. 1, p. 24.

71. *Loc. cit.*

72. *Ibid.*, pp. 23-24.

73. Much the same range of imagery appears in Robert Weir's illustration, 1836, to Bryant's poem (Fig. 170).

74. Seneca, *Letters*, in *The Stoic Philosophy of Seneca*, Moses Hadas trans., "Letter XLI," p. 188.

75. Magoon, *op. cit.*, p. 24.

76. In Sir Roger L'Estrange, op. cit., p. 138, this passage is rendered thus: "We have a veneration for all the works of Nature, the heads of rivers, and the springs of medicinal waters; the horrors of groves and of caves strike us with an impression of religion and worship."

77. Gilpin, op. cit., vol. 1, p. 209.

78. Ibid., vol. 1, pp. 204-205.

79. Cited in Paul Frankl, The Gothic: Literary Sources and Interpretations Through Eight Centuries, Princeton, 1960, p. 458.

80. Friedrich von Schlegel, "Principles of Gothic Architecture," in Aesthetic and Miscellaneous Works, E. J. Millington trans., London: Henry G. Bohn, 1849, p. 185.

81. Daniel March, Our Father's House, or the Unwritten Word, Philadelphia, 1870, pp. 97-98.

82. W. C. Bryant, "A Forest Hymn," (1825) in The Poetical Works, 1883, vol. 1, pp. 130-131.

83. We have already seen that in 1855, the year he exhibited In the Woods, Durand quoted these verses in his comments on the sublime contained in the letter written at North Conway, August 20, 1855, and published in The Crayon, vol. 2, no. 9, Aug. 29, 1855, p. 133.

84. Durand cannot have been unaware of the forest setting of the frontier revivals, which flourished in the first three decades of the nineteenth century and continued thereafter. Frances Trollope described a forest revival in Domestic Manners of the Americans of 1832:

This was the only moment at which I perceived anything like the solemn and beautiful effect, which
I had heard ascribed to this woodland worship.  It
is certain that the combined voices of such a multitude, heard at dead of night, from the depths of
their eternal forests, the many fair, young faces
turned upward, and looking paler and lovelier as
they met the moonbeams, the dark figures of the
officials in the middle of the circle, the lurid
glare thrown by the altar-fires on the woods beyond,
did altogether produce a fine and solemn effect,
that I shall not easily forget, but ere I had enjoyed it, the scene changed, and sublimity gave
place to horror and disgust. . . .

Above a hundred persons, nearly all female,
came forward uttering howlings and groans, so terrible that I shall never cease to shudder when I
recall them.  They appeared to drag each other forward, and on the word being given, "let us pray,"
they all fell on their knees; but this posture was
soon changed for others that permitted greater
scope for the convulsive movements of their limbs;
and they were soon all lying on the ground in an
indescribable confusion of heads and legs. . . .

But how am I to describe the sounds that pro-
ceeded from this strange mass of human beings?
. . . Hysterical sobbings, convulsive groans, shrieks

and screams the most appalling, burst forth on all

sides. I felt sick with horror.

(Quoted in Gilbert Seldes, The Stammering Century,

New York and Evanston: Harper & Row, Harper Colo-

phon Books, 1965, pp. 64-65.)

Worthington Whittredge introduced a far more sedate revival

into a forest picture--the Camp Meeting of 1874 (Metropolitan

Museum of Art). The forest worship to which Durand invites

the spectator, while primitive, is to be as much controlled

by the governing mind as is the delineation of the tree-forms

of the painting itself.

85. See Frankl, op. cit., p. 480.

86. Gilpin, op. cit., vol. 1, pp. 205-206.

87. Quoted in Frankl, op. cit., p. 444.

88. A. B. Durand Durand, Journal, August 25, 1840. A. B. Durand

Papers, NYPL. The west facade and much of the nave of

Cologne Cathedral were completed in the years 1842 to 1880.

89. W. C. Bryant, "A Forest Hymn," (1825), in The Poetical Works,

1883, vol. 1, p. 131. H. T. Tuckerman described the forest

in terms of the cathedral:

As you walk in the shadow of lofty trees, the repose

and awe of hearts that breathe from a sacred temple,

gradually lulls the tide of care and exalts despond-

ency into worship . . . then lifting your gaze to

the canopy beneath which you lovingly stroll, greet

as old and endeared acquaintances the noble trees

in their autumn splendor . . . whose brilliant hues

mingle and glow in the sunshine like the stained
windows of an old gothic cathedral; and you feel
that it is true to fact as to poetry that "the groves
were God's first temples." . . . the withered leaves
rustle like the sighs of penitents, and the lofty
tree-tops send forth a voice like that of prayer.
Fresh vines encumber aged trunks, solitary leaves
quiver slowly to the earth, a twilight hue chastens
the brightness of noon, and, all around, is the
charm of a mysterious quietude and seclusion that
induces a dreamy and reverential mood . . .

("Over the Mountains, or The Western Pioneer," The
Home Book of the Picturesque, pp. 133-134.)

90. Interior of the Church of S. James, Utrecht, 1642, Alte
Pinakothek, Munich.

91. As a sort of temple, the forest would, as we have noted,
qualify as sublime according to Alison:

The Forms . . . which distinguish bodies connected
in our minds with the ideas of Awe or Solemnity,
are in general sublime. The forms of Temples, although very different as Forms, have in all ages,
been accounted as sublime.

(Alison, op. cit., vol. 1, p. 323.)

The other type of Romantic painting in which religious
worship takes place in a landscape setting is that in which
peasants gather or kneel before a way-side shrine. These
thoroughly orthodox expressions of a still institutionalized

Christianity are related to the old tradition of paintings representing holy hermits in the wilderness--e.g., Washington Allston's Elijah Fed by the Ravens (1818, Museum of Fine Arts, Boston)--in that they emphasize more the piety of the people represented than the appropriateness of nature as a place for worship. Among the "way-side shrine" paintings may be counted Samuel F. B. Morse's Chapel of the Virgin at Subiaco (1830, Worcester Art Museum), B. C. Koekkoek's The Way-Side Shrine (1837, Fig. 185), Corot, The Calvary (illus. in E. Meynell, Corot and his Friends, London, 1908, opp. p. 128), Thomas Cole's An Italian Autumn (1844, Walker Art Center, Minneapolis). Paul Gauguin briefly revived this type in his Yellow Christ (1889, Albright Art Gallery, Buffalo). During his European tour Durand encountered way-side shrines:

> As we approached Brussels, observed for the first time those peculiar testimonials of Catholic devotion in the form of shrines or small chapels by the road side dedicated to the Virgin whose image with others is seen within, lights are burning in them at night.
>
> (Journal, August 12, 1840. A. B. Durand Papers, NYPL.)

Regarding these as "testimonials of Catholic devotion," Durand, who sought to excite a different kind of devotion, never painted them.

92. It is noteworthy that Durand returned to the more institu-
    tionalized approach to God when he repeated the 1839
    Sunday Morning (Fig. 74) composition at a moment of extreme
    national crisis in 1860.

93. A. B. Durand, Journal, July 26, 1840. A. B. Durand Papers,
    NYPL.

94. Loc. cit.

95. Ibid., August 2, 1840.

96. Loc. cit.

97. The Old Oak of 1844 (Fig. 184), with its venerable tree before
    a watery plain and sunset sky, may be an earlier attempt to
    combine the sublime and beautiful.

98. W. E. Channing, Journal, July 13-18, 1822, quoted in Memoir,
    vol. 2, p. 218.

99. Alison, op. cit., vol. 2, pp. 3-4.

100. Ibid., vol. 2, p. 4.

101. Ibid., vol. 2, p. 8.

102. Loc. cit.

103. W. E. Channing, "Remarks on the Character and Writings of
     Fénelon, 1829," in Discourses, Reviews, and Miscellanies,
     pp. 203-204.

104. Ibid., p. 204.

105. A. B. Durand, "Letter VII," p. 274.

106. Loc. cit.

107. Joshua Taylor, op. cit., p. 239. The conversation referred
     to was recorded by the artist's wife in her journal. (Ibid.,
     p. 239, n. 13.)

108. George Inness, Jr., The Life, Art, and Letters of George Inness, New York, 1917, pp. 67-68.

109. 1860-1861, Detroit Institute of Art.

110. Taylor, op. cit., p. 239, implies that Page advocated an over-all fusion of light and shade: "One might suppose a more fruitful equilibrium could be established through a pattern of light and dark rather than through . . . a merger . . ." But Page seems to have sought just such a pattern, although a pattern embracing a point of harmony in the limited application of a "middle-tint."

111. A. B. Durand, "Letter VI," p. 210.

CHAPTER SEVEN.

1. Letter to John Casilear, dated Camptown, New Jersey, August 2, 1832. A. B. Durand Papers, NYPL.

2. Letter to Thomas Cole, dated March 30, 1838. A. B. Durand Papers, NYPL.

3. W. C. Bryant, "Thoughts on a Rainy Day," New-York Mirror, vol. 1, no. 5, Aug. 30, 1823, p. 34.

4. W. C. Bryant, "Preface," The American Landscape, no. 1, 1830, p. 5.

5. Thomas Cole, "Essay on American Scenery," p. 5.

6. Colonel David Humphreys, The Life and Heroic Exploits of Israel Putnam, Hartford, Conn., 1853, pp. 43-44. Durand, of course, must have consulted an earlier edition of this frequently printed book.

7. Loc. cit.

8. Loc. cit.

9. This phrase is used twice in "Letter VIII," p. 355.

10. A. B. Durand, "Letter III," p. 66.

11. A. B. Durand, "Letter VIII," p. 354.

12. A. B. Durand, "Letter II," p. 34.

13. Anne C. Lynch, "To the Memory of Channing," in Poems, New York, 1849, p. 67.

14. W. E. Channing, "Discourse on the Evidences of Revealed Religion, Delivered before the University of Cambridge, at the Dudleian Lecture, 14 March, 1821," in <u>Discourses</u>, <u>Reviews</u>, <u>and</u> <u>Miscellanies</u>, pp. 340-342.

15. W. E. Channing, <u>Memoir</u>, vol. 2, pp. 2-3.

16. W. E. Channing, "Sermon, of October, 1814," in <u>Memoir</u>, vol. 2, p. 4.

17. W. E. Channing, <u>Memoir</u>, vol. 2, p. 205. This and the following were written on June 25, 1822, during Channing's voyage to England.

18. <u>Ibid</u>., p. 207.

19. <u>Ibid</u>., p. 208.

20. <u>Ibid</u>., p. 207.

21. William James Stillman, a close friend of John and Asher Durand in the mid-1850's, believed that the emotions of the sublime and beautiful are excited by the signs of Divine Wisdom and Love respectively. These emotions, he wrote, "are alike involuntary and independent of pure, intellectual cognition or examination, alike instantaneous and instinctive in their awakening;--one being, if our theory holds, the intuitive understanding of the signs of the Divine Wisdom in Creation; the other of the Divine Love . . ." ("The Nature and Use of Beauty," <u>The</u> <u>Crayon</u>, vol. 3, no. 7, July, 1856, p. 193.) Durand, of course, did not regard the sublime and beautiful in nature simply as arbitrary symbols of the Divine attributes, but rather as symbols that are fitted to excite those emotions which the attributes of God should

excite were they apprehensible to the physical senses.
Durand, I think, would have admitted that a collection of
ragged, heavy lines might excite a sublime emotion, but
he would object that this sublime emotion is not founded
upon that apprehension of God's justice and power that is
conveyed through the image of the sublime in nature and
therefore must be of an inferior intensity. Durand was
certainly not interested in signs that would only communicate an intellectual apprehension of the Divine attributes.

22. W. E. Channing, "Remarks on the Character and Writings of
Fénelon, 1829," in Discourses, Reviews, and Miscellanies,
pp. 200-201.

23. The following have recently commented on Kindred Spirits:
Virgil Barker, op. cit., p. 432; Bertha Monica Stearns,
"Nineteenth-Century Writers in the World of Art," Art in
America, vol. 40, no. 1, Winter, 1952, p. 30; Evelyn L.
Schmitt, "Two American Romantics--Thomas Cole and William
Cullen Bryant," Art in America, vol. 41, no. 2, Spring,
1953, p. 68; D. A. Ringe, "Kindred Spirits: Bryant and
Cole," American Quarterly, vol. 6, 1954, pp. 234-236; E. P.
Richardson, Painting in America, p. 169; Alexander Eliot,
op. cit., p. 73; Oliver Larkin, op. cit., 1960, p. 204;
Flexner, op. cit., p. 68; and John W. McCoubrey, op. cit.,
p. 26.

24. Bertha M. Stearns, op. cit., p. 30. E. L. Schmitt, op. cit.,
p. 68. E. P. Richardson, Painting in America, p. 166.
Flexner, op. cit., p. 68.

25. Noble, op. cit., p. 408.

26. Type-script of a letter to Maria Cole on behalf of the National Academy of Design, February 18, 1848. Thomas Cole Papers, E. P. Lesley, Jr., ed., NYHS.

27. Letter from Jonathan Sturges to W. C. Bryant, n. d., printed in Parke Godwin, op. cit., vol. 2, p. 37.

28. W. C. Bryant, "Thomas Cole. A Funeral Oration, Delivered before the National Academy of Design, New York, May 4, 1848," in Orations and Addresses, New York, 1873, pp. 39-40.

29. Ibid., pp. 40-41.

30. John Keats, "Sonnet VII," in Poetical Works, H. Buxton Forman ed., New York: Thomas Y. Crowell and Company, 1895, pp. 43-44. The connection between Durand's painting and Keats's sonnet is noted by John W. McCoubrey, op. cit., p. 26.

31. A. B. Durand Papers, NYPL.

32. "The upward and imploring look of the Voyager shows his dependence on a Superior Power; and that faith saves him from the destruction that seems inevitable." (Cole's description of the Voyage of Life, quoted in Noble, op. cit., p. 289.)

33. The Literary World, vol. 3, no. 63, April 15, 1848, pp. 207-208.

34. W. E. Channing, "Immortality," Works, vol. 4, pp. 179-181.

35. W. E. Channing, "Likeness to God. Discourse at the Ordination of the Rev. F. A. Farley, Providence R. I.,1828," Works, vol. 3, p. 230. The Rev. Elias L. Magoon also held

that one may become kindred to God in the contemplation of nature: "In viewing magnificent scenes, the soul, expanded and sublimed, is imbued with a spirit of divinity, and appears, as it were, associated with the Divinity himself. For, as the shepherd feels himself ennobled, while communing with his sovereign, the beholder, in a far nobler degree, feels himself advanced to a higher scale in the creation, in being permitted to see and admire the grandest of nature's works." (Op. cit., p. 7.)

36. W. E. Channing, "Likeness to God," Works, vol. 3, p. 235.

37. That even in this life Cole believed that he saw more in nature then the ordinary mortal eye sees is indicated by a passage in his Journal for November 21, 1835, in which he lamented the lack of a kindred spirit:

> I cannot but consider myself unfortunate in not having found here a companion of congenial soul; one whose spirit would mingle with mine in unreserved communion. . . . How few really love, and live upon the beautiful! How few cast off worldliness, and clear away from their eyes the film which prevents them from beholding the truth and the glory of nature!
>
> (Quoted in Noble, op. cit., p. 208.)

And on Cole's notion of the accessibility of Paradise to man in this world one should note his statement: "We are still in Eden; the wall that shuts us out of the garden is our own ignorance and folly." ("Essay on American Scenery," p. 12.)

38. W. C. Bryant, "Thanatopsis," (1811) in Poetical Works, 1883, vol. 1, pp. 17-20.

39. Ibid., vol. 1, pp. 130-134.

40. In connection with the interpretation of Durand's composite landscapes as "death and resurrection" devices we may notice the meanings attached by Thorwaldsen to the three stages in the making of a statue as reported by Hawthorne in The Marble Faun (published in 1860): "The reader is probably acquainted with Thorwaldsen's three-fold analogy--the clay model, the Life; the plaster cast, the Death; and the sculptured marble, the Resurrection." (Edition cited, p. 432.) These analogies,which are certainly derived from another analogy--that between sculpture and alchemy--may have been familiar to Thomas Cole, whom the sculptor visited on March 19, 1842,in Rome (Noble, op. cit., p. 320). On this occasion Thorwaldsen inspected and praised the second version of Cole's Voyage of Life series. This series (now at "Scarlet Oaks," Bethesda Hospital, Cincinnati, Ohio; ex-coll. G. K. Shoenberger) does in fact, treat successive states of human life, just as, according to Thorwaldsen, the three parts of sculpture are representative of successive phases of life. Perhaps, at this time Thorwaldsen explained his theory to Cole. It seems possible, although I have not sufficient evidence to be certain, that Cole himself experimented with a composite, death and resurrection type of landscape after his interview with Thorwaldsen. We may compare Cole's View near Tivoli (Morning) of 1832 (Metropolitan

Museum of Art) with his <u>Arch</u> <u>of</u> <u>Nero</u> of 1846 (The Newark
Museum)--two paintings that represent the same view, a
ruined arch and ancient bridge in the foreground, a valley
in the middle-ground, and a range of mountains in the distance. Cole has replaced the misty and obscure middle-
ground of the first with a clear delineation of smiling,
rolling, tree-studded meadows in the second, and the distant mountains assume softer and more rounded forms in the
later version. In the first we may discover primarily "a
pleasing and poetic effect, a sentiment of tranquility and
solitude"--as Cole wrote of a similar picture of about the
same date. (See E. I. Seaver, <u>op</u>. <u>cit</u>., p. 24, no. 20.)
But the second might be regarded as an attempt to translate
Thorwaldsen's three-fold analogy into landscape painting.
From this point of view--and this holds true for Durand's
composite landscapes as well--the present condition of the
spectator is the clay-Life, the ruinous foreground is the
plaster-Death, and the beauty of the middle-ground and distance is the marble-Resurrection. We should also note that
Cole painted at least four views of Mount Aetna from Taormina, Sicily (Seaver, <u>op</u>. <u>cit</u>., p. 33, no. 44). In at least
three of these (William Lyman Allyn Museum, New London,
Conn.; The Wadsworth Athenaeum, Hartford, Conn.; and International Business Machines, Inc.), a foreground, strewn with
ruins, gives way to rough terrain, which is superceded by the
smooth curves of the seashore and the slopes of the volcano
softened by mist. The general arrangement of these paint-

ings is similar to Karl Rottmann's view of the same scene--
Taormina mit dem Atna, Neue Staatsgalerie, Munich. Here
again, then, we have a sublime foreground, frought with
images of decay, which is followed by a more beautiful landscape and infinite space through which the resurrected soul
may freely wing its way. It should, also, be noted that
the scene is that associated with the death and resurrection
myth of Proserpina, and that the fourth of Cole's views
(formerly in the collection of Mrs. Florence H. Cole Vincent)
is entitled Proserpina Gathering Flowers. If Cole did,
indeed, concern himself with the death and resurrection,
composite landscape, it may have been he who introduced the
idea to Durand, whose Thanatopsis does recall, in its organization of forms and space, Cole's Mount Aetna paintings.

Hawthorne's The Marble Faun affords ample evidence of
a concern with the death and resurrection idea. In one
incident Kenyon and Donatello climb an ancient Umbrian tower.
Within the tower they encounter an alabaster skull. After
commenting upon this emblem of death, they proceed to the
summit of the tower where Kenyon, at least, in contemplating
the beauty of the Umbrian hills, experiences a sort of
beatific vision:

> The sculptor felt as if his being were suddenly
> magnified a hundred-fold; so wide was the Umbrian
> valley that suddenly opened before him, set in its
> grand framework of nearer and more distant hills

. . . there was the broad, sunny smile of God . . .

(Edition cited, p. 296.)

But the extended scene, comparable to the middle-ground and distance of Durand's composite landscapes, is not merely something to be looked at, but also it is an area into which the resurrected, liberated soul may try a tentative flight:

> They stood awhile, contemplating the scene, but, as inevitably happens after a spiritual flight, it was not long before the sculptor felt his wings flagging in the rarity of the upper atmosphere. He was glad to let himself quietly downward out of the mid-sky, as it were, and alight on the solid platform of the battlemented tower.

(Edition cited, p. 298.)

Hence, if only briefly, Kenyon experiences three phases of human life: he begins at the bottom of the tower in the ordinary, mortal condition; he passes through death and, finally, experiences the vision of God and the liberty of the soul that pertain to the resurrected. But, in broader terms, in respect to Hawthorne's novel, each of the four major characters experience his or her own passage from ordinary life through death to resurrection, so that the novel as a whole, as a work of art, conducts the reader on precisely the same journey as do Durand's composite land-scapes. It is the conception of life as a succession of distinct phases that unites the art of Durand, Cole, Haw-thorne, and Thorwaldsen and that underlies Hawthorne's criticism of sculpture as mainly a static and timeless art and therefore incapable of presenting a valid view of human life.

41. Gilpin, op. cit., vol. 1, p. 105 note. Seneca also found in the cycles of birth and death in nature an argument for the rebirth of the self after death:

> If you're really possessed of such an ardent desire for a longer life, reflect that none of those things which pass from our view and are reabsorbed into nature, from which they issued and are to issue anew hereafter, are annihilated; they cease but don't perish, and death, from which we shrink in dread and rebellion, only suspends life, doesn't rob us of it. A day will come once more which shall restore us to the light. . . . Later on I shall show you in more detail that seeming destruction is only change. He who's destined to return should go forth without repining. Consider nature's recurrent cycles; you'll see that throughout the universe there's no extinction, but an alternate rise and fall. Summer's gone, but next year will bring it back: winter lies low; the months in its good time will restore it; night has swallowed up the sun; a little while and she herself will be flying before day. Yonder stars in their course will traverse their old road again: unceasingly half the sky rises,

half sinks.

(Seneca, _Letters_, E. P. Barker trans., "Letter XXXVI," 10-11.)

42. A. B. Durand, "Letter IX," p. 17. This passage all but concludes his _Letters_.

43. A. B. Durand, "Letter II," p. 34.

44. "Our Private Collections. No. II," _The Crayon_, vol. 3, no. 2, p. 58.

45. W. E. Channing, _Memoir_, vol. 2, p. 3.

46. _Ibid._, vol. 1, p. 257.

47. A. B. Durand, "Letter VI," p. 210.

48. A. B. Durand, "Letter IV," p. 98.

49. Wordsworth, "Lines Composed a Few Miles above Tintern Abbey, on Revisiting the Banks of the Wye during a Tour, July 13, 1798," in _The Poetical Works_, New York, John Wurtele Lovell, 1880, p. 189.

50. W. E. Channing, "The Present Age. An Address Delivered before the Mercantile Library Company of Philadelphia, May 11, 1841," in _Works_, vol. 6, pp. 155-156.

51. A. B. Durand, "Letter VI," pp. 209-210.

CONCLUSION.

1. Seneca, _Letters_, E. P. Barker trans., "Letter XLI," 4-5.

2. A. B. Durand, "Letter IV," p. 98.

3. In the portrait of Durand after Gaston Fay (Fig. 208) on the cover of _Appleton's Journal_, vol. 3, no. 58, May 7, 1870, he is seated looking _into_ one of his landscapes in which the sublime and beautiful are combined in such a way that the soul of the spectator is purified and liberated.

4. Harold Rosenberg, "The American Action Painters," in _The Tradition of the New_, New York: Grove Press, 1961, pp. 25 and 28.

5. Sam Hunter, _Modern American Painting and Sculpture_, New York: Dell Publishing Company, 1959, p. 151.

6. L'Estrange, _op. cit._, pp. 113-114.

7. S. G. W. Benjamin, _op. cit._, p. 69.

BIBLIOGRAPHY.

Note: the following bibliography includes all of the works
quoted in the text and a selection of the works consulted but
not quoted. A list of exhibitions in which paintings by Durand
appeared and a list of catalogues of collections which include
paintings or drawings by Durand may be found in the introduction to Appendix II. Nineteenth-century exhibition reviews
are cited only in the catalogue entries describing the items
reviewed.

I. Asher B. Durand.

Anonymous. "An Aged Artist," The Studio, vol. 2, nos. 31-34,
August, 1883, pp. 60-63.

_____. "Durand's Picture of the Capture of Major André,"
Magazine of American History, vol. 24, no. 4, October, 1890,
pp. 321-322.

_____. Obituary, New-York Daily Tribune, September 18, 1886,
p. 5, column 5.

_____. Obituary, Harper's Weekly, vol. 30, no. 1553, September
25, 1886, p. 619.

Benson, Eugene. "A. B. Durand--Our Veteran Landscape Painter,"
Appleton's Journal, vol. 3, no. 58, May 7, 1870, pp. 520-521.

Blanchard, Julian. "The Durand Engraving Companies," The Essay
Proof Journal, vol. 7, no. 2, April, 1950, pp. 81-89; vol. 7,
no. 3, July, 1950, pp. 147-152; vol. 8, no. 1, January, 1951,
pp. 11-16.

Dresser, Louisa. "The Capture of Major André," Bulletin of the
Worcester Art Museum, vol. 24, no. 3, Autumn, 1933, pp. 73-75.

Durand, Asher B. "Letter to the Editors, North Conway, August
20, 1855," The Crayon, vol. 2, no. 9, August 29, 1855, p. 133.

_____. "Letters on Landscape Painting," The Crayon, vol. 1,
no. 1, January 3, 1855, pp. 1-2; no. 3, January 17, pp. 34-35;
no. 5, January 31, pp. 66-67; no. 7, February 14, pp. 97-98;
no. 10, March 7, pp. 145-146; no. 14, April 4, pp. 209-211;
no. 18, May 2, pp. 273-275; no. 23, June 6, pp. 254-255; vol. 2,
no. 2, July 11, 1855, pp. 16-17.

Durand, John. The Life and Times of A. B. Durand. New York, 1894.

Grolier Club. Catalogue of the Engraved Work of Asher B. Durand.
New York, 1895.

Hart, C. H. "Asher Brown Durand," in The Grolier Club, Catalogue
of the Engraved Work of Asher B. Durand, New York, 1895,
pp. 3-11.

Huntington, Daniel. Asher B. Durand; A Memorial Address. New
York, 1887.

Lee, Francis Bazley, ed. Genealogical and Memorial History of the
State of New Jersey. 3 vols. New York, 1910.

Leeds Art Galleries. Catalogue of Oil Paintings, Executed by
A. B. Durand, Esq. Our Well-known and Distinguished Artist,
Consisting of Finished Pictures and Studies from Nature,

Representing Various American Scenes, to be Sold at Auction
by Henry H. Leeds and Minor. New York, December 5, 1867.

Lewis, E. Anna. "Art and Artists of America, Asher Brown Dur-
and," Graham's Magazine, vol. 45, no. 4, October, 1854,
pp. 318-322.

Libbie, C. F., and Company. Catalogue of the Charles E. Clark
Collection of American Portraiture, Including . . . an Almost
Complete Collection of the Engraved Work of . . . A. B. Durand
. . . to be Sold by Auction . . . January 15, 16, 17, 1901.
Boston, 1900.

Lossing, Benson J. "The National Academy of Design, and its
Surviving Founders," Harper's Monthly Magazine, vol. 66,
no. 396, May, 1883, pp. 852-863.

Newlin, Alice. "Asher B. Durand, American Engraver," The Metropolitan Museum of Art Bulletin, vol. 1, no. 5, January, 1943,
pp. 165-170.

Novak, Barbara. "Asher Durand and European Art," The Art Journal,
vol. 21, no. 4, Summer, 1962, pp. 250-254.

Ortgies' Art Gallery. Executor's Sale . . . Studies in Oil by
Asher B. Durand, N. A., . . . Engravings by Durand, Raphael
Morgan, Turner, W. Sharp, Bartolozzi, Wille, Strange, and
Others; also, a Choice Collection of Fine Illustrated Art
Books. New York, April 13-14, 1887.

Sherman, Frederic F. "Asher B. Durand as a Portrait Painter,"
Art in America, vol. 18, no. 6, October, 1930, pp. 309-316.

Sweet, Frederick A. "Asher B. Durand, Pioneer American Landscape
Painter," The Art Quarterly, vol. 8, no. 2, Spring, 1945,
pp. 141-160.

Tolman, Ruel P. "Asher Brown Durand," Art in America, vol. 11,
no. 4, June, 1923, pp. 197-200.

Unpublished correspondence, manuscripts, and documents.

Asher B. Durand Correspondence. Owned by Miss Bartlett Cowdrey.
A few letters.

Asher B. Durand Correspondence. Owned by The New-York Historical
Society. A small group of letters.

Asher B. Durand Papers. Owned by The New York Public Library.
Microfilmed by the Archives of American Art. This very large
collection was inventoried by Miss Bartlett Cowdrey for the
Archives of American Art and includes a large body of correspondence and Durand's European Journal.

"Asher B. Durand," in American Painters, Colonial and Early Nineteenth Century, scrapbook of reproductions at The New York
Public Library.

II. Classical Literature.

L'Estrange, Sir Roger. Seneca's Morals. By Way of Abstract.
A new edition. London, 1793.

Lucretius. On the Nature of the Universe. Ronald Latham trans.
Harmondsworth, Middlesex: Penguin Books, 1951.

Pliny the Elder. The Natural History. John Bostock and H. T.
Riley trans. 6 vols. London: Henry G. Bohn, 1857.

Plutarch. Lives. John and William Langhorne trans., 4 vols.
New York: Harper and Brothers, 1846.

_____. Miscellanies and Essays. Comprising all his Works
Collected under the Title of "Morals." Translated by several

hands, corrected and revised by W. W. Goodwin, 3 vols. Boston, 1871.

Seneca, L. Annaeus. _Letters to Lucilius._ E. Phillips Barker trans. 2 vols. Oxford, 1932.

_____. _Minor Dialogues._ Aubrey Stewart trans. London, 1889.

_____. _The Stoic Philosophy of Seneca._ Moses Hadas ed. and trans. Garden City, N.Y.: Doubleday and Company, Doubleday Anchor Books, 1958.

III. _English and European Literature, Criticism, and Culture._

Abrams, M. H. _The Mirror and the Lamp: Romantic Theory and the Critical Tradition._ New York: W. W. Norton and Company, 1958.

Addison, Joseph. _The Spectator._ 2 vols. Philadelphia: J. J. Woodward, 1832.

Alison, Archibald. _Essays on the Nature and Principles of Taste._ 2nd ed. 2 vols. Edinburgh, 1811.

Babbitt, Irving. _The New Laokoon, An Essay on the Confusion of the Arts._ London, Boston, and New York, 1910.

_____. _Rousseau and Romanticism._ New York: Meridian Books, 1957.

Babenroth, A. Charles. _English Childhood, Wordsworth's Treatment of Children in the Light of English Poetry from Prior to Crabbe._ New York, 1922.

Barzun, Jacques. _Classic, Romantic, and Modern._ Garden City, N. Y.: Doubleday and Company, Doubleday Anchor Books, 1961.

Bate, Walter Jackson. _From Classic to Romantic: Premises of Taste in Eighteenth-Century England._ New York: Harper and Brothers, Harper Torchbooks, The Academy Library, 1961.

_____. Prefaces to Criticism. Garden City, N.Y.: Doubleday
   and Company, Doubleday Anchor Books, 1959.

Beach, Joseph W. The Concept of Nature in 19th Century English
   Poetry. New York, 1936.

Burke, Edmund. A Philosophical Enquiry into the Origin of Our
   Ideas of the Sublime and Beautiful. A new edition. London:
   printed for F. C. and J. Rivington and others, 1812.

Cassirer, Ernst. The Philosophy of the Enlightenment. Fritz
   C. A. Koelln and James P. Pettegrove trans. Boston: Beacon
   Press, 1955.

Cohn, Norman. The Pursuit of the Millenium: Revolutionary Messian-
   ism in Medieval and Reformation Europe and its Bearing on
   Modern Totalitarian Movements. New York: Harper and Brothers,
   Harper Torchbooks, The Academy Library, 1961.

Frankl, Paul. The Gothic, Literary Sources and Interpretations
   Through Eight Centuries. Princeton, 1960.

Gilpin, William. Observations, Relative Chiefly to Picturesque
   Beauty, Made in the Year 1772, on Several Parts of England;
   Particularly the Mountains, and Lakes of Cumberland and
   Westmoreland. 2nd. ed. 2 vols. London, 1788.

_____. Three Essays: on Picturesque Beauty; on Picturesque
   Travel; and on Sketching Landscape: to Which is Added a Poem
   on Landscape Painting. London, 1792.

Hipple, Walter John, Jr. The Beautiful, The Sublime, and The
   Picturesque in 18th Century British Aesthetic Theory.
   Carbondale, Ill., 1957.

Keats, John. The Poetical Works. H. Buxton Forman ed. New
York: Thomas Y. Crowell and Company, 1895.

Larrabee, Stephen A. English Bards and Grecian Marbles, The
Relationship between Sculpture and Poetry Especially in the
Romantic Period. New York, 1943.

Lovejoy, Arthur O. Essays in the History of Ideas. New York:
G. P. Putnam's Sons, Capricorn Books, 1960.

_____. The Great Chain of Being: A Study in the History of
an Idea. New York: Harper and Brothers, Harper Torchbooks,
The Academy Library, 1960.

Manwaring, Elizabeth W. Italian Landscape in Eighteenth Century
England. New York, 1925.

Mill, John Stuart. "Thoughts on Poetry and its Varieties," in
Dissertations and Discussions, Political, Philosophical, and
Historical. 2 vols. London: John W. Parker and Son, 1859,
vol. 1, pp. 63-94.

Milton, John. "On that Sort Of Dramatic Poem which is Called
Tragedy," preface to Samson Agonistes in Poetical Works.
New York: American Book Exchange, 1880, pp. 348-350.

Monk, Samuel H. The Sublime: A Study of Critical Theories in
XVIII-Century England. Ann Arbor, Mich.: The University of
Michigan Press, Ann Arbor Paperbacks, 1960.

Nicholson, Marjorie. Mountain Gloom and Mountain Glory. Ithaca,
N. Y., 1959.

Schlegel, Friedrich von. "Principles of Gothic Architecture,"
in Aesthetic and Miscellaneous Works. E. J. Millington trans.
London: Henry G. Bohn, 1849, pp. 149-199.

Templeman, William D. The Life and Work of William Gilpin
(1724-1804) Master of the Picturesque and Vicar of Boldre.
Urbana, Ill., 1939.

Thomson, James. The Poetical Works. The Rev. D. C. Tovey ed.
2 vols. London: George Bell and Sons, 1897.

Willey, Basil. The Eighteenth Century Background: Studies on
the Idea of Nature in the Thought of the Period. Boston:
Beacon Press, 1961.

Wordsworth, William. The Poetical Works. Boston: Phillips,
Sampson, and Company, 1859.

_____. The Poetical Works. New York: John Wurtele Lovell,
1880.

IV. English and European Art and Art Theory.

Badt, Kurt. John Constable's Clouds. Stanley Godman trans.
London, 1950.

Bergstrom, D. Dutch Still Life Painting in the Seventeenth
Century. New York, 1956.

Bryan, Michael. Dictionary of Painters and Engravers. New
edition, revised and enlarged under the supervision of George
C. Williamson. 5 vols. New York: The Macmillan Company, and
London: George Bell and Sons, 1903.

Fletcher, A. E. Thomas Gainsborough, R. A. London and New York,
1904.

Gombrich, E. H. Art and Illusion, A Study in the Psychology of
Pictorial Representation. New York, 1960.

Hawley, Henry. Neo-Classicism, Style and Motif. The Cleveland
Museum of Art, 1964.

Hind, Charles Lewis. Landscape Painting from Giotto to the Present Day. 2 vols. London and New York, 1923.

Janson, H. W. and Dora Jane Janson. History of Art, A Survey of the Major Visual Arts from the Dawn of History to the Present Day. New York and Englewood Cliffs, N. J., n. d.

Leslie, Charles R. Memoirs of the Life of John Constable, Composed Chiefly of his Letters. Jonathan Mayne ed. London: The Phaidon Press, 1951.

Michel, Francois Emile. Great Masters of Landscape Painting. Philadelphia and London, 1910.

Muther, Richard. The History of Modern Painting. Rev. ed. 4 vols. London: J. M. Dent and Company, and New York: E. P. Dutton and Company, 1907.

Newhall, Beaumont. The History of Photography from 1839 to the Present Day. New York, 1949.

Novotny, Fritz. Painting and Sculpture in Europe, 1780 to 1880. Baltimore, 1960.

Redgrave, Richard and Samuel. A Century of British Painters. Ruthven Todd ed. London: The Phaidon Press, 1947.

Reynolds, Joshua. Discourses on Art. New York: Collier Books, 1961.

Richardson, Jonathan. Works. A new edition. Printed at Strawberry Hill, 1792.

Röthlisberger, Marcel. Claude Lorrain, the Paintings. 2 vols. New Haven, 1961.

Ruskin, John. Modern Painters. 5 vols. New York: John Wiley and Sons, 1878-1879.

Thieme, Ulrich and Felix Becker. Allgemeines Lexikon der
Bildenden Künstler von der Antike bis zur Gegenwart. 37 vols.
Leipzig, 1907-1950.

Thomas, T. H. French Portrait Engraving of the XVIIth and
XVIIIth Centuries. London, 1910.

Thornbury, Walter. The Life of J. M. W. Turner, R. A. A new
edition. London: Chatto and Windus, 1877.

Townsend, Francis G. Ruskin and the Landscape Feeling; A Critical
Analysis of his Thought during the Crucial Years of his Life,
1843-56. Urbana, Ill., 1951.

Waterhouse, Ellis K. Reynolds. London, 1941.


V. American and New York History: Social, Economic, and Political.

Anonymous, ed. Mind and Spirit. Vol. 9 of the History of the
State of New York. New York, 1937.

Booth, Mary L. History of the City of New York, from its Earliest
Settlement to the Present Time. New York, 1866.

Colden, Cadwallader D. Memoir, Prepared at the Request of a
Committee of the Common Council of the City of New York, and
Presented to the Mayor of the City, at the Celebration of the
Completion of the New York Canals. New York, 1825.

Francis, John W. Old New York; or, Reminiscences of the Past
Sixty Years. New York, 1858.

Headley, J. T. The Great Riots of New York, 1712 to 1873. New
York, 1873.

Hone, Philip. Diary. Bayard Tuckerman ed. 2 vols. New York, 1889.
_____. Diary. Allan Nevins ed. 2 vols. New York, 1927.

Humphreys, Colonel David. The Life and Heroic Exploits of
    Isreal Putnam. A new edition. Hartford, Conn., 1853.

Lamb, Martha J. History of The City of New York: Its Origin,
    Rise, and Progress. 2 vols. New York and Chicago, 1877-1880.

Lanier, H. W. A Century of Banking in New York. New York, 1922.

Lossing, Benson J. History of New York. New York, 1884.

McGrane, Reginald Charles. The Panic of 1837, Some Financial
    Problems of the Jacksonian Era. Chicago and London: The
    University of Chicago Press, Phoenix Books, 1965.

Schlesinger, Arthur M. The Age of Jackson. Boston, 1945.

Trollope, Frances. Domestic Manners of the Americans. London and
    New York, 1832. See also Donald Smalley ed. New York: Alfred
    A. Knopf, 1939.

Wilson, J. G., ed. Memorial History of the City of New York.
    4 vols. New York, 1892-1893.

VI. American Cultural History.

Badeau, Adam. The Vagabond. New York, 1859.

Branch, Edward D. The Sentimental Years: 1836-1860. New York,
    1934.

Brooks, Van Wyck. The Dream of Arcadia. New York, 1958.

_____. The Flowering of New England, 1815-65. New York, 1936.

_____. The World of Washington Irving. Cleveland, Ohio, 1944.

Huth, Hans. Nature and the American, Three Centuries of Changing
    Attitudes. Berkeley and Los Angeles, 1957.

Lewis, R. W. B. The American Adam, Innocence, Tragedy, and
    Tradition in the Nineteenth Century. Chicago: The University
    Press, Phoenix Books, ca. 1959.

Matthiessen, F. O. *American Renaissance, Art and Expression in the Age of Emerson and Whitman.* London, Toronto, and New York, 1941.

Meyers, Marvin. *The Jacksonian Persuasion, Politics and Belief.* New York: Vintage Books, 1960.

Mumford, Lewis. *The Golden Day: A Study in American Literature and Culture.* Boston: Beacon Press, 1957.

Nevins, Allan. *The Evening Post, A Century of Journalism.* New York, ca. 1922.

Newton, A. *Wordsworth in Early American Criticism.* Chicago, 1928.

Parrington, Vernon Louis. *The Romantic Revolution in America 1800-1860.* Vol. 2 of *Main Currents in American Thought.* New York: Harcourt Brace and Company, A Harvest Book, n.d.

Seldes, Gilbert. *The Stammering Century.* New York and Evanston: Harper and Row, Harper Colophon Books, 1965.

Smith, Henry Nash. *Virgin Land, The American West as Symbol and Myth.* New York: Random House, Vintage Books, ca. 1950.

Taft, Kendall B. *Minor Knickerbockers.* New York, 1947.

VII. *Unitarianism and Other Religious Movements in America.*

Allen, Joseph Henry. *Our Liberal Movement in Theology.* Boston, 1882.

Anonymous. "Review of Orville Dewey's *Moral View of Trade, Society, and Politics,*" *The New York Review,* vol. 3, no. 6, October, 1838, pp. 443-456.

Bellows, Henry W. "The Unitarian Traditions of New York," in
Services in Commemoration of the Fifty Fourth Anniversary of
the Founding of the Church of the Messiah, and of the Redemption of the Church from Debt. New York, 1879.

Chadwick, John White. Old and New Unitarian Belief. Boston, 1894.

_____. Unitarianism: its Origin and History, a Course of
Sixteen Lectures. Boston, 1895.

_____. William Ellery Channing. Boston, 1903.

Channing, William Ellery. Discourses, Reviews, and Miscellanies.
Boston, 1830.

_____. Memoir. 3 vols. London: John Chapman, 1848.

_____. Works. Seventh complete edition. 6 vols. Boston:
James Munroe and Company, 1847.

Cooke, George Willis. Unitarianism in America: a History of its
Origin and Development. Boston, 1902.

Davis, Andrew Jackson. The Principles of Nature, Her Divine
Revelations and a Voice to Mankind. 3rd. ed. New York:
S. S. Lyon and William Fishbrough, 1847.

Dewey, Mary E. Life and Letters of Catherine M. Sedgwick. New
York, 1871.

Dewey, Orville. Discourses on Human Nature, Human Life, and the
Nature of Religion. New York, 1868.

_____. Moral Views of Commerce, Society, and Politics, in
Twelve Discourses. New York, 1838.

_____. The Old World and the New; or a Journal of Reflections
and Observations Made on a Tour in Europe. 2 vols. New York,
1836.

Parke, David B. The Epic of Unitarianism, Original Writings from the History of Liberal Religion. Boston: Beacon Press, 1960.

Peck, Thomas Bellows. Henry Whitney Bellows. Keene, N. H., n.d.

Podmore, Frank. Mediums of the 19th Century. 2 vols. New York: University Books, 1963.

Wilbur, Earl M. Our Unitarian Heritage. Boston, 1925.

VIII. American Art: General Works.

Anonymous. "A Review of the Gallery of the American Academy of Fine Arts, as Now Opened for the Exhibition of Dunlap's Painting of Death on the Pale Horse," The Atheneum Magazine, vol. 2, December, 1825, pp. 77-78.

_____. "Fine Arts," The New-York Review, vol. 2, April, 1826, pp. 368-370.

_____. "Our Private Collections, No. 1, John Wolfe," The Crayon, vol. 3, no. 1, January, 1856, pp. 27-28; "No. 2, Jonathan Sturges," no. 2, pp. 57-58; "No. 3, A. M. Cozzens," no. 4, p. 123; "No. 4, C.M. Leupp," no. 6, p. 186; "No. 5, M. O. Roberts," no. 8, p. 249; "No. 6, E. L. Magoon," no. 12, p. 374.

_____. "Notices of Recent Pictures. Bierstadt's Rocky Mountains," The New Path, vol. 1, no. 12, April, 1864, pp. 160-162.

_____. "Review: The Exhibition of the National Academy of Design, 1827," The United States Review and Literary Gazette, vol. 2, no. 4, July, 1827, pp. 241-263.

Barker, Virgil. <u>American</u> <u>Painting</u>: <u>History</u> <u>and</u> <u>Interpretation</u>. New York, 1950.

Benjamin, S. G. W. <u>Art</u> <u>in</u> <u>America</u>: <u>A</u> <u>Critical</u> <u>and</u> <u>Historical</u> <u>Sketch</u>. New York, 1880. Benjamin's account of Durand first appeared in Harper's <u>New</u> <u>Monthly</u> <u>Magazine</u>, vol. 59, no. 350, July, 1879, pp. 254-255.

Bethune, George W. "Art in the United States," in <u>The</u> <u>Home</u> <u>Book</u> <u>of</u> <u>the</u> <u>Picturesque</u>. New York, 1852, pp. 167-188.

Bolton, Theodore. <u>Early</u> <u>American</u> <u>Portrait</u> <u>Draughtsmen</u> <u>in</u> <u>Crayons</u>. New York, 1923.

Born, Wolfgang. <u>American</u> <u>Landscape</u> <u>Painting</u>. New Haven, 1948.

————. "Sentiment of Nature in American Landscape Painting," <u>Gazette</u> <u>des</u> <u>Beaux-Arts</u>, series VI, vol. 36, no. 974, April, 1948, pp. 219-238.

Burroughs, Alan. <u>Limners</u> <u>and</u> <u>Likenesses</u>: <u>Three</u> <u>Centuries</u> <u>of</u> <u>American</u> <u>Painting</u>. Cambridge, Mass., 1936.

Caffin, Charles H. <u>The</u> <u>Story</u> <u>of</u> <u>American</u> <u>Painting</u>, <u>The</u> <u>Evolution</u> <u>of</u> <u>Painting</u> <u>in</u> <u>America</u>. De luxe edition. Garden City, N. Y.: Garden City Publishing Company, 1937.

Clement, Clara Erskine and Laurence Hutton. <u>Artists</u> <u>of</u> <u>the</u> <u>Nine-</u> <u>teenth</u> <u>Century</u>. 2 vols. Boston, 1879.

Cook, Clarence Chatham. <u>Art</u> <u>and</u> <u>Artists</u> <u>of</u> <u>Our</u> <u>Time</u>. 3 vols. New York, 1888.

Dickason, David H. <u>The</u> <u>Daring</u> <u>Young</u> <u>Men</u>: <u>The</u> <u>Story</u> <u>of</u> <u>the</u> <u>American</u> <u>Pre-Raphaelites</u>. Bloomington, Ind., 1953.

Eliot, Alexander. <u>Three</u> <u>Hundred</u> <u>Years</u> <u>of</u> <u>American</u> <u>Painting</u>. New York, 1957.

Flexner, James T. _American Painting: The Light of Distant Skies._ New York, 1954.

———. _That Wilder Image, The Painting of America's Native School from Thomas Cole to Winslow Homer._ Boston and Toronto, 1962.

French, Henry W. _Art and Artists in Connecticut._ Boston and New York, 1879.

Gerdts, William H., Jr. _Painting and Sculpture in New Jersey._ Princeton, New York, Toronto, and London, 1964.

Goodrich, Lloyd. "A Century of American Landscape Painting," _The Carnegie Magazine,_ vol. 13, no. 1, April, 1939, pp. 3-8.

Groce, George C. and David H. Wallace. _The New-York Historical Society's Dictionary of Artists in America, 1564-1860._ New Haven and London, 1957.

Hamilton, Sinclair. _Early American Book Illustrators and Wood Engravers, 1670-1870._ Princeton, 1958.

Hamlin, Talbot. _Greek Revival Architecture in America: Being an Account of Important Trends in American Architecture and American Life prior to the War between the States._ London, New York, and Toronto, 1944.

Hartmann, Sadakichi. _A History of American Art._ 2 vols. Boston, 1902.

Hunter, Sam. _Modern American Painting and Sculpture._ New York: Dell Publishing Company, 1959.

Isham, Samuel. _The History of American Painting._ New edition with supplemental chapters by Royal Cortissoz. New York: The Macmillan Company, 1927.

714

Killner, Sydney. "The Beginnings of Landscape Painting in
America," <u>Art in America</u>, vol. 26, no. 4, October, 1938,
pp. 158-169.

Lanman, Charles. "Our Landscape Painters," <u>Southern Literary
Messenger</u>, vol. 16, May, 1850, pp. 272-280.

Larkin, Oliver W. <u>Art and Life in America</u>. Revised and enlarged
edition. New York, 1960.

Longacre, James B. and James Herring, eds. <u>The National Portrait
Gallery of Distinguished Americans</u>. 4 vols. Philadelphia,
New York, and London, 1834-1840.

McCoubrey, John W. <u>American Tradition in Painting</u>. New York,
1963.

Mather, Frank Jewett, Jr., Charles Rufus Morey, and William James
Henderson. <u>The American Spirit in Art</u>. New Haven, Toronto,
and London, 1927.

Matthews, Mildred B. "Paintings of the Hudson River School in
the Philadelphia Centennial of 1876," <u>Art in America</u>, vol. 34,
no. 3, July, 1946, pp. 143-160.

Mendelowitz, Daniel M. <u>A History of America Art</u>. New York, 1960.

Rice, Foster Wild. "Antecedents of the America Bank Note Company
of 1858," <u>The Essay-Proof Journal</u>, vol. 18, nos. 71-72, 1961.

Richardson, Edgar P. <u>American Romantic Painting</u>. Robert Freund
ed. New York, 1944.

_____. <u>Painting in America</u>. New York, 1956.

_____. <u>The Way of Western Art</u>. Cambridge, Mass., 1939.

Ringe, Donald A. "Horatio Greenough, Archibald Alison, and the
Functionalist Theory of Art," <u>College Art Journal</u>, vol. 19,
no. 4, Summer, 1960, pp. 314-321.

Rosenberg, Harold. The Tradition of the New. New York: Grove Press, 1961.

Rowland, Benjamin, Jr. "Popular Romanticism: Art and the Gift Books," The Art Quarterly, vol. 20, no. 4, Winter, 1957, pp. 364-381.

Schmitt, Evelyn L. "Two American Romantics--Thomas Cole and William Cullen Bryant," Art in America, vol. 41, no. 2, Spring, 1953, pp. 61-68.

Sears, Clara Endicott. Highlights among the Hudson River Artists. Boston, 1947.

Sheldon, G. W. American Painters. New York, 1879.

Sherman, Frederic Fairchild. Early America Portraiture. New York, 1930.

Slatkin, Charles E. and Regina Shoolman. Treasury of American Drawings. New York, 1947.

Stauffer, David McN. American Engravers on Copper and Steel. 2 vols. New York, 1902.

Stearns, Bertha M. "Nineteenth Century Writers in the World of Art," Art in America, vol. 40, no. 1, Winter, 1952, pp. 29-33.

Stein, Roger Breed. Art, Nature, and Morality: John Ruskin and Aesthetic Controversy in America. Unpublished doctoral dissertation in the history of American civilization, Harvard University, 1960.

Sweet, Frederick A. The Hudson River School and the Early American Landscape Tradition. Chicago and New York, 1945.

Thompson, Ralph. American Literary Annuals and Gift Books, 1825-1865. New York, 1936.

Tuckerman, Henry T.  Artist-Life:  or Sketches of American
    Painters. New York and Philadelphia, 1847.

_____. Book of the Artists.  American Artist Life, Comprising
    Biographical and Critical Sketches of American Artists:
    Preceded by an Historical Account of the Rise and Progress of
    Art in America. New York and London, 1867.

IX.  Art Organizations and Museums in America.

The Century Association. The Century Association Year-Book,
    1957. New York, 1957.

Clark, Eliot. History of the National Academy of Design, 1825-
    1953. New York, 1954.

Cowdrey, Mary Bartlett. American Academy of Fine Arts and American
    Art-Union. 2 vols. New York, 1953.

_____. National Academy of Design Exhibition Record, 1826-
    1860. 2 vols. New York, 1943.

Cummings, Thomas S. Historic Annals of the National Academy of
    Design, New York Drawing Association, etc., with Occasional
    Dottings by the Way-side, from 1825 to the Present Time.
    Philadelphia, 1865.

Durand, John. Prehistoric Notes of the Century Club. New York,
    1882.

Howe, Winifred. E. A History of the Metropolitan Museum of Art.
    2 vols. New York, 1913.

Rutledge, Anna Wells. Cumulative Record of Exhibition Catalogues,
    The Pennsylvania Academy of the Fine Arts, 1807-1870; The

Society of Artists, 1800-1814; The Artists Fund Society,
1835-1845. Philadelphia, 1955.

Swan, Mabel Munson. The Athenaeum Gallery 1827-1873; The Boston
Athenaeum as an Early Patron of Art. Boston, 1940.

Vail, R. W. G. Knickerbocker Birthday: a Sesquicentennial
History of the New-York Historical Society, 1804-1954. New
York, 1954.

Unpublished Manuscripts.

Louis Lang. "Art History of the Century Association." Owned by
The Century Association, New York.

The Sketch Club. "Minutes of XXI, 1835" and "Minutes of XXI.
Sketch Club, January 12, 1844 to April 9, 1869." Owned by
The Century Association, New York.

X. American Artists and Writers: 1760-1880.

Allston, Washington.

Anonymous. "Allston the Painter," American Monthly Magazine,
new series, vol. 1, May, 1836, pp. 435-446.

Flagg, Jared B. The Life and Letters of Washington Allston.
New York, 1892.

Richardson, Edgar P. Washington Allston, A Study of the
Romantic Artist in America. Chicago, 1948.

Ware, William. Lectures on the Works and Genius of Washington
Allston. Boston, 1852.

Bancroft, George.

Bancroft, George. Literary and Historical Miscellanies. New
York, 1855.

Bryant, William Cullen.

   Bigelow, John. William Cullen Bryant. Boston and New York,
      1890.

   Bryant, William Cullen. "Lake George," New-York Mirror,
      vol. 1, no. 21, December 20, 1823, pp. 164-165.

   _____. Orations and Addresses. New York, 1873.

   _____. The Poetical Works. Parke Godwin ed. 2 vols.
      New York, 1883.

   _____. Prose Writings. Parke Godwin ed. 2 vols. New
      York, 1889.

   _____. "Thoughts on a Rainy Day," New-York Mirror, vol. 1,
      no. 5, August 30, 1823, pp. 34-35.

   Bryant et al. The American Landscape, no. 1., 1830.

   Bryant, W. C. and Sydney Howard Gay. A Popular History of the
      United States. 4 vols. New York, 1883.

   Godwin Parke. A Biography of William Cullen Bryant, with
      Extracts from his Private Correspondence. 2 vols. New
      York, 1883.

   Peckham, Harry Houston. Gotham Yankee, A Biography of William
      Cullen Bryant. New York, ca. 1950.

   Ringe, Donald A. "Kindred Spirits: Bryant and Cole,"
      American Quarterly, vol. 6, 1954, pp. 234-236.

   Wilson, James Grant. Bryant and his Friends: Some Reminis-
      cences of the Knickerbocker Writers. New York, 1886.

Unpublished Manuscripts.

   William Cullen Bryant Papers, microfilmed for The New York
      Public Library.

Champney, Benjamin.

 Champney, Benjamin. <u>Sixty</u> <u>Years</u>: <u>Memoirs</u> <u>of</u> <u>Art</u> <u>and</u> <u>Artists</u>.
  Woburn, Mass., 1900.

Cole, Thomas.

 Bryant, William C. <u>A</u> <u>Funeral</u> <u>Oration</u>, <u>Occasioned</u> <u>by</u> <u>the</u> <u>Death</u>
  <u>of</u> <u>Thomas</u> <u>Cole</u>, <u>Delivered</u> <u>before</u> <u>the</u> <u>National</u> <u>Academy</u> <u>of</u>
  <u>Design</u>, <u>New</u> <u>York</u>, <u>May</u> <u>4</u>, <u>1848</u>. New York and Philadelphia,
  1848; also in <u>Orations</u> <u>and</u> <u>Addresses</u>. New York, 1873,
  pp. 1-41.

 Cole, Thomas. "Essay on American Scenery," <u>American</u> <u>Monthly</u>
  <u>Magazine</u>, new series, vol. 1, January, 1836, pp. 1-12.

 Homer, William I. "Thomas Cole and Field's 'Chromatography,'"
  <u>Record</u> <u>of</u> <u>the</u> <u>Art</u> <u>Museum</u> <u>Princeton</u> <u>University</u>, vol. 19,
  1960, pp. 26-30.

 Noble, Louis L. <u>The</u> <u>Course</u> <u>of</u> <u>Empire</u>, <u>Voyage</u> <u>of</u> <u>Life</u>, <u>and</u>
  <u>Other</u> <u>Pictures</u> <u>of</u> <u>Thomas</u> <u>Cole</u>, <u>N.</u> <u>A</u>. New York, 1853.

 Seaver, Esther Isabel. <u>Thomas</u> <u>Cole</u>, <u>1801-1848</u>, <u>One</u> <u>Hundred</u>
  <u>Years</u> <u>Later</u>. Hartford and New York, 1948.

 <u>Unpublished</u> <u>Manuscripts</u>.

  Lesley, E. P., Jr. ed. "Thomas Cole Papers," unpublished
   type-scripts and photostats in The New-York Historical
   Society.

Cooper, James Fenimore.

 Cooper, James Fenimore. <u>The</u> <u>Spy</u>, <u>a</u> <u>Tale</u> <u>of</u> <u>the</u> <u>Neutral</u>
  <u>Ground</u>. New York: Charles Scribner's Sons, 1931.

Cranch, Christopher P.

 Scott, Leonora Cranch. <u>The</u> <u>Life</u> <u>and</u> <u>Letters</u> <u>of</u> <u>Christopher</u>
  <u>Pearse</u> <u>Cranch</u>. Boston and New York, 1917.

Cummings, Thomas S.

   Unpublished Manuscripts.

      Correspondence of Thomas Seir Cummings. Owned by the
         Century Association, New York.

Dunlap, William.

   Dunlap, William. Diary. Dorothy C. Barck ed. 3 vols. New
      York, 1931.

   _____. History of the Rise and Progress of the Arts of
      Design in the United States. 2 vols. New York, 1834.

Emerson, Ralph Waldo.

   Emerson, Ralph Waldo. The Complete Essays and Other Writings.
      New York: The Modern Library, 1950.

   Hopkins, Vivian C. Spires of Form; A Study of Emerson's
      Aesthetic Theory. Cambridge, Mass., 1951.

Ferrer, Thomas Charles.

   Ferrer, Thomas Charles. "A Few Questions Answered. An Essay
      Read before The Society /for the Advancement of Truth in
      Art7, Tuesday, March 31, 1863," The New Path, vol. 1,
      no. 2, June, 1863, pp. 14-15.

Fisher, Alvan.

   Burroughs, Alan. "A Letter from Alvan Fisher, Reprinted with
      Notes," Art in America, vol. 32, no. 3, July, 1944,
      pp. 117-126.

   Johnson, Charlotte Buel. "The European Tradition and Alvan
      Fisher," Art in America, vol. 41, no. 2, Spring, 1953,
      pp. 79-87.

Halleck, Fitz-Greene.

    Adkins, Nelson F. _Fitz-Greene Halleck, an Early Knickerbocker Wit and Poet_. New Haven, 1930.

    Wilson, James G. _Life and Letters of Fitz-Greene Halleck_. New York, 1869.

Harding, Chester.

    Harding, Chester. _A Sketch of Chester Harding, Artist, Drawn by his Own Hand_. Margaret E. White ed. New edition, annotated by W. P. G. Harding. Boston and New York, 1929.

Hawthorne, Nathaniel.

    Hawthorne, Nathaniel. _The Complete Works_. With introductory notes by George Parsons Lathrop. 13 vols. Boston and New York: Houghton Mifflin Company, 1914.

Irving, Washington.

    Irving, Washington. _Works_. Many vols. New York and London: The Co-operative Publication Society, n.d.

Jarves, James Jackson.

    Jarves, James Jackson. _The Art-Idea_. Benjamin Rowland, Jr. ed. Cambridge, Mass., 1960.

Lynch, Anne C. (Mrs. Vincenzo Botta).

    Anonymous. _Memoirs of Anne C. L. Botta, Written by her Friends, with Selections from her Correspondence and from her Writings in Prose and Poetry_. New York, 1894.

    Gardner, Albert Ten Eyck. "The Arts and Mrs. Botta," _The Metropolitan Museum of Art Bulletin_, vol. 6, no. 3, November, 1947, pp. 105-108.

    Lynch, Anne C. _Poems_. New York, 1849.

Magoon, Elias L.

    Magoon, Elias L. "Report of the Committee on the Art Gallery
       of Vassar Female College," Vassar College Art Gallery,
       1939, pp. 19-24.

    _____. Republican Christianity. Boston, 1849.

    _____. "Scenery and Mind," in The Home Book of the Pictures-
       que. New York, 1852, pp. 1-48.

Maverick, Peter.

    Stephens, Stephen DeWitt. The Mavericks, American Engravers.
       New Brunswick, N. J., 1950.

Morse, Samuel F. B.

    Morse, Edward Lind. Samuel F. B. Morse, His Letters and
       Journals. 2 vols. Boston and New York, 1914.

Mount, William Sidney.

    Cowdrey, Bartlett and Hermann Warner Williams, Jr. William
       Sidney Mount, 1807-1868, An American Painter. New York,
       1944.

Page, William.

    Taylor, Joshua C. William Page, The American Titian. Chicago,
       1957.

Poe, Edgar Allan.

    Poe, Edgar Allan. "The Poetic Principle," in Complete Works.
       10 vols. New York, Fred de Fau and Company, n.d., vol. 1,
       pp. 164-197.

Pratt, Matthew.

    Sawitzky, William. Matthew Pratt, 1734-1805. New York, 1942.

Sartain, John.

    Sartain, John. <u>The</u> <u>Reminiscences</u> <u>of</u> <u>a</u> <u>Very</u> <u>Old</u> <u>Man</u>, <u>1808-</u>
       <u>1897</u>. New York, 1900.

Stillman, William James.

    Stillman, William J. <u>The</u> <u>Autobiography</u> <u>of</u> <u>a</u> <u>Journalist</u>.
       2 vols. London, 1901.

    _____. "The Nature and Use of Beauty," <u>The</u> <u>Crayon</u>, vol. 3,
       no. 1, January, 1856, pp. 1-4; no. 2, February, pp. 33-36;
       no. 3, March, pp. 65-67; no. 4, April, pp. 97-99; no. 5,
       May, pp. 129-132; no. 7, July, pp. 193-195.

Stuart, Gilbert.

    Mason, George C. <u>The</u> <u>Life</u> <u>and</u> <u>Works</u> <u>of</u> <u>Gilbert</u> <u>Stuart</u>. New
       York, 1879.

Trumbull, John.

    Morgan, John Hill. <u>Paintings</u> <u>by</u> <u>John</u> <u>Trumbull</u> <u>at</u> <u>Yale</u> <u>University</u>
       <u>of</u> <u>Historic</u> <u>Scenes</u> <u>and</u> <u>Personages</u> <u>Prominent</u> <u>in</u> <u>the</u> <u>American</u>
       <u>Revolution</u>. New Haven, 1926.

    Sizer, Theodore, ed. <u>The</u> <u>Autobiography</u> <u>of</u> <u>Colonel</u> <u>John</u> <u>Trum-</u>
       <u>bull</u>, <u>Patriot-Artist</u>, <u>1756-1843</u>. New Haven, 1953.

    Weir, John F. <u>John</u> <u>Trumbull</u>, <u>A</u> <u>Brief</u> <u>Sketch</u> <u>of</u> <u>his</u> <u>Life</u> <u>to</u>
       <u>Which</u> <u>is</u> <u>Added</u> <u>a</u> <u>Catalogue</u> <u>of</u> <u>His</u> <u>Works</u>. New York, 1901.

Tuckerman, Henry T.

    Bellows, H. W. <u>Address</u> <u>at</u> <u>the</u> <u>Funeral</u> <u>of</u> <u>Mr.</u> <u>Henry</u> <u>T.</u> <u>Tucker-</u>
       <u>man</u>, <u>At</u> <u>All</u> <u>Souls'</u> <u>Church</u>, <u>New</u> <u>York</u>, <u>December</u> <u>21</u>, <u>1871</u>.
       New York, 1872.

    Tuckerman, Henry T. <u>The</u> <u>Criterion</u>; <u>or</u> <u>the</u> <u>Test</u> <u>of</u> <u>Talk</u> <u>about</u>
       <u>Familiar</u> <u>Things</u>. New York, 1866.

_____. The Optimist. New York, 1850.

_____. "Over the Mountains, or the Western Pioneer," in
The Home Book of the Picturesque. New York, 1852, pp. 115-
135.

Verplanck, Gulian Crommelin.

July, Robert W. The Essential New Yorker, Gulian Crommelin
Verplanck. Durham, 1951.

Verplanck, Gulian C. The Advantages and the Dangers of the
American Scholar. A Discourse Delivered on the Day Preceding the Annual Commencement of Union College, July 26,
1836. New York, 1836.

_____. Discourses and Addresses. New York, 1833.

West, Benjamin.

Galt, John. The Life of Benjamin West. Nathalia Wright ed.
2 vols. in one. Gainesville, Fla.: Scholars' Facsimiles
and Reprints, 1960.

APPENDIX.


In all notations of dimension, height precedes width.

The following abbreviations are used in the Appendices:

Century 1943      The Century Association, New York, "Exhibition of Paintings by Asher B. Durand, 1796-1886," Jan. 14-Feb. 12, 1943.

Dunlap      William Dunlap, History of the Rise and Progress of the Arts of Design in the United States, 2 vols., New York, 1834.

FARL      Frick Art Reference Library.

Grolier Club      The Grolier Club, The Engraved Work of Asher B. Durand, New York, 1895.

HRS 1945      Frederick A. Sweet, The Hudson River School and the Early American Landscape Tradition, Chicago and New York, 1945.

Huntington 1887      Daniel Huntington, Asher B. Durand; a Memorial Address, New York, 1887.

JD      John Durand, The Life and Times of A. B. Durand, New York, 1894.

Lay and Bolton    Charles Downing Lay and Theodore
          Bolton, Works of Art, Silver, and
          Furniture Belonging to The Century
          Association, New York, 1943.

Lewis 1854      E. Anna Lewis, "Art and Artists of
          America, Asher Brown Durand,"
          Graham's Magazine, vol. 45, no. 4,
          Oct., 1854, pp. 318-322.

MMA 1965       Albert Ten Eyck Gardner and Stuart
          P. Feld, American Paintings, A
          Catalogue of the Collection of the
          Metropolitan Museum of Art, 3 vols.,
          Greenwich, Conn., 1965-?, vol. 1.

NAD          National Academy of Design, Annual
          Exhibition.

NYHS 1885      Catalogue of the Gallery of Art of the
          New-York Historical Society, New York,
          1885.

NYHS 1903      Catalogue of the Gallery of Art of the
          New-York Historical Society, New York,
          1903.

NYHS 1915      Catalogue of the Gallery of Art of the
          New-York Historical Society, New York,
          1915.

NYHS 1941      Catalogue of American Portraits in the
          New-York Historical Society, New York,
          1941.

NYPL                    Asher B. Durand Papers, New York
                       Public Library.

Ortgies 1887           Ortgies' Art Gallery, New York,
                       "Executor's Sale . . . Studies in
                       Oil by Asher B. Durand, N. A.,
                       Deceased. . .," April 13-14, 1887.

Tuckerman 1847         Henry T. Tuckerman, Artist-Life: or
                       Sketches of American Painters, New
                       York, 1847.

Tuckerman 1867         Henry T. Tuckerman, Book of the
                       Artists, New York, 1867.

APPENDIX I.  ITINERARY.

| | |
|---|---|
| October, 1829 | Mendham, N. J. (Letter, Durand, Oct. 9, 1829, to a sister--NYPL). Delaware Water Gap (Letter, Elias Wade, Jr., Oct. 9, 1829, to Durand--NYPL). |
| Feb., 1830 | Charleston, S. C., and St. Augustine, Fla. (Letter, Elias Wade, Jr., Feb. 11, 1830, to Durand--NYPL). |
| July-Aug., 1832 | Campton, N. J. (Letters, Elias Wade, Jr., July 16, 1832, and Casilear, Aug. 2, 1832, to Durand--both NYPL). |
| Oct., 1832 | Boston (Letter, Durand, Oct. 9, 1832, to John Casilear--NYPL). |
| Sept., 1833 | "Montpelier," Va. (Letter, Durand, Sept. 24, 1833, to Casilear--NYPL). |
| Feb.-March, 1835 | Washington, D. C. to paint portraits of Henry Clay and Andrew Jackson (JD, pp. 107-108). |
| June, 1835 | Boston with Luman Reed and Theodore Allen (Letters, Durand, June 14, 1835, to Casilear and Reed, June 18, 1835, to Durand--both, NYPL; also JD, pp. 109-114). |
| Sept., 1835 | Pine Orchard, N. Y. (App. IV, no. 11, fol. 1). |

| | |
|---|---|
| Oct., 1835 | Brunswick and Portland, Me. (Letter, Durand, Oct. 21, 1835, to Casilear-- NYPL; and App. IV, no. 11, fol. 22). |
| May, 1836 | Catskill, N. Y. (Letter, Durand, June 5, 1836, to Cole--NYPL). |
| July, 1836 | Connecticut with Jonathan Sturges (Letter, Durand, July 7, 1836, to Cole--NYPL). |
| Sept., 1836 | Hudson, Saugerties, Catskill, Albany, Utica, Boston, Trenton Falls, and Madison, N. Y., in part with Casilear (Letter, Durand, July 7, 1836, to Cole--NYPL; and App. IV, nos. 10, fol. 12 v., 11, fols. 29, 36, 37, 39, 40, and 43 v.). |
| June 22-July 8, 1837 | Schroon Lake with Mrs. Durand, Thomas Cole and Mrs. Cole (Louis Noble, _The Course of Empire_, New York, 1853, pp. 238-242; and App. IV, nos. 14, 15, 17, and 18). |
| July 12, 1838 | Hyde Park, N. Y. (App. IV, no. 24). |
| Sept., 1838 | Long Pond, Shawangunk Mts., Kingston, Rhinebeck, and Saugerties, N. Y., with Casilear (Letters, Durand, Sept. 2 and Sept. 5, 1838, to Cole--both NYPL; and App. IV, no. 25). |

June and July, 1839    Boston, Salem, Portsmouth, Winnepesaukee
Lake, White Mts., Rutland (Vt.), Green
Mountains, with Cole. (Letter, Durand,
June 30, 1839, to his wife--NYPL; and
App. IV, no. 35).

June 1, 1840    "Left N. York in the Steamer British
Queen for London in Company with my
Friends J. W. Casilear & Messrs.
Kensett and Rossiter . . ." (Ms.
Journal, p. 1--NYPL. On Durand's
European tour see also Letters to Mrs.
Durand, John Durand, Baring Brothers and
Company, Charles R. Leslie, and Thomas
Cole, dated June 21, 1840 to July 8,
1841--NYPL; and JD, pp. 143-166.)
Durand borrowed money at interest from
Jonathan Sturges for his trip to
Europe and other expenses in 1841 and
1842. Sturges received at least six-
teen paintings by Durand in partial
repayment of the sum of $5,469. This
sum was repaid by June 1, 1850 (See
"A. B. Durand in acc. with Jon. Sturges
to June 1, 1850." There are two copies
in the A. B. Durand Papers, NYPL.) On

the eve of Durand's departure,
Sturges requested him to write
" . . . as often as you can giving me
an account of the galleries and pictures you see, and what you are doing,
and any other information you think
will interest me--If you paint any
pictures send them to me before you
return--do not sacrifice any time that
can be more usefully employed to paint
for me--I leave it to you what to
paint" (Letter from Sturges May 3,
1840, to Durand--NYPL).

| | |
|---|---|
| June 17, 1840 | Arrived at London (<u>Journal</u>, p. 13). |
| July 14 | Visit to Windsor Castle (<u>Journal</u>, pp. 34-41). |
| July 15-16 | Visit to Hampton Court (<u>Journal</u>, pp. 41-42). |
| July 20 | Visit to Strawberry Hill, Richmond (Journal, p. 45). |
| July 26 | Visit to the park at Windsor "for the sole object of sketching from the old oaks and Elms . . ." (<u>Journal</u>, p. 55 and see App. IV, no. 37). |
| July 31 | Set out from London for Paris by way of Southampton and Le Havre (<u>Journal</u>, p. 57). |

| | |
|---|---|
| Aug. 1, 1840 | Le Havre and arrived at Rouen (Journal, p. 58). |
| Aug. 3 | Left Rouen and arrived at Paris (Journal, pp. 67 and 71). |
| Aug. 9 | Visit to Versailles (Journal, p. 78). |
| Aug. 12-13 | Left Paris and arrived at Brussels (Journal, pp. 80-82). |
| Aug. 14 | Visit to Waterloo battlefield (Journal, p. 85). |
| Aug. 15 | Arrived at Antwerp (Journal, p. 87). |
| Aug. 18 | Arrived at Rotterdam (Journal, p. 97). |
| Aug. 19 | Passed through The Hague, Leyden, and Haarlem on the way to Amsterdam (Journal, p. 100). |
| Aug. 21 | Returned to The Hague (Journal, p. 108). |
| Aug. 22 | To Rotterdam (Journal, p. 111). |
| Aug. 23 | Set out on a voyage up the Rhine (Journal, p. 111). |
| Aug. 24 | Arrived at Cologne (Journal, p. 111). |
| Aug. 25 | To Bonn (Journal, p. 117). |
| Aug. 26 | To Godesberg (Journal, p. 118). |
| Aug. 27 | Stopped at Konigswinter and went on to the Island of Nonnenwerth (Journal, p. 120). |
| Aug. 28 | To Coblenz (Journal, p. 121). |
| Aug. 29 | Along the Moselle River to Cochem (Journal, p. 122). |

Aug. 30, 1840        To Carden (<u>Journal</u>, p. 126).

Aug. 31        To Cobern (<u>Journal</u>, p. 123).

Sept. 1        To Coblenz (<u>Journal</u>, p. 127).

Sept. 2        To Mayence (<u>Journal</u>, p. 128).

Sept. 3        Visited Wiesbaden (<u>Journal</u>, p. 129).

Sept. 4        Visited St. Goar and Oberwesel (<u>Journal</u>, p. 130 and see App. IV, no. 194).

Sept. 5        To Frankfort (<u>Journal</u>, p. 130).

Sept. 6        To Heidelberg (<u>Journal</u>, p. 131).

Sept. 7        To Kehl (<u>Journal</u>, p. 132).

Sept. 8        To Strasburg and set out for Basle (<u>Journal</u>, p. 132).

Sept. 9        Arrived at Basle (<u>Journal</u>, p. 133).

Sept. 10        To Zurich (<u>Journal</u>, p. 135).

Sept. 11        To Lucerne (<u>Journal</u>, p. 136 and see App. IV, no. 38, fols. 1-7).

Sept. 18        To Berne (<u>Journal</u>, p. 140).

Sept. 19        To Fribourg (<u>Journal</u>, p. 141).

Sept. 20        To Lausanne (<u>Journal</u>, p. 141).

Sept. 21        To Geneva (<u>Journal</u>, p. 142).

Sept. 22        To Chamonix (<u>Journal</u>, p. 143 and App. IV, fols. 8-11).

Sept. 24        To St. Martin (<u>Journal</u>, p. 145 and App. IV, no. 38, fol. 12).

Sept. 25        Return to Geneva (<u>Journal</u>, p. 145).

| | |
|---|---|
| Sept. 26, 1840 | Visit to the house of Voltaire at Ferney (Journal, p. 146 and App. IV, no. 38, fols. 13 and 14). |
| Sept. 27 | To Vevey (Journal, p. 146 and App. IV, no. 38, fol. 15). |
| Sept. 28. | Visit to the Castle of Chillon (Journal, p. 147 and App. IV, no. 38, fols. 16 and 17). |
| Sept. 29 | Visited Castle of Blonay, Vevey (Journal, p. 147 and App. IV, no. 38, fols. 18 and 19). |
| Sept. 30 | To Berne and Thun (Journal, p. 148 and App. IV, no. 38, fols. 20-29). |
| Oct. 3 | To Interlaken (Journal, p. 149 and App. IV, no. 38, fol. 31). |
| Oct. 4 | To Lauterbrunner (Journal, p. 150 and App. IV, no. 38, fols. 32 and 33). |
| Oct. 5 | To Grindelwald (Journal, p. 150). |
| Oct. 6 | Ascended the Faulhorn and passed the night at Rosenlaui (Journal, p. 151 and App. IV, no. 38, fols. 34 and 35). |
| Oct. 7 | To Meiringen (Journal, p. 153 and App. IV, no. 38, fols. 30, 35 and 38-40). |
| Oct. 9 | Visited Brienz (Journal, p. 153). |
| Oct. 10-11 | Ascent to the Susten Pass (Journal, pp. 155-156 and App. IV, no. 38, fol. 41). |

The Manuscript <u>Journal</u> ends with the entry for Sunday,
October 11, 1840, the concluding words of which are: "set
off after 8 o ck. passing the fan-shape glacier of Stein
and in an hour or two arrived at the summit." Durand's
travels in Italy and his steps homeward may be traced in
letters to his family (NYPL) and from the inscriptions on
the extant drawings. John W. Casilear accompanied Durand as
far as Naples. The banker-painter Francis W. Edmunds joined
Durand in Rome in February, 1841, accompanied him to Naples,
and returned with him as far as Paris.

| | |
|---|---|
| Nov. 11, 1840 | In Florence (App. IV, no. 38, fol. 42). |
| Jan. 8, 1841 | In Rome (Letter to his wife, Rome, Jan. 15, 1841--NYPL). |
| Feb. 27-28 | Tivoli and Hadrian's Villa (App. IV, no. 38, fols. 42, 43, 45, and 47-50). |
| March 9 | Albano (App. IV, no. 39, fols. 2 and 4. In a letter to his wife from Rome, March 6, 1841--NYPL--Durand states that he plans to visit Naples, Pompeii, Herculaneum, and Paestum. In a letter to John Durand, April 12, 1841--NYPL--Durand states that he has been to Naples, Paestum, Amalfi, Capri, Sorrento, Pompeii, and Herculaneum). |
| March 10 | Terracina (App. IV, no. 39, fols. 5 and 6). |

| | |
|---|---|
| March 11, 1841 | S'Agata and Capua (App. IV, no. 39, fols. 7 and 8). |
| March 13 | Capri (App. IV, no. 39, fols. 9 and 10). |
| March 16 | Paestum (App. IV, no. 39, fols. 14 and 15). |
| March 17-18 | Amalfi (App. IV, no. 39, fols. 16, 19, and 20). |
| March 18-19 | Capri (App. IV, no. 39, fols. 21, 22, 23, 25, and 26). |
| March 19 | Sorrento (App. IV, no. 39, fol. 24 and nos. 41-43). |
| March 20 | Naples (App. IV, no. 44). |
| March 22 | Ascent to crater of Mount Vesuvius (App. IV, no. 45 and letter to John Durand, Rome, April 12, 1841--NYPL). |
| March 25 | Pompeii (App. IV, no. 39, fol. 27). |
| March 27 | Capua (App. IV, no. 39, fol. 28). |
| March 29 | Velletri (App. IV, no. 46). |
| March 30 | Albano (App. IV, no. 39, fols. 32 and 40). |
| March 31 | Back in Rome (App. IV, no. 40). |
| April 13 | Left Rome to start homeward (Letter to John Durand, April 12, 1841--NYPL). |
| April 14 | Viterbo (App. IV, no. 40, fol. 8). |
| April 15 | Radicofani (App. IV, no. 40, fols. 10-14). |

| | |
|---|---|
| April 16, 1841 | Siena (App. IV, no. 40, fol. 12). |
| April 17-19 | Florence (App. IV, no. 40, fols. 16-19). |
| April 23 | Monselice (App. IV, no. 40, fol. 20). |
| April 24 | Pianoro (App. IV, no. 40, fol. 22). |
| April 26 | Monselice (App. IV, no. 40, fol. 23). |
| April 27-29 | Venice (App. IV, no. 40, fol. 25). |
| May 1 | Villeneuve (App. IV, no. 40, fol. 28). |
| May 4 | Milan (Letter to his wife from Milan, May 4, 1841--NYPL). |
| May 10 | Geneva (App. IV, no. 40, fol. 32). |
| May 15 | Arrived in Paris having come from Milan by way of the Simplon Pass, Geneva, and Lyons (Letter to his wife from Paris, May 22, 1841--NYPL). |
| June 17 | Stratford-on-Avon (App. IV, no. 48), Warwick Castle (App. IV, no. 49), and Kenilworth Castle (App. IV, no. 50). |
| July 8 | By this time Durand was back in New York (Letter to Thomas Cole, New York, July 8, 1841 --NYPL). |
| Aug.-Sept., 1842 | Hyde Park, Newburgh, and possibly Lake Mahopac, N. Y. (Letter, Durand, Aug. 30, 1842, to John Durand--NYPL). |
| Aug., 1843 | Saugerties, N. Y. (Letter, Durand and |

Caroline Durand, Aug. 17, 1843, to
John Durand--NYPL).

June 28, 1844  Willacomack Creek, N. Y. (App. IV, no.
63, fols. 1-4).

June 29  Big Beaver Kill, N. Y. (App. IV, no.
63, fols. 5-7).

July 27-29  Monroe and Barker, N. Y. (App. IV, no.
65, fols. 13-16).

July 29-30  Pelham, N. Y. (App. IV, no. 73, fols.
17-19).

Aug. and Sept.  Kingston, N. Y., with Casilear (Letters,
Lucy Durand, Aug. 20, 1844, to Durand
and Durand, Sept. 17, 1844, to Francis
W. Edmonds--both NYPL; and App. IV,
no. 63, fols. 21-22).

July 4, 1845  Rye Pond (App. IV, no. 63, fol. 31).

July and Aug.  Valley of the Mohawk River (App. IV,
no. 63, fols. 35, 39, and 40).

Late June-Early Aug.,
1846  Cornwall, N. Y. (Letters, Edmonds,
June 29, 1846, to Durand and Durand,
Aug. 2, 1846, to John Durand--both
NYPL).

Aug. and Sept.  Marbletown, N. Y. (Letters, Durand,
Aug. 13 and Sept. 18, 1846, to John
Durand--NYPL).

| | |
|---|---|
| Mid-Sept., 1846 | Big Hollow, Pine Hill, and Kingston, N. Y. (Letter, Durand, Sept. 16, 1846, to John Durand--NYPL). |
| 1847 | Dover Plains, N. Y. (App. IV, nos. 66 and 67). |
| Sept. | Marbletown, N. Y. with Casilear (Letters, John Durand, Sept. 8, 1847, to Durand and Durand, Sept. 18, 1847, to John Durand--both NYPL). |
| Late June-late July, 1848 | Albany, Saratoga, Troy, Whitehall, Lake Champlain, Port Kent, Kerseville, Essex, Elizabethtown, N. Y. (by June 22) with Casilear and Kensett (Letter, Durand, June 22, 1848, to John Durand--NYPL). |
| Late July | Burlington, Vt., with Casilear and Kensett, to meet Sturges (Letter, Durand, July 14, 1848, to John Durand--NYPL). |
| Sept. | Catskill Mountain House (to Sept. 23) and Pine Orchard, N. Y. (Letter, Durand, Sept. 10, 1848, to John Durand--NYPL; and App. IV, no. 87). |
| Sept.-Oct. | Palensville, Catskill Clove, N. Y. (Letters, Durand, Sept. 24, and Oct. 2, |

|          |                                             |
|----------|---------------------------------------------|
|          | 1848, to John Durand--NYPL; and             |
|          | App. IV, no. 85).                           |
| 1849     | Durand purchased a house at Newburgh,       |
|          | in which he did not remain long             |
|          | (JD, pp. 184-185).                          |
| Sept.    | Tannersville, N. Y., with Casilear          |
|          | and Kensett and next door to Joseph         |
|          | Vollmering, a German painter (Letter,       |
|          | Durand, Sept. 28, 1849, to Caroline         |
|          | Durand--NYPL).                              |
| Sept.-Oct., 1850 | Tannersville, N., Y., with Cristopher |
|          | P. Cranch and near a painter named          |
|          | Williams--probably Frederick D.             |
|          | Williams. (Letters, Durand, Sept. 18,       |
|          | 1850, to Caroline Durand, Oct. 4            |
|          | and 9, 1850, to John Durand--all            |
|          | NYPL; and L. C. Scott, The Life and         |
|          | Letters of Christopher Pearse Cranch,       |
|          | Boston and New York, 1917, p. 179.          |
|          | Cranch wrote to his brother Edward,         |
|          | Aug. 25, 1850, that he expected to          |
|          | join Durand at Catskill Clove about         |
|          | the first of September.)                    |
| Oct. 7   | Catskill Clove, N. Y. (App. IV, no.         |
|          | 96).                                        |

| | |
|---|---|
| July, 1851 | Saratoga Springs, N. Y. (Letters, Durand, July 19, 1851, to John Durand and John Durand, July 21, 1851, to Durand--both NYPL). |
| Aug.-Sept. | Manchester, Factory Point, and Dorset, Vt. (Letters, Durand, Aug. 23 and Sept. 14, 1851, to John Durand and John Durand, Sept. 18, 1851, to Durand-- all NYPL; and App. IV, nos. 97 and 98). |
| Aug.-Sept., 1852 | Factory Point, Pawlet, and Hay Stack Mt., Vt., with his nephew Elias Durand (Letter, Durand, Aug. 29, 1852, to John Durand--NYPL). |
| Sept. | Shandaken (?), N. Y., with E. D. Nelson (Letter, Durand, Aug. 29, 1852, to John Durand--NYPL). |
| June-Aug., 1853 | Olive City, N. Y., with W. Kemble, E. D. Nelson, Strang, and Elias Durand (Letter, Caroline Durand, June 12, 1853, to Mrs. Durand--NYPL; and Durand, July 7, 1853, to Nelson--New-York Historical Society; and App. IV, no. 102). |
| 1853 | Stratton Notch, Vt. (App. III, Sect. C, no. 25). |

| | |
|---|---|
| June-Sept., 1854 | Olive Bridge, N. Y. (Letter, Caroline Durand, June 28, and Durand, Aug. 6, 1854, to John Durand--both NYPL). |
| June, 1855 | Passed through Springfield, Windsor, and St. Johnsbury, Vt., with E. D. Nelson (Letter, Durand, June 19, 1855, to John Durand--NYPL). |
| July | Littleton, N. H. (Letter, Durand, July 20, 1855, to John Durand--NYPL). |
| July-Aug. | Franconia, White Mountain Notches, Mt. Lafayette, and North Conway, N. H. Benjamin Champney, Albert G. Hoit, Samuel Coleman, James M. or William Hart, Alvan Fisher, John F. Kensett, and Daniel Huntington also worked at North Conway during the summer of 1855 (Letters, Durand, July 23 and Aug. 25, 1855, to John Durand--NYPL; and App. IV, nos. 106, 107, and 109-111). |
| Sept. 25 | Thornhill and Mt. Washington, N. H. (App. IV, no. 114). |
| Oct. | Compton and West Compton, N. H. (App. IV, nos. 115-117). |
| July-Sept., 1856 | West Compton, N. H. Frederick D. (?) Williams, Alfred T. Ordway, and Samuel |

W. Griggs worked at West Compton in
the summer of 1856 (Letters, Caroline
Durand, July 19, and Durand, Sept. 8,
1856, to John Durand--both NYPL; and
App. IV, nos. 121-123).

Oct. 4, 1856  Bulls Ferry (App. IV, no. 124).

June 13, 1857  Tamaqua (App. IV, no. 125).

July  Catskill Mountains (App. IV, no. 126
and 127).

Aug.-Sept.  Woodstock, Vt. (App. IV, nos. 128-
130).

Sept. 10  West Compton, N. H. (App. IV, nos. 132-
133).

Aug. 22, 1858  Kaaterskill Clove, N. Y. (App. IV, no.
135).

June-July, 1859  Geneseo, N. Y. (App. IV, nos. 136-
139).

July-Sept., 1860  Fishkill Landing, N. Y. (App. IV, nos.
142-144).

June-Oct., 1861  Hillsdale, N. Y. (Letters, Caroline
Durand, June 26, and Durand, Sept. 20,
1861, to John Durand--both NYPL).

July-Aug., 1862  Hague, N. Y., on Lake George (Letter,
Durand, July 20, 1862, to John Durand--
NYPL; and App. IV, nos. 150, 151, and
156).

| | |
|---|---|
| June-Oct., 1863 | Bolton, N. Y., on Lake George (App. IV, nos. 163-170; and Letter, Durand, Oct. 1, 1863, to E. D. Nelson--New-York Historical Society). |
| June, 1864 | Meninhingog (?) (App. IV, nos. 180 and 181). |
| July 25 | Catskill Clove, N. Y. (App. IV, no. 182). |
| June and July, 1865 | Barrytown, N. Y. (App. IV, nos 183 and 184). |
| July 26 | Livingston, N. Y. (App. IV, no. 185). |
| Aug. | Santa Cruz, N. Y. (App. IV, no. 186). |
| July and Aug., 1866 | East Kill, N. Y. (App. IV, nos. 187 and 190, fol. 23). |
| Aug. 22, 1867 | Parker Mountains, N. Y. (App. IV, nos. 191 and 197, fol. 2). |
| Aug. 24 | East Kill Woods, N. Y. (App. IV, no. 197, fol. 7). |
| Oct. 2 | Rip Van Winkle Hollow, N. Y. (App. IV, no. 192). |
| Oct. 3 | Parkers, N. Y. (App. IV, no. 197, fol. 12). |
| July-Sept., 1868 | Keene, N. Y., on Lake George (App. IV, nos. 197, fols. 13 and 33, and 198). |
| Summer, 1869 | Berkshire Mts. (?) (Letter, E. D. Nelson, June 16, 1869, to Durand--NYPL). |

| | |
|---|---|
| Sept., 1869 | Lake Placid, N. Y. (App. IV, no. 200). |
| Aug. 17, 1870 | Martins, N. Y. (App. IV, no. 197, fol. 23). |
| Sept. 4 | S. Bebe's, N. Y. (App. IV, no. 197, fol. 24). |
| Sept., 1871 | Lake George, N. Y. (App. IV, nos. 201-203). |
| Oct. 1 | Harbor Islands, Lake George, N. Y (App. IV, no. 204). |
| Sept. 21, 1872 | Odell Islands, Lake George, N. Y. (App. IV, no. 205). |
| Sept. 12, 1873 | Mother Bunch, N. Y. (App. IV, no. 208). |
| Sept. 12, 1874 | Lake George, N. Y. (App. IV, nos. 210 and 211). |

APPENDIX II. CATALOGUE OF PAINTINGS OTHER THAN OIL
STUDIES FROM NATURE.

In view of the fairly large number of paintings
by Durand which have so far eluded notice, the following
catalogue is necessarily far from definitive. In it I have
attempted to list all of Durand's portraits, copies, figure
paintings, and landscape compositions--that is, works
executed in the studio, in contrast to the oil studies from
nature, which were painted out-of-doors and are described
in Appendix III. In every case where one recorded work
cannot positively be identified with another recorded
work, each is listed as a separate item. For example, all
paintings exhibited at the National Academy of Design under
the title "Portrait of a Gentleman" have been listed as
separate items although it is probable that some of these
are the same as portraits known today and listed elsewhere.
Additional documentary evidence and the discovery of more
of Durand's paintings must tend to abbreviate the present
list somewhat. Yet, I believe that with a large part of
the documentation codified, the process of identifying
and,perhaps,of locating additional paintings will be
facilitated.

The arrangement of the catalogue is roughly
chronological. However, the reader may note that a large

number of undated portraits have been inserted between the
years 1839 and 1840.  Also, a number of dated and undated
paintings, noticed too late for inclusion in the body of
the catalogue, have been recorded following the year 1878.
Each item has been listed under the year indicated by a
date on the painting or under the year in which its existence is first documented.  Fortunately, Durand dated most
of his studio paintings, and those that have been located
constitute the basis of any chronology of his work.  In
addition, the Durand Papers in the New York Public Library
frequently provide sufficient evidence for assigning an
absolute date to a particular painting, as does the brief
list of paintings (apparently based largely on the Durand
Papers) given by John Durand in his _Life and Times of A. B.
Durand_, pages 173-178.  Few other documents are of much
assistance in establishing absolute dates.  Nevertheless,
the National Academy of Design exhibition catalogues afford
good evidence for the approximate dates of those of Durand's
paintings exhibited there during his lifetime.  In most
cases these were executed during the year preceding the
late spring exhibitions.  Also, those paintings included in
the distributions of the American Art-Union were usually
the product of the preceding twelve to fifteen months.
When no concrete evidence for the date of a painting is
given, it has been assigned to a particular year merely

upon the basis of its stylistic similarity to others of
that year.

Under each year, the several types of paintings
are listed in the following order:

1. Portraits of children.

2. Portraits of ladies.

3. Portraits of gentlemen.

4. Genre, literary, and historical paintings.

5. Landscape paintings.

For each item I have, as far as possible, indicated media,
dimensions, name of its present owner, exhibition and/or
sale record, relevant literature, and the names of past
owners. While I have sought to include as much information as possible, the notations remain incomplete, particularly in respect to exhibition and sale records and the
reviews of Durand's work in the periodical literature of
the period. Further study of these is probably the most
expedient path toward a clearer view of the extent and
character of Durand's work. Paintings by Durand appeared in
the following special exhibitions:

1853      American Art-Union, N. Y., "The Washington
          Exhibition, in Aid of the New-York Gallery
          of the Fine Arts."

1859      Young Men's Association, Troy, N. Y., "Second
          Annual Art Exhibition."

1867          Paris, "Exposition Universelle."

1876          Philadelphia, "Centennial Exhibition."

Metropolitan Museum of Art and the National
Academy of Design, "Centennial Loan Exhibition of Paintings."

1893          Chicago, "Columbian Exposition."

1915          San Francisco, "Panama-Pacific-International
Exposition."

1916          The Cleveland Museum of Art, "The Inaugural
Exhibition," June 6-Sept. 20.

1917          Brooklyn Institute of Arts and Sciences,
"Exhibition of Early American Paintings,"
Feb. 3-March 12.

Brooklyn Institute of Arts and Sciences,
"A Special Historical Exhibition to Celebrate
the Opening of the Catskill Aqueduct,"
Nov. 1-21.

1918          Ehrich Galleries, N. Y., "One Hundred Early
American Paintings."

1924          Union League Club, N. Y., "Exhibition of
Pictures by Early American Portrait
Painters," Feb. 14-15 and 21-22.

1925-1926   National Gallery of Art, Washington, D. C.,
"Exhibition of Early American Paintings
and Miniatures," Dec. 5, 1925-Jan. 31, 1926.

1928      Philadelphia Museum of Art, "Portraits by
Early American Artists of the 17th, 18th,
and 19th Centuries Collected by Thomas
B. Clarke."

1930-1931      Newark Museum, "Development of American
Painting, 1700-1900," Nov. 13, 1930-
Feb. 1, 1931.

1932      John Herron Art Museum, Indianapolis, Ind.,
"Exhibition of American Paintings."

Macbeth Gallery, N. Y., "Hudson River School,"
Jan. 25-Feb. 13.

National Society of Colonial Dames of America,
Dumbarton House, Washington, D. C., April
20-May 29.

1934      National Academy of Design, N. Y., "Selection
of Paintings from the Permanent Collection
of the National Academy of Design,"
Nov. 16-30.

1935      M. H. DeYoung Memorial Museum, California
Palace of the Legion of Honor, San
Francisco, Calif., "Exhibition of American
Painting," June 7-July 7.

1936      Virginia Museum of Fine Arts, Richmond, Va.,
"Inaugural Exhibition; The Main Currents
in the Development of American Painting,"
Jan. 16-March 1.

| | |
|---|---|
| 1937 | The Century Association, N. Y., "Exhibition of Portraits owned by Clubs of New York," Jan. 9-Feb. 3. |
| | Washington County Museum of Fine Arts, Hagerstown, Md., "American Paintings before 1865," Sept. 4-26. |
| 1937-1938 | The Corcoran Gallery of Art, Washington, D. C., "150th Anniversary of the Constitution of the United States," Nov. 27, 1937-March 1, 1938. |
| 1938 | Whitney Museum of American Art, N. Y., "A Century of American Landscape Painting, 1800-1900," Jan. 19-Feb. 25. |
| | Springfield Museum of Fine Art, Springfield, Mass., "A Century of American Landscape Painting, 1800-1900," March 8-28. |
| 1939 | Carnegie Institute, Pittsburgh, Pa., "A Century of American Landscape Painting," March 22-April 30. |
| | Metropolitan Museum of Art, N. Y., "Life in America," April 24-Oct. 29. |
| | National Academy of Design, N. Y., "Special Exhibition," May 8-June 25. |
| 1939-1940 | The New-York Historical Society, N. Y., "Anniversary Exhibition," Nov. 20, 1939-Feb. 25, 1940. |

1940            The Century Association, N. Y., "Fifty
Years of American Painting: Landscape
and Genre, 1825-1875," March 3-31.

Baltimore Museum of Art, "Romanticism in
America, 1812-1865," May 10-June 10.

Carnegie Institute, Pittsburgh, Pa.,
"Survey of American Painting," Oct. 24-
Dec. 15.

1941            C. W. Lyon Gallery, N. Y., "Benefit Exhibition for Bundles for Britain," March 26-
April 25.

Victor D. Spark, N. Y., "Exhibition of Early
American Genre and Still Life Painting,"
May 5-June 5.

Albany Institute of History and Art, "Thomas
Cole Exhibition," Nov. 1-Dec. 15.

1942            National Academy of Design, N. Y., "Our
Heritage, a Selection from the Permanent
Collection of the National Academy,"
Jan. 8-Feb. 7.

1943            Museum of Modern Art, N. Y., "Romantic
Painting in America."

The Century Association, N. Y., "Exhibition
of Paintings by Asher B. Durand, 1796-
1886," Jan. 14-Feb. 12.

Robert C. Vose Galleries, Boston, "The Art

of Colonial America and of the Early
Republic, Primitives, Hudson River
School, and Their Contemporaries," April 7-
May 1.

M. Knoedler and Co., Inc., N. Y., "Exhibition
of American Landscape Paintings Dating
from 1750," May 17-June 1.

1944    Montclair Art Museum, Montclair, N. J., "Early
American Paintings," Feb. 4-29.

Lyman Allyn Museum, New London, Conn.,
"Exhibition of Paintings by John Trumbull
and his Contemporaries," March 6-April 16.

George Chapellier Gallery, N. Y., "American
and European Old Masters," Autumn.

Kennedy and Co., N. Y., "The Hudson River
School," Oct. 1-Nov. 5.

Ferargil Galleries, N. Y., "Annual Exhibition
of Early American Paintings," Oct. 3-28.

1944-1945    The Newark Museum, "Exhibition of American
Paintings and Sculpture from the Museum's
Collections," Oct. 31, 1944-Jan. 31, 1945.

The Detroit Institute of Arts, "The World of
the Romantic Artist, a Survey of American
Culture from 1800-1875," Dec. 28, 1944-
Jan. 28, 1945.

1945    Montclair Art Museum, "Art in New Jersey,
          1776-1876," Jan. 1-28.

        The Art Institute of Chicago, "The Hudson
          River School  and the Early American
          Landscape Tradition," Feb. 15-March 25.

        Whitney Museum of American Art, "The Hudson
          River School and the Early American
          Landscape Tradition," April 17-May 18.

        Robert C. Vose Galleries, Boston, "American
          Landscape Art, Hudson River School," Summer.

        Ferargil Galleries, N. Y., "Nineteenth Annual
          Exhibition of Early American Painting,"
          Oct. 3-27.

        Akron Art Institute, "40 American Painters,"
          December.

1946    Metropolitan Museum of Art, "The Taste of the
          Seventies," April.

        Tate Gallery, London, "American Painting,"
          June-July.

        Robert C. Vose Galleries, Boston, "Third
          Annual Summer Exhibition of Early American
          Landscapes, Featuring the Hudson River
          School," Summer.

        M. Knoedler and Company, N. Y., "Washington
          Irving and his Circle," Oct. 8-26.

Grand Central Art Galleries, N. Y., "60 Americans Since 1800," Nov. 19-Dec. 5.

1946-1947    Walters Art Gallery, Baltimore, "Hudson River School," Dec., 1946-Jan., 1947.

1947    Kennedy and Co., N. Y., "Picturesque America."

Washington County Museum of Fine Arts, Hagerstown, Md., "American Romantic Painting," March 30-April 27.

Colorado Springs Fine Arts Center, "Twenty-one Great Paintings," July 20-Aug. 30.

Ca. 1947    United States Department of State, "Exhibition of Paintings from the Collection of the Department of Fine Arts of the International Business Machines Corporation; 60 Americans Since 1800."

1948    Saginaw Museum, Saginaw, Mich., "Exhibition of American Painting from Colonial Times until Today," Jan. 1--Feb. 15.

1948-1949    Wadsworth Atheneum, Hartford, Conn., "Thomas Cole, 1801-1848, One Hundred Years Later," Nov. 12, 1948-Jan. 2, 1949.

The New-York Historical Society, N. Y., "Up from the Cradle," Nov. 14, 1948-Jan. 16, 1949.

1949    Whitney Museum of American Art, "Thomas Cole, 1801-1848,One Hundred Years Later," Jan. 8-Jan. 30.

| | |
|---|---|
| 1951 | The Detroit Institute of Arts and The Toledo Museum of Art, "Travelers in Arcadia, American Artists in Italy, 1830-1875." |
| | The Hill School, Pottstown, Pa., "A Century of American Painting, 1851-1951," April 5-April 25. |
| | National Academy of Design, N. Y., "The American Tradition, 1800-1900," Dec. 3-16. |
| 1953 | Wildenstein and Co., N. Y., "A Loan Exhibition of Great American Paintings: Landmarks in American Art, 1670-1950, for the Benefit of the American Federation of Arts," Feb. 26-March 28. |
| 1954 | The Hudson River Museum at Yonkers, Inc., "A Loan Exhibition of Paintings, Hudson River School," June 20-Sept. 12. |
| 1957 | The Newark Museum, "Early New Jersey Artists, 18th and 19th Centuries," March 7-May 19. |
| 1958-1959 | Metropolitan Museum of Art, "Fourteen American Masters." |
| 1960-1961 | Pasadena Art Museum, "American Paintings of the Nineteenth Century; The George F. McMurray Collection," Nov. 30, 1960-Jan. 4, 1961. |

1962        Vassar College Art Gallery, Poughkeepsie,
            N. Y., "The Hudson River School," Nov.
            19-Dec. 16.

1963        The Newark Museum, "Classical America,
            1815-1845," April 26-Sept. 2.

Paintings, drawings, and engravings by Durand are recorded
in the following catalogues of institutional collections:

Addison Gallery of American Art:

Handbook of Paintings, Sculpture, Prints, and Drawings in
the Permanent Collection, Andover, 1939.

Albany Institute and Historical and Art Society:

Catalogue of the Albany Institute and Historical and Art
Society, Albany, 1924.

Boston Museum of Fine Arts:

M. & M. Karolik Collection of American Paintings 1815
to 1865, Cambridge, Mass.,

M. & M. Karolik Collection of American Water Colors and
Drawings, 1800-1875, 2 vols., Boston, 1962.

Brooklyn Institute of Arts and Sciences:

Catalogue of Paintings, Brooklyn, 1910.

The Century Association:

Charles Downing Lay and Theodore Bolton, Works of Art,
Silver, and Furniture Belonging to The Century Association, New York, 1943.

Chamber of Commerce of the State of New York:

Catalogue of Portraits, New York, 1924.

Corcoran Gallery of Art:

Handbook of Paintings and Sculpture, Washington, D. C., 1926.
Handbook of American Paintings, Washington, D. C., 1947.

The Detroit Institute of Arts:

Catalogue of Paintings, 2nd ed., Detroit, 1944.

Masterpieces of Painting and Sculpture from The Detroit
Institute of Arts, Detroit, 1949.

John Herron Art Museum:

Complete List of European and American Paintings in the
Permanent Collection of the John Herron Art Museum,
Indianapolis, 1942.

The Metropolitan Museum of Art:

Catalogue of the Paintings, New York, 1905.

Bryson Burroughs, Catalogue of Paintings, New York,
1914; 2nd ed., 1916; 6th ed., 1922; etc.

Catalogue, New York, 1931.

A. T. E. Gardner, A Concise Catalogue of the American
Paintings, New York, 1957.

Albert Ten Eyck Gardner and Stuart P. Feld, American
Paintings, a Catalogue of the Collection of the Metropolitan Museum of Art, 3 vols., Greenwich, Conn.,
1965--?, vol. 1.

The New York Hospital:

Catalogue of Paintings, New York, 1909.

New York Public Library:

Catalogue of Paintings in the Picture Galleries at the
New York Public Library--Astor, Lenox, and Tilden Foundations,
New York, 1941.

New York State Historical Association:

Clifford L. Lord, _The Museum and Art Gallery of the New York State Historical Association_, Cooperstown, 1942.

The Rochester Memorial Art Gallery of the University of Rochester:

_Handbook_, Rochester, 1961.

Smithsonian Institution, National Collection of Fine Arts:

_The Opening of the Adams-Clement Collection_, Washington, D. C., n.d. /ca. 1951/.

The Toledo Museum of Art:

_American Paintings: A Checklist_, mimeograph, Toledo, n.d.

Vassar College Art Gallery:

_Vassar College Art Gallery, 1939_, Poughkeepsie, N. Y., n.d.

The Walters Art Gallery:

_The Walters Collection_, Baltimore, n.d.

E. S. King and M. C. Ross, _Catalogue of the American Works of Art Including French Medals Made for America_, Baltimore, 1956.

Whitney Museum of American Art:

_History, Purpose, and Activities, with a Complete List of Works in its Permanent Collection to June, 1937_, New York, n.d.

William Rockhill Nelson Gallery of Art and Mary Atkins Museum of Fine Arts:

_Handbook of the Collections_, 4th ed., Kansas City, 1959.

Worcester Art Museum:

Catalogue of Paintings and Drawings, Worcester, 1922.

Yale University:

Yale University Portrait Index, 1701-1951, New Haven, 1951.

Fig. 1. Durand. Original Design. Ca. 1815.

Fig. 2. Durand. Theodore Clark, Business Card.
1817-1820.

Fig. 3. Durand (after Waldo). Old Pat. Ca. 1819.

Fig. 4. Durand (after Trumbull). The Declaration of
Independence of the United States of America.
1820-1823.

Fig. 5. Durand (after Waldo and Jewett). Rev. James
Milnor, D.D. 1819.

Fig. 6. Durand (after Waldo and Jewett). Rev. J.B.
Romeyn, D.D.  1820.

Fig. 7. Durand (after Ingham). William Fuller.
1823.

Fig. 9. Durand. Musidora.
1825.

Fig. 10. Durand. Musidora.
1825.

Fig. 8. Durand. ΑΠΟΛΛΩΝ. 1825.

Fig. 12. Durand. Musidora. 1819.

*VENERE*

*Anch'esso esistente in Londra presso il Sig.r Enrico Iomanne*

Fig. 11. Cavaceppi. Venere. 1768–1772.

Fig. 13. Durand (after Cole). Winnipiseogee Lake. 1830.

Fig. 14. Durand. Delaware Water Gap. 1830.

Fig. 15. Durand. Catskill Mountains. 1830.

Fig. 16. Smillie and Durand (after Weir). Fort Putnam. 1830.

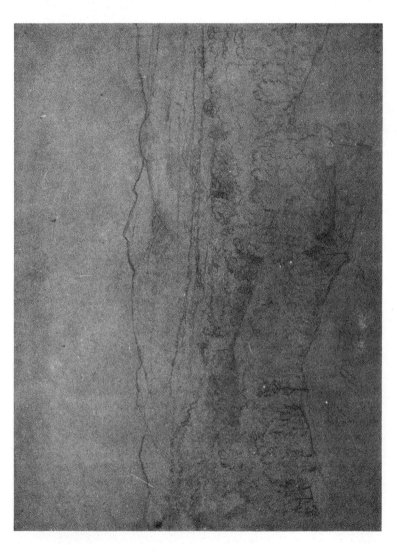

Fig. 17. Durand. Valley with the Catskill Mountains beyond. 1830.

Fig. 18. Cole. River in the Catskills. 1843.

Fig. 19. Cole. In the Catskills. 1837.

Fig. 20. Durand. Catskill Mountains. Ca. 1831.

Fig. 21. Durand (after Inman). The Sisters. No date.

Fig. 22. Durand (after Morse). Sisters. No date.

Fig. 23. Durand (after Morse). The Wife. No date.

Fig. 24. Durand (after Leslie). Gipsying Party.

No date.

Fig. 25. Durand. Hagar. 1827-1829.

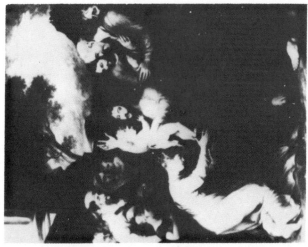

Fig. 27. Trumbull. Our
Savior with Little
Children. 1812.

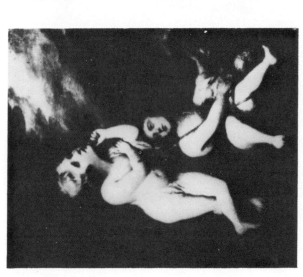

Fig. 26. Trumbull. The
Savior and St. John
Playing with a Lamb.   1801.

Fig. 28. Durand. Portrait of Caroline Durand.
Ca. 1828.

Fig. 29. Durand. Children of the Artist. 1832.

Fig. 30. Earlom   (after Gainsborough).

Girl with Pigs. 1783.

Fig. 31. Durand. Portrait of Mary and Jane
Cordelia Frank.  1834.

Fig. 32. Gainsborough. Elizabeth and Mary Linley.
Ca. 1772.

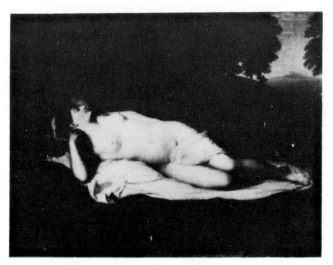

Fig. 33. Durand (after Vanderlyn). Ariadne Asleep
On the Island of Naxos.  Ca. 1835.

Fig. 34. Durand (after Vanderlyn). Ariadne. 1835.

Fig. 35. Durand. Ideal Head.
A Suggestion from Life.
1836.

Fig. 36. Durand. Mrs. Asher B.
Durand (Mary Frank).
Ca. 1837.

Fig. 37. Durand. Il Pappagallo. 1840.

Fig. 38. Flagg. Lady and Parrot. Ca. 1835.

Fig. 40. Durand. Portrait
of Andrew Jackson. 1835.

Fig. 39. Casilear.
The Presidents. 1834.

Fig. 42. Durand. Portrait of George Washington. 1835.

Fig. 41. Durand. Portrait of James Madison. 1833

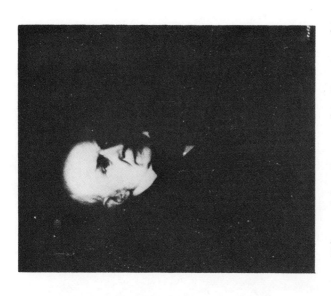

Fig. 44. Durand. Portrait of John Quincy Adams. 1835.

Fig. 43. Durand. Portrait of John Quincy Adams. 1835.

Fig. 46. Durand. Portrait of
Aaron Ogden. 1834.

Fig. 45. Longacre. Portrait
of William Wirt. Ca. 1836.

Fig. 47. Durand. Portrait
of Luman Reed. 1836.

Fig. 48. Durand. Portrait
of Joseph Hoxie. 1839.

Fig. 49. Durand. Portrait of John Fessenden. 1830's.

Fig. 50. Portrait of William Cullen Bryant. 1854.
Courtesy of Sleepy Hollow Restorations,
Tarrytown, New York.

Fig. 51. Durand. Head of a Roman. 1841.

Fig. 52. Durand. Head of a Roman. 1841.

Fig. 53. Durand. The Capture of Major Andre. 1834.

Fig. 54. Durand. The Capture of Major Andre. 1833.

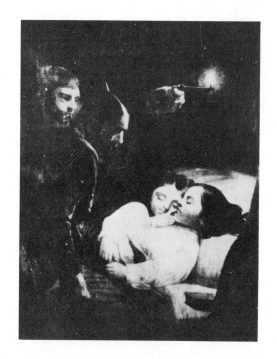

Fig. 55. Flagg. The Murder of the Princes
in the Tower. Ca. 1834.

Fig. 56. Durand. The Pedlar Displaying His Wares.
1836.

Fig. 57. Rowlandson. Doctor Syntax Turned Nurse.
1821.

Fig. 58. Mount. The Truant Gamblers. 1836.

Fig. 59. Flagg. Falstaff Enacting Henry IV Ca. 1834.

Fig. 61. Rowlandson. The Death of Punch. 1821.

Fig. 60.Durand. The Wrath of Peter Styvesant. 1836.

Fig. 63. Durand.
School Let Out. 1836.

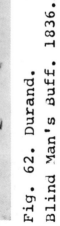

Fig. 62. Durand.
Blind Man's Buff. 1836.

Fig. 64. Durand. Boys Playing Marbles. 1836.

Fig. 65. Durand. Boy Chasing a Pig. 1836.

Fig. 66. Baumann (after Webster). Children on a See-Saw. No date.

Fig. 67. Mount. Farmers Nooning. 1836.

Fig. 68. Mount. Bargaining for a Horse. 1835.

Fig. 69. Flagg. The Chess-Players, Check-Mate.
Ca. 1835.

Fig. 70. Cole. Dream of Arcadia. 1838.

Fig. 71. Durand. Dance on the Battery
in the Presence of Peter Styvesant.
1838.

Fig. 72. Rowlandson. Rural Sports. 1812.

Fig. 73. Durand. Sunday Morning. 1839.

Fig. 74. Hinshelwood (after Durand). Sunday Morning.
1869.

Fig. 75. Durand. Landscape with Children.
1837.

Fig. 76. Smillie (after Durand). Dover Plains. 1850.

Fig. 77. Durand. Landscape: View of Rutland,
Vermont. 1840.

Fig. 78. Durand. Landscape, Sunset. 1838.

Fig. 79. Cole. Summer Sunset. Ca. 1834.

Fig. 80. Durand. An Old Man's Reminiscences. 1845.

Fig. 81. Inman. Dismissal of School on an October Afternoon. 1845.

Fig. 83. Durand. Morning Ride. 1851.

Fig. 84. Cole. The Valley of Vaucluse.
1841.

Fig. 85. Durand. The Morning of Life. 1840.

Fig. 86. Durand. The Evening of Life. 1840.

Fig. 87. Durand. Farm Yard on the Hudson. 1843.

Fig. 88. Durand. View of Oberweisal on the Rhine. 1843.

Fig. 89. Durand. Landscape with Covered Wagon.
1847.

Fig. 90. Hooper. (after Durand). Progress. 1853.

Fig. 91. Durand. The First Harvest. 1855.

Fig. 92. Fenner Sears and Company (after Cole).
A View near Conway, N. Hampshire. 1831.

Fig. 93. Durand. Hudson River. 1847.

Fig. 94. Claude. Landscape. 1636.

Fig. 95. Durand. Last Interview between Harvey
Birch and Washington. 1843.

Fig. 96. Durand. Study of a Tree. 1837.

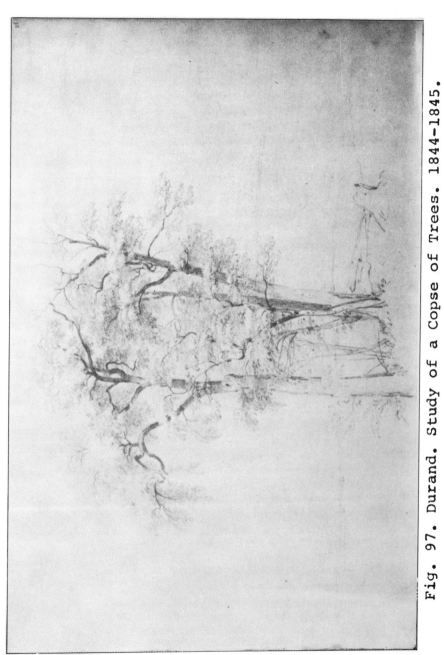

Fig. 97. Durand. Study of a Copse of Trees. 1844-1845.

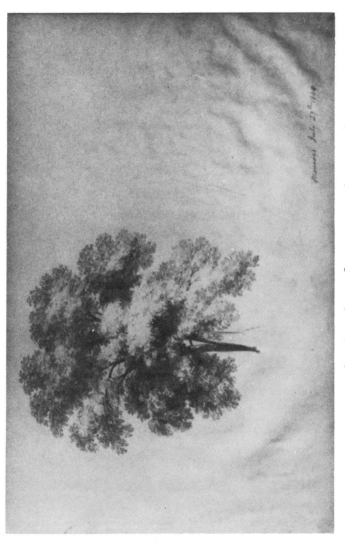

Fig. 98. Durand. Study of a Tree in Foliage. 1844.

Fig. 99. Durand. Study of Trees. 1848.

Fig. 100. Durand. Study of a Group of Trees.
1853.

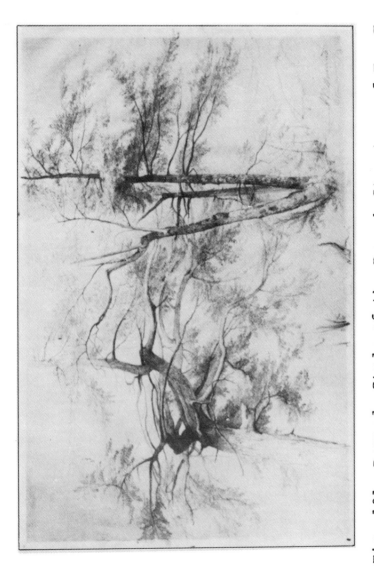

Fig. 101. Durand. Study of the Branch Structure of Two Trees.
1863.

Fig. 102. Durand. Study of a Tree. 1865.

Fig. 103. Durand. Rural Scene. 1827.

Fig. 103A. Durand. Brook, Rocks and Trees. 1836.

Fig. 103B. Durand. Castle of Blonay. 1840.

Fig. 103C. Durand. Tivoli. 1841.

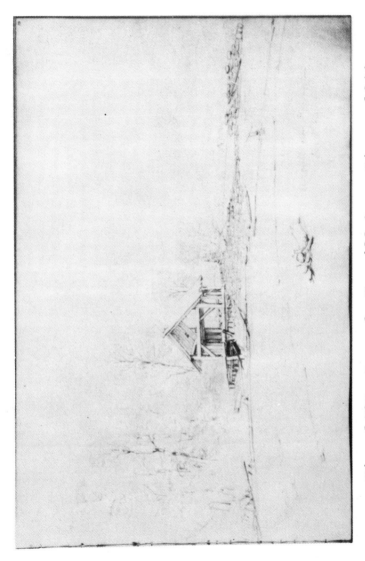

Fig. 103D. Durand. Sawmill by a River. 1844.

Fig. 103E. Durand. Plain and Mountain Range. 1855.

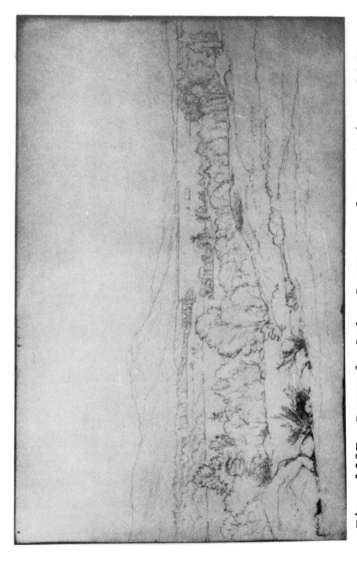

Fig. 103F. Durand. Lake George and Mountains. 1863.

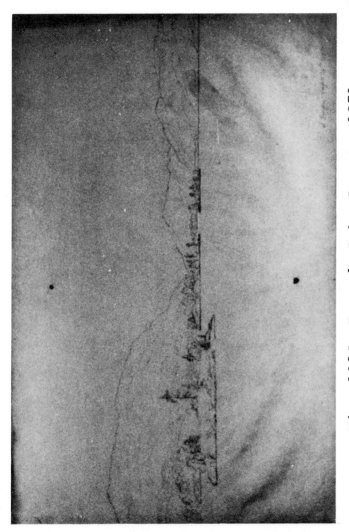

Fig. 103G. Durand. Lake George. 1871.

Fig. 103H. Durand. Trees and Rocks. Ca. 1849.

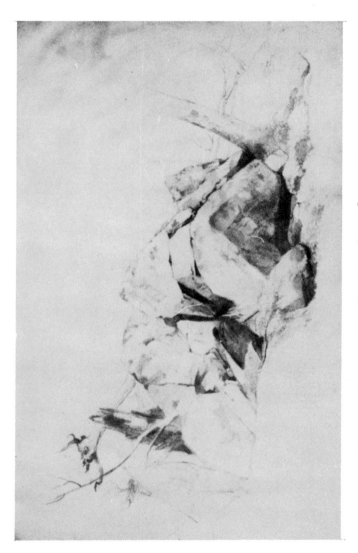

Fig. 1031. Durand. Study of Rocks. 1863.

Fig. 103J. Durand. Study of the Upturned Roots of a Tree. 1870.

Fig. 104. Durand. Study from Nature. Ca. 1834.

Fig. 106 Durand. Study at Marbletown, N.Y. Ca. 1845.

Fig. 105. Durand. Study from Nature. Ca. 1834.

Fig. 107. Durand. Landscape with a Beech Tree.
1844.

Fig. 108. Durand. The Beeches.          1845.

Fig. 109. Durand. Trees by the Brookside,
Kingston, N.Y. 1846.

Fig. 110. Durand. Forenoon. 1847.

Fig. 111. Durand. In the Woods. 1847.

Fig. 112. Durand. Woodland Scene. 1850.

Fig. 113. Durand. On the Wissahickon. 1850.

Fig. 114. Durand. Where the Streamlet Sings
in Rural Joy. 1850.

Fig. 115. Vollmering. Landscape. No Date.

Fig. 116. Vollmering. Winter Scene. No date.

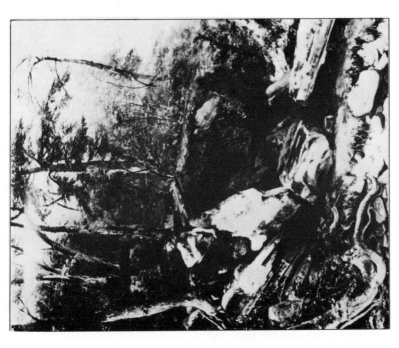

Fig. 118. Durand. Trees and Rocks. 1856.

Fig. 117. Durand. Study from Nature: Bronxville. 1856.

Fig. 119. Durand. Rocks and Trees. 1856.

Fig. 120. Durand. Study of the Interior
of a Wood. 1856.

Fig. 122. Durand. Landscape with Figures. 1861.

Fig. 121. Durand.

Bash-Bish Falls. 1861.

Fig. 123. Durand. Chappel Pond, Keene Flats, Adirondacks. 1870.

Fig. 124. Durand. Chappel Brook. 1871.

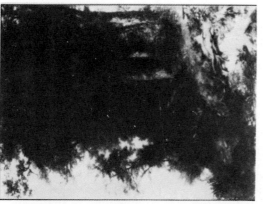

Fig. 127. Durand. Landscape:
Study from Nature. 1855-1857.

Fig. 126. Durand. Group
of Trees. 1855-1857.

Fig. 125. Durand.
Landscape. 1855-1857.

Fig. 128. Durand. Landscape. 1859.

Fig. 129. Durand. Forest Landscape. 1859.

Fig. 130. Durand. Mountains and Stream. 1853.

Fig. 131. Durand. View of the Shandaken Mountains.
1853.

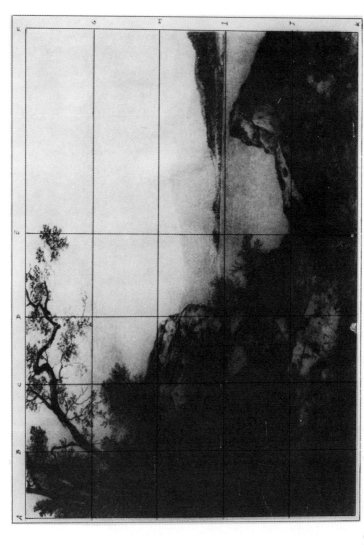

Fig. 132. Durand. Lake George, N.Y. 1862. H. 16 3/4 x w. 23 3/4 inches.

A-D, E-F, F-I + = 3/5 height of painting.

A-B, B-C, C-D, F-G, H-I, I-J, J-K = 1/5 height of painting.

Fig. 133. Durand. The Old Oak. 1844.

H. 34 x W. 46 3/4 inches.

AB=CE=FG=¼ h. of painting.

AD=DG

PH and OD cross BN at

the same point

CD=DE= ½AB=1/8 h. of painting.

Fig. 134. Durand. Vermont Scenery. 1852.
        AB, BC, CE, EF, FG, GI
        = 1/5 width of painting.
        AD, DG = ½ width.
        RJ and AN cross CD at the same point
        RQ = AT.

Fig. 135. Durand. In the Woods. 1855.
H. 60 3/4 x w. 48 5/8.
The painting is divided into twenty
one-foot squares.

Fig. 136. Durand. Harbor Island, Lake George. 1872.

Fig. 137. Durand. Harbor Island, Lake George. 1872.
H. 17 x w. 24 inches.
AB and EO = ¼ width of painting.
NG and ME cross BL at the same point.
DK and AH cross NG at the same point.
BC = ½ AB
FI and CH cross NG at the same point.

Fig. 138. Durand. Black Mountain, Lake George. 1878.

Fig. 139. Durand. Black Mountain, Lake George. 1878.

H. 15 x w. 24 inches.

DL = EF = ¼ width of painting.

DE = IH and GF.

LF = DE.

Fig. 140. Durand. Black Mountain, Lake George. 1874.

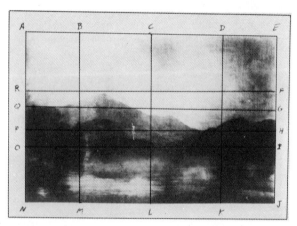

Fig. 141. Durand. Black Mountain, Lake George. 1874.
H. 16 x w. 24 inches.
AB, DE, EF, FI = 1/3 height of painting.
NL, LJ = ½ width of painting.
ML=LK=AQ=PN

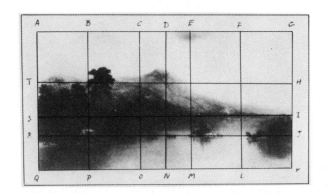

Fig. 142. Durand. View of Black Mountain from the Harbor
Islands, Lake George. 1875

H. 32 x w. 60 inches.
AB, BC, CE, EF, FG, GH, HJ, IK
= 1/5 width of picture.
QN =NK.

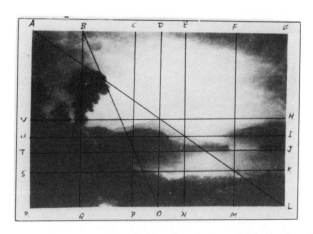

Fig. 143. Durand. Souvenir of the Adirondacks. 1878.
H. 25 x w. 37 inches.
AB, BC, CE, EF, FG = 1/5 width of painting.
AD =DG
VH and AL cross DO at the same point.
UI and AL cross EN at the same point.
TJ and BO cross CP at the same point.
SK and AL cross FM at the same point.

Fig. 144. Cole. Tornado in the Wilderness. 1835.

Fig. 145. Smillie (after Durand). Cover to The
American Landscape. 1830.

Fig. 146. Durand. Trompe-l'oeil Drawing. 1837.

Fig. 147. Cole. Dream of Arcadia. 1838.

Fig. 148. Durand. Landscape, Sunday Morning. 1850.

Fig. 149. Rolph (after Durand). Evening. 1845.

Fig. 150. Durand. View in the Catskills. 1847.

Fig. 151. Durand. Vermont Scenery. 1852.

Fig. 152. Durand. Brook, Trees and Mountains, Manchester, Vt. 1851.

Fig. 153. Durand. Trees, a Valley and Mountains. 1851.

Fig. 154. Durand. High Point:
Shandaken Mountains. 1853.

Fig. 155. Smillie (after Durand). A Glimpse
in New Hampshire. 1857.

Fig. 157.   Durand. The Pedestrian. 1858.

Fig. 158. Durand. River Scene. 1861.

Fig. 159. Durand. Summer Afternoon. 1865.

Fig. 160. Durand. Landscape. 1866.

Fig. 161. Durand. Landscape. 1867.

Fig. 162. Durand. Scene among the Berkshire Hills. 1872.

Fig. 163. Durand. View of Black Mountain from the
Harbor Islands, Lake George. 1875.

Fig. 164. Durand. Souvenir of the Adirondacks.
1878.

Fig. 165. Koekkoek  Woodland Scenery
with Water on
a Normal Day. 1849.

Fig. 166. Walters. Pool in the Catskills.
No date.

Fig. 167. Hart. At the Ford. No date.

Fig. 169. Durand. In the Woods. 1855.

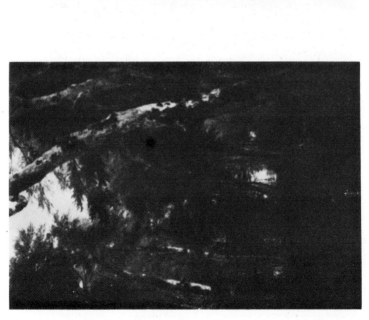

Fig. 168. Durand. Primeval Forest. 1854.

Fig. 170. Cushman (after Weir). "... enter
this wild wood, / And view the haunts
of Nature."m      1836.

Fig. 171. Rice (after John). The First Temples. 1870.

Fig. 172. Constable. Salisbury Cathedral from the
Bishop's Grounds. 1823. Crown Copyright.
Victoria and Albert Museum.

Fig. 173. Friedrich. Cloister Graveyard
in the Snow. 1810.

Fig. 174. Carus. The Churchyard on the Oybin
in Winter. Ca. 1828.

Fig. 175. Durand. A Primeval Forest. Ca. 1855.

Fig. 176. Durand. Trees and Brook. Ca. 1855.

Fig. 177. Durand. Trees and Brook. 1858.

Fig. 178. Durand. Woodland Brook. 1859.

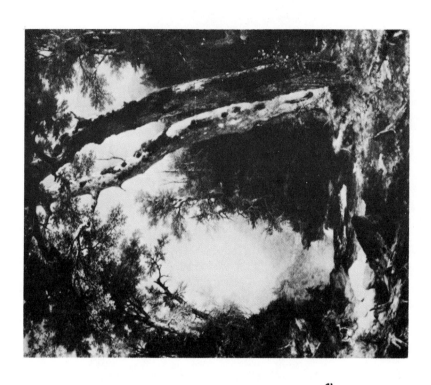

Fig. 180. Durand. The Catskills. 1859.

Fig. 179. Durand. A Sycamore
Tree. 1858.

Fig. 181. Durand. Landscape. 1858.

Fig. 182. Durand. Valley Landscape. 1859.

Fig. 183. Durand. Primeval Forest. 1869.

Fig. 184. Durand. The Old Oak. 1844.

Fig. 185. Koekkoek    The Way-side Shrine.
1837.

Fig. 186. Smillie (after Durand).
My Own Green Forest Land. 1847.

Fig. 187. Durand. Study of Trees. 1848.

Fig. 188. Durand. Landscape. 1849.

Fig. 189. Durand. View Toward the Hudson Valley. 1851.

Fig. 189A. Durand. Study of Trees. 1848.

Fig. 190. Koekkoek. Small Town on a River. 1840.

Fig. 191. Durand. Shandaken Range, Kingston, N.Y.
1854.

Fig. 192. Durand. Landscape. 1855.

Fig. 193. Durand. Fishkill Mountains, N.Y. 1856.

Fig. 194. Durand. Hudson River, View of the Fishkill
Mountains. 1856.

Fig. 195. Durand. Franconia, White Mountains. 1857.

Fig. 196.Durand. Franconia Notch. 1857.

Fig. 197. Durand. Catskill Clove. 1866.

Fig. 199. Bobbet and Edmonds (after Durand). To the Memory of Channing. 1849.

Fig. 198. Durand. Escape of General Putnam. 1844.

Fig. 200. Durand. A Tree and A Limb. 1848.

Fig. 201. Durand. Kindred Spirits. 1849.

Fig. 202. Cole. Expulsion from Eden. 1828.

Fig. 203. Durand. Study for Thanatopsis. 1850.

Fig. 204. Durand. Thanatopsis. 1850.

Fig. 205. Huntington. Portrait of Asher B. Durand. 1857.

Fig. 206. Fay. Portrait of Asher B. Durand. 1870.